People and Places

Grade 2
Teacher's Edition

Editorial Offices: Glenview, Illinois • Parsippany, New Jersey • New York, New York
Sales Offices: Parsippany, New Jersey • Duluth, Georgia • Glenview, Illinois • Coppell, Texas • Ontario, California

ISBN: 0-328-01887-2

2 3 4 5 6 7 8 9 10 V064 11 10 09 08 07 06 05 04 03 02

What makes this program different and better?

People make the difference. The people behind Scott Foresman *Social Studies* share a personal commitment to this program. They believe it can change students' lives and help build a better future.

PROGRAM AUTHORS

Dr. Candy Dawson Boyd
Professor, School of Education
Director of Reading Programs
St. Mary's College
Moraga, California

Dr. C. Frederick Risinger
Director, Professional Development and Social Studies Education
Indiana University
Bloomington, Indiana

Dr. Allen D. Glenn
Professor and Dean Emeritus
College of Education
Curriculum and Instruction
University of Washington
Seattle, Washington

Dr. Geneva Gay
Professor of Education
University of Washington
Seattle, Washington

Sara Miranda Sanchez
Elementary and Early Childhood Curriculum Coordinator
Albuquerque Public Schools
Albuquerque, New Mexico

Dr. Carole L. Hahn
Professor, Educational Studies
Emory University
Atlanta, Georgia

CONTRIBUTING AUTHORS

Rita Geiger
Director of Social Studies and Foreign Languages
Norman Public Schools
Norman, Oklahoma

Dr. Carol Berkin
Professor of History
Baruch College and the Graduate Center
The City University of New York
New York, New York

Dr. M. Gail Hickey
Professor of Education
Indiana University-Purdue University
Fort Wayne, Indiana

Dr. James B. Kracht
Associate Dean for Undergraduate Programs and Teacher Education
College of Education
Texas A&M University
College Station, Texas

Lee A. Chase
Staff Development Specialist
Chesterfield County Public Schools
Chesterfield County, Virginia

Dr. Bonnie Meszaros
Associate Director
Center for Economic Education and Entrepreneurship
University of Delaware
Newark, Delaware

Dr. Valerie Ooka Pang
Professor of Teacher Education
San Diego State University
San Diego, California

Dr. Jim Cummins
Professor of Curriculum
Ontario Institute for Studies in Education
University of Toronto
Toronto, Canada

CONTENT CONSULTANTS

Catherine Deans-Barrett
World History Specialist
Northbrook, Illinois

Dr. Michael Frassetto
Studies in Religions
Independent Scholar
Chicago, Illinois

Dr. Gerald Greenfield
Hispanic-Latino Studies
History Department
University of Wisconsin, Parkside
Kenosha, Wisconsin

Dr. Frederick Hoxie
Native American Studies
University of Illinois
Champaign, Illinois

Dr. Cheryl Johnson-Odim
Dean of Liberal Arts and Sciences and Professor of History
African American History Specialist
Columbia College
Chicago, Illinois

Dr. Michael Khodarkovsky
Eastern European Studies
University of Chicago
Chicago, Illinois

Robert Moffet
U.S. History Specialist
Northbrook, Illinois

Dr. Ralph Nichols
East Asian History
University of Chicago
Chicago, Illinois

CLASSROOM REVIEWERS

Diana Vicknair Ard
Woodlake Elementary School
St. Tammany Parish
Mandeville, Louisiana

Dr. Charlotte R. Bennett
St. John School
Newburgh, Indiana

Sharon Berenson
Freehold Learning Center
Freehold, New Jersey

Betsy Blandford
Pocahontas Elementary School
Powhatan, Virginia

Gloria Cantatore
Public School #5
West New York, New Jersey

LuAnn Curran
Westgate Elementary School
St. Petersburg, Florida

Louis De Angelo
Office of Catholic Education
Archdiocese of Philadelphia
Philadelphia, Pennsylvania

Dr. Trish Dolasinski
Paradise Valley School District
Arrowhead Elementary School
Glendale, Arizona

Dr. John R. Doyle
Director of Social Studies Curriculum
Miami-Dade County Schools
Miami, Florida

Dr. Roceal Duke
District of Columbia Public Schools
Washington, D.C.

Peggy Flanagan
Roosevelt Elementary School
Community Consolidated School District #64
Park Ridge, Illinois

Mary Flynn
Arrowhead Elementary School
Glendale, Arizona

Sue Gendron
Spring Branch ISD
Houston, Texas

Su Hickenbottom
Totem Falls Elementary School
Snohomish School District
Snohomish, Washington

Sally Hunter
Highland Park Elementary School
Austin ISD
Austin, Texas

Allan Jones
North Branch Public Schools
North Branch, Minnesota

Brandy Bowers Kerbow
Bettye Haun Elementary School
Plano ISD
Plano, Texas

Sandra López
PSJA Service Center
San Juan, Texas

Martha Sutton Maple
Shreve Island School
Shreveport, Louisiana

Lyn Metzger
Carpenter Elementary School
Community Consolidated School District #64
Park Ridge, Illinois

Marsha Munsey
Riverbend Elementary School
West Monroe, Louisiana

Christine Nixon
Warrington Elementary School
Escambia County School District
Pensacola, Florida

Liz Salinas
Supervisor
Edgewood ISD
San Antonio, Texas

Beverly Scaling
Desert Hills Elementary
Las Cruces, New Mexico

Madeleine Schmitt
St. Louis Public Schools
St. Louis, Missouri

Barbara Schwartz
Central Square Intermediate School
Central Square, New York

Ronald Snapp
North Lawrence Community Schools
Bedford, Indiana

Lesley Ann Stahl
West Side Catholic Consolidated School
Evansville, Indiana

Carolyn Moss Woodall
Loudoun County of Virginia Public Schools
Leesburg, Virginia

Suzanne Zaremba
J. B. Fisher Model School
Richmond Public Schools
Richmond, Virginia

How do I teach my students key content?

Children need to explore their world and see how they can contribute as individuals. Scott Foresman *Social Studies* helps every child become an active, involved, and informed citizen.

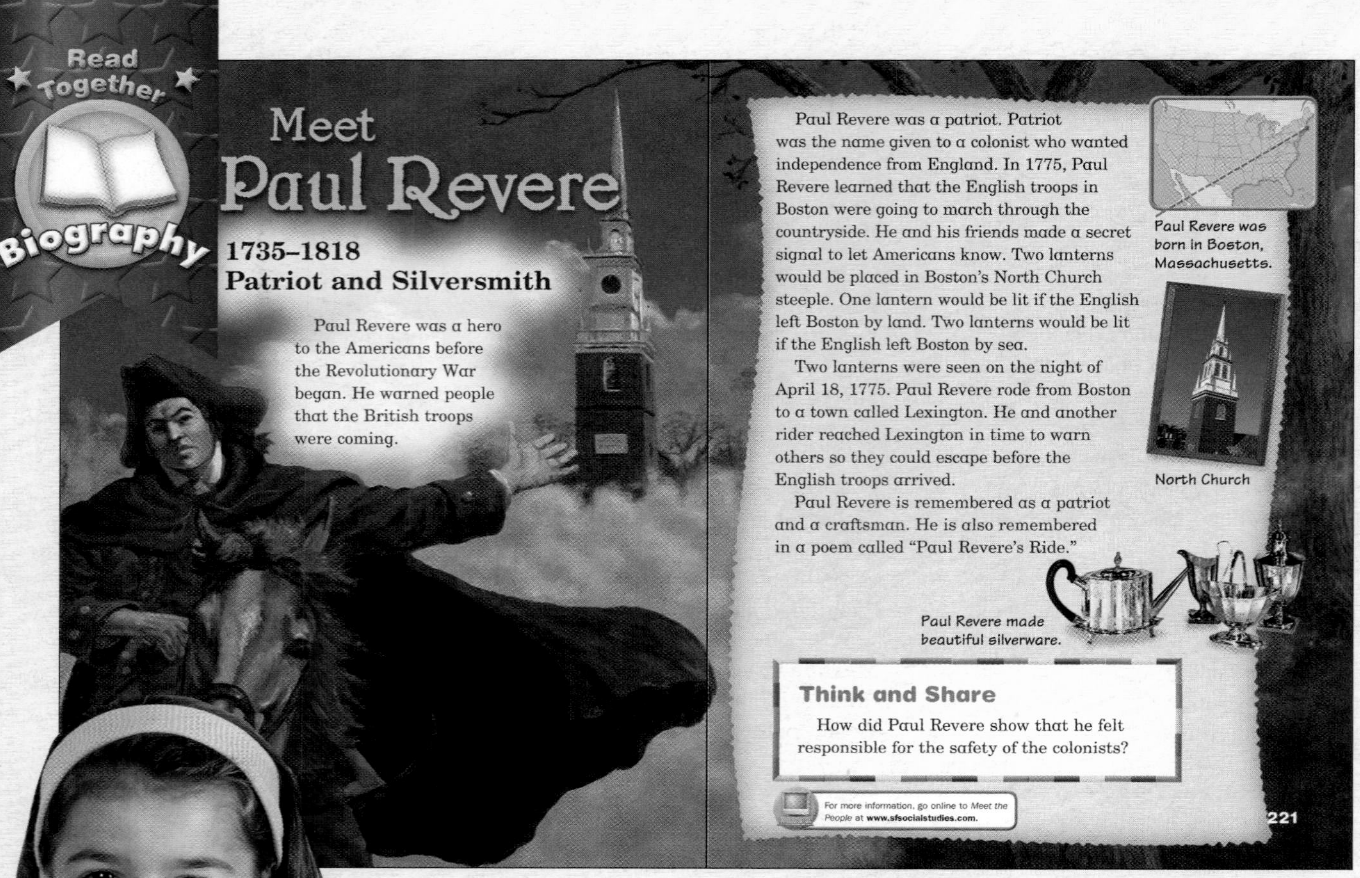

HISTORY TO ENGAGE AND INSPIRE

- Up-to-date, accurate, and comprehensive
- Fully aligned to curriculum standards
- Biographies that bring key figures to life
- Museum-quality artwork, photographs, and diagrams
- Web-based updates and activities
- Interactive multimedia

GEOGRAPHY TO LINK PEOPLE AND PLACES

- Exclusive maps that are custom built for Scott Foresman by MapQuest™
- Maps that show change and movement
- Beautifully illustrated map adventures
- Lessons to help children read maps and understand directional terms
- Online atlas with up-to-the-minute maps and current information

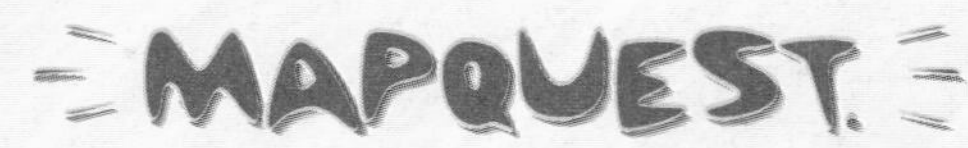

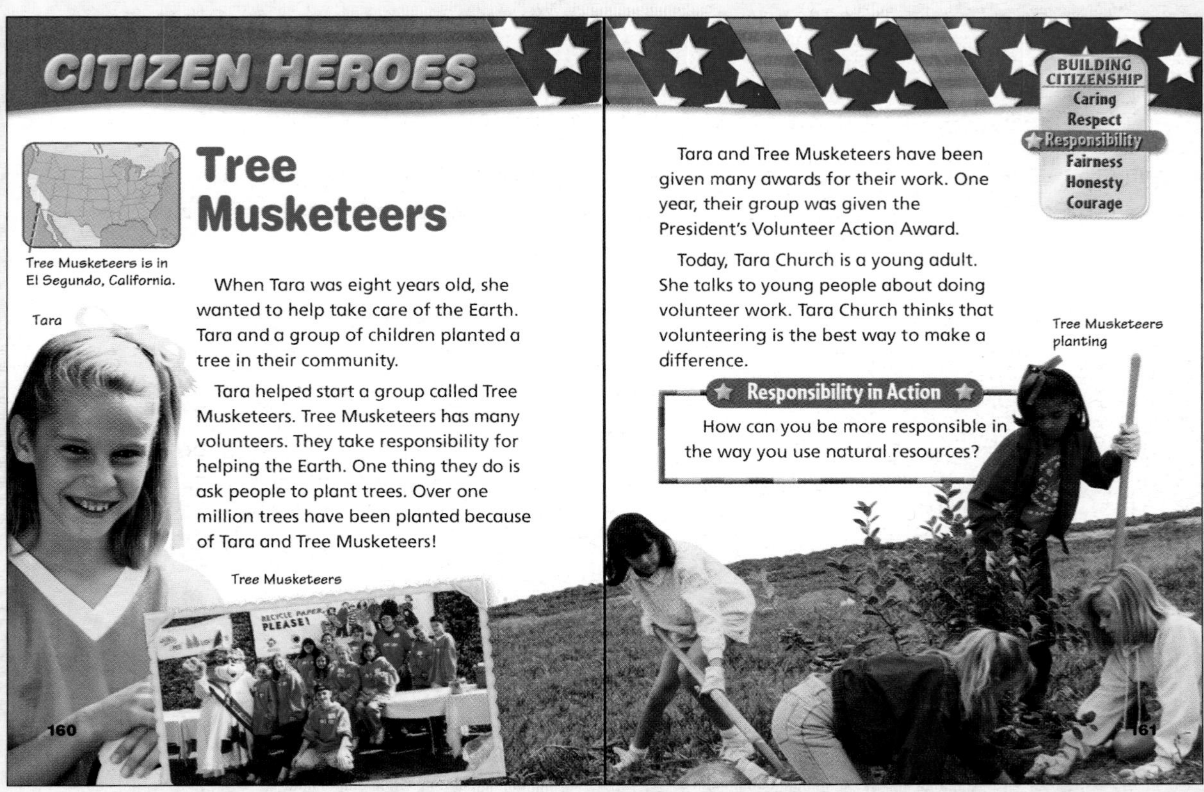

CITIZEN HEROES

BUILDING CITIZENSHIP
Caring
Respect
Responsibility
Fairness
Honesty
Courage

Tree Musketeers

Tree Musketeers is in El Segundo, California.

Tara

When Tara was eight years old, she wanted to help take care of the Earth. Tara and a group of children planted a tree in their community.

Tara helped start a group called Tree Musketeers. Tree Musketeers has many volunteers. They take responsibility for helping the Earth. One thing they do is ask people to plant trees. Over one million trees have been planted because of Tara and Tree Musketeers!

Tree Musketeers

160

Tara and Tree Musketeers have been given many awards for their work. One year, their group was given the President's Volunteer Action Award.

Today, Tara Church is a young adult. She talks to young people about doing volunteer work. Tara Church thinks that volunteering is the best way to make a difference.

Responsibility in Action

How can you be more responsible in the way you use natural resources?

Tree Musketeers planting

161

CITIZENSHIP LESSONS TO HELP CHILDREN MAKE A DIFFERENCE

- ★ Built-in lessons in the student book teach good citizenship skills and a positive self concept: Caring, Respect, Responsibility, Fairness, Courage, and Honesty.
- ★ Historic figures and everyday citizen heroes inspire students.
- ★ Engaging, real-life applications

Content that covers the key social studies strands

SOCIAL STUDIES STRAND **Citizenship**

SOCIAL STUDIES STRAND **Culture**

SOCIAL STUDIES STRAND **Economics**

SOCIAL STUDIES STRAND **Geography**

SOCIAL STUDIES STRAND **Government**

SOCIAL STUDIES STRAND **History**

SOCIAL STUDIES STRAND **Science • Technology**

Content organized for the way you teach

If time is short, use the Quick Teaching Plan to cover the core content and skills.

QUICK Teaching Plan

If time is short, write the vocabulary words on the board.

- Have volunteers suggest words related to each vocabulary word.
- List the responses on the board.

OR

To add depth and richer enjoyment, use the wealth of information in each lesson.

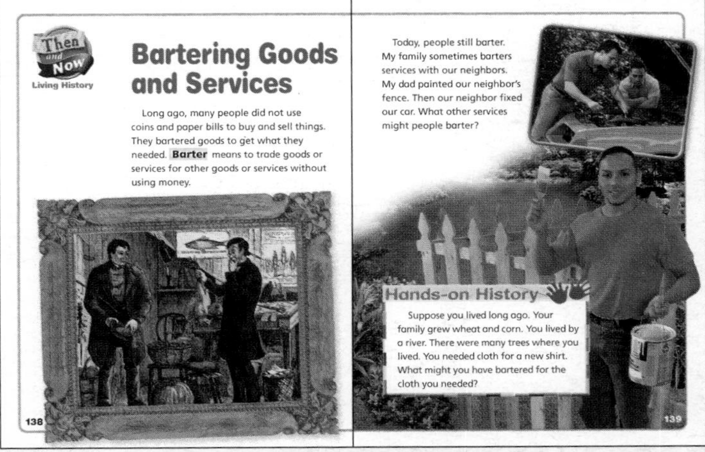

Then and Now Living History

Bartering Goods and Services

Long ago, many people did not use coins and paper bills to buy and sell things. They bartered goods to get what they needed. **Barter** means to trade goods or services for other goods or services without using money.

138

Today, people still barter. My family sometimes barters services with our neighbors. My dad painted our neighbor's fence. Then our neighbor fixed our car. What other services might people barter?

Hands-on History

Suppose you lived long ago. Your family grew wheat and corn. You lived by a river. There were many trees where you lived. You needed cloth for a new shirt. What might you have bartered for the cloth you needed?

139

What can I do to reach all my students?

If children are going to be successful, they need to practice and apply effective reading strategies. Scott Foresman *Social Studies* provides systematic instruction to improve comprehension and to reach out to all learners.

UNIT 3

Reading Social Studies

Ben at Work

Put Things in Order

Target Skill

Hi! I'm Ben. Someday I want to own a pizza shop.

Saturday I had a lemonade stand. These pictures show the order in which things happened. Use your own words to tell what I did.

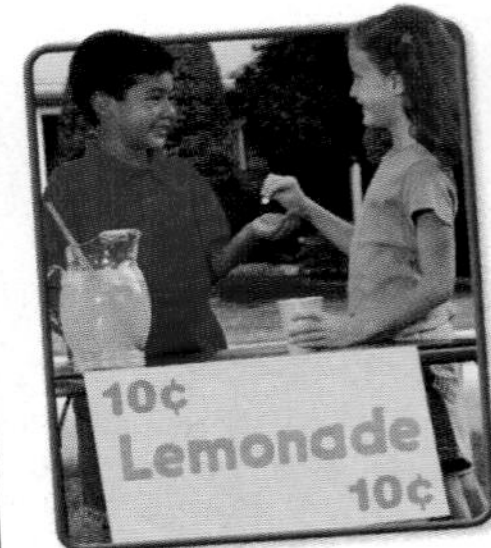

First

Next

92

Did you use words like **first, next,** and **last?** Those words tell the order in which things happened.

First, I made the lemonade.

Next, I set up my stand.

Last, I sold a cup to my friend.

Look for **first, next,** and **last** as you learn more about people at work.

10¢ Lemonade 10¢

Last

Try it!

Tell or write about how Ben could make a pizza. Use the words **first, next,** and **last.** Draw pictures to show the order in which things happen.

93

DEVELOPING READING SKILLS WITH SOCIAL STUDIES

- ★ Built-in comprehension skill lessons in every unit
- ★ Preteach a target comprehension skill, then apply the same skill throughout the unit for sustained practice
- ★ Graphic organizers provide support for every skill.

LOOK FOR THE TARGET SKILL ICON!

- ★ At the beginning of lessons
- ★ In Lesson Reviews
- ★ Throughout the units
- ★ In Unit Reviews

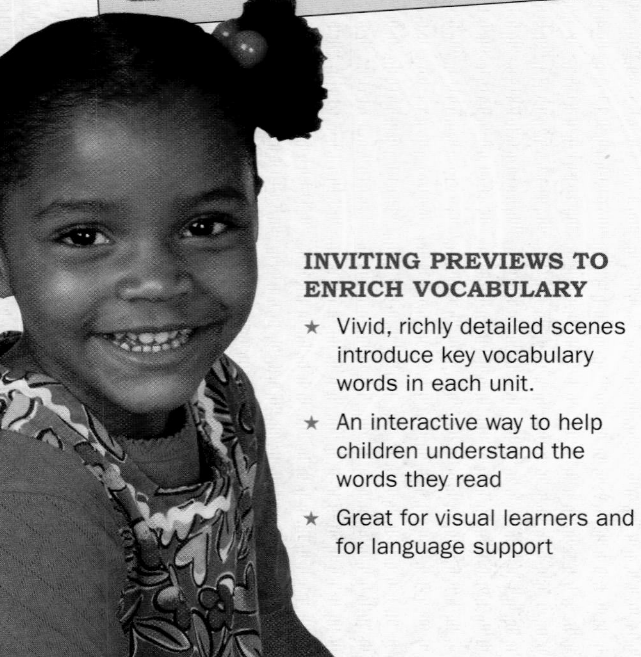

INVITING PREVIEWS TO ENRICH VOCABULARY

- ★ Vivid, richly detailed scenes introduce key vocabulary words in each unit.
- ★ An interactive way to help children understand the words they read
- ★ Great for visual learners and for language support

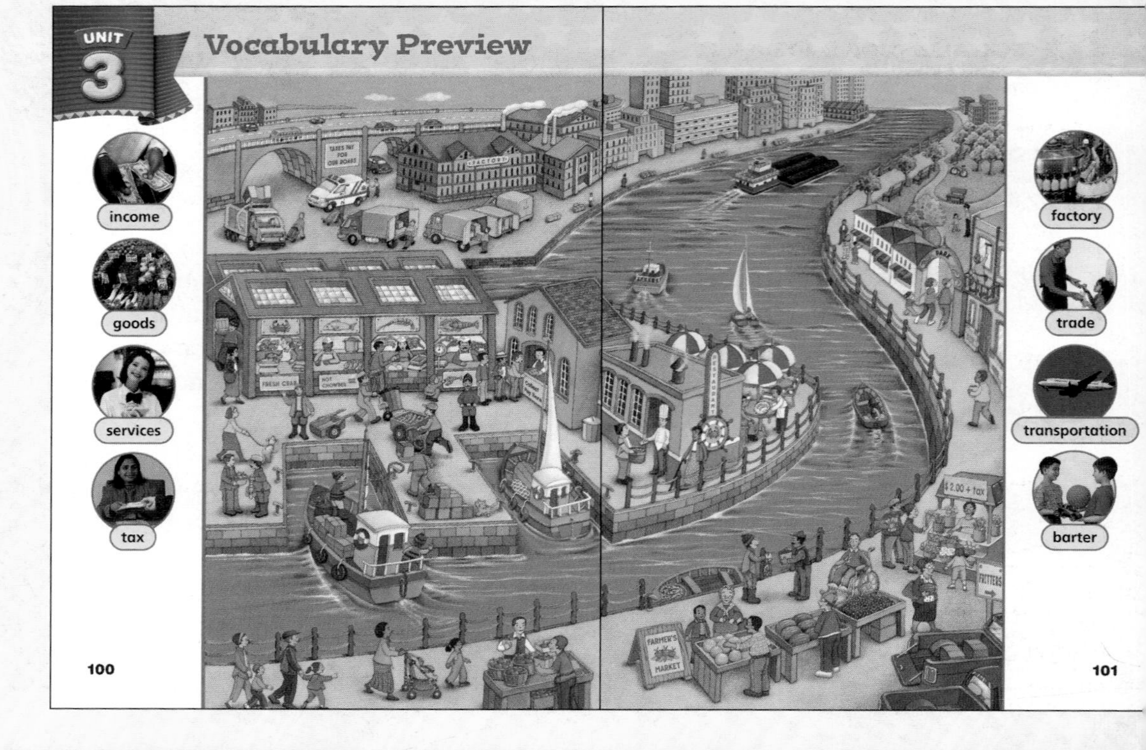

MEETING INDIVIDUAL NEEDS
Leveled Practice

Interviews

Children choose a service worker they want to find out more about by writing interview questions.

Easy Have children write one interview question they would like to ask a service worker. **Reteach**

On-Level Children write three or four questions for an interview. Questions can be about the duties performed, how the worker uses tools to perform his or her job, who pays the worker, and the challenges the worker faces every day. **Extend**

Challenge Have pairs of children take turns interviewing and being interviewed, using their questions. Encourage children to preview the questions they will be asked and find answers as needed. **Enrich**

LEVELED PRACTICE TO MATCH CHILDREN'S ABILITIES

* The same activity at three instructional levels to reach all learners
* Specific strategies for various learning styles
* Promotes active participation and learning in every lesson

ESL Support

Using Pictures Show children pictures of modern-day soup kitchens or other places people can go for help in the community.

Beginning Ask children to point to the pictures as they repeat the names of jobs of the workers pictured on pp. 108–111. Then show other job pictures and help children brainstorm a list of other jobs.

Intermediate Have children follow along as you read the sentences in speech balloons on pp. 108–110. Then have children name the workers pictured on p. 111 and dictate sentences the workers might say.

Advanced After children identify the workers pictured in the book, they can find pictures of other workers and use them to talk about the jobs these people do and the goods or services they provide.

For additional ESL support, use Every Student Learns Guide, pp. 50–53.

AUDIO TEXT AND VOCABULARY CARDS TO HELP ALL STUDENTS ACCESS CONTENT

* All lessons are recorded so students can listen and read along.
* Vocabulary cards for all key terms include picture and definition.

LANGUAGE STRATEGIES AT POINT OF USE

* Effective strategies for Beginning, Intermediate, and Advanced language learners in every lesson
* Explore word meanings, usage, and form as well as cognates, etymologies, and more

Every Student Learns

* Access prior knowledge/build background: poster discussions, read alouds, word banks, word webs, and activity ideas
* Access content: lesson summaries, graphic organizers, and blackline practice worksheets
* Extend language: activities that use the language and content of the lesson

How can I engage and motivate my students?

Scott Foresman *Social Studies* is brimming with compelling visuals, intriguing facts, and exciting real-world learning. It makes every child an interested social studies student who feels, knows, and thinks.

SMITHSONIAN VISUAL LESSONS

- ★ Developed exclusively for Scott Foresman in cooperation with the Smithsonian Institution
- ★ Brilliant visual lessons that bring children up close to national treasures and fascinating artifacts
- ★ A museum in every student book

LOOK INSIDE THE SMITHSONIAN

Native American Clothing

The beautiful Native American clothing shown here represents many different tribes.

Apache Moccasins
The round toe of these moccasins protected the toes from sharp cactuses, rocks, sticks, and snakes.

What materials do you think the Apache used to make these moccasins?

Crow Dance Dress
This child's dress is made of red and blue wool and decorated with carved copies of elk teeth. Elk teeth represented love and long life.

Ojibwe Beaded Bag
Most of these bags were made by women and worn by men. Each bag took as long as a year to make!

Tlingit Hat
Many Tlingit people gathered spruce roots from nearby forests. This hat was woven from spruce roots and decorated with a painted design.

Seminole Boy's Shirt
Women and girls sewed these big shirts for the men and boys in their families. Great care was taken in making the patchwork designs.

Artifacts are from the Smithsonian Institution.

208 209

DORLING KINDERSLEY VISUAL LESSONS

- ★ Recognized around the world for its visually stunning informational books and resources
- ★ Bold, large-as-life photographs with interesting, easy-to-read expository captions
- ★ Helps children visualize their world and its past

DORLING KINDERSLEY

DK CELEBRATIONS

Spring

Springtime festivals celebrate new life, energy, and growth. For many children, these are happy, colorful festivals with flowers, music, and dancing.

Chinese New Year starts on the first day of the Chinese calendar and lasts for 15 days. Man Po and her family feast, visit friends, and watch colorful street parades.

The N'cwala ceremony is held each February to celebrate the harvest. Groups of dancers perform their warrior dance. M'sangombe is the youngest dancer in his group.

Fête des Mères is celebrated on the last Sunday in May. Matilde calls this day Mommy's Festival. Matilde brings her mother breakfast in bed and recites the poem she has learned.

Hina Matsuri is celebrated March 3. This is a day dedicated to dolls. During the festival, Sayo displays her dolls in the best room of the house.

Man Po from Hong Kong

M'sangombe from Zambia

Matilde from France

Sayo from Japan

Sophie from England

The children in Sophie's village celebrate May Day on May 1. They listen to music, pick spring flowers, and dance around a maypole.

260 261

A Note from the Smithsonian
Viewing treasures of the past

What makes us want to see the flag that inspired the national anthem? Why do we stand in awe before George Washington's historic uniform?

These are treasured icons of our nation. They tell the story of America, our story. It is a story filled with great courage and sacrifice, with heartfelt convictions and a lasting belief in liberty and justice for all. These treasured icons, these priceless relics, bring us closer to who we are and what we believe as a nation.

The mission of the Smithsonian Institution is "the increase and diffusion of knowledge." Nowhere is the knowledge of our past more useful than in the minds and hearts of our children. Museum objects and their unique stories bring history alive and make it more exciting for children to learn. It is an honor to fulfill our mission this way by sharing these objects with a new generation of students.

BEGIN WITH A SONG FOR LIVELY, ENGAGING LEARNING

- ★ Introduce important concepts and vocabulary in each unit with fun rhymes and rhythms
- ★ Promote interaction and social participation
- ★ Delightful recordings of each song on audio

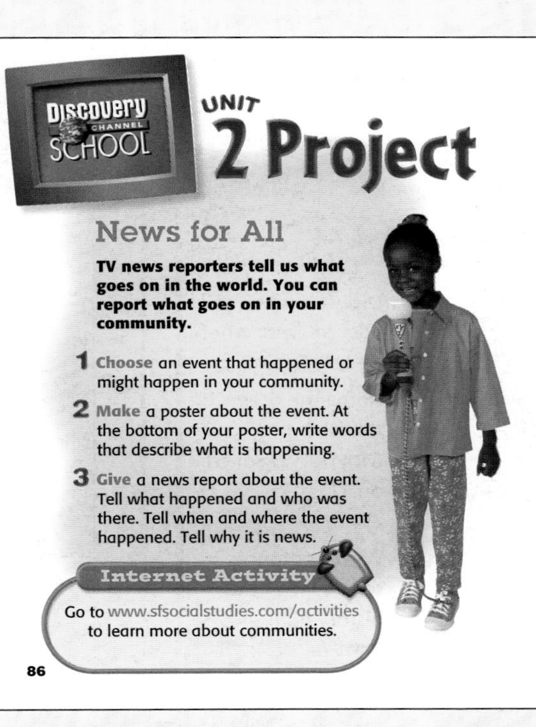

Social Studies Plus!

A HANDS-ON APPROACH

- ★ Long-term and short-term projects and activities to extend lessons
- ★ Social Studies Fair ideas, Readers Theater, learning center themes, holiday celebrations, writing and research activities, and more
- ★ Inspires hands-on, mind-on learning

DISCOVERY CHANNEL SCHOOL PROJECTS

- ★ From one of the world's leading providers of educational multimedia
- ★ Exclusive, hands-on unit projects synthesize and enhance learning.
- ★ Exciting Web-based activities extend lessons.

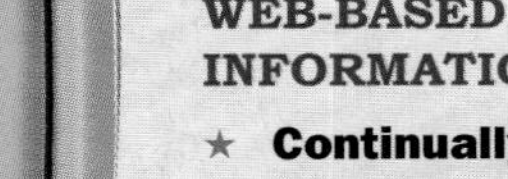

WEB-BASED INFORMATION CENTER

- ★ **Continually updated information, maps, and biographies**
- ★ Exclusive, customized **Fact Monster™** from **Information Please®**
- ★ Motivating, interactive learning games

How will I know my students are successful?

Children need to become critical thinkers who can solve problems, work together, and make decisions. Scott Foresman *Social Studies* provides built-in skill lessons and multiple assessment tools to develop thinking citizens.

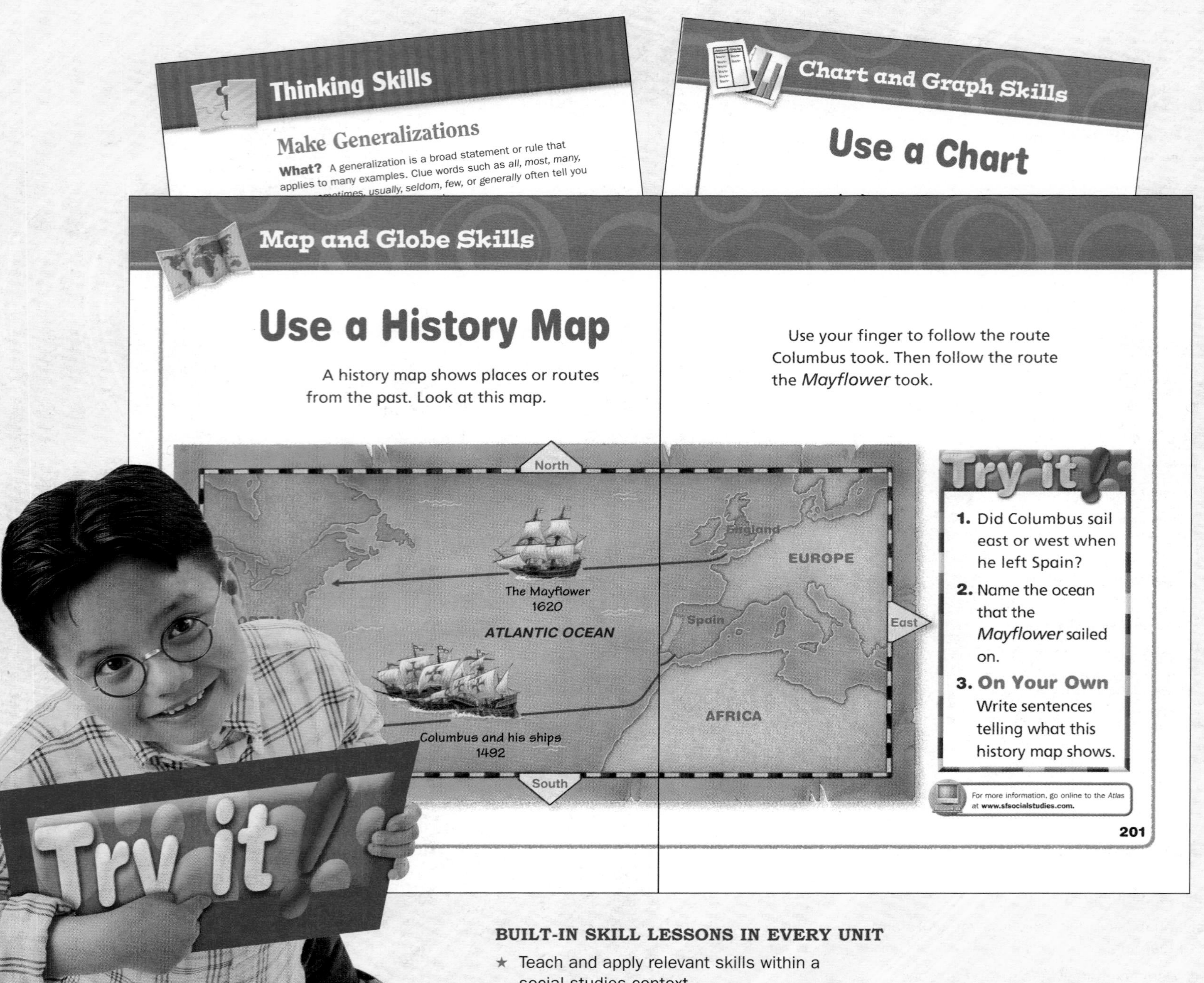

BUILT-IN SKILL LESSONS IN EVERY UNIT

- Teach and apply relevant skills within a social studies context
- Graphics that support the content

✓ Ongoing Assessment

If... children do not know if what a particular worker provides is a good or a service,

then... remind them that goods are what workers make or grow and services are what workers do to help others.

INFORMAL ASSESSMENT OPPORTUNITIES

- ★ Monitor children's learning as you teach
- ★ If/then guidelines with specific reteaching strategies and effective practice
- ★ Assess instruction and make adjustments

Test Talk

TEST-TAKING STRATEGY LESSONS

- ★ Develop test-taking strategies right in the student book
- ★ Test preparation for national and state tests
- ★ Transparencies and worksheets to support instruction

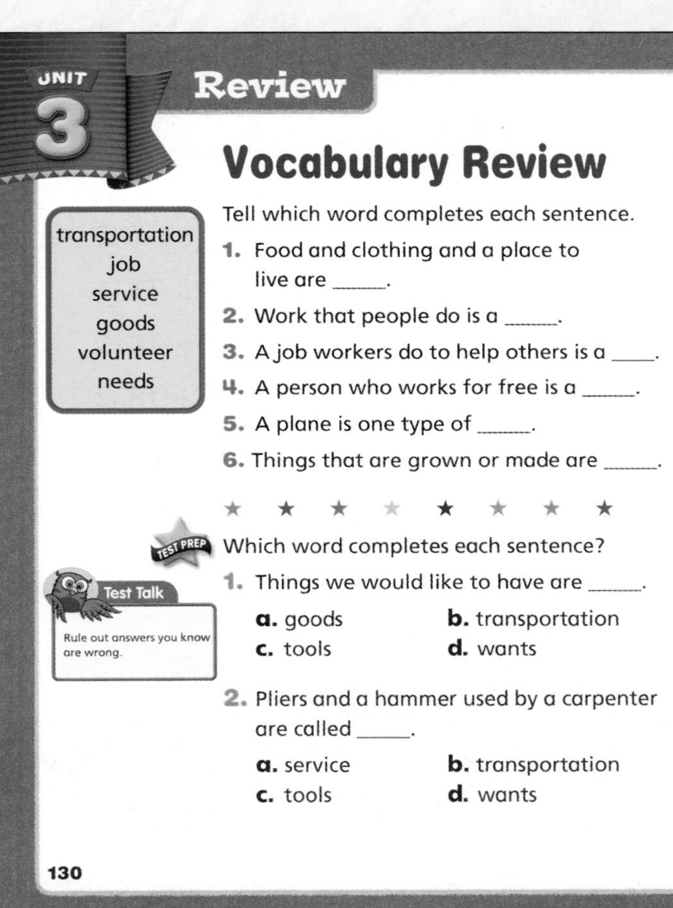

UNIT 3 Review

Vocabulary Review

transportation
job
service
goods
volunteer
needs

Tell which word completes each sentence.

1. Food and clothing and a place to live are _____.
2. Work that people do is a _____.
3. A job workers do to help others is a _____.
4. A person who works for free is a _____.
5. A plane is one type of _____.
6. Things that are grown or made are _____.

★ ★ ★ ★ ★ ★ ★ ★

TEST PREP

Which word completes each sentence?

Test Talk
Rule out answers you know are wrong.

1. Things we would like to have are _____.
   - **a.** goods
   - **b.** transportation
   - **c.** tools
   - **d.** wants
2. Pliers and a hammer used by a carpenter are called _____.
   - **a.** service
   - **b.** transportation
   - **c.** tools
   - **d.** wants

130

Skills Review

Put Things in Order

Write about a job you want to do some day. Tell what you would do **first, next,** and **last.**

★ ★ ★ ★ ★ ★ ★ ★ ★

Follow a Route

1. What buildings are east of the store?
2. Follow the route with your finger. Whe
   does Pat's route begin?
3. Tell what direction Pat goes on each

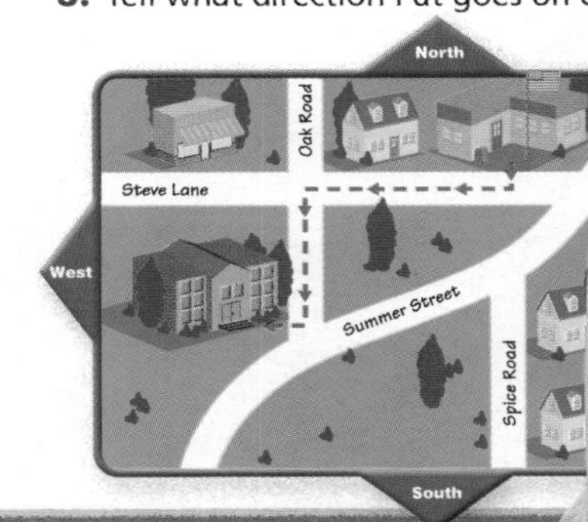

FORMAL ASSESSMENT OPPORTUNITIES

- ★ Assess children's learning and provide practice for key test-taking skills
- ★ Built-in Lesson, Chapter, and Unit Reviews in the student book
- ★ Chapter Tests and Unit Tests in the Assessment Handbook
- ★ Standardized test format with multiple-choice, open-ended, and written responses
- ★ Performance-based assessments

People and Places

Teacher's Edition Table of Contents

Teacher Resources

I want to be a great leader!

People and Places

Program Authors

Dr. Candy Dawson Boyd
Professor, School of Education
Director of Reading Programs
St. Mary's College
Moraga, California

Dr. Geneva Gay
Professor of Education
University of Washington
Seattle, Washington

Rita Geiger
Director of Social Studies and Foreign Languages
Norman Public Schools
Norman, Oklahoma

Dr. James B. Kracht
Associate Dean for Undergraduate Programs and Teacher Education
College of Education
Texas A&M University
College Station, Texas

Dr. Valerie Ooka Pang
Professor of Teacher Education
San Diego State University
San Diego, California

Dr. C. Frederick Risinger
Director, Professional Development and Social Studies Education
Indiana University
Bloomington, Indiana

Sara Miranda Sanchez
Elementary and Early Childhood Curriculum Coordinator
Albuquerque Public Schools
Albuquerque, New Mexico

Contributing Authors

Dr. Carol Berkin
Professor of History
Baruch College and the Graduate Center
The City University of New York
New York, New York

Lee A. Chase
Staff Development Specialist
Chesterfield County Public Schools
Chesterfield County, Virginia

Dr. Jim Cummins
Professor of Curriculum
Ontario Institute for Studies in Education
University of Toronto
Toronto, Canada

Dr. Allen D. Glenn
Professor and Dean Emeritus
Curriculum and Instruction
College of Education
University of Washington
Seattle, Washington

Dr. Carole L. Hahn
Professor, Educational Studies
Emory University
Atlanta, Georgia

Dr. M. Gail Hickey
Professor of Education
Indiana University-Purdue University
Fort Wayne, Indiana

Dr. Bonnie Meszaros
Associate Director
Center for Economic Education and Entrepreneurship
University of Delaware
Newark, Delaware

Editorial Offices: Glenview, Illinois • Parsippany, New Jersey • New York, New York
Sales Office: Parsippany, New Jersey • Duluth, Georgia • Glenview, Illinois • Coppell, Texas • Ontario, California

www.sfsocialstudies.com

Content Consultants

Catherine Deans-Barrett
World History Specialist
Northbrook, Illinois

Dr. Michael Frassetto
Studies in Religions
Independent Scholar
Chicago, Illinois

Dr. Gerald Greenfield
Hispanic-Latino Studies
History Department
University of Wisconsin, Parkside
Kenosha, Wisconsin

Dr. Frederick Hoxie
Native American Studies
University of Illinois
Champaign, Illinois

Dr. Cheryl Johnson-Odim
Dean of Liberal Arts and Sciences and Professor of History
African American History Specialist
Columbia College
Chicago, Illinois

Dr. Michael Khodarkovsky
Eastern European Studies
University of Chicago
Chicago, Illinois

Robert Moffet
U.S. History Specialist
Northbrook, Illinois

Dr. Ralph Nichols
East Asian History
University of Chicago
Chicago, Illinois

Classroom Reviewers

Diana Vicknair Ard
Woodlake Elementary School
St. Tammany Parish
Mandeville, Louisiana

Dr. Charlotte R. Bennett
St. John School
Newburgh, Indiana

Sharon Berenson
Freehold Learning Center
Freehold, New Jersey

Betsy Blandford
Pocahontas Elementary School
Powhatan, Virginia

Gloria Cantatore
Public School #5
West New York, New Jersey

LuAnn Curran
Westgate Elementary School
St. Petersburg, Florida

Louis De Angelo
Office of Catholic Education
Archdiocese of Philadelphia
Philadelphia, Pennsylvania

Dr. Trish Dolasinski
Paradise Valley School District
Arrowhead Elementary School
Glendale, Arizona

Dr. John R. Doyle
Director of Social Studies Curriculum
Miami-Dade County Schools
Miami, Florida

Dr. Roceal Duke
District of Columbia Public Schools
Washington, D.C.

Peggy Flanagan
Roosevelt Elementary School
Community Consolidated School District #64
Park Ridge, Illinois

Mary Flynn
Arrowhead Elementary School
Glendale, Arizona

Sue Gendron
Spring Branch ISD
Houston, Texas

Su Hickenbottom
Totem Falls Elementary School
Snohomish School District
Snohomish, Washington

Sally Hunter
Highland Park Elementary School
Austin ISD
Austin, Texas

Allan Jones
North Branch Public Schools
North Branch, Minnesota

Brandy Bowers Kerbow
Bettye Haun Elementary School
Plano ISD
Plano, Texas

Sandra López
PSJA Service Center
San Juan, Texas

Martha Sutton Maple
Shreve Island School
Shreveport, Louisiana

Lyn Metzger
Carpenter Elementary School
Community Consolidated School District #64
Park Ridge, Illinois

Marsha Munsey
Riverbend Elementary School
West Monroe, Louisiana

Christine Nixon
Warrington Elementary School
Escambia County School District
Pensacola, Florida

Liz Salinas
Supervisor
Edgewood ISD
San Antonio, Texas

Beverly Scaling
Desert Hills Elementary
Las Cruces, New Mexico

Madeleine Schmitt
St. Louis Public Schools
St. Louis, Missouri

Barbara Schwartz
Central Square Intermediate School
Central Square, New York

Ronald Snapp
North Lawrence Community Schools
Bedford, Indiana

Lesley Ann Stahl
West Side Catholic Consolidated School
Evansville, Indiana

Carolyn Moss Woodall
Loudoun County of Virginia Public Schools
Leesburg, Virginia

Suzanne Zaremba
J. B. Fisher Model School
Richmond Public Schools
Richmond, Virginia

2 3 4 5 6 7 8 9 10 V057 11 10 09 08 07 06 05 04 03 02

Contents

Social Studies Handbook

Unit 1

Where We Live

Unit 2
Our Earth

Unit 3
Working Together

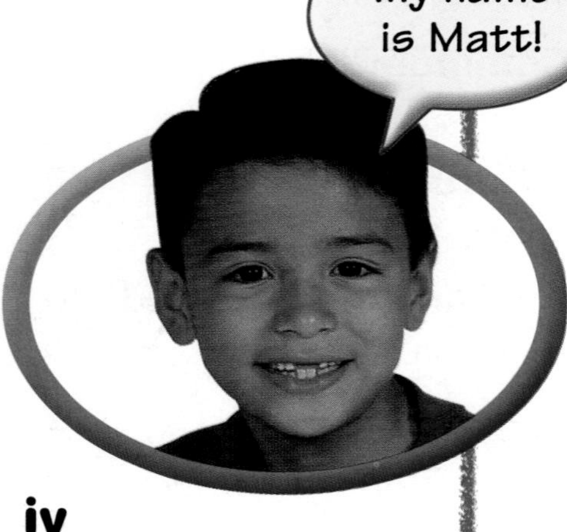

Unit 4

Our Country Today

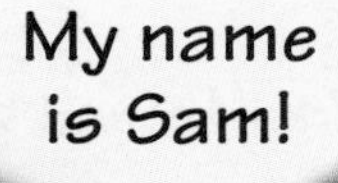

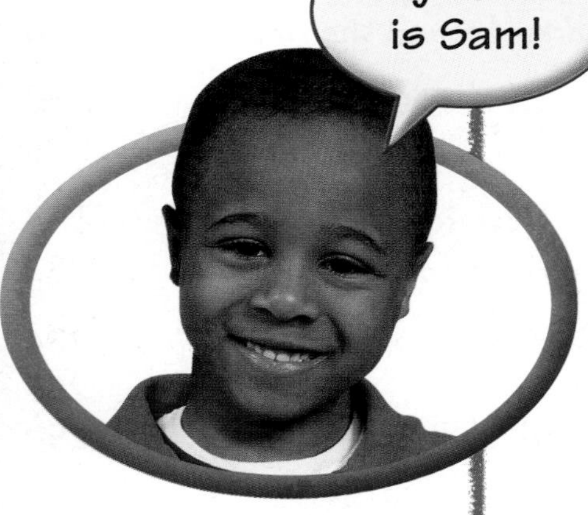

Unit 5

Our Country Long Ago

Unit 6

People and Places in History

Reference Guide

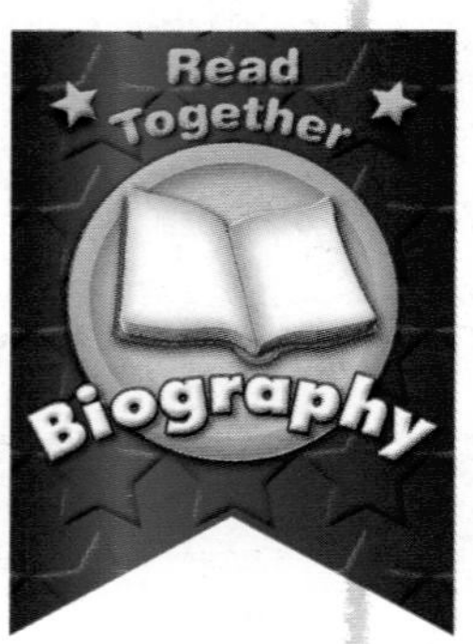

Biographies

Maps

Skills

Reading Social Studies

Map and Globe Skills

Chart and Graph Skills

Thinking Skills

Then and Now

Here and There

Citizen Heroes

Let the Discovery Begin

Fireworks

After reading the text, invite students to talk about the picture of the fireworks.

To begin discussion, you may want to ask questions similar to the following:

- What do you think of when you look at the picture?
- How do you feel when you see fireworks?
- In what ways do fireworks help a neighborhood celebrate?
- What celebrations usually include fireworks?
- Why are fireworks seen as a symbol of celebrations?
- What are other ways neighborhoods celebrate?

Hands-on Unit Projects

The Hands-on Unit Projects at the end of each unit provide you with ongoing performance assessment projects to enrich students' learning throughout Grade 2. You can find Hands-on Unit Projects at the end of each unit in this book on the following pages:

- **Unit 1**: ***Travel Channel,*** p. 48
- **Unit 2**: ***Guess My Place,*** p. 96
- **Unit 3**: ***Business Basics,*** p. 146
- **Unit 4**: ***Get Out the Vote,*** p. 194
- **Unit 5**: ***Do an Interview,*** p. 242
- **Unit 6**: ***My Hero,*** p. 290

Let the Discovery Begin

Bright colors flash and fill the dark sky. People celebrate the Fourth of July everywhere in the United States. At night they watch fireworks with family, friends, and neighbors. During the day, many people have parades and picnics in their neighborhoods.

How do people in your neighborhood celebrate? Read on to discover more about celebrations!

Practice and Extend

About Fireworks

- By the time of the American Revolution in 1776, people used fireworks to celebrate important events, including their independence. An annual event that joins Americans as one large neighborhood is the fireworks show in Washington, D.C. Put on by the National Parks Service, the display is televised to millions of people.
- One of the most spectacular fireworks displays in the United States was the celebration of the 100th anniversary of the Statue of Liberty, held on July 4, 1986. This show used 22,000 aerial fireworks launched from 30 barges and other places, as well as 18,000 ground displays.

Discovery Channel School

Discovery Channel School educational products include award-winning videos, CD-ROMs, and print resources covering curriculum topics in science, social studies, literature, and more. They are created specifically for use in the classroom and are correlated to National Education Standards.

Web Site

- Discovery Channel Education's online service, **DiscoverySchool.com**, provides cutting-edge resources for teachers and students, featuring a lesson plan library, teacher's guide, and a variety of tools—*Puzzlemaker, Worksheet Generator, Quiz Center, Lesson Planner, Glossary Builder*—that allow teachers to create customized resources.
- The site remains one of the top ten Web sites used by teachers.

Videos

- Certain units in this book contain suggestions for using videos from Discovery Channel School.
- Please check the teacher's page containing bibliography suggestions at the beginning of each unit. If a Discovery Channel School video is suggested for the unit, it will be listed there.
- To order Discovery Channel School videos, please call the following toll-free number: 1-888-892-3484.

CURRICULUM CONNECTION
Writing

Write Poems

- Ask children to close their eyes and visualize a fireworks display. Then have them each write a poem about how the fireworks make them feel. This poem could be organized as a picture that looks like a fireworks display.

SOCIAL STUDIES STRAND
Geography

Locate Washington, D.C.

- Use a large map of the United States to show the location of Washington, D.C. Engage children in a discussion of how the fireworks in Washington on July 4th make the entire country one large neighborhood.

Building Citizenship Skills

Read the introductory text to children as they follow along. Then read aloud the definitions of the six citizenship characteristics and talk briefly about the photographs.

Use the following questions to guide children to understand that they can demonstrate each of the characteristics in their own daily lives.

Respect

1 **The girl in the photo is showing and telling the woman about something. How do you think the girl is speaking to show that she respects the woman?** Possible answer: The girl is speaking in a soft, kind, and patient way. She is not shouting or turning away as she speaks. **Analyze Pictures**

Caring

2 **If a friend of yours were sad, how might you show that you cared about his or her feelings?** Possible answer: Give a hug or talk over what is making the friend sad **Express Ideas**

Responsibility

3 **What do you think the boy is doing to show that he is responsible?** Possible answer: He is doing his homework. **Analyze Pictures**

Fairness

4 **Why is taking turns an important part of playing fairly?** When people take turns, each one has a chance to take part in a game or sport. No one is left out. **Draw Conclusions**

Honesty

5 **Listen to this saying, "Finders keepers, losers weepers." How is the message of the saying the opposite of honesty?** People who are honest do not keep what does not belong to them. **Compare and Contrast**

Courage

6 **What are some things children your age do that takes courage?** Possible answers: They go to school in a new place; learn to swim; act in the class play. **Apply Information**

Building Citizenship Skills

There are many ways to show good citizenship. In your textbook, you will learn about people who are good citizens in their community, state, and country.

Respect means treating others as you want to be treated. 1

Caring means understanding how someone feels and being thoughtful. 2

Responsibility means doing what is expected of you. 3

Fairness means taking turns and playing by the rules. 4

Honesty means giving back what isn't yours and telling the truth. 5

Courage means doing what is right even when it is hard. 6

Practice and Extend

CURRICULUM CONNECTION
Reading

Using a Table of Contents

- Talk briefly with children about the purpose of the Table of Contents at the front of their books. Explain that it lists all the names of all the lessons and special features they will read.
- Note that the entries are arranged in page order.
- Work with children to use the Table of Contents to find the names of some of the Citizen Heroes they will learn about.

★ Citizenship in Action ★

Good citizens make careful decisions. They learn to solve problems. Help these children act like good citizens. Here are the steps they follow.

Problem Solving

It is time to go inside, but we cannot find one of the soccer balls. What can we do?

1. Name the problem.
2. Find out more about the problem.
3. List ways to solve the problem.
4. Talk about the best way to solve the problem.
5. Solve the problem.
6. How well is the problem solved?

Decision Making

We are planning a class party. Which games should we play?

1. Tell what decision you need to make.
2. Gather information.
3. List your choices.
4. Tell what might happen with each choice.
5. Make a decision.

Social Studies Handbook H5

SOCIAL STUDIES STRAND
Citizenship

In Grade 2, children will read about the following Citizen Heroes:

- Kids Care Clubs: Caring
- The Earth Angels: Responsibility
- Phoenix Kids Pride Program: Respect
- Anna Beavers: Fairness
- Ella Cara Deloria: Honesty
- Ellen Ochoa: Courage

★ Citizenship in Action ★

Read aloud the introductory paragraph and then focus children's attention on the two activities. Have children listen and follow along as you read each numbered step in each process.

As you discuss each step individually, encourage children to express a range of ideas they may have. Aside from identifying the problem or decision to be made, make it clear that there is no one correct response to each step.

Problem Solving

Guide children through the problem-solving steps.

1. The problem is that the children cannot find the soccer ball.
2. Talk about what might cause a ball to be missing—kicked out of the area accidentally.
3. Possible ways to solve the problem: re-count the balls to be certain one truly is missing; search the play area
4. If a ball truly is missing, try the second solution.
5. Search carefully until the ball is found.
6. Discuss why a careful search was the right solution, or tell why another solution may have been better.

Decision Making

Guide children through the decision-making steps.

1. The decision to be made is which games to play.
2. Children might take a poll among themselves or they might ask the teacher which games would work best in a classroom setting.
3. Choices might include: Musical Chairs, I Spy, Pin the Tail on the Donkey.
4. Have children decide which games would be most fun and most appropriate to the setting.
5. Have children talk about their reasons for making their decision.

The United States

Read aloud the information about the national flag. Then share the following information with children.

Taking Care of Our Flag

- The colors of the flag have special meanings. White stands for liberty, blue stands for loyalty, and red stands for courage. Since the flag represents our American spirit, it must be treated with special respect.
- When a flag passes by in a parade or is raised or lowered, everyone should face the flag and stand at attention. People who are not in the military should salute by placing their right hand over their heart. Men wearing hats should remove them.
- The flag should be displayed every day except when bad weather conditions might damage it. The flag is displayed usually from sunrise to sunset, but it may be shown at night as long as there is a light shining on it.
- The flag should never touch anything beneath it, such as the ground, the floor, or water.

Saying the Pledge

Share the following with children before reading aloud the pledge.

- The Pledge of Allegiance was first used more than 100 years ago. It was recited by school children during a Columbus Day celebration.
- Explain that the words "pledge of allegiance" mean a "solemn promise to be loyal."
- While saying the pledge, people face the flag and place the right hand over the heart to show honor and respect.

Building Citizenship Skills

The United States

The American flag is a symbol of our country. The number of stripes on the flag stands for the number of states there were when the country first began. There is one star for each of the 50 states.

The Pledge of Allegiance

I pledge allegiance to the Flag of the United States of America, and to the Republic for which it stands, one Nation under God, indivisible, with liberty and justice for all.

H6 Social Studies Handbook

Practice and Extend

FYI SOCIAL STUDIES **Background**

The Pledge of Allegiance

- Francis Bellamy (1855–1931) probably wrote the original pledge.
- The original wording of the pledge has been changed more than once. In 1923 and again in 1924, the National Flag Conferences of the American Legion added words. In 1954, Congress added more words.

The Star-Spangled Banner

Oh, say! can you see, by the dawn's early light,
What so proudly we hailed at the twilight's last gleaming?
Whose broad stripes and bright stars, through the
perilous fight,
O'er the ramparts we watched were so gallantly
streaming?
And the rockets' red glare, the bombs bursting in air,
Gave proof through the night that our flag was still there.
O say, does that Star-Spangled Banner yet wave,
O'er the land of the free and the home of the brave?

Social Studies Handbook H7

AUDIO CD Technology

- Play the CD, *Songs and Music,* to listen to other patriotic songs with children.
- Help children compare and contrast the lyrics, as well as the feelings the music brings out.

Our National Anthem

Before guiding children through the text of the song, discuss the following:

- An anthem is the official song of a country. It is meant to make people feel proud of and loyal to their country.
- Some national anthems, including "The Star-Spangled Banner," remember important events in history.
- An American lawyer, Francis Scott Key, wrote the words to the song as a poem. Key saw the British attack an American fort near Baltimore. At dawn, he saw a large American flag flying over the fort. He knew then that the fort was safe. He then wrote the words to the song.
- Beginning in Baltimore, the words were published with a note to sing them to a tune that was already familiar to many people. Soon the song was published in other cities.
- Congress officially approved the song as our country's national anthem in 1931.

Read aloud the words to the song, stopping to discuss words that will be unfamiliar to children. On a second reading, have them close their eyes to try and "see" the events described.

The Five Themes of Geography

From "*Guidelines for Geographic Education: Elementary and Secondary Skills*," prepared by the Joint Committee on Geographic Education of the National Council for Geographic Education and the Association of American Geographers

Location

Describing a *location* involves finding the relative or exact place where something is. You may wish to have children use the Big Book Atlas to complete the following.

- Have children locate a country. They should tell what countries and oceans are east, west, north, and south of their selected country.
- Have children locate your city/town (or a large neighboring one) and tell which other states are nearby and faraway.

1 **Look at the first picture. What avenues is the park near?** Fifth Avenue and Sam Houston Avenue **Analyze Pictures**

Place

Place is what makes one location different from another. When describing a place, it is useful to compare the features of an area (human-made and natural) with the features of other areas.

2 **In the second picture, how is the park like and different from a park you visit?** Possible response: My park also has trees and grass, but my park has benches and big water fountains. **Compare and Contrast**

Movement

Talk with children about *movement*—the ways in which people and goods move from place to place.

3 **What are some ways people and goods move from city to city, state to state, or country to country?** Car, truck, bus, train, plane, ship **Generalize**

Practice and Extend

SOCIAL STUDIES Background

The Essential Elements of Geography
From the National Council for Geographic Education

- **The World in Spatial Terms** Geography studies the spatial relationships between people, places, and environment.
- **Places and Regions** The identities of individuals and cultures can be found in particular places and regions.
- **Physical Systems** Physical processes shape Earth's surface and create, sustain, and change ecosystems.
- **Human Systems** Human activities help shape Earth's surface.
- **Environment and Society** The physical environment is modified by human activities. Human activities are also influenced by Earth.
- **The Uses of Geography** Knowledge of geography enables people to understand the relationships between people, places, and environments over time.

Places and People Change Each Other

Discuss the interaction between *people and places.* Note that people change places by building roads, cutting down trees, and constructing buildings. People who move to big cities learn to live and work in noisy urban environments.

4 **How did the artists' work change the park?** It gave people new pretty things to look at. **Recall and Retell**

Region

A *region* is a large area that can be described by features such as climate, landforms, or bodies of water. Regions are different from each other.

5 **How do you think other regions of our country may differ from the region where the park is?** Possible answer: In other regions, leaves on the trees may not change color. **Make Inferences**

Additional Resources

The following resources can be used throughout Grade 2 to teach and reinforce geography skills.

- Big Book Atlas
- Outline Maps
- Desk Maps
- Map Resources CD-ROM

CURRICULUM CONNECTION
Art

I Know a Place

- Have children think about a place they know well. It might be a park, a shopping mall, or their own neighborhood.
- Ask children to draw a series of pictures with captions beneath them to show and tell: the location of the area, what makes it different from other places, how people get to and from the area, and what people have done to change the area.
- Discuss children's finished drawings. Then use a map to show the region children live in.
- Talk about characteristics of your region.

Map and Globe Skills Review

Talk About the Picture

- Before reading the text on page H10, talk with children about the picture. Ask them what it shows. (Earth) Ask if they know from where the picture was taken. (space) Then read the introductory text.
- Have children tell if there is more land or more water on Earth. Ask how they know. Confirm that Earth has about three times as much water as land.
- Have children point to land areas and areas of water other than those marked by the captions and the lead lines.

From the Earth to a Globe

Our Earth is like a ball floating in space. This picture of Earth was taken from deep space. The Earth is made up of land and water.

The areas with green on them are called land. The largest green areas are called continents.

The blue areas are called water. The largest blue areas are called oceans.

Practice and Extend

About the Earth

- Earth makes a complete turn, or rotation, about every 24 hours. As it turns, the part of the Earth facing the sun has daylight. The part turned away has nighttime.
- Earth completes an orbit, or revolution, around the sun about every 365 days (actually 365.3 days).
- People on Earth cannot feel the Earth moving either when it rotates on its axis or when it revolves around the sun.
- People, land, and water do not fly or "spill" off the Earth because of gravity. Gravity pulls things toward the center of the Earth.

You can hold a globe in your hands!

A model of Earth is called a globe. Globes show the continents and oceans of Earth. You can turn a globe and get an idea of how far away Earth's seven continents are from each other. You can also see how big the oceans are as you turn a globe.

A model is a small copy of something.

Use a Globe

- Have children talk about how the picture of the Earth and the globe are similar.
- Have a globe available for use with children. Ask volunteers to point out continents and bodies of water, including oceans, on the globe. As each is pointed out, read its name. Then have children locate the United States and, if possible, their community on the globe.
- Call on individuals to close their eyes as you spin the globe in front of them. With closed eyes, have them point to a place on the globe. Then have them open their eyes and say if the place is a landmass or a body of water. Ask how they know.

Map and Globe Skills Review

Talk About the Picture

- Ask children where they think the picture was taken from—a car passing by, a rooftop, a plane. Have them explain their thinking.
- Have children tell if they can see a lot of details in the photograph. Help them notice that they can see houses, streets, and trees, but they cannot tell much about them because the photo is taken from a distance overhead. The photograph just gives a general idea of places and their location in the neighborhood.
- To sum up the discussion, call on volunteers to read sentences in the text. Be certain a child reads the speech bubble, too.

Building Geography Skills

Map and Globe Skills Review

Reading a Map

Not all pictures of Earth show the whole planet. The picture below shows only a small part of Earth. This is a city neighborhood as seen from above.

It has streets, sidewalks, and buildings. A drawing of this picture is called a map. Look at the map on the next page.

How are the picture and map alike? How are they different?

Practice and Extend

CURRICULUM CONNECTION
Writing

Write Descriptions

- Have children select one building or one prominent object in their neighborhood.
- Ask them to write to describe their selected object as they would see it from ground level.
- Then have them write to describe how the same object would look from above.

Sometimes you need help in reading a map. A symbol is a shape, a color, or a line that stands for something. Knowing what the symbols stand for can help you read a map.

A map key is a box that is part of the map. It is where you will find the symbols. The map key also tells you what the symbols mean.

What things on the map do the symbols stand for?

CURRICULUM CONNECTION
Art

Make a Playground Map

Help children make a playground map.

- Ask children to name playground equipment. List the equipment on the board.
- Ask volunteers to draw symbols next to the items on the list. Remind them that a map symbol is a simple shape.
- Work with the class to outline and cut out playground symbols from different colored paper. Have children glue the shapes on construction paper.
- Ask children to include a map key using the list and symbols on the board. Have them title their map "Playground Map."

Talk About the Map

- After reading aloud the text on page H13 to the children, focus attention on the map. Ask children how the map on page H13 and the photograph on page H12 are alike. Discuss with them that both show the neighborhood and its roads, trees, and houses. Explain that often photographs are used to help someone draw a map.
- Have children identify the map key by pointing to it. Ask what they think its purpose is. As needed, explain that a map key helps someone understand symbols on a map.
- Read aloud the question. Call on volunteers to supply answers. Then have children match each symbol in the key to its occurrence on the map.

Map and Globe Skills Review

Read a History Map

- Talk about kinds of maps children may have seen—neighborhood map, map of the United States, road map, map of locations in a theme park or zoo. Have them identify the common function of all maps. (to help someone find places)
- Show children a current map of the United States. Have them compare and contrast it with the map on the page. (**Like**: The United States has the same shape and size on both maps; the bodies of water around it are the same; Canada is north of the United States, and Mexico is south of it. **Different**: The current map shows the names of our fifty states; the history map does not show states; the only labels on the history map show dates.)
- Read aloud the title of the map on the page and the labels written on it. Explain that this history map gives a picture of how our country grew from one time period to another.

Answers

1. West

2. Atlantic Ocean, Gulf of Mexico, Pacific Ocean

3. Mexico

Read a History Map

A history map shows places and events from the past. The map below shows the size of the United States in 1853. You can see how the country grew in the years between 1783 and 1853.

The United States in 1853

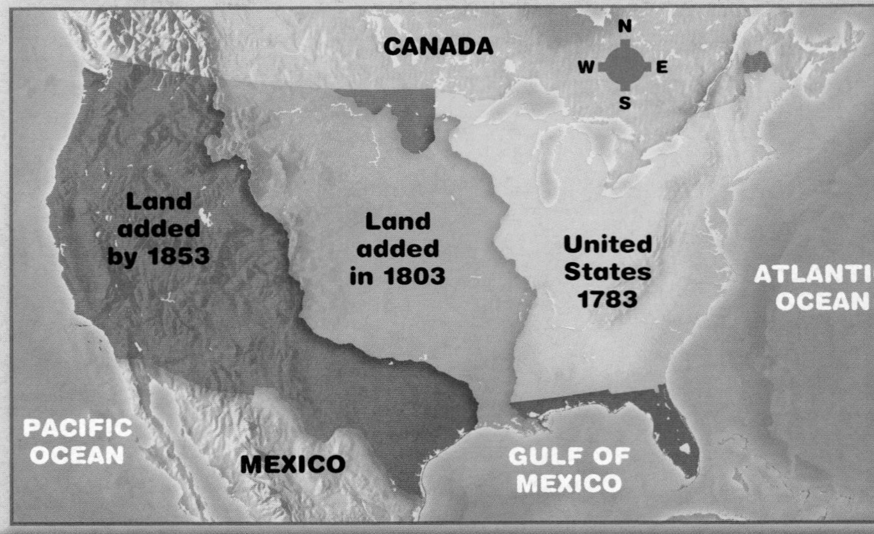

1. In what direction did the United States grow?
2. What bodies of water did the United States touch?
3. What country is south of the land added by 1853?

Practice and Extend

SOCIAL STUDIES Background

About the History Map

- In 1783, the Revolutionary War ended, and America became its own country, free of British rule. Lands were acquired as part of the treaty that ended the war.
- In 1803, President Thomas Jefferson bought land that was owned by France. The sale was called the *Louisiana Purchase*. The new land made the country almost twice as big.
- In the mid-1800s, Mexico sold the United States some land for ten million dollars. With this *Gadsden Purchase*, as the sale was called, our country grew to be the size and shape we recognize it to be today. The land acquired was the last piece in the puzzle to bring our country from ocean to ocean.

UNIT 1

Where We Live

UNIT 1

Unit 1 Planning Guide

Unit 1 • Where We Live

Begin with a Song pp. 2–3 **Vocabulary Preview** pp. 4–5

 **Reading Social Studies, Context and Picture Clues** pp. 6–7

Lesson Titles	Pacing	Main Ideas
Lesson 1 **Living in a Neighborhood** pp. 8–11 **Citizen Heroes: Caring Kids Care Clubs** pp. 12–13 **Problem Solving at the Library** pp. 14–15	3 days	• People live, work, and play in places called neighborhoods. Like rules at school, which can be amended through voting, laws help keep order in a neighborhood. • Kids Care Clubs in the U.S. and Canada help people in need. • Solving a problem is a multi-step process that involves cooperative behaviors.
Lesson 2 **A Walk Through a Community** pp. 16–19 **Map and Globe Skills: Read a City Map** pp. 20–21 **Then and Now: How a Community Changes** pp. 22–23	3 days	• Little Italy and Chinatown are just two of New York City's many diverse communities. • Cardinal directions and a map key are important parts of a map. • Like all communities, cities change over time. New York City has grown upward as it has gotten bigger and busier.
Lesson 3 **Comparing Communities** pp. 24–27 **Biography: Henrietta King** pp. 28–29	2 days	• Urban, rural, and suburban communities differ in some ways, but are alike in other ways. • Henrietta King was a Texas rancher who donated land for the benefit of the community.
Lesson 4 **Our State and Our Country** pp. 30–33 **Biography: Benjamin Banneker** pp. 34–35	2 days	• The United States is made up of fifty states and a capital city, Washington. D.C. Its neighbor to the north is Canada; to the south, Mexico. • Benjamin Banneker was a surveyor and inventor who helped in the building of Washington, D.C.
Lesson 5 **Our Country Is Part of Our World** pp. 36–39 DK **Children of the World** pp. 40–41	2 days	• The Earth has seven continents and four oceans; it is divided by an imaginary line called the equator. • Children around the world are alike in many ways: they go to school, play games, and wish for peace.

✓ **End with a Poem** pp. 42–43 ✓ **Unit 1 Review** pp. 44–47 ✓ **Unit 1 Project** p. 48

✓ = Assessment Options

Scott Foresman Social Studies
Indiana Academic Standards

Grade 2 Unit 1 • *Where We Live*

Lesson Title	Indiana Academic Standards Social Studies
Lesson 1 Living in a Neighborhood pp. 8-11	**IN Academic Standard 2.5.1** Identify responsibilities that individuals have. **(Also 2.2.1, 2.2.2, 2.2.5, 2.4.6, 2.5.2, 2.5.5)**
Citizen Heroes: Kids Care Clubs pp. 12-13	**IN Academic Standard 2.2.4** Identify good leaders and good citizens, and explain the qualities that make them admirable. **(Also 2.5.1, 2.5.2)**
Problem Solving at the Library pp. 14-15	**Previews IN Academic Standard 4.4.10** Explain how money helps people to save. Develop a savings plan.
Lesson 2 A Walk Through a Community pp. 16-19	**IN Academic Standard 2.5.5** Identify people of different backgrounds and explain how they contribute to the community.
Map and Globe Skills: Read a City Map pp. 20-21	**IN Academic Standard 2.3.6** Identify map symbols of cultural or human features. **(Also 2.3.1, 2.3.2, 2.3.3, 2.3.4, 2.3.5, 2.4.6)**
Then and Now: How a Community Changes pp. 22-23	**IN Academic Standard 2.1.2** Identify changes that have occurred in the community.
Lesson 3 Comparing Communities pp. 24-27	**IN Academic Standard 2.5.5** Identify people of different backgrounds and explain how they contribute to the community.
Biography: Henrietta King pp. 28-29	**IN Academic Standard 2.2.4** Identify good leaders and good citizens, and explain the qualities that make them admirable.
Lesson 4 Our State and Our Country pp. 30-33	**IN Academic Standard 2.3.3** Locate the local community and the U.S.
Biography: Benjamin Banneker pp. 34-35	**IN Academic Standard 2.2.4** Identify good leaders and good citizens, and explain the qualities that make them admirable.
Lesson 5 Our Country is Part of Our World pp. 36-39	**IN Academic Standard 2.3.3** Locate the local community and the U.S.
Children of the World pp. 40-41	**Reviews IN Academic Standard 1.5.5** Compare customs, foods, play, recreation, and celebrations.

Insert between pages 1b - 1c
For complete standards listing, please see front tab.

Continued on other side →

Scott Foresman Social Studies to the Indiana Academic Standards for English/Language Arts

Grade 2 Unit 1 • *Where We Live*

Lesson Title	Indiana Academic Standards English/Language Arts
Begin with a Song, pp. 2-3 *Vocabulary Preview, pp. 4-5* *Reading Social Studies, Context and Picture Clues, pp. 6-7*	**2.3.4** Identify the use of rhythm, rhyme, and alliteration (using words with repeating consonant sounds) in poetry. See also 2.1.1, 2.1.10, 2.2.7
Lesson 1 Living in a Neighborhood, pp. 8-11	**2.2.4** Ask and respond to questions to aid comprehension about important elements of informational texts. See also 2.1.1, 2.1.2, 2.1.3, 2.4.2
Citizen Heroes: Kids Care Clubs, pp. 12-13	**2.4.1** Create a list of ideas for writing. See also 2.4.2, 2.4.3, 2.4.5, 2.4.6, 2.4.7, 2.4.8, 2.5.2, 2.6.2, 2.6.3, 2.6.4, 2.6.5, 2.6.7, 2.6.8, 2.6.9, 2.7.11
Problem Solving at the Library, pp. 14-15	**2.2.4** Ask and respond to questions to aid comprehension about important elements of informational texts. See also 2.1.1, 2.1.2, 2.1.3, 2.1.5, 2.1.8, 2.2.5, 2.4.1, 2.4.2, 2.4.6, 2.4.7, 2.4.8
Lesson 2 A Walk Through the Community, pp. 16-19	**2.2.5** Restate facts and details in the text to clarify and organize ideas. See also 2.1.1, 2.1.2, 2.1.3, 2.1.5
Map and Globe Skills: Read a City Map, pp. 20-21	**2.2.7** Interpret information from diagrams, charts, and graphs. See also 2.4.6, 2.4.7, 2.4.8, 2.5.3, 2.5.5, 2.5.6, 2.6.1, 2.6.2, 2.6.3, 2.6.4, 2.6.5, 2.6.7, 2.6.8
Then and Now: How a Community Changes, pp. 22-23	**2.2.4** Ask and respond to questions to aid comprehension about important elements of informational texts. See also 2.4.6, 2.4.7, 2.4.8, 2.5.3, 2.5.5, 2.5.6, 2.6.1, 2.6.2, 2.6.3, 2.6.4, 2.6.5, 2.6.7, 2.6.8
Lesson 3 Comparing Communities, pp. 24-27	**2.2.4** Ask and respond to questions to aid comprehension about important elements of informational texts. See also 2.4.1, 2.4.2, 2.4.5, 2.4.6, 2.4.7, 2.4.8, 2.5.3, 2.5.5, 2.5.6, 2.6.1, 2.6.2, 2.6.3, 2.6.4, 2.6.5, 2.6.7, 2.6.8
Biography: Henrietta King, pp. 28-29	**2.2.6** Recognize cause-and-effect relationships in a text. See also 2.7.8, 2.7.10
Lesson 4 Our State and Our Country, pp. 30-33	**2.78** Retell stories, including characters, setting, and plot. See also 2.2.7
Biography: Benjamin Banneker, pp. 34-35	**2.2.4** Ask and respond to questions to aid comprehension about important elements of informational texts. See also 2.5.6, 2.6.1, 2.6.3, 2.6.7, 2.6.9
Lesson 5 Our Country Is Part of Our World, pp. 36-39	**2.2.7** Interpret information from diagrams, charts, and graphs. See also 2.2.4
DK Children of the World, pp. 40-41	**2.2.7** Interpret information from diagrams, charts, and graphs. See also 2.2.4
End with a Poem, pp. 42-43 *Unit 1 Review, pp. 44-47* *Unit 1 Project, p. 48*	**2.5.4** Write rhymes and simple poems. See also 2.5.5, 2.5.6, 2.6.1, 2.6.3, 2.6.4, 2.6.7, 2.6.8, 2.6.9

ocabulary	Resources	Meeting Individual Needs
law **vote**	• Workbook, pp. 3–4 • Transparencies 6, 10 • Vocabulary Cards: law, vote • Every Student Learns Guide, pp. 2–5	• ESL Support, TE p. 10 • Leveled Practice, TE p. 15a
community **history**	• Workbook, pp. 5–6 • Transparencies 5, 11 • Vocabulary Cards: community, history • Every Student Learns Guide, pp. 6–9	• ESL Support, TE pp. 18 • Leveled Practice, TE p. 23a
rural **suburb** **urban**	• Workbook, p. 7 • Transparency 4 • Vocabulary Cards: rural, suburb, urban • Every Student Learns Guide, pp. 10–13	• ESL Support, TE p. 27 • Leveled Practice, TE p. 29a
capital	• Workbook, p. 8 • Transparencies 8, 12 • Vocabulary Card: capital • Every Student Learns Guide, pp. 14–17	• ESL Support, TE p. 32 • Leveled Practice, TE pp. 35a
	• Workbook, p. 9 • Transparency 13 • Every Student Learns Guide, pp. 18–21	• ESL Support, TE p. 39 • Leveled Practice, TE p. 41a

Providing More Depth

Multimedia Library

- ***Building*** **by Philip Wilkinson**
- ***Night on Neighborhood Street*** **by Jan Spivey Gilcrest**
- **Songs and Music**
- **Video Field Trips**
- **Software**

Additional Resources

- Family Activities
- Vocabulary Cards
- Daily Activity Bank
- Desk Maps
- Big Book Atlas
- Outline Maps
- Social Studies Plus!

ADDITIONAL Technology

- AudioText
- The test maker
- Teacher Resources CD-ROM
- Map Resources CD-ROM
- **www.sfsocialstudies.com**

To establish guidelines for childrens' safe and responsible use of the Internet, use the **Scott Foresman Internet Guide.**

Additional Internet Links
To find out more about:

- participating in community life, visit **www.pbs.org**
- character development, visit **www.charactercounts.org**

Key Internet Search Terms

- citizenship
- pillars of character

Unit 1 Objectives

Beginning of Unit 1

- **Use music to learn about a topic.** (pp. 2–3)
- **Use pictures to obtain information.** (pp. 4–5)
- **Determine the meanings of words.** (pp. 4–5)
- **Use context clues to develop meanings of new words.** (pp. 6–7)

Lesson 1
Living in a Neighborhood pp. 8–11

- **Identify ways people can work together in the classroom and community by obeying rules and laws.**
- **Explain how rules can be made and changed by voting.**
- **Identify people who model good citizenship.** (pp. 12–13)
- **Use a problem-solving process.** (pp. 14–15)

Lesson 2
A Walk Through a Community
pp. 16–19

- **Recognize diversity in communities.**
- **Use symbols, find locations, and determine directions on maps.** (pp. 20–21)
- **Draw maps to show places.** (pp. 20–21)
- **Use vocabulary related to chronology, including *past, present*, and *future*.** (pp. 22–23)
- **Name several sources of information about a given period.** (pp. 22–23)

Lesson 3
Comparing Communities pp. 24–27

- **Compare rural, urban, and suburban communities.**
- **Identify contributions of historical figures.** (pp. 28–29)

Lesson 4
Our State and Our Country pp. 30–33

- **Locate communities, states, and countries on maps.**
- **Identify state and national symbols.**
- **Identify individuals of past and present significance to the community and nation.** (pp. 34–35)

Lesson 5
Our Country Is Part of Our World
pp. 36–39

- **Demonstrate map and globe skills.**
- **Obtain information from visual sources—photographs and maps.** (pp. 40–41)

End of Unit 1

- **Create poems to express ideas.** (pp. 42–43)

Assessment Options

✓ Formal Assessment

- **What did you learn?** PE/TE pp. 11, 19, 27, 33, 39
- **Unit Review,** PE/TE pp. 44–47
- **Unit 1 Tests, Assessment Book,** pp. 1–4
- **The test maker,** (test generator software)

✓ Informal Assessment

- **Teacher's Edition Questions,** throughout Lessons and Features
- **Close and Assess,** TE pp. 7, 11, 13, 15, 19, 21, 23, 27, 29, 33, 35, 39, 41, 43
- **Try it!** PE/TE pp. 7, 15, 21
- **Think and Share,** PE/TE pp. 11, 19, 27, 29, 33, 35, 39
- **Caring in Action,** PE/TE p. 13
- **Hands-on History,** PE/TE p. 23

Ongoing Assessment

Ongoing Assessment is found throughout the Teacher's Edition lessons using an **If...then** model.

If = students' observable behavior,

then = reteaching and enrichment suggestions

✓ Portfolio Assessment

- **Portfolio Assessment,** TE pp. 1, 46
- **Leveled Practice,** TE pp. 4, 15a, 23a, 29a, 35a, 41a
- **Workbook,** pp. 1–11
- **Unit Review: Skills on Your Own,** PE/TE p. 46
- **Curriculum Connection: Writing,** TE pp. 13, 15a, 19, 23, 26, 29a, 35a, 41a, 42

✓ Performance Assessment

- **Hands-on Unit Project** (Unit 1 Performance Assessment), PE/TE pp. 1, 48
- **Internet Activity,** PE p. 48
- **Unit Review: Write and Share,** PE/TE p. 47
- **Scoring Guides,** TE pp. 45, 46

Test Talk

Test-Taking Strategies

Understand the Question

- **Locate Key Words in the Question,** TE p. 10
- **Locate Key Words in the Text,** TE p. 38

Understand the Answer

- **Choose the Right Answer, Test Talk Practice Book**
- **Use Information from the Text,** TE p. 17
- **Use Information from Graphics,** TE p. 32
- **Write Your Answer,** TE p. 29

For additional practice, use the Test Talk Practice Book.

Featured Strategy

Locate Key Words in the Question

Children will:

- Find the key words in the question.
- Turn the key words into a statement that begins "I need to find out...."

PE/TE p. 47, **TE** p. 10

Curriculum Connections

Integrating Your Day

The lessons, skills, and features of Unit 1 provide many opportunities to make connections between social studies and other areas of the elementary curriculum.

Social Studies

Reading

"My Word Book," TE pp. 15a, 29a

Reading Skill—Context and Picture Clues, PE/TE pp. 6–7

Reading Skill—Main Idea and Details, TE p. 16

Crossword Puzzle, TE p. 23a

Reading Skill—Compare and Contrast, TE p. 24

Reading Skill—Recall and Retell, TE p. 30

Question and Answer Game, TE p. 35a

Reading Skill—Context Clues, TE p. 36

Writing

Write Project Plans, TE p. 13

Neighborhood Questions, TE p. 15a

Write a Journal Entry, TE p. 19

Timely Descriptions, TE p. 23

A Friendly Letter, TE p. 26

Writing Questions, TE p. 35

Interview, TE p. 35a

Pen Pal Letters, TE p. 41a

Adding Lines to the Poem, TE p. 42

Math

Counting Heads, TE p. 7

Adding and Subtracting, TE p. 33

Count the Kids!, TE p. 40

Literature

Read Together, TE p. 23a

Books About the City and the Country, TE p. 43

Read About Where You Live! TE p. 47

Science

Solving Environmental Problems, TE p. 15

Posters, TE p. 29a

The Solar System, TE p. 38

Music/Drama

Create a Skit, TE p. 29

"The More We Get Together," TE p. 41

'Round the World, TE p. 41a

Art

Make a Postcard, TE p. 21

Draw a Neighborhood, TE p. 23a

Build a Diorama, TE p. 29a

A "My Neighborhood" Poster, TE p. 42a

Look for this symbol throughout the Teacher's Edition to find **Curriculum Connections.**

Professional Development

Reading the Social Studies Textbook

by Candy Dawson Boyd, Ph.D.
St. Mary's College of California

The pedagogical and learning demands of reading social studies text with both understanding and engagement has daunted elementary teachers for too long. It is important to devote real time to the teaching of social studies, with the textbook as a core part of the active curriculum.

A critical first step is for the teacher to carefully explore both the Teacher's Edition and Pupil's Edition in the social studies textbook series. A perusal of the table of contents offers the structure of content in the form of units and lessons. Examining how individual components are structured at the lesson, special feature, unit, and overall textbook levels aids in assessing the reading strategies and skills readers need. Critical questions to ask include:

- How are lessons organized?
- Is vocabulary labeled in clear ways?
- Are illustrations and photographs presented where they need to be to serve as support for the reader?
- Are visuals presented in a way that informs the reader without being overwhelming?
- Are there a variety of clear, focused maps?

The answers to these questions will impact how easily the reader will be able to engage text. Below are some ways Scott Foresman *Social Studies* structures its program to help students read with understanding and engagement.

Every unit has a ***Vocabulary Preview*** *that introduces unit vocabulary and relates each word to a photograph. Students then are asked to find in an illustration examples that relate to each vocabulary word.*

Every unit has a ***Reading Social Studies*** *feature that highlights a target reading skill. Students are then encouraged to apply that strategy throughout the unit.*

Map and Globe Skills *features are found in many lessons. This allows students to connect visually to the content of the lesson while using map skills.*

ESL Support

by Jim Cummins, Ph.D.
University of Toronto

There is general agreement among cognitive psychologists that we learn by integrating new input into our existing cognitive structures. Our prior experience provides the foundation for interpreting new information. No learner is a blank slate. In reading, for example, we construct meaning by bringing our prior knowledge of language and of the world to the text. For example, a child who knows a lot about baseball will find it much easier to understand a story about baseball than a child who has very little prior knowledge about the game. The same holds true for social studies. The more a child already knows about a particular topic in the text, the more of the text he/she is likely to understand. And, the more of the text a child understands, the more new knowledge he/she can acquire.

Activate Prior Knowledge/ Build Background

The following examples in the Teacher's Edition will help you to activate children's prior knowledge and build background for the concepts developed in the lessons.

- ***Talking About Rules*** *on p. 10 helps English Language Learners articulate and develop further their understanding of the function of rules.*
- ***Recall Solving a Problem*** *on p. 14 encourages English Language Learners to share their personal experiences in problem-solving situations.*

Read Aloud

Sing a Song of People

By Lois Lenski

Sing a song of people
Walking fast or slow;
People in the city,
Up and down they go.

People on the sidewalk,
People on the bus;
People passing, passing,
In back and front of us.

Sing a song of people
Who like to come and go!

Build Background

- Ask children to tell about places where they might find many people walking, riding in cars or buses, hurrying here and there.
- Ask children to share their experience of being in a crowded place with lots of people moving around them.

Read Alouds and Primary Sources

Read Alouds and Primary Sources contains additional selections to be used with Unit 1.

Bibliography

Alphabet City, by Stephen T. Johnson (Puffin, ISBN 0-140-55904-3, 1999) **Easy** ***Caldecott Honor Book***

The Paperboy, by Dav Pilkey (Orchard, ISBN 0-531-07139-1, 1999) **Easy** ***Caldecott Honor Book***

Trashy Town, by Andrea G. Zimmerman and David Clemesha; Dan Yaccarino (illlustrator), (HarperCollins, ISBN 0-060-27139-6, 1999) **Easy** ***ALA Notable Book***

What Is a Community from A to Z? by Bobbie Kalman (Crabtree, ISBN 0-86505-384-7, 2000) **Easy**

Mama & Papa Have a Store, by Amelia Lau Carling and Amelia Lau (illustrator), (Dial Books for Young Readers, ISBN 0-803-72044-0, 1998) **On-Level**

Smoky Night, by Eve Bunting and David Diaz (illustrator), (Harcourt Brace, ISBN 0-152-01884-0, 1999) **On-Level** ***Caldecott Medal Winner***

Century Farm: One Hundred Years on a Family Farm, by Cris Peterson and Alvis Upitis (photographer), (Boyds Mills, ISBN 1-563-97710-9, 1999) **Challenge**

Island Boy, by Barbara Cooney (Puffin, ISBN 0-140-50756-6, 1991) **Challenge** ***Boston Globe/Horn Book Award***

Pioneer Church, by Carolyn Otto and Megan Lloyd (illustrator), (Henry Holt and Co., ISBN 0-805-02554-5, 1999) **Challenge** ***Notable Social Studies Book***

Uncle Willie and the Soup Kitchen, by DyAnne DiSalvo-Ryan (Mulberry Books, ISBN 0-688-15285-6, 1997) **Challenge** ***Reading Rainbow Book***

My Backyard History Book, by David Weitzman (Little Brown and Company, ISBN 0-316-92902-6, 1995) **Teacher Reference**

***Discovery Channel School* Videos**
Two Children, Two Cultures. Meet Koumba from Congo, in Africa, and Yeye from Shanghai, China, and get a taste of two different cultures; 25 minutes.

Look for this symbol throughout the Teacher's Edition to find **Award-Winning Selections**. Additional book references are suggested throughout this unit.

Practice and Extend

✓ **Unit 1 Performance Assessment**

- The Unit 1 Project, found on p. 48, is an ongoing performance assessment project to enrich children's learning throughout this unit.
- This project, which has children make a "Travel Channel" booklet, may be started now or at any time during this unit of study.
- A performance assessment scoring guide is located on p. 48.

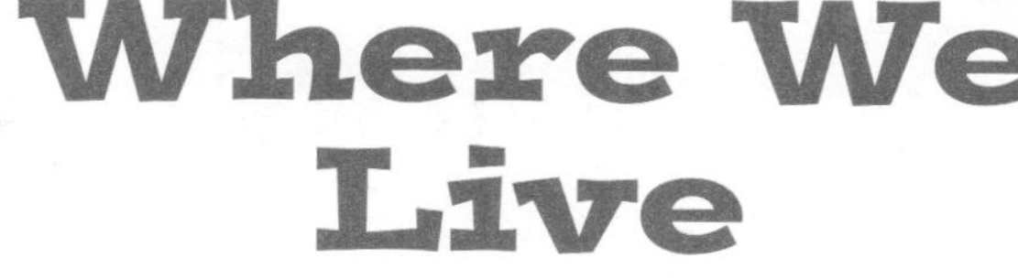

Unit Overview

This unit introduces children to the different places in which people live and describes the characteristics of each of these different places.

Introduce Joanna

Read the unit title and then introduce the featured child for this unit as a second grader named Joanna. Talk about where Joanna lives as shown on her favorite snow globe.

Unit Question

- Ask children the question on this page.
- Ask children to describe the places in which they live. Are the buildings big or small? Are there many people living there or few people? Is there a lot of street traffic or little traffic?
- To activate prior knowledge, list on the board the words or phrases children use to describe the places in which they live.

✓ **Portfolio Assessment** Keep a copy of this list for the Portfolio Assessment at the end of the unit.

Places Where We Live

Objective

- Use music to learn about a topic.

Resources

- *Songs and Music* CD "Places Where We Live"
- Poster 1
- Social Studies Plus!

Introduce the Song

Preview Tell children that they will be singing a song about places where people live. Focus first on the picture of Joanna, and then on the photo of New York City in the background.

Warm Up To activate prior knowledge, use the list generated in response to the Unit question (p. 1). Ask children if any words or phrases on the list could also be used to describe the place where Joanna lives.

Sing the Song

- Have children sing the song "Places Where We Live."
- Suggest that children add sound effects to the song. Brainstorm ideas for sound effects for each kind of community: a big city, a suburb, a town. Then sing the song again, adding the sound effects.
- Help children write a new verse that tells about where they live. Suggest that they use words and phrases from the list that describe where they live.

Practice and Extend

SOCIAL STUDIES Background

About New York City

New York City has several famous landmarks.

- The Brooklyn Bridge connects the boroughs of Manhattan and Brooklyn. Designed by John Roebling, it was the world's largest suspension bridge when it opened in 1883.
- Until the tragic events of September 11, 2001, the World Trade Center's twin towers were a landmark in the New York skyline. The towers, each 110 stories, were designed by Minoru Yamasaki and were completed between 1973 and 1974. Children who live in New York City or who are familiar with the cityscape through personal experience or media exposure may have a need to talk about what happened the day the towers fell. Allow children to do so.
- You may wish to use the suggestions in the special section, pp. TR1–TR2, in this Teacher's Guide to help children deal with fear and loss.

Talk About the Picture

Identify the city in the photo as New York City. Point out all the skyscrapers, and ask children what they think it would be like to live in a place with so many tall buildings.

1 **How do you think Joanna feels about New York City?** She looks very happy in the photo. She probably likes living in New York City. **Make Inferences**

2 **Many of the tall buildings you see in the photo are offices where people work. Where do you think these people may live?** Answers will vary but may include in apartments in the city or in houses in the suburbs. **Draw Conclusions**

3 **How do you think people who live in the areas outside the city get to their jobs in the city?** Some probably travel by car. Others may take trains or buses. **Hypothesize**

4 **What else do the buildings in the picture suggest about New York City?** Answers will vary but may include that New York is a busy, crowded city. **Draw Conclusions**

AUDIO CD
Technology

Play the CD, *Songs and Music*, to listen to "Places Where We Live."

Vocabulary Preview

Objectives

- Use pictures to obtain information.
- Determine the meanings of words.

Resources

- Workbook, p. 1
- Vocabulary Cards
- Poster 2

Introduce the Vocabulary

Read aloud and point to each vocabulary word and the photograph illustrating it. Have volunteers give the meanings of the words. Then have children find several examples of vocabulary words in the illustration. Write these examples on the board.

Vocabulary Word	Illustrated Examples
law	Signs: stop, no bike riding, put trash here
vote	Show-of-hands vote, voting box
community	Wall pictures of city, farm area, suburb
history	Victrola, old photos, old-fashioned toy car
urban	City picture with tall buildings
suburb	Picture of family homes
rural	Picture of farm
capital	Map of Indiana showing Indianapolis

Social Studies Strand
Citizenship

Listed below are some basic principles of citizenship for young children. Direct your discussion of the illustration toward the further development of these concepts.

- rules and laws and their purpose
- need for participation in the neighborhood or community
- qualities of citizenship: belief in truth, justice, equality, and responsibility
- people in the past and present contribute to community and nation
- respect for different cultures and traditions

Practice and Extend

MEETING INDIVIDUAL NEEDS
Leveled Practice

Visit the Classroom

Have children suppose it is visitors' day in the classroom shown. Take a look around together.

Easy Talk first about the classroom setting, using the appropriate vocabulary words. Call on volunteers to follow your lead. Then talk about the action that children see. Focus on the meaning of *vote*. Have children raise their hands to show one way to vote. **Reteach**

On-Level Have children describe one part of the illustration. Encourage use of appropriate new vocabulary. Ask listeners to point to that part of the picture. **Extend**

Challenge Have children take turns writing a vocabulary word on the board that matches a volunteer's description of part of the illustration. **Enrich**

urban

suburb

rural

capital

5

Talk About the Illustration

Allow children time to study the illustration. Ask if there are more boys, more girls, or the same number of boys and girls in the classroom.

Encourage children to tell how the classroom shown is like and different from their classroom. Call attention to the board. Read aloud what the children are voting on and the choices listed.

1 **What are three different kinds of communities the children are learning about? Tell how you know.** Urban, suburb, and rural; from the pictures in the classroom **Analyze Pictures**

2 **What do you see that shows a state and its capital city?** Map **Analyze Pictures**

3 **What do the signs on the wall next to the board show?** Rules; what to do and what not to do **Draw Conclusions**

Look Ahead

Tell children they will learn more about each of the vocabulary words as they study Unit 1.

You may want to revisit the picture with children to review the concepts and vocabulary in the unit.

4 **Why are some children raising their hands?** They are showing that they want to do one of the things listed on the board at recess; they are voting. **How is the teacher keeping track of the vote?** She is making a mark for each vote someone makes for one of the choices. **Analyze Pictures**

WEB SITE
Technology

You can look up vocabulary words online. Click on *Social Studies Library* and select the dictionary at **www.sfsocialstudies.com.**

Workbook, p. 1

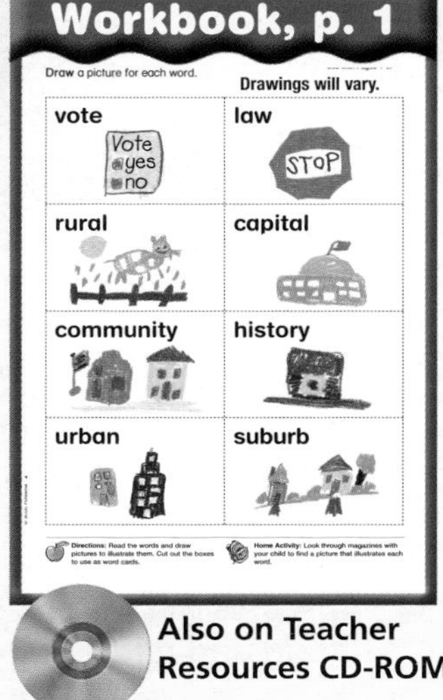
Draw a picture for each word.

Drawings will vary.

vote	law
rural	capital
community	history
urban	suburb

Also on Teacher Resources CD-ROM.

We Belong to Groups

Use Context and Picture Clues

Objective

- Use context clues to develop meanings of new words.

Resource

- Workbook, p. 2

About the Unit Target Skill

- The target reading skill for this unit is Context Clues.
- Children are introduced to the unit target skill here and are given an opportunity to practice it.
- Further opportunities to find context clues are found throughout Unit 1.

1 Introduce and Motivate

Preview To determine if children understand the concept of context clues, ask children to pretend that you don't know what the word *chair* means. Ask them to make up oral sentences that would help you figure out what *chair* means. List responses on the board. Review the responses and conclude that a chair is something on which to sit.

Warm Up To activate prior knowledge, write on the board: *The robin flapped its wings. It flew to a tree branch*. Read the sentences with children. Have them say what a robin is. Ask what words in the sentences could have helped them know that a robin is a bird.

Reading Social Studies

We Belong to Groups

Use Context and Picture Clues

Hi! I'm Joanna. I belong to many groups. A **group** is a gathering of people or things. People in a group can do activities together.

If you don't know what a word means, look at the words around it to find some clues. These clues will help you find its meaning.

Mrs. Ward asked the singers to stand together as a group.

6

Practice and Extend

BUILD BACKGROUND ESL Support

Use Clues Model drawing pictures of a person alone and of several people in a group, labeling each *alone* or *group*. Have each child make two similar drawings.

Beginning Point to the picture of the person alone and say *alone*. Have children do the same. Repeat for the picture of the group. Say *Point to the group of people* and *Point to the person alone*.

Intermediate Write sentences about the pictures, such as *This person is alone*. Have children read the sentences aloud and name the context clues for *alone* and *group*.

Advanced Have children turn their drawings facedown and take turns picking a drawing and creating two sentences with context clues about it.

Pictures can also help you learn the meaning of a word. Look at these pictures. How do they help you learn the meaning of **group?**

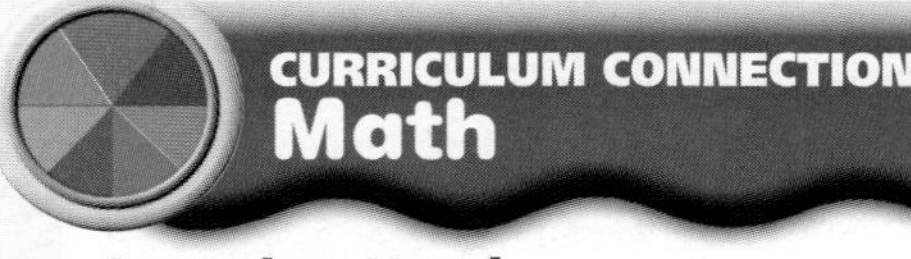

Draw a picture of two groups. Tell or write about what people do in each group.

7

2 Teach and Discuss

- Read aloud pp. 6–7 to the class. Review the word *group.* Ask children to identify any groups to which they belong. Make a quick list.
- Direct children's attention to the pictures on p. 7. Have children describe what they see in each one. Immediately after talking about each picture, ask: *Who is in this group?*
- Help children summarize by noting that by looking for clues in the pictures they have learned that a group can be a family, friends, or a swimming class.

3 Close and Assess

Try it!

Children's drawings or sentences should include details or clues that would help someone figure out the meaning of the word *group.*

CURRICULUM CONNECTION Math

Counting Heads

Have children count the people shown in each group. Then ask them to add the numbers to get a total. Tell children to add to or subtract from the total to solve the following:

- Another teacher and one more child join the swim class group.
- Grandma joins the family group.
- One friend in the friends' group goes home.

Have children share and compare their answers.

Workbook, p. 2

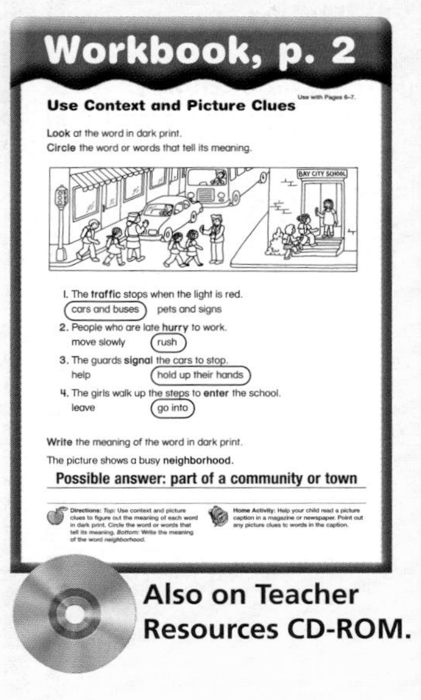

Use Context and Picture Clues Use with Pages 6–7.

Look at the word in dark print.
Circle the word or words that tell its meaning.

1. The **traffic** stops when the light is red.
   (cars and buses) pets and signs
2. People who are late **hurry** to work.
   move slowly (rush)
3. The guards **signal** the cars to stop.
   help (hold up their hands)
4. The girls walk up the steps to **enter** the school.
   leave (go into)

Write the meaning of the word in dark print.

The picture shows a busy **neighborhood.**

Possible answer: part of a community or town

Directions: *Top:* Use context and picture clues to figure out the meaning of each word in dark print. Circle the word or words that tell its meaning. *Bottom:* Write the meaning of the word *neighborhood.*

Home Activity: Help your child read a picture caption in a magazine or newspaper. Point out any picture clues to words in the caption.

Also on Teacher Resources CD-ROM.

Workbook Support

Use the following Workbook pages to support content and skills development as you teach Unit 1. You can also view and print Workbook pages from the Teacher Resources CD-ROM.

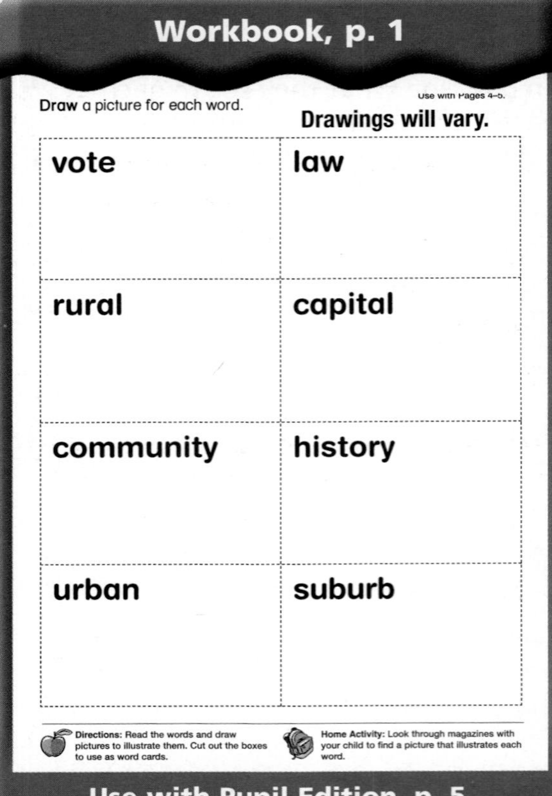

Workbook, p. 1

Use with Pages 4–5.

Draw a picture for each word. **Drawings will vary.**

vote	law
rural	capital
community	history
urban	suburb

Directions: Read the words and draw pictures to illustrate them. Cut out the boxes to use as word cards.

Home Activity: Look through magazines with your child to find a picture that illustrates each word.

Use with Pupil Edition, p. 5.

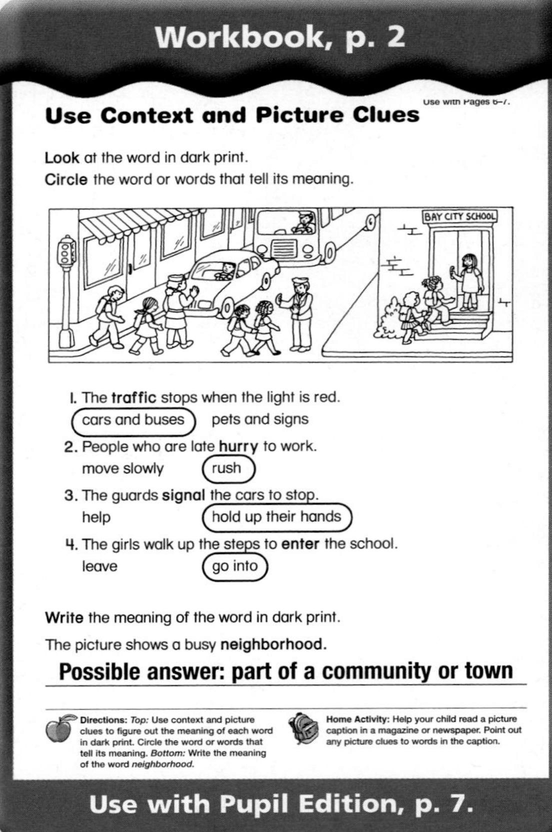

Workbook, p. 2

Use with Pages 6–7.

Use Context and Picture Clues

Look at the word in dark print.
Circle the word or words that tell its meaning.

1. The **traffic** stops when the light is red.
   cars and buses — pets and signs
2. People who are late **hurry** to work.
   move slowly — rush
3. The guards **signal** the cars to stop.
   help — hold up their hands
4. The girls walk up the steps to **enter** the school.
   leave — go into

Write the meaning of the word in dark print.

The picture shows a busy **neighborhood.**

Possible answer: part of a community or town

Directions: *Top:* Use context and picture clues to figure out the meaning of each word in dark print. Circle the word or words that tell its meaning. *Bottom:* Write the meaning of the word *neighborhood.*

Home Activity: Help your child read a picture caption in a magazine or newspaper. Point out any picture clues to words in the caption.

Use with Pupil Edition, p. 7.

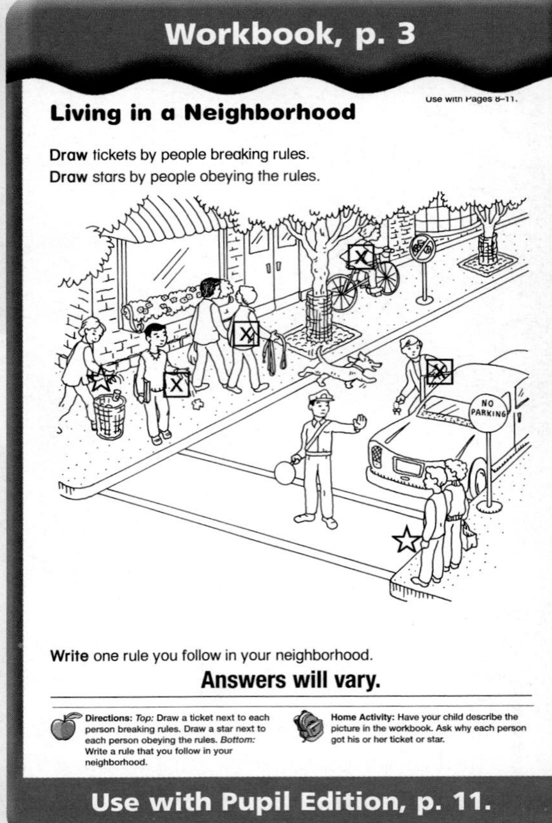

Workbook, p. 3

Use with Pages 8–11.

Living in a Neighborhood

Draw tickets by people breaking rules.
Draw stars by people obeying the rules.

Write one rule you follow in your neighborhood.

Answers will vary.

Directions: *Top:* Draw a ticket next to each person breaking rules. Draw a star next to each person obeying the rules. *Bottom:* Write a rule that you follow in your neighborhood.

Home Activity: Have your child describe the picture in the workbook. Ask why each person got his or her ticket or star.

Use with Pupil Edition, p. 11.

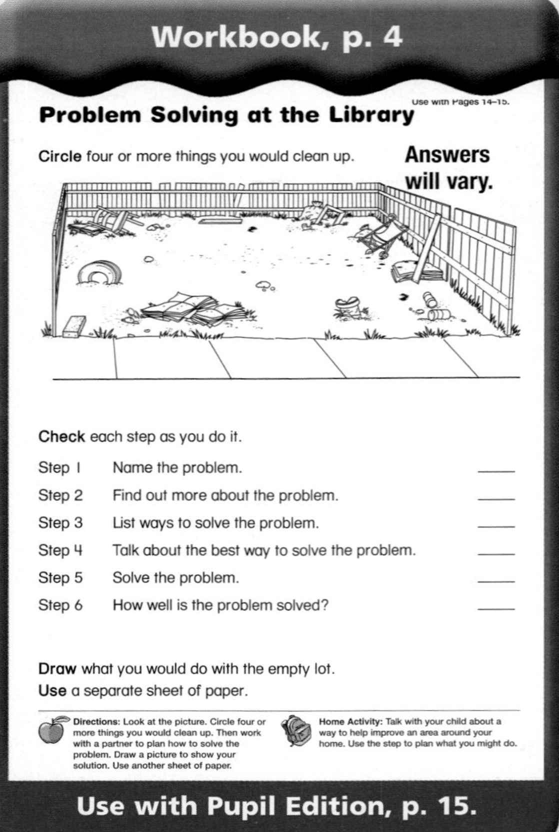

Workbook, p. 4

Use with Pages 14–15.

Problem Solving at the Library

Circle four or more things you would clean up. **Answers will vary.**

Check each step as you do it.

Step 1	Name the problem.	___
Step 2	Find out more about the problem.	___
Step 3	List ways to solve the problem.	___
Step 4	Talk about the best way to solve the problem.	___
Step 5	Solve the problem.	___
Step 6	How well is the problem solved?	___

Draw what you would do with the empty lot.
Use a separate sheet of paper.

Directions: Look at the picture. Circle four or more things you would clean up. Then work with a partner to plan how to solve the problem. Draw a picture to show your solution. Use another sheet of paper.

Home Activity: Talk with your child about a way to help improve an area around your home. Use the step to plan what you might do.

Use with Pupil Edition, p. 15.

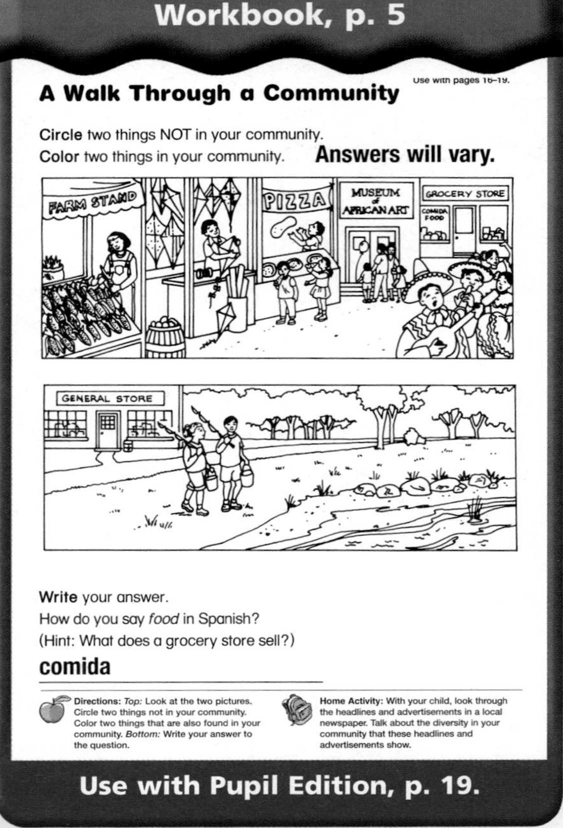

Workbook, p. 5

Use with pages 16–19.

A Walk Through a Community

Circle two things NOT in your community.
Color two things in your community. **Answers will vary.**

Write your answer.
How do you say *food* in Spanish?
(Hint: What does a grocery store sell?)

comida

Directions: *Top:* Look at the two pictures. Circle two things not in your community. Color two things that are also found in your community. *Bottom:* Write your answer to the question.

Home Activity: With your child, look through the headlines and advertisements in a local newspaper. Talk about the diversity in your community that these headlines and advertisements show.

Use with Pupil Edition, p. 19.

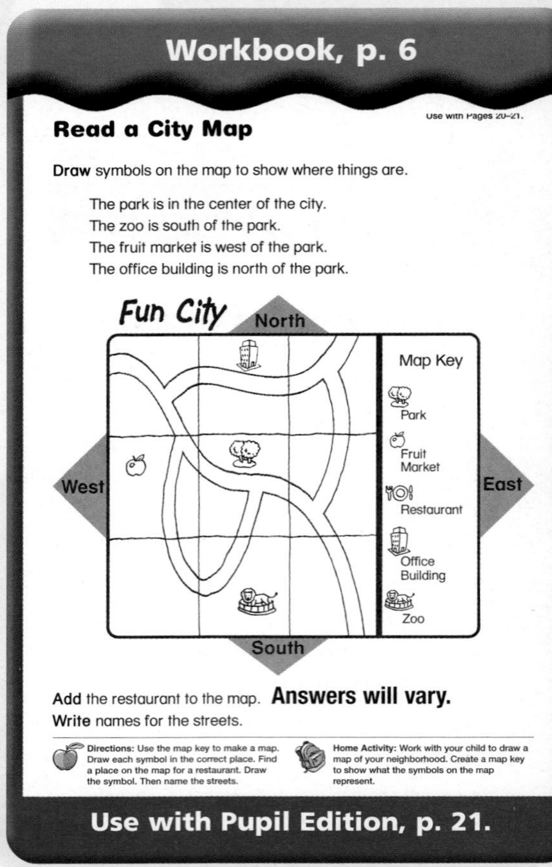

Workbook, p. 6

Use with Pages 20–21.

Read a City Map

Draw symbols on the map to show where things are.

The park is in the center of the city.
The zoo is south of the park.
The fruit market is west of the park.
The office building is north of the park.

Add the restaurant to the map. **Answers will vary.**
Write names for the streets.

Directions: Use the map key to make a map. Draw each symbol in the correct place. Find a place on the map for a restaurant. Draw the symbol. Then name the streets.

Home Activity: Work with your child to draw a map of your neighborhood. Create a map key to show what the symbols on the map represent.

Use with Pupil Edition, p. 21.

Workbook Support

Workbook, p. 7

Use with Pages 24–27.

Comparing Communities

Circle the correct answers.

What two things do you find in an urban community?

cows (skyscrapers) (subway)

What two things would you NOT find in a suburb?

(farms) houses (corn fields)

Draw a picture of a rural community. **Drawings will vary.**

Directions: *Top:* Circle the answers to each question. *Bottom:* Draw a picture of a rural community.

Home Activity: Talk with your child about the type of community in which you live. Make a list of the features that identify your community as urban, suburban, or rural.

Use with Pupil Edition, p. 27.

Workbook, p. 8

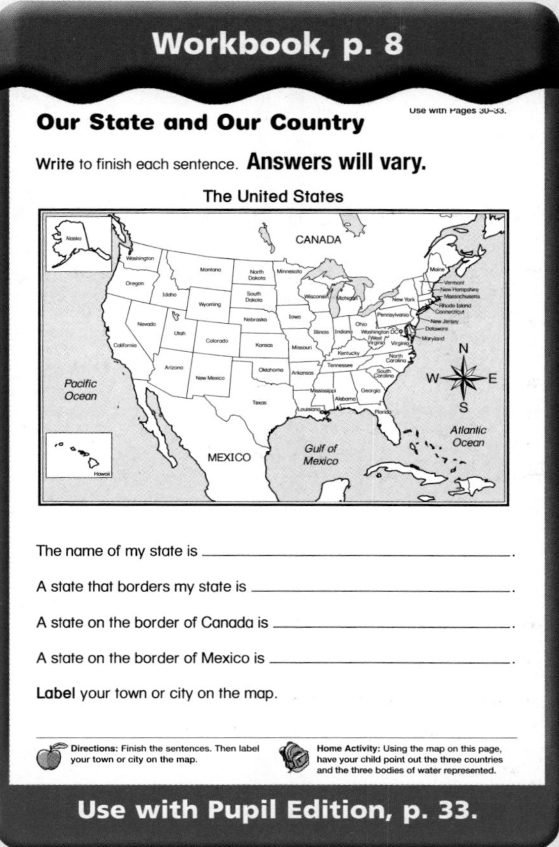

Use with Pages 30–33.

Our State and Our Country

Write to finish each sentence. **Answers will vary.**

The United States

The name of my state is ______.

A state that borders my state is ______.

A state on the border of Canada is ______.

A state on the border of Mexico is ______.

Label your town or city on the map.

Directions: Finish the sentences. Then label your town or city on the map.

Home Activity: Using the map on this page, have your child point out the three countries and the three bodies of water represented.

Use with Pupil Edition, p. 33.

Workbook, p. 9

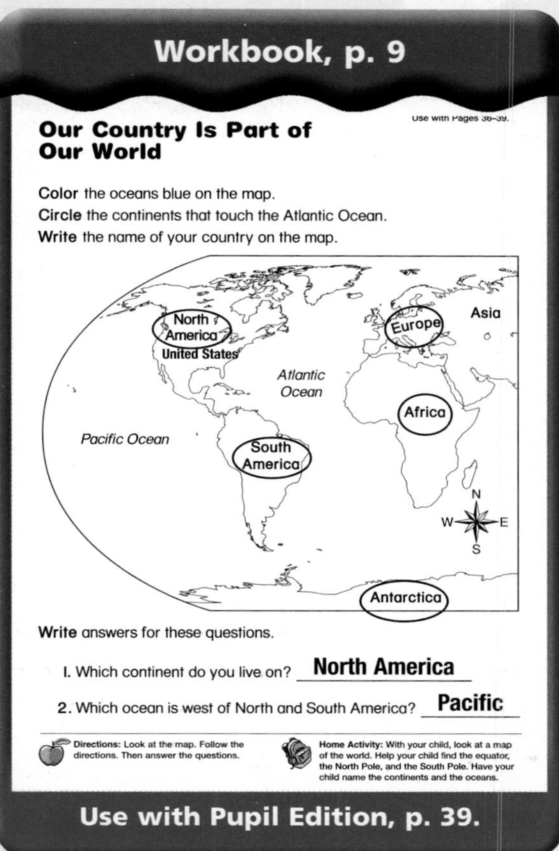

Use with Pages 36–39.

Our Country Is Part of Our World

Color the oceans blue on the map.
Circle the continents that touch the Atlantic Ocean.
Write the name of your country on the map.

Write answers for these questions.

1. Which continent do you live on? **North America**
2. Which ocean is west of North and South America? **Pacific**

Directions: Look at the map. Follow the directions. Then answer the questions.

Home Activity: With your child, look at a map of the world. Help your child find the equator, the North Pole, and the South Pole. Have your child name the continents and the oceans.

Use with Pupil Edition, p. 39.

Workbook, p. 10

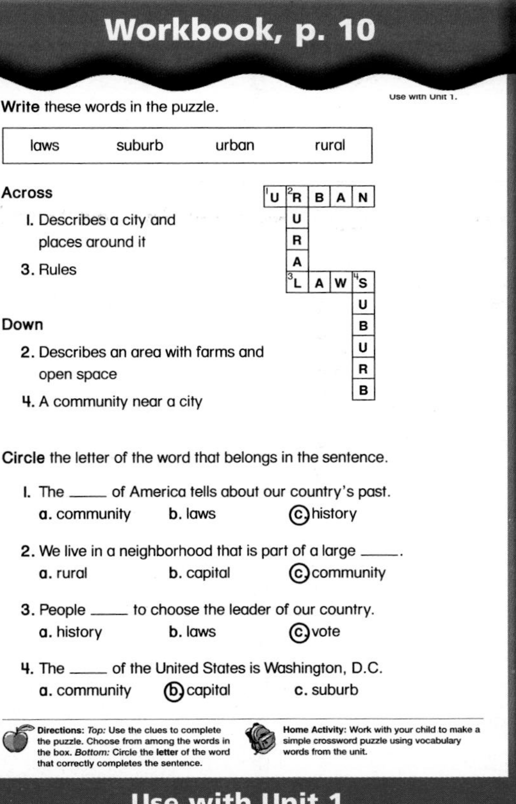

Use with Unit 1.

Write these words in the puzzle.

laws	suburb	urban	rural

Across

1. Describes a city and places around it
3. Rules

Down

2. Describes an area with farms and open space
4. A community near a city

Puzzle answers: 1 Across URBAN; 2 Down RURAL; 3 Across LAWS; 4 Down SUBURB

Circle the letter of the word that belongs in the sentence.

1. The ____ of America tells about our country's past.
   a. community b. laws (c.) history
2. We live in a neighborhood that is part of a large ____.
   a. rural b. capital (c.) community
3. People ____ to choose the leader of our country.
   a. history b. laws (c.) vote
4. The ____ of the United States is Washington, D.C.
   a. community (b.) capital c. suburb

Directions: *Top:* Use the clues to complete the puzzle. Choose from among the words in the box. *Bottom:* Circle the letter of the word that correctly completes the sentence.

Home Activity: Work with your child to make a simple crossword puzzle using vocabulary words from the unit.

Use with Unit 1.

Workbook, p. 11

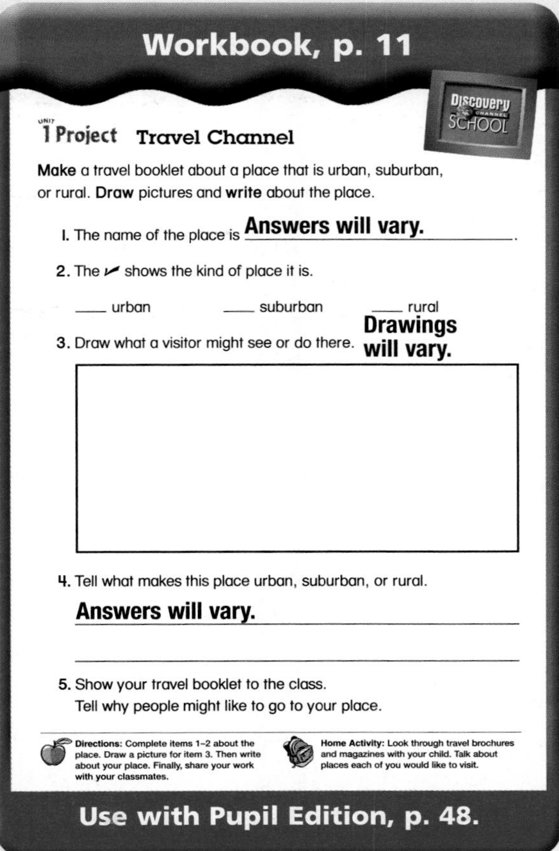

Discovery Channel School

Unit 1 Project **Travel Channel**

Make a travel booklet about a place that is urban, suburban, or rural. **Draw** pictures and **write** about the place.

1. The name of the place is **Answers will vary.**
2. The ✔ shows the kind of place it is.
   ___ urban ___ suburban ___ rural
3. Draw what a visitor might see or do there. **Drawings will vary.**
4. Tell what makes this place urban, suburban, or rural.
   Answers will vary.
5. Show your travel booklet to the class.
   Tell why people might like to go to your place.

Directions: Complete items 1–2 about the place. Draw a picture for item 3. Then write about your place. Finally, share your work with your classmates.

Home Activity: Look through travel brochures and magazines with your child. Talk about places each of you would like to visit.

Use with Pupil Edition, p. 48.

Assessment Support

Use these Assessment Book pages and the test maker to assess content and skills in Unit 1. You can also view and print Assessment Book pages from the Teacher Resources CD-ROM.

Assessment Book, p. 1

Unit 1: Content Test

Circle a word to finish each sentence.

1. My cousin lives on a very large farm in a _____ area.
   (rural) urban community
2. Reading stories about the past is a good way to learn about _____.
   law (history) community
3. Who will you _____ for the next time we choose a class president?
   capital law (vote)
4. I visited the White House during my trip to the _____ of our country.
   community suburb (capital)

TEST PREP Which word completes each sentence?

1. A suburb is a kind of _____.
   a. law b. history
   c. capital (d.) community
2. Our town has a _____ against jaywalking.
   a. vote b. rural
   (c.) law d. history

Use with Pupil Edition, p. 44.

Assessment Book, p. 2

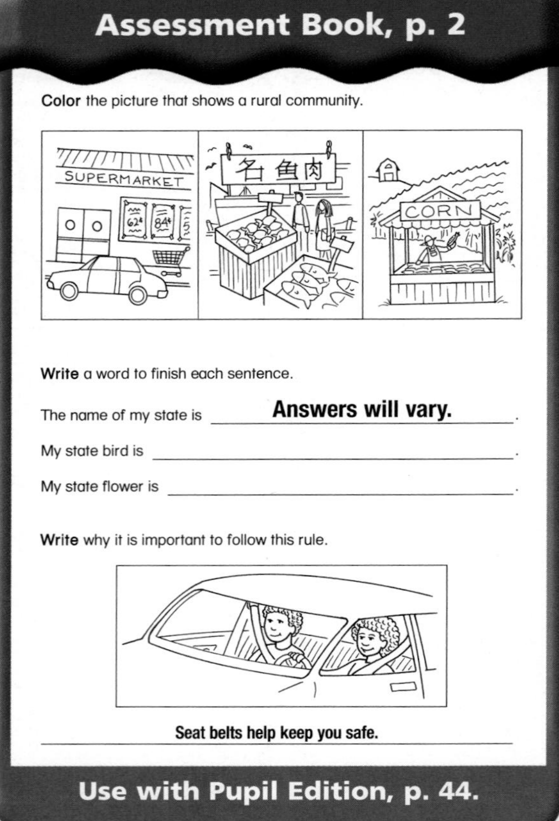

Color the picture that shows a rural community.

Write a word to finish each sentence.

The name of my state is **Answers will vary.**

My state bird is _____________.

My state flower is _____________.

Write why it is important to follow this rule.

Seat belts help keep you safe.

Use with Pupil Edition, p. 44.

Assessment Book, p. 3

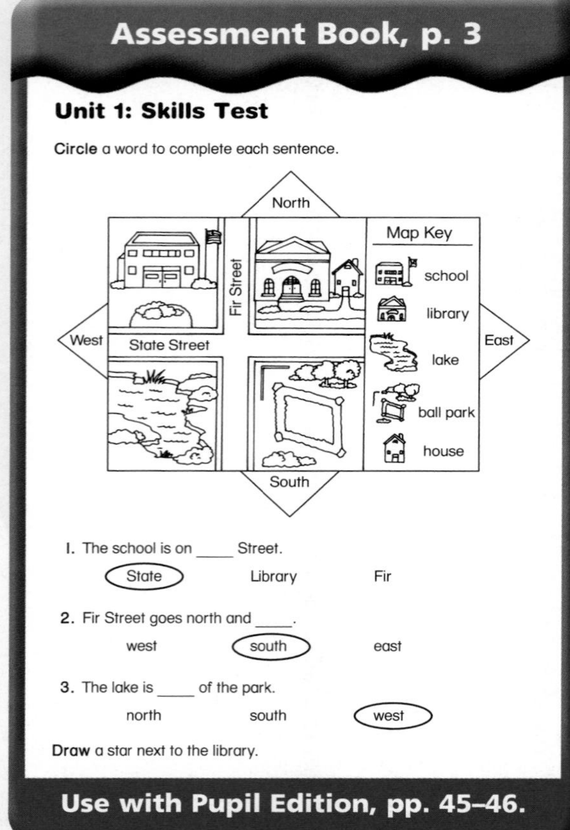

Unit 1: Skills Test

Circle a word to complete each sentence.

1. The school is on _____ Street.
   (State) Library Fir
2. Fir Street goes north and _____.
   west (south) east
3. The lake is _____ of the park.
   north south (west)

Draw a star next to the library.

Use with Pupil Edition, pp. 45–46.

Assessment Book, p. 4

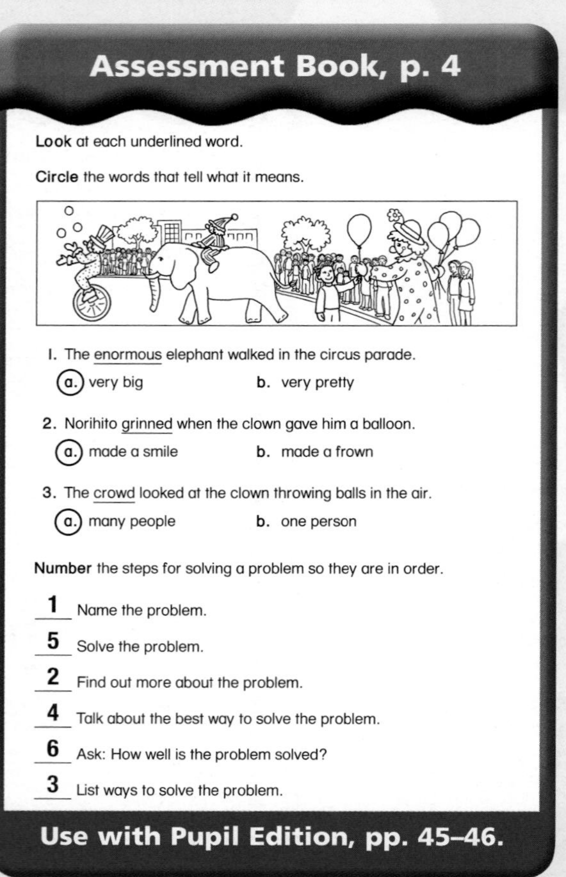

Look at each underlined word.

Circle the words that tell what it means.

1. The enormous elephant walked in the circus parade.
   (a.) very big b. very pretty
2. Norihito grinned when the clown gave him a balloon.
   (a.) made a smile b. made a frown
3. The crowd looked at the clown throwing balls in the air.
   (a.) many people b. one person

Number the steps for solving a problem so they are in order.

1 Name the problem.
5 Solve the problem.
2 Find out more about the problem.
4 Talk about the best way to solve the problem.
6 Ask: How well is the problem solved?
3 List ways to solve the problem.

Use with Pupil Edition, pp. 45–46.

Lesson 1 Overview

Lesson	Objective	Time and Resources
Living in a Neighborhood pages 8–11	Children will learn meanings for the words *law* and *vote*. They will recognize how laws and rules keep the people who live in a neighborhood safe.	 Time 20–30 minutes Resources • Workbook, p. 3 • Vocabulary Cards law vote • Every Student Learns Guide, pp. 2–5
Kids Care Clubs pages 12–13	Children will learn how Kids Care Clubs organize projects that benefit the community.	Time 15–20 minutes
Problem Solving at the Library pages 14–15	Children will learn how to solve a problem by following a series of steps.	 Time 15–20 minutes Resource • Workbook, p. 4

Build Background

Activity

The Sign Says ___?

 **Time** 15–20 minutes

Have children make a neighborhood sign that they see every day or create a design for a new street sign they think would protect or benefit the neighborhood. Have children begin by cutting out a shape for their sign. Children then write words or draw a picture on their shape that states or shows the rule or law.

If time is short, have children brainstorm ideas for important signs. List their ideas on the board. When the list is complete, choose one of the ideas. On the board sketch out children's suggestions for a sign to go along with the idea.

Read Aloud

In Our Neighborhood

by Christopher Erickson

On our busy streets,
Above and to the side,
In every shape and size,
There are signs to help and guide.

The red one says to STOP!
A green light signals go.
An arrow tells us "turn."
A warning sign says NO!

In our neighborhood,
We safely work and play
Because we all obey
The safety signs and rules.

Living in a Neighborhood

Objectives

- Identify ways people can work together in the classroom and community by obeying rules and laws.
- Explain how rules can be made and changed by voting.

Vocabulary

law a rule that everyone must follow (p. 9)

vote to make a choice about something (p. 11)

QUICK Teaching Plan

If time is short, have children look at the pictures and name some of the things they do in their neighborhood every day.

- Have children brainstorm a list of the rules and laws they follow in their neighborhood.

1 Introduce and Motivate

Preview Read aloud the title of the lesson. Ask children what a neighborhood is. Then ask volunteers to name a building in their neighborhood. Do they or their family members visit this building? Why or why not?

Warm Up To activate prior knowledge, ask children to name some of the things they did this week in their neighborhoods. Tell them to think about the people they saw, the places they visited, and the games they played. Then have volunteers act out one thing they did in their neighborhood such as played baseball, shopped in a store, or planted a garden.

Living in a Neighborhood

My home and school are in my neighborhood. A neighborhood is a place where people live, work, play, and help each other. Look at these pictures of my neighborhood. My neighborhood is a very busy place! What is your neighborhood like?

8

Practice and Extend

READING SKILL Context Clues

Display the graphic below.

- Have children help you complete it to show the words or phrases in the text that helped them better understand the meaning of one of the lesson's vocabulary words.

WEB SITE Technology

You can look up vocabulary words online. Click on *Social Studies Library* and select the dictionary at **www.sfsocialstudies.com.**

We have many rules in our busy neighborhood. Rules tell us what to do and what not to do. Rules help keep us safe.

A rule that everyone must follow is called a **law.** When people follow laws, they keep our neighborhood safe and clean.

A sign often tells us what to do to follow a law. What laws do these signs show? ❸

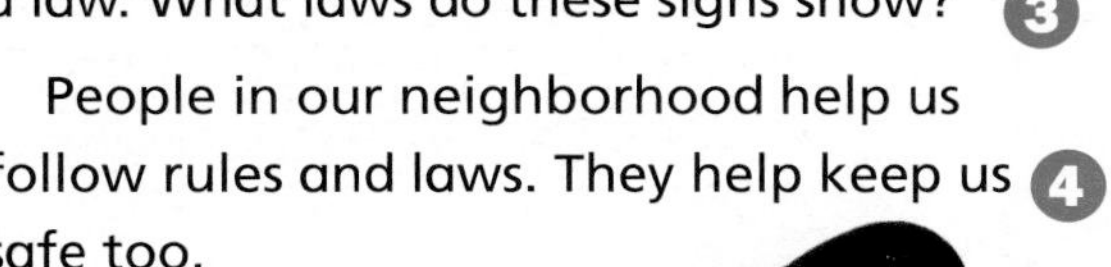

People in our neighborhood help us follow rules and laws. They help keep us ❹ safe too.

9

2 Teach and Discuss

Tell children that the photos show Joanna's neighborhood. Ask children to name the things they see in the photos.

Page 8

❶ **What makes Joanna's neighborhood a busy place?** Possible answer: People in the photo are shopping, walking, and driving. **Analyze Pictures**

❷ **Compare and contrast what you see in the photographs with things you see in your own neighborhood. Are they the same or similar? Are they different?** Possible answer: They are different. My neighborhood has a big playground. **Compare and Contrast**

Ongoing Assessment

If... children need help comparing and contrasting,	**then...** use a Venn diagram to graph the similarities and differences.

Page 9

Display the Vocabulary Card **law** and share its meaning as "a rule that people must obey or follow." Ask volunteers to name a rule they follow every day. Then, discuss the importance of following laws and rules. Discuss how laws can help maintain order and provide safety and security.

❸ **What signs do you see on your way to school every day? How do these signs protect people in the neighborhood?** Possible answer: There is a sign that reads *Children at Play*. It reminds drivers that they should watch out for children playing. **Apply Information**

❹ **Who do you think helps the people in your neighborhood follow the laws?** Answers may include: police officers, crossing guards **Make Inferences**

FYI SOCIAL STUDIES Background

Possible Misconceptions

- Children may think that all neighborhoods are the same size and are comprised of the same things.
- Neighborhoods can vary in size from one block to several blocks to even a small town.
- Some neighborhoods contain a school, several stores, and different places in which people live, while other neighborhoods contain only houses or small apartment buildings. Large cities usually contain several different neighborhoods.

continued

Page 10

Tell children to look at the photo on this page. Ask volunteers to describe the photo and explain why rules on a school bus are important.

Begin an ongoing classroom list of ways children currently participate responsibly in neighborhood life. As you read through the unit, have children add to the list.

Test Talk

Locate Key Words in the Question

5 What other rules do you follow when riding the bus? Possible answers: I speak quietly with others. I don't shout or make the bus driver turn around because I am noisy.

Have children ask themselves, "What is this question about?" Tell children that words that tell what the question is about are key words.
Apply Information

6 What rules do you follow when riding a bicycle? Possible answers: I wear a helmet. I never make sudden stops. **Express Ideas**

Every morning, I ride the bus to school. Our bus driver makes sure that we stay in our seats. This is an important rule. What do you think might happen if we did not follow this rule? 5 6

10

Practice and Extend

ESL
ACTIVATE PRIOR KNOWLEDGE
ESL Support

Talking About Rules Ask children to think about a rule they followed this morning before they came to school.

Beginning Have children pantomime the activity they performed as they followed the rule.

Intermediate Ask children to draw a picture of the rule they followed and to label the rule.

Advanced Have children write about the rule they followed. Encourage children to write several sentences.

For additional ESL support, use Every Student Learns Guide, pp. 2–5.

7 We also follow rules in school. Our principal, the leader of our school, makes some of these rules. These rules help us work and play together.

8 We help our teacher make some of the classroom rules. Today, we voted on a new rule.
9 To **vote** is to make a choice about something. Sometimes, we vote to change a rule to make it better.

What did you learn?

1. Make a list of rules that you follow at home or at school.
2. How do people in your neighborhood follow laws? Tell what might happen if people did not follow these laws.
3. **Think and Share** Explain what the word *neighborhood* means. Use words and pictures from the lesson to tell about the meaning of neighborhood.

11

Workbook, p. 3

Living in a Neighborhood

Draw tickets by people breaking rules.
Draw stars by people obeying the rules.

Write one rule you follow in your neighborhood.
Answers will vary.

Also on Teacher Resources CD-ROM.

Page 11

Make the point with children that they have a right to feel safe at school and traveling to and from school, but they have the responsibility to follow safety rules.

7 **Why are school rules important?** They help us work and play together. They keep us safe in the school. **Cause and Effect**

8 **Who helps you follow rules in other places you go to?** Possible answer: On a team, coaches explain the rules because they understand how to play the game. **Draw Conclusions**

9 **What kinds of things have you voted on?** Possible answers: Where we should go on a class field trip, what game to play at recess **Recall and Retell**

3 Close and Assess

Discuss with children the rules you have for your classroom. Ask if there is one rule they would like to vote to change in some way. Have children explain how they think the change would improve life in the classroom.

What did you learn?

1. Children's answers should include the rules they follow daily at home or in school.
2. Answers will vary. Possible answers: People don't park their cars near fire hydrants. If they did not follow this law, fire trucks could not get water to put out fires.
3. **Think and Share** Children's answers should reflect their understanding that neighborhoods are places in which they work, live, play, and help each other.

CITIZEN HEROES

Kids Care Clubs

Objective

- Identify people who model good citizenship.

1 Introduce and Motivate

Preview Have children look at the photos to see what citizen heroes they will read about. On p. 13, point out that *Caring* is starred in the Citizenship logo. Have children identify some caring behaviors.

Warm Up To activate prior knowledge, have volunteers tell about ways they help others in their neighborhood. Then introduce Kids Care Clubs as an organization that works within a neighborhood to help the people who live there.

2 Teach and Discuss

Pages 12–13

Read p. 12 to the class. Have a volunteer read the map caption. Add to children's geography awareness by pointing out Connecticut on a map of the United States.

❶ **Who do the Kids Care Clubs help?** Possible answers: Older people who need help with their yards, neighbors in need, people who have lost their homes due to earthquakes or storms.
Analyze Information

❷ **How have the Kids Care Clubs helped people?** Possible answers: They have made snacks for children in homeless shelters, collected books for children who need them, collected food, blankets, and toys for earthquake victims.
Recall and Retell

CITIZEN HEROES

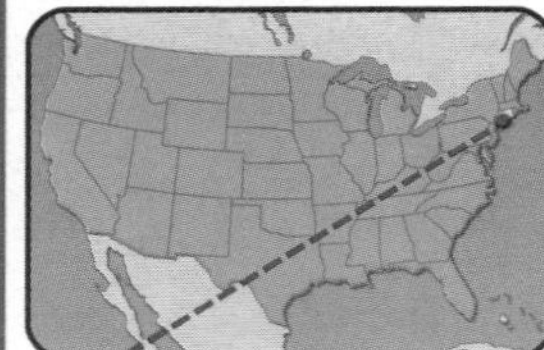

The Kids Care Clubs started in New Canaan, Connecticut.

Kids Care Clubs

Kids Care Clubs first began when a group of children decided to rake a lawn for a neighbor who was old. Later, these children ❶ made lunches to give to a soup kitchen. The children felt good because they were able to help neighbors in need.

Today, more than 25,000 children are part of Kids Care Clubs in the United States and Canada. These children have learned how important it is to help others.

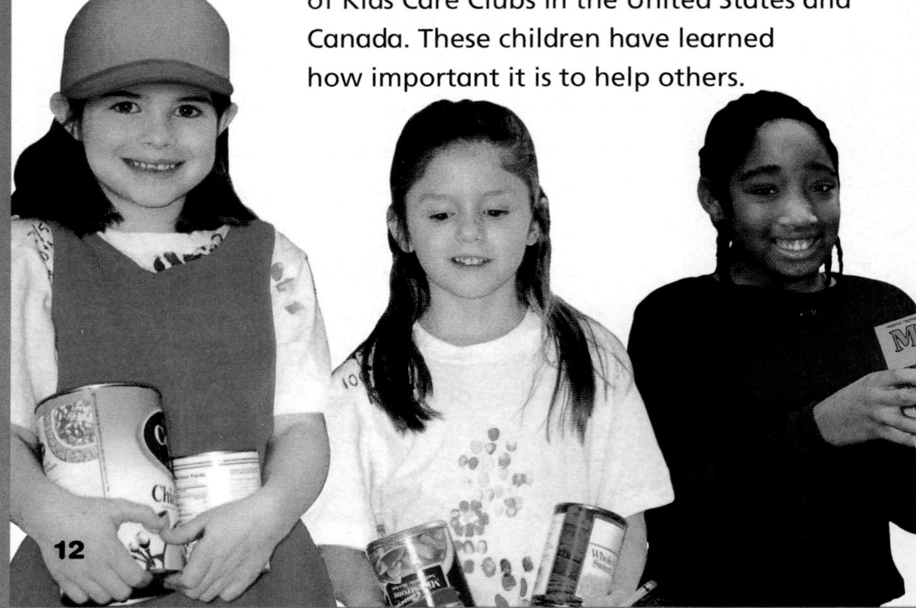

12

Practice and Extend

SOCIAL STUDIES STRAND
Citizenship

Caring

- Tell children that Kids Care Clubs help people within a neighborhood in many different ways. Explain that there are many other organizations, both large and small, that help people around the world.
- Mention that many charitable organizations raise money to provide needy people across the United States and in different countries with such things as food and medicine.
- Have children think about a club, organization, or group in their school or community that helps people. Ask volunteers to talk about how the club or group benefits the neighborhood.

Children in Kids Care Clubs show they care by working on special projects. Some clubs collected food, toys, and blankets for people who lost their homes in an earthquake. One club made bedtime snacks for children in a homeless shelter.

A Kids Care Club at Holmes School in Darien, Connecticut, collected books for other children who needed them. They did this to share their love of reading with others. 2 3 4

Caring in Action

Think of ways to show that you care about people in your school and neighborhood.

13

CURRICULUM CONNECTION

Writing

Write Project Plans

- Have children think about their own neighborhood. Is there a project or a service that would benefit their neighborhood?
- Form small groups. Have each group brainstorm, develop, and write a plan for a neighborhood or community project. Suggest possible projects such as providing a friendly visitor service to senior citizens or painting all of the benches in the schoolyard.
- Have each group present their completed plans to the class.

Make the point with children that their school is a kind of "little neighborhood." They and all who work in the school are "neighbors." Talk about how each day children demonstrate good-neighbor behaviors. Touch on respect, fairness, sharing, and caring.

3 **How might a Kids Care Club help a neighborhood after a hurricane?** Possible answers: They might give away bottled water or food. They might help with cleanup efforts. **Solve Problems**

4 **Why do you think people join groups?** Answers may include: They share the same interests. They like working with others to get things done. **Draw Conclusions**

3 Close and Assess

Caring in Action

Read the question and have children discuss possible answers. Responses might include: *I show I care for my neighborhood by using trash bins; I show I care for my school by sharing books and art supplies with other students.*

Encourage children to put their understanding of good citizenship into action. Encourage them, for example, to take the initiative when a new student comes to class. Children can introduce the newcomer and explain the school and classroom rules.

Problem Solving at the Library

Objective

- Use a problem-solving process.

1 Introduce and Motivate

Preview Tell children that sometimes libraries do not have enough books for all the people who like to read. Explain that books cost money and that some libraries do not have a lot of money.

Warm Up To activate prior knowledge, ask children to think about what they do when they have a problem. Do they talk to someone about the problem? Do they try to solve it themselves? Tell children they will read about a problem at a community library and learn a step-by-step method for solving the problem.

2 Teach and Discuss

Pages 14–15

Have children read pp. 14–15. Then review each step in the problem-solving process with the class.

1 **Why do you think it's important for the library to get more books?** Possible answers: Many people like to read. There should be enough books for everyone. **Make Inferences**

2 **Why are Steps 1 and 2 important?** They name and explain the problem. **Analyze Information**

Thinking Skills

Problem Solving at the Library

Joanna's class read a newspaper story about a problem at their community library. Here are the steps the class took to help solve the problem.

1

Step 1 Name the problem.

Neighborhood News
Library Needs Books
Our community library does not have enough children's books.
Kids Love to Read

Step 2 Find out more about the problem. 2

Let's talk to the librarian.

Step 3 List ways to solve the problem.

- **Bring books from home.**
- **Have a bake sale to make money for books.**
- **Collect pennies to buy books.**

14

Practice and Extend

ACTIVATE PRIOR KNOWLEDGE
ESL Support

Recall Solving a Problem Pantomime and name a problem children may have had during a typical school day, such as forgetting to bring lunch or losing a pencil or notebook.

Beginning Have children pantomime or draw a picture that reflects a similar problem and how they solved it. Name the actions or label the pictures for children.

Intermediate Have partners tell each other about a problem they once experienced and how they solved it.

Advanced Have individual children write about a problem they experienced and the steps they used to solve it.

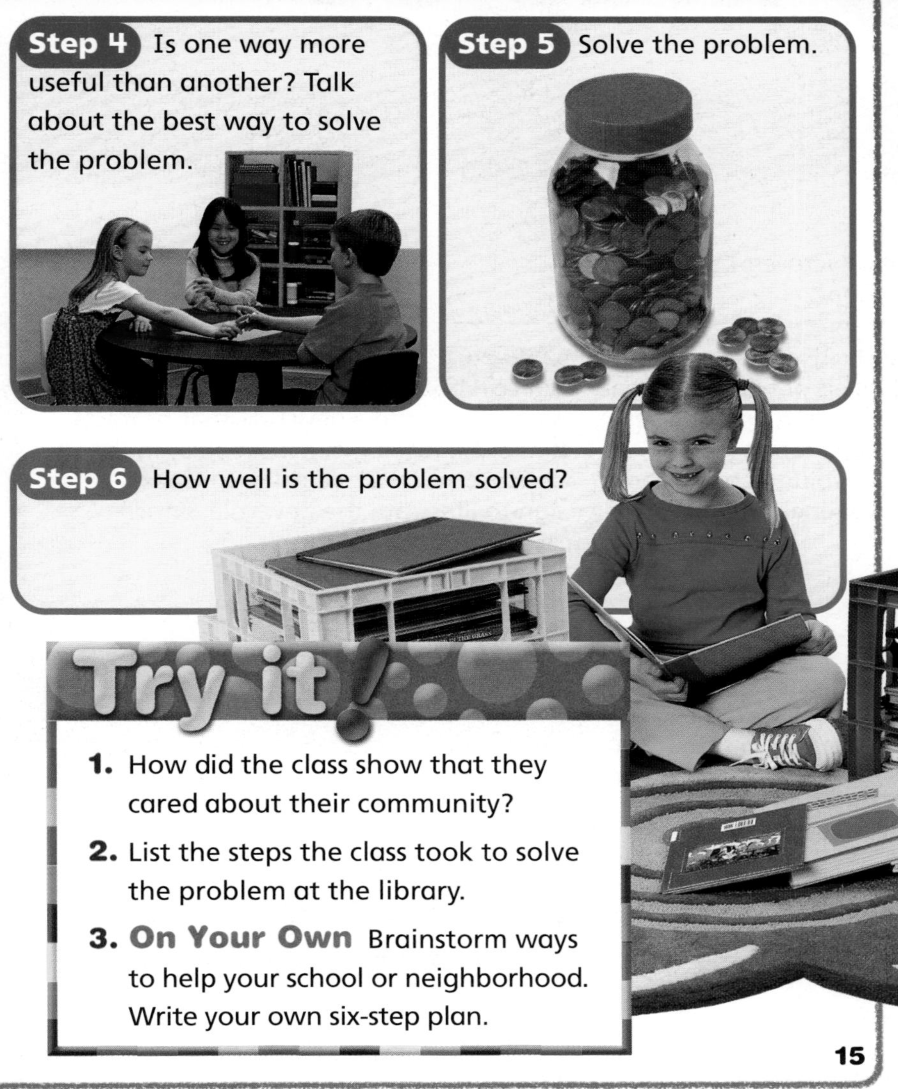

Step 4 Is one way more useful than another? Talk about the best way to solve the problem.

Step 5 Solve the problem.

Step 6 How well is the problem solved?

Try it!

1. How did the class show that they cared about their community?
2. List the steps the class took to solve the problem at the library.
3. **On Your Own** Brainstorm ways to help your school or neighborhood. Write your own six-step plan.

15

❸ **Why do you think it's helpful to list different ways to solve a problem?** Possible answer: Because then you can choose the best solution **Make Inferences**

❹ **In which step do you think Joanna's class could have voted? Why?** Step 4; If they couldn't all agree on the best solution, they could choose the solution with the most votes. **Make Inferences**

❺ **How will Joanna know if she and her class solved the library books problem well?** Answers may include: They will see their books being read and enjoyed at the library. **Hypothesize**

3 Close and Assess

Try it!

1. They tried to solve a problem that the community faced.
2. The class named a problem. They found out more about the problem. They listed possible solutions. They talked about each solution and decided on the best one. They solved the problem. They evaluated how well the problem had been solved by going to the library and looking at the new books.
3. **On Your Own** Answers will vary. Make sure each step in the problem-solving plan is clearly identified.

CURRICULUM CONNECTION Science

Solving Environmental Problems

- Tell children that air pollution, water pollution, and littering hurt the environment.
- Discuss how one of these problems might be solved. Record children's ideas. Reread the listed ideas.
- Model how to rewrite the ideas in the form of a clear, step-by-step problem-solving program. Have children add to the final plan by contributing any necessary steps.

Workbook, p. 4

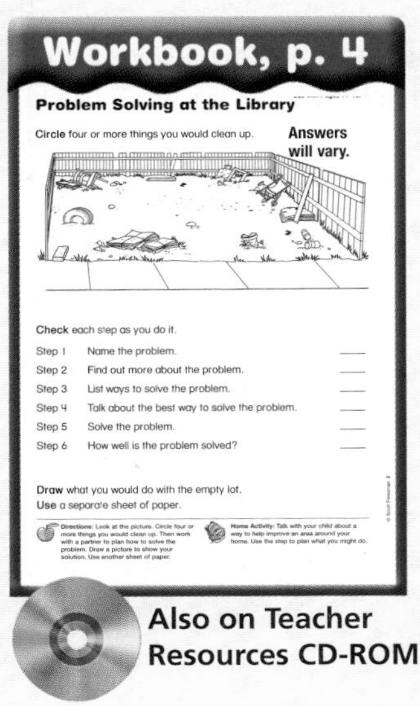

Problem Solving at the Library

Circle four or more things you would clean up. **Answers will vary.**

Check each step as you do it.

Step 1	Name the problem.	___
Step 2	Find out more about the problem.	___
Step 3	List ways to solve the problem.	___
Step 4	Talk about the best way to solve the problem.	___
Step 5	Solve the problem.	___
Step 6	How well is the problem solved?	___

Draw what you would do with the empty lot.
Use a separate sheet of paper.

Directions: Look at the picture. Circle four or more things you would clean up. Then work with a partner to plan how to solve the problem. Draw a picture to show your solution. Use another sheet of paper.

Home Activity: Talk with your child about a way to help improve an area around your home. Use the step to plan what you might do.

Also on Teacher Resources CD-ROM.

Use with pages 8–13

Lesson 1 Wrap-Up

MEETING INDIVIDUAL NEEDS

Leveled Practice

Find Important Signs

Provide newspapers and magazines. Have each child cut out a picture of a sign that shows a rule or law that protects people living in a neighborhood.

Easy Have children use their signs to make a classroom bulletin board. Help children arrange their signs on the board and draw a long roadway that loops around and about the signs. **Reteach**

On-Level Have each child create a label that briefly explains his or her sign. *What does it mean? Who does it protect?* Tell children to attach their labels next to their signs. Then ask volunteers to read aloud their labels. **Extend**

Challenge Review the completed bulletin board with children. Then have each child write a new rule that protects him or her at home, at school, or in the neighborhood. Have children create a sign to illustrate the new rule. **Enrich**

Hands-on Activities

CURRICULUM CONNECTION

Reading

"My Word Book"

Objective Define and illustrate the words *law* and *vote*.

Resources Vocabulary Cards: **law, vote**

Materials crayons, pencils

Learning Style Visual

Individual

Time 10–15 minutes

1. Display the Vocabulary Cards. Have children make "L" and "V" pages for a word book and have them write the words *law* and *vote* on those pages.

2. Have children draw pictures to illustrate the words and write a sentence below or next to each picture using the vocabulary word.

SOCIAL STUDIES STRAND

Citizenship

Rule Book

Objective Make a school rule book.

Materials construction paper, pencils, crayons

Learning Style Linguistic/Visual

Individual

Time 15–20 minutes

1. Have each child choose a rule he or she follows in school.

2. Tell each child to create a page for that rule by writing and illustrating the rule.

3. Collect the finished pages and organize them into a booklet. Review the finished rule book in class or set aside time for children to review the book on their own.

CURRICULUM CONNECTION

Writing

Neighborhood Questions

Objective Write questions for a questionnaire. Gather and interpret information.

Materials paper, pencils

Learning Style Verbal

Partners

Time 10–15 minutes

1. Assign partners. Tell children to think of laws that might help cut down noise and littering and make streets safe for walkers.

2. Have partners choose a topic. They should write two questions using these patterns: Do you think there is (too much horn honking) in the neighborhood? (Yes/No) Would you vote for a law that says: ____?

3. Have children get responses to their questions and report back.

Lesson 2 Overview

A Walk Through a Community **pages 16–19**	Children will learn the meaning of the word *community*. They will learn about some of the different neighborhoods that make up a city.	 Time 20–30 minutes Resources • Workbook, p. 5 • Vocabulary Card **community** • Transparency 2 • Every Student Learns Guide, pp. 6–9
Read a City Map **pages 20–21**	Children will learn how to read a city map.	 Time 15–20 minutes Resource • Workbook, p. 6
How a Community Changes **pages 22–23**	Children will learn how communities change over time.	 Time 15–20 minutes Resources • Workbook, p. 7 • Vocabulary Card **history**

Build Background

Activity

Make a Cityscape

 **Time** 20-30 minutes

Talk with children about what they might see in a big city. Give examples such as buses, tall buildings, and train stations. Then have children draw a place or a thing they think would be in a city. Collect children's drawings in a Cityscape Bulletin Board.

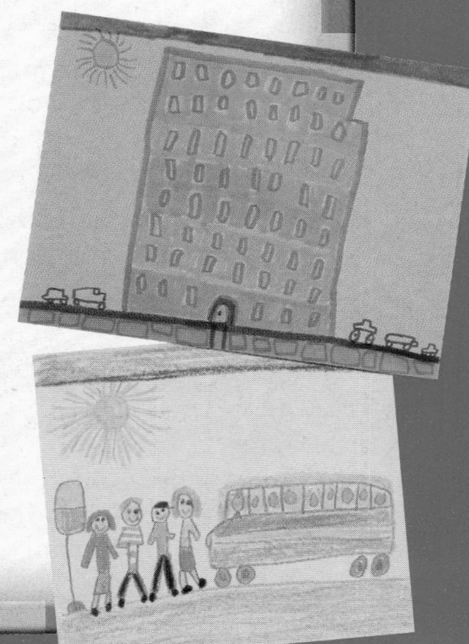

If time is short, ask each child in turn to name something he or she would see in a big city. Then have children explain why their thing or place is important.

Read Aloud

Community Life

by Hannah Meyer

Cars and buses
Honk and beep.
People and trains,
No time to sleep!

Buildings reach
Up to the sky.
Dream in the park
As time passes by.

Places to go,
Things to see.
Community life
Is right for me!

A Walk Through a Community

Objective

- Recognize diversity in communities.

Vocabulary

community a place that is made up of many neighborhoods (p. 16)

QUICK Teaching Plan

If time is short, have children look through the pictures and make a list of the different things they see in the community of New York.

- Have children make a list of the different things they see in their own community.

1 Introduce and Motivate

Preview Display the Vocabulary Card **community** and share its meaning "as a place that is made up of many neighborhoods." Have children locate the word as they preview the lesson. Explain that the pictures in the lesson show some of the things that people can see and do in a community.

Warm Up To activate prior knowledge, tell children to think of the community in which they live. What do they see in their community? What kinds of things do they do in their community? Who lives in their community?

Have children choose one of the things they see or do in their community and draw a picture of it. Display the pictures in class for children to review.

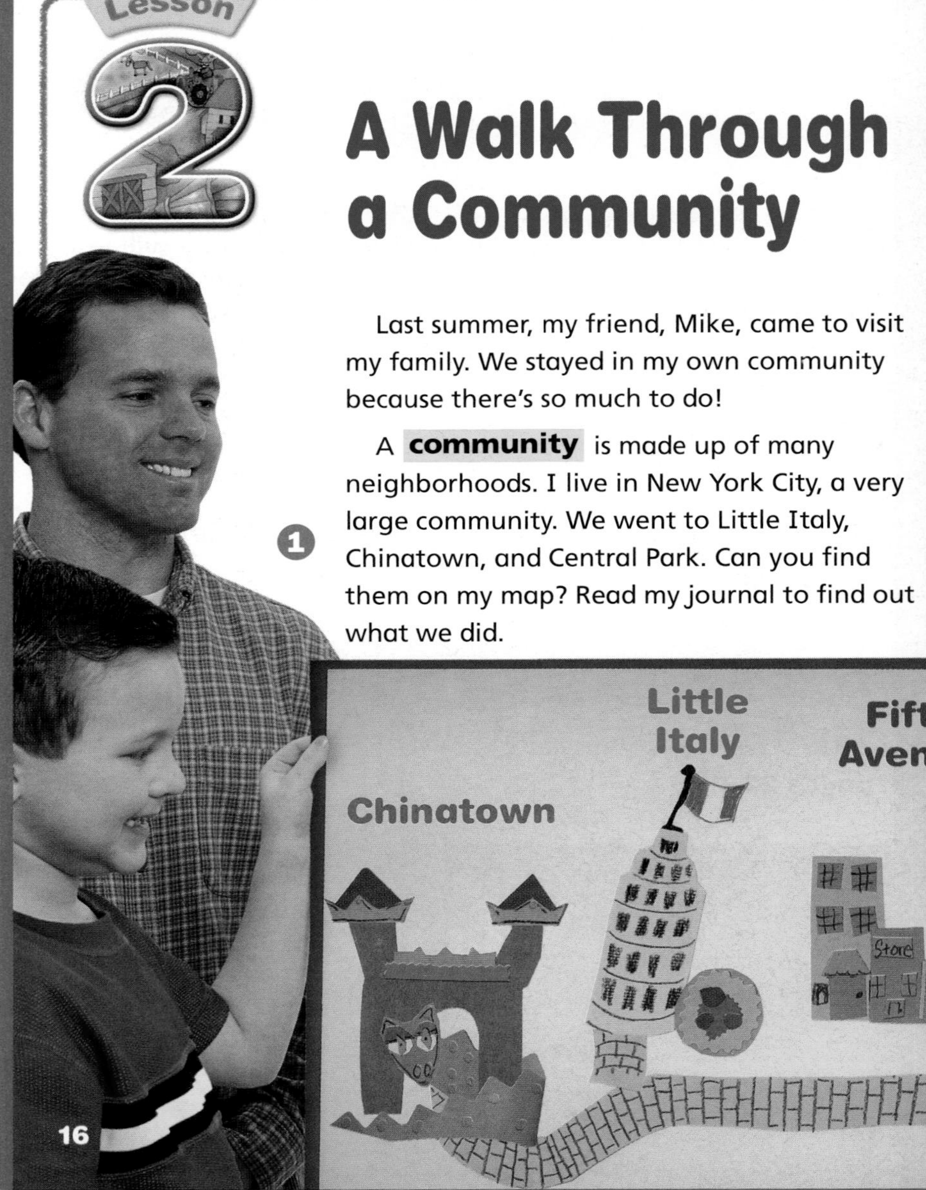

Practice and Extend

READING SKILL Main Idea and Details

- Tell children that the main idea of the lesson is that "Communities are made up of many neighborhoods."
- After they read pp. 16–19, give children a copy of Transparency 5.
- Have them complete it to show the "details" or information in the lesson that "supports" the main idea.

WEB SITE Technology

You can look up vocabulary words online. Click on *Social Studies Library* and select the dictionary at **www.sfsocialstudies.com.**

Cafe in Little Italy

Italian ice

SOCIAL STUDIES
Background

Possible Misconceptions

- Some children may think that *only* Chinese people live in Chinatown and that *only* Italian people live in Little Italy.
- In the past this was largely true.
- In the present each neighborhood includes people from other ethnic/cultural groups.

2 Teach and Discuss

Page 16

Tell children to look at Joanna's map. Explain that it shows only a small part of the city. Point out Little Italy and Chinatown. If possible, display a map of New York City. Point out Little Italy and Chinatown on the map.

1 **Why do you think the neighborhoods are called "Little Italy" and "Chinatown"?** Possible answer: Because people from Italy and China live in the neighborhoods **Make Inferences**

Page 17

Say the word *ciao* (chou). Have children repeat the word after you. Ask children what words from other languages they hear in their community.

2 **What do you think *ciao* means?** Hello **Make Inferences**

3 **What can you learn about Little Italy from the pictures?** Possible answer: There is a nice place to eat in Little Italy. **Analyze Pictures**

Test Talk

Use Information from the Text

4 **How is Little Italy like your community? How is Little Italy different from your community?** Possible answer: My community also has good places to eat. My community does not have places with outdoor eating.

Children should look back at the text to see that they have correct information to answer the question. **Compare and Contrast**

continued

Page 18

Have children discuss the pictures on p. 18.

Write the word *museum* on the board and ask children what they think a museum is. Then provide a definition.

5 **Why do you think people like to live in Chinatown?** Possible answer: Chinatown has many interesting shops. You can see examples of Chinese American culture everywhere.
Draw Conclusions

6 **What museum have you visited? How is it like the museum in Chinatown? How is it different?** Possible answer: I went to a science museum. It is like the museum in Chinatown because it shows many interesting things. It is different because it shows things such as dinosaur bones that are related to science. **Compare and Contrast**

GEOGRAPHY
Place

7 **How is Chinatown different from Little Italy?** You can eat in an Italian restaurant in Little Italy. Some of the people there speak Italian. In Chinatown, there are shops that sell Chinese goods.
Analyze Pictures

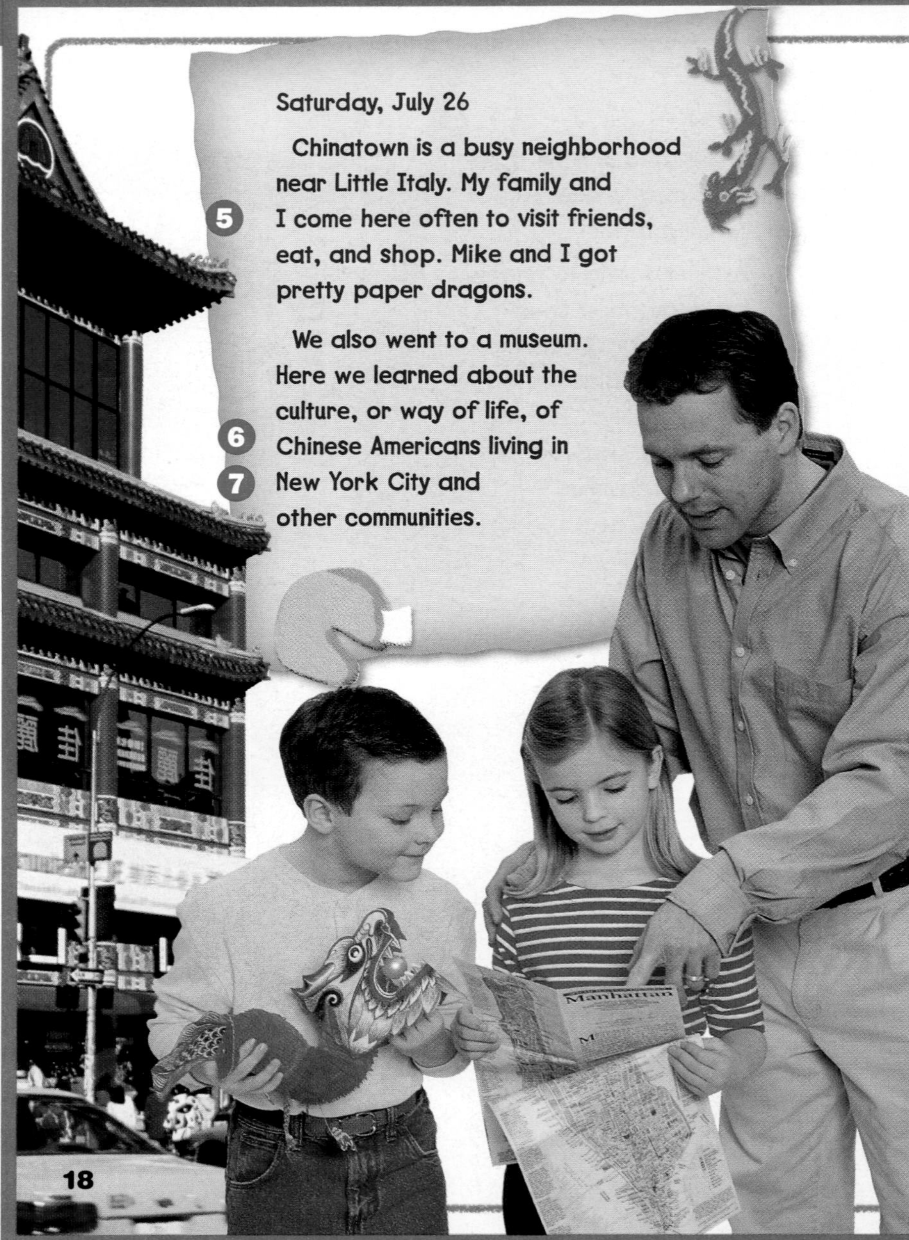

Practice and Extend

SOCIAL STUDIES STRAND
Culture

Celebrations

- In Chinatown—as in other communities in the United States—people have the freedom to celebrate their culture and who they are in many different ways.
- Ask volunteers if there are any celebrations in their community that celebrate their culture. Talk briefly about children's experiences.

ESL Support

For additional ESL support, use Every Student Learns Guide, pp. 6–9.

Sunday, July 27

Today was a busy day! First we walked along Fifth Avenue. We saw many tall buildings called skyscrapers. We also saw many old buildings.

Next we went to Central Park. We saw people jogging, playing baseball, and having picnics. While we were at the park, we visited the zoo. Our last stop for the day was the museum. At the end of the day, we were very tired! 9 10

Fifth Avenue 8

Central Park

What did you learn?

1. Describe two neighborhoods in Joanna's community.
2. Make a list of things you would enjoy doing in New York City.
3. **Think and Share** Draw a picture of Joanna's community. Now draw a picture of your community. How are these two communities alike? How are they different?

CURRICULUM CONNECTION Writing

Write a Journal Entry

- Tell children that what they read on pp. 17–19 were journal entries. Explain that many people keep a journal to record what they do every day.
- Have children think about what they did yesterday or last Saturday in their community.
- Have them write their own journal entry that describes their day.

Workbook, p. 5

A Walk Through a Community

Circle two things NOT in your community.
Color two things in your community. **Answers will vary.**

Write your answer.
How do you say *food* in Spanish?
(Hint: What does a grocery store sell?)
comida

Directions: *Top:* Look at the two pictures. Circle two things not in your community. Color two things that are also found in your community. *Bottom:* Write your answer to the question.

Home Activity: With your child, look through the headlines and advertisements in a local newspaper. Talk about the diversity in your community that these headlines and advertisements show.

Also on Teacher Resources CD-ROM.

Page 19

Discuss the photographs on the page.

8 **Look at the photo of Fifth Avenue. How does what you see compare to an important street in your community?** Possible answer: There are no skyscrapers in my community. But there are many people in my community. **Analyze Pictures**

9 **What are parks like in most communities?** Possible answer: They are places where people play and get together for fun. **Generalize**

10 **What would your community be like without such things as parks and places to shop?** Possible answers: We would have to travel farther to find parks and places to shop. It would not be as nice a place to live. **Hypothesize**

3 Close and Assess

Have children brainstorm a list of important places in the community such as a park, a swimming pool, or a shopping center. Record children's ideas on the board. Ask volunteers to explain why the places are important.

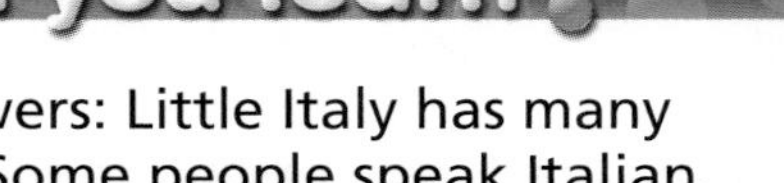

✓ **What did you learn?**

1. Possible answers: Little Italy has many restaurants. Some people speak Italian. Chinatown has a museum that tells about Chinese culture.
2. Possible answer: I would like to see the skyscrapers and have a picnic in Central Park.
3. **Think and Share** Answers will vary. Guide children to include such things as buildings, parks, and homes in their drawings.

Read a City Map

Objectives

- Use symbols, find locations, and determine directions on maps.
- Draw maps to show places.

Vocabulary

map a map that shows where places are (p. 20)

symbols picures that stand for things on a map (p. 20)

map key tells what the symbols on a map mean (p. 20)

1 Introduce and Motivate

Preview Ask children how people are able to travel to a place they have never been before without getting lost. How do they know where to turn? How do they know what highways and roads to travel on? After children respond, share the meanings of the vocabulary words.

Warm Up To activate prior knowledge, tell children to refer back to Joanna's community map. What did the map show them? Then ask children to think about how they got to school this morning. What streets or roads did they travel on? What buildings and other things did they see?

2 Teach and Discuss

Pages 20–21

Tell children that a map can show a small area such as a community or it can show a larger area such as a whole city. Maps can help us get to where we want to go.

Map and Globe Skills

Read a City Map

Here is a map and map key of one part of New York City that Joanna and Mike visited. A **map** is a drawing that shows you where
1 places are located. **Symbols** are pictures that stand for things on a map. A **map key** tells what the symbols on a map mean. 2

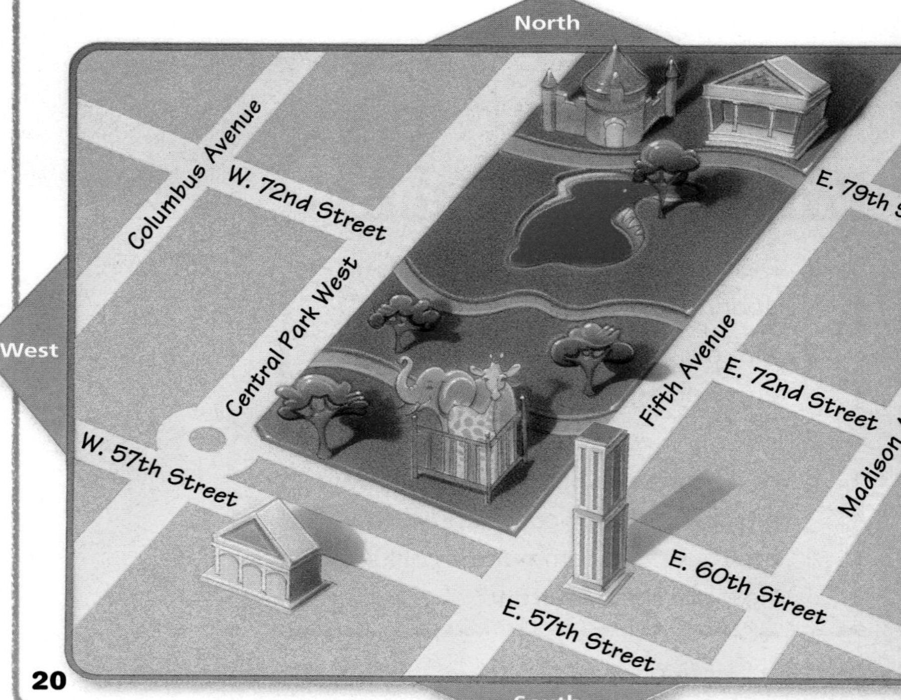

Practice and Extend

Trace a Neighborhood Route

- Tell children to think again about the route they traveled to school this morning.
- Have children draw a simple map that shows the major features of their neighborhood. Tell them to include cardinal directions and a map key.
- Encourage children to include on their maps their homes, stores, library, parks, other important places, and their school.
- Show the finished maps. Have children use them to trace their routes from home to school.

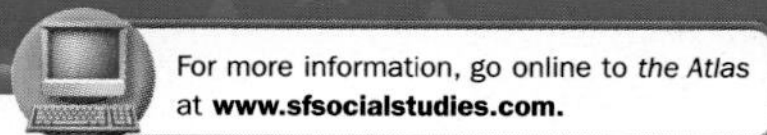

Look at the symbols on the map key. Find the symbol for the zoo. Now find the zoo on the map.

Maps have four main directions. The directions are north, south, east, and west. Find the arrows that show north and south on the map. Find the arrows that show east and west.

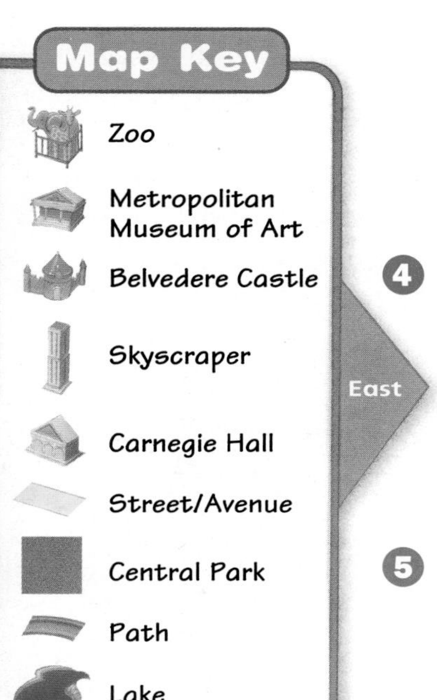

East

4

5

1. Tell what a map shows.
2. Is the [castle] north or south of the [skyscraper] ?
3. **On Your Own** Draw a map of a park. Include a map key and arrows on the map that show the directions.

21

1 Why might a visitor to New York City need a city map? Possible answer: Someone visiting for the first time would not know where to go without a map to help him or her. **Make Inferences**

2 What is the purpose of the map key? It tells what each thing on the map is. **Interpret Maps**

If ... children do not understand the function of a map key,	**then...** explain that the pictures show where such things as streets, lakes, parks, and buildings are.

3 Why do you think arrows are used to show directions on a map? The tip of the arrow can point to each different direction. **Interpret Maps**

4 On the map, what direction is shown by the arrow pointing right? East **Interpret Maps**

5 What symbol would you draw to show a playground? Why? Possible answers: A swing, a slide, a seesaw **Apply Information**

3 Close and Assess

Try it!

1. A map shows where places are.
2. The castle is north of the skyscraper.
3. **On Your Own** Tell children to include such things as pathways, a ball field, park benches, a lake, and a playground on their map.

CURRICULUM CONNECTION Art

Make a Postcard

- Have children use the map of New York City to create a postcard. Tell them to look for interesting places on the map that they would like to draw and write about.
- Provide unlined index cards. On one side, children draw a picture of something, such as the zoo.
- On the flip side, they should write a message to a friend, telling about New York City.

Workbook, p. 6

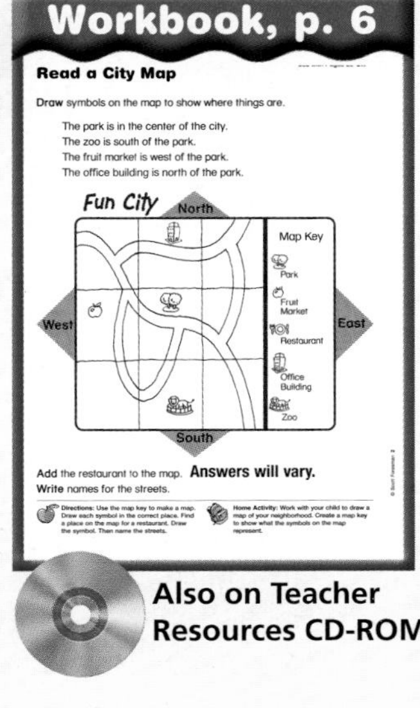
Read a City Map

Draw symbols on the map to show where things are.

The park is in the center of the city.
The zoo is south of the park.
The fruit market is west of the park.
The office building is north of the park.

Add the restaurant to the map. **Answers will vary.**
Write names for the streets.

Also on Teacher Resources CD-ROM.

How a Community Changes

Objectives

- Use vocabulary related to chronology, including *past, present,* and *future*.
- Name several sources of information about a given period.

Vocabulary

history the story of people and places from the past (p. 22)

1 Introduce and Motivate

Preview Display the Vocabulary Card **history** and share its meaning. Have children locate the word as they preview the lesson.

Warm Up To activate prior knowledge, ask children to talk about how they looked and behaved when they were babies. Have them confirm that they have *changed* over time. Now they look different and can do many more things. Then tell children they will learn how a very large community has changed over time.

2 Teach and Discuss

Page 22

Tell children that the photos are primary sources. They were taken by people who lived at the time and reflect changes that have occurred in a community. Other primary sources are letters, diaries, and maps.

1 What clues in the picture tell you that it shows part of New York's history? Possible answer: Buildings that are not very tall and there are trolley tracks and trolleys on the street instead of modern buses and taxis and lots of cars. **Analyze Pictures**

How a Community Changes

Look at this picture taken of New York City long ago. It shows part of the city's history. **History** tells the story of people and places from the past. Pictures can tell you about history.

Practice and Extend

SOCIAL STUDIES Background

About New York City History

- About 400 years ago, a man named Henry Hudson explored the lands alongside a great river. It would later be called the Hudson River. The lands near the mouth of the Hudson River would become New York City.
- Soon, ships brought people and goods from around the world to New York City. Streets and houses were built. People from all over learned to live and work together in the city.
- Over 100 years ago, the Statue of Liberty was placed in New York Harbor. It welcomes newcomers to New York and the United States.

This is a picture of New York City at the present time. How does this picture look different from the picture taken in the past? How has the city changed?

Hands-on History

Find out what your community was like 100 years ago. What is it like today? How might your community change in the future?

Broadway North from 45th Street, New York City.

CURRICULUM CONNECTION
Writing

Timely Descriptions

- Refer children back to the photos on pages 22 and 23.
- Have children choose one of the pictures and write a few sentences about what it may be like to be there. Tell them to use their five senses to describe the city. What do they see? What do they hear? What do they smell? and so on.
- Have volunteers read their stories to the class.

2 How are the people in the photo dressed? Possible answer: The people are wearing old-fashioned clothing. **Analyze Pictures**

Page 23

Tell children that the picture on this page shows how the same street looks today. Point out that even though New York City has grown over time, some cities become smaller over time. Talk with children about possible reasons for growth or decline.

3 How do the pictures look alike and different? Possible answer: There are more buildings, more lights, and more vehicles in the second picture. **Compare and Contrast**

4 Why do you think many of the things in New York City have changed from the way they looked in the past? Possible answers: More people require more space. Larger buildings provide more space. More people require more ways of moving around, more and faster ways to travel. **Draw Conclusions**

5 How do you think New York City will look in the future? Possible answers: The buildings may be even taller. They may be connected so people will not have to go outdoors. **Predict**

3 Close and Assess

Hands-on History

Guide children in researching the history of their community in the library, the town hall, or a local museum. Help them use primary sources such as newspapers, photos, and period maps. Help children develop a list of questions such as: *How many buildings were in this area?*

Have children speculate on what their chosen community area will look like in the future.

Use with pages 16–23

Lesson 2 Wrap-Up

MEETING INDIVIDUAL NEEDS

Leveled Practice

Draw a Neighborhood

Children draw one of the neighborhoods—Chinatown or Little Italy—they have read about.

Easy Have children make a list of the places and activities in the neighborhood they drew. **Reteach**

On-Level Have children write sentences about the neighborhood's places and activities. **Extend**

Challenge Have children write a paragraph that would make people want to visit the neighborhood they selected. **Enrich**

Hands-on Activities

CURRICULUM CONNECTION

Reading

Crossword Puzzle

Objective Review vocabulary.

Resources Vocabulary Cards: **law, vote, community, history**

Materials chart paper, marker

Learning Style Visual/Verbal

Group

Time 10–15 minutes

1. Display the puzzle grid below.

2. Display the Vocabulary Cards. Read these clues and have children tell you what word to write. *Down*/1. The story of people and places from the past; *Across*/2. A place made up of many neighborhoods; 3. Rules that people must obey or follow; 4. To make a choice about something.

Remind children to add pages for *community* and *history* to their glossaries.

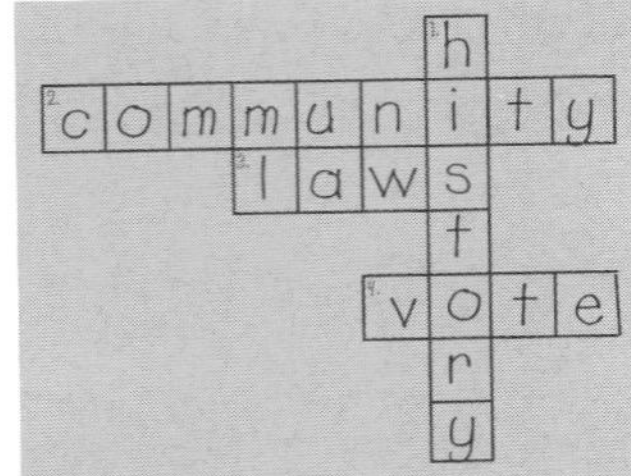

SOCIAL STUDIES STRAND

Geography

Map Keys

Objective Understand map symbols.

Materials paper, crayons, pencils

Learning Style Visual/Kinesthetic

Individual

Time 15–20 minutes

1. Tell children they will draw a map key with three symbols.

2. Explain that each symbol should represent something in a city such as a mall, store, museum, park, bike path, theater, skating rink, public pool, bus station, aquarium, and so on. Have children label the symbols on the reverse side of the map key.

3. Display the finished map keys in class. Ask volunteers to name the map key symbols. Turn the map keys over to check their responses.

SOCIAL STUDIES STRAND

Culture

Read Together

Objective Obtain information from visual sources—print, photos.

Materials *Lion Dancer: Ernie Wan's Chinese New Year,* by Kate Waters and Madeline Slovenz-Low (Scholastic, ISBN 0-590-43047-5, 1990)

Learning Style Visual/Verbal

Group

Time 15–20 minutes

1. Read the book and show the photos.

2. Talk with children about the characters, setting, and story events.

3. Have children draw pictures to show their favorite part of the book.

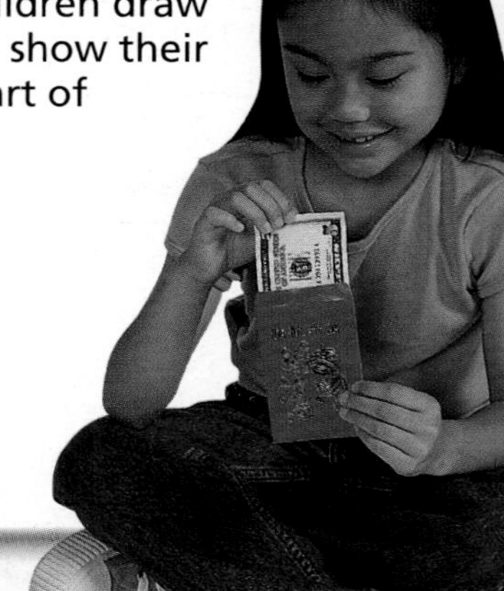

Lesson 3 Overview

Comparing Communities **pages 24–27**	Children will learn meanings for the words *urban, suburb*, and *rural*. They will learn to describe what living in each area is like. 	Time 20–30 minutes Resources • Workbook, p. 7 • Vocabulary Cards urban suburb rural • Every Student Learns Guide, pp. 10–13
Meet Henrietta King **pages 28–29**	Children will learn about the rancher and community donor, Henrietta King.	 Time 20–30 minutes

Build Background

Activity

Where Do You Want to Live?

 **Time** 10-15 minutes

Show children a picture of an apartment building, a group of houses, and a farmhouse. Ask children which place they would like to live in and why. Then have children draw pictures of themselves in the home environment of their choice.

If time is short, discuss in class what it would be like to live in a city, near a city, or out in the countryside.

Read Aloud

What Do You See?

by Christopher Erickson

In a city you'll find
Tall buildings and buses.
People are rushing.
Everyone fusses

Around the cities
People live and play.
They travel by train
To work every day.

At night on a farm
You can see many stars.
And across the hills,
The lights of passing cars.

Comparing Communities

Objective

- Compare rural, urban, and suburban communities.

Vocabulary

urban a city and the places around it (p. 24)

suburb an area located near a city (p. 25)

rural an area with small communities called towns that are far apart (p. 26)

QUICK Teaching Plan

If time is short, have children look at the pictures to learn about urban, suburban, and rural areas.

- Have children write two sentences about each type of community.

1 Introduce and Motivate

Preview Display the Vocabulary Cards **urban**, **suburb**, and **rural**. Ask children what they think each word means. Then define the words for children and use each in a sentence.

Warm Up To activate prior knowledge, ask children to recall what they have learned about the community of New York City. Tell them that New York City is an urban area. Explain that the places near New York City are suburban areas and the places beyond the suburban areas are rural areas. Then ask children to say whether they live in an urban area, a suburb, or a rural area.

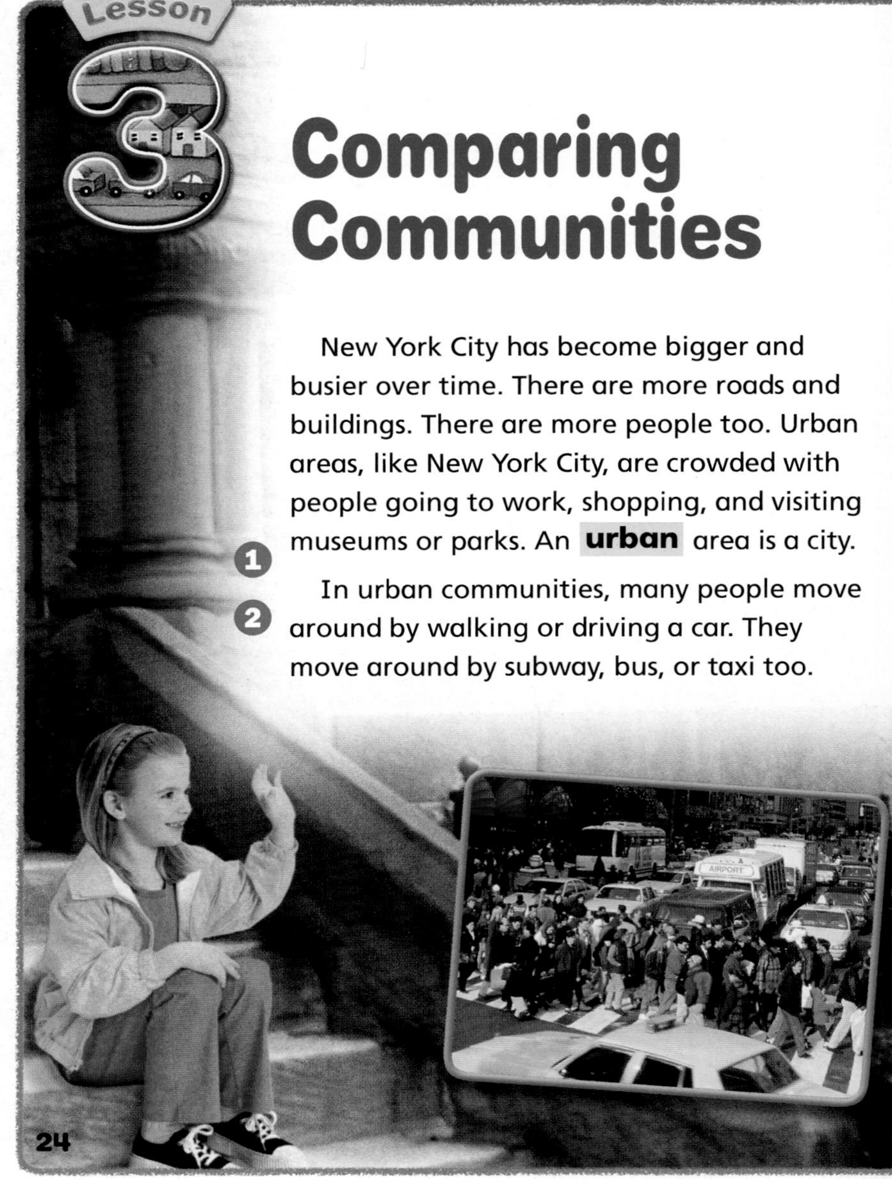
Lesson 3

Comparing Communities

New York City has become bigger and busier over time. There are more roads and buildings. There are more people too. Urban areas, like New York City, are crowded with people going to work, shopping, and visiting
1 museums or parks. An **urban** area is a city.

In urban communities, many people move
2 around by walking or driving a car. They move around by subway, bus, or taxi too.

24

Practice and Extend

READING SKILL
Compare and Contrast

Have children read Lesson 3.

- Have them fill in a chart similar to the one below with words or sentences that describe each type of area described in the lesson.
- When children have completed their charts, talk about how the areas are alike and how they are different.

Urban	Suburb	Rural

Many people live in a kind of community called a suburb. A **suburb** is an area located near a city. My friend, Mike, lives in a suburban area. His neighborhood is quieter than mine!

Mike's family moved to a suburb when his mom became the principal of a school there. His dad rides the train to the city to work. 3 4 Mike's family shops at a shopping mall. Different kinds of stores sell many things they need.

25

SOCIAL STUDIES STRAND
History

Suburbs

- Tell children that in the early 1900s cars were first mass-produced; this gave many people the opportunity to live farther from urban areas.
- Explain that in the 1950s, the U.S. suburbs grew quickly, due to more people and highways.
- Help children find out when a city and a suburb were established. Children can plot the dates on a time line.

WEB SITE
Technology

You can look up vocabulary words online. Click on *Social Studies Library* and select the dictionary at **www.sfsocialstudies.com.**

2 Teach and Discuss

Page 24

Name several large urban areas other than New York in the United States such as Dallas, Los Angeles, Chicago, and Tampa. Mention that in the United States many urban areas continue to grow in population, or the number of people who live there.

1 **Why are urban areas usually noisy places?** There are many people living and working there. The streets are crowded with buses, trucks, and taxis. **Draw Conclusions**

2 **Why do people in urban areas need buses, subways, and taxis to help them move around?** Possible answer: There isn't enough room to drive or park many cars in urban areas, so people find other ways to get from place to place. **Make Inferences**

Page 25

Tell children that most people living in the suburbs need to use their cars to get from place to place because suburban areas usually do not have many forms of public transportation.

3 **Why do you think some people like to live in suburbs? Why do some like living in the city?** Possible answer: The people living in suburbs are close enough to the city to work there, and they have more living space in the suburbs. People living in the city like being close to work and city activities. **Draw Conclusions**

4 **Compare the city and suburb described and pictured on pp. 24–25. How are they alike? How are they different?** Possible answers: Both have homes where people live. In the city, Joanna lives in an apartment building. Mike lives in a house with a garage for the family car. It is quieter in the suburb where Mike lives. **Compare and Contrast**

Lesson 3 continued

Page 26

Tell children that in the United States there are many rural areas. Explain that rural areas are a lot quieter than urban and suburban areas. Note that rural areas have the fewest cars, buildings, and people.

5 **Why is a rural area a good place for someone who wants to raise animals?** Rural areas have lots of land and open space, which are needed for raising animals. **Make Inferences**

6 **Why do people in rural areas farm the land?** To grow food for themselves and people in other places **Make Inferences**

7 **How do you think Kim's and Joanna's after-school activities may differ?** Possible response: Kim may ride her horse or help with farm chores. Joanna may go to the playground or a park. **Compare and Contrast**

Other people live in rural areas. A **rural** area has small communities called towns that are far apart. There is open space used for growing plants for food and raising animals. My cousin, Kim, lives in a rural area. 5 6

When I visited Kim, we drove for a long time before we came to her town. I saw cows and horses in the fields. I also saw roadside stands with fruits and vegetables.

When we got to Kim's house, I helped her brush and feed her horse. That night, Kim's family had a big barbecue. It was fun to cook dinner over an open fire. 7

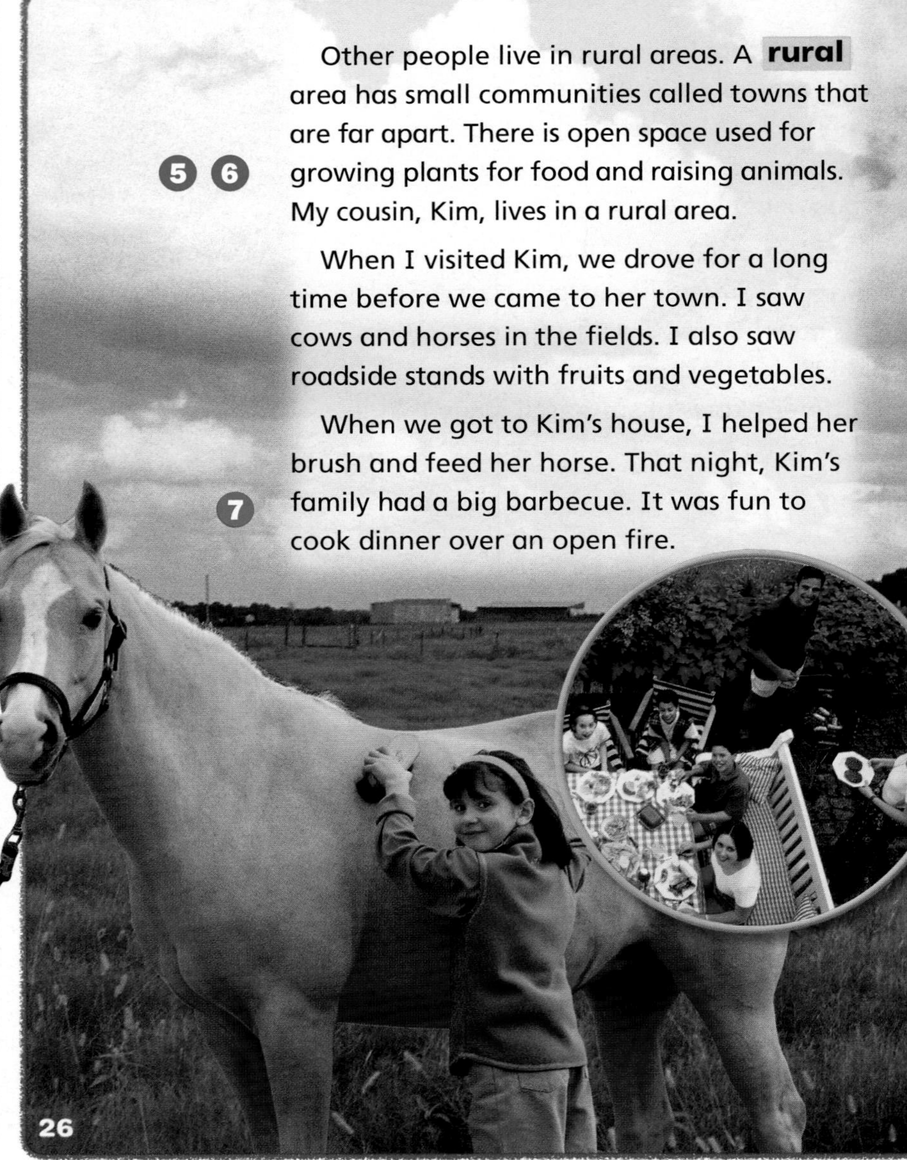

26

Practice and Extend

SOCIAL STUDIES STRAND

Geography

The Three Regions

- On the board draw a circle and label it *Urban*.
- Then draw a circle around the first circle. Next, draw an even larger circle around the first two circles. (Do not label the second and third circles.)
- Have children draw the graphic with the label *Urban* on a piece of paper. Tell them to label the other circles appropriately as *Suburb* and *Rural*. Tell children to review the lesson if they need help naming each circle.

CURRICULUM CONNECTION

Writing

A Friendly Letter

- Have children choose one of the three areas—urban, suburb, and rural—and write a letter to a friend describing what they do in their chosen community.
- Tell children to talk about the places they visit, the things they see, and the buildings where people live and work.
- Ask volunteers to share their letters with the class.

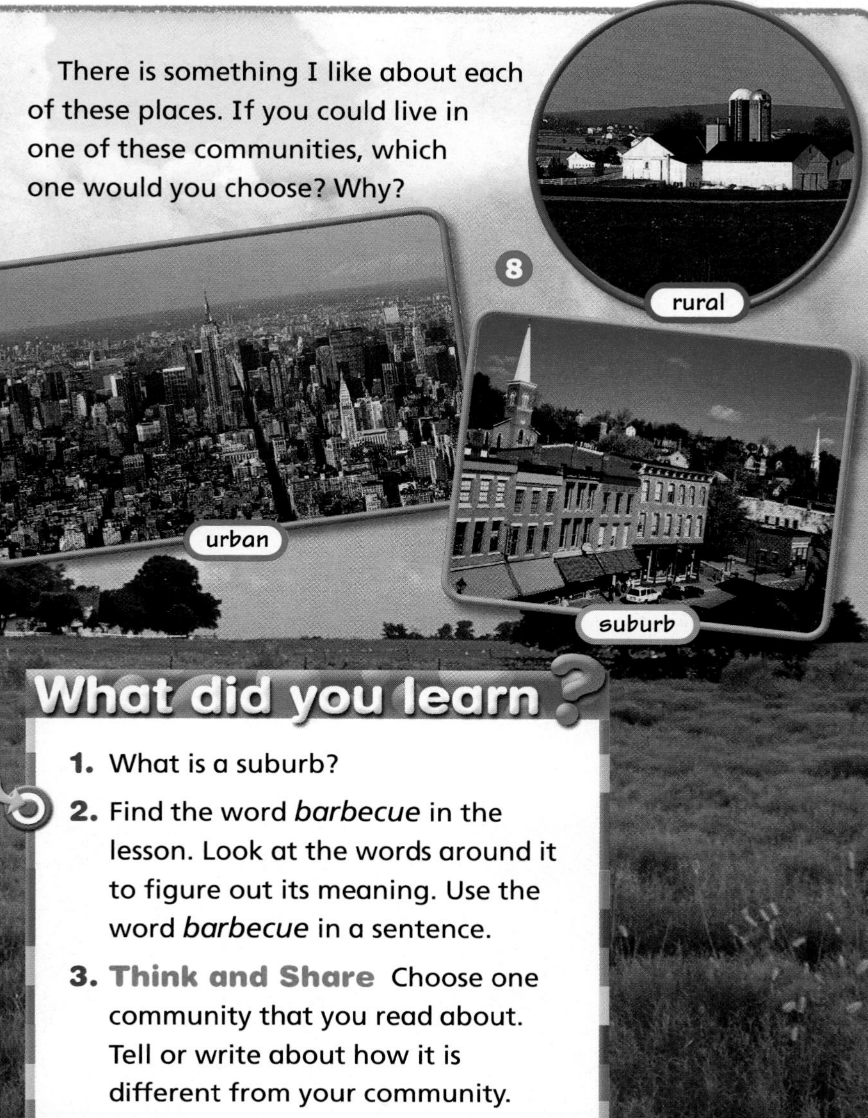
There is something I like about each of these places. If you could live in one of these communities, which one would you choose? Why?

What did you learn?

1. What is a suburb?
2. Find the word *barbecue* in the lesson. Look at the words around it to figure out its meaning. Use the word *barbecue* in a sentence.
3. **Think and Share** Choose one community that you read about. Tell or write about how it is different from your community.

27

Page 27

Have children answer the questions at the end of the paragraph at the top of p. 27. Check that children give logical reasons for the type of community they chose.

You may wish to discuss how the area where the children in your class live has changed over time in terms of physical development and population. Children may be surprised to learn that their bustling city or growing suburb was once a rural area!

8 How are suburbs and rural areas alike? Use the photos. Possible response: Both areas are away from the city. Neither has very tall buildings or crowded streets. **Compare and Contrast**

3 Close and Assess

Assign children to three groups: people who live in an urban community, a suburban community, and a rural community. Have the members of each group take turns telling something about the place they live.

1. An area that is located near a city
2. The word *barbecue* is found on p. 26. Context clue for *barbecue*: cook dinner over an open fire. Sentences will vary. Possible sentence: We ate hot dogs at a barbecue in the country.
3. **Think and Share** Children's responses should reflect their understanding of urban, suburban, and rural communities.

ESL ACCESS CONTENT ESL Support

Drawing and Writing Have children draw pictures that reflect an urban area, a suburb, and a rural area. They should label their pictures appropriately.

Beginning Have children cut and paste magazine pictures of things found in each of the three areas.

Intermediate Children should write a definition sentence in each square.

Advanced Have children write a short paragraph about what they could do in each area.

For additional ESL Support, use Every Student Learns Guide, pp. 10–13.

Workbook, p. 7

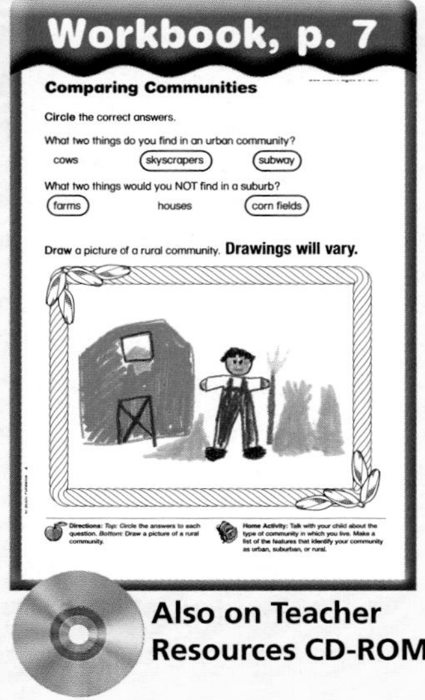
Comparing Communities

Circle the correct answers.

What two things do you find in an urban community?

cows (skyscrapers) (subway)

What two things would you NOT find in a suburb?

(farms) houses (corn fields)

Draw a picture of a rural community. **Drawings will vary.**

Also on Teacher Resources CD-ROM.

Henrietta King

Objective

- Identify contributions of historical figures.

1 Introduce and Motivate

Preview Tell children they are going to read a biography—information about a person's life. Identify the subject as Henrietta King and say that she is someone who made a contribution to her community. Define *contribution* as "the act of giving or doing something." Have children look at the photo. Ask them to tell what they know about Henrietta King by looking at details in the photo.

Warm Up To activate prior knowledge, have children recall the three kinds of communities they have learned about—urban, suburban, and rural. Focus on rural communities briefly. Ask children what they think are some things a rural community would have to have to attract people to live there. Ask: **Would good roads make people want to come to a new rural community? Would it be important to have schools?**

2 Teach and Discuss

Read aloud the subtitle of the biography. Explain the meaning of *donor*, saying that a donor is someone who gives away money or other things to people.

1 The Kings lived and built their ranch in a place where few people lived. Why? They needed a lot of land to raise their animals. **Draw Conclusions**

2 Do you think living in such a place was easy or difficult? Why? Possible answer: It was difficult. If the Kings needed help, there would not be others around. It may have been lonely too. **Make Inferences**

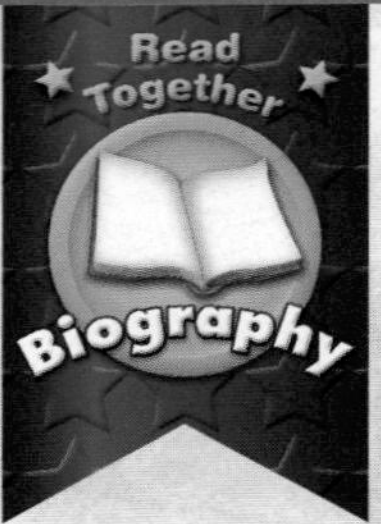

Meet Henrietta King

1832–1925
Rancher and Community Donor

Henrietta Chamberlain King helped build one of the largest ranches in Texas. She also donated land for a rural community.

28

Practice and Extend

SOCIAL STUDIES Background

About Henrietta King

- The Kings moved to their land in 1854. Richard King died in 1885, leaving his family in debt. Mrs. King paid off that debt with the help of her son-in-law.
- In the next 10 years, Henrietta King, with the help of her son-in-law, would make the ranch very successful.
- Mrs. King experimented with ways of improving livestock that greatly helped the Texas cattle industry.
- Mrs. King founded many companies, creating many jobs at a time when the country really needed them.
- At the time of Mrs. King's death, the ranch had grown to more than $1\frac{1}{2}$ million acres and stretched from Corpus Christi to Brownsville.

When Henrietta married Richard King, they moved to a ranch in Texas. A ranch is a place with a large area of land used to raise cattle and horses. Mr. and Mrs. King had five children. (1)

Mrs. King helped families of the ranch workers go to school and find homes. When Richard King died, Mrs. King took over the ranch. She helped King Ranch grow very large in size. (2) (3)

Mrs. King donated land to people in charge of building a railroad. Then she donated land to help build towns along the railroad. One town was named (4) Kingsville, after her husband, Richard King. As the town grew, Mrs. King (5) helped build churches and schools.

Today, many people visit King Ranch in Texas. Henrietta King is remembered as a rancher and a person who cared for the land and its people.

Henrietta Chamberlain King was born in Boonville, Missouri.

King Ranch building

Henrietta King

Think and Share

How did Henrietta King help build the community of Kingsville, Texas?

For more information, go online to *Meet the People* at **www.sfsocialstudies.com.**

29

(3) **Who did Mrs. King help to educate?** The families of the workers **Main Idea and Details**

(4) **What are some things Mrs. King wanted people to do with the land she gave them?** Build homes on the land; build a railroad to bring more people to the area **Recall/Retell**

Decision Making

(5) **Why did Mrs. King decide to continue to give away land and money instead of keeping the land and money for herself?** Possible answer: She saw the need for more schools, churches, libraries. **Cause and Effect**

SOCIAL STUDIES STRAND Citizenship

Tell children that one of the characteristics of good citizenship is concern about the common good; that is, feeling that the people around you are important and that you have a responsibility to make their lives better as well as your own. Ask: **How did Mrs. King practice good citizenship?**

3 Close and Assess

Think and Share

Test Talk

Write Your Answer
Tell children to write their answer to the question.

Children's responses should reflect their knowledge of Henrietta King's motivational as well as tangible contributions to the community such as land and money to build schools and churches.

Have children exchange their written answers with a partner. Children should evaluate each other's answers and say what might be added.

CURRICULUM CONNECTION Drama

Create a Skit

- Organize children into small groups. Have each group plan, rehearse, and perform a skit about the life of Henrietta King.
- Tell children they can play Henrietta, her husband Richard, a ranch hand, or a newcomer to the Kingsville area.
- Help children create props and scenery to use in their skits.

WEB SITE Technology

You may help children find out more about Henrietta King by going online. Click on *Meet the People* at **www.sfsocialstudies.com.**

Use with pages 24–29

Lesson 3 Wrap-Up

MEETING INDIVIDUAL NEEDS
Leveled Practice

Create a Travel Brochure
Have children label three pieces of construction paper *Urban, Suburb,* and *Rural.* Then have them draw pictures on the pages that reflect each type of community.

Easy Have children bind the pages together. Then have them label each picture. **Reteach**

On-Level At the bottom of each page children can write two sentences about the type of community pictured. **Extend**

Challenge Provide children with reference books to learn more about one specific urban area, suburb, or rural area. Show them how to use table of contents and index to find information. Then have them include a chart on which they list the attributes for each community. **Enrich**

Hands-on Activities

CURRICULUM CONNECTION
Reading

Add to "My Word Book"

Objective Define and illustrate the words *urban, suburb,* and *rural.*

Resources Vocabulary Cards: **urban, suburb, rural**

Materials crayons, pencils

Learning Style Visual/Verbal

Individual

Time 15–20 minutes

1. Display the Vocabulary Cards. Direct children to create "U," "S," and "R" pages in their word books and have them write *urban, suburb,* and *rural* on the correct pages.

2. Have children draw pictures to illustrate each word and write a sentence below or next to each picture.

CURRICULUM CONNECTION
Art

Build a Diorama

Objective Visually describe urban areas.

Materials shoe boxes or other small boxes, pencils, pens, scissors, glue, construction paper

Learning Style Visual/Kinesthetic

Partners

Time 25–30 minutes

1. Tell children to draw and cut out pictures of small buildings and other things they might see in an urban area.

2. Have them glue or tape their drawings to the inside of their box.

3. Tell them to add small drawings to their dioramas to add to the "urban feel" of their work.

CURRICULUM CONNECTION
Science

Posters

Objective Learn about some of the resources of rural areas.

Materials construction paper, pencils, crayons

Learning Style Kinesthetic/Social

Group

Time 20–30 minutes

1. As a class, brainstorm a list of crops and animals that are important in rural communities.

2. Organize children into small groups. Have each group choose one crop or animal to research in books or on the Internet.

3. Have children within a group collaborate on a poster. Posters should include a drawing of the food or animal they studied and a short paragraph that presents their findings.

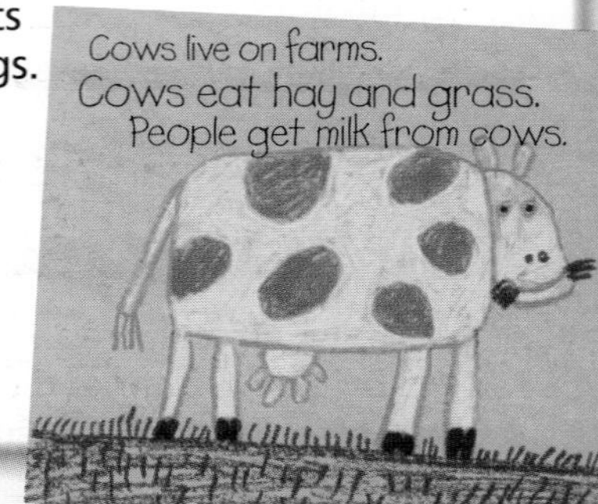

Lesson 4 Overview

Our State and Our Country **pages 30–33**	Children will learn the meaning of the word *capital*. They will also learn that they live in a state and a country and that both places have capitals. 	Time 20–30 minutes **Resources** • Workbook, p. 8 • Vocabulary Card **capital** • Every Student Learns Guide, pp. 14–17
Meet Benjamin Banneker **pages 34–35**	Children will learn about Benjamin Banneker, the man who helped measure the land for Washington, D.C.	 Time 15-20 minutes

Build Background

Activity

Make a *State*ment

 **Time** 10–15 minutes

Ask a volunteer to name the state that he or she lives in. Record the state name on the board. Then ask children to name other states that they have visited, lived in, or read about. Add those state names to the list. Have children tell what they know about the states listed.

If time is short, show children a classroom map of the United States. Ask volunteers to come forward, point out one state, and say that state's name.

California
Virginia
New York
North Carolina
Florida
Michigan

Read Aloud

It's on the Map!

by Dana Marshall

What is the name of our country?

How many states can you find?

Where is the nation's capital?

Can you picture it in your mind?

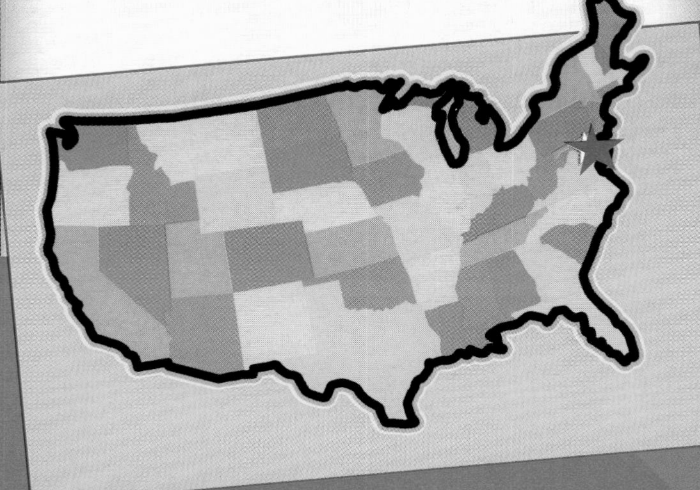

Our State and Our Country

Objectives

- Locate communities, states, and countries on maps.
- Identify state and national symbols.

Vocabulary

capital the place where the leaders of a state work (p. 33)

QUICK Teaching Plan

If time is short, have children look at the art in the lesson, specifically the map on p. 31. Help children read the names of the states that border Texas. Point to each name and have children do the same as you read it.

- On the map on p. 32, have children locate their home state. Have them compare the location and size of their state to Texas.

1 Introduce and Motivate

Preview Display the Vocabulary Card **capital** and ask children what they think the word means. Use the word in sentence context to give children clues to its meaning. Then share the meaning of the word. Make the point that every state has a capital and that the United States has a capital.

Warm Up To activate prior knowledge, ask children the name of their city, state, and country. List their information on the board.

Lesson 4

Our State and Our Country

1 Our class is learning about the fifty states. These states make up our country, the United States of America. I did a report on Texas, the place where Henrietta King lived.

In my report, I wrote a poem about Texas. It includes symbols, or pictures that stand for this state. 2 3

30

Practice and Extend

READING SKILL Recall and Retell

- Tell children that when they recall what they have read and want to retell what they have learned, they should include just the big ideas.
- After children read Lesson 4, recall and discuss the big ideas of the lesson.
- Then model how to retell the information. You may wish to write your retelling on chart paper and have children compare it to the lesson text.

WEB SITE Technology

You can look up vocabulary words online. Click on *Social Studies Library* and select the dictionary at **www.sfsocialstudies.com.**

Texas is a very large state. Look at its border. A border is a line that divides one state or country from another. Trace the border around Texas. What are the four states that share its border? 4 5

Look at the map key. Tell what symbols are shown on the map key.

Five States

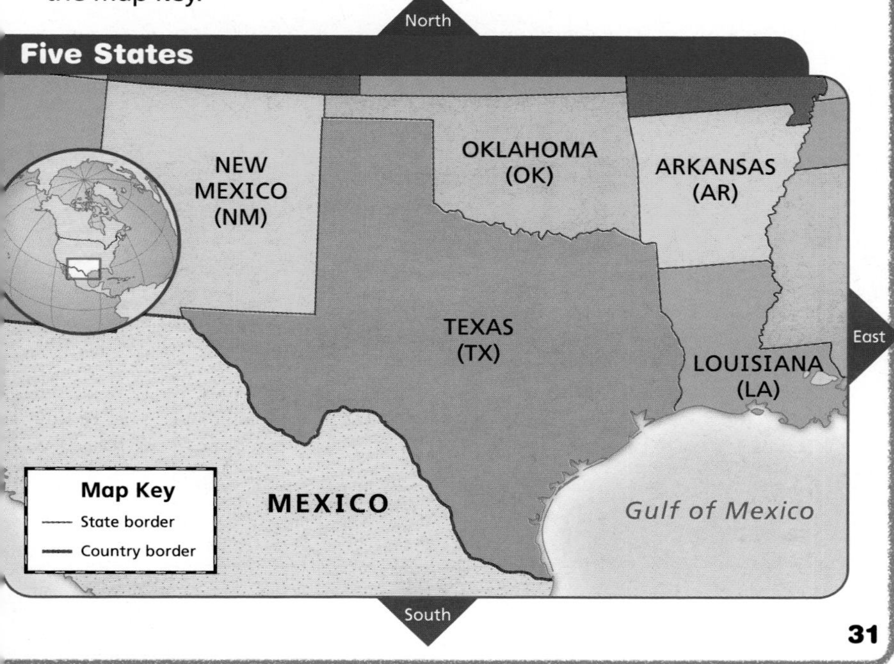

31

FAST FACTS

The "Lone Star State"

These may have been among the facts Joanna found as she prepared her report. Share with children.

- The name *Texas* comes from *techas* or *tejas*, a Caddo Indian word that means "allies" or "friends"—thus the state motto "friendship."
- Texas has a state animal—the armadillo. It also has a state dish—chili.
- Camels once lived in Texas. An experiment was tried to have camels carry supplies across the Southwest Desert to settlers in California after the gold rush.
- Texas has more festivals, fairs, and exhibits every year than any other state—over 500!

2 Teach and Discuss

Page 30

Call attention to the symbols of Texas. Ask children to describe what they see. Name the bird—mockingbird—and flower—bluebonnet. All states have symbols. The American flag and bald eagle are familiar symbols of the United States. The official flower of the United States is the rose.

1 **How is a state different from a country?** A state is a small part of a country. Our country is made up of 50 states. **Main Idea and Details**

2 **If you were in Texas, do you think you might see a mockingbird or a bluebonnet flower? Why?** Answers may include: Yes. That's why they are the symbols of Texas. **Draw Conclusions**

3 **Think about your own community. What bird and flower would you choose to be your community's symbols?** Children's responses should reflect flowers and birds local to your area. **Apply Information**

Page 31

As needed, help children read the names of the states bordering Texas. Tell children that borders are not something that someone would see as he or she crossed from one state into another. Say that borders are lines that appear on a map.

4 **What do borders on a map tell you?** They tell where one state ends and another begins. **Interpret Maps**

5 **Does Texas border on any water? How do you know?** Yes; an area south and east of Texas is colored blue on the map. **Interpret Maps**

Lesson 4 continued

Page 32

As needed, write the name of your state on the board to facilitate children's finding it on the map.

Introduce children in a general way to the concept of scale. Note that the inset maps of Hawaii and Alaska make them appear much smaller than many other states. Use state maps of Hawaii and Alaska in conjunction with other state maps to compare relative size.

6 Why do some people say that the states on the map look like pieces of a jigsaw puzzle? Possible answer: The states are different shapes; all fit together to make a picture.
Make Inferences

7 Name a large state shown on the map. What states share its border? Have children check their responses against the map.
Interpret Maps

8 What two states do not share a border with any other states? Hawaii and Alaska
Interpret Maps

Test Talk

Use Information from Graphics

9 What is the name of a state that shares a border with Canada? Have children find the name *Canada* on the map to identify correctly one or more bordering U.S. states.

Possible answers: Washington, North Dakota, Michigan, New York **Interpret Maps**

Our country has fifty states. Find your state on this map. What are the states that share a border with your state?

Canada and Mexico are two countries that share borders with the United States. Trace the border that the United States shares with our neighbor to the south, Mexico. Trace the border that the United States shares with Canada, our neighbor to the north.

6 7 8 9

The United States

North
West
South

CANADA
MEXICO
PACIFIC OCEAN
ATLANTIC OCEAN
Gulf of Mexico
ARCTIC OCEAN
ALASKA
HAWAII

Map Key
National capital
State border
Country border

32

Practice and Extend

EXTEND LANGUAGE
ESL Support

Make Maps Provide children with outline maps of the countries from which their families originated. Write the English name of each child's country on the board.

Beginning Have children copy the English name for their country on their map. Have children find out the name of the state or region their family lived. Help them write its name on the map in the correct location.

Intermediate Have children add bordering states or regions to their maps. Help them write labels.

Advanced Have children write to tell about the country and states or regions their map represents.

For additional ESL support, use Every Student Learns Guide, pp. 14–17.

In my report, I learned that Austin is the capital of Texas. A **capital** is a city where the leaders of a state work. What is the name of your state's capital? (10) (11)

Our country has a capital too. It is Washington, D.C. This is the home of the President, who is our country's leader. Washington, D.C., is the place where people chosen from each state vote to make our country's laws. These lawmakers work with the President to help make the United States a better place to live. (12)

Washington, D.C.

What did you learn?

1. What two countries share a border with the United States?
2. Where is our country's capital located?
3. **Think and Share** Draw an outline map of your state. Include its capital. Put a title on the map. Around the map, draw symbols that stand for your state.

33

CURRICULUM CONNECTION Math

Adding and Subtracting

Tell children that in its history the number of states in the United States has changed. Then have children write a math problem for each bulleted item.

- If the United States added one more state, how many states would there be?
- Before Alaska and Hawaii were added to the United States in 1959, how many states were there?

Workbook, p. 8

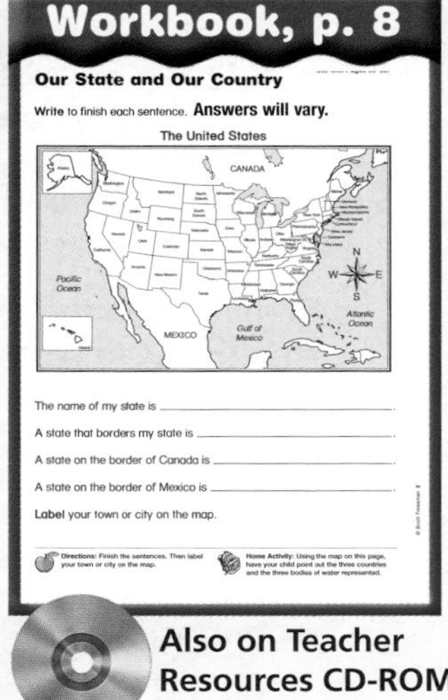

Our State and Our Country

Write to finish each sentence. **Answers will vary.**

The United States

The name of my state is ____

A state that borders my state is ____

A state on the border of Canada is ____

A state on the border of Mexico is ____

Label your town or city on the map.

Also on Teacher Resources CD-ROM.

Page 33

Use your state map to point out the state capital. Have children help you locate your community on the map in relation to the capital. Ask if it is north, east, south, or west of the capital. Then on a U.S. map, point out other state capitals. Last, point out the U.S. capital, Washington, D.C., and note that it is not in any state.

(10) **What is a state capital?** A capital is a city where the leaders of a state work.
Main Idea and Details

(11) **Why do you think it's important for a state to have a capital?** The capital city is one place people can come to from all across the state to discuss laws and other important state business.
Draw Conclusions

(12) **What do the lawmakers from all the states do in Washington, D.C.?** They vote to pass laws. They help the President make our country a better place to live. **Recall and Retell**

3 Close and Assess

Have children identify their state, name its capital city, and then identify at least one state that shares a border with their state.

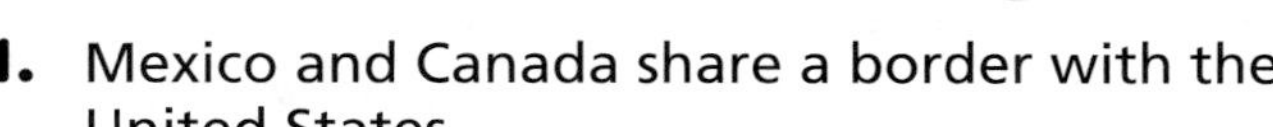

✓ What did you learn?

1. Mexico and Canada share a border with the United States.
2. Washington, D.C., is our country's capital.
3. **Think and Share** Provide children with reference materials, if necessary. Check that children have written the correct capital city and symbols.

Benjamin Banneker

Objective

- Identify individuals of past and present significance to the community and nation.

1 Introduce and Motivate

Preview Read aloud the title of the feature and then read the subtitle. Focus on the word *surveyor,* which most children will be unfamiliar with. Explain that a surveyor examines and measures land to decide how to plan its use and decide on borders. Have volunteers tell what an inventor does.

Warm Up To activate prior knowledge, have children close their eyes for a moment or two and try to visualize their neighborhood or community. Ask if children think someone planned how their community would look. Ask if they think the parks and schools were built in appropriate places. Encourage discussion.

2 Teach and Discuss

Before children read with you, talk about these terms: *pocket watch, boundary,* and *almanac*. Tell children pocket watches predated wristwatches, a boundary is like a border (a term they already know), and, if possible show an almanac to supplement the definition in the text.

1 What subject that you study in class helped Benjamin Banneker do his surveying job? Math
Recall and Retell

Practice and Extend

About Benjamin Banneker

- Benjamin Banneker was one of the first African Americans to work officially (as part of the survey team) for the United States.
- A picture of Banneker was featured on a U.S. postage stamp.

You may help children find out more about Benjamin Banneker by clicking on *Meet the People* at **www.sfsocialstudies.com.**

Benjamin Banneker grew up on a farm in Maryland. His grandmother taught him to read. Benjamin also studied math. He attended school until he was old enough to spend his days working on the farm.

As a young man, Benjamin Banneker had never seen a clock. He was shown a pocket watch. He carefully looked at the watch. Then he built a wooden clock that kept the correct time for many years.

President Washington wanted to build a new capital city for our nation. The city was to be named Washington, District of Columbia. Many people worked together to build this new city. Benjamin Banneker was part of a team of surveyors. Surveyors measure an area of land. Benjamin Banneker helped measure the land for Washington, D.C. 1 2 3 4

Benjamin Banneker returned to the farm. He wrote an almanac, or booklike calendar, that included information about the sun, moon, and stars.

Benjamin Banneker was born near Baltimore, Maryland.

Benjamin Banneker, 1795

Think and Share

How did Benjamin Banneker help build the capital city of our nation, Washington, D.C.?

For more information, go online to *Meet the People* at **www.sfsocialstudies.com.**

2 How did he use math skills as a surveyor? He measured the land. Measuring correctly is a math skill. **Draw Conclusions**

3 In what way did Benjamin Banneker show that he was a good citizen? Possible answer: He helped to build a capital city that would be good for everyone in the country. He worked for the good of all the people. **Make Inferences**

4 Why do you think people remember Benjamin Banneker? Possible answer: He made a contribution to our country by helping to build an important and beautiful capital city. **Make Inferences**

3 Close and Assess

Think and Share

Benjamin Banneker worked with a team of surveyors. He helped measure the land for the new capital city and decide on boundaries.

CURRICULUM CONNECTION

Writing

Writing Questions

- Encourage children to write on index cards questions they would like to ask Benjamin Banneker.
- Create a classroom question box and have children place their cards in the box.
- As time permits, have children select one or more question cards and then do research individually or with a partner to try to answer the question.
- Have children write the answers they find on the reverse side of the index cards.

Use with pages 30–35

Lesson 4 Wrap-Up

MEETING INDIVIDUAL NEEDS

Leveled Practice

Adopt a State

Using a map, children choose a state they want to "adopt." Children trace the outline of the state.

Easy Have children label the map with the state name. Help children find the state's capital and have them write it in the correct location on their own maps. **Reteach**

On-Level Have children add one or more state symbols beside the map, drawing the symbols and labeling them. If necessary, help children find that state's symbols in an encyclopedia or other reference work. **Extend**

Challenge Have children find out more about the state and then write several sentences that compare and contrast the adopted state with either their home state or Texas. **Enrich**

Hands-on Activities

CURRICULUM CONNECTION

Reading

Question and Answer Game

Objective Use the word *capital* in various contexts.

Resources Vocabulary Card: **capital**

Materials United States map (showing state capitals)

Learning Style Visual/Verbal

Partners

Time 15–20 minutes

1. Display the Vocabulary Card. Ask a volunteer to say what the word means.
2. Assign children partners.
3. Model how to use the map to ask questions and give answers using the word *capital*: *What is the capital of Utah? Is Austin the capital of California?* Have partners take turns following your model. Remind children to add *capital* to their "My Word Book" glossaries.

SOCIAL STUDIES STRAND

Geography

U. S. Capital

Objective Identify the monuments in Washington, D.C.

Materials drawing paper, pencils, crayons

Learning Style Visual/Kinesthetic

Partners

Time 15–20 minutes

1. Organize children in pairs.
2. Provide reference materials that show the monuments of the National Mall.
3. Have partners choose, draw, and label a poster of one of monuments, statues, or buildings.

CURRICULUM CONNECTION

Writing

Interview

Objective Interview someone who has demonstrated good citizenship.

Materials paper, pencil

Learning Style Verbal/Auditory

Individual

Time 15–20 minutes

1. Children can interview firefighters, police officers, or volunteer workers.
2. Tell children to ask the people to describe what they do. Children should take notes.
3. Children can give oral reports about their interview, including opinions of how their subject demonstrates good citizenship.

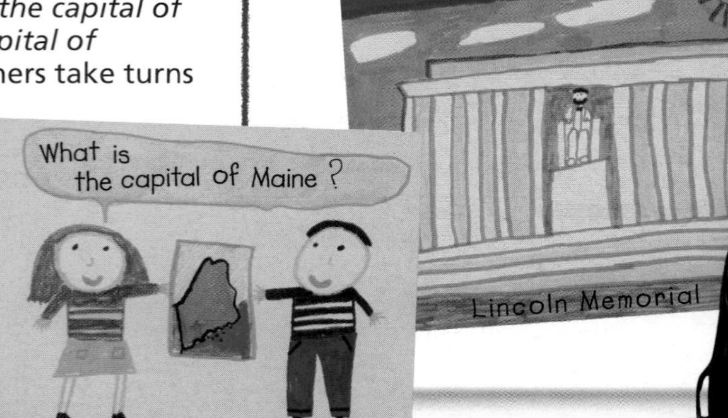

Lesson 5 Overview

Our Country Is Part of Our World **pages 36–39**	Children will learn that they live on Earth, a world that has landmasses called continents on it. They will learn, too, that they live on the continent of North America.	Time 20–30 minutes Resources • Workbook, p. 9 • Every Student Learns Guide, pp. 18–21
Children of the World **pages 40–41**	Children will learn that children around the world have much in common.	Time 15–20 minutes

Build Background

Activity

Where Do We Live?

Time 10–15 minutes

Have children turn paper circles into pictures of Earth. Have them show in a general way landmasses and bodies of water. One by one, have children pin their pictures on a bulletin board. As they do, they should introduce themselves and say where they live on Earth. Model the pattern: *I am Mrs. Meyer. I live in Clarkson in the state of Michigan in the United States.*

If time is short, have children introduce themselves using the pattern.

Read Aloud

Home Sweet Home

by Betsy King

We all live in many places,
Some small and some big spaces.

We share neighborhoods
with friends.

We follow the laws of our
communities.

We are proud of our states.

And we pledge allegiance to
our COUNTRY!

Our Country Is Part of Our World

Objective

- Demonstrate map and globe skills.

QUICK Teaching Plan

If time is short, have children look at the picture on page 37. Help them identify the object that Joanna is holding as a globe. Have children tell what a globe shows. Write the term Earth on the chalkboard. Then read the speech balloon and define continent as it is in the text—a large body of land.

- Have children take turns finding North America on a classroom globe. Then as children look on, point out and name the remaining continents.

1 Introduce and Motivate

Preview Guide children on a picture preview of the lesson. Encourage them to describe what they see. Introduce the terms *continent* and *Earth*. Tell children they will learn on which continent on Earth they live.

Warm Up To activate prior knowledge, display a globe and a large rubber ball. Ask children how the globe and the ball are alike and different. Ask if they know which one shows a very small model of Earth. Encourage children to examine the globe, distinguishing between land and water. Point out symbols such as the equator line, and show children how to tell north from south. Have volunteers explain how a globe is like a map.

Our Country Is Part of Our World

Where do you live? There are many ways to answer the question. Look at my picture to see how I answered the question.

How would you answer the question?

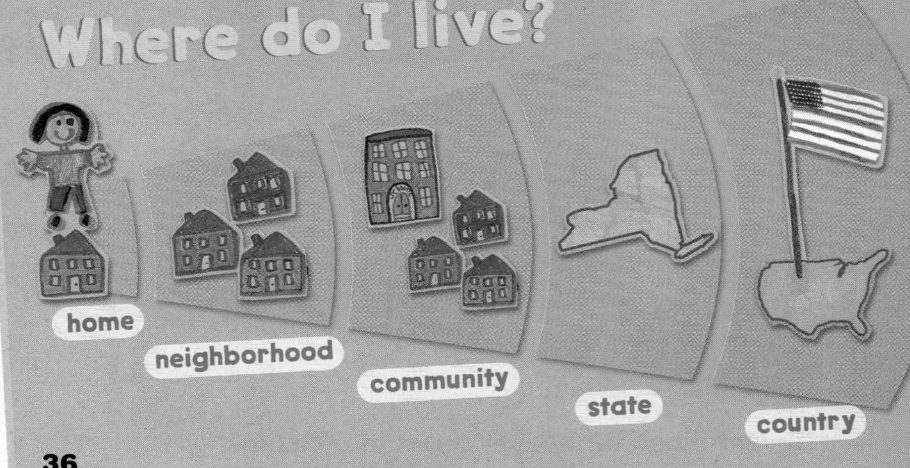

36

Practice and Extend

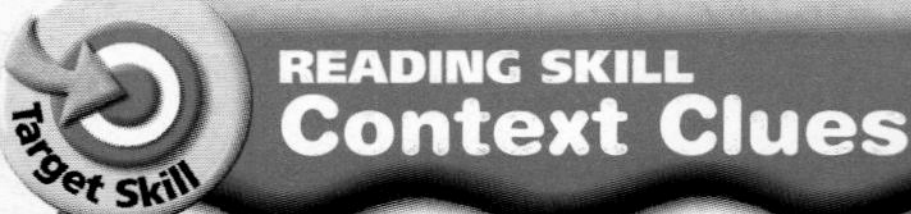

READING SKILL
Context Clues

- Tell children that in this lesson they will encounter the words *continent, equator, globe,* and *ocean*.
- Show children how to fold a sheet of paper into quadrants. Tell them to open up the paper.
- Have children write each of the four words, one to a quadrant.
- After they read pp. 36–39, have children go back and reread to find words in the text that give the meaning of each word. Have them write those words.

There are more ways I can tell about where I live. Remember when we looked at borders that the United States shares with Canada and Mexico? These three countries are part of a continent, or large body of land, called North America. 

A globe is a model of Earth. Look on this globe to find North America. What are the names of the oceans, or large bodies of salt water, around North America?

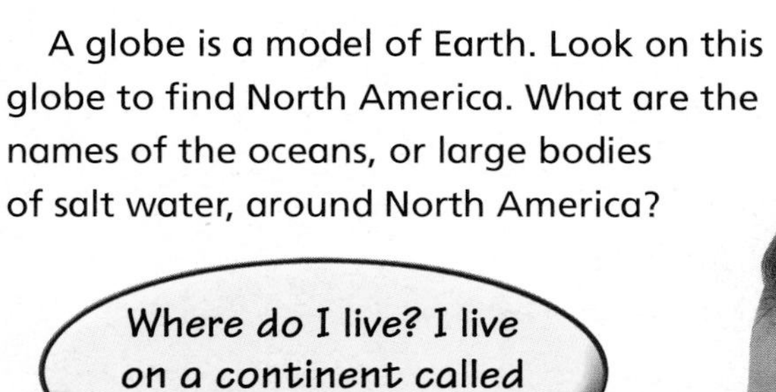

37

2 Teach and Discuss

Page 36

Review with children the labels in the diagram. Have volunteers use each of the words in a sentence.

1 **How are a neighborhood and a community alike? Different?** People live in both places. Communities are larger than neighborhoods.
Compare and Contrast

2 **Which is larger—your home state or our country?** Our country is larger.
Compare and Contrast

Page 37

After reading the page with children, help them use a globe to answer the question posed in the last sentence. Make the point that oceans are the largest bodies of water on Earth.

3 **Is a continent usually bigger than a country? How do you know?** Three countries make up the continent of North America.
Draw Conclusions

Ongoing Assessment

If... children get the concepts of country and continent confused,

then... show a map of South America. Identify it as a continent as you trace the outline of it with your finger. Point out countries within South America. Call on children to trace each outline. Ask: **Is this country bigger or smaller than the continent of South America?**

SOCIAL STUDIES STRAND
Culture

The Language of Mexico

- Point out Mexico on the globe. Tell children that most of the people in Mexico speak Spanish as their first language.
- Explain that children in Mexico learn counting rhymes and songs too. Teach the following Mexican counting rhyme. If there are children in the class who speak Spanish, have them read and lead the rhyme.

  Uno, dos, tres, cho-
  Uno, dos, tres, co-
  Uno, dos, tres, la-
  Uno, dos, tres, te.
  Chocolate, chocolate,
  ¡bate, bate, el chocolate!

continued

Page 38

Preview the content of pp. 38 and 39. Tell children that Earth has seven continents and four major oceans. Use a globe to point out and name the continents and oceans. Point out the Philippine islands off the coast of the continent of Asia. Tell children all of those islands together—about 7,000 of them—make up the country called the Republic of the Philippines. The islands are considered to be part of Asia.

Locate Key Words in the Text

4 What can you see on a map of the world? Tell children to look back at the text to find the correct answer.
Continents, oceans, the equator
Main Idea and Details

5 Do the children live on the same or different continents? Different **Analyze Pictures**

6 Which continent is south of North America? South America **Interpret Maps**

7 Is Africa closer to Asia or North America? Asia **Interpret Maps**

This is a map of the world. You can see continents and oceans on this map. You can also see the equator. The equator is a line 4 found on a map of the world that divides the world in half.

Practice and Extend

SOCIAL STUDIES Background

About Africa

- Some children may think that Africa is a country.
- Africa is the second largest continent and contains over 50 countries. The people have different languages, religions, and ways of life.

CURRICULUM CONNECTION Science

The Solar System

- Show children Earth's place in the solar system. Display a picture and name the planets in the order from nearest to the Sun to farthest from the Sun: Mercury, Venus, Earth, Mars, Jupiter, Saturn, Uranus, Neptune, and Pluto.

9 Meet some children from different countries around the world. What can you tell about where each child lives?

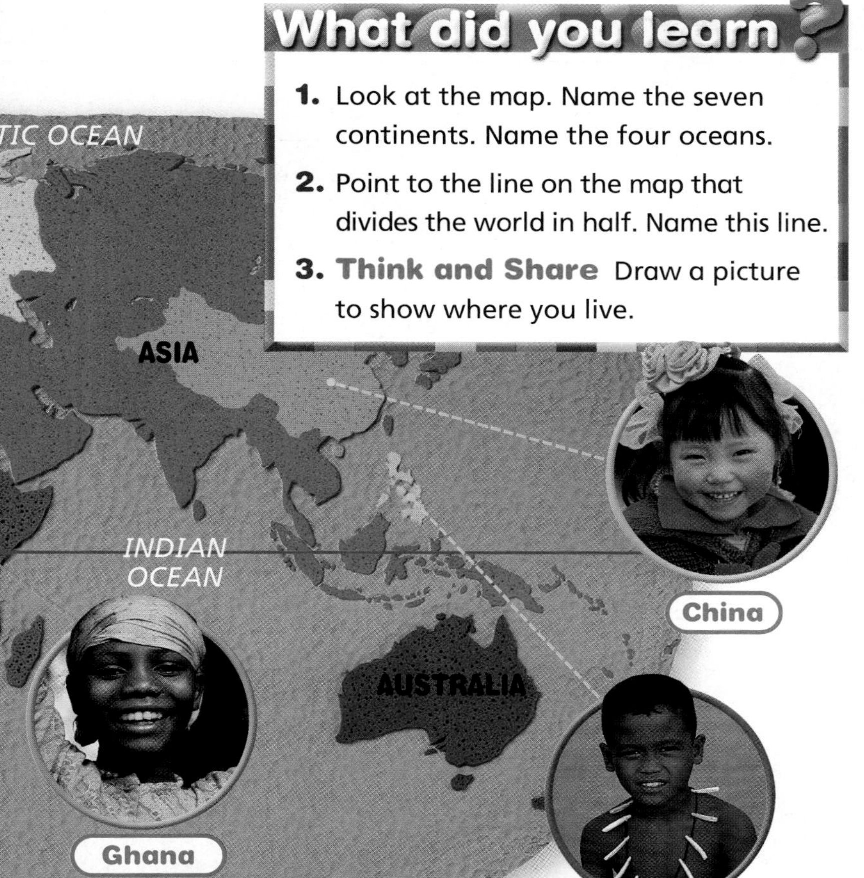

What did you learn?

1. Look at the map. Name the seven continents. Name the four oceans.
2. Point to the line on the map that divides the world in half. Name this line.
3. **Think and Share** Draw a picture to show where you live.

39

Page 39

Ask children who were born in other countries to identify their birth countries. If most of the children were born in the United States, have volunteers say where their ancestors were born. Make a list on the board. Next to each country's name, write the name of the continent it is on.

8 **What are some things you think most children do no matter where they live?** Children may respond: I think children everywhere play and go to school. **Generalize**

9 **What would you tell a child from another country about where you live?** Answers will vary but should include accurate information. Possible answer: I live in the state of Iowa in the country of the United States on the continent of North America. I live on a big farm. **Express Ideas**

3 Close and Assess

Ask children what information they can find on a globe, or a model of Earth. Have children write the name of the continent they live on. As needed, review/reteach these key concepts.

✓ What did you learn?

1. The seven continents are: North America, South America, Asia, Europe, Africa, Australia, Antarctica. The four oceans are: Atlantic, Pacific, Indian, and Arctic Oceans.
2. Observe children to check that they point to the equator.
3. **Think and Share** Review children's drawings with them individually. Children should understand that they are part of a larger world.

ACCESS CONTENT ESL Support

Knowing North America
Children focus attention on North America. Children use the map on pp. 38–39 to trace North America.

Beginning Have children label the continent and the Atlantic and Pacific Oceans.

Intermediate Have children write two facts about North America.

Advanced Have children write to say where North America is in relation to the other continents.

For additional ESL support, use Every Student Learns Guide, pp. 18–21.

Workbook, p. 9

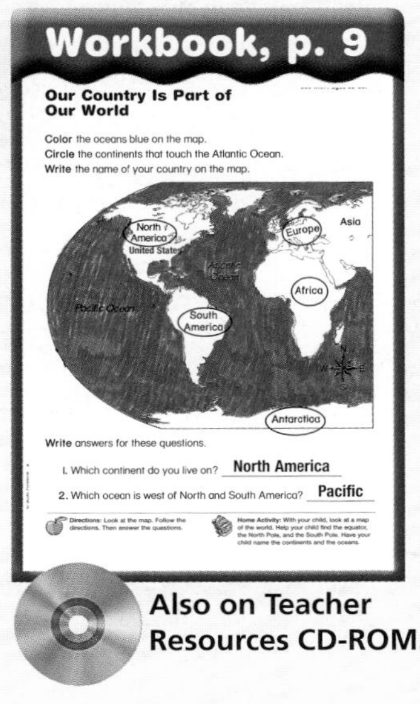

Our Country Is Part of Our World

Color the oceans blue on the map.
Circle the continents that touch the Atlantic Ocean.
Write the name of your country on the map.

Write answers for these questions.

1. Which continent do you live on? North America
2. Which ocean is west of North and South America? Pacific

Directions: Look at the map. Follow the directions. Then answer the questions.

Home Activity: With your child, look at a map of the world. Help your child find the equator, the North Pole, and the South Pole. Have your child name the continents and the oceans.

Also on Teacher Resources CD-ROM.

Big Book/Pupil Book pp. 40–41
DORLING KINDERSLEY

Children of the World

Objective

- Obtain information from visual sources—photographs and maps.

1 Introduce and Motivate

Preview Read the title of the feature while children look at the photographs. Ask what information is given about each child. Have children say what they notice is the same about all the children. (All are about the same age; all are smiling.)

Warm Up To activate prior knowledge, have children identify some things they think children all over the world do. Make a quick list.

2 Teach and Discuss

Have children follow along as you read the text. Read aloud the children's names and their home countries.

1 Why do you think a map is included on these pages? To help readers find the countries the children come from **Make Inferences**

2 Point to each of these continents as I say their names: *North America, South America, Europe, Africa, Asia and Australia*. Observe children to be certain they are locating each continent. Note: Antarctica, a continent around or near the South Pole, is not shown on this map. You may want to help children locate Antarctica on a globe or world map. **Interpret Maps**

CHILDREN

Children of the World

Oscar
Bolivia

Carlitos
Argentina

Mohammed
Egypt

Tadesse
Ethiopia

Children all around the world are busy doing the same things. They love to play games and they enjoy going to school. They wish for peace. They think that adults should take good care of the Earth. How else do you think these children are like each other? How else do you think they are like you?

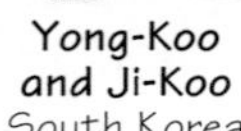

Aseye
Ghana

Esta
Tanzania

Sarala
India

Yong-Koo and Ji-Koo
South Korea

Ngawaiata
New Zealand

40

Practice and Extend

CURRICULUM CONNECTION
Math

Count the Kids!

- Have children count all the children shown.
- Have boys in the class count the boys shown.
- Have girls in the class count the girls.
- Take the gender counts and have children add them to see if they come up with the number of their original total group count.

CURRICULUM CONNECTION
Music

The More We Get Together

Have children sing the song with you.

The More We Get Together
The more we get together,
The more we get together, together, together,
the happier we'll be.
For your friends, and my friends
are your friends.
The more we get together,
the happier we'll be.

3 Describe how the children are dressed. Point out children whose clothing looks the most different from your clothing. Possible answer: Some children are dressed in sweaters, pants, and skirts like those we wear. Other children are wearing the special clothing of their country. **Analyze Picture/Compare and Contrast**

4 If your picture were added to these pages, what would it say below your picture? It would say my name and that I live in the United States. **Draw Conclusions**

3 Close and Assess

- Have children say what message they get from the words and pictures on the pages.
- Ask children to think about a message they would like to send children around the world. Call on volunteers to share their ideas.
- Read the names of the children and their countries. Ask children to say which child they might like to have as a pen pal. Encourage children to explain their selections.

Use with pages 36–41

Lesson 5 Wrap-Up

MEETING INDIVIDUAL NEEDS
Leveled Practice

Make a Map of the World
Have children trace the outline of a simple world map. Then have them indicate the cardinal directions north, south, east, and west on their maps.

Easy Have children label each of the continents and the four major oceans on their world maps. **Reteach**

On-Level Have children do what is described for the Easy level and indicate the borders of the United States, Mexico, and Canada on the map. Have children label each country. **Extend**

Challenge Have children work with partners. Have each partner write three questions about the map, such as *Is Europe east or west of North America?* Have children exchange papers and answer the questions. **Enrich**

Hands-on Activities

SOCIAL STUDIES STRAND
Culture

A World of Words

Objective Identify examples of cultural heritage (language).

Materials self-stick notes, world map

Learning Style Linguistic

Group

Time 15–20 minutes

1. Have children suggest words they know from other languages—*mother, father, hello, goodbye,* animal names, everyday objects.

2. Write children's suggestions on self-stick notes. Have them stick the words on the map to show the countries from which the words came.

konnichiwa

hola

mamá

CURRICULUM CONNECTION
Drama

'Round the World

Objective Participate in a game to identify the continents.

Learning Style Kinesthetic/Verbal

Group

Time 15–20 minutes

1. Tell children they will play a circle game about the continents.

2. Have children stand in a circle. Model how to play the game. You are "it." You walk around the circle several times saying: "Go round and round the world, go round and round the world, go round and round the world, as we have done before."

3. Choose a child and say as you lead him or her away: "Now follow me to (continent name). Now follow me to (continent name). Now follow me to (continent name). As we have done before." The game continues with a new child who is "it."

CURRICULUM CONNECTION
Writing

Pen Pal Letters

Objective Write to tell about self.

Materials paper, pencils

Learning Style Verbal/Kinesthetic

Partners

Time 15–20 minutes

1. Have each child choose one of the children featured on pp. 38–39 to have as a pen pal.

2. Children should use a friendly letter form to tell their pen pals about where they live—continent, country, state, city, or town—and some personal information.

3. Children may include pictures of themselves.

Dear Milo,
How are you?
I went to the circus. The clowns were funny.

Ending Unit 1

End with a Poem **pages 42–43**	Children will listen to and talk about a poem titled "In the Country, In the City" by Charles Wood. The poem contrasts the sights and sounds of country and city living.	
Unit 1 Review **pages 44–47**	Children will review unit vocabulary words and the unit skills of using context clues, using a problem-solving process, and reading and making a map. Children will answer questions about what they learned in the unit. Children will learn about several books that describe places people live.	Resources • Workbook, p. 10 ✓• Assessment Book, pp. 1–4
Unit 1 Project **page 48**	Children will learn how to make a travel booklet. They will also be directed to a Web site where they can learn more about different kinds of communities.	Resource • Workbook p. 11

Wrap-up

Activity

A "My Neighborhood" Poster

Have children use sheets of oaktag or stiff paper to make posters about their neighborhoods.

- The posters should include five places that are important to children. Children should draw a picture of each place and beside the picture write the purpose or function of the place and why it is important to them.
- Children should label their posters with *My (urban, suburban, rural) Neighborhood.*

Performance Assessment
You can use the activity on this page as a performance assessment.

✓ Assessment Scoring Guide

Make a "My Neighborhood" Poster	
4	Identifies five distinct places and explains their importance. Correctly identifies the type of neighborhood.
3	Identifies fewer than five distinct places. Sometimes explains their importance. Correctly identifies the type of neighborhood.
2	Identifies five distinct places. Neglects identifying their importance. Correctly identifies the type of neighborhood.
1	Identifies fewer than five places. Does not identify the type of neighborhood.

In the Country, In the City

Objective

- Create poems to express ideas.

1 Introduce and Motivate

Preview Point to and read the title, then identify the author of the poem. From the title and art, ask children what they think the poem might be about. Explain that country here refers to a rural community, not a nation.

Warm Up To activate prior knowledge, write a "T" chart on the board. Label the columns *Country* and *City*. Ask children to suggest words or phrases that describe each place. Record their responses.

2 Teach and Discuss

Invite children to listen as you read the poem. Encourage them to "hear in their own minds" some of the sounds described in the poem. Also have them picture in their minds some of the settings described.

Help children realize that page 42 describes the country, while page 43 describes the city.

1 What others sounds would you hear in the country? Answers will vary, but possible responses include: pig squealing, horses neighing, and tractors being driven. **Express Ideas**

Practice and Extend

Adding Lines to the Poem

- Refer children's attention to the "T" chart on the board.
- Have each child choose one of the words or phrases on the chart and write a complete sentence about the city or the country.
- Then have children use their sentences as the basis for creating two new lines for either verse of the poem.

Books About the City and the Country

Use the following books for children to learn more about life in the city and life out in the country.

The Last Dragon, by Susan Miho Nunes and Chris K. Soentpiet (illustrator), (Clarion Books, ISBN 0-395-67020-9, 1995) Easy ***Notable Social Studies Book***

My Grandma's the Mayor: A story for children about community spirit and pride, by Marjorie White Pellegrino and John Lund (illustrator), (Magination, ISBN 1-557-98608-8, 1999) Challenge

2 **Where is it busier—the country or the city? What words let you know?** The city; trains zoom, buses go, runners run. **Compare and Contrast**

3 **Does the poet, or the person who wrote the poem, like the city or the country better?** Possible answer: He probably likes them both equally. **Draw Conclusions**

3 Close and Assess

- Divide children into two groups.
- Have children do a choral reading of the selection, with each group reading alternate stanzas. Groups can take turns beginning the reading.
- After children have read the poem aloud, invite them to share what they like most about the poem.

For variety, you can also assign one line of the poem to each child in class or several lines to small groups of children. Instead of having the child or group read aloud the line or lines, have them either pantomime the action or repeat the sound mentioned in the rhyming pairs.

Review

Resources

- Assessment Book, pp. 1–4
- Workbook, p. 10: Vocabulary Review

Vocabulary Review

1. vote
2. law
3. community
4. history
5. suburb

Answers to Test Prep

1. urban
2. rural

Review

Vocabulary Review

community
history
law
vote
suburb

Tell which word completes each sentence.

1. You make a choice when you ________.
2. A rule that everyone must follow is called a _______.
3. Many neighborhoods make up a __________.
4. The story of people and places from the past is ________.
5. A community located near a city is a ________.

★ ★ ★ ★ ★ ★ ★ ★

Which word completes each sentence?

1. A city is called an ________ area.
   a. rural b. community
   c. urban d. suburb
2. A lot of open space and towns that are far apart is called a ________ area.
   a. rural b. community
   c. urban d. capital

44

Practice and Extend

Assessment Options

✓ Unit 1 Assessment

- Unit 1 Content Test: Use Assessment Book, pp. 1–2
- Unit 1 Skills Test: Use Assessment Book, pp. 3–4

Standardized Test Prep

- Unit 1 tests contain standardized test formats.

✓ Unit 1 Performance Assessment

- See p. 48 for information about using the Unit 1 Project as a means of performance assessment.
- A scoring guide for the Unit 1 Project is provided in the teacher's notes on p. 48.

Test Talk

- Test Talk Practice Book

Skills Review

Use Context Clues

Read the following passage.

A capital is a city where leaders of a state make laws and work. Leaders from North Carolina work in the capital city of Raleigh.

Tell the meaning of *capital*. If you don't know what the word means, look at the words around it to help you find its meaning.

Solve a Problem

Think of a problem that you want to solve. Tell or write about it, using this six-step plan:

1. Name the problem.
2. Find out more about the problem.
3. List ways to solve the problem.
4. Talk about the best way to solve the problem.
5. Solve the problem.
6. How well is the problem solved?

45

WEB SITE Technology

For more information you can select the dictionary or encyclopedia from *Social Studies Library* at **www.sfsocialstudies.com.**

Workbook, p. 10

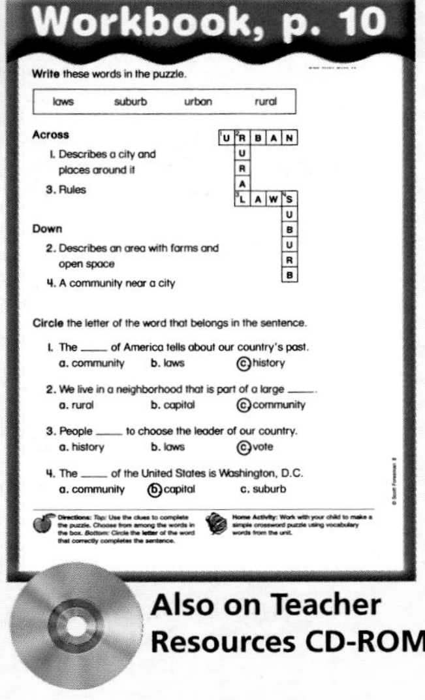

Write these words in the puzzle.

laws suburb urban rural

Across

1. Describes a city and places around it
3. Rules

Down

2. Describes an area with farms and open space
4. A community near a city

(Puzzle answers: 1 Across URBAN; 2 Down RURAL; 3 Across LAWS; 4 Down SUBURB)

Circle the letter of the word that belongs in the sentence.

1. The ____ of America tells about our country's past.
   a. community b. laws (c.) history
2. We live in a neighborhood that is part of a large ____.
   a. rural b. capital (c.) community
3. People ____ to choose the leader of our country.
   a. history b. laws (c.) vote
4. The ____ of the United States is Washington, D.C.
   a. community (b.) capital c. suburb

Directions: *Top:* Use the clues to complete the puzzle. Choose from among the words in the box. *Bottom:* Circle the **letter** of the word that correctly completes the sentence.

Home Activity: Work with your child to make a simple crossword puzzle using vocabulary words from the unit.

Also on Teacher Resources CD-ROM.

Skills Review

Context Clues

- Children's sentences should show an understanding of the word *capital* as it relates to a city where the government of a state is located.

Use the following scoring guide.

✓ Assessment Scoring Guide

Write a Sentence After Using Context Clues	
4	Sentence details show recognition and application of context clues.
3	Sentence details show some application of context clues.
2	Sentence details show little understanding of how to use context clues.
1	Sentence reiterates the model.

Solve a Problem

Problems will differ. Children's responses should demonstrate understanding and inclusion of all the steps in the problem-solving skill.

Review

continued

Skills Review

Read a Map

1. South
2. Park Street
3. Answers will vary. Children may respond that the schools in their community are also large buildings, that the courthouse has a flag on top of it or outside it. Some children may say their community library is more like an office building and larger than the one shown.

Skills on Your Own

- Children's maps should be clear, accurate, and inclusive of the elements identified.

Use the following scoring guide.

✓Assessment Scoring Guide

Make a Map	
4	Represents the community accurately and includes all required elements.
3	Represents the community accurately but includes only some required elements.
2	Represents the community with some inaccuracies and excludes some required elements.
1	Misrepresents the community due to many errors and excludes some required elements.

Review

Read a Map

This map shows a courthouse, a library, and other buildings that you might have in your community. Use the map key and direction arrows to help you answer these questions.

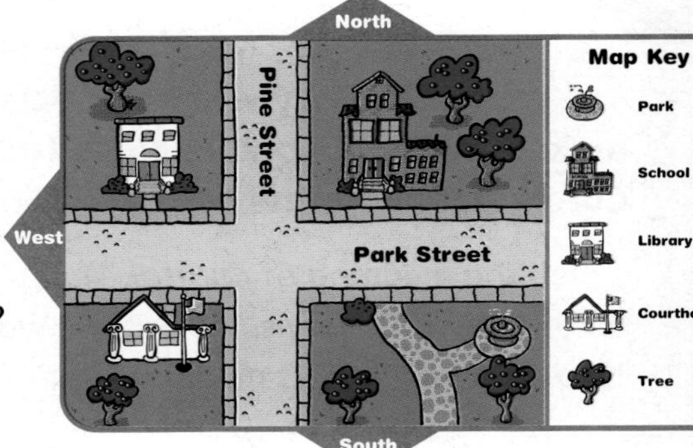

1. What direction would you go if you were walking from the library to the courthouse?
2. What street is in front of the [school symbol]?
3. Tell how these buildings are like the ones in your community. Tell how they are different.

Skills On Your Own

Draw your own map of a community. Include a map key with symbols that stand for a library, a post office, a hospital, a courthouse, and other buildings.

46

Practice and Extend

Revisit the Unit Question

✓Unit 1 Portfolio Assessment

- Have children write notes to tell what they would say now about where they live.
- Encourage children to put a check mark next to ideas they got while reading the unit.
- Have children use their notes to write complete sentences.
- Suggest children draw a picture or pictures to go with their final sentences.
- Have children add their drawings and sentences to their Social Studies Portfolio.

What did you learn?

1. Describe two neighborhoods in your community.
2. Why are laws important?
3. How are urban, suburban, and rural communities alike? How are they different?
4. **Write and Share** Tell or write about where you live. Tell something about your community, state, and country.

Look for key words in the question.

Read About Where You Live

Look for books like these in the library.

47

What did you learn?

1. Children's responses should be detailed and show an understanding of comparing and contrasting.
2. Laws are important because they keep our community clean and safe.
3. Urban communities have many people, big buildings, and lots of cars and buses. Suburban communities are near cities. They have houses and small buildings. Rural areas have lots of land. Many farms are in rural areas. People live in all three kinds of communties.
4. **Write and Share** Check children's responses for inclusiveness and clarity.

Locate Key Words in the Question
Use What did you learn?, Question 3, to model the Test Talk strategy.

Find the key words in the question.
Have children ask themselves, "What key words in the question will help me answer it?"

Reread the question.
Children should identify the key words *alike* and *different*.

Read About Where You Live

Communities, by Gail Saunders-Smith (Pebble Books, ISBN 1-560-65494-5, 1997). **Easy**

Houses and Homes, by Ann Morris (Mulberry Books, ISBN 0-688-13578-1, 1995). A world map is included at the back of the book. **On-Level**

City Green, by DyAnne DiSalvo-Ryan (Morrow, ISBN 0-688-12786-X, 1994). A young girl works with neighbors to change an empty lot into a community garden. **Challenge**

Unit 1 Project

Travel Channel

Objective

- Compare and contrast rural, suburban, and urban communities.

Resource

- Workbook, p. 11

Materials

construction paper, pencils, coloring materials, magazine pictures, postcards, travel brochures

Follow This Procedure

- Review the differences between rural, urban, and suburban places.
- Have children make a travel brochure for a rural, urban, or suburban location. Share travel brochures.
- Have children fold a sheet of paper into three parts. The name or type of location can go on the front and the illustrations inside.
- Have children work individually or in pairs. The brochure should describe the place as rural, urban, or suburban and tell why it is a good place to visit.
- Invite children to present their brochures in class.

✓ **Assessment Scoring Guide**

	Travel Channel
4	Describes and illustrates a location using elaborate details to explain why it is rural, urban, or suburban and gives reasons why it is a good place to visit.
3	Describes and illustrates a location using several details to explain why it is rural, urban, or suburban and gives at least one reason why it is a good place to visit.
2	Describes and illustrates a location using few details to explain why it is rural, urban, or suburban and uses vague word choices to tell why it is a good place to visit.
1	Describes and illustrates a location using few or no details, is unable to explain why the location is rural, urban, or suburban, uses limited or incorrect word choices to tell about the location and why it is a good place to visit.

Travel Channel

Travel reporters share their thoughts about places to visit.

1 **Choose** a place to visit that is urban, suburban, or rural.

2 **Make** a travel booklet about the place you chose. Draw pictures of what a visitor might see or do there.

3 **Write** words to describe your pictures. Tell what makes your place rural, urban, or suburban.

4 **Present** your booklet to the class. Tell why people might like to go to your place.

Internet Activity

Go to www.sfsocialstudies.com/activities to learn more about communities.

Practice and Extend

✓**Performance Assessment**

- The Unit Project can also be used as a performance assessment activity.
- Use the scoring guide to assess each group's work.

Children can launch the activity by clicking on *Grade 2, Unit 1* at **www.sfsocialstudies.com/ activities**.

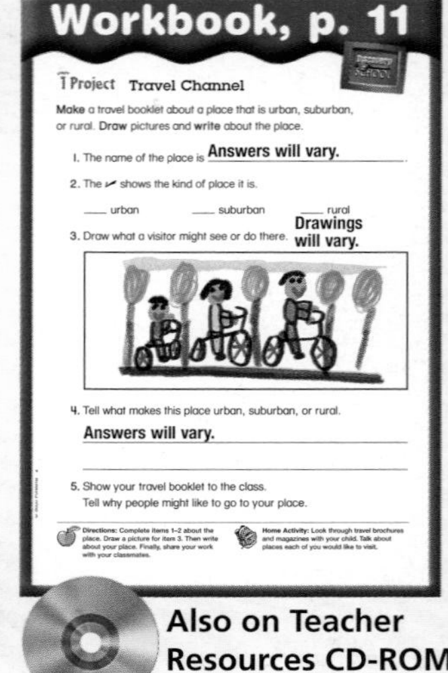

Workbook, p. 11

1 Project Travel Channel

Make a travel booklet about a place that is urban, suburban, or rural. **Draw** pictures and **write** about the place.

1. The name of the place is **Answers will vary.**
2. The ✓ shows the kind of place it is.
   ___ urban ___ suburban ___ rural
3. Draw what a visitor might see or do there. **Drawings will vary.**
4. Tell what makes this place urban, suburban, or rural.
   Answers will vary.
5. Show your travel booklet to the class.
   Tell why people might like to go to your place.

Directions: Complete items 1–2 about the place. Draw a picture for item 3. Then write about your place. Finally, share your work with your classmates.

Home Activity: Look through travel brochures and magazines with your child. Talk about places each of you would like to visit.

Also on Teacher Resources CD-ROM.

Our Earth
UNIT
2

Unit 2 Planning Guide

Our Earth

Begin with a Song pp. 50–51 **Vocabulary Preview** pp. 52–53

 **Reading Social Studies, Cause and Effect** pp. 54–55

Lesson Titles	Pacing	Main Ideas
Lesson 1 **Interview with a Geographer** pp. 56–59 **Map and Globe Skills: Landforms and Water on a Map** pp. 60–61	2 days	• In the study of geography, one learns about such landforms as mountains and plains, and about such bodies of water as oceans and rivers. • Some maps show landforms.
Lesson 2 **Where People Live** pp. 62–65 **Then and Now: How and Where People Lived** pp. 66–67	2 days	• People live in different kinds of communities and in different environments. • Climate affected the way people lived in the past, just as it affects people today.
Lesson 3 **From My Orchard to You** pp. 68–71 **Smithsonian Institution: Harvest Time** pp. 72–73 **Biography: Cesar Chavez** pp. 74–75	3 days	• Producers make or grow goods; consumers buy and use them. • Vintage seed packets and catalogs and crate advertising tell about our agricultural past. • Cesar Chavez organized farm workers and fought for their rights; he helped many such workers become U.S. citizens.
Lesson 4 **Our Earth's Resources** pp. 76–79 **Chart and Graph Skills: Read a Bar Graph** pp. 80–81	2 days	• Since all living things depend on the Earth's natural resources, those resources must be used wisely. • A bar graph can be used to compare information.
Lesson 5 **Caring for Our Resources** pp. 82–85 **Biography: Rachel Carson** pp. 86–87 **Citizen Heroes: Responsibility The Earth Angels** pp. 88–89	3 days	• Yellowstone National Park is a place where conservation is put into practice. • Rachel Carson, a biologist and writer, dedicated her life to conserving the Earth's resources. • Children, too, can help save the Earth and its resources, as demonstrated by the Earth Angels.

✓ **End with a Song** pp. 90–91 ✓ **Unit 2 Review** pp. 92–95 ✓ **Unit 2 Project** p. 96

✓ = Assessment Options

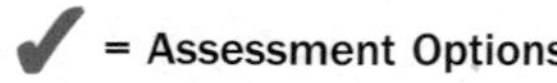

Scott Foresman Social Studies
Indiana Academic Standards

Grade 2 Unit 2 • *Our Earth*

Lesson Title	Indiana Academic Standards Social Studies
Lesson 1 Interview with a Geographer pp. 56-59	**IN Academic Standard 2.4.1** Define productive resources and identify resources used to produce goods and services.
Map and Globe Skills: Landforms and Water on a Map pp. 60-61	**IN Academic Standard 2.3.5** Identify map symbols for land and water forms.
Lesson 2 Where Poeple Live pp. 62-65	**IN Academic Standard 2.3.7** Identify ways that the physical environment influences human activities. **(Also 2.3.3, 2.3.4)**
Then and Now: How and Where People Lived pp. 66-67	**IN Academic Standard 2.1.1** Listen to historical stories and compare life in the past and present. **(Also 2.1.2, 2.3.7)**
Lesson 3 From My Orchard to You pp. 68-71	**IN Academic Standard 2.4.1** Define productive resources and identify resources used to produce goods and services. **(Also 2.1.1, 2.1.2, 2.4.4)**
Smithsonian Institution: Harvest Time pp. 72-73	**Reviews IN Academic Standard K.1.1** Compare people, objects, and events of today and long ago.
Biography: Cesar Chavez pp. 74-75	**IN Academic Standard 2.2.4** Identify good leaders and good citizens, and explain the qualities that make them admirable. **(Also 2.3.3, 2.5.5)**
Lesson 4 Our Earth's Resources pp. 76-79	**IN Academic Standard 2.4.1** Define productive resources and identify resources used to produce goods and services. **(Also 2.3.7)**
Chart and Graph Skills: Read a Bar Graph pp. 80-81	**Reviews IN Academic Standard 1.5.1** Identify talents, interests, and hobbies.
Lesson 5 Caring for Our Resources pp. 82-85	**Previews IN Academic Standard 3.3.7** Identify environmental issues and ways to solve these problems.
Biography: Rachel Carson pp. 86-87	**IN Academic Standard 2.2.4** Identify good leaders and good citizens, and explain the qualities that make them admirable, such as honesty. **(Also 2.3.3, 2.3.7, 2.4.1)**
Citizen Heroes: The Earth Angels pp. 88-89	**IN Academic Standard 2.1.3** Identify individuals who had an impact on communities. **(Also 2.2.1, 2.2.4, 2.3.3, 2.5.5)**

Insert between pages 49b - 49c
For complete standards listing, please see front tab.

Continued on other side →

Scott Foresman Social Studies to the Indiana Academic Standards for English/Language Arts

Grade 2 Unit 2 • *Our Earth*

Lesson Title	Indiana Academic Standards English/Language Arts
Begin with a Song, pp. 50-51 *Vocabulary Preview, pp. 52-53* *Reading Social Studies, Cause and Effect, pp. 54-55*	**2.2.6** Recognize cause-and-effect relationships in a text. See also 2.2.4, 2.2.7, 2.3.4
Lesson 1 Interview with a Geographer, pp. 56-59	**2.1.3** Decode (sound out) regular words with more than one syllable (dinosaur, vacation). See also 2.1.5, 2.1.8, 2.2.2, 2.2.4, 2.2.5, 2.6.2, 2.6.3, 2.6.5, 2.6.6, 2.6.7, 2.6.8, 2.6.9
Map and Globe Skills: Landforms and Water on a Map, pp. 60-61	**2.2.7** Interpret information from diagrams, charts, and graphs. See also 2.1.1, 2.1.3, 2.2.2, 2.2.4
Lesson 2 Where People Live, pp. 62-65	**2.2.6** Recognize cause-and-effect relationships in a text. See also 2.4.4, 2.4.5, 2.4.6, 2.4.7, 2.4.8, 2.5.2, 2.5.5, 2.5.6, 2.6.2, 2.6.3, 2.6.4, 2.6.7, 2.6.8, 2.6.9
Then and Now: How and Where People Lived, pp. 66-67	**2.2.6** Recognize cause-and-effect relationships in a text. See also 2.4.4, 2.4.5, 2.4.6, 2.4.7, 2.4.8, 2.5.2, 2.5.5, 2.5.6, 2.6.2, 2.6.3, 2.6.4, 2.6.7, 2.6.8, 2.6.9
Lesson 3 From My Orchard to You, pp. 68-71	**2.2.6** Recognize cause-and-effect relationships in a text. See also 2.1.3, 2.2.4, 2.2.5, 2.7.8
Smithsonian Institution: Harvard Time, pp. 72-73	**2.2.7** Interpret information from diagrams, charts, and graphs. See also 2.1.3, 2.2.4
Biography: Cesar Chavez, pp. 74-75	**2.7.8** Retell stories, including characters, setting, and plot. See also 2.7.11
Lesson 4 Our Earth's Resources, pp. 76-79	**2.1.3** Decode (sound out) regular words with more than one syllable. See also 2.2.4, 2.2.6, 2.4.6, 2.4.7, 2.4.8, 2.5.2, 2.6.2, 2.6.4, 2.6.8
Chart and Graph Skills: Read a Bar Graph pp. 80-81	**2.2.7** Interpret information from diagrams, charts, and graphs. See also 2.2.4, 2.4.2, 2.5.6, 2.6.1, 2.6.2, 2.6.4, 2.6.8, 2.7.4
Lesson 5 Caring for Our Resources, pp. 82-85	**2.2.6** Recognize cause-and-effect relationships in a text. See also 2.2.4, 2.7.8
Biography: Rachel Carson, pp. 86-87	**2.2.4** Ask and respond to questions to aid comprehension about important elements of informational texts. See also 2.7.8
Citizen Heroes: The Earth Angels, pp. 88-89	**2.2.6** Recognize cause-and-effect relationships in a text. See also 2.2.4, 2.7.8
End with a Song, pp. 90-91 *Unit 2 Review, pp. 92-95* *Unit 2 Project, p. 96*	**2.2.6** Recognize cause-and-effect relationships in a text. See also 2.1.3, 2.1.5, 2.2.4, 2.2.7, 2.4.2, 2.4.4, 2.4.5, 2.4.6, 2.4.7, 2.4.8, 2.5.5, 2.5.6, 2.6.1, 2.6.2, 2.6.3, 2.6.4, 2.6.5, 2.6.8

Please don't litter.

Smell the flowers, but don't pick them!

Vocabulary	Resources	Meeting Individual Needs
geography **landform**	• Workbook, pp. 14–15 • Transparencies 3, 14 • Vocabulary Cards: geography, landform • Every Student Learns Guide, pp. 22–25	• ESL Support, TE p. 58 • Leveled Practice, TE p. 61a
	• Workbook, p. 16 • Transparency 13 • Every Student Learns Guide, pp. 26–29	• ESL Support, TE p. 63 • Leveled Practice, TE p. 67a
ancestor **producer** **consumer**	• Workbook, pp. 17–18 • Transparency 2 • Vocabulary Cards: ancestor, producer, consumer • Every Student Learns Guide, pp. 30–33	• ESL Support, TE p. 71 • Leveled Practice, TE p. 75a
natural resource **crop**	• Workbook, pp. 19–20 • Transparency 15 • Vocabulary Cards: natural resource, crop • Every Student Learns Guide, pp. 34–37	• ESL Support, TE p. 78 • Leveled Practice, TE p. 81a
conservation	• Workbook, p. 21 • Vocabulary Card: conservation • Every Student Learns Guide, pp. 38–41	• ESL Support, TE p. 85 • Leveled Practice, TE p. 89a

Providing More Depth

Multimedia Library

- ***Earth*** **by Susanna Van Rose**
- ***Miss Rumphius*** **by Barbara Cooney**
- **Songs and Music**
- **Video Field Trips**
- **Software**

Additional Resources

- Family Activities
- Vocabulary Cards
- Daily Activity Bank
- Social Studies Plus!
- Big Book Atlas
- Outline Maps
- Desk Maps

ADDITIONAL Technology

- Audio Text
- The test maker
- Teacher Resources CD-ROM
- Map Resources CD-ROM
- **www.sfsocialstudies.com**

To establish guidelines for children's safe and responsible use of the Internet, use the **Scott Foresman Internet Guide.**

Additional Internet Links
To find out more about:

- Yellowstone National Park, visit **www.nps.gov**

Key Internet Search Terms

- Yellowstone/national parks
- apples

Unit 2 Objectives

Beginning of Unit 2

- **Use music to learn about a topic.** (pp. 50–51)
- **Use pictures to obtain information.** (pp. 52–53)
- **Determine the meanings of words.** (pp. 52–53)
- **Identify cause-and-effect relationships.** (pp. 54–55)

Lesson 1
Interview with a Geographer pp. 56–59

- **Identify landforms and bodies of water.**
- **Obtain information through interviews.**
- **Identify major landforms and bodies of water on a map.** (pp. 60-61)

Lesson 2
Where People Live pp. 62–65

- **Compare similarities and differences among families in different communities.**
- **Understand how physical characteristics of places and regions affect people's activities and settlement patterns.** (pp. 66-67)

Lesson 3
From My Orchard to You pp. 68–71

- **Distinguish between producing and consuming.**
- **Trace the development of a product from a natural resource to a finished product.**
- **Obtain information from a variety of sources such as photographs of artifacts.** (pp. 72-73)
- **Identify characteristics of good citizenship such as a belief in justice, truth, equality, and responsibility for the common good.** (pp. 74-75)

Lesson 4
Our Earth's Resources pp. 76–79

- **Learn how people depend on the physical environment and its resources to meet their needs.**
- **Identify ways to conserve and replenish natural resources.**
- **Interpret and construct bar graphs.** (pp. 80-81)

Lesson 5
Caring for Our Resources pp. 82–85

- **Identify ways people can conserve and replenish natural resources.**
- **Identify ways people can conserve and replenish natural resources.** (pp. 86-87)
- **Identify characteristics of good citizenship such as belief in justice, truth, equality, and responsibility for the common good.** (pp. 86-87)
- **Identify ordinary people who exemplify good citizenship.** (pp. 88-89)

End of Unit 2

- **Identify selected patriotic songs.** (pp. 90-91)

Assessment Options

✓ Formal Assessment

- **What did you learn?** PE/TE pp. 59, 65, 71, 79, 85, 95
- **Unit Review,** PE/TE pp. 92–95
- **Unit 2 Tests, Assessment Book,** pp. 5–8
- **The test maker,** (test-generator software)

✓ Informal Assessment

- **Teacher's Edition Questions,** throughout Lessons and Features
- **Close and Assess,** TE pp. 55, 59, 61, 65, 67, 71, 73, 75, 79, 81, 85, 87, 89, 91
- **Try it!** PE/TE pp. 55, 61, 81
- **Think and Share,** PE/TE pp. 59, 65, 71, 75, 79, 85, 87
- **Responsibility in Action,** PE/TE p. 89
- **Hands-on History,** PE/TE p. 67

Ongoing Assessment

Ongoing Assessment is found throughout the Teacher's Edition lessons using an **If... then** model.

If = students' observable behavior,	**then** = reteaching and enrichment suggestions

✓ Portfolio Assessment

- **Portfolio Assessment,** TE pp. 49, 94
- **Leveled Practice,** TE pp. 52, 61a, 67a, 75a, 81a, 89a
- **Workbook,** pp. 12–23
- **Unit Review: Skills on Your Own,** p. 94
- **Curriculum Connection: Writing,** TE pp. 57, 61a, 65, 81, 81a, 89a

✓ Performance Assessment

- **Hands-on Unit Project** (Unit 2 Performance Assessment), PE/TE pp. 49, 96
- **Internet Activity,** PE p. 96
- **Unit Review: Write and Share,** PE/TE p. 95
- **Scoring Guides,** TE pp. 90a, 94, 96

Test Talk

Test-Taking Strategies

Understand the Question

- **Locate Key Words in the Question,** TE p. 61
- **Locate Key Words in the Text,** TE pp. 59, 79, 95

Understand the Answer

- **Choose the Right Answer, Test Talk Practice Book**
- **Use Information from the Text,** TE p. 67
- **Use Information from Graphics,** TE p. 81
- **Write Your Answer,** TE p. 65

For additional practice, use the Test Talk Practice Book.

Featured Strategy

Locate Key Words in the Text

Children will:

- Make sure they understand the key words in the question.
- Find key words in the text that match key words in the question.

PE/TE p. 95, **TE** pp. 59, 79

Curriculum Connections

Integrating Your Day

The lessons, skills, and features of Unit 2 provide many opportunities to make connections between social studies and other areas of the elementary curriculum.

Social Studies

Reading

Reading Skill—Cause and Effect, PE/TE pp. 54–55, TE pp. 56, 62, 68, 82

Words to Keep!, TE p. 67a

Word Search, TE p. 75a

Reading Skill—Categorize, TE p. 76

Reading Skill—Cause and Effect, TE p. 82

Writing

Write Interview Questions, TE p. 57

Riddles, TE p. 61a

Pen Pal Letters, TE p. 65

Write a Recipe for Fruit Salad, TE p. 81

Earth Chants, TE p. 81a

Terrific Trees, TE p. 81a

Slogans, TE p. 89a

My Book About Our Earth, TE p. 90a

Math

Apple Math, TE p. 69

Apple Seeds, TE p. 75a

Literature

Desert Life, TE p. 67a

Field Trip, TE p. 75a

Share a Classic, TE p. 87

Read About Our Earth and Its Resources, PE/TE p. 95

Science

Parts of a Plant, TE p. 55

Fact Detectives, TE p. 61a

Hairy Heads, TE p. 81a

Neighborhood Plants and Animals, TE p. 83

Animal Facts, TE p. 89a

Music/Drama

Re-create the Interview, TE p. 59

Sing a Song About Maps, TE p. 61

Dramatizing, TE p. 67a

Sing a Song, TE p. 77

Art

Picture It!, TE p. 51

Draw Geography Pictures, TE p. 61a

Clay Forms, TE p. 61a

A Class Mural, TE p. 67a

In the Marketplace, TE p. 75a

Make a Collage, TE p. 81a

Earth Day T-shirts, TE p. 89a

Picture the Song, TE p. 91

Look for this symbol throughout the Teacher's Edition to find **Curriculum Connections.**

Professional Development

Why Study the Social Studies?

by Dr. M. Gail Hickey, Ed.D.
Indiana University/Purdue University

Adults often think of social studies as an unending stream of names, dates, and events to be memorized. Children study social studies in schools for purposes far more vital than simple memorization. Studying social studies helps students develop into well-rounded persons equipped to understand the world around them. Social studies also helps students comprehend their own abilities to contribute to and shape their environments—whether these environments be social or geographic.

People, Places, and Environments

The study of people, places, and human-environment interactions assists students as they create their spatial views and geographic perspectives of the world beyond their personal locations. Students need the knowledge, skills, and understanding to answer questions such as: Where are things located? Why are they located where they are? What do we mean by "region"? How do landforms change? What implications do these changes have for people?

Tarry Lindquist, recipient of the Elementary Social Studies Teacher of the Year Award and author of SEEING THE WHOLE THROUGH SOCIAL STUDIES (1995), believes "making learning meaningful is the core of teaching." If young students cannot connect what is happening in the classroom with their own homes and lives, she writes, "then it seems to me that not much learning is going to occur."

- *The Citizen Heroes feature "The Earth Angels" (pp. 88–89) discusses a group of children who help protect the Earth's resources by implementing a number of wildlife conservation projects.*

ESL Support

by Jim Cummins, Ph. D.
University of Toronto

Accessing the Language of Social Studies

There is general agreement among applied linguists that sufficient *comprehensible input* is a necessary condition for acquisition of a second or third language. The notion of comprehensible input refers to the processing of meaning in the target language. Exposure by itself is not enough—it must be exposure that learners can understand.

Dramatization/Acting Out

For beginning ESL students, *Total Physical Response*, where students act out commands, can be highly effective. Additionally, the meanings of individual words can be demonstrated through gestures and pantomime. The teacher can do this or call on students who know the meanings to act them out for other students to guess. This can also be a group activity that generates a lot of fun in the classroom. At more advanced levels, history can come alive in the classroom by having students *dramatize historical events and characters*. This kind of dramatization is especially effective for ESL students as it enables them to take on another "persona" in the classroom.

The following examples in the Teacher's Edition will help you to enable ESL students to access the content:

Desert Pantomime *(p. 63) helps English Language Learners learn the concept of the types of places in which people live, such as desert. This approach will help them understand the similarities and differences among a variety of communities.*

Taking Roles *(p. 71) has children acting out the roles of the consumer and producer to distinguish between the two concepts. This activity will also help children understand the process of getting a good, such as apples, from the farm to the store and finally to the consumer.*

Read Aloud

This Land Is Your Land

by Woody Guthrie

This land is your land.
This land is my land.
From California
To the New York island;
From the redwood forest
To the Gulf Stream waters;
This land was made for you and me.

Build Background

- Use a U.S. map to point out California, New York, the Pacific Northwest, and the Gulf of Mexico. Tell children the land the song refers to is all of the United States—all of the land between those four points.
- Ask children who may have traveled cross country or from state to state to tell about their experiences.

Read Alouds and Primary Sources

Read Alouds and Primary Sources contains selections to be used with Unit 2.

Bibliography

I Am Water, by Jean Marzollo and Judith Moffatt (Illustrator) (Cartwheel Books, ISBN 0-590-26587-3, 1996). **Easy**

Time Flies, by Eric Rohmann (Dragonfly, ISBN 0-517-88555-7, 1997). A bird flies through a museum exhibit and back into the land of the dinosaurs in this imaginative picture book tale. **Easy** ***Caldecott Honor Book***

The Butterfly House, by Eve Bunting and Greg Shed (Illustrator) (Scholastic, ISBN 0-590-84884-4, 1999). A girl rescues a caterpillar and cares for it. **On-Level** ***Notable Social Studies Book***

Water, Water Everywhere: A Book About the Water Cycle, by Melvin Berger and Gilda Berger, Bobbi Tull (Illustrator) (Ideals, ISBN 1-571-02042-X, 1995). **On-Level**

The Way to Start a Day, by Byrd Baylor and Peter Parnall (Illustrator) (Aladdin, ISBN 0-689-71054-2, 1986). The importance of being in tune with nature and the Earth is the message of this desert-setting book. **On-Level** ***Caldecott Honor Book***

A Child's Calendar, by John Updike and Trina Schart Hyman (Holiday, ISBN 0-823-41445-0, 1999). A year's worth of poems about nature. **Challenge** ***Caldecott Honor Book***

Time of Wonder, by Robert McCloskey (Puffin, ISBN 0-140-50201-7, 1989). **Challenge** ***Caldecott Medal Winner***

Mapmaking with Children: Sense of Place Education for the Elementary Years, by David Sobel (Heinemann, ISBN 0-325-00042-5, 1980). **Teacher Reference**

***Discovery Channel School* Videos**

Africa: People and Places. Four segments cover the continent's geography; traditional culture of two equatorial countries; people living along the Nile; and the making of a wildlife film in the Serengeti; 19 minutes.

China: People and Places. Three segments introduce the culture and history of China: visit the Forbidden City, learn about the Chinese alphabet characters, and meet young athletes; 34 minutes.

Two Children, Two Cultures. Two segments feature children from Congo, in Africa, and Shanghai, China, who give insight to their cultures and traditions; 25 minutes.

Invention: Recycling. Learn about how people reuse materials and help save our enviroment; 27 minutes.

Look for this symbol throughout the Teacher's Edition to find **Award-Winning Selections**. Additional book references are suggested throughout this unit.

Practice and Extend

✓ **Unit 2 Performance Assessment**

- The Unit 2 Project, *Guess My Place*, found on p. 96, is an ongoing performance assessment project to enrich children's learning throughout the unit.
- This project, which has children creating their own geography-related game show, may be started now or at any time during this unit of study.
- A performance assessment scoring guide is located on p. 96.

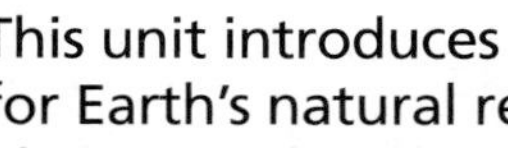

Our Earth

Unit Overview

This unit introduces children to the concept of caring for Earth's natural resources—its land, water, air, and plants—and explores different ways children can conserve and protect them.

Introduce Sara

Read the unit title and then introduce the featured child for this unit as a second grader named Sara. Talk about what Sara is doing in the photo and how she might help care for Earth.

Unit Question

- Ask children the question on this page.
- Initiate a discussion of things people can do to keep the Earth beautiful.
- To activate prior knowledge, make a list on the board of ideas children have for keeping the Earth beautiful.

✓ **Portfolio Assessment** Keep a copy of this list for the Portfolio Assessment at the end of the unit.

Show You Care

Objective

- Use music to learn about a topic.

Resources

- *Songs and Music CD*, "Show You Care"
- Poster 3
- Social Studies Plus!

Introduce the Song

Preview Tell children that they will be singing a song about caring about the Earth. Ask children to look at the picture of Sara and name the different features they see surrounding Sara. (sky, hills, meadows, lake)

Warm Up To activate prior knowledge, invite children to name one of Earth's features they would like to care for. Then ask children to think of ways to care for these features. Remind children that people can care for the land, water, and air just by doing simple, everyday things when they are in school, at home, or even walking on the street.

Sing the Song

- Have children sing the song "Show You Care."
- Have children name the things on Earth that the song says to care for.
- You may want to have children act out the ways they suggested to practice conservation.

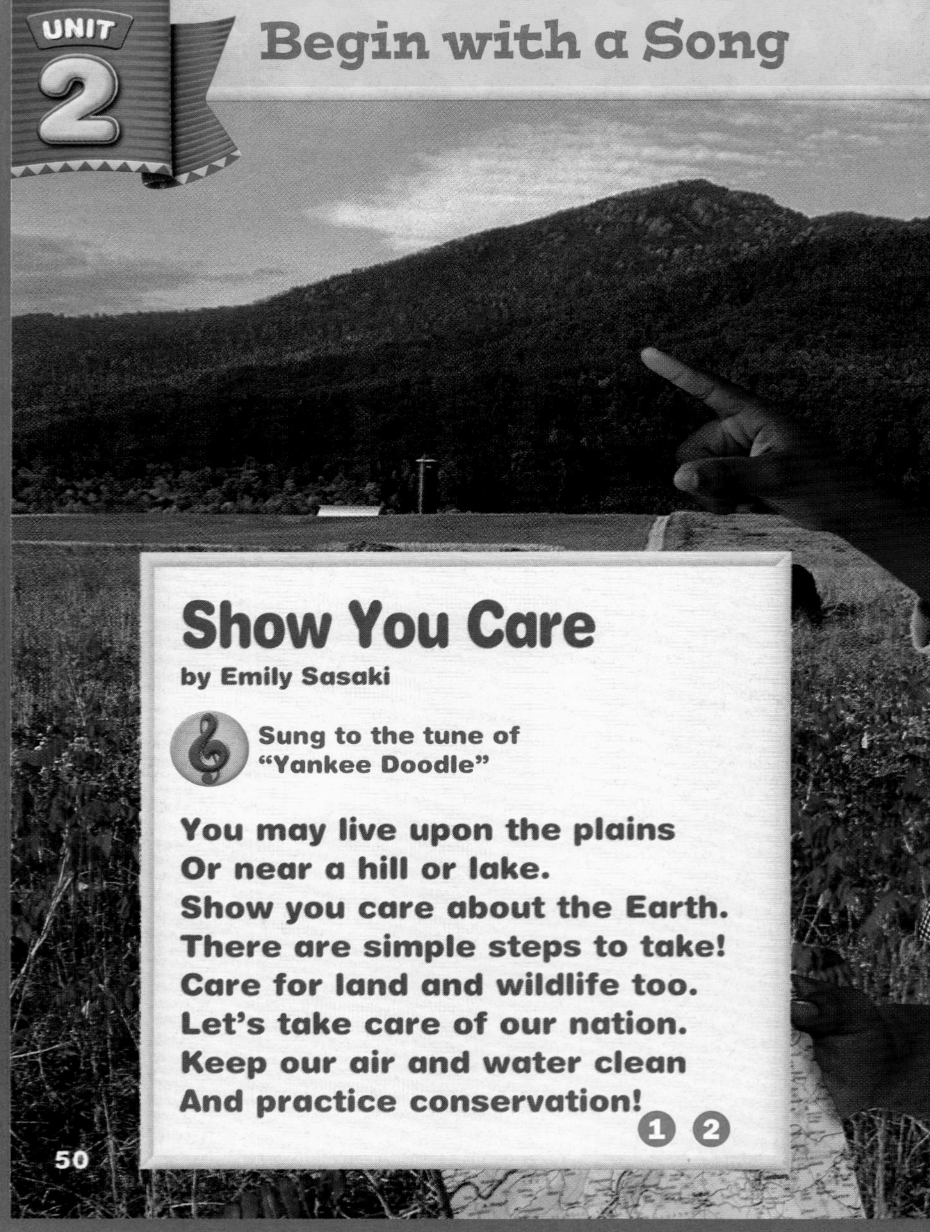

Practice and Extend

SOCIAL STUDIES Background

Possible Misconceptions

- Children may think that people can only care for the Earth if they live in the country.
- Remind children that caring for the land, air, water, and animals is an effort everyone needs to do together, no matter if someone lives in an apartment building in the city or on a farm in the country.

AUDIO CD Technology

Play the CD, *Songs and Music*, to listen to the song "Show You Care."

CURRICULUM CONNECTION
Art

Picture It!

- Have children draw pictures of themselves enjoying nature and Earth's resources.
- Before children draw, help them brainstorm activities people enjoy outdoors—swimming, boating, gardening, hiking, picnicking, and so on.
- Encourage children to caption and share their drawings.

Talk About the Picture

1 **How do the details in the photograph tell more about the message of the song?** Possible answer: The photo shows the resources people can enjoy if they remember to take care of Earth—the land, water, and air.
Main Idea and Details

2 **What do you think Sara and her brother are doing in the photo? What clues are in the photo?** Hiking, taking a walk; Sara's backpack, the fact that she is surrounded by a clear, blue sky, green grass, fields, hills, and streams
Interpret Pictures

Vocabulary Preview

Objectives

- Use pictures to obtain information.
- Determine the meanings of words.

Resources

- Workbook, p. 12
- Vocabulary Cards
- Poster 4

Introduce the Vocabulary

Read aloud and point to each vocabulary word and the photograph illustrating it. Have volunteers give the meanings of the words. Then have children find several examples of vocabulary words in the illustration. Write these examples on the board.

Vocabulary Word	Illustrated Examples
geography	Woman holding map, farm directory
landform	Hills, river, small island, pond
ancestor	Pictures on farm entrance gate
producer	Farmer with cows, vegetable farmers
consumer	People at pumpkin stand, man leaving with pumpkin
natural resource	Water, soil, trees
crop	Barrels of apples, pumpkins
conservation	Recycling bins

SOCIAL STUDIES STRAND

Geography

Listed below are some basic principles of geography for young children. Use them to direct your discussion of the illustration.

- Earth's surface consists of landforms and bodies of water.
- Maps and globes show land and water.
- People use natural resources to live.
- Different areas have different natural resources, climate, and weather.
- Natural resources along with climate and weather affect where people decide to live.
- People need to conserve natural resources for the future.

Vocabulary Preview

geography

landform

ancestor

producer

Practice and Extend

MEETING INDIVIDUAL NEEDS

Leveled Practice

Visit a Farm

Have children suppose they are on a class trip to a large farm. Lead them on a "picture walk" tour of the farm.

Easy Talk in detail about the left part of the illustration, taking children from the top of the page to the bottom. Use the new vocabulary words in your descriptions. Then repeat with the right part of the illustration. Point to particular things and ask questions such as: *Is this a landform or a crop?* **Reteach**

On-Level Ask volunteers to describe one part of the illustration. Encourage use of appropriate new vocabulary. Ask listeners to point to that part of the picture. **Extend**

Challenge Have children repeat the vocabulary word you say and then find the designated number of examples, for example: *Natural resource/Find and name three natural resources.* **Enrich**

consumer

natural resource

crop

conservation

53

WEB SITE
Technology

You can look up vocabulary words online. Click on *Social Studies Library* and select the dictionary at **www.sfsocialstudies.com.**

Workbook, p. 12

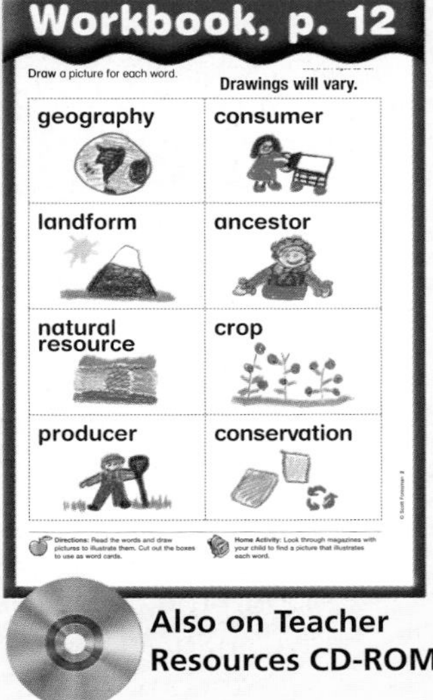

Draw a picture for each word. Drawings will vary.

geography	consumer
landform	ancestor
natural resource	crop
producer	conservation

Also on Teacher Resources CD-ROM.

Talk About the Illustration

Allow children time to study the illustration. Ask children why they think a trip to a farm like the one shown might make an interesting class trip.

Encourage children to identify some of the activities they see people involved in.

1 **What would looking at a map of the farm help visitors do?** Possible answer: The map would show where different places on the farm are. **Draw Conclusions**

2 **What can consumers buy at the three stands near the gate?** Apple juice, pie, pumpkins **Analyze Pictures**

3 **What crop do you think was used to produce the juice one woman sells?** Apples **What clue do you have?** There are apples right in front of the stand. **Draw Conclusions**

Look Ahead

Tell children they will learn more about each of the vocabulary words as they study Unit 2.

You may want to revisit the picture with children to review the concepts and vocabulary in the unit.

4 **What landform do you see rising up high?** Hills **Analyze Pictures**

Sara Helps Plants Grow

Cause and Effect

Objective

Identify cause-and-effect relationships.

Resource

- Workbook, p. 13

About the Unit Target Skill

- The target reading skill for this unit is Cause and Effect.
- Children are introduced to the unit target skill here and are given an opportunity to practice it.
- Further opportunities to practice cause and effect are found throughout Unit 2.

1 Introduce and Motivate

Preview To determine whether children understand the concept of cause and effect, present them with this scenario: A child turns a glass of water upside down. The water spills out. Ask: *What caused the water to spill out of the glass? What happened because the child turned the glass upside down?* Help children state that the cause is that the child turned the glass upside down. The effect is that the water spilled out.

Warm Up To activate prior knowledge, ask children to tell about their experiences growing things. Ask what a plant needs in order to live. (water, sunlight, soil to grow in) Ask what might happen if someone didn't water a plant for a long time.

Reading Social Studies

Sara Helps Plants Grow

Cause and Effect

Hi, I'm Sara. My family and I live on a farm in Virginia. We grow apples. In school, I am learning about growing other fruits and vegetables. In my classroom, I am in charge of watering the plants. When I water the plants, they grow.

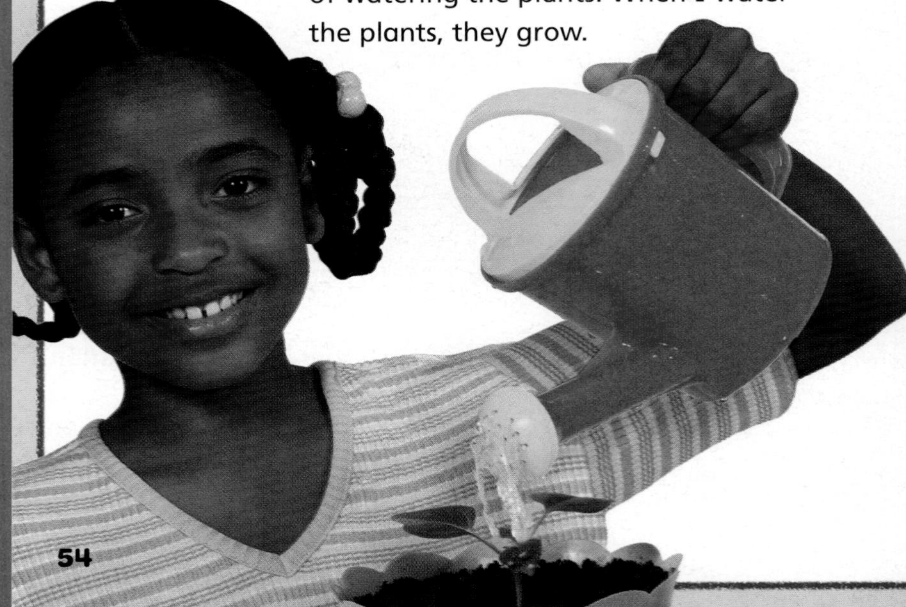

54

Practice and Extend

BUILD BACKGROUND
ESL Support

Cause and Effect Pantomime opening a window. Then shiver. Identify the actions as a cause and an effect, respectively.

Beginning Have children pantomime with you. Help them name the actions as cause and effect. Then call out one or the other term and have children pantomime the correct action.

Intermediate Label a T-chart *Cause* and *Effect*. Model writing the cause (*open window*) and effect (*shiver*). Then have children give other examples of cause/effect and write the appropriate words in the columns.

Advanced Do the Intermediate activity, but have children write complete sentences to identify the causes and effects.

A **cause** is what makes something happen. An **effect** is what happens. One cause is watering a plant. The effect is that a plant will grow.

Try it!

Write the words **cause** and **effect.** Ask the teacher to switch off the lights. What caused the lights to go off? Write this under **cause.** What happened when the lights were switched off? Write this under **effect.**

55

2 Teach and Discuss

Have children read page 54 and examine the photograph. Invite volunteers to identify Sara's classroom job and to tell what she is doing.

Then have children read page 55. Help them find the words *cause* and *effect* under the photographs. Have children use the words *cause* and *effect* as they describe what they see happening in the photos.

Cause and Effect is an important skill for understanding social studies. Knowing why things happen will be invaluable as children explore and learn about their world.

Ongoing Assessment

If... children get the terms *cause* and *effect* mixed up,

then... point out that *cause* begins with *c*. The letter *c* comes before e, the first letter in *effect*. Say that there has to be a *cause* for something to happen. The *cause* comes first.

3 Close and Assess

Try it!

Have children write *cause* and *effect* at the top of a sheet of paper. Turn off the lights. Then proceed with the activity as a class. Have children write their answers on their papers.

Have children talk with partners about what happened in the light-switch activity and why.

CURRICULUM CONNECTION Science

Parts of a Plant

- Help children name the three basic parts of a plant—roots, stem, leaves.
- Have them say which part soaks up the water when Sara waters the plant.
- Talk about the functions of stems and leaves, too. Stems carry water from the soil. Leaves make food for the plant. Ask children what they think the effect might be if one or more of the plant parts got damaged.

Workbook, p. 13

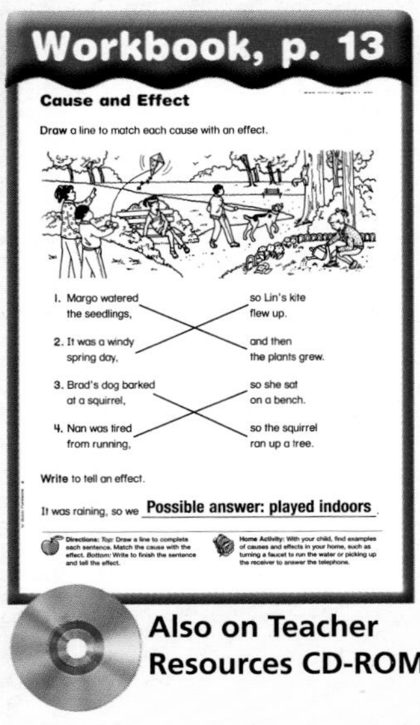

Cause and Effect

Draw a line to match each cause with an effect.

1. Margo watered the seedlings, — and then the plants grew.
2. It was a windy spring day, — so Lin's kite flew up.
3. Brad's dog barked at a squirrel, — so the squirrel ran up a tree.
4. Nan was tired from running, — so she sat on a bench.

Write to tell an effect.

It was raining, so we **Possible answer: played indoors**.

Directions: *Top:* Draw a line to complete each sentence. Match the cause with the effect. *Bottom:* Write to finish the sentence and tell the effect.

Home Activity: With your child, find examples of causes and effects in your home, such as turning a faucet to run the water or picking up the receiver to answer the telephone.

Also on Teacher Resources CD-ROM.

Workbook Support

Use the following Workbook pages to support content and skills development as you teach Unit 2. You can also view and print Workbook pages from the Teacher Resources CD-ROM.

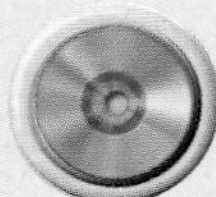

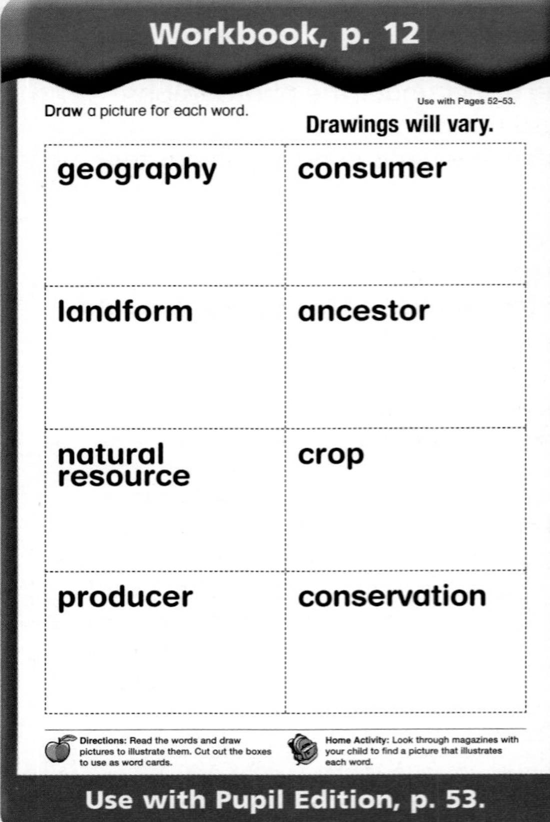

Workbook, p. 12

Use with Pages 52–53.

Draw a picture for each word. Drawings will vary.

geography	consumer
landform	ancestor
natural resource	crop
producer	conservation

Directions: Read the words and draw pictures to illustrate them. Cut out the boxes to use as word cards.

Home Activity: Look through magazines with your child to find a picture that illustrates each word.

Use with Pupil Edition, p. 53.

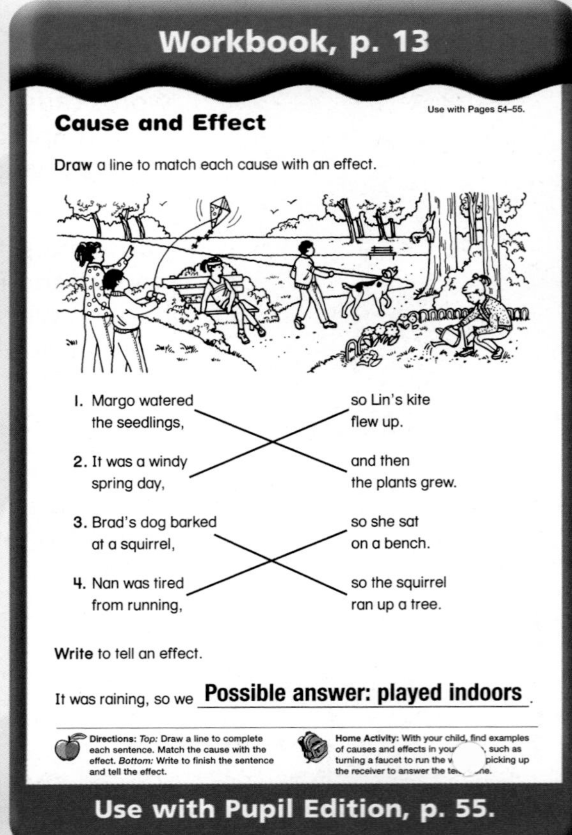

Workbook, p. 13

Use with Pages 54–55.

Cause and Effect

Draw a line to match each cause with an effect.

1. Margo watered the seedlings, — and then the plants grew.
2. It was a windy spring day, — so Lin's kite flew up.
3. Brad's dog barked at a squirrel, — so the squirrel ran up a tree.
4. Nan was tired from running, — so she sat on a bench.

Write to tell an effect.

It was raining, so we Possible answer: played indoors.

Directions: *Top:* Draw a line to complete each sentence. Match the cause with the effect. *Bottom:* Write to finish the sentence and tell the effect.

Home Activity: With your child, find examples of causes and effects in your ..., such as turning a faucet to run the ..., picking up the receiver to answer the te...ne.

Use with Pupil Edition, p. 55.

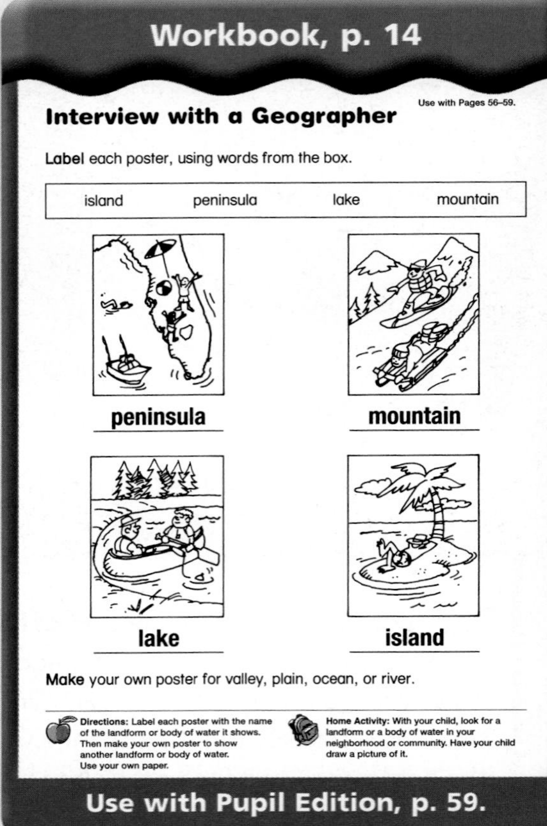

Workbook, p. 14

Use with Pages 56–59.

Interview with a Geographer

Label each poster, using words from the box.

island peninsula lake mountain

peninsula — mountain

lake — island

Make your own poster for valley, plain, ocean, or river.

Directions: Label each poster with the name of the landform or body of water it shows. Then make your own poster to show another landform or body of water. Use your own paper.

Home Activity: With your child, look for a landform or a body of water in your neighborhood or community. Have your child draw a picture of it.

Use with Pupil Edition, p. 59.

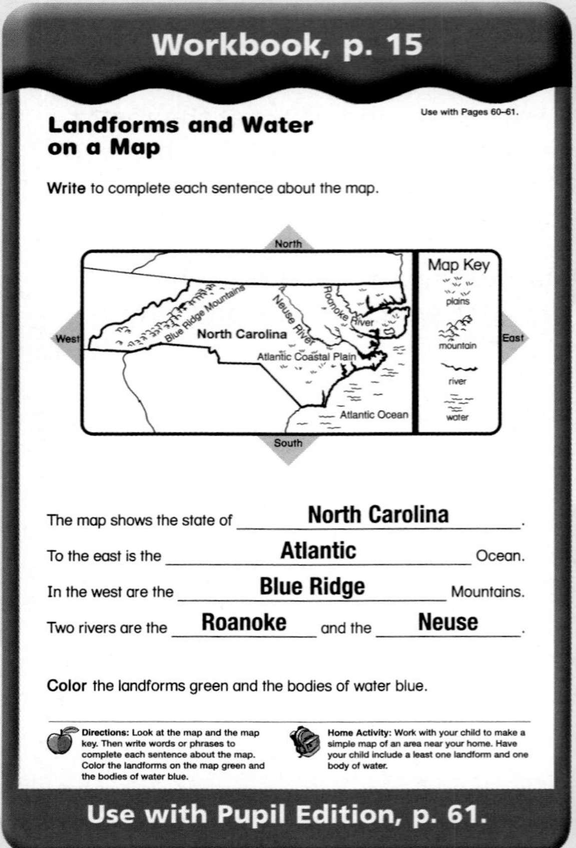

Workbook, p. 15

Use with Pages 60–61.

Landforms and Water on a Map

Write to complete each sentence about the map.

The map shows the state of North Carolina.

To the east is the Atlantic Ocean.

In the west are the Blue Ridge Mountains.

Two rivers are the Roanoke and the Neuse.

Color the landforms green and the bodies of water blue.

Directions: Look at the map and the map key. Then write words or phrases to complete each sentence about the map. Color the landforms on the map green and the bodies of water blue.

Home Activity: Work with your child to make a simple map of an area near your home. Have your child include at least one landform and one body of water.

Use with Pupil Edition, p. 61.

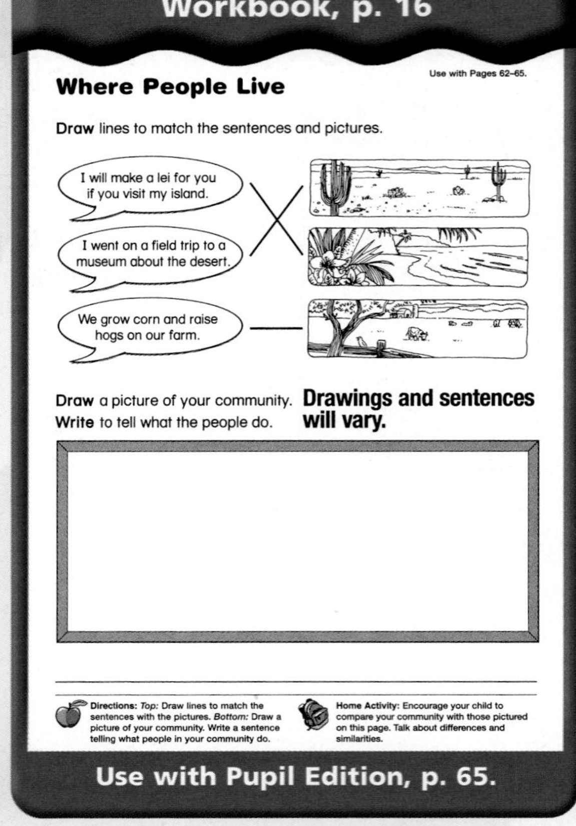

Workbook, p. 16

Use with Pages 62–65.

Where People Live

Draw lines to match the sentences and pictures.

I will make a lei for you if you visit my island.

I went on a field trip to a museum about the desert.

We grow corn and raise hogs on our farm.

Draw a picture of your community. **Write** to tell what the people do. Drawings and sentences will vary.

Directions: *Top:* Draw lines to match the sentences with the pictures. *Bottom:* Draw a picture of your community. Write a sentence telling what people in your community do.

Home Activity: Encourage your child to compare your community with those pictured on this page. Talk about differences and similarities.

Use with Pupil Edition, p. 65.

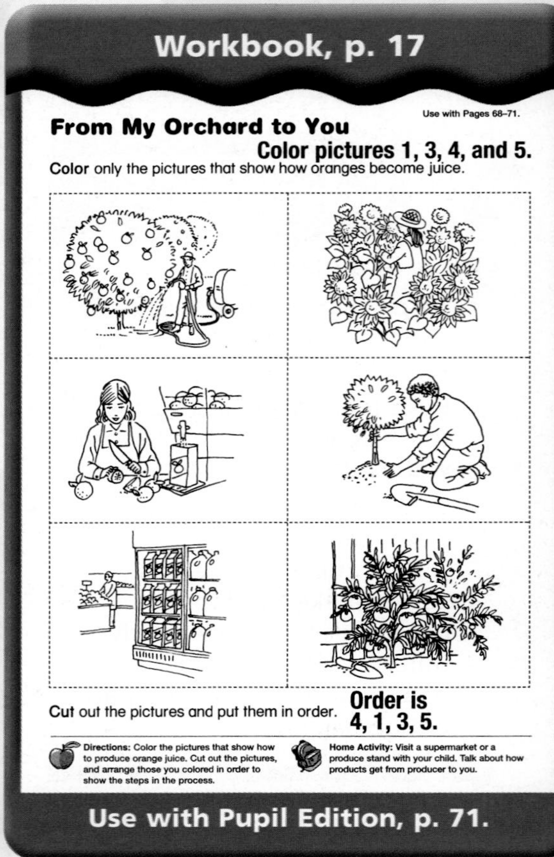

Workbook, p. 17

Use with Pages 68–71.

From My Orchard to You

Color pictures 1, 3, 4, and 5.

Color only the pictures that show how oranges become juice.

Cut out the pictures and put them in order. Order is 4, 1, 3, 5.

Directions: Color the pictures that show how to produce orange juice. Cut out the pictures, and arrange those you colored in order to show the steps in the process.

Home Activity: Visit a supermarket or a produce stand with your child. Talk about how products get from producer to you.

Use with Pupil Edition, p. 71.

Workbook Support

Workbook, p. 18

Harvest Time

Look at "Harvest Time" on pages 72–73 as you do this page.

1. Look again at the fruit crate labels.
   Which apples would you buy? **Answers will vary.**
   Why? **Answers will vary.**
2. Draw a modern fruit crate label. **Drawings will vary.**
3. Look again at the seed packets.
   What kinds of seeds were in the packets?
   fruit and vegetable seeds
4. Choose a fruit or vegetable you like.
   Design a label for the seed packet.
   Include words and pictures. **Designs will vary.**

Directions: Look at pages 72–73 in your books as you complete this page. For item 4, draw a picture and write words to show what kind of seeds are in the packet.

Home Activity: Look with your child at labels on food products. Talk about what is on the labels, and how pictures can be used to help sell the products.

Use with Pupil Edition, p. 73.

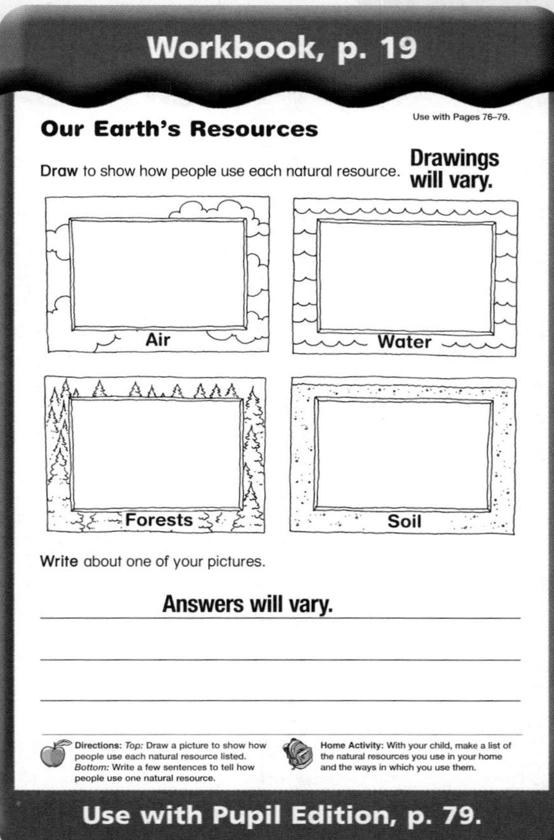

Workbook, p. 19

Use with Pages 76–79.

Our Earth's Resources

Draw to show how people use each natural resource. **Drawings will vary.**

Write about one of your pictures.

Answers will vary.

Directions: *Top:* Draw a picture to show how people use each natural resource listed. *Bottom:* Write a few sentences to tell how people use one natural resource.

Home Activity: With your child, make a list of the natural resources you use in your home and the ways in which you use them.

Use with Pupil Edition, p. 79.

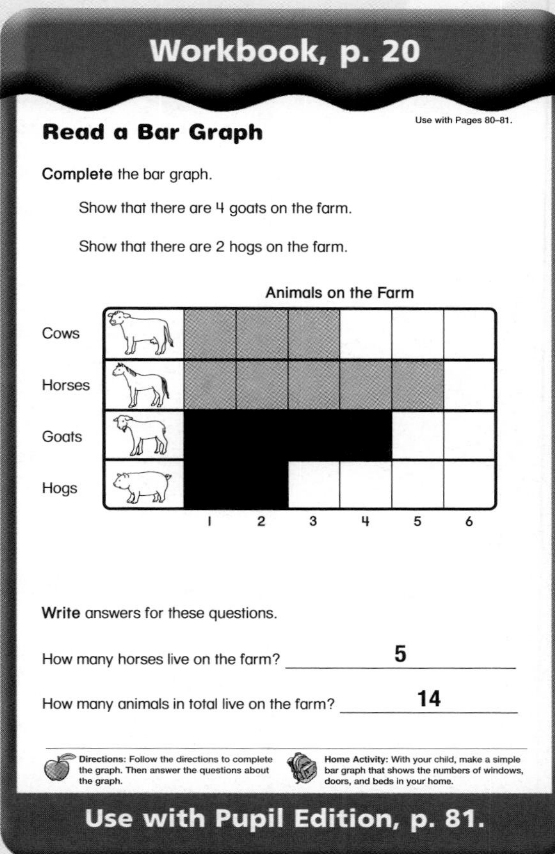

Workbook, p. 20

Use with Pages 80–81.

Read a Bar Graph

Complete the bar graph.

Show that there are 4 goats on the farm.

Show that there are 2 hogs on the farm.

Write answers for these questions.

How many horses live on the farm? **5**

How many animals in total live on the farm? **14**

Directions: Follow the directions to complete the graph. Then answer the questions about the graph.

Home Activity: With your child, make a simple bar graph that shows the numbers of windows, doors, and beds in your home.

Use with Pupil Edition, p. 81.

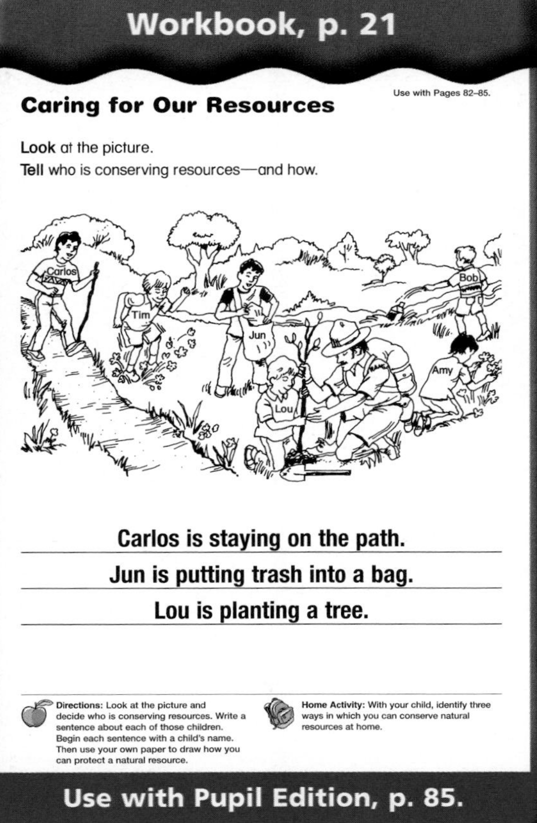

Workbook, p. 21

Use with Pages 82–85.

Caring for Our Resources

Look at the picture.
Tell who is conserving resources—and how.

Carlos is staying on the path.

Jun is putting trash into a bag.

Lou is planting a tree.

Directions: Look at the picture and decide who is conserving resources. Write a sentence about each of those children. Begin each sentence with a child's name. Then use your own paper to draw how you can protect a natural resource.

Home Activity: With your child, identify three ways in which you can conserve natural resources at home.

Use with Pupil Edition, p. 85.

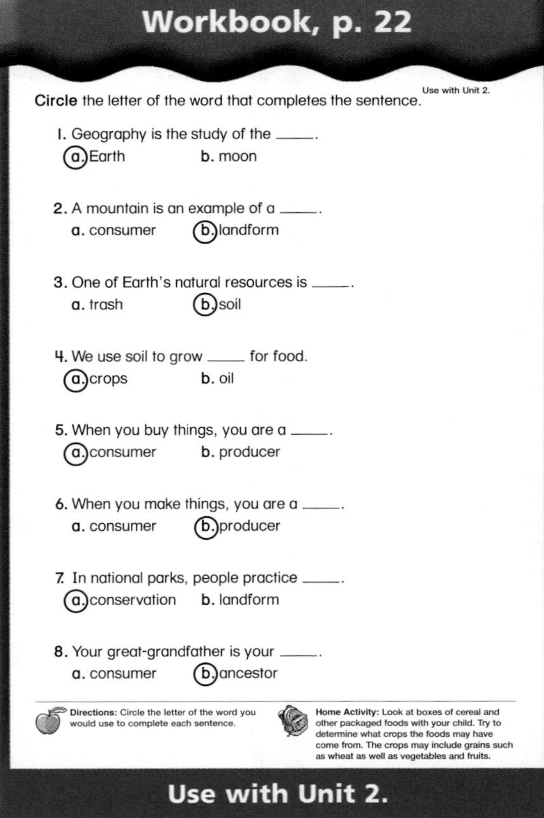

Workbook, p. 22

Use with Unit 2.

Circle the letter of the word that completes the sentence.

1. Geography is the study of the ____.
   (a.) Earth b. moon
2. A mountain is an example of a ____.
   a. consumer (b.) landform
3. One of Earth's natural resources is ____.
   a. trash (b.) soil
4. We use soil to grow ____ for food.
   (a.) crops b. oil
5. When you buy things, you are a ____.
   (a.) consumer b. producer
6. When you make things, you are a ____.
   a. consumer (b.) producer
7. In national parks, people practice ____.
   (a.) conservation b. landform
8. Your great-grandfather is your ____.
   a. consumer (b.) ancestor

Directions: Circle the letter of the word you would use to complete each sentence.

Home Activity: Look at boxes of cereal and other packaged foods with your child. Try to determine what crops the foods may have come from. The crops may include grains such as wheat as well as vegetables and fruits.

Use with Unit 2.

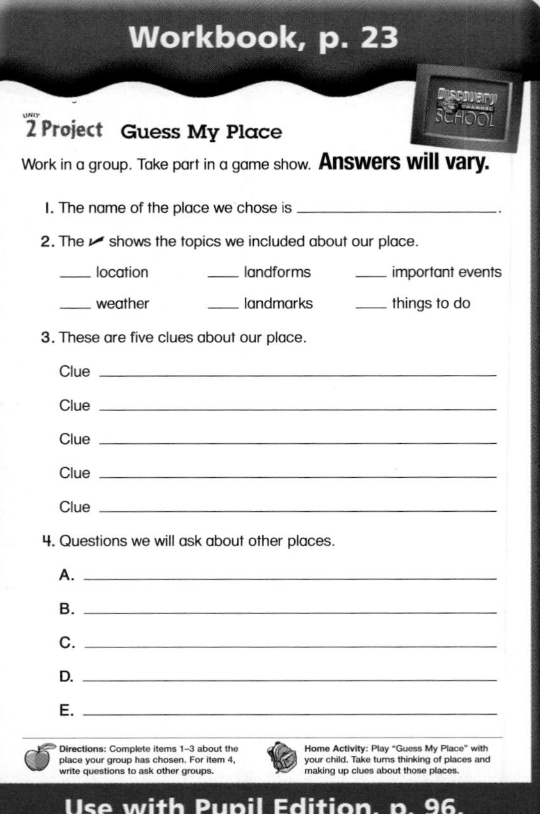

Workbook, p. 23

Unit 2 Project Guess My Place

Work in a group. Take part in a game show. **Answers will vary.**

1. The name of the place we chose is ______.
2. The ✔ shows the topics we included about our place.
   ____ location ____ landforms ____ important events
   ____ weather ____ landmarks ____ things to do
3. These are five clues about our place.
   Clue ______
   Clue ______
   Clue ______
   Clue ______
   Clue ______
4. Questions we will ask about other places.
   A. ______
   B. ______
   C. ______
   D. ______
   E. ______

Directions: Complete items 1–3 about the place your group has chosen. For item 4, write questions to ask other groups.

Home Activity: Play "Guess My Place" with your child. Take turns thinking of places and making up clues about those places.

Use with Pupil Edition, p. 96.

Assessment Support

Use these Assessment Book pages and the test maker to assess content and skills in Unit 2. You can also view and print Assessment Book pages from the Teacher Resources CD-ROM.

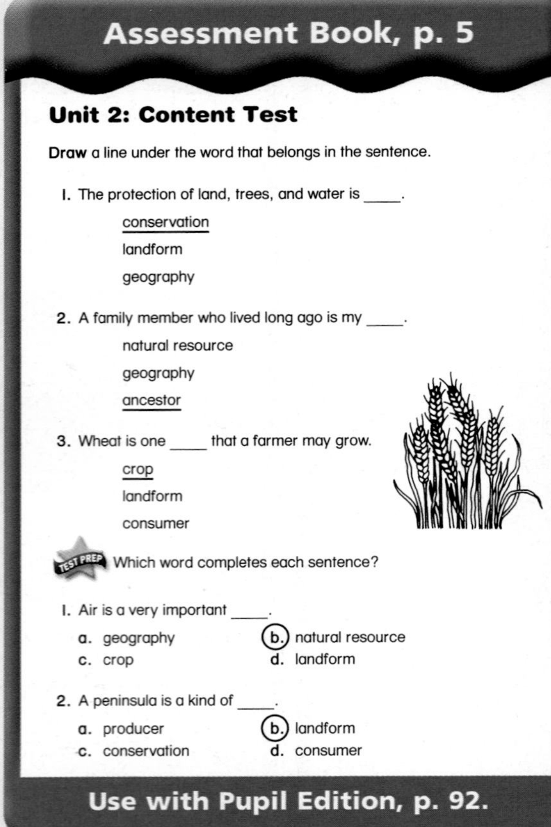

Assessment Book, p. 5

Unit 2: Content Test

Draw a line under the word that belongs in the sentence.

1. The protection of land, trees, and water is ____.
   - <u>conservation</u>
   - landform
   - geography
2. A family member who lived long ago is my ____.
   - natural resource
   - geography
   - <u>ancestor</u>
3. Wheat is one ____ that a farmer may grow.
   - <u>crop</u>
   - landform
   - consumer

TEST PREP Which word completes each sentence?

1. Air is a very important ____.
   - a. geography
   - (b.) natural resource
   - c. crop
   - d. landform
2. A peninsula is a kind of ____.
   - a. producer
   - (b.) landform
   - c. conservation
   - d. consumer

Use with Pupil Edition, p. 92.

Assessment Book, p. 6

Think about how natural resources are used.

Write *soil*, *forests*, or *water* under the picture.

water — soil — forests

Look at the picture.

Write two ways to show conservation.

walk on the path,

take care of animals and plants

Use with Pupil Edition, p. 92.

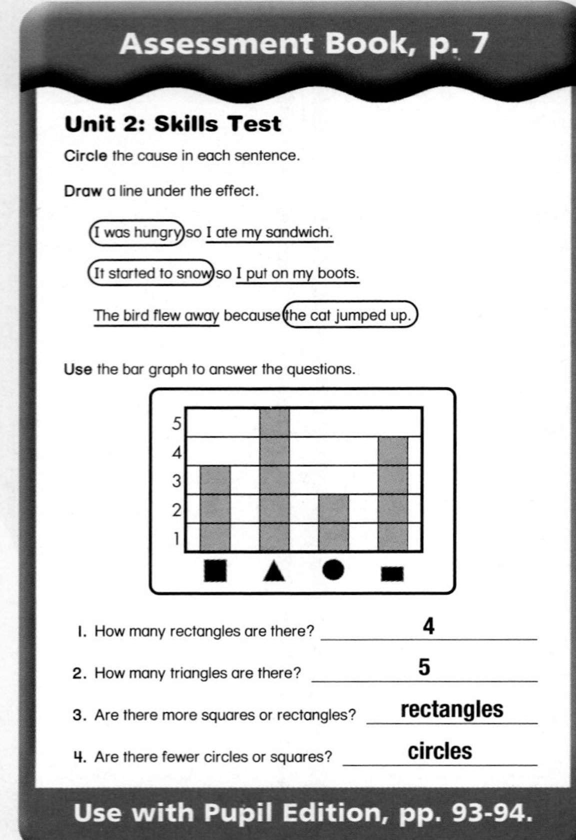

Assessment Book, p. 7

Unit 2: Skills Test

Circle the cause in each sentence.

Draw a line under the effect.

(I was hungry) so <u>I ate my sandwich.</u>

(It started to snow) so <u>I put on my boots.</u>

<u>The bird flew away</u> because (the cat jumped up.)

Use the bar graph to answer the questions.

1. How many rectangles are there? **4**
2. How many triangles are there? **5**
3. Are there more squares or rectangles? **rectangles**
4. Are there fewer circles or squares? **circles**

Use with Pupil Edition, pp. 93-94.

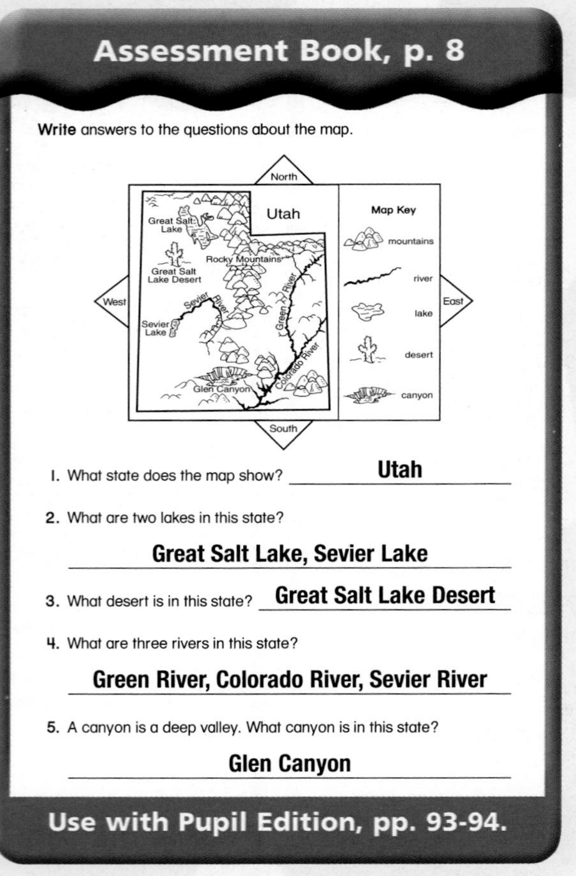

Assessment Book, p. 8

Write answers to the questions about the map.

1. What state does the map show? **Utah**
2. What are two lakes in this state? **Great Salt Lake, Sevier Lake**
3. What desert is in this state? **Great Salt Lake Desert**
4. What are three rivers in this state? **Green River, Colorado River, Sevier River**
5. A canyon is a deep valley. What canyon is in this state? **Glen Canyon**

Use with Pupil Edition, pp. 93-94.

Lesson 1 Overview

Interview with a Geographer **pages 56–59**	Children will learn the meanings of the words *geography* and *landform*, and they will explore different kinds of landforms and bodies of water.	 Time 20–30 minutes Resources • Workbook, p. 14 • Vocabulary Cards geography landform • Every Student Learns Guide, pp. 22-25
Landforms and Water on a Map **pages 60–61**	Children will learn how to use a map key to locate different types of land and water on a map.	 Time 15–20 minutes Resource • Workbook, p. 15

Build Background

Activity

Land or Water?

 **Time** 15–20 minutes

Brainstorm lists of land formations and bodies of water children know about through their experiences. Get them started by suggesting hills and lakes.

Next have children fold a large sheet of drawing paper in half. At the top of each half, children should write *Land* or *Water*. Have them draw and label pictures of landforms and bodies of water they have already identified.

Have children share their drawings and add them to a bulletin board display entitled *Our Earth.*

If time is short, just do the brainstorming portion of the activity described above.

Read Aloud

Fly with Me

by Nina Evans

Fly with me, and we will see
A world as beautiful as can be!
High lands and low lands are all
around.
Oceans, rivers, and lakes abound.
Fly with me, and we will see
A world that needs care from
you and me!

Lesson 1

Interview with a Geographer

Objectives

- Identify landforms and bodies of water.
- Obtain information through interviews.

Vocabulary

geography the study of Earth and the ways people use it (p. 56)

landform a kind of shape on the surface of the Earth (p. 56)

QUICK Teaching Plan

If time is short, define *geography*, and explain that a *geographer* is someone who studies and works in the field of geography. Have children suggest some specific things they think a geographer studies.

- Have children study the photographs and generate a list of words that describe the different landforms and bodies of water.

1 Introduce and Motivate

Preview Display the Vocabulary Cards **geography** and **landform**. Ask children what they think each word means. Share the meaning of each word. Have children locate the terms as they preview the lesson with you.

Warm Up To activate prior knowledge, have children talk about their experiences with landforms and bodies of water. Prompt them with questions such as: *Have you ever hiked up a hill? How was being at the top of a hill different from being on flat land? Have you ever gone swimming in the ocean? Did you taste the water? Did you see and feel waves?*

Lesson 1

Interview with a Geographer

Sara What does a geographer do? 1

Mrs. Bond I study geography. **Geography** is the study of Earth and the ways people use it. 2 3

Sara What else does a geographer do?

Mrs. Bond I study the Earth's surface. The surface of the Earth has many different shapes. Each kind of shape is a **landform.** For example, a hill is a landform. A hill is a high place on the Earth's surface.

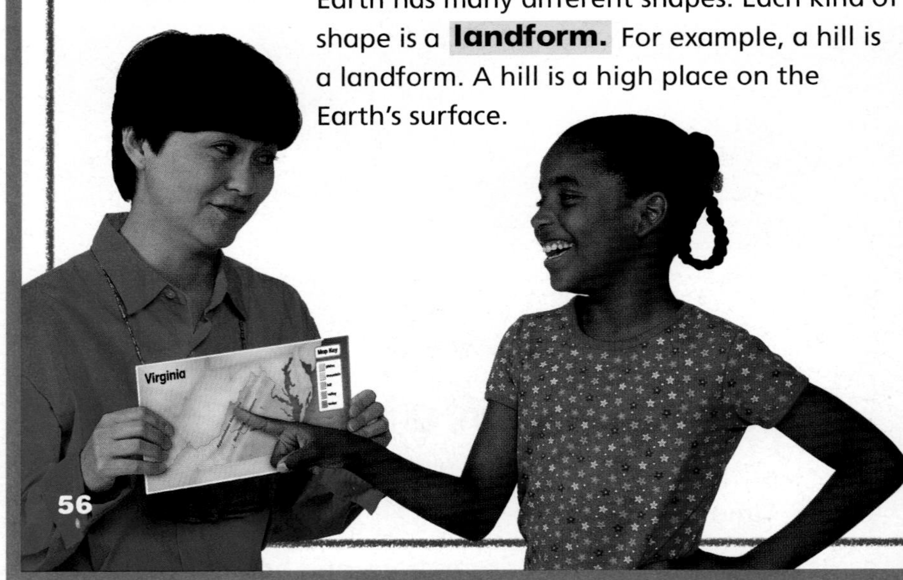

56

Practice and Extend

READING SKILL
Compare and Contrast

Mountains and Plains After children read p. 57, draw a Venn diagram on the board. Label the two circles *Mountains* and *Plains*.

- Ask children how mountains and plains are alike. Write *landform* where the circles overlap.
- Ask how mountains and plains are different. Write *high* for *mountains* and *mostly flat* for *plains*.

Use the Venn diagram to help children compare and contrast other features of the Earth.

WEB SITE
Technology

You can look up vocabulary words online. Click on *Social Studies Library* and select the dictionary at **www.sfsocialstudies.com.**

Mrs. Bond

A mountain is a landform. A mountain is the highest kind of land.

4

Mrs. Bond

This is a plain. A plain is a large, mostly flat, area of land. Many farms are found on plains. 5

Mrs. Bond

This is a valley, or a low area of land. A valley is usually found between mountains or hills.

57

SOCIAL STUDIES
Background

Young and Old Mountains

- The shape of a mountain tells whether it is young or old.
- Young mountains have jagged tops with rough sides.
- Older mountains are more rounded. Over the years, the weather has worn them down.

CURRICULUM CONNECTION
Writing

Write Interview Questions

Have partners work together to generate a list of interview questions they might like to ask Mrs. Bond about her job as a geographer. Tell children the list should have complete sentences and correct punctuation.

2 Teach and Discuss

Page 56

Read the lesson title and define *interview*. Identify Sara and Mrs. Bond in the photograph. Invite volunteers to suggest what Sara and Mrs. Bond might be saying.

1 **What is Mrs. Bond's job?** She is a geographer. **Main Ideas and Details**

2 **What does a geographer do?** Studies the Earth and how people use it **Main Ideas and Details**

3 **How does your family use the Earth's land and water?** Possible answers: We grow plants in the soil. We use water for drinking and to help the plants live. **Apply Information**

Page 57

Discuss each landform in the photographs.

4 **What words can you think of to describe each landform?** Words should tell about shape, texture, colors, size, and so on. **Analyze Pictures**

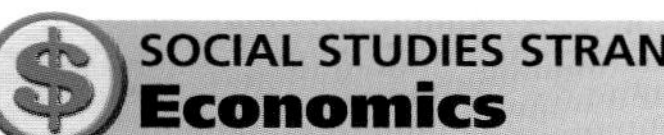

SOCIAL STUDIES STRAND
Economics

Food Producers Point out that many people depend on farmers to grow their food. Ask children to name foods that can be grown on a farm and sold in stores.

5 **Why is a plain a good place for a farm?** Possible answer: It is easier to plant on a flat area than on a mountain. When it rains, the water soaks into the soil. It doesn't slide off as it would on a mountain. **Make Inferences**

continued

Page 58

Help children note the change of focus to water and landforms near water.

6 How is an island different from a peninsula? An island is surrounded by water on all sides; a peninsula is almost but not completely surrounded by water. **Compare and Contrast**

Ongoing Assessment

If...children cannot keep straight the definitions of an island and a peninsula, **then...**have them point their index fingers and note that *point* and *peninsula* begin with *p*. Ask how a pointing finger looks like a peninsula.

7 What did Sara learn about ocean water in school? It is salty. **Recall and Retell**

Sara
Can you tell me about land that is near water?

Mrs. Bond
An island is land that is surrounded by water.

Mrs. Bond
A peninsula is land that is almost surrounded by water. 

Sara
In school, we learned that an ocean is a huge body of salt water.

7

58

Practice and Extend

ACTIVATE PRIOR KNOWLEDGE
ESL Support

Bodies of Water Write the names of bodies of water—*ocean, river, lake*—and read them. Then ask children about bodies of water they have seen or know about.

Beginning Have children divide a sheet of paper into three columns labeled *ocean, river, lake*. Then have them work with partners to generate at least one example of each.

Intermediate Children can work in pairs to generate examples of oceans, rivers, and lakes. Then they should write three sentences describing the characteristics of oceans, rivers, and lakes.

Advanced Children, working in pairs, can generate examples of oceans, rivers, and lakes and then write several sentences comparing their characteristics.

For additional ESL support, use Every Student Learns Guide, pp. 22–25.

FAST FACTS

Oceans of the Earth

- Most of the Earth's surface is covered by water.
- There is really one "world ocean," but the continents divide it. Geographers see the world ocean in terms of four great oceans: the Pacific, Atlantic, Indian, and Arctic Oceans.
- The ocean floor has many of the features found on land—plains, mountain chains, and deep valleys.

Mrs. Bond

That's right! Bodies of water also have different sizes and shapes. A river is a stream of fresh water. Rivers usually flow toward a lake or an ocean.

Mrs. Bond

This is a lake. It is a large body of water surrounded by land. 8

Sara

Thank you for teaching me about geography. 9

What did you learn?

1. What is geography?
2. Name a landform and a body of water. Draw a picture of each.
3. **Think and Share** It is cold at the top of the mountain so the snow does not melt. Tell the **cause** and the **effect.**

59

CURRICULUM CONNECTION
Drama

Re-create the Interview

- Have partners take on the roles of Sara and Mrs. Bond to dramatize the interview for the class.
- Allow time for children to prepare their presentations.
- Encourage children to make their interviews sound natural—as though they are having a real conversation with the other person.

Workbook, p. 14

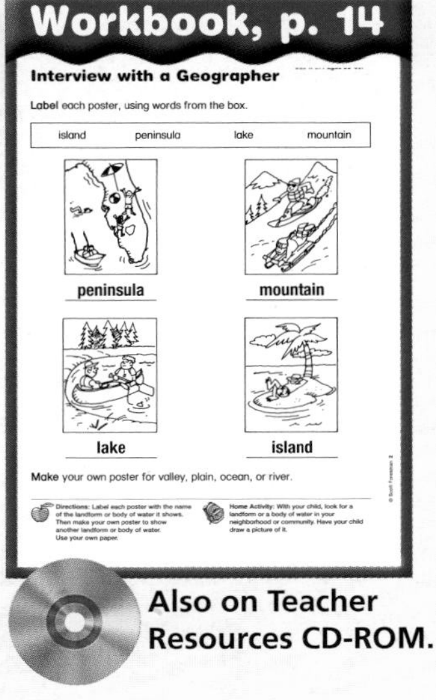
Interview with a Geographer

Label each poster, using words from the box.

island	peninsula	lake	mountain

peninsula

mountain

lake

island

Make your own poster for valley, plain, ocean, or river.

Also on Teacher Resources CD-ROM.

Page 59

8 **How is a lake different from a river?** A lake is surrounded by land. A river is not.
Compare and Contrast

9 **In your own words, tell what Sara learned by interviewing Mrs. Bond.** Children should include details about the different landforms and bodies of water that a geographer studies.
Recall and Retell

3 Close and Assess

Have children recall the landforms and bodies of water they learned about in this lesson. Children should be able to identify each landform or body of water, say its name, and briefly describe it.

✓ What did you learn?

Test Talk

Locate Key Words in the Text
Help children locate the key word *geography* in the text.

1. Geography is the study of the Earth and the ways people use it.
2. Answers will vary but should include both a landform and a body of water.
3. **Think and Share** The cause is that it is cold. The effect is that snow does not melt.

Landforms and Water on a Map

Objective

- Identify major landforms and bodies of water on a map.

1 Introduce and Motivate

Preview Have children look at the map as you read its title. Point out the map key. Ask children to tell how Sara might use the map key to learn about Virginia.

Warm Up To activate prior knowledge, have children tell why people use maps. Discuss the kinds of maps they see in their everyday lives at school, at home, or in their community.

2 Teach and Discuss

Page 60

Ask whether children can tell which parts of the map show land and which parts show water. Then read p. 60 with them.

1 Why do you think Mrs. Bond showed this map to Sara? To give Sara a real-life example of what she was talking about during their interview
Make Inferences

Map and Globe Skills

Landforms and Water on a Map

1 Mrs. Bond showed Sara a map of Virginia. This map will help Sara find different types of land and water in the state where she lives.

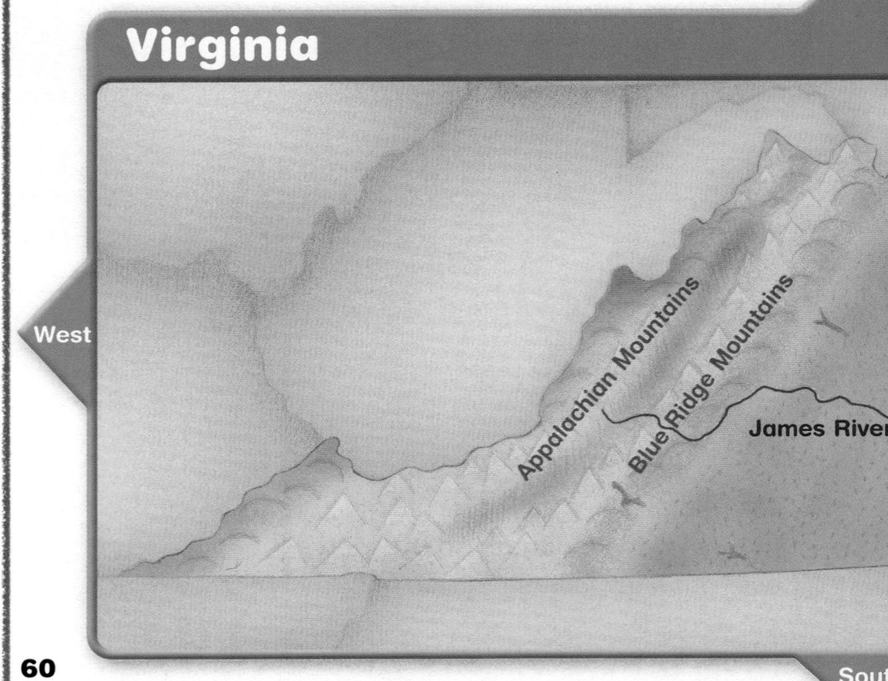

60

Practice and Extend

SOCIAL STUDIES STRAND
Geography

Local Maps

- Using an atlas, show children a map of your own state. Point out the map key.
- Work together to identify and name the different landforms and bodies of water in your state.
- Record children's findings on a two-column chart labeled *Land* and *Water*.

WEB SITE
Technology

You may help children go online to learn more about your state. Click on *Social Studies Library* and select the Atlas at **www.sfsocialstudies.com.**

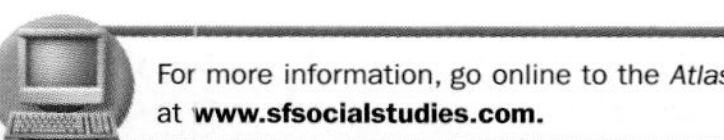

For more information, go online to the *Atlas* at **www.sfsocialstudies.com.**

Look at the map key. Find the colors and symbols that stand for landforms and bodies of water.

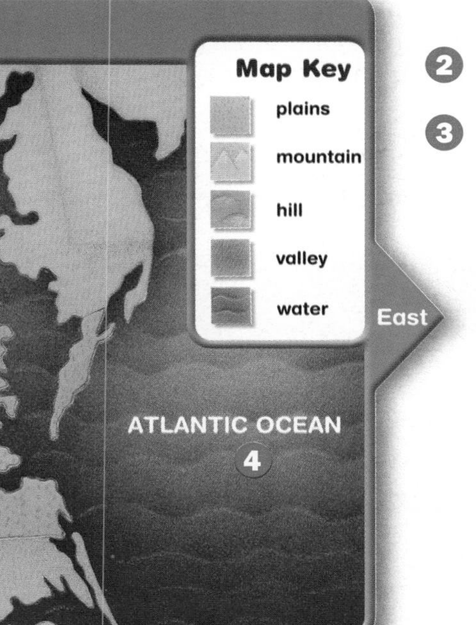

1. Find the symbol for mountain. What mountain ranges do you see on the map?

2. Into what body of water does the James River flow?

3. On Your Own Make your own land and water map. Include colors and symbols for a mountain, hill, lake, and river.

Page 61

Help children use the symbols and colors in the map key to locate various landforms and bodies of water in Virginia.

2 How many symbols are shown in the map key? Five **Interpret Maps**

3 How many different kinds of landforms are shown on the map? Four **What are they?** Mountain, hill, plains, valley **Interpret Maps**

4 What is the biggest body of water you see on the map? Atlantic Ocean **Interpret Maps**

3 Close and Assess

Have children tell what Sara probably learned about her state by looking at the map. Ask children how the colors and symbols helped them read the map.

Try it!

1. Appalachian; Blue Ridge

Locate Key Words in the Question
Ask children to look for key words in the question to determine that the answer is *Atlantic Ocean.*

2. Atlantic Ocean

3. On Your Own Maps will vary but should include a map key (colors and symbols) and the four specified kinds of landforms (mountain, hill, lake, river).

CURRICULUM CONNECTION Music

Sing a Song About Maps

Teach children to sing this song to the tune of "Matchmaker, Matchmaker."

Mapmaker, mapmaker,
Make me a map!
Show me mountains high
And plains so flat!
Mapmaker, mapmaker,
Make me a map.
Show me this, too.
Rivers and oceans colored in blue.
Mapmaker, mapmaker,
What would we do,
If we didn't have someone
like you?

Workbook, p. 15

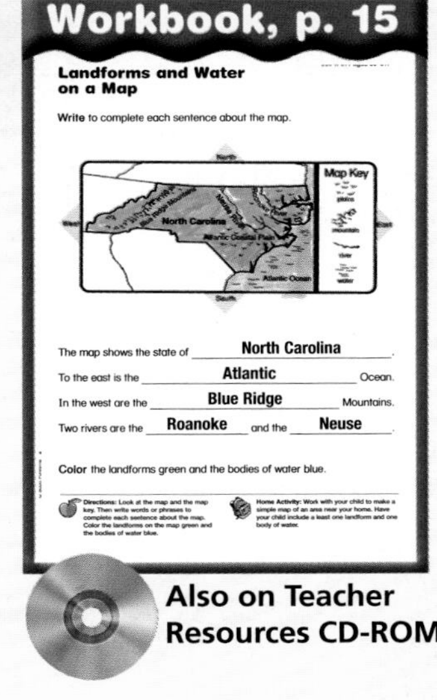

Landforms and Water on a Map

Write to complete each sentence about the map.

The map shows the state of North Carolina.
To the east is the Atlantic Ocean.
In the west are the Blue Ridge Mountains.
Two rivers are the Roanoke and the Neuse.

Color the landforms green and the bodies of water blue.

Also on Teacher Resources CD-ROM.

Use with pages 56–61

Lesson 1 Wrap-Up

MEETING INDIVIDUAL NEEDS

Leveled Practice

Draw Geography Pictures
Have children draw and share pictures of landforms and bodies of water.

Easy Have children sort the pictures into two groups labeled *Landforms* and *Bodies of Water*. If there are two or more pictures of the same thing, children should clip them together. Encourage children to name what is shown in their pictures. **Reteach**

On-Level Have children determine the type of landform or body of water in each picture and write a caption for each picture. **Extend**

Challenge Have children refer to a map of the United States and then write on each picture they drew the name of a place where that feature can be found, such as *Florida* on a peninsula picture. **Enrich**

Hands-on Activities

CURRICULUM CONNECTION
Writing

Riddles

Objective Write riddles to demonstrate an understanding of new vocabulary.

Resources Vocabulary Cards: **geography landform**

Materials paper, pencils

Learning Style Verbal/Linguistic

Individual/Group

Time 10–15 minutes

1. Display the Vocabulary Cards. Review the meanings of the words.

2. Help children make a list of landforms and bodies of water.

3. Model how to make a riddle about one entry on the list. For example, *Sometimes I'm deep and sometimes I'm not. You can swim in me when you're hot. Land is all around me. What am I? (lake)*

4. Have children choose an entry from the list and write a riddle.

Remind children to add the two new vocabulary words to their "My Word Book" glossaries.

CURRICULUM CONNECTION
Science

Fact Detectives

Objective Locate and record scientific facts about water.

Materials paper, pencils, nonfiction books about water

Learning Style Linguistic/Verbal

Partners

Time 20–25 minutes

1. Have partners use the books to find five interesting facts about water to share with the class.

2. Encourage children to check glossaries in the books, so they understand the terms.

3. Ask pairs to create a visual aid of some kind to present their findings. Allow time for sharing.

4. Create a wall display entitled *Wonderful Water!*

CURRICULUM CONNECTION
Art

Clay Forms

Objective Make clay representations of land and water forms.

Materials modeling clay, newspaper

Learning Style Visual/Kinesthetic

Individual

Time 20–25 minutes

1. Have children revisit the pictures of the landforms and bodies of water on pp. 57–59.

2. Children can spread newspaper and then use the clay to make visual representations of land and water forms.

3. Suggest that each child choose one landform and one body of water to model.

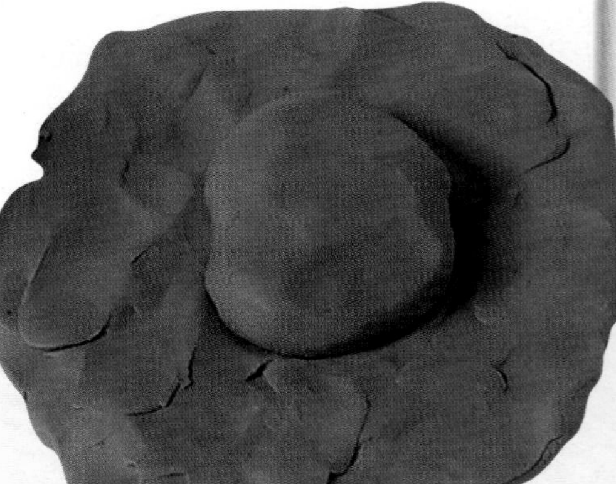

Lesson 2 Overview

Where People Live **pages 62–65**	Children will learn about how people live in three different communities.	 Time 20–30 minutes **Resources** • Workbook, p. 16 • Transparency 13 • Every Student Learns Guide, pp. 26-29
How and Where People Lived **pages 66–67**	Children will learn how Native Americans—the first people to live in what is now the United States—used the Earth's resources to meet their needs.	 Time 15–20 minutes

Build Background

Activity

Where We Live

 **Time** 20–25 minutes

Write on the board: ***I ♥ (name of your city/town), (name of your state).*** Have children copy it in the center of a large sheet of drawing paper. Then have children draw small pictures that communicate what they like best about where they live. Model a few ideas at the board by drawing a radiant sun to show good weather, a little sailboat to represent water activities, or tall, tall buildings. Have children label each picture.

Encourage volunteers to display and talk about their work. Then collect children's work in a book format, making it available for leisure time review.

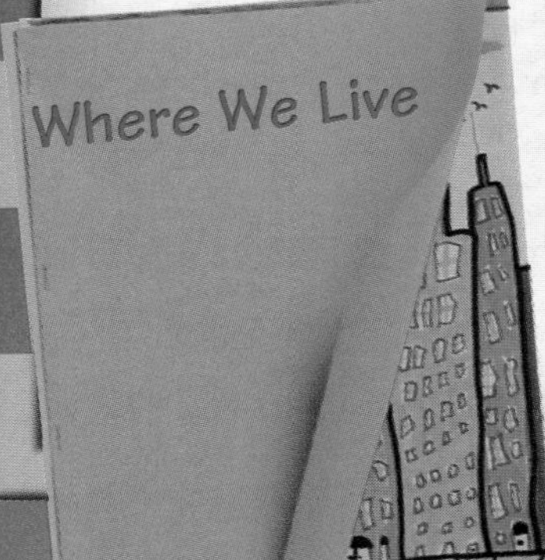

If time is short, have children choose partners. Have partners tell one or two things they like best about where they live.

Read Aloud

People Live Everywhere

by Kim Franklyn

People live ...

near an ocean,
by a river,
on the plain,
in a desert,
on an island,
in a valley,
on a mountain,
beside a lake.

There can be no mistake.
People live in homes everywhere!

Where People Live

Objective

- Compare similarities and differences among families in different communities.

QUICK Teaching Plan

If time is short, write these phrases on the board: *near a desert, on an island, on a farm.* Read the phrases with children. Have them use prior knowledge and their experiences to tell what life would be like in each setting.

- Have children use the maps and photographs on pp. 62–64 to formulate oral descriptions of each different place.

1 Introduce and Motivate

Preview Have children scan the lesson and look at the maps and photographs. Point out the three friendly letters and have children predict what they will be reading about. Show children photographs in books or brochures of Arizona, Hawaii, and Indiana. Encourage them to compare those images with the descriptions in the letters.

Warm Up To activate prior knowledge, ask children to share what they know about pen pals. Discuss what kinds of information children like to share in letters to friends and family. If time allows, discuss how children would describe their own community to a pen pal.

Where People Live

Our class has pen pals who live in three different places. Come and meet our new friends.

Tucson, Arizona

Juan

Hi!

I live in Tucson, Arizona. My city is near a hot and dry desert.

Last week, my class took a field trip to a really great museum about the desert. Did you know that many animals and plants live in the desert?

Rabbits, snakes, and even coyotes live here. The cactuses grow in many shapes and sizes. A cactus can store water and live through months of dry weather.

What kind of plants and animals live around you?

Write back soon.

Juan

P.S. I like bike riding, baseball, and swimming. What do you like to do?

1 2 5 8

Sonoran Desert

62

Practice and Extend

READING SKILL Compare and Contrast

- Explain that this lesson talks about three different places in the United States.
- After children read pp. 62–65, display Transparency 3.
- Ask children to choose two of the places and to use a Venn diagram to tell how the places are alike and different.
- If necessary, remind children that they can write how the two places are alike in the space where the two circles overlap.

ESL ACCESS CONTENT ESL Support

Desert Pantomime Write *desert* on the board. Say: *I'm in the desert. The desert is hot. The desert is dry.* Pantomime being in the desert—wipe your brow, fan your face with your hand, indicate that you are thirsty.

Beginning Have children follow your model of pantomiming. Ask: *Is the desert hot? Is the desert dry?* Prompt children to respond with *Yes*, followed by a full sentence.

Intermediate As children pantomime being in the desert, have them tell about the conditions there and how they are feeling.

Advanced In addition to pantomiming and telling how they are feeling, children should describe what they are likely to see in a desert.

For additional ESL support, use Every Student Learns Guide, pp. 26–29.

2 Teach and Discuss

Page 62

After reading the page, tell children that a desert is an example of an *ecosystem*, or a place where living and nonliving things interact successfully. The animals and plants do well in the hot, dry desert conditions.

1 **Describe the area around Juan's home. What is the desert like? What kinds of plants and animals would you see in the desert?** Hot and dry; rabbits, snakes, coyotes, cactuses **Main Idea and Details**

2 **Why can a cactus live for months without rain?** It stores up water for a long time, so it doesn't need rain very often. **Cause and Effect**

Page 63

To assure that children clearly understand that Hawaii is a group of islands in the Pacific Ocean, show an atlas map to supplement the inset.

3 **What is Leilani's community like?** Possible answers: It is very green because it rains almost every day. It has beautiful rainbows. It is by the ocean, and it has white sand beaches and hiking trails. **Main Idea and Details**

4 **Kauai is an island. On how many sides of an island is there water?** Children should recall that an island has water on all sides. **Apply Information**

Ongoing Assessment

If...children don't recall the definition of *island*,	**then...**refer them back to Lesson 1, p. 58.

5 **How are Juan's and Leilani's communities alike and different?** Answers will vary but should use details in both letters, including rainfall, plants, animals, etc. **Compare and Contrast**

continued

Page 64

Help children read Matt's letter. Repeat that he lives in Kokomo (kō'•kə•mō), Indiana. Explain that a Ferris wheel is an amusement ride and that a corn dog is a hot dog on a stick, wrapped in a corn meal batter, and deep fried.

6 How does Matt's family get money to buy things such as clothing, furniture, a car? Possible answer: They sell some of the corn and soybeans they grow. **Make Inferences**

7 What kinds of chores do you think Matt's family does on the farm every morning and evening? Ideas might include feeding the animals, milking cows, gathering eggs from chickens, watering the corn and soybeans, etc. **Make Inferences**

SOCIAL STUDIES STRAND
Geography

8 How are Matt's and Juan's communities alike and different? Matt's and Leilani's communities? Possible answers: Matt and Juan both live in places where there are plants and animals. Matt lives on a farm, though, and Juan lives in a city near a desert. The plants and animals are different. Leilani lives on an island that has sand beaches and beautiful flowers. Matt's farm has crops of soybeans and corn. **Compare and Contrast**

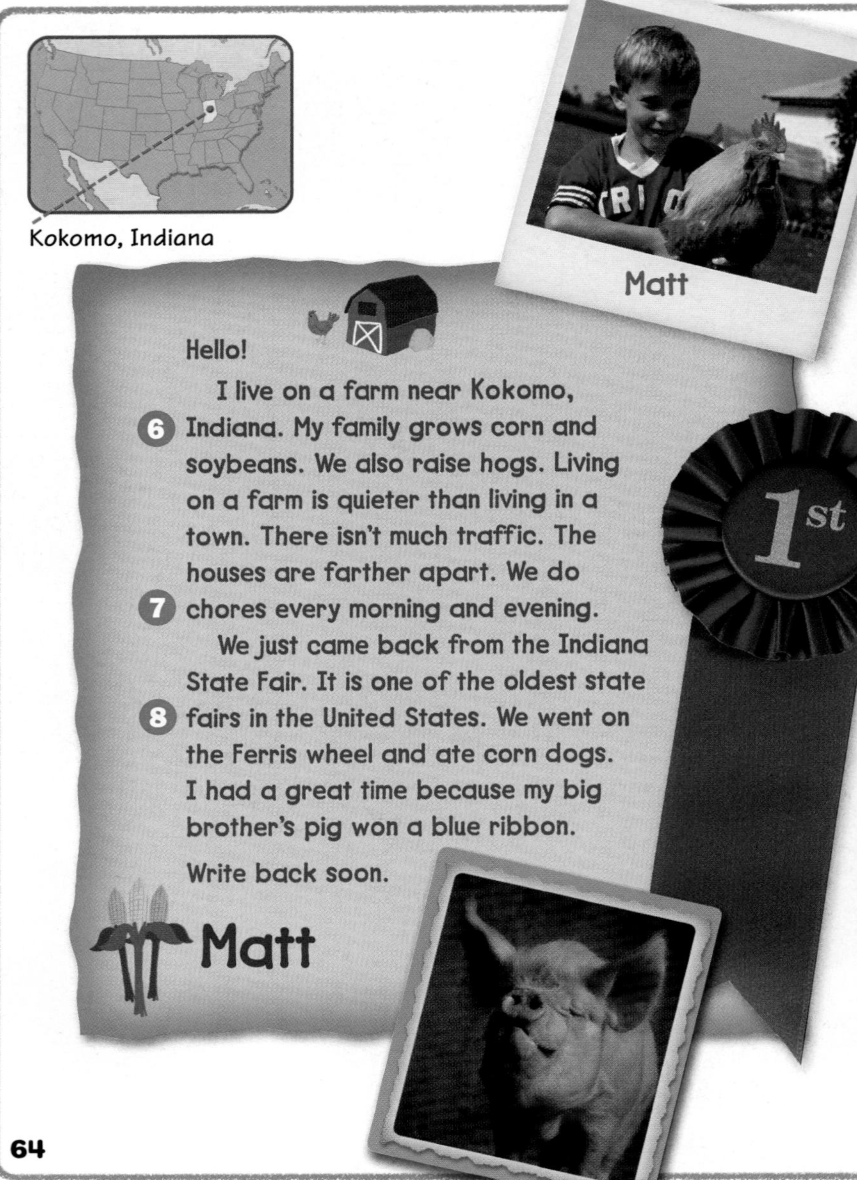

Practice and Extend

SOCIAL STUDIES
Background

The Hoosier State

- People from Indiana are called *Hoosiers*. No one is certain about the origin of the term, but some suggest the name comes from pioneers on the plains calling out "Who's here?"
- Indiana's rich soil is a great resource for the state. There are more than 60,000 farms in Indiana.
- Corn, soybeans, and tomatoes are important crops. Indiana also leads in the production of popcorn!

WEB SITE
Technology

You may go online to learn more about Arizona, Indiana, and Hawaii. Click on the *Atlas* at **www.sfsocialstudies.com.**

North

United States

10 ARCTIC OCEAN

CANADA

PACIFIC OCEAN

CANADA

INDIANA

ARIZONA

PACIFIC OCEAN

ATLANTIC OCEAN

East

HAWAII

PACIFIC OCEAN

MEXICO

Gulf of Mexico

9 Map Key
Country border
State border

South

Look at the map. Find Arizona, Indiana, and Hawaii.

What did you learn?

1. Which of the three states in this lesson shares a border with Mexico?
2. Which state is a group of islands in the Pacific Ocean?
3. **Think and Share** Compare the place you live with one of the communities you read about in the pen pal letters.

65

Page 65

Ask children to locate Arizona, Indiana, and Hawaii. Mention that both Hawaii and Alaska are part of the United States even though they are not connected geographically with the rest of the United States.

Using an atlas, have children look at state maps of Arizona, Indiana, and Hawaii to compare and contrast prominent landforms.

9 What map key symbol shows a country border? Thick dark line **Interpret Maps**

10 What oceans are shown on the map? Atlantic, Pacific, and Artic Oceans **Interpret Maps**

3 Close and Assess

Have children make a three-column chart on drawing paper and write the name of each community described in the lesson at the top of a column. Children can use their charts to record details about each place and then use their charts to discuss how all three places are alike and different.

✓ What did you learn?

1. Arizona
2. Hawaii

Test Talk

Write Your Answer
Children should make sure that their written answer is correct and complete.

3. **Think and Share** Children's comparisons should include specific details about how the two places are alike and different.

CURRICULUM CONNECTION Writing

Pen Pal Letters

- Place children's names in a hat or bag. Have each child draw the name of a class pen pal.
- Have children write to each other, telling some of the things they enjoy doing.
- Encourage them to follow the letter form used by Juan, Leilani, and Matt.
- Provide envelopes.
- Collect and deliver children's letters for them to enjoy.

Workbook, p. 16

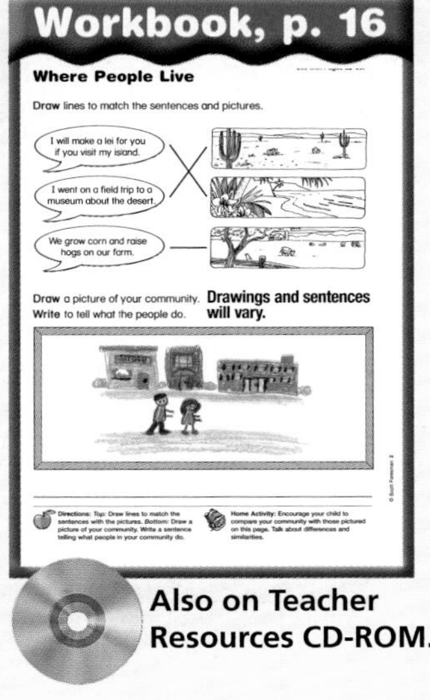
Where People Live

Draw lines to match the sentences and pictures.

I will make a lei for you if you visit my island.

I went on a field trip to a museum about the desert.

We grow corn and raise hogs on our farm.

Draw a picture of your community. Write to tell what the people do. **Drawings and sentences will vary.**

Also on Teacher Resources CD-ROM.

Living History

How and Where People Lived

Objective

- Understand how physical characteristics of places and regions affect people's activities and settlement patterns.

1 Introduce and Motivate

Preview Ask children to scan the lesson, noting illustrations and photographs that capture their attention. Have children predict what they will be reading about. Tell children Native Americans had and still have a great respect for nature and its resources.

Warm Up To activate prior knowledge, initiate a discussion about people's basic needs—food, water, clothing, shelter. Ask children if they think people's needs are different today from what they were long ago.

2 Teach and Discuss

The terms *Native American* and *American Indian* are often used interchangeably. Preference as to the use of these terms is mixed even among tribal groups.

Page 66

1 What did the Native Americans need in order to live? Food, clothing, and a place to live
Main Idea and Details

2 What kinds of materials found in nature do you think they used to make their homes? Possible answers include tree branches, bark, grass-like plants, rocks and stones, dirt mixed with water.
Make Inferences

Living History

How and Where People Lived

Some Native Americans made canoes, or narrow boats, to travel on the rivers.

Native Americans, also known as American Indians, were the first people to live in what is now the United States. They used land, water, plants, and animals to meet their needs. A need is something that people must have to live. Food, clothing, and a place to live are needs. 1

Native Americans lived in areas with different climates. Climate is the kind of weather a place usually has. Native Americans built homes to suit the climate. They used things found in nature to make their homes. 2

66

Practice and Extend

CURRICULUM CONNECTION
Science

- Ask children to tell what the weather is like today. Ask if the weather stays the same year round where they live.
- Point out that the *climate* of a place refers to the weather in that place over a long period of time.
- Ask children to draw and write to describe the *climate* where they live. You may want to share with children what an almanac says about the climate where they live.

Many groups of Native Americans lived in an area called the Great Plains. These Native Americans were called Plains Indians. Some Plains Indians were farmers. They planned their lives around
3 the changing seasons. Spring was the time to plant. Fall was the time to harvest.

Painted animal skin

Sometimes terrible storms and floods happened on the plains. How would these very bad weather conditions have affected the crops? How might bad weather conditions affect the activities of farmers today?

4 Many Plains Indians hunted animals for food. They used animal skins to keep warm. Some lived in a kind of tent called a tepee.

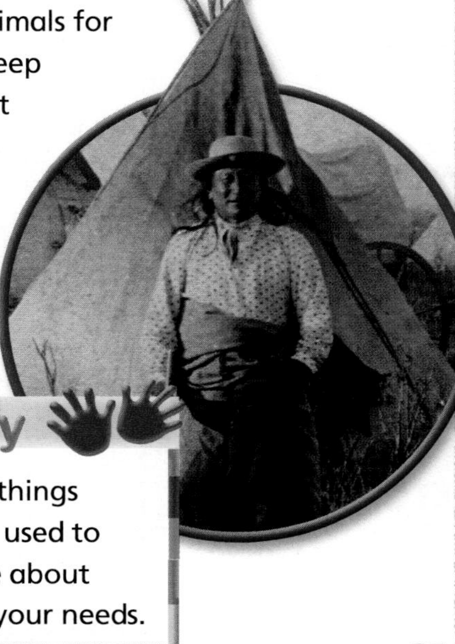

Today life has changed for many Native Americans. Some are still farmers while others have jobs in towns or cities.

Hands-on History

Draw and label pictures of things Native Americans might have used to meet their needs. Tell or write about some things you use to meet your needs.

67

SOCIAL STUDIES STRAND

Culture

Tribes

- Explain that Native Americans lived together in tribes—groups of people who lived in the same area, spoke the same language, and shared the same customs and heritage.
- Tell children a few things about one or two Native American groups you have learned about, such as the Cherokee or the Navajo.
- Have children ask questions about the tribe, which you or another expert can answer.

Page 67

As you read with children, define *harvest* and *crops*, if necessary. Have children answer each of the questions in the second paragraph.

Talk briefly with children about the state where you live. Gather information from encyclopedia articles and maps to discuss distribution of population and how it may relate to available natural resources such as fertile soil, minerals, water sources for irrigation, transportation, and energy. Talk, too, about climate and seasonal weather and how they may motivate where people choose to live.

3 **Why did the Plains Indians who were farmers plan their lives around the changing seasons?** Certain jobs and activities could be done only in certain kinds of weather. Planting was done in the spring; harvesting was done in the fall.
Draw Conclusions

4 **Why did many Plains Indians hunt animals?** For food, for skins to help keep them warm
Cause and Effect

3 Close and Assess

Hands-on History

Test Talk

Use Information from the Text
Help children look for details in the text to support their answer.

Before children draw, have them recall how Native Americans used land, water, plants, and animals to meet their needs. Check that their labeled drawings are accurate and that children's descriptions of meeting their own needs are logical.

Use with pages 62–67

Lesson 2 Wrap-Up

MEETING INDIVIDUAL NEEDS

Leveled Practice

A Class Mural

Have children cut out from magazines and other sources pictures that relate generally to what they know about a desert area, an island, and a plains farm.

Easy Have children sort the pictures according to place and paste them on a large sheet of paper to make a three-part mural. Children should create labels for the three parts of the mural. **Reteach**

On-Level Have children write a few sentences about each of the three parts of the mural. **Extend**

Challenge Have children look at the mural pictures and recall what they have learned about each place. Ask them to write a short paragraph about the place they like best. **Enrich**

Hands-on Activities

CURRICULUM CONNECTION

Reading

Words to Keep!

Objective Identify key words from the lesson.

Materials chart paper, marker

Learning Style Visual/Verbal

Group

Time 15–20 minutes

1. Explain that you will give children clues about words they have met in the lesson. Consider: *desert, cactus, rainbow, island, chores, fair, need, season names, harvest, crops.* Give clues such as: *A hot and dry place; an outdoor show of farm products and animals.*

rainbow
fair

2. As each word is identified, write it on a chart. If children hesitate, refer them to the section of the lesson that includes the word you want them to recall.

CURRICULUM CONNECTION

Drama

Dramatizing

Objective Express information from a text in a different way.

Materials stiff paper for making name tags, markers or crayons

Learning Style Visual/Verbal

Group

Time 20–30 minutes

1. Precut the paper to make name tags. Distribute the tags and tell children to write the name of a child they met in the lesson—Juan, Matt, or Leilani—on their tags.

2. Explain that when children put on their name tags, they will become the character they chose.

3. Call on volunteers to tell about themselves—in character.

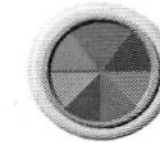

CURRICULUM CONNECTION

Literature

Desert Life

Objective Describe and appreciate one place where people live—near a desert.

Resources Vocabulary Cards: **geography landform**

Materials *Listen to the Desert/¿Qué dice el desierto?* by Pat Mora (Clarion Books, ISBN 0-395-67292-9, 1994)

Learning Style Auditory/Visual/Verbal

Group

Time 15–20 minutes

1. Preview the book with a quick picture walk. Then read the text and show the pictures.

2. Call on volunteers to compare and contrast the information in Juan's letter with information given in the book.

Lesson 3 Overview

From My Orchard to You pages 68–71	Children will learn the meanings of the words *ancestor, producer,* and *consumer.* They will explore how one family uses and changes the land through the seasons to grow apple trees.	 Time 20–30 minutes Resources • Workbook, p. 17 • Vocabulary Cards ancestor producer consumer • Every Student Learns Guide, pp. 30-33
Smithsonian Institution: Harvest Time pages 72–73	Children will view agricultural artifacts.	 Time 15–20 minutes
Cesar Chavez pages 74–75	Children will read how Cesar Chavez worked to make life better for migrant farm workers.	 Time 15–20 minutes

Build Background

Activity

Make, Grow, or Buy?

 **Time** 15–20 minutes

- Begin a list with children of things their families buy at the store. Title the list *What do we buy?* Start children off by suggesting that families buy clothes, vegetables, bread.
- Then talk with children about who makes or grows the items on the list. Make an entry next to each item. Show, for example, the entry *clothing makers* next to *clothes.* Label the second column entries as *Who makes or grows it?*
- Note that people buy things because they don't make or grow those things themselves.

If time is short, have partners name things made or grown by a baker, a fruit farmer, and a carpenter. Ask: *Why do others buy what these people make?*

Read Aloud

All in a Day's Work

by Bob Geary

A toy maker makes toys.
A baker makes pies.
A dairy farmer collects milk.
An artist makes pictures.

So that we can . . .
Play with the toys,
Eat the pies,
Drink the milk,
And enjoy
the pictures!

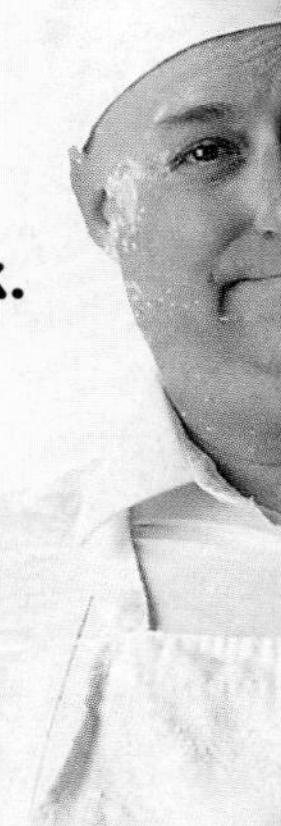

From My Orchard to You

Objectives

- Distinguish between producing and consuming.
- Trace the development of a product from a natural resource to a finished product.

Vocabulary

ancestor a person in our family who lived before we were born (p. 68)

producer someone who makes or grows something (p. 68)

consumer someone who buys goods (p. 71)

QUICK Teaching Plan

If time is short, discuss some of the predictable steps in growing and producing apples.

- Introduce the terms *producer* and *consumer.* Have children describe what is happening in the photos on pp. 69–71. Associate what they see with the concept of producing.

1 Introduce and Motivate

Preview Display the Vocabulary Cards **producer** and **consumer**. Ask children what they think each word means. Share the meaning of each word. Tell children that the word *orchard* in the title of the lesson is another way of saying "apple farm." Ask whether the owners of an orchard are producers or consumers.

Warm Up To activate prior knowledge, ask children to tell what they may know about apple orchards or other types of fruit or vegetable farms. Have them tell what happens when the crop is ready. Ask what happens after the crop is picked.

From My Orchard to You

A long time ago, my great-grandfather had a small apple orchard. My great-grandfather is my ancestor. An **ancestor** is a person in our family who lived before we were born. This picture shows some of my ancestors. 1

The people in my family are producers of apples. A **producer** is someone who makes or grows something. We use and change the land to grow our tasty apples. Here's what we do to get the apples from the orchard to you!

2

68

Practice and Extend

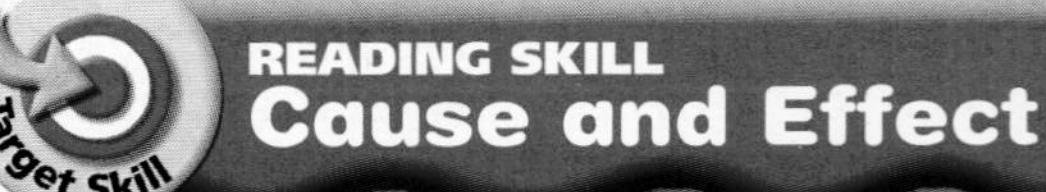

READING SKILL
Cause and Effect

Target Skill

- As you read this lesson, have children look for causes and effects to find out why Sara's family performs certain jobs during each season of the year.
- Direct their attention to the question at the bottom of p. 69 and have them answer it.
- Encourage children to note other examples of cause-and-effect relationships in the lesson as they read.

winter

Workers prune, or cut, the branches of the trees. This lets more sunlight reach the trees so the apples ripen. Pruning also makes it easier to pick the apples. 3

4

We clear some of the land to make room for new trees to be planted. We cut tall grass to keep away harmful insects. Sometimes we spray to protect the trees and fruit from insects.

spring

5

summer

We irrigate if we don't get enough rain. Irrigate means to bring water to the land. Irrigation can be done by using ditches or sprinkling. When we irrigate the land, the crops grow well. Irrigation is the **cause.** What is the **effect?**

69

CURRICULUM CONNECTION
Math

Apple Math

Have children do some "apple math" to figure out the following.

- Meg and Fran picked 5 apples each. How many did they have all together?
- Damal picked 6 apples but ate 2 before he got home. How many were left?
- Andy picked 4 apples and then bought 3 more from Will. How many apples does Andy have?

WEB SITE
Technology

You can look up vocabulary words online. Click on *Social Studies Library* and select the dictionary at **www.sfsocialstudies.com.**

2 Teach and Discuss

Page 68

Display the Vocabulary Card **ancestor**. Say the word aloud and have children repeat it.

1 Who is Sara's ancestor? Her great-grandfather; anyone in her family who lived before she was born **Context Clues**

2 Why do you think Sara's family produces apples? The orchard was probably handed down to her family, so that is why they still grow apples. It wouldn't make sense to grow something else if they already have apple trees. **Make Inferences**

Page 69

Have children read the label under each photograph. Ask what information the labels give.

3 Why do Sara and her family prune the apple trees? To let more sunlight reach the trees, to make the apples easier to pick
Cause and Effect

GEOGRAPHY
People and Places Change Each Other

4 Why do they clear the land? How will this affect Sara and her family? They clear the land to make room for new trees, and to keep away harmful insects. In the future, the new trees will provide more apples to pick and then to sell.
Cause and Effect

5 What are two ways to irrigate the land? Using ditches and sprinkling **Recall and Retell**

continued

Page 70

6 Why does Sara think that fall is the best season of all? It's time to harvest and sort the apples. **Main Idea and Details**

7 Why can't apples be harvested in the spring or early summer? They wouldn't be full-grown; apples form in the spring and ripen during the summer. **Make Inferences**

ECONOMICS
Jobs

Explain that producing apples involves many different jobs. Have children reread p. 70 and identify some of the jobs Sara describes. (picking the apples; sorting the apples; packing them in boxes; driving the trucks; selling the apples; making some apples into pies, sauce, and juice; and so on)

Page 71

8 What do you do that makes you and your family producers? Possible answer: We make cookies for bake sales. **Apply Information**

If... children don't understand that they can be called producers,

then... ask them if they ever bake cookies, make a card for a friend, or lemonade to sell. Say that someone who makes things is a producer.

9 How can someone be both a producer and a consumer? A person who makes or grows something also needs to buy goods as a consumer. **Analyze Information**

Fall is the best season of all! That's because it's time to harvest and sort the apples. We hire workers to help us pick the apples by hand. Next we pack the apples into boxes. Then we load the boxes into trucks.

fall

Some trucks take fresh apples to stores or farm stands. Other trucks take apples to an apple factory, or plant. Here, factory workers make the apples into sauce, pies, or juice. Then these apple products are shipped to stores around the country.

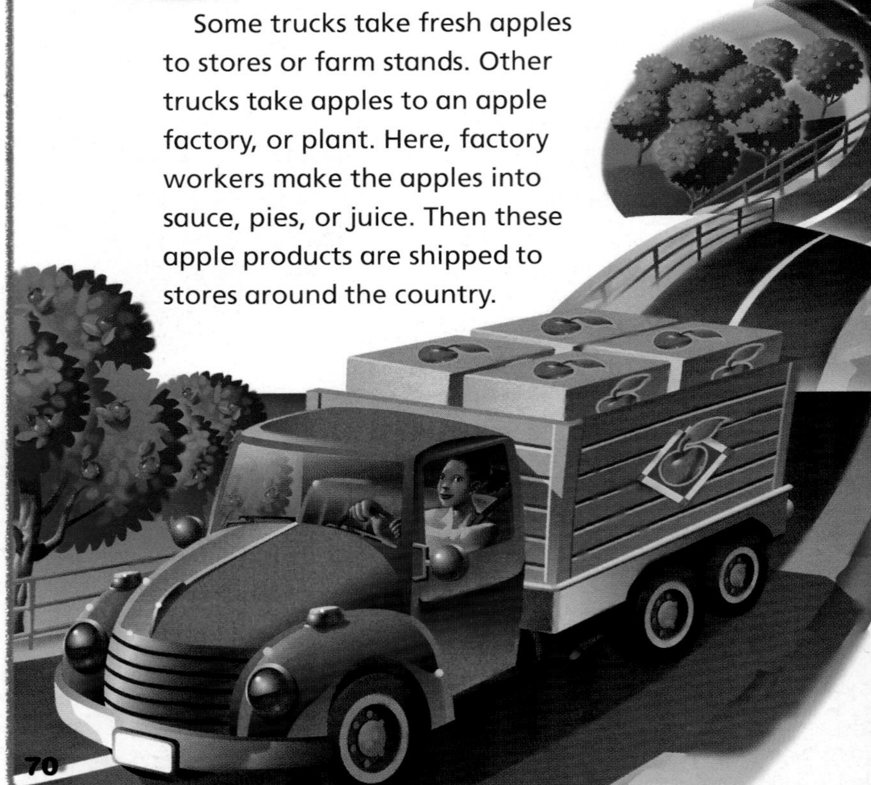

70

Practice and Extend

SOCIAL STUDIES STRAND
History

Yesterday and Today

Have children compare and contrast apple farming at the time of Sara's ancestors and today. Help children find answers to these questions:

- Did Sara's ancestors have the same tools and machines (sprinklers, pruning tools, mowers) to keep the trees healthy? How did they do these jobs?
- Did they have superhighways to send their apples long distances to stores and markets?
- How did they keep track of how many apples they grew each year and how much money they made? Did they have computers and fax machines?

Make the point that science and technology have changed the way farmers do business. They have also given farmers more free time to do other things.

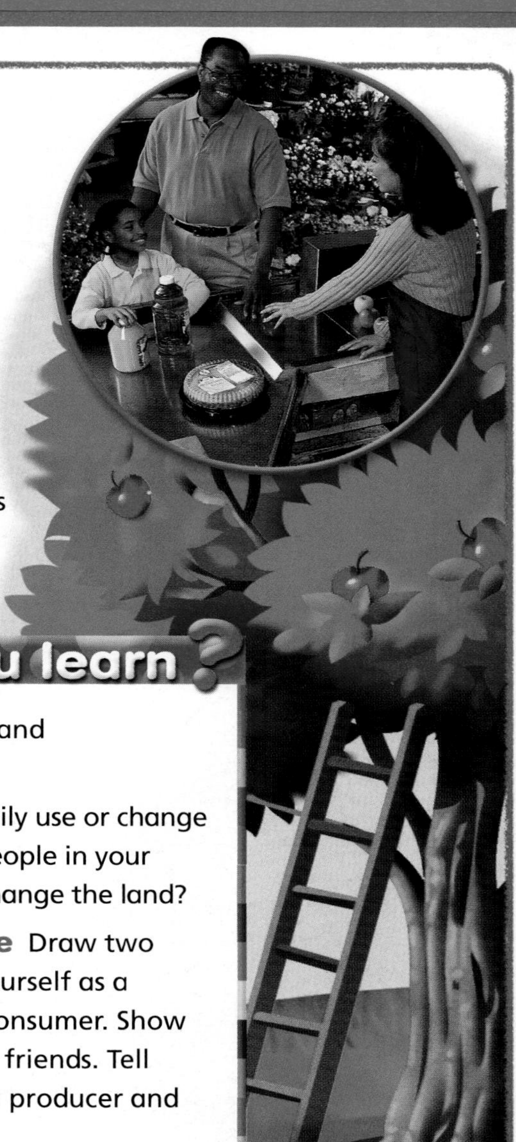

8 At the store, workers put the apples and apple products on shelves for consumers just like you.
9 A **consumer** is someone who buys and uses goods. Goods are things that people make or grow. What other goods do consumers buy at the store?

What did you learn?

1. What do producers and consumers do?
2. How does Sara's family use or change the land? How do people in your community use or change the land?
3. **Think and Share** Draw two pictures showing yourself as a producer and as a consumer. Show the pictures to your friends. Tell them about being a producer and a consumer.

71

ACCESS CONTENT ESL Support

Taking Roles Have volunteers draw pictures that show what a producer or consumer does.

Beginning Have children act out parallel activities such as picking an apple (producer) and eating an apple (consumer).

Intermediate Have children in small groups take the roles of producers and consumers, saying what they produce or what they buy and why.

Advanced Have children dramatize the steps of getting a good from the farm to the store and finally to consumers.

For additional support, use Every Student Learns Guide, pp. 30–33.

Workbook, p. 17

Also on Teacher Resources CD-ROM.

3 Close and Assess

Ask children how Sara's family gets money to spend as consumers.

Sum up by saying that Sara's family uses three kinds of resources to grow apples—*natural resources,* the land and water; *human resources,* their work and that of the workers they hire; and *capital resources,* their tools and machines.

✓ What did you learn?

1. Producers make and grow things; consumers buy the things producers make or grow.
2. Sara's family uses the land to grow the apple trees; the family changes the land by clearing the land, planting new trees, and irrigating. Look for specific details in children's ideas about how people in their community use or change the land.
3. **Think and Share** Observe children as they talk with partners. Prompt them to talk about specific details in their pictures. As needed, suggest details they might add.

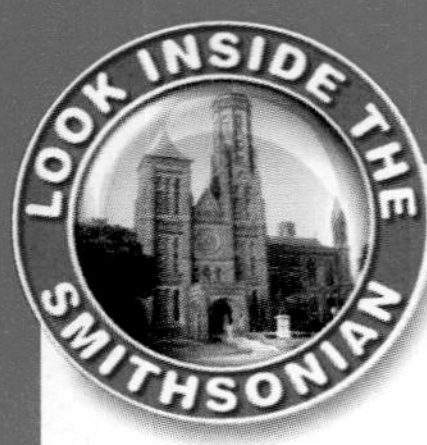

Harvest Time

Objective

- Obtain information from visual sources such as photographs of artifacts.

Resource

- Workbook, p. 18

1 Introduce and Motivate

Preview Read the title and the introduction aloud. Guide children to talk about the objects they see. Note the orchard setting for the painting, asking children to describe some features of an orchard. Ask children to describe the apples they see on the different fruit crate labels. Which apples look like ones they have eaten and enjoyed? Call on volunteers to identify other fruits and vegetables depicted.

Warm Up To activate prior knowledge, have children think about products they see in the supermarket. Ask what the purposes of the labels on the products are. Guide children to realize that product labels include the brand name, or which company makes or sells the product; a list of ingredients; pictures of the product; and, sometimes, pictures of people enjoying the product. Talk briefly with children about the kinds of colors they see used on product labels. Ask if labels are usually bold and bright or light and pale. Talk, too, about the size of the lettering that names the product. It it large or small? Is it easy to read if the product is on a shelf?

Ask children to visualize products they are very familiar with, such as breakfast cereals or juice bottles or boxes. Call on volunteers to describe the colors, type size, and pictures that are parts of the labels.

FYI Social Studies Background

About Crate Labels

- Fruit and vegetable growers put thought into their labels. The labels had to communicate the quality and freshness of a product buyers could not see inside the crates. The labels also had to communicate an appeal for the product. Growers often tried to associate their products with a love of family and wholesomeness.
- Between 1880 and 1956, millions of labels were produced.
- Today crate labels are collectibles. There is a network of about 2,000 serious collectors across the United States.

Seed Packets
Many people used to grow their own fruits and vegetables from seeds. The seeds came in small packets. On some of the packets, artists drew beautiful pictures. 2

Seed Catalog
Seeds could be ordered from catalogs such as these. These catalogs had many pages.

3

Fruit Crate Labels
Long ago, fruits and vegetables were packed into wooden crates for shipping. Then brightly colored labels were pasted to the ends of the crates. These labels told people what was inside each crate.

Artifacts are from the Smithsonian Institution. 73

2 Teach and Discuss

Have children follow along as you read the captions for the objects.

1 What does the painting "Apple Pickers" show you that lets you know that apple picking is hard work? Possible answers: Pickers must climb up and stand on ladders to reach the apples. They pick the apples by hand and put them in big boxes. The boxes look heavy to lift or move. **Analyze Pictures**

2 Look very closely at the seed packets. What information do you get by looking at the pictures and reading the words? The kinds of seeds inside the packets; what the grown products will look like; the names of the seed companies; how long one company has been in business. **Analyze Pictures**

3 Why do you think one crate label shows a child eating an apple? Possible answers: The child eating the apple might make people think that apples are tasty. The child looks healthy, so people might think that apples are good for a person's health. **Make Inferences**

3 Close and Assess

Allow time for partners or small groups of children to take a closer look at the objects. Tell children to look for as many details as possible. Ask them to focus on colors, pictures, size of lettering, and kinds of information. Then encourage children to respond to the following:

- At what time of year do you think the apple pickers are doing their work? Why?
- Which seed company had pointed out that they had been in business for 55 years?
- How does a company let people know that some animals find apples tasty?
- According to the seed catalog cover, who should plant apple seeds?

You may wish to close by inviting children to design a crate label for apples. Encourage volunteers to explain why they included the words and images they did.

WEB SITE Technology

You can visit the Smithsonian Institution online. Click on Smithsonian at **www.sfsocialstudies.com** or go to **www.si.edu.**

Workbook, p. 18

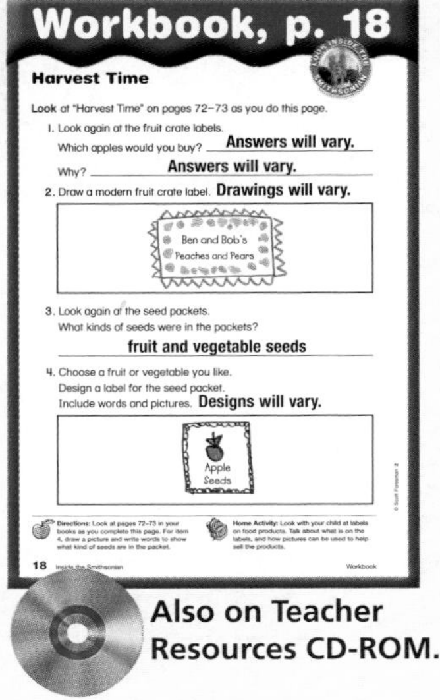

Harvest Time

Look at "Harvest Time" on pages 72–73 as you do this page.

1. Look again at the fruit crate labels.
   Which apples would you buy? **Answers will vary.**
   Why? **Answers will vary.**
2. Draw a modern fruit crate label. **Drawings will vary.**
   Ben and Bob's Peaches and Pears
3. Look again at the seed packets.
   What kinds of seeds were in the packets?
   fruit and vegetable seeds
4. Choose a fruit or vegetable you like.
   Design a label for the seed packet.
   Include words and pictures. **Designs will vary.**
   Apple Seeds

18 Inside the Smithsonian Workbook

Also on Teacher Resources CD-ROM.

Cesar Chavez

Objective

- Identify characteristics of good citizenship such as a belief in justice, truth, equality, and responsibility for the common good.

1 Introduce and Motivate

Preview Allow time for children to look at the words, illustrations, and photographs. Ask them to predict what they will be reading about in the lesson.

Warm Up To activate prior knowledge, write the word *leader* on the board. Ask children what they think of when they hear the word *leader*. Talk about the qualities a leader needs. Record children's ideas. Then invite them to name people—today and throughout history—who they think are leaders.

2 Teach and Discuss

Pages 74-75

Help children with the correct pronunciation of Cesar Chavez's name (sā'• zär chä'• vez). Then read the biography together. You may wish to have children use context clues to determine the meaning of the word *migrant*.

1 What work did Cesar Chavez and his family do on the farms? They picked crops that other farmers had grown. **Recall and Retell**

Practice and Extend

SOCIAL STUDIES Background

About Cesar Chavez

- Cesar Chavez is well known for his efforts to organize the grape pickers in California during the 1960s.
- In 1962, he established the National Farm Workers Association, which later merged with another union and eventually became the United Farm Workers of America. The union was dedicated to getting labor contracts and improved conditions for agricultural workers.
- After Chavez's death, President Clinton awarded him the Medal of Freedom, America's highest civilian honor.

WEB SITE Technology

You may help children find about more about Cesar Chavez by clicking on *Meet the People* at **www.sfsocialstudies.com.**

As a child, Cesar Chavez lived on a small farm in Arizona. When Cesar was ten, his family had to give up their farm. The Chavez family became migrant farm workers. They followed the harvest in California. They picked crops that other
1 farmers had grown. Cesar attended more than thirty different schools as the family moved from place to place.

After eighth-grade graduation, Cesar ended his education. He began working full-time in the fields. Life for Cesar, and other migrant workers, was very hard.
2 They worked long hours for low pay. They often lived in their cars or trucks.

Cesar Chavez wanted to make life better for farm workers. He began to teach Mexican farm workers to read and write. He helped
3 them become citizens so they could vote. Cesar organized the farm workers into a group called a *union*. He became their leader. He helped farm workers get fair pay and better working conditions.

4

Cesar Chavez was born near Yuma, Arizona.

Cesar Chavez School in San Francisco, CA

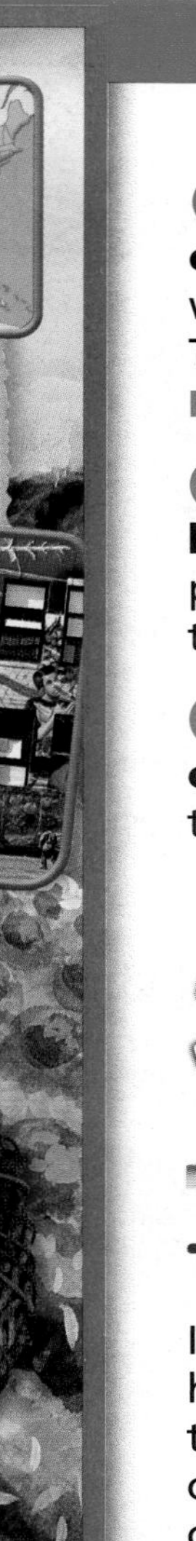

Think and Share

How did Cesar Chavez help farm workers?

For more information, go online to *Meet the People* at **www.sfsocialstudies.com.**

75

SOCIAL STUDIES STRAND
Citizenship

Unions in Action

- Discuss the function of a union—to identify unfair practices on the job, to say what things need to be changed.
- Explain that leaders in a union go to a boss to tell what the workers talk about.
- Have children role-play a situation in which a union leader presents a "problem" to a boss. Remind children of the steps of the problem-solving process as they plan their role-plays.

2 What was life like for Cesar Chavez and other migrant workers? Possible answer: Life was hard. They worked long hours for little pay. They sometimes lived in their cars and trucks. **Main Idea and Details**

3 Why did Cesar Chavez help workers to become citizens? Only citizens can vote. He probably wanted them to be able to make choices that would affect their lives. **Cause and Effect**

4 How did Chavez show that he was a good citizen? He worked hard to make life better for the farm workers. **Draw Conclusions**

3 Close and Assess

Think and Share

In their own words, children should be able to tell how Chavez helped farm workers by teaching them basic skills, encouraging them to become citizens, and organizing them into a union that could get them rights and benefits that workers in other kinds of jobs already had.

Use with pages 68–75

Lesson 3 Wrap-Up

MEETING INDIVIDUAL NEEDS

Leveled Practice

In the Marketplace

Have children draw or cut out pictures of goods that will be sold in a class market. Then have children label their pictures and group them by category on the bulletin board.

Easy Have children act as producers to tell about some of the goods they "brought to market." **Reteach**

On-Level Have children act as consumers to shop at the market. They should identify things they wish to buy and draw pictures of themselves using the good. Then have them write sentences to describe their pictures. **Extend**

Challenge Have children write to describe what would happen if they, as consumers at the market, did not want to buy some or all of the goods producers showed. **Enrich**

Hands-on Activities

CURRICULUM CONNECTION
Reading

Word Search

Objective Identify and use new vocabulary words.

Resources Vocabulary Cards: **ancestor producer consumer**

Materials paper, pencils

Learning Style Visual

Individual/Partner

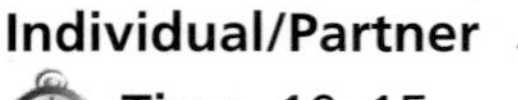

Time 10–15 minutes

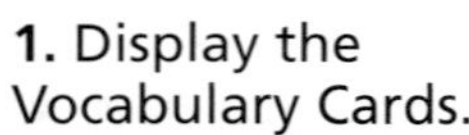

1. Display the Vocabulary Cards. Tell children they will make word search puzzles. They will hide the three new vocabulary words. Say they can hide the words in a horizontal row or a vertical row.

2. As needed, show a puzzle sample. Tell children they can hide each word as many times as they like.

3. Have partners exchange puzzles and then circle the hidden words.

Remind children to add the new words and definitions to their "My Word Book" glossaries.

CURRICULUM CONNECTION
Math

Apple Seeds

Objective Estimate the number of seeds in an apple.

Materials apples (several), a paring knife, paper towels

Learning Style Kinesthetic/Visual

Group

Time 20 minutes

1. Give each group an apple.

2. Have children estimate how many seeds are inside their apple. Ask them to record their estimate.

3. Visit each group to cut open the apple to reveal its seeds. Have children count the seeds to check their estimates. Children should record the true number of seeds.

4. Collect the data from the groups and make a chart with the headings *Estimates/Real Counts.*

CURRICULUM CONNECTION
Literature

Field Trip

Objective Listen and respond to a contemporary story.

Materials *Albert's Field Trip,* by Leslie Tryon (Atheneum, ISBN 0-689-31821-9, 1993)

Learning Style Visual/Verbal

Group

Time 15–20 minutes

1. Guide children on a picture walk through the book. Have them tell where the characters go on their field trip.

2. Read the book through once. Then reread it and talk with children about the characters' experiences.

3. Encourage volunteers to say whether they would enjoy going on a similar field trip.

Lesson 4 Overview

Our Earth's Resources **pages 76–79**	Children will learn the meaning of the terms *natural resource* and *crop*. They will explore how people use the resources—air, water, forests, and soil—to live.	Time 20–30 minutes Resources • Workbook, p. 19 • Vocabulary Cards natural resource crop • Every Student Learns Guide, pp. 34–37
Read a Bar Graph **pages 80–81**	Children will use a bar graph to compare preferences for different kinds of fruit.	Time 15–20 minutes Resource • Workbook, p. 20

Build Background

Activity

Earth's Stamp of Approval!

Time 15–20 minutes

Tell children they will design special postage stamps. Write *air, water, soil*, and *forests* on the board. Read the words with children, pointing out that these things come from nature.

Ask children to draw pictures that celebrate one or more of nature's gifts. Suggest that their pictures be simple. After all, there isn't much room on a postal stamp for many details!

Encourage volunteers to show and tell about their stamps. Collect and display all the stamps.

If time is short, display *air, water, soil*, and *forests*, identifying them as nature's gifts. Have children tell which gift they think is most useful to people and why.

Read Aloud

I'm Glad . . .

Anonymous

I'm glad the sky is painted blue,
And the Earth is painted green,
With such a lot of nice fresh air
All sandwiched in between.

Lesson 4 Our Earth's Resources

Objectives

- Explain how people depend on the physical environment and its resources to meet their needs.
- Identify ways to conserve and replenish natural resources.

Vocabulary

natural resource a useful material that comes from the Earth (p. 76)

crop a kind of plant grown by people for food and other uses (p. 78)

QUICK Teaching Plan

If time is short, write *natural resources* on the board. Below it list *air, water, soil, trees, oil, coal, gas.* Explain that these are some examples of natural resources. Talk briefly with children about how people use each resource.

- Have children think and talk about how animals use some of the same natural resources.

1 Introduce and Motivate

Preview Display the Vocabulary Cards **natural resource** and **crop**. Then read aloud the definitions. Ask children what crop Sara's family grows. (apples) Have children tell what natural resources enable the family to grow their apples.

Warm Up To activate prior knowledge, have children make word associations related to *air, water, soil*, and *trees*. Record children's ideas in four different word webs. Review the finished webs with children. Retain the word webs so children can add to them as they read the lesson.

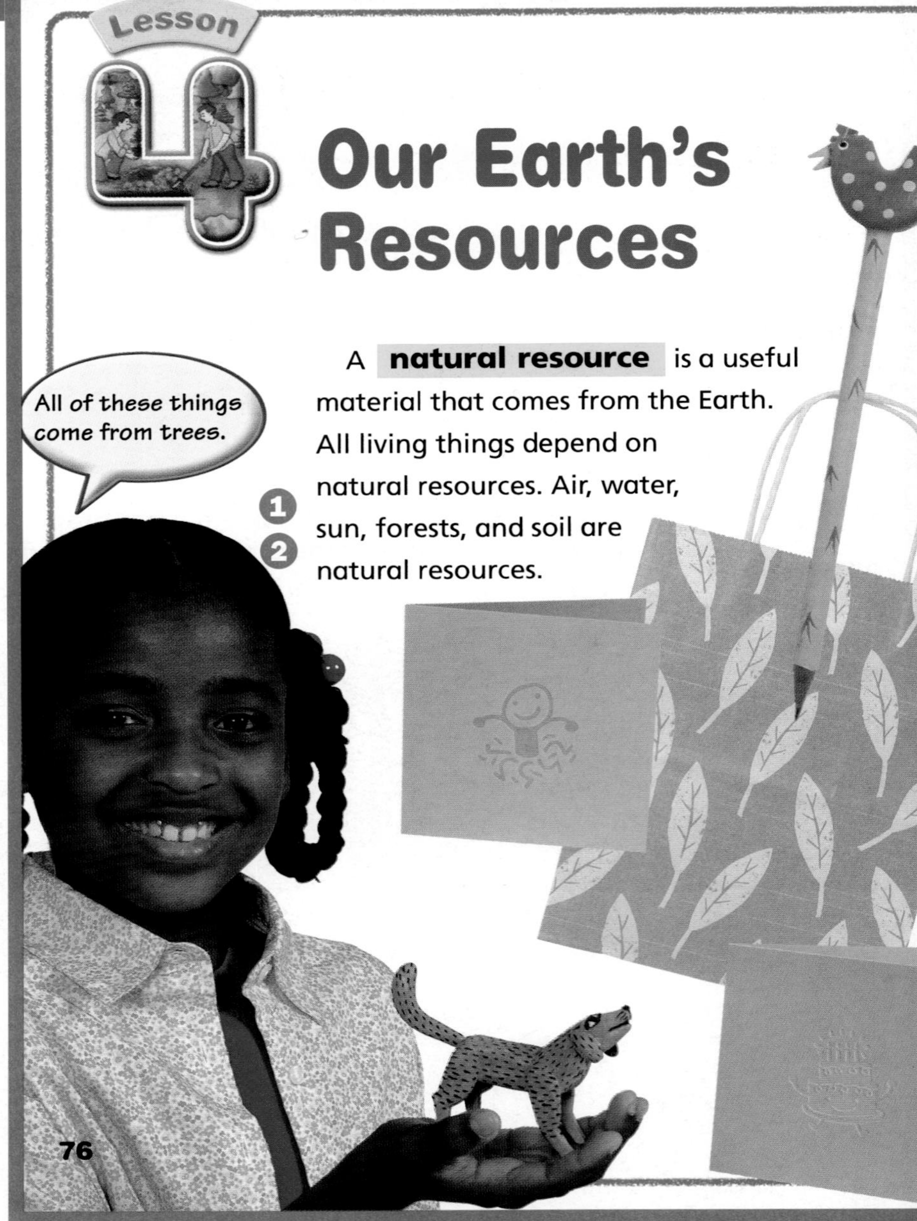

Practice and Extend

READING SKILL Categorize

- Have children make a three-column chart with these headings: *Made from Trees, Made from Wool, Made from Wheat.*
- Children can look through the lesson and write the names of objects that would belong in each category.
- Encourage children to add their own ideas of things that would belong in each category.

WEB SITE Technology

You can look up vocabulary words online. Click on *Social Studies Library* and select the dictionary at **www.sfsocialstudies.com.**

Farmers use natural resources to raise animals such as sheep. Sheep give us wool. During the winter, a sheep's coat of wool grows. When springtime comes, the sheep's wool gets cut. Luckily, it grows back, just like our hair!

Shearing sheep for wool

4

All of these things are made from sheep's wool.

77

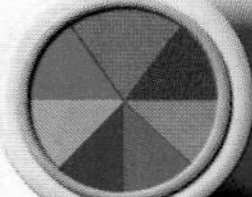

CURRICULUM CONNECTION
Music

Sing a Song

Tell children that people have been raising sheep for their wool for hundreds of years. Sing this familiar Mother Goose rhyme/song from long ago with children.

Baa, Baa, Black Sheep

Baa, baa, black sheep,
Have you any wool?
Yes, sir, yes, sir,
Three bags full;
One for my master,
And one for the dame,
And one for the little boy
Who lives down the lane.

2 Teach and Discuss

Page 76

Have children identify Sara and read the words in the speech bubble. Ask what things Sara is referring to.

1 **What are four kinds of natural resources?** Air, water, forests, and soil **Recall and Retell**

2 **How do you think living things depend on natural resources?** Possible answers: People depend on natural resources to satisfy their basic needs. They use water for drinking and transportation, forests for wood, air to breathe, and soil to plant food. **Draw Conclusions**

Ongoing Assessment

If...	then...
If...children have difficulty understanding what natural resources are,	**then...**explain that natural resources come from the Earth. They are not made by humans. However, humans use them to meet their needs.

Page 77

3 **Which natural resources do farmers use to raise sheep?** They use soil, water, and air. The sheep feed on foods that are grown in soil. The sheep drink water and breathe air. **Generalize**

4 **What things in the pictures are made from sheep's wool?** Scarf, mittens, yarn, coat, sweater **Analyze Pictures**

continued

Page 78

Have children read p. 78 and identify the foods on Sara's table.

5 **How are all these foods alike?** They are all made from wheat. **Compare and Contrast**

6 **Find the photograph of the wheat stalk. Why are seeds an important part of the plant?** The seeds are the part of wheat that is used to make foods, like those pictured. In addition, they can be used to start new plants. **Analyze Pictures**

SOCIAL STUDIES STRAND
Geography

Point out the words *Great Plains*. Have children revisit p. 57 to look at the picture and define a plain as a large, mostly flat area of land. Use a map of the U.S. to point out the location of the Great Plains.

7 **Why do you think the Great Plains is a good place to grow wheat?** Possible answer: The land is flat, and the soil is good for growing wheat. **Apply Information**

Practice and Extend

ACCESS CONTENT
ESL Support

More About Crops Write on the board: *wheat, corn, hogs, tomatoes, chickens, apples.* Point to each and read it aloud. Ask: *Is this a kind of crop?* Then have each child select one crop and draw a picture of it. Have children label their pictures with the crops' names.

Beginning Have children also draw things that come from the crop, such as catsup and tomato sauce from tomatoes. Help children label each item.

Intermediate Have children use their pictures to tell partners what they know about the crops they selected.

Advanced Have each child write two sentences about how the crop is grown and used by people.

For additional ESL support, use Every Student Learns Guide, pp. 34–37.

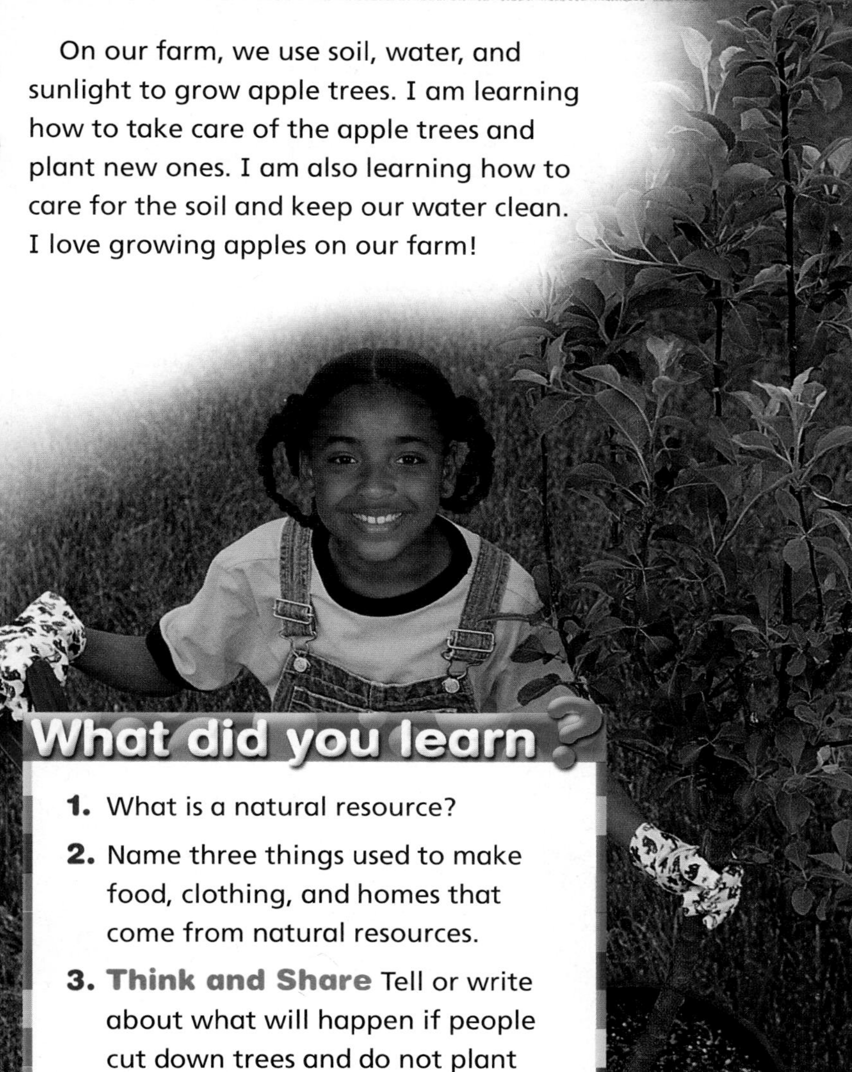

On our farm, we use soil, water, and sunlight to grow apple trees. I am learning how to take care of the apple trees and plant new ones. I am also learning how to care for the soil and keep our water clean. I love growing apples on our farm!

What did you learn?

1. What is a natural resource?
2. Name three things used to make food, clothing, and homes that come from natural resources.
3. **Think and Share** Tell or write about what will happen if people cut down trees and do not plant new ones.

79

Workbook, p. 19

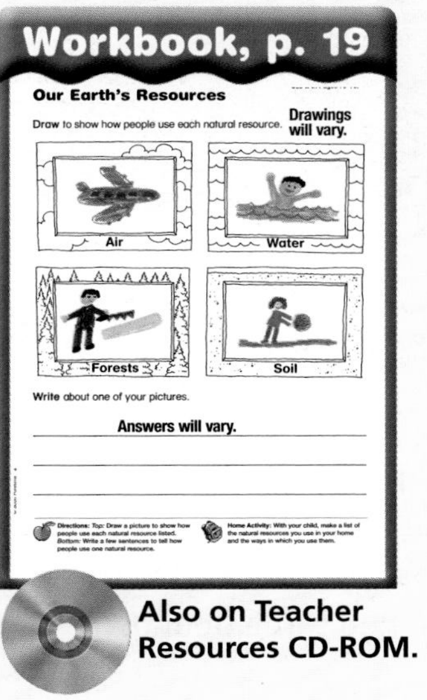

Our Earth's Resources

Draw to show how people use each natural resource. **Drawings will vary.**

Air | Water | Forests | Soil

Write about one of your pictures.

Answers will vary.

Also on Teacher Resources CD-ROM.

Page 79

Have children look at the photo and tell what Sara is doing.

8 How are wheat and apple trees both helped by natural resources? Both crops are planted in the soil and helped by air and water. **Draw Conclusions**

9 Why does Sara want to take care of the trees and plant new ones? Some older trees may die. Taking care of others will make them last. New trees will take the place of those that die. **Cause and Effect**

3 Close and Assess

Have children identify some of the Earth's natural resources (air, water, forests, soil) and give three examples of how people use each resource to make products they need.

✓ What did you learn?

Test Talk

Locate Key Words in the Text
Help children locate key words, such as *natural* and *resource*, in the text.

1. A natural resource is a useful material that comes from the Earth.
2. Possible answers: Wheat, wool, wood
3. **Think and Share** Children's responses may include: There would be no more trees for people to use for shade or to use to make paper and to build houses and furniture.

Read a Bar Graph

Objective

- Interpret and construct bar graphs.

Vocabulary

bar graph helps to compare groups (p. 80)

1 Introduce and Motivate

Preview Have children look at the graph as you read its title. Then read the text on p. 80. Have children point to the term *bar graph* and then tell what the purpose of a bar graph is.

Warm Up To activate prior knowledge, direct attention to any charts (such as job charts) on display in the classroom. Point out that someone can get information quickly from a visual such as a chart. Ask children whether they could get the same information as quickly if it were written as a paragraph. Point out that a graph, like a chart, is a way to show information visually.

2 Teach and Discuss

Page 81

Have children answer the questions posed on p. 81 as they read.

1 How many different kinds of fruit do the children in Sara's class like? Four
Interpret Graphs

Chart and Graph Skills

Read a Bar Graph

Sara's class made a bar graph of different kinds of fruit. A **bar graph** helps you compare groups. Look at the bar graph.

80

Practice and Extend

SOCIAL STUDIES Background

About Apples

Since apples turned out to be the favorite fruit in Sara's class, children may enjoy knowing the following:

- There are more than 7,500 different kinds of apples worldwide; 2,500 kinds in the U.S.
- Some apple trees live to be more than 100 years old and may grow to more than 40 feet high.
- The Pilgrims planted the first apple trees in the U.S.
- The largest apple ever picked weighed three pounds—as much as nine medium apples.

The title of the graph is "Our Favorite Fruit." On the side of the bar graph, find the name of each fruit. 1 What kinds of fruit does the class like? The bottom of the bar graph shows the number of children. Look at the bar next to the oranges. How many children picked oranges? 2 3 4

1. What is the favorite fruit in Sara's class?
2. Name the two fruits that got the same number of votes.
3. **On Your Own** Make a bar graph of other foods that you like. Ask classmates to vote on which food they like the best.

CURRICULUM CONNECTION
Writing

Write a Recipe for Fruit Salad

- Tell children to use the favorite fruits of Sara's class to write a recipe for fruit salad.
- Point out that the recipe should be in two parts. Write on the board: *What do I need? What should I do?*
- Encourage children to draw a picture to show the finished product—or to illustrate each step.
- Have children share and compare recipes.

Workbook, p. 20

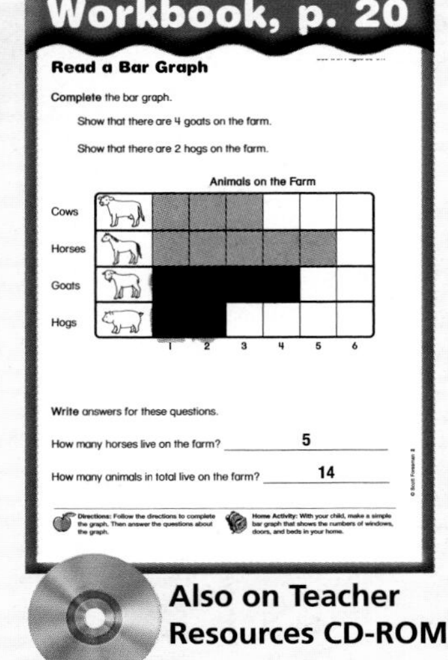

Read a Bar Graph

Complete the bar graph.

Show that there are 4 goats on the farm.

Show that there are 2 hogs on the farm.

Animals on the Farm

Cows, Horses, Goats, Hogs; 1 2 3 4 5 6

Write answers for these questions.

How many horses live on the farm? 5

How many animals in total live on the farm? 14

Also on Teacher Resources CD-ROM.

Test Talk

Use Information from Graphics

2 **How many children voted for apples as their favorite?** Eight **Interpret Graphs**

Have children find and point to the place on the graph that helped them answer the question.

3 **Which two fruits got the fewest votes?** Oranges and strawberries **Interpret Graphs**

4 **Which fruit on the graph would you cast your vote for?** Answers will vary but should be one of the fruits shown on the chart. **Express Ideas**

3 Close and Assess

Have children tell what Sara's class learned by looking at their bar graph.

Try it!

1. Apples
2. Oranges and strawberries
3. **On Your Own** Children's graphs will vary, but they should follow the form of the graph on p. 80. Check children's graphs for accurate labeling.

Use with pages 76–81

Lesson 4 Wrap-Up

MEETING INDIVIDUAL NEEDS

Leveled Practice

Make a Collage
Have children cut out pictures to make a collage representing the Earth's natural resources.

Easy Have children show and talk about their collages. Be sure they name at least four natural resources as they share their artwork. **Reteach**

On-Level As children share their collages, have them describe each picture that is part of the collage and tell why they chose it to represent a natural resource. **Extend**

Challenge Have children describe what is shown in their collages. Have them suggest ways people can make sure that others will have access to the same natural resources in the future. **Enrich**

Hands-on Activities

CURRICULUM CONNECTION
Writing

Earth Chants

Objective Express ideas creatively in writing.

Materials paper, pencils

Learning Style Verbal

Individual

Time 15–20 minutes

1. Tell children they will write chants about natural resources.
2. Model how to create a short chant. On the board, write this sample:

   Air, air! We must care!
   About the freshness of our air!
3. Have children write their own chants. Some children may like to collaborate with partners.

Remind children to add *natural resources* to the "My Word Book" they keep.

CURRICULUM CONNECTION
Writing

Terrific Trees

Objective Illustrate trees and write sentences about the illustrations.

Materials nonfiction picture books about trees, drawing paper, crayons

Learning Style Kinesthetic/Verbal/Visual

Individual

Time 15–20 minutes

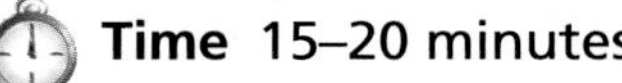

1. Children should look through the books to find interesting "tree facts" to share.
2. Children draw pictures that relate to the fact they wish to share. Then they write sentences about the pictures.
3. Encourage children to include information that tells why trees are important to the Earth.

CURRICULUM CONNECTION
Science

Hairy Heads

Objective Plant grass seeds and observe growth.

Materials styrofoam cups, potting soil, grass seeds, spoons, markers

Learning Style Kinesthetic/Visual

Individual

Time 25–30 minutes

1. Have each child draw a funny face on the front of a cup and then write his or her name on the back.
2. Have children spoon soil into their cups, sprinkle grass seeds on top of the soil, and water.
3. Place the cups in a sunny window.
4. As children watch seeds grow, they will also see hair grow on their cup characters!
5. Have children record daily observations of their plants in a chart.

Lesson 5 Overview

Lesson	Description	Time and Resources
Caring for Our Resources **pages 82–85**	Children will learn the meaning of the word *conservation.* They will explore ways they can protect and conserve the Earth.	Time 20–30 minutes Resources • Workbook, p. 21 • Vocabulary Card **conservation** • Every Student Learns Guide, pp. 38–41
Rachel Carson **pages 86–87**	Children will read about biologist and writer Rachel Carson and identify her contributions to the environment.	Time 15–20 minutes
The Earth Angels **pages 88–89**	Children will read about a group of youngsters who help protect and conserve the Earth's resources.	Time 15–20 minutes

Build Background

Activity

Spread the Word!

Time 20–25 minutes

Brainstorm a list of things children can do to protect the land, water, plants, trees, animals. Make a suggestion: Don't pull leaves or branches off trees. Then tell children they will make greeting cards to spread the word about protecting the Earth.

Have available a variety of art materials. Have each child make a card to send to a friend or family member that shows one or two ways to protect our natural environment. Children can fold a sheet of construction paper in half, draw a picture on the front and then write a message on the inside.

If time is short, just do the brainstorming part of the activity described above.

pretty flowers!

Just look and sniff.

Don't pick the flowers!

Read Aloud

Please!

by Bonnie Flynn

Please don't pick the flowers!
Please don't squash the plants!
Please don't let the water run!
Please don't step on ants!
Please DO protect our Earth!

Lesson 5 Caring for Our Resources

Objective

- Identify ways people can conserve and replenish natural resources.

Vocabulary

conservation the care and protection of land, water, plants, trees, and animals (p. 82)

QUICK Teaching Plan

If time is short, write *Save the Earth!* on the board. Have children look at the photos in the lesson.

- Then ask children to name things in nature people should work together to save. Guide children to identify land, water, plants, trees, animals, and air.

1 Introduce and Motivate

Preview Display the Vocabulary Card **conservation**. Use the word in a sentence. Ask children to tell what the word means. Then define the word for them. Tell children to look for the word as they preview the lesson.

Warm Up To activate prior knowledge, ask children to tell how people in their own neighborhoods take care of a park or other green space. Make a list and display it. Encourage children to add to the list as they learn about caring for the Earth.

SOCIAL STUDIES STRAND Government

National Parks Explain that national parks in the U.S. are areas that are set aside by the government for protection. Yellowstone National Park was the first national park in the world. It was established by Congress and President Grant in 1872.

Encourage children to tell why they think the government sets aside land as national parks.

Lesson 5 Caring for Our Resources

3

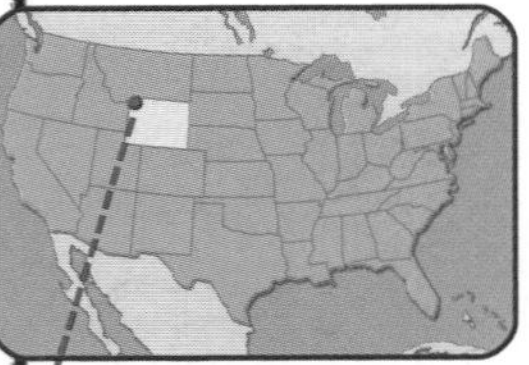

Yellowstone National Park, Wyoming

Last summer, I visited Yellowstone National Park in Wyoming. Yellowstone is the oldest national park in the United States. In national parks, conservation is very important. **Conservation** is the care and protection of land, water, plants, and animals. In the park, people are not allowed to cut down trees, litter, or take away any of the plants or animals. 2

1

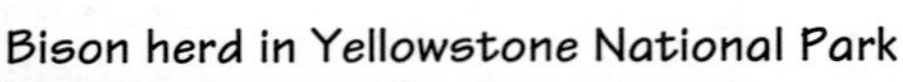

Bison herd in Yellowstone National Park

82

Practice and Extend

READING SKILL Cause and Effect

Target Skill

Remind children that it is important to look for cause-and-effect relationships as they read. Recall that the *effect* is what happens and the *cause* is why it happens.

- After children read pp. 82–85, make a cause-and-effect T-chart on the board. Under *Effect* write: *The natural resources in Yellowstone are safe.*
- Ask volunteers to name causes for the effect.
- Write their answers on the board.

4 When I grow up, I hope to become a park ranger. It would be my job to protect the plants and animals. I would help workers plant new trees.

While visiting Yellowstone, I was in the Junior Ranger program. We learned about important park rules. One rule is to stay on the trails. We do this so we do not get lost. We also do this so we do not step on plants or disturb the animals. The park ranger reminds us not to tease

5 or feed the animals.

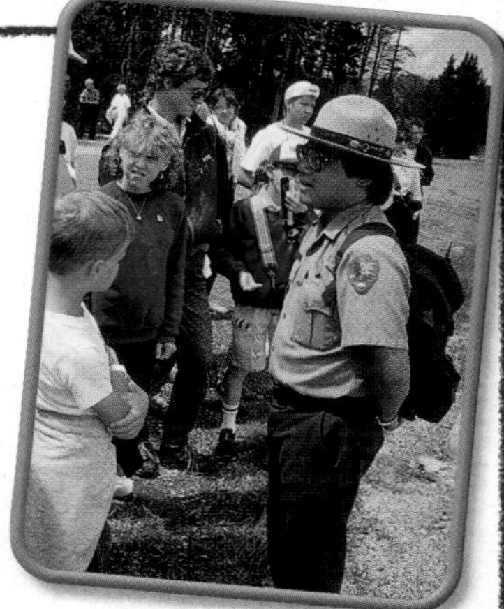

Yellowstone Park Ranger

The track of the grizzly bear is the symbol for the Junior Ranger program.

83

CURRICULUM CONNECTION
Science

Neighborhood Plants and Animals

- Take your class on a nature walk around the school. Tell children to draw pictures of or write notes about interesting plants and animals they see.
- When you return to the classroom, collect children's drawings and notes and display them under the title *Plants and Animals in Our Neighborhood.* Discuss children's observations.

WEB SITE
Technology

You can look up vocabulary words online. Click on *Social Studies Library* and select dictionary at **www.sfsocialstudies.com**.

2 Teach and Discuss

Page 82

Read the lesson title and have children read the page.

1 Use the photographs to tell about Yellowstone's natural resources and wildlife. Encourage children to cite specific details from the photos in their descriptions. **Analyze Pictures**

2 What would be the effect if there were no conservation in the park? Possible answers: Trails might be littered. Plants and shrubs might be trampled or pulled out. Animals might depend on people for food. **Cause and Effect**

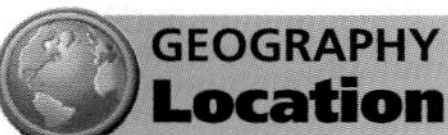

GEOGRAPHY
Location

3 In what part of the United States is Yellowstone National Park located? It is north and toward the west. **Interpret Maps**

Page 83

Decision Making

4 Why do you think Sara decided to become a Park Ranger instead of thinking about an indoor job? Which kind of job would you prefer? Possible answers: Sara enjoyed her time as a Junior Ranger. She wants to help people think about conservation. Children's personal responses will vary but should include an explanation of their choice. **Express Ideas**

5 Do you agree that the park rules are important? Why? Children are likely to say yes because the rules help keep people from getting lost and from disturbing plants and animals. **Evaluate**

continued

Page 84

Point out the geyser in the photo. Tell children that Old Faithful "erupts" about every 76 minutes. It has not missed an eruption in 80 years!

6 **Why do you think Sara drew the route in her Junior Ranger newspaper?** To remember all the places she had seen **Draw Conclusions**

7 **What did Sara learn about geysers?** They are underground springs. They blast hot water and steam into the air. There are more than 300 geysers in Yellowstone. **Recall and Retell**

8 **Why do you think the geyser in the photo is named "Old Faithful"?** Answers will vary, but children may suggest that the geyser has been shooting into the air for a long time. **Make Inferences**

Page 85

Reminder: If you began a chart in Unit 1, Lesson 1, that records ways in which children can act as responsible citizens, revisit that chart now. Have children add ideas about how they can help conserve and replenish local natural resources.

9 **What do you think Sara and her class will do to conserve a park or green place in their own neighborhood?** Possible answer: They may pick up litter. **Make Inferences**

Ongoing Assessment

If... children are not sure of the meaning of *conservation*, **then...** relate it to "protecting" the natural resources people and animals need to live.

I got a Junior Ranger newspaper on my first day at the park. In my newspaper, I drew the route my family took through 6 Yellowstone Park. In my journal, I wrote about favorite things I saw.

Yellowstone has more than 300 geysers. Geysers are underground springs that throw hot water and steam into the air. I've never seen anything like them before!

7

8

84

Practice and Extend

MEETING INDIVIDUAL NEEDS

Learning Styles

Describe Yellowstone National Park

Using their individual learning styles, children can review what they've learned so far about Yellowstone National Park.

Visual Learning Have children draw pictures to represent various things they would see in the park.

Linguistic Learning Have children write journal entries as if they were in Yellowstone Park.

Kinesthetic/Verbal Learning Have children dramatize hiking through the park and seeing things described in the lesson.

When I got back from my trip, I told my class about being a Junior Ranger. We talked about things we can do to help protect and conserve
9 the park in our neighborhood.

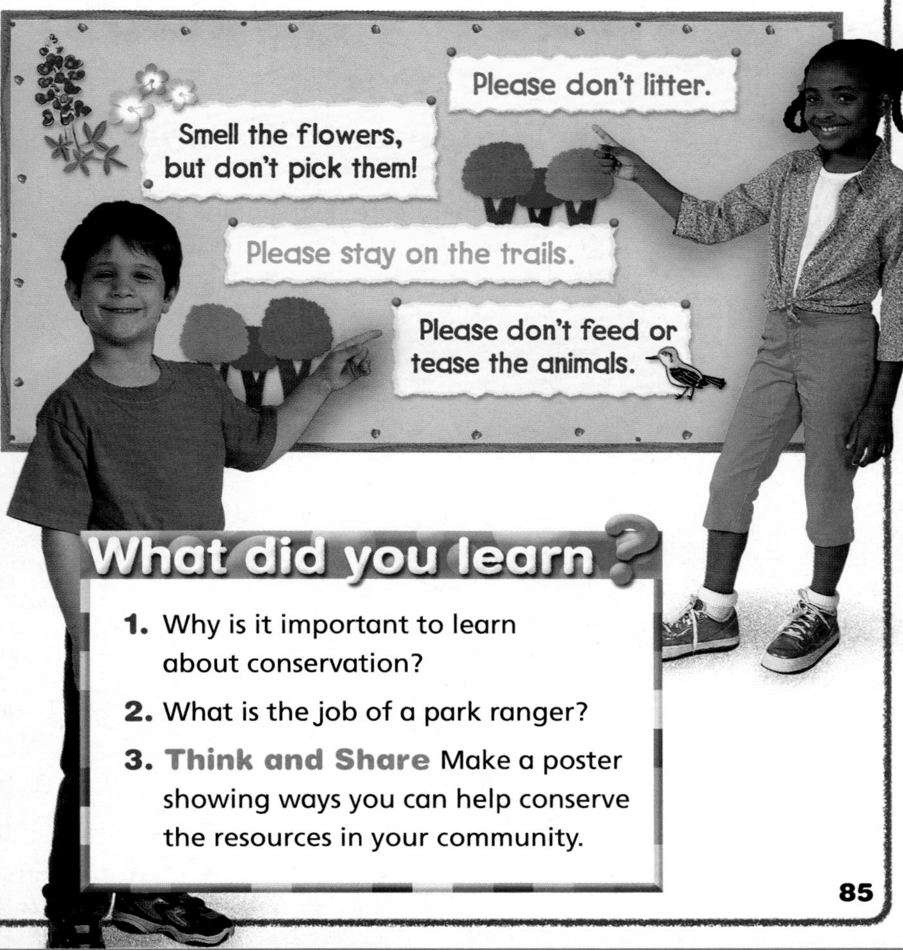

What did you learn?

1. Why is it important to learn about conservation?
2. What is the job of a park ranger?
3. **Think and Share** Make a poster showing ways you can help conserve the resources in your community.

85

ACCESS CONTENT ESL Support

Conservation Talk with children about good conservation practices.

Beginning Tell children what to pantomime. After they pantomime, ask if the action is good or bad—conservation-wise.

Intermediate Have children write two sentences—one that describes a good conservation practice and one that describes an anti-conservation practice.

Advanced Have partners talk about the consequences of two or three anti-conservation practices.

For additional ESL support, use Every Student Learns Guide, pp. 38–41.

Workbook, p. 21

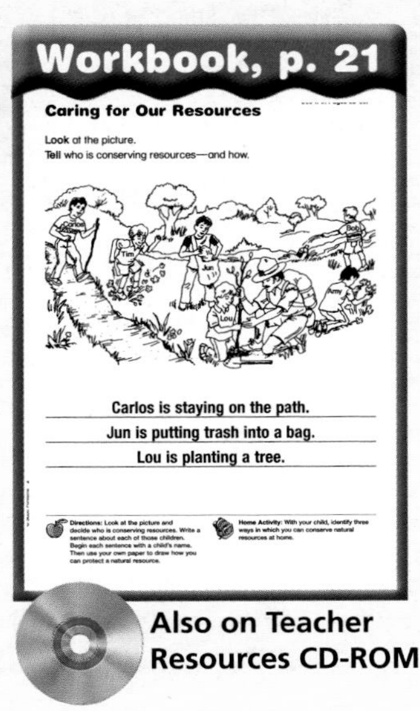

Caring for Our Resources

Look at the picture.
Tell who is conserving resources—and how.

Carlos is staying on the path.
Jun is putting trash into a bag.
Lou is planting a tree.

Also on Teacher Resources CD-ROM.

3 Close and Assess

Check children's understanding of the lesson ideas by having them identify two rules of conservation people must follow. Ask children if they would like to visit Yellowstone someday. Encourage them to express why or why not.

✓ What did you learn?

1. It is important to learn how we can care for and protect the Earth's land, water, plants, trees, and animals—so that they don't disappear from the Earth.
2. A park ranger protects the plants, animals, and trees of a national park. He or she makes sure people follow the park's rules.
3. **Think and Share** Children's responses may reflect ideas such as using a hose to water a tree, cleaning up litter, riding a bike or walking places to avoid polluting the air.

Rachel Carson

Objectives

- Identify ways people can conserve and replenish natural resources.
- Identify characteristics of good citizenship such as a belief in justice, truth, equality, and responsibility for the common good.

1 Introduce and Motivate

Preview Read aloud the title of the biography and then the subtitle. Have children scan pp. 86–87 and note things that capture their interest, such as maps, words, names, and photographs. Ask children to predict what they will be reading about, citing specific clues on the pages.

Warm Up To activate prior knowledge, write the word *biologist* in the center of a word web. Below it, write *studies living things.* Have children name some living things a biologist might study. Record their ideas on the web. As needed, prompt children with questions such as: *Would a biologist study birds?* As children read, have them notice if any of their ideas are mentioned in the text as being of special interest to Rachel Carson.

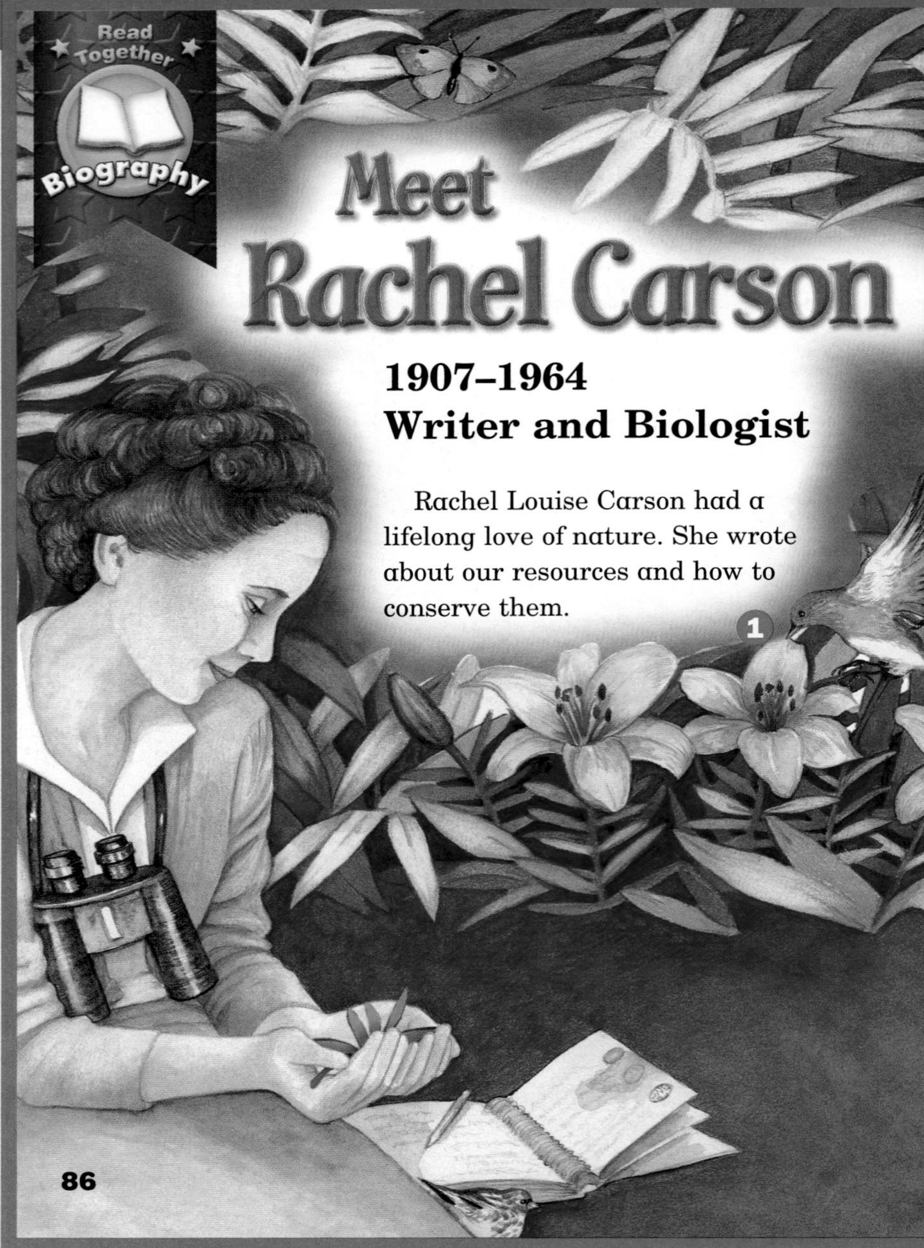

Practice and Extend

FYI SOCIAL STUDIES Background

About Rachel Carson

- In her writings, Rachel Carson stressed the interrelation of all living things.
- *The Sea Around Us*, published in 1951, describes the biology, chemistry, geography, and history of the sea.
- *Silent Spring,* published in 1962, called public attention to the destructive uses of pesticides.
- Carson warned that pesticides poison the food supplies of animals and kill birds and fish. She also pointed out that pesticides could contaminate human food supplies.
- Her arguments led to restrictions on pesticide use in many parts of the world.

As a child, Rachel loved books. When she was ten, she published her first story. Rachel's mother encouraged her to write and introduced her to nature.

When she grew older, Rachel could not decide whether she wanted to become a writer or a biologist. One of her teachers convinced Rachel that she could be both.

As a biologist and writer, Rachel Carson dedicated her life to conserving the Earth's resources. ❸ She was especially interested in protecting birds, fish, and other wildlife. She wrote newspaper articles and books to help this cause. Rachel Carson also worked to have laws passed to protect our resources.

Rachel Carson wrote books to teach people about the beauty of the Earth. Two of her books, *The Sea Around Us* and *Silent Spring,* were bestsellers. One article she wrote was turned into a book for parents. It is called *The Sense of Wonder.* ❹

Rachel Carson was born in Springdale, Pennsylvania. ❷

Rachel Carson looking through a microscope.

Think and Share

Tell how Rachel Carson helped protect the Earth's resources.

For more information, go online to *Meet the People* at **www.sfsocialstudies.com.**

87

2 Teach and Discuss

Read the biography together. Tell children that Rachel Carson worked hard to protect and care for the Earth's resources.

❶ **Look at the illustration on page 86. What kinds of things do you think Rachel Carson is writing in her journal?** Notes about nature **Make Inferences**

❷ **Where was Rachel Carson born?** Springdale, Pennsylvania **Recall and Retell**

❸ **A biologist studies living things. How would Rachel Carson's life have been different if she had chosen only to be a biologist?** If she were just a biologist, not so many people would know about protecting wildlife and resources. **Draw Conclusions**

❹ **Why do you think her book *The Sense of Wonder* was turned into a book parents could share with their children?** The book had important information in it for parents to teach children about the environment. **Draw Conclusions**

3 Close and Assess

Think and Share

In their own words, children should be able to tell how Rachel Carson helped protect the Earth's resources. (Possible answers: She worked to protect fish, birds, and wildlife; she wrote articles and books so others could learn about conserving and protecting our resources.)

CURRICULUM CONNECTION
Literature

Share a Classic

Share excerpts and show pictures from Rachel Carson's *The Sense of Wonder* (HarperCollins, ISBN 0-06-757520-X, 1998) with your class. This award-winning classic asks readers and listeners to open their eyes and ears to the astonishing variety of life that exists all around us—to study birds, listen to the winds, observe the stars, and listen to the "living music" of insects.

WEB SITE
Technology

You may help children learn more about Rachel Carson by clicking on *Meet the People* at **www.sfsocialstudies.com.**

CITIZEN HEROES

The Earth Angels

Objective

- Identify ordinary people who exemplify good citizenship.

1 Introduce and Motivate

Preview Initiate a discussion about responsibility. Talk about what responsibility is and what it means to be responsible. Invite children to tell how they show that they are responsible. Ideas include helping with the family chores, doing homework for school, recycling, and following rules. Write children's ideas on the board.

Warm Up To activate prior knowledge, have children respond to this question: *What things do animals need to live?* Guide children to realize that animals need food, water, air, and a safe home, or place to live.

Tell children that they will read about some children who make sure that animals have what they need in order to live, as well as doing other things to take care of and protect the Earth.

2 Teach and Discuss

Read p. 88, including the caption for the map. You may wish to add to children's geography awareness by having them locate Missouri on your classroom map.

1 Why did the Earth Angels win the President's Environmental Youth Award? They built special nesting boxes for birds.
Cause and Effect

2 How do the Earth Angels raise money? They raise money by recycling and by selling pins.
Recall and Retell

CITIZEN HEROES

The Earth Angels of the Guardian Angel Settlement are located in St. Louis, Missouri.

The Earth Angels

The Earth Angels is a group of children from St. Louis, Missouri. They are responsible for many projects that help protect the Earth's resources.

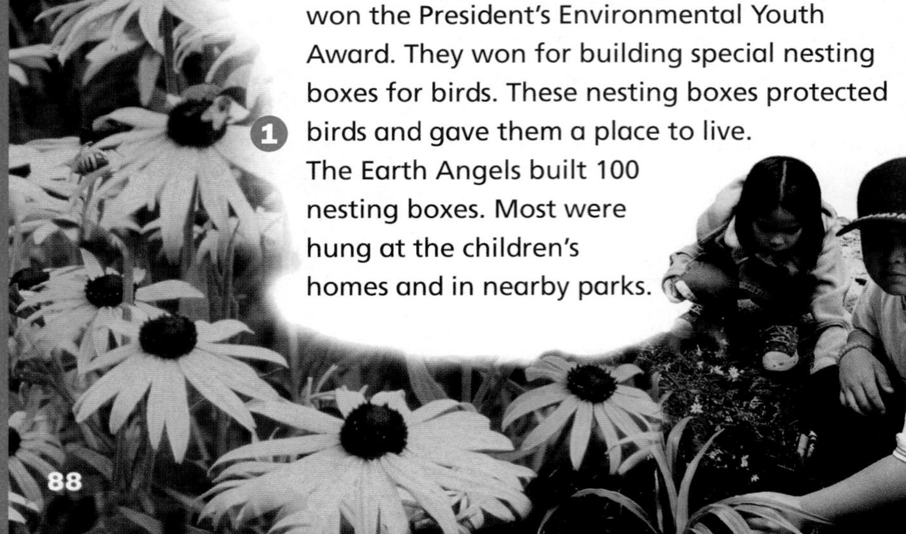

In 1999, the Earth Angels won the President's Environmental Youth Award. They won for building special nesting boxes for birds. These nesting boxes protected birds and gave them a place to live. **1** The Earth Angels built 100 nesting boxes. Most were hung at the children's homes and in nearby parks.

88

Practice and Extend

FYI SOCIAL STUDIES Background

About the Earth Angels

- The Earth Angels was founded in 1987.
- It is an inner-city environmental group composed of "at risk" children, ages 7–12.
- The group has received over 105 environmental awards.
- The Earth Angels have a goal of collecting and recycling one million aluminum cans.
- At the beginning of the year 2000, the group had recycled over 881,222 cans!

BUILDING CITIZENSHIP
Caring
Respect
Responsibility
Fairness
Honesty
Courage

The Earth Angels also have made wildlife habitats in the city. Habitats are places where plants and animals live. The habitats include a prairie garden and butterfly gardens.

The Earth Angels raise money to pay for their projects. They raise money through recycling. They
2 also sell Earth Angel buttons.

The Earth Angels rescue animals and find homes for them. They plant trees in parks. These children are always thinking of new ways to take responsibility for helping the
3 world around them.
4 5 6

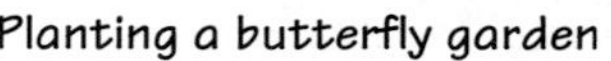
Planting a butterfly garden

Responsibility in Action

How do the Earth Angels show they are responsible citizens in their community? How can you be a responsible citizen in your community?

89

SOCIAL STUDIES STRAND
Citizenship

We're Responsible

- Point out that the Earth Angels prove that they are responsible and caring citizens by volunteering their time to help protect their neighborhood and the Earth's resources.
- Remind children of the discussion they had to preview the lesson. Help them recall some of their ideas about how they are responsible members of a community.
- Have children draw pictures of themselves doing something that shows their sense of responsibility. Have them label their pictures *Responsibility starts at* ____, filling in the last word.

3 How do the Earth Angels protect the world around them? They protect birds and give them a place to live; make wildlife habitats; recycle; rescue animals; plant trees in parks. **Main Idea and Details**

4 What can the Earth Angels do as a group that one child cannot do? A group can accomplish more by working together than one person can do alone. **Draw Conclusions**

5 Why do you think these children are called Citizen Heroes? Sample response: Heroes take action. They are leaders. They help those who are needy in some way. They are unselfish. **Make Inferences**

Problem Solving

6 Think of a problem with natural resources in your community. If you were in the Earth Angels, what would you do to solve it? Answers will vary but should reflect practical, citizen-based solutions to a local problem. **Express Ideas**

3 Close and Assess

Responsibility in Action

Read the question with children. Responses may include: The Earth Angels look around the community to see where help is needed. They work together to think of possible solutions to problems. They choose one, and then they go out to solve the problem. They raise money or do whatever it takes. In response to the second question, children may say that they can recycle more or look for ways to keep their community clean and safe.

Use with pages 82–89

Lesson 5 Wrap-Up

MEETING INDIVIDUAL NEEDS Leveled Practice

Help Save Earth's Resources
Have children cut out magazine pictures showing land, water, air, trees, animals.

Easy Have children sort the pictures by category and use them to make a large poster display. **Reteach**

On-Level Have children do the easy activity. Then have each select a picture to talk about more. Make a word web on the board. Ask children to supply words and phrases that relate to conservation of the resource depicted. **Extend**

Challenge Have children do both the Easy and On-Level activities. Then have them use the information in the word web to write a short paragraph about ways to conserve the resource. **Enrich**

Hands-on Activities

CURRICULUM CONNECTION
Writing

Slogans

Objective Express ideas about conservation in writing.

Resources Vocabulary Card: **conservation**

Materials paper, pencils, crayons or markers

Learning Style Linguistic

Individual

Time 10–15 minutes

1. Write *conservationist* on the board, and compare it with *conservation.* Explain that a conservationist is someone who cares about conservation issues.

2. Tell children that conservationists often have slogans. Give an example such as: *Don't waste the water!* Have children write one-line slogans of their own.

Remind children to add *conservation* to their word books.

CURRICULUM CONNECTION
Science

Animal Facts

Objective Investigate endangered animals.

Materials nonfiction books about endangered animals, paper, crayons, pencil

Learning Style Visual/Verbal

Partners

Time 30 minutes

1. Partners can choose an animal and make a fact sheet showing a picture of the animal, five interesting facts about it and what people can do to protect it.

2. As partners share their findings, have them add their fact sheets to a classroom display entitled *How Can We Help?*

CURRICULUM CONNECTION
Art

Earth Day T-shirts

Objective Use visuals to express ideas about the environment.

Materials paper T-shirt outlines, crayons, markers

Learning Style Visual/Verbal/Kinesthetic

Individual

Time 20–25 minutes

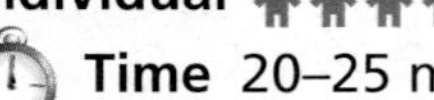

1. Tell children that Earth Day is celebrated on April 22. On Earth Day people get together to clean up parks, beaches, and local neighborhoods. They may also protest against behaviors that damage the environment.

2. Distribute a paper T-shirt to each child. Have children create designs that support the environment or protest negative behaviors.

3. Collect the T-shirts and create a bulletin board or wall display.

4. Invite children from other classes to view and comment on the display.

Ending Unit 2

End with a Song **pages 90–91**	Children will listen to, sing, and talk about the patriotic song "America, the Beautiful" by Katharine Lee Bates.	Resource • *Songs and Music* CD
Unit 2 Review **pages 92–95**	Children will review unit vocabulary words and the unit skills of cause and effect, locating land and water on a map, and reading and constructing a bar graph. Children will answer questions about what they learned in the unit. Children will learn about several books about the Earth and its resources.	Resources • Workbook, p. 22 ✓• Assessment Book, pp. 5–8
Unit 2 Project **page 96**	Children will learn how to create a game show. They will also be directed to a Web site where they can learn more about some famous places.	Resource • Workbook, p. 23

Wrap-up

Activity

My Book About Our Earth

Have children make a small book by folding two sheets of paper in half. The front should show the title *My Book About Our Earth*.

- On the first few pages, children should draw and label three landforms and three bodies of water.
- On subsequent pages, children should draw and write what they learned about the Earth's natural resources.
- The last page of the book should carry an Earth-friendly message or slogan.

Performance Assessment
You can use the activity on this page as a performance assessment.

✓ Assessment Scoring Guide

Make a Book About Our Earth	
4	Includes all four parts of the activity. Drawings are clear and labeled; natural resources are accurately described; and slogan is appropriate.
3	Includes all four parts, but either the physical features section or the natural resources section is incomplete or inaccurate.
2	Includes only three of the four required parts, or has significant inaccuracies in more than one part.
1	Is incomplete and/or contains significant inaccuracies in most parts.

America, the Beautiful

Objective

- Identify selected patriotic songs.

1 Introduce and Motivate

Preview Point to and read the title. Identify the name of the person who wrote the song. Allow time for children to look at the illustration on pp. 90–91 and talk about what they see. Ask children to predict what the song will be about.

Warm Up Have children look back at the photos on pp. 82–85. Ask if they think the photos show a "beautiful America." If possible, show children other photos of American landscapes, and ask them to respond with descriptive words.

2 Teach and Discuss

Explain that "America, the Beautiful" was originally written as a poem and then later set to music. Invite children to listen as you read the song aloud. Pause to explain that *amber* means light brown in color. Note, too, that the phrase *waves of grain* refers to stalks of wheat moving in the wind. Explain that the *fruited plain* is another way of referring to the wheat and other crops in the fields.

Use a map to point out the two shining seas—the Atlantic and Pacific Oceans that sandwich the United States.

① **What landforms and bodies of water does the poet describe?** Mountains, plains, seas
Recall and Retell

② **Do you think the poet is proud of America? What clues help you to know?** Yes; she calls it beautiful and describes her favorite colors and sights. **Make Inferences**

Practice and Extend

FYI SOCIAL STUDIES Background

About "America, the Beautiful"

- Katharine Lee Bates (1859–1929) wrote the poem in 1893.
- Bates was an English professor and always kept a diary of her observations and poetry.
- The poem "America, the Beautiful" was inspired by her view from the top of Pikes Peak—a 14,000-foot mountain in Colorado—on July 22, 1893.

Close and Assess

- Reread the song. Have children listen for rhyming words.
- Sing the song for children or play a recording. Then have them join in singing the song.
- Have children tell why they like the song's title.

CURRICULUM CONNECTION
Art

Picture the Song

- Have children read the words to the song with you. Then have them draw patriotic pictures that incorporate the images mentioned in the song.
- Collect and display the pictures.

Review

Resources

- Assessment Book, pp. 5–8
- Workbook, p. 22: Vocabulary Review

Vocabulary Review

1. landform
2. geography
3. natural resource
4. ancestor
5. conservation

Answers to Test Prep

1. consumer
2. producer

Test Talk

Locate Key Words in the Text
Use Test Prep, Question 2, to model the Test Talk strategy.

Decide where you will look for the answer
Have children make notes about details from the text that answer the question.

Use information from the text
Have children check their notes and then ask themselves, "Do I have the right information?"

For additional practice, use the Test Talk Practice Book.

UNIT 2 Review

Vocabulary Review

natural resource
landform
geography
conservation
ancestor

Find the correct meaning for each word.

1. a shape on the surface of the Earth
2. the study of the Earth and the ways people use it
3. something useful that comes from the Earth
4. a person in our family who lived before we were born
5. the care and protection of land, water, plants, and animals

★ ★ ★ ★ ★ ★ ★ ★

Which word completes each sentence?

1. Someone who buys and uses goods is called a _______.
   a. producer **b.** consumer
   c. geography **d.** conservation

Test Talk
Find key words in the text.

2. Someone who makes or grows something is called a _______.
   a. producer **b.** consumer
   c. crop **d.** conservation

92

Practice and Extend

Assessment Options

✓ Unit 2 Assessment

- Unit 2 Content Test: Use Assessment Book, pp. 5–6
- Unit 2 Skills Test: Use Assessment Book, pp. 7–8

Standardized Test Prep

- Unit 2 tests contain standardized test formats.

✓ Unit 2 Performance Assessment

- See p. 96 for information about using the Unit 2 Project as a means of performance assessment.
- A scoring guide for the Unit 2 Project is provided in the teacher's notes on p. 96.

Test Talk

- Test Talk Practice Book

Skills Review

Cause and Effect

Tell the **cause** and **effect** in each sentence.

1. We irrigated, so the corn grew tall.
2. I feel warm because I am wearing a wool sweater.

Landforms and Water on a Map

1. The Rio Grande is part of the border between what two countries?
2. What mountains do you see west of the Mississippi River?
3. What bodies of water do you see on the map between Canada and the United States?

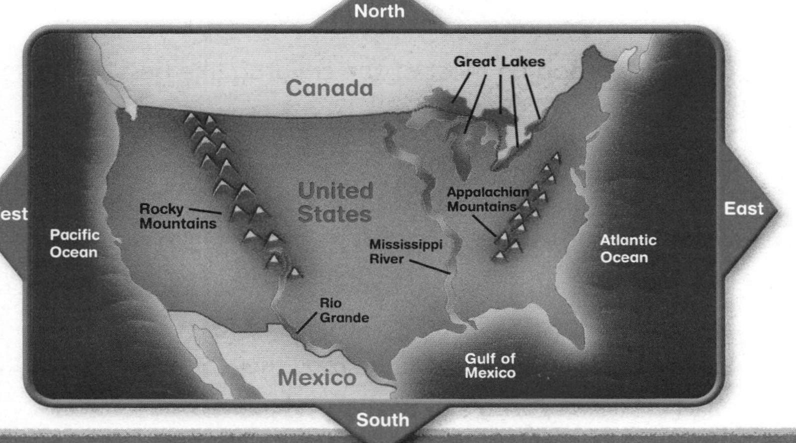

93

For more information, you can select the dictionary or encyclopedia from *Social Studies Library* at **www.sfsocial studies.com.**

Workbook, p. 22

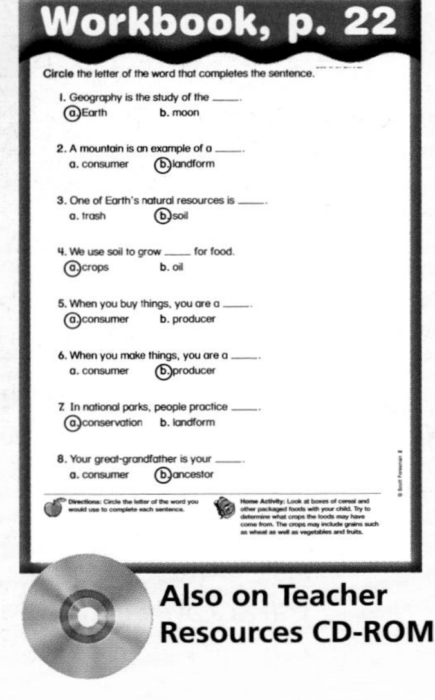
Circle the letter of the word that completes the sentence.

1. Geography is the study of the ____. (a) Earth b. moon
2. A mountain is an example of a ____. a. consumer (b) landform
3. One of Earth's natural resources is ____. a. trash (b) soil
4. We use soil to grow ____ for food. (a) crops b. oil
5. When you buy things, you are a ____. (a) consumer b. producer
6. When you make things, you are a ____. a. consumer (b) producer
7. In national parks, people practice ____. (a) conservation b. landform
8. Your great-grandfather is your ____. a. consumer (b) ancestor

Also on Teacher Resources CD-ROM.

Skills Review

Cause and Effect

1. **cause**—irrigated; **effect**—corn grew tall
2. **cause**—wearing a wool sweater; **effect**—feeling warm

Landforms and Water on a Map

Observe children's responses for accuracy and the ease with which they are made. Children should be able to:

- Locate and name the Rio Grande as part of the border between the United States and Mexico.
- Locate and name the Rocky Mountains.
- Locate and name the Great Lakes.

Review

continued

Skills Review

Read a Bar Graph

1. apple sauce

2. six

3. apple juice

Skills On Your Own

- Children's bar graphs should be clearly labeled and accurately reflect the information obtained.

Use the following scoring guide.

✓ Assessment Scoring Guide

Use a Bar Graph	
4	Format, results, and spelling are completely correct.
3	Format and results are completely correct but not spelling.
2	Format is completely correct but not results and spelling.
1	Format, results, and spelling are only partially correct.

Review

Skills Review

Read a Bar Graph

Sara's class voted for their favorite foods made from apples. Use the bar graph to answer the questions.

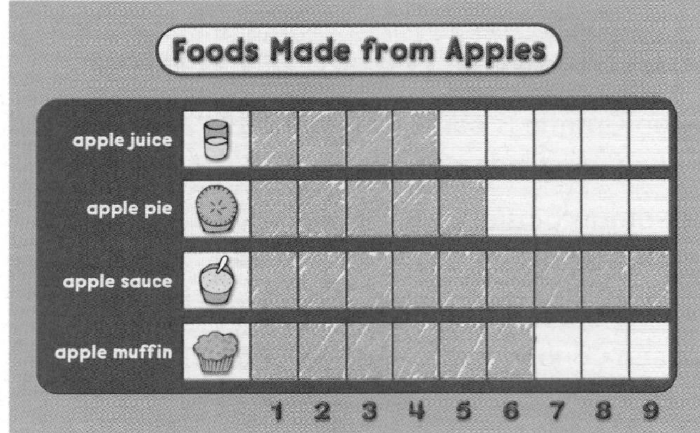

1. Which food do most of the children like best?

2. How many children picked apple muffins?

3. Which food was picked the fewest times?

Skills On Your Own

Make a bar graph of foods made from wheat, such as bread, pasta, and crackers. Write a name for your graph. Ask some friends to vote on the food they like the best.

Practice and Extend

Revisit the Unit Question

✓ Portfolio Assessment

Ask children to look back at the list of ways to keep the Earth beautiful they generated on page 49.

- Ask children to write sentences to say what they would tell others now about keeping the Earth beautiful.
- Encourage children to put a check mark next to ideas they got while reading the unit.
- Ask children to use their sentences to write a short paragraph.
- Suggest children paste their paragraphs on "globes" of blue construction paper.
- Have children add their drawings and sentences to their Social Studies portfolio.

What did you learn?

1. Draw and label three landforms.
2. Identify ways people depend on natural resources to meet their needs.
3. What are two ways of irrigating land?
4. **Write and Share** Tell or write about what could happen if we do not take care of our resources.

Read About Our Earth and Its Resources

Look for books like these in the library.

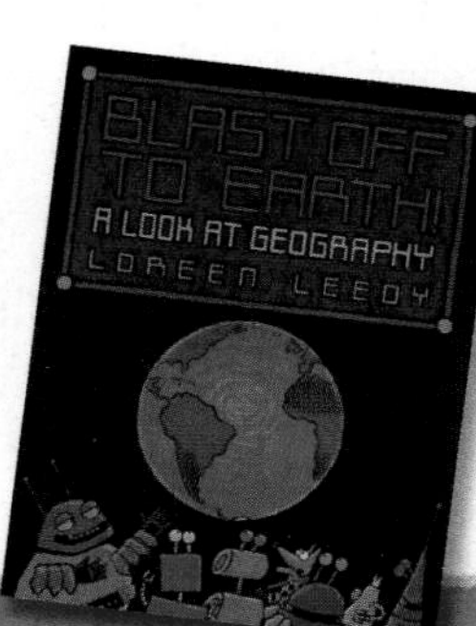

What did you learn?

1. Children's pictures should show *three* of the following: mountain, plain, valley, island, peninsula. Each should be correctly labeled.
2. People depend on natural resources for food and water, for clothing, and for shelter.
3. Irrigation can be done by using ditches or sprinklers.
4. **Write and Share** Possible answer: If we don't take care of our resources, they may not be there for people to use in the future. Then people would not be able to get the things to meet their needs.

Locate Key Words in the Text
Use What did you learn?, Question 2, to model the Test Talk strategy.

Make sure you understand the question
Have children finish the statement "I need to find out . . ."

Read About Our Earth and Its Resources

You might want to have these or other books about Earth and its resources available in the classroom.

Bread Is for Eating, by David and Phillis Gershator, (Henry Holt, ISBN 0-805-05798-6, 1998) **Easy**

Blast Off to Earth!: A Look at Geography, by Loreen Leedy (Holiday House, ISBN 0-823-40973-2, 1992) **On-Level**

Somewhere in the World Right Now, by Stacey Schuett (Dragonfly, ISBN 0-679-88549-8,1997) **Challenge**

Unit 2 Project

Guess My Place

Objective

- Describe different aspects of a specific place, including geographical location, landforms, weather, and popular activities.

Resource

- Workbook, p. 23

Materials

paper, writing materials, magazines for cutting out pictures, poster board

Follow This Procedure

- Tell children they're going to make up their own game show. Have children work in small groups to present clues and answer questions about a place as the class tries to guess the location.
- As an example, choose a famous or familiar place, and review what children know about it.
- Invite each group to choose a place to visit. Tell them to keep the place a secret.
- Have children find facts and use them to write five clues about their places. Children may also draw clues.
- Groups write five questions. Suggest for example: *Is it nearby or far away? Are there tall mountains there?*
- Groups take turns asking questions. They may forfeit a question by asking for a clue. A round is over when children have asked all their questions or a group has guessed correctly.

✓ Assessment Scoring Guide

	Guess My Place
4	Writes five clues and five questions that relate to location, well-known landforms, bodies of water, and so on.
3	Writes fewer than five clues and five questions, but those are complete and specific.
2	Writes five or fewer clues and/or questions that are vague or misleading.
1	Responds randomly, writing neither clear clues nor questions.

UNIT 2 Project

Guess My Place

On this game show, you will try to guess a place!

1. **Work** in a group to choose an interesting, fun, or famous place.
2. **Write** five clues about your place. Then write five questions to ask the other groups about their places.
3. **Form** a team. Take turns giving clues to the other teams. Let the other teams ask questions.
4. **Give** clues until a team guesses your place or until all teams have asked all their questions.

Internet Activity

Go to www.sfsocialstudies.com/activities to learn more about Earth.

96

Practice and Extend

✓ Performance Assessment

- The Unit Project can also be used as a performance assessment activity.
- Use the scoring guide to assess each group's work.

Children can launch the activity by clicking on *Grade 2, Unit 2* at **www.sfsocialstudies.com/activities**.

Workbook, p. 23

2 Project Guess My Place

Work in a group. Take part in a game show. **Answers will vary.**

1. The name of the place we chose is
2. The ✓ shows the topics we included about our place.
   location, landforms, important events, weather, landmarks, things to do
3. These are five clues about our place.
   Clue / Clue / Clue / Clue / Clue
4. Questions we will ask about other places.
   A. / B. / C. / D. / E.

Also on Teacher Resources CD-ROM.

Working Together

UNIT 3

Unit 3 Planning Guide

Working Together

Begin with a Song pp. 98–99 **Vocabulary Preview** pp. 100–101

Reading Social Studies, Predict pp. 102–103

Lesson Titles	Pacing	Main Ideas
Lesson 1 Choosing Goods and Services pp. 104–107 **Thinking Skills: Make a Decision** pp. 108–109 **Citizen Heroes: Respect Phoenix Kids Pride Program** pp. 110–111	2 days	• People make choices about earning, spending, and saving money. • Making a decision is based on a step-by-step process. • The Phoenix Kids Pride Program encourages children to make Phoenix a "better place to live."
Lesson 2 Services in Our Community pp. 112–115 **Biography: Florence Nightingale** pp. 116–117 **DK Fire Engine** pp. 118–119	3 days	• Taxes are used to pay for services provided to the community. • Florence Nightingale exemplified good citizenship by devoting her life to training nurses and improving the care of sick and injured people. • By reading a diagram of a fire engine, people understand the importance of its many parts.
Lesson 3 Goods from the Factory to You pp. 120–123 **Map and Globe Skills: Use a Compass Rose** pp. 124–125	2 days	• A factory is a building where people produce goods. • The development of goods sold to consumers can be traced from natural resources, which producers turn into finished products. • Using a compass rose helps people understand direction and follow a route.
Lesson 4 A Trip to the Bank pp. 126–129 **Chart and Graph Skills: Read a Pie Chart** pp. 130–131 **Biography: Linda Alvarado** pp. 132–133	3 days	• People spend and save their money in different ways; people pay for goods and services in different ways. • A pie chart is a good way to show information. • Linda Alvarado is a community leader and company president whose success shows why it is important to get a good education.
Lesson 5 Countries Trade and Move Goods pp. 134–137 **Then and Now: Bartering Goods and Services** pp. 138–139	2 days	• Countries exchanges goods by using different means of transportation, such as trains, trucks, boats, and planes. • People in the past bartered goods and services instead of using money to get what they needed.

✓ **End with Riddles** pp. 140–141 ✓ **Unit 3 Review** pp. 142–145 ✓ **Unit 3 Project** p. 146

 = Assessment Options

Scott Foresman Social Studies
Indiana Academic Standards

Grade 2 Unit 3 • *Working Together*

Lesson Title	Indiana Academic Standards Social Studies
Lesson 1 Choosing Goods and Services pp. 104-107	**IN Academic Standard 2.4.7** Explain why people trade for goods and services. **(Also 2.4.1, 2.4.2, 2.4.3, 2.4.4, 2.4.5, 2.4.6)**
Thinking Skills: Make a Decision pp. 108-109	**IN Academic Standard 2.4.5** Explain that people must make choices and incur opportunity costs. **(Also 2.2.1, 2.4.3, 2.5.1)**
Citizen Heroes: Phoenix Kids Pride Program pp. 110-111	**IN Academic Standard 2.2.4** Identify good leaders and good citizens, and explain the qualities that make them admirable. **(Also 2.1.3, 2.2.1, 2.3.3, 2.4.2, 2.5.5)**
Lesson 2 Services in Our Community pp. 112-115	**IN Academic Standard 2.4.2** Identify community workers who provide goods and services. **(Also 2.4.1, 2.4.4, 2.4.6)**
Biography: Florence Nightingale pp. 116-117	**IN Academic Standard 2.2.4** Identify good leaders and good citizens, and explain the qualities that make them admirable.
Fire Engine pp. 118-119	**Previews IN Academic Standard 3.4.2** Give examples of goods and services provided by local government.
Lesson 3 Goods from the Factory to You pp.120-123	**IN Academic Standard 2.4.1** Define productive resources and identify resources used to produce goods and services. **(Also 2.4.2, 2.4.4)**
Map and Globe Skills: Use a Compass Rose pp. 124-125	**IN Academic Standard 2.3.1** Use cardinal and intermediate directions to locate places on maps. **(Also 2.3.2, 2.3.4, 2.4.1)**
Lesson 4 A Trip to the Bank pp. 126-129	**IN Academic Standard 2.4.7** Explain why people trade for goods and services.
Chart and Graph Skills: Read a Pie Chart pp. 130-131	**Reviews IN Academic Standard 1.4.5** Explain that people make choices because of scarcity.
Biography: Linda Alvarado pp. 132-133	**IN Academic Standard 2.1.3** Identify individuals who had an impact on communities. **(Also 2.3.3, 2.5.5)**
Lesson 5 Countries Trade and Move Goods pp. 134-137	**Previews IN Academic Standard 3.4.3** Give examples of trade in the community.
Then and Now: Bartering Goods and Services pp. 138-139	**IN Academic Standard 2.1.1** Listen to historical stories and compare life in the past and present. **(Also 2.1.2)**

Insert between pages 97b - 97c
For complete standards listing, please see front tab.

Continued on other side →

Scott Foresman Social Studies to the Indiana Academic Standards for English/Language Arts

Grade 2 Unit 3 • *Working Together*

Lesson Title	Indiana Academic Standards English/Language Arts
Begin with a Song, pp. 98-99 **Vocabulary Preview, pp. 100-101** **Reading Social Studies, Predict, pp. 102-103**	**2.2.4** Ask and respond to questions to aid comprehension about important elements of informational texts. See also 2.1.2, 2.1.3, 2.1.5, 2.2.5, 2.2.7
Lesson 1 Choosing Goods and Services, pp. 104-107	**2.1.2** Recognize and use knowledge of spelling patterns when reading. See also 2.1.2, 2.1.3, 2.1.5, 2.2.2, 2.2.4
Thinking Skills: Make a Decision, pp. 108-109	**2.2.6** Recognize cause-and-effect relationships in a text. See also 2.2.4, 2.2.8, 2.4.2, 2.4.6, 2.4.8, 2.5.1, 2.5.5, 2.5.6, 2.6.1, 2.6.2, 2.6.3, 2.6.4, 2.6.8
Citizen Heroes: Phoenix Kids Pride Program, pp. 110-111	**2.2.2** State the purpose for reading. See also 2.2.6, 2.4.6, 2.4.7, 2.4.8, 2.5.5, 2.5.6, 2.6.1, 2.6.2, 2.6.3, 2.6.7, 2.6.8
Lesson 2 Services in Our Community, pp. 112-115	**2.2.5** Restate facts and details in the text to clarify and organize ideas. See also 2.2.4, 2.7.9
Biography: Florence Nightingale, pp. 116-117	**2.7.8** Retell stories, including characters, setting and plot. See also 2.2.2, 2.2.3
DK Fire Engine, pp. 118-119	**2.2.4** Ask and respond to questions to aid comprehension about important elements of informational texts. See also 2.1.2, 2.1.3, 2.2.2, 2.2.3, 2.2.5
Lesson 3 Goods from the Factory to You, pp. 120-123	**2.2.4** Ask and respond to questions to aid comprehension about important elements of informational texts. See also 2.1.2, 2.1.3, 2.1.5, 2.2.2, 2.2.3, 2.2.5
Map and Globe Skills: Use a Compass Rose, pp. 124-125	**2.2.7** Interpret information from diagrams, charts, and graphs. See also 2.2.4, 2.2.5, 2.2.8
Lesson 4 A Trip to the Bank, pp. 126-129	**2.7.8** Retell stories, including characters, setting and plot. See also 2.1.2, 2.1.3, 2.1.5, 2.2.2, 2.2.3
Chart and Graph Skills: Read a Pie Chart, pp. 130-131	**2.2.7** Interpret information from diagrams, charts, and graphs. See also 2.2.2, 2.2.4, 2.7.8
Biography: Linda Alvarado, pp. 132-133	**2.2.4** Ask and respond to questions to aid comprehension about important elements of informational texts. See also 2.1.2, 2.1.3, 2.1.5, 2.2.2, 2.2.3, 2.4.1, 2.4.2, 2.4.4, 2.4.5, 2.4.6, 2.4.7, 2.4.8, 2.5.5, 2.5.6, 2.6.1, 2.6.2, 2.6.3, 2.6.7, 2.6.8, 2.6.9
Lesson 5 Countries Trade and Move Goods, pp. 134-147	**2.2.6** Recognize cause-and-effect relationships in a text. See also 2.1.2, 2.1.3, 2.1.5, 2.2.2, 2.2.3, 2.4.1, 2.4.2, 2.4.4, 2.4.5, 2.4.6, 2.4.7, 2.4.8, 2.5.5, 2.5.6, 2.6.1, 2.6.2, 2.6.3, 2.6.7, 2.6.8, 2.6.9
Then and Now: Bartering Goods and Services, pp. 138-139	**2.2.4** Ask and respond to questions to aid comprehension about important elements of informational texts. See also 2.1.3
End with Riddles, pp. 140-141 *Unit 3 Review, pp. 142-145* *Unit 3 Project, p. 146*	**2.2.5** Restate facts and details in the text to clarify and organize ideas. See also 2.4.1, 2.4.2, 2.4.4, 2.4.5, 2.4.6, 2.4.7, 2.4.8, 2.5.5, 2.5.6, 2.6.1, 2.6.2, 2.6.3, 2.6.7, 2.6.8, 2.6.9

Vocabulary	Resources	Meeting Individual Needs
income **goods** **services**	• Workbook, pp. 26–27 • Transparencies 7, 16 • Vocabulary Cards: income, goods, services • Every Student Learns Guide, pp. 42–45	• Leveled Practice, TE p. 111a
tax	• Workbook, p. 28 • Transparencies 3, 17 • Vocabulary Card: tax • Every Student Learns Guide, pp. 46–49	• ESL Support, TE p. 114 • Leveled Practice, TE p. 119a
factory	• Workbook, pp. 29–30 • Transparencies 9, 18 • Vocabulary Card: factory • Every Student Learns Guide, pp. 50–53	• ESL Support, TE p. 122 • Leveled Practice, TE p. 125a
	• Workbook, pp. 31–32 • Transparencies 5, 19 • Every Student Learns Guide, pp. 54–57	• ESL Support, TE p. 130 • Leveled Practice, TE p. 133a
trade **transportation**	• Workbook, p. 33 • Transparency 7 • Vocabulary Cards: trade, transportation • Every Student Learns Guide, pp. 58–61	• ESL Support, TE p. 135 • Leveled Practice, TE p. 139a

Providing More Depth

Multimedia Library

- ***Money*** **by Joe Cribb**
- ***I Want to Be*** **by Jerry Pinkney**
- **Songs and Music**
- **Video Field Trips**
- **Software**

Additional Resources

- Family Activities
- Vocabulary Cards
- Daily Activity Bank
- Social Studies Plus!
- Big Book Atlas
- Outline Maps
- Desk Maps

ADDITIONAL Technology

- AudioText
- The test maker
- Teacher Resources CD-ROM
- Map Resources CD-ROM
- **www.sfsocialstudies.com**

To establish guidelines for children's safe and responsible use of the Internet, use the **Scott Foresman Internet Guide.**

Additional Internet Links
To find out more about:

- being a smart consumer, visit **www.zillions.org**
- opportunity cost, trade, visit **www.thinkquest.org**

Key Internet Search Terms

- money
- economics

Unit 3 Objectives

Beginning of Unit 3

- **Obtain information about a topic using oral sources such as music.** (pp. 98–99)
- **Determine the meanings of words.** (pp. 100–101)
- **Interpret print material by predicting.** (pp. 102–103)

Lesson 1
Choosing Goods and Services
pp. 104–107

- **Explain how work provides income to purchase goods and services.**
- **Explain the choices people make about earning, spending, and saving money.**
- **Make predictions.**
- **Use a decision-making process.** (pp. 108–109)
- **Explain that scarcity requires people to make choices.** (pp. 108–109)
- **Identify ordinary people who exemplify good citizenship.** (pp. 110–111)

Lesson 2
Services in Our Community
pp. 112–115

- **Identify people who provide services to our community.**
- **Identify historic figures who have exemplified good citizenship.** (pp. 116–117)
- **Obtain information from visual materials—diagram.** (pp. 118–119)

Lesson 3
Goods from the Factory to You
pp. 120–123

- **Distinguish between producing and consuming.**
- **Identify ways people are both producers and consumers.**
- **Trace the development of a product from natural resources to finished product.**
- **Use a map to follow a route.** (pp. 124–125)

Lesson 4
A Trip to the Bank
pp. 126–129

- **Explain the choices people can make about earning, spending, and saving money.**
- **Obtain information from a pie chart.**
- **Construct a pie chart.**
- **Identify ordinary people who exemplify good citizenship.** (pp. 132–133)

Lesson 5
Countries Trade and Move Goods
pp. 134–137

- **Explain how countries are linked by trade and transportation.**
- **Distinguish between the use of barter and money in the exchange of goods and services.** (pp. 138–139)

End of Unit 3

- **Obtain information from visual sources, such as printed text and pictures.** (pp. 140–141)

Assessment Options

✓ Formal Assessment

- **What did you learn?** PE/TE pp. 107, 109, 115, 123, 129, 137, 145
- **Unit Review,** PE/TE pp. 142–145
- **Unit 3 Tests, Assessment Book,** pp. 9–12
- **The test maker,** (test-generator software)

✓ Informal Assessment

- **Teacher's Edition Questions,** throughout Lessons and Features
- **Close and Assess,** TE pp. 103, 107, 109, 111, 115, 117, 119, 123, 125, 129, 131, 133, 137, 139, 141
- **Try it!** PE/TE pp. 103, 109, 125, 131
- **Think and Share,** TE p. 107, PE/TE pp. 115, 117, 123, 129, 131, 133, 137
- **Respect in Action,** PE/TE p. 111
- **Hands-on History,** PE/TE p. 139

Ongoing Assessment

Ongoing Assessment is found throughout the Teacher's Edition lessons using an **If . . . then** model.

If = students' observable behavior, **then =** reteaching and enrichment suggestions

✓ Portfolio Assessment

- **Portfolio Assessment,** TE pp. 97, 144
- **Leveled Practice,** TE pp. 100, 111a, 119a, 125a, 133a, 139a
- **Workbook,** pp. 24–35
- **Unit Review: Skills on Your Own,** PE/TE p. 144
- **Curriculum Connection: Writing,** TE pp. 111, 111a, 133, 133a, 140

✓ Performance Assessment

- **Hands-on Unit Project** (Unit 3 Performance Assessment), PE/TE pp. 97, 142, 146
- **Internet Activity,** PE p. 146
- **Unit Review: Write and Share,** PE/TE p. 145
- **Scoring Guides,** TE pp. 143, 144, 146

Test Talk

Test-Taking Strategies

Understand the Question

- **Locate Key Words in the Question,** TE p. 106
- **Locate Key Words in the Text,** TE p. 137

Understand the Answer

- **Choose the Right Answer,** TE p. 142
- **Use Information from the Text,** TE p. 123
- **Use Information from Graphics,** TE p. 119
- **Write Your Answer,** TE p. 133

For additional practice, use the Test Talk Practice Book.

Featured Strategy

Choose the Right Answer

Children will:

- Narrow the answer choices and rule out answers they know are wrong.
- Choose the best answer.

PE/TE p. 142

Curriculum Connections

Integrating Your Day

The lessons, skills, and features of Unit 3 provide many opportunities to make connections between social studies and other areas of the elementary curriculum.

Social Studies

Reading

Reading Skill—Predict, PE/TE pp. 102–103, TE p. 104, 134

Reading Skill—Compare and Contrast, TE p. 112

Tax Time, TE p. 119a

Reading Skill—Put Steps in Order, TE p. 120

What's Inside? TE p. 125a

Reading Skill—Main Idea and Details, TE p. 126

Sentence Trade, TE p. 139a

Math

How Does It Add Up? TE p. 99

Is the Price Right? TE p. 109

Count the Cash, TE p. 128

Another Pie Chart, TE p. 131

Make a Bar Graph, TE p. 137

Writing

Mottoes, TE p. 111

Make a Jobs Booklet, TE p. 111a

Perform an Interview, PE p. 133

Diagram Leadership, TE p. 133a

Create Riddles, TE p. 140

Literature

More About Community Workers, TE p. 115

From Start to Finish—More to Read, TE p. 123

Read About Work, PE/TE p. 145

Science

Magnets, TE p. 103

Music/Drama

Sing a Song, TE p. 119a

Perform an Interview, TE p. 133

Sing a Song, TE p. 133a

Play a Variation on a Game, TE p. 141

Art

Word Pictures, TE p. 111a

Safety Posters, TE p. 119

Hats, Hats, Hats, TE p. 119a

Paper T-shirts, TE p. 122

 Look for this symbol throughout the Teacher's Edition to find **Curriculum Connections.**

Professional Development

Economics in the Elementary Classroom

Why? How? When? Where?

by Bonnie Meszaros
University of Delaware

Children live in an economic world and bring economic knowledge and experience into the classroom. Some of the economic knowledge children bring to school is correct and teachers can build upon it in their instruction. Some of the knowledge is wrong and fraught with misconceptions. Teachers have a responsibility to understand and correct children's confusion and misconceptions about economics.

Some children assume that income is used only to buy goods—tangible things that can be carried away. In Lesson 1 of Unit 3, pp. 104–107, children learn how work provides income to purchase both goods and services.

To teach young children economics, students need to be taught in developmentally appropriate ways. The keys to successful teaching and learning economics include:

- making economic learning meaningful through experienced-based instruction; and
- providing for teacher-child and child-child communication exchanges so students can verbalize economic ideas.

The Thinking Skills feature "Make a Decision" on pp. 108–109 helps children understand how to make a wise economic decision by considering and discussing a range of economic choices.

ESL Support

by Jim Cummins, Ph. D.
University of Toronto

Academic Language Proficiency

Academic language proficiency includes knowledge of the less frequent vocabulary of English as well as the ability to interpret and produce increasingly complex written language. The development of academic language proficiency, for both ESL and non-ESL students, requires specific instructional strategies designed to enable students to harvest the language they encounter in the content areas.

Extend Language

Students extend their command of academic language by reading extensively from texts that contain this form of language and by systematically studying how academic language is put together.

The following examples in the Teacher's Edition will help you enable ESL students to extend their understanding and production of language:

- ***Matching Game*** *on p. 114 expands understanding of what specific community workers do. Children are asked to match an object with the particular worker who uses that object—matching a thermometer with a nurse. This aids in expanding understanding of what specific community workers do.*
- ***Draw and Write*** *on p. 135 helps children understand how trade and transportation link countries by inviting English Language Learners to draw pictures, label them, and write sentences about goods and ways to move them.*

Read Aloud

General Store

by Rachel Field

Some day I'm going to have a store
With a tinkly bell hung over the door,
With real glass cases and counters wide
And drawers all spilly with things inside.

I'll fix the window and dust each shelf,
And take the money in all myself.
It will be my store and I will say,
"What can I do for you today?"

Build Background

- Ask children to talk about stores they have visited. Have them name the type of store and ways in which the merchandise was displayed—on shelves, on racks, in cases, freestanding.
- Ask children what happens in a store. (Store owners sell things; shoppers buy things.)

Read Alouds and Primary Sources

Read Alouds and Primary Sources contains additional selections to be used with Unit 3.

Bibliography

Frederick, by Leo Lionni (Knopf, ISBN 0-394-82614-0, 1987) **Easy** ***Caldecott Honor Book***

Joseph Had a Little Overcoat, by Simms Taback (Viking, ISBN 0-670-87855-3, 1999) **Easy** ***Caldecott Medal Winner***

Zin! Zin! Zin!: A Violin, by Lloyd Moss and Marjorie Priceman (Illustrator) (Aladdin Paperbacks, ISBN 0-689-83524-8, 2000). **Easy** ***Caldecott Honor Book***

Ferryboat, by Betsy Maestro and Giulio Maestro (Illustrator) (HarperCollins, ISBN 0-690-04520-4, 1987) **On-Level** ***Notable Social Studies Book***

Granddaddy's Street Songs, by Monalisa Degross and Floyd Cooper (Illustrator) (Hyperion, ISBN 0-786-80160-3, 1999) A one-time street vendor tells his stories. **On-Level** ***Notable Social Studies Book***

What Do Illustrators Do?, by Eileen Christelow (Houghton Mifflin, ISBN 0-395-90230-4, 1999) **On-Level** ***ALA Notable Book***

Love as Strong as Ginger, by Lenore Look and Stephen T. Johnson (Illustrator) (Atheneum, ISBN 0-689-81248-5, 1999) Katie's wish is to see her Chinese grandmother at work. **Challenge** ***Notable Social Studies Book***

Nim and the War Effort, by Milly Lee and Yangsook Choi (Illustrator) (Farrar Straus & Giroux, ISBN 0-374-35523-1, 1997) **Challenge** ***ALA Notable Book***

Economics and Children's Literature: Supplement, by B. Flowers and B. Meszaros (SPEC Publishing/ St. Louis, 1998) **Teacher Reference**

Discovery Channel School Videos

Technology at Work. Take a look at how the forces of technology affect our world—and the universe; 2 videos. 60 minutes.

Inventors and Inventions. Explore how and why some inventions were created and then meet some famous inventors; 2 videos. 49 minutes.

Look for this symbol throughout the Teacher's Edition to find **Award-Winning Selections**. Additional book references are suggested throughout this unit.

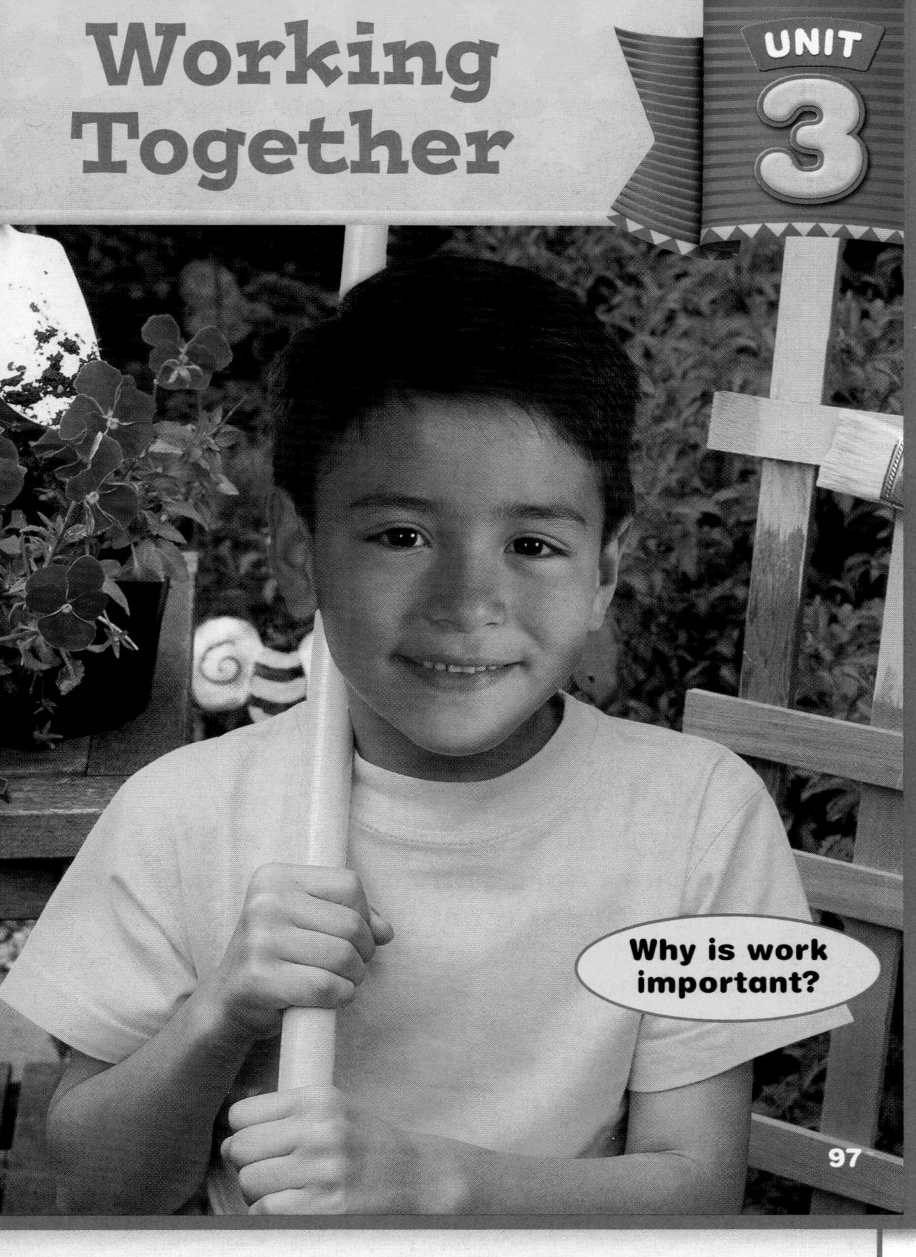

Working Together

Unit Overview

In this unit, children will learn about work in the community. They will discuss income as it relates to spending and saving. They will differentiate between goods and services and will follow the process of taking a product from farm to factory to consumer. As the unit concludes, they will investigate and discuss trade and barter.

Introduce Matt

Read the unit title and then introduce the featured child for this unit as a second grader named Matt. Talk about what Matt and his family are doing in the garden.

Unit Question

- Read the question on this page.
- Initiate a discussion about reasons work is important in the home and in the community.
- To activate prior knowledge, make a list on chart paper of children's reasons why work is important.

✓ **Portfolio Assessment** Keep a copy of this list for the Portfolio Assessment at the end of the unit on p. 144.

Hands-on Unit Project

✓ **Unit 3 Performance Assessment**

- The Unit 3 Project, *Business Basics,* on p. 146, is an ongoing performance assessment project to enrich children's learning.
- This project which has children select a good or service to advertise may be started now or at any time during this unit of study.
- A performance assessment scoring guide is located on p. 146.

I'll Work Hard!

Objective

- Obtain information about a topic using oral sources, such as music.

Resources

- *Songs and Music CD,* "I'll Work Hard!"
- Poster 5
- Social Studies Plus!

Introduce the Song

Preview Tell children they will sing about working hard to earn money. Ask children what kind of work they see being done in the photo.

Warm Up To activate prior knowledge, ask children to name jobs and chores that they can perform around the house or in their neighborhood to earn extra money. List their responses on the chalkboard. Then ask children to tell what they would do with the money they earn.

Sing the Song

- Have children sing the song "I'll Work Hard!"
- Have children draw pictures of themselves doing a job at home. Jobs might include working in the garden, baby-sitting a sibling, or cleaning their room.
- Ask volunteers to act out the scene they drew. Invite children to guess the job or chore that is being performed.

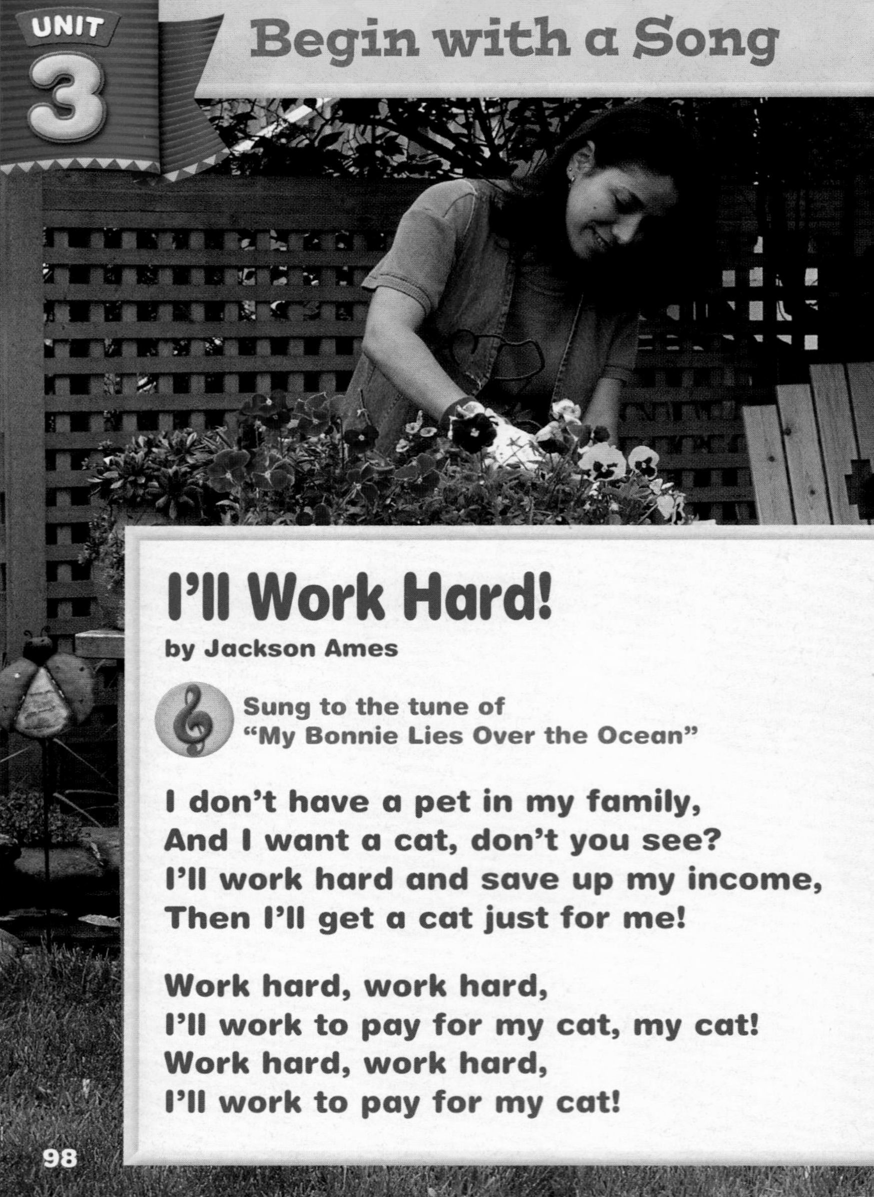

Practice and Extend

Make Job Coupons

- Tell children they are going to make job coupons.
- Begin by distributing two index cards to each child in class. Have children write the name of a job, task, or chore they know someone at home would appreciate help with on each index card. Tell them to include the amount of time they will spend on the job.
- Have children bring home their completed coupons and give them to a parent or other family member.
- When the parent needs one of the specific jobs completed, he or she can attach that coupon to the refrigerator (or other place) to let their child know that his or her help is needed and welcomed.

Talk About the Picture

Direct children's attention to the photograph on pages 98–99. Ask volunteers to talk about what they see in the scene. Then ask children to talk about experiences they have had helping in a garden.

1 **Who are working together?** Members of a family—Matt and his parents **Analyze Pictures**

2 **Why is it important for families to work together?** Possible answer: Working together helps families stay close and have a good time together. **Draw Conclusions**

3 **Do you think Matt will earn money for the work he is doing?** Possible answer: No; he's helping with a family chore. **Predict**

CURRICULUM CONNECTION
Math

How Does It Add Up?

- Have children suppose that Matt and some friends worked to earn money. Write these children's names on the board with the amounts they earned.
- Matt helped paint a fence. He earned $2.00.
- Jen watered her neighbor's garden. She got $1.00.
- Pete washed his grandpa's car. He was paid $2.00.

Have children decide what operation to use to figure out how much the children earned altogether. Then have them do the math. ($5.00)

AUDIO CD
Technology

Play the CD, *Songs and Music,* to listen to "I'll Work Hard!"

Vocabulary Preview

Objective

- Determine the meanings of words.

Resources

- Workbook, p. 24
- Vocabulary Cards
- Poster 6

Introduce the Vocabulary

Read aloud and point to each vocabulary word and the photograph illustrating it. Have volunteers give the meaning of the words. Then have children find several examples of vocabulary words in the illustration. Write these examples on the board.

Vocabulary Word	Illustrated Examples
income	people doing jobs and buying goods
goods	boxes on trucks, goods in shops
services	storekeepers, workers unloading goods
tax	tax sign in front of highway
factory	building near the highway
trade	ships at dock with goods
transportation	trucks, carts, boats, cars, buses
barter	people exchanging goods

SOCIAL STUDIES STRAND
Economics

Listed below are some basic principles of economics for young children. Direct your discussion of the illustration toward the further development of these concepts.

- choices people make about jobs
- goods and services
- choices people make about how they spend the money they earn
- how workers who serve the community are paid
- where goods are made
- how goods are moved from place to place
- the different ways that people acquire goods

income

goods

services

tax

MEETING INDIVIDUAL NEEDS
Leveled Practice

Take a Walk

Invite children to take a walk with you through the community shown in the illustration.

Easy Describe in detail the three sections of the illustration—the harbor, the marketplace, and the area around the factory—using the vocabulary words. After each section is reviewed have children recall the vocabulary words that were illustrated in that scene. List their responses on the chalkboard. **Reteach**

On-Level Have children take turns describing specific scenes in the illustration. Have children use the vocabulary word that names the scene or activity. **Extend**

Challenge Have children take turns writing a vocabulary word on the board. Then have volunteers use the vocabulary word in an oral sentence that relates to the picture. **Enrich**

You can look up vocabulary words online. Click on *Social Studies Library* and select the dictionary at **www.sfsocialstudies.com.**

Workbook, p. 24

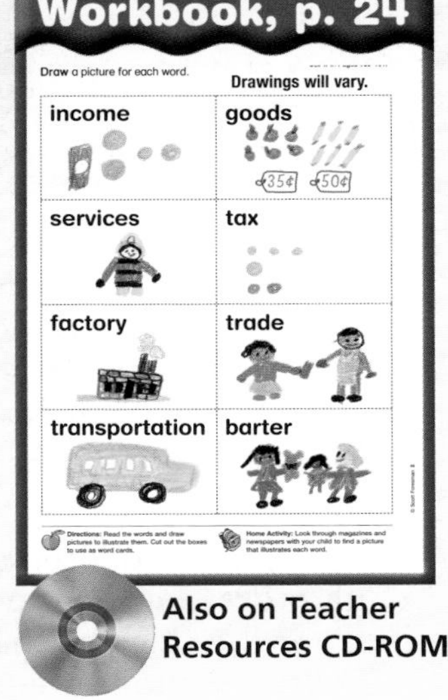

Also on Teacher Resources CD-ROM.

Talk About the Illustration

Allow children time to study the illustration. Explain that the picture shows people performing different jobs within a community. Ask children to discuss some things the workers are doing and name some places in which people are working.

1 What are some of the jobs shown in the illustration? Possible answers: Workers unloading trucks and ships, shopkeepers, boat captains, food cart operators **Analyze Pictures**

2 How are goods being moved from place to place? Possible answers: By trucks, carts, and boats **Analyze Pictures**

3 How are the types of transportation shown in the picture alike and different? Possible answer: Some types of transportation move goods and people on land; other types move goods and people across water. **Compare and Contrast**

Look Ahead

Tell children they will learn more about each of the vocabulary words as they study Unit 3.

You may want to revisit the picture with children to review the concepts and vocabulary in the unit.

4 Name some of the goods in the illustration that are being bought and sold. Possible answers: Seafood, fruits, and vegetables **Analyze Pictures**

5 What do you think would happen if there were no workers in the community pictured? Possible answer: Goods would not be unloaded from the boats and trucks; goods would not get to the stores and markets. **Predict**

What Will Matt Do?

Predict

Objective

Interpret print material by predicting.

Resource

- Workbook, p. 25

About the Unit Target Skill

- The target reading skill for this unit is Predict. Children are introduced to the unit target skill here and given an opportunity to practice it.
- Further opportunities to predict are found throughout Unit 3.

1 Introduce and Motivate

Preview To determine whether children understand what a prediction is, use the following activity:

- Ask children to think about weather.
- Ask them what season this is.
- Then ask them what month it is.
- Next, ask them what the weather is like today.
- Finally, tell children to think about their answers to each question and to use that information to think about what the weather might be like tomorrow. List children's responses on the chalkboard.

Warm Up To activate prior knowledge, have children talk about times they have thought about what might happen next. Initiate children's discussion by asking: *When your birthday is coming, do you try to guess what gifts you may get? When you visit the dentist, do you think about what he or she may do and say?*

UNIT 3 Reading Social Studies

What Will Matt Do?

Predict

I'm Matt. I want to get my very own cat. If I get a cat, I will feed it and play with it every day.

How can I get a cat? Here are some things I might do.

I can save money to buy a cat at the pet store.

My grandma wants to give me a present. Maybe I can ask her for a cat.

I can ask my parents to take me to an animal shelter to find a cat.

102

Practice and Extend

BUILD BACKGROUND
ESL Support

Children draw and write to make predictions.

Beginning Draw two simple sketches—an egg and an egg with obvious cracks in it and a little chick beak poking through. Have children draw a picture to show what will happen next.

Intermediate Children draw the picture and write a caption for their picture.

Advanced Children do both activities above. Then they draw another picture to show what will happen after the chick has hatched. Have children write a sentence about the picture. Ask children to use complete sentences to describe the sequence of events in the four pictures.

Cats at the animal shelter need good homes. Workers at the animal shelter help people choose the cat that is best for them.

Now it's time for you to predict! **Predict** means to tell what you think will happen next. Think about the things I might do to get a cat. What do you think I will do next?

I decided to ask my mom and dad to take me to the animal shelter. I hope I find a friendly cat! Did I do what you thought I would do?

Try it!

What would happen if the animal shelter did not have any cats? What if Matt's grandmother had already bought him another present? **Predict** what Matt might do next.

103

2 Teach and Discuss

- Read p. 102. Review each of the three things that Matt might do. Have children discuss the possibilities.

- Poll the class to see what they predict. Record children's responses on the chalkboard in a tally chart.
- Read p. 103 with children.
- Ask: *Was your prediction correct? Do you think Matt made a good choice? Why or why not?*

Ongoing Assessment

If... children have difficulty with the concept of predicting,

then... link the concept to weather forecasting. Note that people use information they gather to predict or say what they think the weather will be the next day and on days that follow.

3 Close and Assess

Try it!

Children's answers may include the following: Matt could look in the newspaper for an ad related to giving away a free cat. Matt could ask friends or relatives whether they knew of anyone who had a cat to give away.

CURRICULUM CONNECTION
Science

Magnets

- Have a magnet and some small paper clips available. Demonstrate how the magnet attracts the clips. Note that magnets attract objects made of certain metals such as iron.
- Place an array of small objects on a table. Have children look at and handle them.
- As you point to each object, have children predict whether the magnet will attract it. Have children use the magnet to test their predictions.

Workbook, p. 25

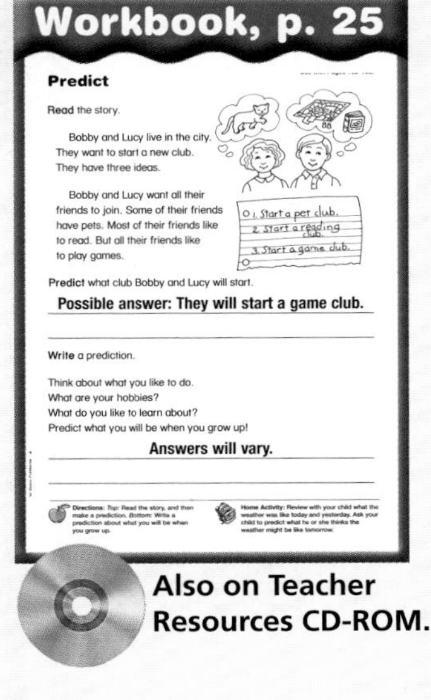

Predict

Read the story.

Bobby and Lucy live in the city. They want to start a new club. They have three ideas.

Bobby and Lucy want all their friends to join. Some of their friends have pets. Most of their friends like to read. But all their friends like to play games.

1. Start a pet club.
2. Start a reading club.
3. Start a game club.

Predict what club Bobby and Lucy will start.

Possible answer: They will start a game club.

Write a prediction.

Think about what you like to do. What are your hobbies? What do you like to learn about? Predict what you will be when you grow up!

Answers will vary.

Also on Teacher Resources CD-ROM.

Workbook Support

Use the following Workbook pages to support content and skills development as you teach Unit 3. You can also view and print Workbook pages from the Teacher Resources CD-ROM.

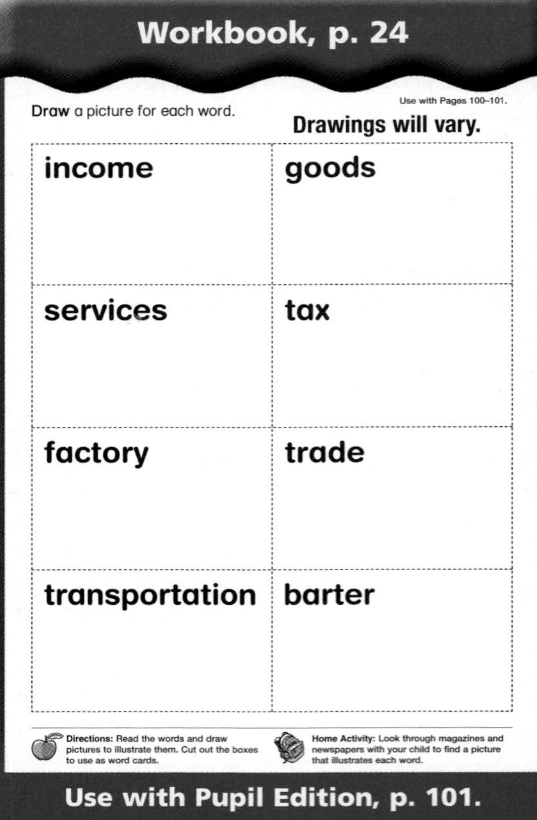

Workbook, p. 24

Use with Pages 100–101.

Draw a picture for each word. **Drawings will vary.**

income	goods
services	tax
factory	trade
transportation	barter

Directions: Read the words and draw pictures to illustrate them. Cut out the boxes to use as word cards.

Home Activity: Look through magazines and newspapers with your child to find a picture that illustrates each word.

Use with Pupil Edition, p. 101.

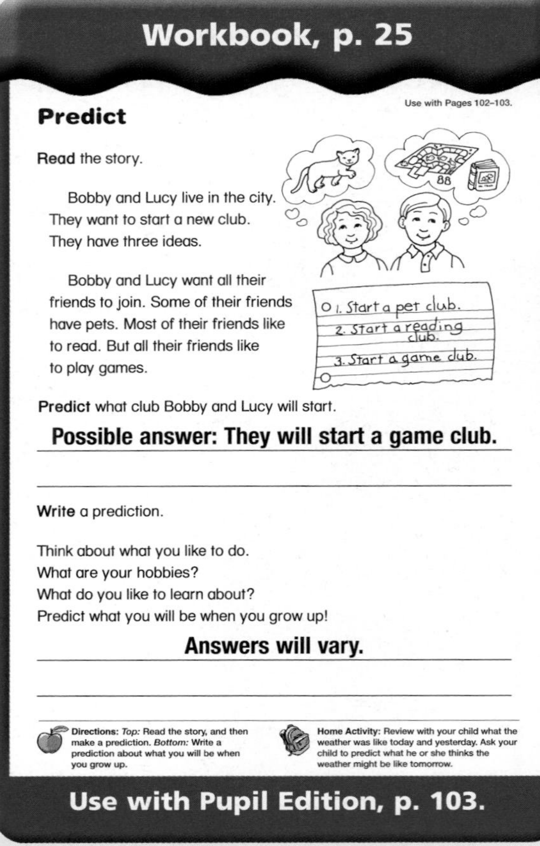

Workbook, p. 25

Use with Pages 102–103.

Predict

Read the story.

Bobby and Lucy live in the city. They want to start a new club. They have three ideas.

Bobby and Lucy want all their friends to join. Some of their friends have pets. Most of their friends like to read. But all their friends like to play games.

Predict what club Bobby and Lucy will start.

Possible answer: They will start a game club.

Write a prediction.

Think about what you like to do.
What are your hobbies?
What do you like to learn about?
Predict what you will be when you grow up!

Answers will vary.

Directions: *Top:* Read the story, and then make a prediction. *Bottom:* Write a prediction about what you will be when you grow up.

Home Activity: Review with your child what the weather was like today and yesterday. Ask your child to predict what he or she thinks the weather might be like tomorrow.

Use with Pupil Edition, p. 103.

Workbook, p. 26

Use with Pages 104–107.

Choosing Goods and Services

Circle the correct answers.

What are jobs that people do to help others?
goods needs (services)

What are things that people make or grow?
income (goods) wants

What do we call the money that people earn?
savings budget (income)

Show what you can do with money.
Write *earn*, *spend*, or *save* under each picture.

save **earn** **spend**

Directions: *Top:* Circle the answer to each question. *Bottom:* Look at the pictures. Write *earn*, *spend*, or *save* to show a choice each child is making.

Home Activity: Talk with your child about choices your family makes in terms of choosing goods and services.

Use with Pupil Edition, p. 107.

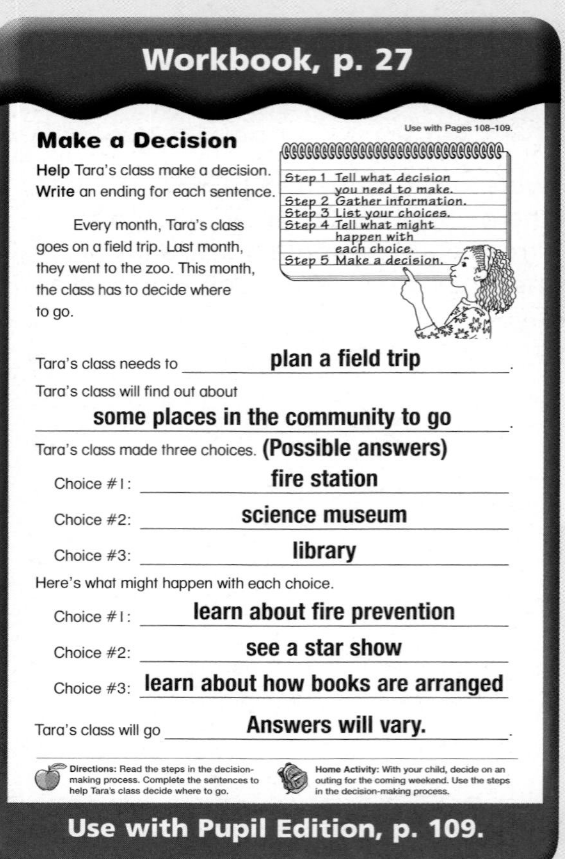

Workbook, p. 27

Use with Pages 108–109.

Make a Decision

Help Tara's class make a decision.
Write an ending for each sentence.

Every month, Tara's class goes on a field trip. Last month, they went to the zoo. This month, the class has to decide where to go.

Tara's class needs to **plan a field trip**.

Tara's class will find out about **some places in the community to go**.

Tara's class made three choices. **(Possible answers)**

Choice #1: **fire station**

Choice #2: **science museum**

Choice #3: **library**

Here's what might happen with each choice.

Choice #1: **learn about fire prevention**

Choice #2: **see a star show**

Choice #3: **learn about how books are arranged**

Tara's class will go **Answers will vary.**

Directions: Read the steps in the decision-making process. Complete the sentences to help Tara's class decide where to go.

Home Activity: With your child, decide on an outing for the coming weekend. Use the steps in the decision-making process.

Use with Pupil Edition, p. 109.

Workbook, p. 28

Use with Pages 112–115.

Services in Our Community

Write what each worker does.

Nurses help care for people who are sick.

Police officers make sure people obey laws.

Firefighters help keep people safe from fires.

School teachers help children learn.

Draw a worker who serves your community. **Drawings will vary.**

Directions: *Top:* Look at the pictures. Write about each worker's job. *Bottom:* Draw a picture of a worker who provides a service in your community.

Home Activity: Point out to your child some of the people who provide services in your community.

Use with Pupil Edition, p. 115.

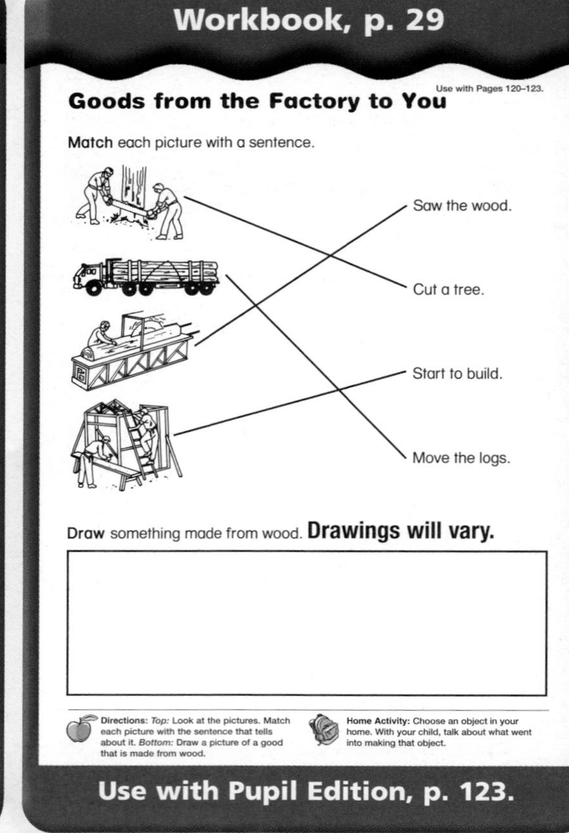

Workbook, p. 29

Use with Pages 120–123.

Goods from the Factory to You

Match each picture with a sentence.

Saw the wood.

Cut a tree.

Start to build.

Move the logs.

Draw something made from wood. **Drawings will vary.**

Directions: *Top:* Look at the pictures. Match each picture with the sentence that tells about it. *Bottom:* Draw a picture of a good that is made from wood.

Home Activity: Choose an object in your home. With your child, talk about what went into making that object.

Use with Pupil Edition, p. 123.

Workbook Support

Workbook, p. 30

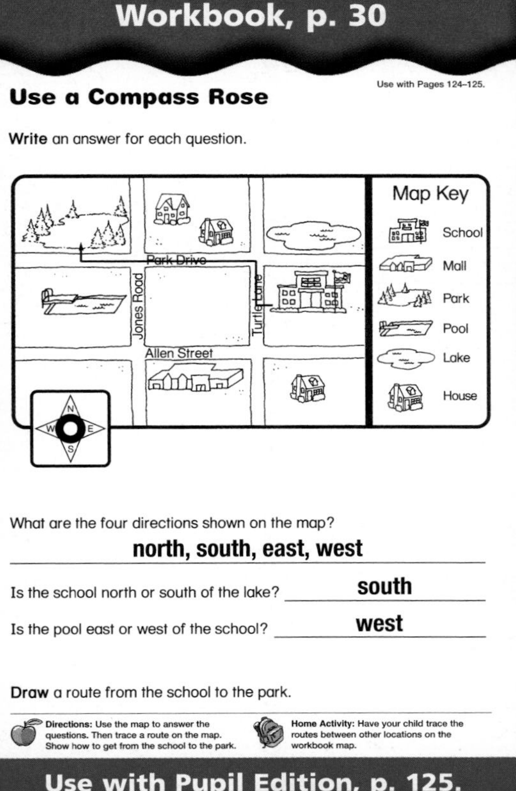

Use a Compass Rose

Use with Pages 124–125.

Write an answer for each question.

What are the four directions shown on the map? **north, south, east, west**

Is the school north or south of the lake? **south**

Is the pool east or west of the school? **west**

Draw a route from the school to the park.

Directions: Use the map to answer the questions. Then trace a route on the map. Show how to get from the school to the park.

Home Activity: Have your child trace the routes between other locations on the workbook map.

Use with Pupil Edition, p. 125.

Workbook, p. 31

A Trip to the Bank

Use with Pages 126–129.

Draw to show a way you might earn money. **Drawings will vary.**

Write answers to these questions.

What are two kinds of bank accounts? **savings account, checking account**

How might people pay for goods and services? **with money, with a check or credit card**

Directions: *Top:* Draw a picture to show a way that you might earn money. *Bottom:* Write an answer for each question.

Home Activity: Visit a local bank with your child. Demonstrate how to use an ATM machine or write a deposit slip.

Use with Pupil Edition, p. 129.

Workbook, p. 32

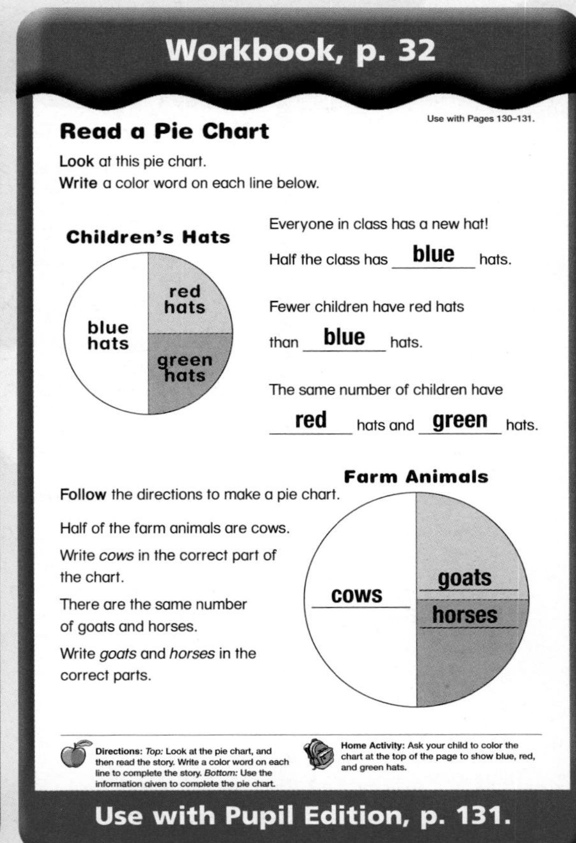

Read a Pie Chart

Use with Pages 130–131.

Look at this pie chart.
Write a color word on each line below.

Everyone in class has a new hat!

Half the class has **blue** hats.

Fewer children have red hats than **blue** hats.

The same number of children have **red** hats and **green** hats.

Follow the directions to make a pie chart.

Half of the farm animals are cows. Write *cows* in the correct part of the chart.

There are the same number of goats and horses. Write *goats* and *horses* in the correct parts.

Directions: *Top:* Look at the pie chart, and then read the story. Write a color word on each line to complete the story. *Bottom:* Use the information given to complete the pie chart.

Home Activity: Ask your child to color the chart at the top of the page to show blue, red, and green hats.

Use with Pupil Edition, p. 131.

Workbook, p. 33

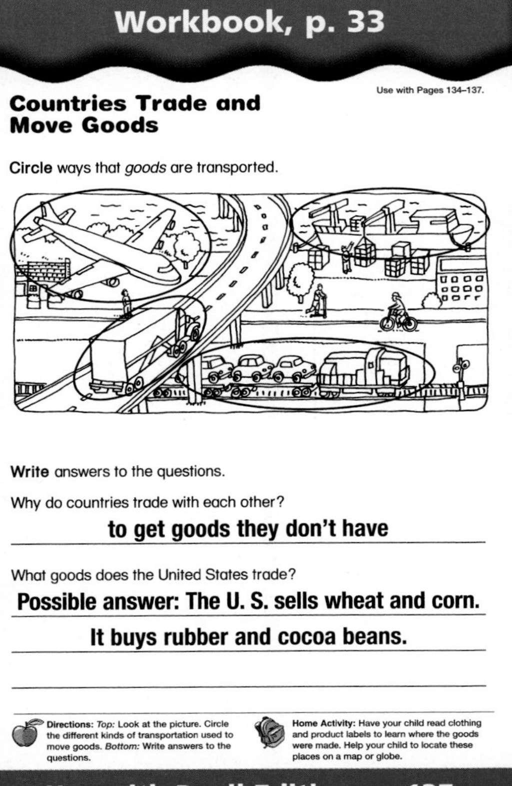

Countries Trade and Move Goods

Use with Pages 134–137.

Circle ways that *goods* are transported.

Write answers to the questions.

Why do countries trade with each other? **to get goods they don't have**

What goods does the United States trade? **Possible answer: The U. S. sells wheat and corn. It buys rubber and cocoa beans.**

Directions: *Top:* Look at the picture. Circle the different kinds of transportation used to move goods. *Bottom:* Write answers to the questions.

Home Activity: Have your child read clothing and product labels to learn where the goods were made. Help your child to locate these places on a map or globe.

Use with Pupil Edition, p. 137.

Workbook, p. 34

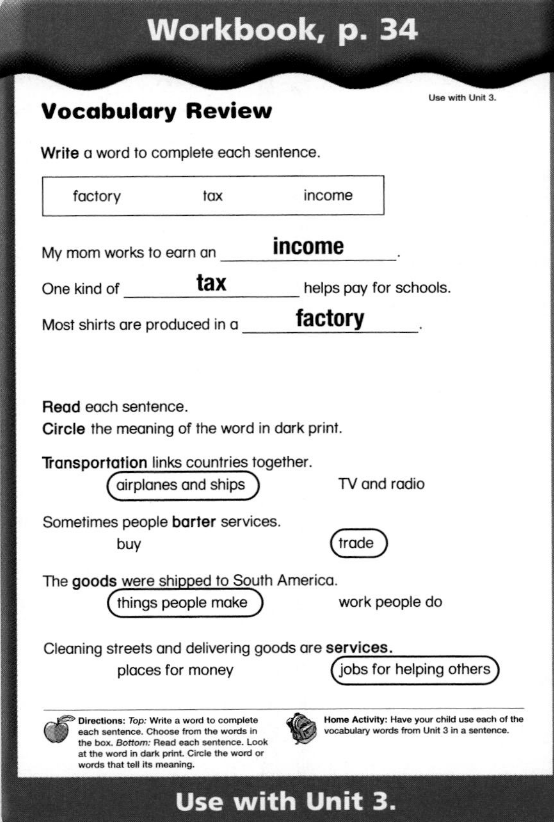

Vocabulary Review

Use with Unit 3.

Write a word to complete each sentence.

factory	tax	income

My mom works to earn an **income**.

One kind of **tax** helps pay for schools.

Most shirts are produced in a **factory**.

Read each sentence.
Circle the meaning of the word in dark print.

Transportation links countries together.
(airplanes and ships) TV and radio

Sometimes people **barter** services.
buy (trade)

The **goods** were shipped to South America.
(things people make) work people do

Cleaning streets and delivering goods are **services.**
places for money (jobs for helping others)

Directions: *Top:* Write a word to complete each sentence. Choose from the words in the box. *Bottom:* Read each sentence. Look at the word in dark print. Circle the word or words that tell its meaning.

Home Activity: Have your child use each of the vocabulary words from Unit 3 in a sentence.

Use with Unit 3.

Workbook, p. 35

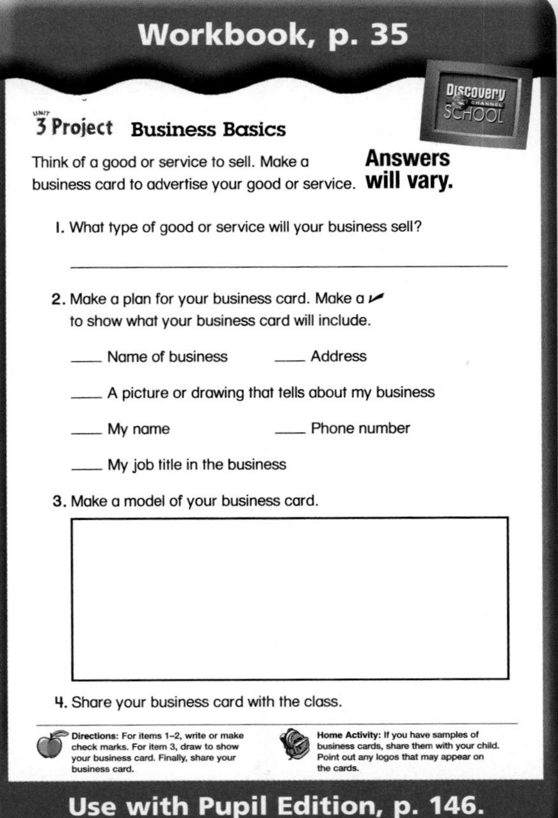

Unit 3 Project **Business Basics**

Think of a good or service to sell. Make a business card to advertise your good or service. **Answers will vary.**

1. What type of good or service will your business sell?
2. Make a plan for your business card. Make a ✔ to show what your business card will include.
   - ____ Name of business ____ Address
   - ____ A picture or drawing that tells about my business
   - ____ My name ____ Phone number
   - ____ My job title in the business
3. Make a model of your business card.
4. Share your business card with the class.

Directions: For items 1–2, write or make check marks. For item 3, draw to show your business card. Finally, share your business card.

Home Activity: If you have samples of business cards, share them with your child. Point out any logos that may appear on the cards.

Use with Pupil Edition, p. 146.

Assessment Support

Use these Assessment Book pages and the test maker to assess content and skills in Unit 3. You can also view and print Assessment Book pages from the Teacher Resources CD-ROM.

Assessment Book, p. 9

Unit 3: Content Test

Write the word that goes with each definition.

trade	services	income	factory

1. the money that someone earns **income**
2. a building where people produce goods **factory**
3. jobs that people do to help others **services**
4. to buy, sell, or exchange goods **trade**

TEST PREP Which word completes each sentence?

1. Trains and trucks are a means of ____.
   - a. services
   - b. taxes
   - c. goods
   - (d.) transportation
2. In some places, there is a sales ____ on goods you buy.
   - (a.) tax
   - b. factory
   - c. trade
   - d. barter

Use with Pupil Edition, p. 142.

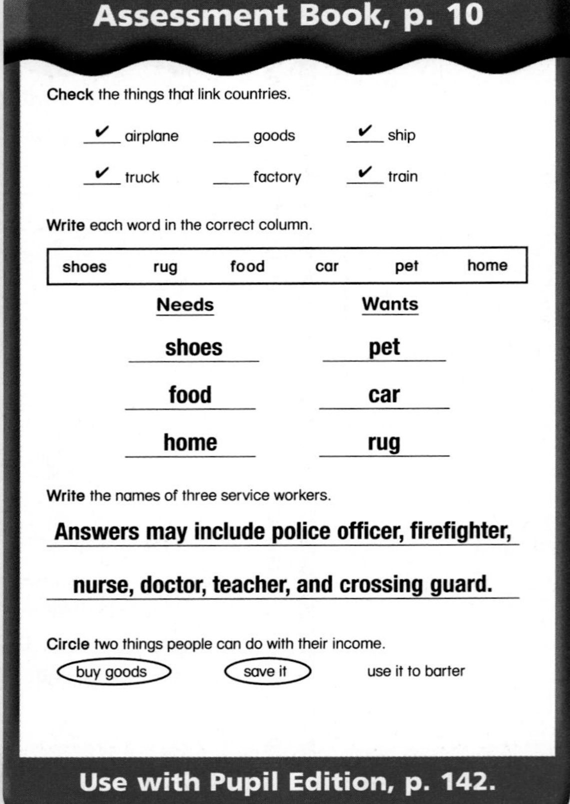

Assessment Book, p. 10

Check the things that link countries.

✔ airplane ____ goods ✔ ship

✔ truck ____ factory ✔ train

Write each word in the correct column.

shoes	rug	food	car	pet	home

Needs	Wants
shoes	pet
food	car
home	rug

Write the names of three service workers.

Answers may include police officer, firefighter, nurse, doctor, teacher, and crossing guard.

Circle two things people can do with their income.

(buy goods) (save it) use it to barter

Use with Pupil Edition, p. 142.

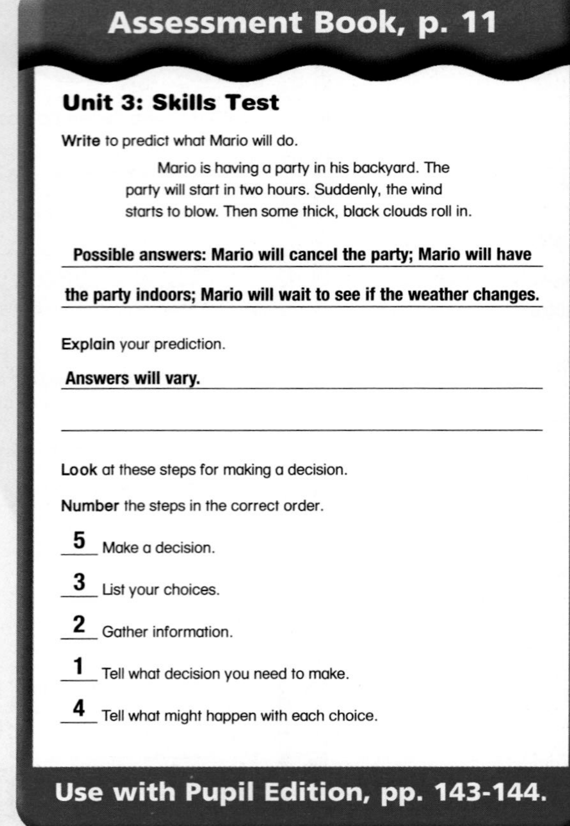

Assessment Book, p. 11

Unit 3: Skills Test

Write to predict what Mario will do.

Mario is having a party in his backyard. The party will start in two hours. Suddenly, the wind starts to blow. Then some thick, black clouds roll in.

Possible answers: Mario will cancel the party; Mario will have the party indoors; Mario will wait to see if the weather changes.

Explain your prediction.

Answers will vary.

Look at these steps for making a decision.

Number the steps in the correct order.

5 Make a decision.

3 List your choices.

2 Gather information.

1 Tell what decision you need to make.

4 Tell what might happen with each choice.

Use with Pupil Edition, pp. 143-144.

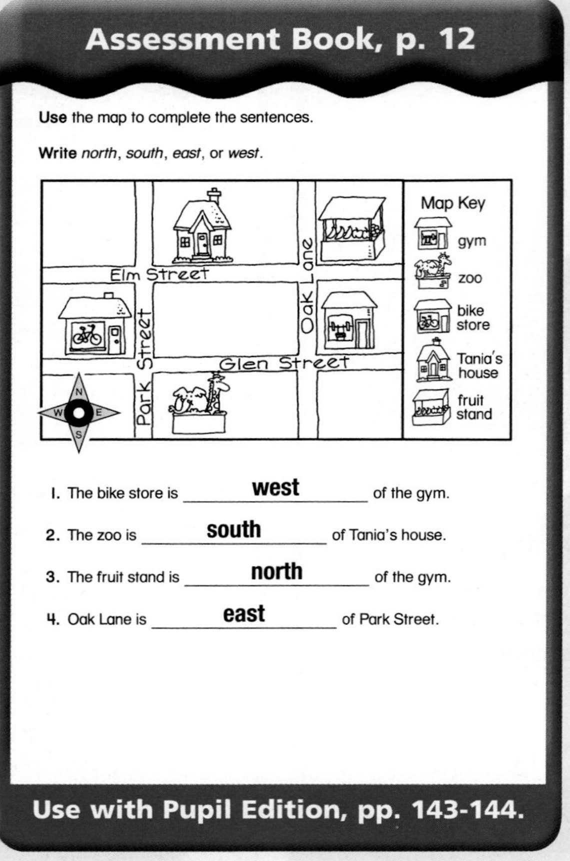

Assessment Book, p. 12

Use the map to complete the sentences.

Write *north*, *south*, *east*, or *west*.

1. The bike store is **west** of the gym.
2. The zoo is **south** of Tania's house.
3. The fruit stand is **north** of the gym.
4. Oak Lane is **east** of Park Street.

Use with Pupil Edition, pp. 143-144.

Lesson 1 Overview

Choosing Goods and Services **pages 104–107**	Children will learn the meaning of the words *income, goods*, and *services*. They will learn that people can make choices about earning, spending, and saving money. 	 Time 20–30 minutes Resources • Workbook, p. 26 • Vocabulary Cards income goods services • Every Student Learns Guide, pp. 42–45
Make a Decision **pages 108–109**	Children will learn to use a step-by-step procedure to make a decision.	 Time 15–20 minutes Resource • Workbook, p. 27
Phoenix Kids Pride Program **pages 110–111**	Children will learn how the Phoenix Kids Pride Program encourages children to make Phoenix "a better place to live."	Time 15–20 minutes

Build Background

Activity

A Classroom Store

 **Time** 20–30 minutes

Have children bring in empty containers, such as cereal boxes, cans, and plastic soda bottles (or use newspaper ads for different products). Arrange the items on a table. Have children take turns choosing the three products that they need to grow and be healthy and three products that they want even though they may not be healthful. Ask children to explain their choices.

If time is short, talk with children about visits they have made to the supermarket with a parent or family member. Ask what foods or household products were bought. Discuss why particular choices might have been made.

Read Aloud

What Should I Buy?

by Christopher Erickson

There are things we want
and things we need.
Deciding which is which
can be hard indeed!

We work so hard
for our money
to buy different goods
such as milk, bread, and honey.

So when we shop
we start with a plan,
to spend our money wisely
as often as we can!

Lesson 1 Choosing Goods and Services

Objectives

- Explain how work provides income to purchase goods and services.
- Explain the choices people make about earning, spending, and saving money.

Vocabulary

income money that people earn (p. 104)

goods things people make or grow (p. 104)

services jobs that people do to help others (p. 105)

QUICK Teaching Plan

If time is short, write the vocabulary words on the board. Have volunteers suggest words related to each vocabulary word. List the responses on the board. For example, a child might suggest *money* as a word related to *income,* or *firefighter* and *teacher* as words related to services.

1 Introduce and Motivate

Preview Display the Vocabulary Cards **income**, **goods**, and **services**. Have children work with partners to write and discuss a definition for each word. Then have children preview the lesson to see whether their definitions are accurate.

Warm Up To activate prior knowledge, ask children how they prepare for a new school year every fall. Do they buy anything? Do they visit someone who provides them with an important service? Copy the chart below on the board and add children's responses.

Goods	Services
notebook raincoat	doctor barber

Lesson 1 Choosing Goods and Services

1 In the United States, people can make choices about earning, spending, and saving money. People can choose where to work and where to live. Many people choose to live near their jobs. 2

My mom and dad have jobs. They work hard to earn money. The money that people earn is called **income.** People use their 3 income to pay for different kinds of goods. **Goods** are things people make or grow. Look at the goods in the picture.

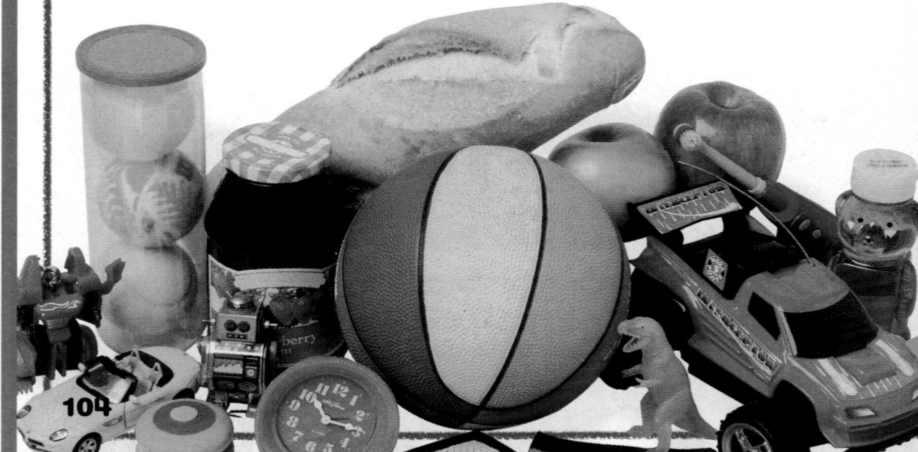

104

Practice and Extend

READING SKILL Predict

- Before children read p. 105, have them pause and close their texts while you read the first sentence on that page.
- Ask children to predict what Matt and his dad will do at the grocery store.
- Then have children reopen their books to read p. 105 to find out whether their predictions were correct.

WEB SITE Technology

You can look up vocabulary words online. Click on *Social Studies Library* and select the dictionary at **www.sfsocialstudies.com.**

Every Saturday, my dad and I go to the grocery store. We buy the food we need.

My dad also uses some of his income to buy services that workers provide. **Services** are jobs that people do to help others. Today (4) we will stop at the barber shop. What does the barber do to help my dad? (5)

105

2 Teach and Discuss

Page 104

Discuss the choices people make about earning, spending, and saving money. For example, people can earn money by working in a large company or in a small business they have in their home; people can spend money on a house or on braces for their teeth; people can save money in a bank.

(1) **How do some of the people in your neighborhood earn money?** Possible answers: They have small stores; they build new buildings; they work in offices. **Draw Conclusions**

(2) **Why do some people like to live near their job?** Possible answers: They save money by walking, riding bikes; they save time. **Make Inferences**

(3) **Why do you think money earned is called income? Look closely at the word for clues.** The money comes into the person's possession. **Draw Conclusions**

Page 105

(4) **What are some examples of service jobs? Tell what kind of service each job provides.** Possible answer: A dentist takes care of your teeth **Draw Conclusions**

(5) **When the barber is finished helping Matt's dad, what do you predict Matt's dad will do before leaving the barbershop?** Possible answer: He will pay the barber for his services. **Predict**

SOCIAL STUDIES STRAND Citizenship

Volunteering

- Tell children that some service jobs are volunteer jobs—the workers are not paid for the work they do. Ask children to identify some of the volunteer workers in their neighborhood or community (readers for the blind, people who collect food and clothes for the needy).
- Make the connection between volunteering and being a responsible citizen.
- Have children think about different ways in which they could volunteer in their neighborhood.
- Ask children what would happen if no one in a neighborhood volunteered.

Page 106

Ask children to review the definitions of *needs* and *wants*. Explain that there are three basic needs: food, clothing, and shelter. Point out that people work for and exchange money for such needs as food, clothing, and shelter.

6 What are some goods that people might want, but do not need to survive? Children's answers should reflect their understanding of the difference between needs and wants. **Express Ideas**

Ongoing Assessment

If... children do not understand the difference between needs and wants,	**then...** explain that food and water, clothes, and a place to live are needs.

Test Talk

Locate Key Words in the Question

Have children turn the question into a statement. Children should use the key words in a sentence that begins "I need to find out. . . ."

7 Why is having a budget important for a family? Possible answer: It helps a family plan how to spend their income. Families should make sure they have enough money to pay for things they need before they purchase things they want. **Draw Conclusions**

SOCIAL STUDIES STRAND
Economics

Have children gather information from oral sources such as conversations with family members about services they might receive in one day. Ask volunteers to share their information.

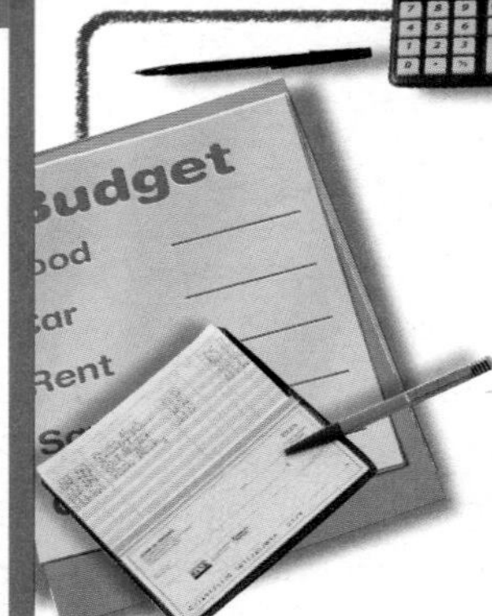

Each month, my parents make a budget, a plan for spending and saving their money. First they put aside money to pay for our needs. Needs are things we must have to live.

My family spends some income on wants. Wants are goods and services that people would like to have. We do not need these goods and services to live. 6 7

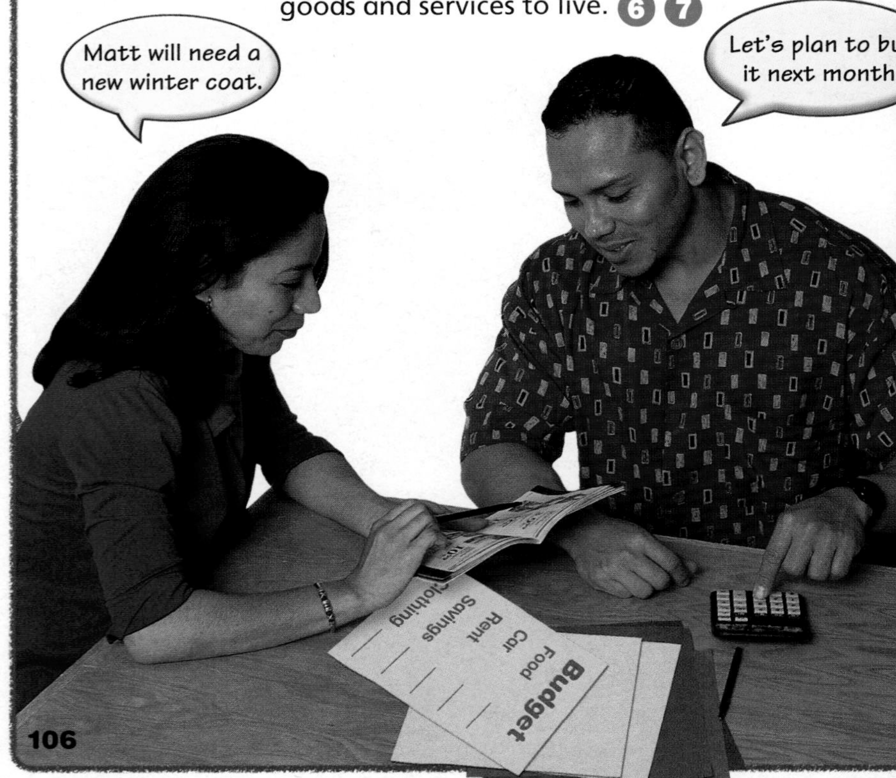

106

Practice and Extend

FYI SOCIAL STUDIES Background

Possible Misconceptions

- Children may assume that income is used only to buy goods—tangible things that can be carried away.
- Help them think of some services they receive but may not think about, such as services offered by the counter clerks at a fast food restaurant, the librarian in the neighborhood library, and the crossing guard.
- Note that the money they or their families pay for a quick meal helps to pay the counter clerks. The taxes their families pay help to buy the services of the librarian and the crossing guard near their school.

My family makes choices about what we can buy. After planning for the things we need, my parents figure out how much money is left. 8

Then we talk about things we want. We don't have enough money to buy all the things we want. We decide what we want the 9 most. We are going to get a cat!

My family sets aside money to take care of a cat. Then we pick out a cat at the animal shelter. I name her Tabby.

What did you learn?

1. How can jobs help people purchase goods and services?
2. Explain choices people can make about earning, spending, and saving money.
3. Suppose a person wants to earn income. This person likes working outdoors and enjoys taking care of animals. **Predict** where this person might live and work.

107

SOCIAL STUDIES STRAND
Economics

The Flow of Money

Display the flowchart. Use the graphic to illustrate the flow of money.

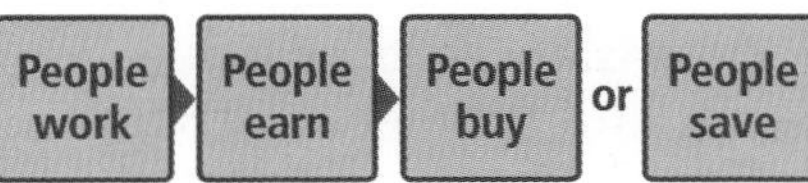

Ask volunteers to use the chart to talk about where people in their community work and the goods and services those people buy with the money they earn.

You may wish to have children copy the chart to use as a study/review tool.

Workbook, p. 26

Choosing Goods and Services

Circle the correct answers.

What are jobs that people do to help others?
goods needs (services)

What are things that people make or grow?
income (goods) wants

What do we call the money that people earn?
savings budget (income)

Show what you can do with money.
Write *earn*, *spend*, or *save* under each picture.

save earn spend

Also on Teacher Resources CD-ROM.

Page 107

8 **What does Matt's family do before they go out to buy things they want?** They figure out how much money they have left to spend. They talk about what they want most. **Sequence**

9 **Why can't people buy everything they need and want?** Possible answer: Most people don't earn enough money to buy everything they need and want. **Make Inferences**

3 Close and Assess

Conclude by saying that people have choices about where they will work and live, how they will spend their money, and if they will save money.

Check children's understanding of lesson concepts with the end-of-lesson questions.

✓ What did you learn?

1. Jobs provide people with income that they can use to buy goods and services.
2. People can often make choices about where they want to work and live. They can choose what goods and services to spend their money on. They can decide whether they want to save any money or to spend all of it on things they need to live and other things they want.
3. Children may predict that a person would choose a job such as dog walker or zookeeper that can be done in the city or the suburbs. They may also suggest the job of farmer that is done in rural areas.

Make a Decision

Objectives

- Use a decision-making process.
- Explain that scarcity requires people to make choices.

1 Introduce and Motivate

Preview Read aloud the title of the feature. Have children look at the series of photographs and tell who will make a decision. Ask children to tell how many steps are involved in the decision-making process.

Warm Up To activate prior knowledge, ask children to identify some decisions they make every day. Offer prompts as needed: *Do you decide what clothes you will wear? Do you decide what you will do on Saturday?*

Encourage children to talk about some of the reasons or factors they use to make their decisions.

2 Teach and Discuss

Pages 108–109

Make the point that although this decision-making scenario is about spending money, people make different kinds of decisions all the time, such as what to eat for dinner, which doctor to see, how to spend daily leisure time.

Have children talk about each photo. Read the speech bubbles and captions with them.

1 Why did Matt's class make and sell flower pots? They wanted to get money to buy something for the class. **Cause and Effect**

Thinking Skills

Make a Decision

Matt's class painted flower pots and sold them at the craft fair. They made money to buy something for the class. These are the steps they followed when deciding what
1 to buy.

What should we buy?

Step 1 Tell what decision you need to make.

2

Step 2 Gather information.

3

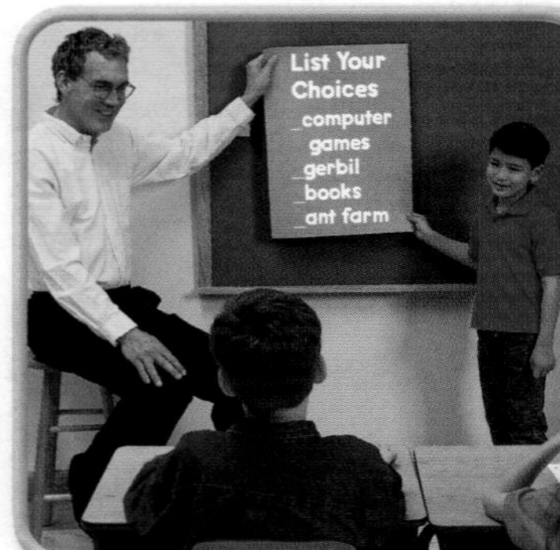

Step 3 List your choices.

Practice and Extend

SOCIAL STUDIES STRAND
Economics

Scarcity

- Introduce the term *scarcity*. Write the word on the board and define it as "not having enough of something." Say that if there is a scarcity of a new and popular toy, there isn't enough for everyone to buy one. Ask children what it means if there is a scarcity of books in the library.
- Tell children that when there is not enough of something, people may have to give up something else to get what they want or need. For example, if there is a scarcity of space in someone's backpack, he or she may have to give up taking along an extra toy on a trip.
- Explain that when there is a scarcity of money, people need to make decisions about what they will buy. They decide how much to spend on the different things they need.

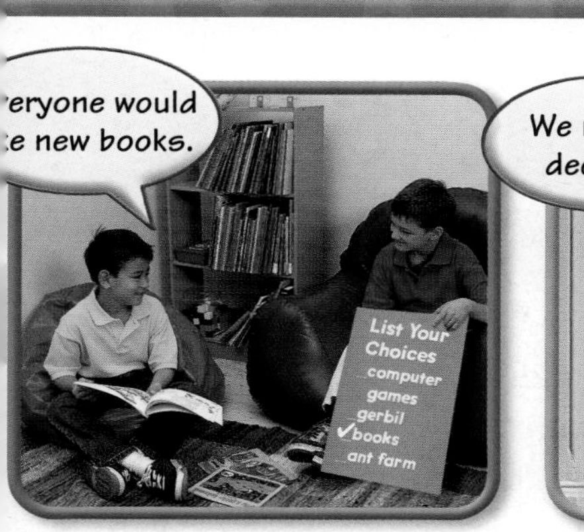

We made a decision.

Step 4 Tell what might happen with each choice.

Step 5 Make a decision.

Matt's class decided to buy books for ❹ the class library. They made a list of the books they want. Now they will buy the books with the money they earned.

What did you learn?

1. What did Matt's class need to decide?
2. Look at the list of choices. What did Matt's class have to give up when they made their decision to buy books?
3. **On Your Own** If you were in Matt's class, what choice would you make? Tell or write about why you think this is the best choice.

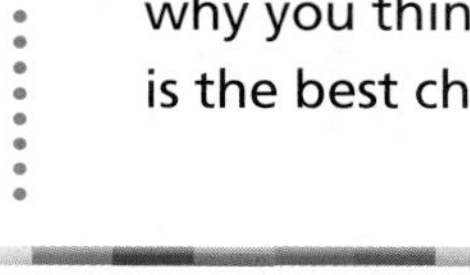

109

❷ **Who might help the children gather information?** Their teacher **What information do you think he might share with them?** How much money they have to spend; some things that may be nice to have in the classroom **Make Inferences** ↻ **Predict**

❸ **How many choices of things to buy do the children have?** Four **Is it important for them to know how much each thing on the list costs? Why?** Yes; then they can make a good decision. **Interpret Graphics/Evaluate**

❹ **What did the class do before going to buy their books?** They made a list of books they wanted. **Sequence**

3 Close and Assess

What did you learn?

1. Matt's class needed to decide how to spend the money they raised.
2. They gave up the computer games, gerbil, and ant farm.
3. **On Your Own** Possible answer: I would choose the ant farm. It is fun to watch ants make tunnels and move around. It would be like having pets but without having to take a lot of care of them.

CURRICULUM CONNECTION Math

Is the Price Right?

- Tell children Matt's class sold each flower pot for $2.00. They sold 11 pots.
- Have children create 11 sets of 2 (dollars). They can use dollar signs to represent the money in each set. Have children count to find how much the class made altogether.
- Say that three new storybooks cost $20.00. Can they afford to buy them? Can they afford a gerbil and a cage that cost $25.00?

Workbook, p. 27

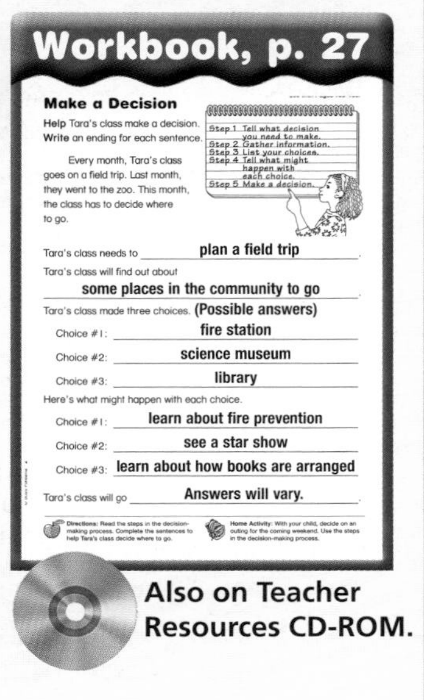

Make a Decision

Help Tara's class make a decision. Write an ending for each sentence.

Step 1 Tell what decision you need to make.
Step 2 Gather information.
Step 3 List your choices.
Step 4 Tell what might happen with each choice.
Step 5 Make a decision.

Every month, Tara's class goes on a field trip. Last month, they went to the zoo. This month, the class has to decide where to go.

Tara's class needs to plan a field trip

Tara's class will find out about some places in the community to go

Tara's class made three choices. (Possible answers)

Choice #1: fire station

Choice #2: science museum

Choice #3: library

Here's what might happen with each choice.

Choice #1: learn about fire prevention

Choice #2: see a star show

Choice #3: learn about how books are arranged

Tara's class will go Answers will vary.

Also on Teacher Resources CD-ROM.

CITIZEN HEROES

Phoenix Kids Pride Program

Objective

- Identify ordinary people who exemplify good citizenship.

1 Introduce and Motivate

Preview Read the title of the feature. Point to the word *Pride*. Ask children what it means to be proud of someone or something. Draw attention to the starred word in the logo on p. 111. Tell children they will read about some children who respect others and have pride in themselves and their school.

Warm Up To activate prior knowledge, ask children how they show respect for people. Have them identify some people they show respect for in school, at home, and in their neighborhood.

2 Teach and Discuss

Pages 110–111

Read the pages with children. Briefly talk with children about times they may have seen disagreements at the playground or other places in the neighborhood.

1 **Why did Celso want to have the "respect" program in his school?** Possible answer: He wanted school to be a safer place. **Cause and Effect**

2 **What is one way to show respect for others?** Possible answers: Speak kindly to others; don't shout or call names; don't interrupt when people speak. **Express Ideas**

CITIZEN HEROES

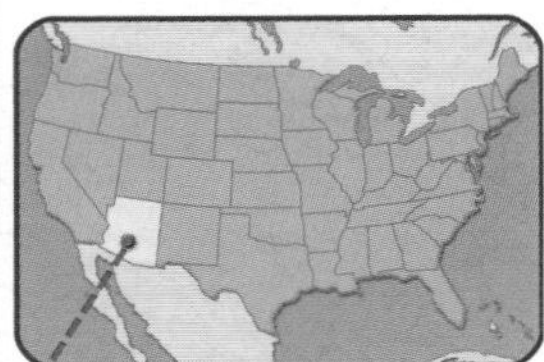

The Phoenix Kids Pride program is found in Phoenix, Arizona.

Phoenix Kids Pride Program

Meet some children from Phoenix, Arizona. They won a Phoenix Kids Pride Award for helping others in their community and school.

1 Celso and some of his classmates wanted their school to be a safe place. They talked about how important it is for people to respect each other. 2

110

Practice and Extend

FYI SOCIAL STUDIES **Background**

About Phoenix Kids Pride Awards

Share the following with children:

- Each year young people in the Phoenix area are chosen to receive a Phoenix Kids Pride Award for the volunteer work they've performed.
- Winners are honored at an awards ceremony; some winners receive $500 prizes.
- The 2000 winners included Anthony, age 10, who led a coat drive; and Elizabeth, age 7, who, along with her Brownie troop, raised money for the Phoenix Crisis Nursery Angel project.

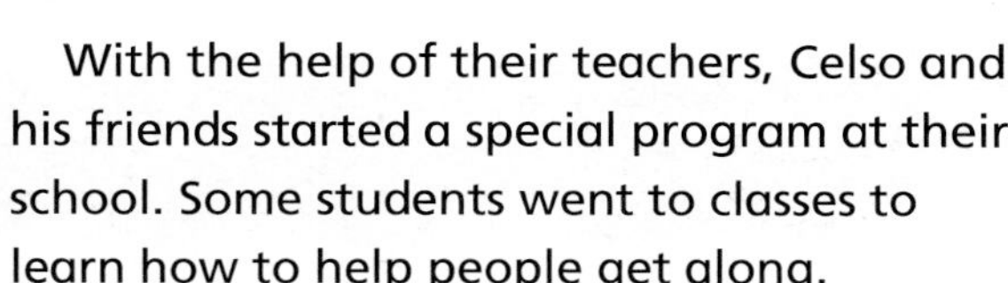

BUILDING CITIZENSHIP
Caring
Respect
Responsibility
Fairness
Honesty
Courage

With the help of their teachers, Celso and his friends started a special program at their school. Some students went to classes to learn how to help people get along.

Now when students have arguments in the school or on the playground, they spend time with the students who have been trained to help people get along. These students teach other students how to show more respect. They teach them how to settle arguments peacefully.

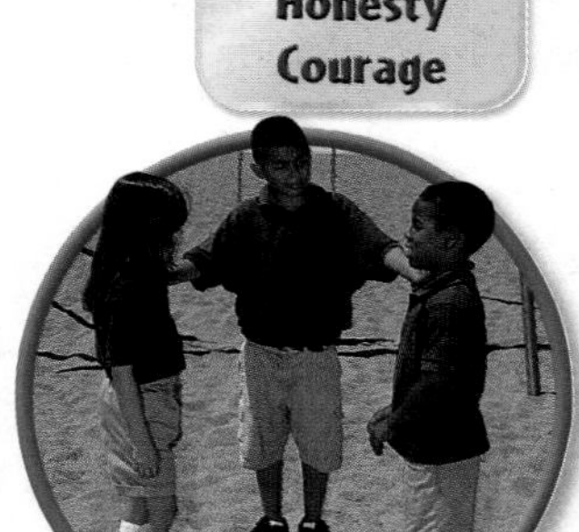

Good citizens practice respect for others.

Since Celso and his friends started their program, there have been fewer fights and arguments in the school. Students are learning to show respect for each other even when they disagree. 3 4

Respect in Action

How do these students show that they respect other people? How can you show that you respect the rights of others?

111

CURRICULUM CONNECTION
Writing

Mottoes

- Have children create mottoes that might be appropriate for a school or class practicing respect and peaceful conflict resolution.
- Model writing some mottoes on the board. For example: *Stop! Think! Talk it over!; Shake hands, not fists!; Don't shout. Don't pout. Chill out!*
- Children may enjoy working with partners.
- Agree to adopt one or more of the mottoes for your class.

3 **What is the effect of Celso's special program at his school?** Students are showing more respect for one another and are resolving problems peacefully. **Cause and Effect**

4 **Do you think all schools should have similar programs for their students? Why?** Possible answer: Yes; it is easier to do your work and learn in a school where people get along. **Express Ideas**

3 Close and Assess

Respect in Action

Children should respond similarly: The students at Celso's school settle arguments peacefully. Answers to the second question will vary but may include: talk things over instead of fighting, treat others as you would like to be treated.

Use with pages 104–111

Lesson 1 Wrap-Up

MEETING INDIVIDUAL NEEDS

Leveled Practice

What Would You Buy?

Have children write the word *goods* and its definition at the top of a piece of poster paper.

Easy Have children cut out pictures of different goods from magazines and newspapers. Encourage them to collect at least ten pictures. **Reteach**

On-Level Have children separate their pictures into two piles: needs and wants. Then have them make a two-column chart on poster paper, heading the columns *Needs* and *Wants*. Tell children to paste their pictures in the appropriate columns. **Extend**

Challenge Tell children to imagine that they are going on a trip and that they can only take along five of the things pictured on their posters. Have them circle their choices. Ask volunteers to explain how they made their decisions of what to take on their trip. **Enrich**

Hands-on Activities

CURRICULUM CONNECTION

Art

Word Pictures

Objective Demonstrate an understanding of the lesson vocabulary through art.

Resources Vocabulary Cards: **income, goods, services**

Materials drawing paper, crayons, pencils

Learning Style Visual/Kinesthetic

Individual

Time 20 minutes

1. Have children choose one of the words. Have them draw a picture to illustrate the word. On the back of the picture, ask them to write the word.

2. Collect and display the pictures. Have children say what they think each one illustrates. Turn over the pictures to reveal the word to show if children were correct or not.

3. Remind children to include the new words in their "My Word Book" glossaries.

CURRICULUM CONNECTION

Writing

Make a Jobs Booklet

Objective Identify and understand different jobs.

Materials construction paper, crayons, markers

Learning Style Linguistic/ Kinesthetic

Partners

Time 20–30 minutes

1. Have partners collaborate to illustrate a job or work situation.

2. Have children write sentences under their pictures to describe their worker's duties.

3. Collect the pages into a "Jobs Booklet." Set aside class time for children to review the different ways in which some day they might earn an income.

SOCIAL STUDIES STRAND

Citizenship

Being a Good Citizen

Objective Identify ways of being a good citizen in different settings.

Materials construction paper, crayons, markers

Learning Style Visual/Kinesthetic

Group

Time 20–30 minutes

1. Assign children to small groups. Have group members create a three-column chart on a sheet of paper. Children should label the chart *Being a Good Citizen*. Tell them to label the columns *At School, At Home, In the Community.*

2. Have children list three ways in which they can demonstrate good citizenship in each of the three places.

Lesson 2 Overview

Services in Our Community **pages 112–115**	Children will learn the meaning of the word *tax*. They will also learn how taxes are used to pay for services provided to the community.	 Time 20–30 minutes Resources • Workbook, p. 28 • Transparency 13 • Vocabulary Card tax • Every Student Learns Guide, pp. 46–49
Florence Nightingale **pages 116–117**	Children will learn about the life and work of Florence Nightingale.	 Time 15–20 minutes
Fire Engine **pages 118–119**	Children will learn about fire engines by looking at and reading a diagram.	 Time 15–20 minutes

Build Background

Activity

Who Will Help?

 **Time** 15–20 minutes

- Have children make up "problem" scenarios that can be solved by the services of a community worker.
- Model at least two scenarios. Say: *My cat is sick and needs someone to help it get better. Who will help me? I need someone to deliver a letter I wrote to my grandma in the next town. Who will help me?*
- Encourage as many children as possible to create scenarios that the class can match workers in the community with.

If time is short, help children brainstorm a list of community workers. Have them give a quick description of what each worker does.

I need someone to deliver a letter I wrote to my grandma in the next town. Who will help me?

Read Aloud

Helpers

by Christopher Erickson

Teachers teach,
And firefighters answer the alarm.
Police protect us
From danger and harm.

Street cleaners clean,
And librarians lend books to read.
In community parks,
The gardeners weed.

The mayor runs our town with flair.
All these workers
Do their work with care!

Services in Our Community

Objectives

- Identify people who provide services to our community.
- Identify some governmental services in the community.

Vocabulary

tax money that is collected by a government (p. 113)

QUICK Teaching Plan

If time is short, have children look at the pictures in the lesson and identify each of the service workers shown.

- Have children choose one of the pictured workers in the lesson who they think is especially important to the community. Children should say why they admire that worker.

1 Introduce and Motivate

Preview Tell children they will talk about two topics in this lesson. Help them read the titles on pages 112 and 114 to identify the topics. Then have children locate the vocabulary word **tax** on page 113. Display the matching Vocabulary Card. Then have children read aloud the word's definition.

Warm Up To activate prior knowledge, have children listen as you name the following: doctor, plumber, barber, teacher, bus driver, librarian. Have children tell what all the people named have in common. Help children articulate that they are all workers in a community.

Services in Our Community

Our community depends on many people to provide us with important services. Some people teach us, some people care for us, and some people keep us safe. 1 2

We are learning about the work people do in our community.

112

Practice and Extend

READING SKILL
Compare and Contrast

- In this lesson, children will learn about some of the people who provide services for the community.
- After children read pp. 112–115, give them a copy of Transparency 3, a Venn diagram. Have them choose two different types of service workers and explain how their jobs are alike and how they are different.

WEB SITE
Technology

You can look up vocabulary words online. Click on *Social Studies Library* and select the dictionary at **www.sfsocialstudies.com.**

Money that is collected by a government is a **tax.** Taxes help pay for building and repairing schools and other community buildings. Tax money is used to buy fire trucks and police cars too. ③ ④

Taxes also help pay many of the people who work in our community. We are making a class bulletin board about some of these workers. You can see our bulletin board on the next page. ⑤

SOCIAL STUDIES STRAND History

Paying Taxes in the Past

Tell children that people did not always pay taxes with money.

- Long ago in European countries, people paid their taxes "in kind," that is, a farmer who grew grain would pay part of his harvest—the crops he picked—to the king.
- In the United States in the late 1800s, people who did not have cash to pay taxes paid what they owed by working for the government. For example, they built roads or bridges.

Ask children to use the information above to tell if they think it was easier or harder to collect taxes in the past.

2 Teach and Discuss

Page 112

After children respond to the second question, discuss *specialization*. Note that it is the action of becoming a specialist, or someone who has trained or studied to be very knowledgeable about a job. Say, for example, that veterinarians and airline pilots have jobs that require special training and skills.

① **Are teachers the only workers in our school? Who are some other workers who provide services in our school?** Possible answers: No; principal, lunchroom workers, librarian, custodian, secretary, nurse **Draw Conclusions**

② **Why do people choose to do different kinds of work in the community?** Possible answers: Different people have different interests and abilities. People have gone to school to learn special skills that help them on the job. **Make Inferences**

Page 113

Have children describe what they see in the photo.

③ **Is tax money useful to the community? in what ways?** Yes; tax money pays some community workers and for community building repairs. **Main Idea and Details**

④ **Who pays taxes?** People in the community **Make Inferences**

SOCIAL STUDIES STRAND Citizenship

⑤ **Why is paying taxes an important part of being a good citizen?** Possible answer: By paying taxes, citizens are making sure there are services to keep everyone in the community safe and well. **Make Inferences**

Lesson 2 continued

Page 114

Have children identify the workers pictured on the class bulletin board.

6 The mayor is the chief community leader. What is something a mayor might do? Possible answer: He or she would help decide how to use tax money. **Draw Conclusions**

7 Why do you think many service workers wear a special uniform? Possible answer: So people can identify them easily **Make Inferences**

8 Why do you think most nurses chose that job? Possible answers: They like to work with people. They like to help people get better. They want to learn more about medicines and treatments. **Generalize**

9 If you could be a community service worker, which would you be? Why? Accept all reasonable answers. Encourage children to use complete sentences. **Express Ideas**

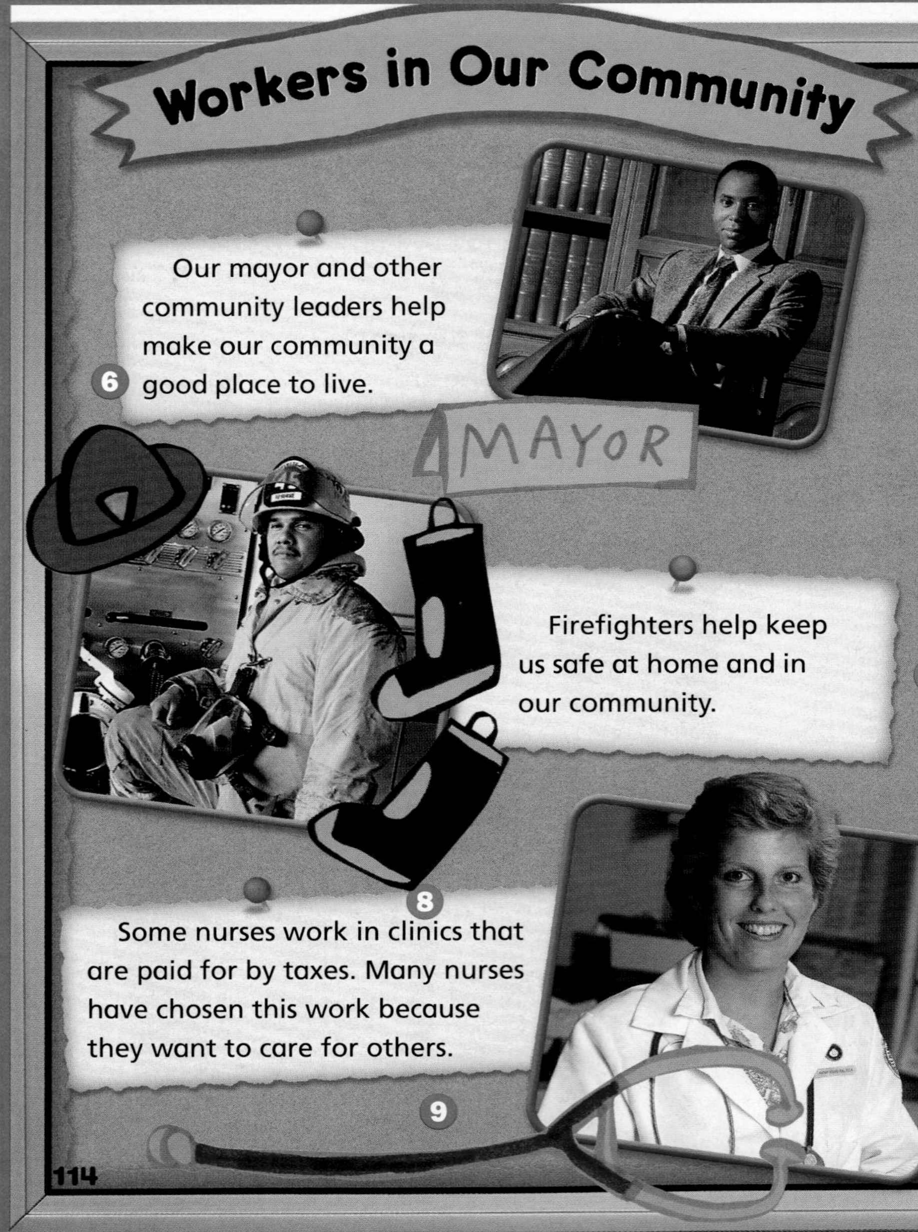

Practice and Extend

ESL ACCESS CONTENT ESL Support

Matching Game Ahead of time, cut out and paste on index cards magazine pictures of the following: thermometer, fire hose, police badge, book.

Beginning From the cards, have children select one and match the object with one of the workers shown on the bulletin board. When the worker is pointed out, ask children if they know the name of the job in their home language. Then have them say the word in English.

Intermediate Have children make oral sentences that link the picture card to the worker, for example: *A nurse uses a thermometer.*

Advanced Children write a sentence that identifies the function of the picture card object: *A firefighter uses a hose to spray water on a fire.*

For additional ESL support, use Every Student Learns Guide, pp. 46–49.

Police officers remind people of important laws that help us live together. 10

Teachers help us learn. Most teachers work in schools. 11

What did you learn?

1. Who are some of the people we depend on in our community? What services do they provide?
2. **Predict** what might happen to services and workers in our community if people did not pay their taxes.
3. **Think and Share** Write about a job you would like to do. Then draw a picture of a service you would provide or goods you would make for others.

115

Page 115

Point out to children the differences in how the community helpers on this page got their jobs: a mayor is elected by people in the community; teachers and lifeguards are hired to do a job.

10 **How are the responsibilities of a firefighter and a police officer alike?** Possible answer: Both firefighters and police officers protect people from harm; both rescue people from dangerous situations; both protect property. **Compare and Contrast**

11 **What do you and your family depend on your community for?** Answers may include: health care, protection, schools. **What do you depend on your family for?** Basic needs such as food, clothing, and shelter **Main Idea and Details**

3 Close and Assess

Have children share what they have learned by explaining the advantages of living in a community. **Recall and Retell**

✓ What did you learn?

1. Police officers, crossing guards, firefighters, and ambulance drivers are people we depend on in our community. They provide protection.
2. Possible answer: There would be no money to pay workers in the community who provide services.
3. **Think and Share** Children's drawings should show that they understand the meaning of goods and services.

CURRICULUM CONNECTION Literature

More About Community Workers

Children may enjoy reading one or more of these books.

- ***Community Helpers from A to Z,*** by Bobbie Kalman, Niki Walker (Crabtree Pub., ISBN 0-865-05404-5, 1997)
- ***School Principals,*** by Tracey Boraas (Bridgestone Books, ISBN 0-736-80074-3, 1999)
- ***We Need Mail Carriers,*** by Lola M. Schaefer (Pebble Books, ISBN 0-736-80392-0,1999)

Workbook, p. 28

Services in Our Community

Write what each worker does.

Nurses help care for people who are sick.

Police officers make sure people obey laws.

Firefighters help keep people safe from fires.

School teachers help children learn.

Draw a worker who serves your community. **Drawings will vary.**

Also on Teacher Resources CD-ROM.

Florence Nightingale

Objective

- Identify historic figures who have exemplified good citizenship.

1 Introduce and Motivate

Preview Have children read aloud the title of the feature with you. Then have children look at the illustrations to learn as much as they can about Florence Nightingale. Note that Florence Nightingale took care of soldiers. Have children tell why nurses would be particularly important during a war or when many, many people in a community are sick or injured.

Warm Up To activate prior knowledge, have children discuss what nurses do on the job. Ask if they think the duties of a nurse are the same today as they were a hundred years ago.

Practice and Extend

SOCIAL STUDIES Background

Florence Nightingale

- At a young age, Florence Nightingale became interested in becoming a nurse.
- Despite the disapproval of her family, Nightingale went on to receive nursing training in Germany.
- Soon after her training, she was sent to Turkey to oversee nurses in local military hospitals. She took 38 nurses with her. In the beginning, the doctors did not want the nurses there.
- In 1860, the year she opened her nursing school, Nightingale published *Notes on Nursing*. The book has been translated into 11 languages and is still available today.

WEB SITE Technology

You may help children find out more about Florence Nightingale by clicking on *Meet the People* at **www.sfsocialstudies.com.**

Long ago, Florence Nightingale was a leader of nurses. She was in charge of caring for army soldiers during a war. **2** When she arrived at the army hospital, she found it too crowded. The soldiers' clothing was dirty. There were not enough beds. **3**

Florence Nightingale was born in Florence, Italy. **1**

Florence Nightingale was determined to give the soldiers the best care possible. She bought supplies. She worked day and night at the army hospital to care for the soldiers.

After the war, Florence Nightingale started the world's first school of nursing. She wanted nurses to be educated and trained properly.

Florence Nightingale wrote the first textbook for nurses. Florence Nightingale is remembered as the person who trained and **4** encouraged people to be nurses.

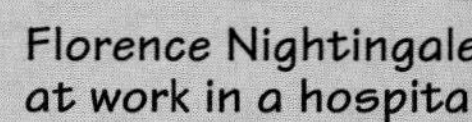

Florence Nightingale at work in a hospital

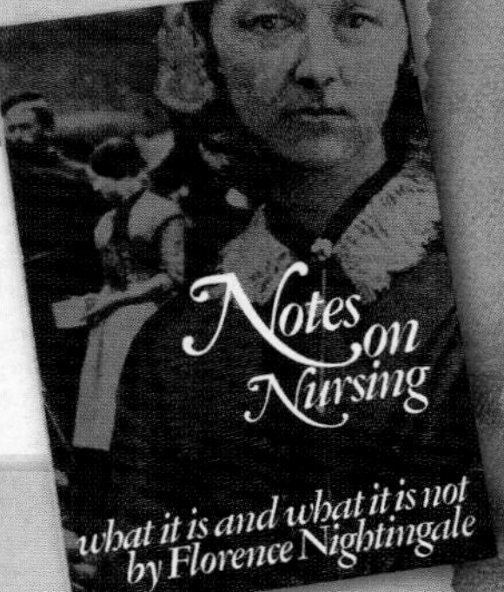

Think and Share

How did Florence Nightingale set an example of good citizenship?

For more information, go online to *Meet the People* at **www.sfsocialstudies.com.**

SOCIAL STUDIES STRAND

Citizenship

Doctors Without Borders

Doctors Without Borders is a medical relief organization. It was founded in 1971. Share the following and have children listen to identify characteristics of citizenship exemplified by the group.

- *Doctors Without Borders* is a group of doctors who travel to countries all over the world that need help. They volunteer their time and skills.
- The doctors treat people with diseases or those who have been injured in wars.
- They work in more than 80 countries in the world and they are often in danger themselves.

Help children recall what a border is. Ask if they think this group's name is a good one based on the work they do.

2 Teach and Discuss

Read the biography as children follow along.

GEOGRAPHY

Location

1 **Where was Florence Nightingale born?** (Show a world map.) Florence, Italy **Which continent is Italy on?** Europe **Interpret Maps**

2 **Do you think Florence Nightingale was brave?** Possible answer: Yes; she went to another country to help others. She was working during a war. She could have been injured herself. **Make Inferences**

3 **What problems did Florence Nightingale have to solve when she arrived at the hospital?** Overcrowding, dirty clothing, not enough beds **Recall and Retell**

4 **How did Florence Nightingale contribute to the nursing profession?** She opened a school and wrote a book to train other nurses. **Draw Conclusions**

3 Close and Assess

Think and Share

Florence Nightingale provided a service to others by caring for sick and injured army soldiers during a war. She also trained other nurses.

Fire Engine

Objective

- Obtain information from a variety of visual sources, such as diagrams.

1 Introduce and Motivate

Preview Have children look at the illustration as you read the first sentence. Have children discuss why fire engines are usually bright red or another very bright color.

Warm Up To activate prior knowledge, have children talk about some of the skills a person needs to become a firefighter. Ask: *Why are firefighters important to have in a community?*

2 Teach and Discuss

Help children read the labels. Explain unfamiliar terms as needed. Tell children that firefighters who drive fire trucks must be specially trained. Not every firefighter can drive a fire truck.

1 What is the ladder used for? Possible answer: Firefighters use the ladder to reach people trapped on high floors of buildings. They use the ladder to reach roofs and other high places where there is fire. **Make Inferences**

COMMUNITY SERVICES

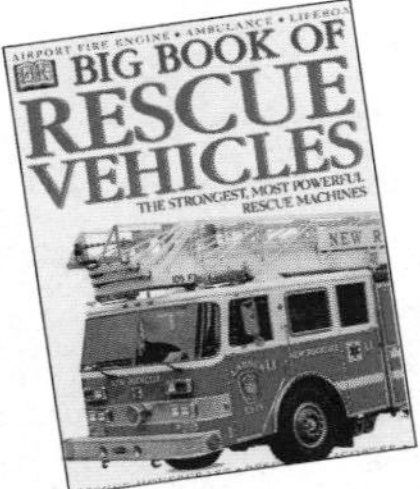

Fire Engine

Everyone knows the sound of a fire engine's siren. It warns drivers to move out of the way. There may be a fire, or somebody may be stuck in a tree. Why else might a fire engine be in a hurry?

118

Practice and Extend

SOCIAL STUDIES STRAND
Citizenship

To the Rescue!

- Remind children that firefighters are not the only people who respond to the needs of others who are in danger or who face disaster. Help children identify other community "rescuers"—police, ambulance teams, doctors, nurses, members of volunteer organizations, counselors, and neighbors on the street.
- Encourage children to talk about times they know of when people such as those mentioned came to the rescue of others. Some children may want to discuss the way firefighters and other rescue workers helped people in response to the tragic events of September 11, 2001.
- For activities to help children understand feelings of fear and loss, see pp. TR1–TR2 of this Teacher's Edition.

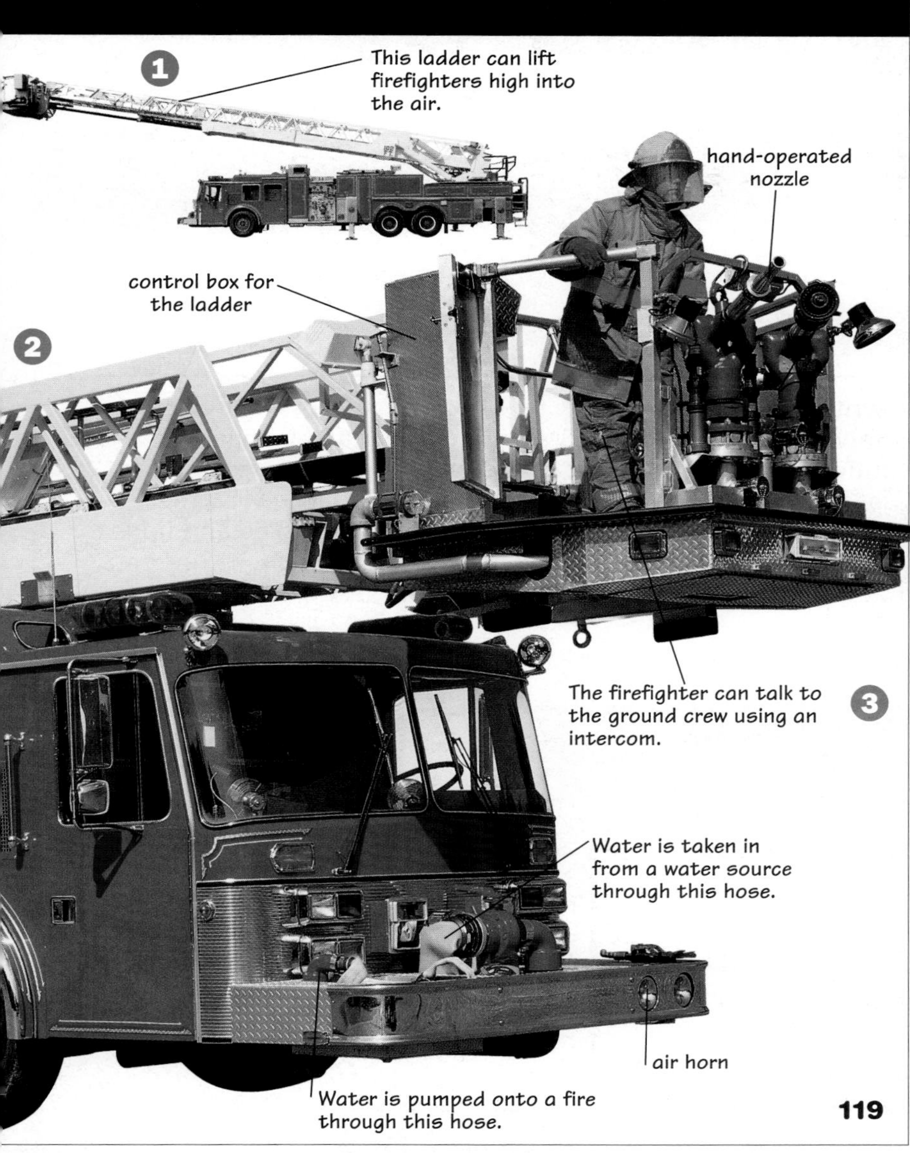

Use Information from Graphics

Tell children to use details from the illustration to support their answer.

2 How is a fire truck different from other trucks? Possible answer: It has special equipment to help put out fires. **Compare and Contrast**

3 Why do firefighters need to have a way to communicate with each other? Possible answers: They need to report what is happening. They may need help from other firefighters. Other firefighters need to know if there is danger before they move into a building. **Make Inferences**

3 Close and Assess

- Have children tell the purpose of a fire truck.
- Ask children to name some of the most important features of a fire truck.
- Have children tell why it is important that fire trucks be kept in good repair.

CURRICULUM CONNECTION
Art

Safety Posters

- Discuss with children basic fire safety rules such as: Leave the building immediately if there is fire; notify the fire department and those in the area; crawl in smoky conditions; don't open a door that is hot to the touch; don't run if clothing catches fire; don't go back into the building for any reason.
- Discuss the *Stop, Drop, and Roll* strategy with children.
- Have children create posters that highlight safety rules you have discussed.
- Talk about and display the posters.

Use with pages 112–119

Lesson 2 Wrap-Up

MEETING INDIVIDUAL NEEDS
Leveled Practice

Interviews
Children choose a service worker they want to find out more about by writing interview questions.

Easy Have children write one interview question they would like to ask a service worker. **Reteach**

On-Level Children write three or four questions for an interview. Questions can be about the duties performed, how the worker uses tools to perform his or her job, who pays the worker, and the challenges the worker faces every day. **Extend**

Challenge Have pairs of children take turns interviewing and being interviewed, using their questions. Encourage children to preview the questions they will be asked and find answers as needed. **Enrich**

Hands-on Activities

CURRICULUM CONNECTION
Reading

Tax Time

Objective Demonstrate understanding of the new vocabulary word.

Resources Vocabulary Card: **tax**

Materials paper, pencils, markers

Learning Style Kinesthetic/ Verbal

Individual

Time 10–15 minutes

1. Display the Vocabulary Card **tax**. Review its meaning.

2. Have children write the word on a sheet of paper in a bright color. Suggest they draw dollar signs all around the word.

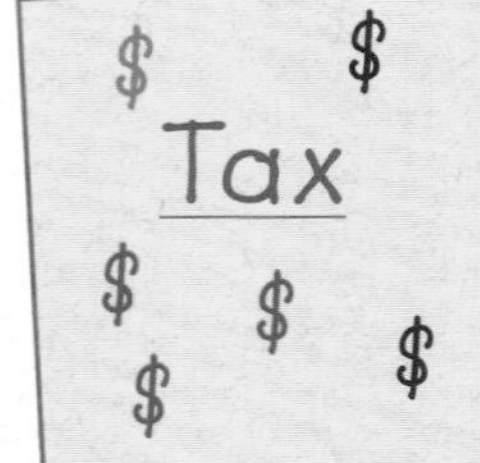

3. On the reverse side of the paper, children should write a sentence that tells how taxes benefit a community.

4. Collect the "taxes" from children. Read aloud their sentences to the group.

Remind children to add *tax* to their "My Word Book" glossaries.

CURRICULUM CONNECTION
Art

Hats, Hats, Hats

Objective Create paper hats that represent service jobs.

Materials construction paper strips, paste, drawing paper, scissors, crayons

Learning Style Kinesthetic/Visual

Individual

Time 20–30 minutes

1. Show children how to use the strips to make hat bands, taping the ends together. Tell them they will draw pictures of different service workers' hats on sheets of drawing paper and then cut them out. Children can color or draw on the shapes and paste them to the hat bands.

2. Have children wear their worker hats in a classroom parade of jobs!

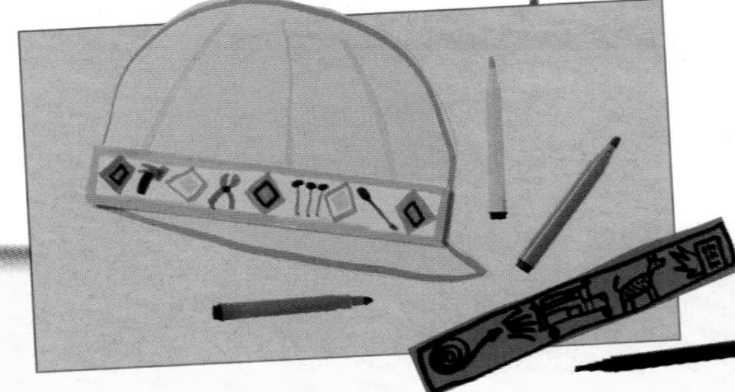

CURRICULUM CONNECTION
Music

Sing a Song

Objective Sing songs about service jobs people do in the community.

Learning Style Aural/Oral

Group

Time 10–15 minutes

1. Sing the first verse of "I've Been Working on the Railroad" for children. Explain that they will substitute different words to sing about different places service workers do their work.

2. Model making substitutions:

I've been working in the firehouse/
All the live-long day.
<repeat>
I've been working in the firehouse/
Just to earn a day's fair pay.

3. Have children suggest and then sing their own new lyrics.

Lesson 3 Overview

Goods from the Factory to You

pages 120–123

Children will learn the meaning of the word *factory*. They will trace the development of a product from a natural resource to a finished product.

Time 20–30 minutes

Resources

- Workbook, p. 29
- Vocabulary Card **factory**
- Every Student Learns Guide, pp. 50–53

Use a Compass Rose

pages 124–125

Children will learn how to use a compass rose to follow a route.

Time 15–20 minutes

Resource

- Workbook, p. 30

Build Background

Activity

From Farm to Table

Time 15–20 minutes

Tell children they will talk about the process of making an apple pie—from farm to table.

- Copy the chart without the answers. Have children supply the answers.
- Have children use the finished chart to draw pictures that show the steps in the process.

If time is short, omit the picture drawing part of the activity.

From Farm to Table

1. Farmers use (soil) and water to (grow) apples.
2. When ready, the apples are (picked)
3. The apples are (packed) in boxes.
4. Trucks take the apples to (stores).
5. A family (buys) some apples.
6. The family uses the apples to make (pies).

Read Aloud

Coming Soon!

by Meg Bloom

Plant. Water.
Watch them grow!

Pick. Pack.
Don't be late.
Get them on the truck.
Factory workers wait.

Machines hum.
And soon out come
Goods for you and me!

Goods from the Factory to You

Objectives

- Distinguish between producing and consuming.
- Identify ways people are both producers and consumers.
- Trace the development of a product from natural resources to finished product.

Vocabulary

factory A building where people produce goods (p. 120)

QUICK Teaching Plan

If time is short, have children look at the photos on pp. 121 and 122. Have them describe what is happening in each photo.

- Have children use the photos on pp. 121 and 122 to answer the questions at the end of p. 123.

1 Introduce and Motivate

Preview Read the title of the lesson with children. Have children look at the photos to tell what will be made at the factory. Ask them to name what plant is the starting point for the making of the T-shirts.

Warm Up To activate prior knowledge, display the Vocabulary Card **factory**. Read the word and ask whether children can tell what a *factory* is. Have them identify some different kinds of factories they know about. Ask them to say what kinds of things they would expect to see in a factory.

Goods from the Factory to You

Today, my class is going on a field trip to visit a T-shirt factory. A **factory** is a building where people produce goods. We will (1) learn how people make T-shirts for consumers (2) (3) who will buy them. I get to ask Ken, our tour guide at the factory, questions that my class wrote down.

120

Practice and Extend

READING SKILL
Put Steps in Order

Sequence

- Have children read p. 121.
- Then have them write the steps involved in getting cotton ready to go to the factory.
- Tell children to write a sentence to tell more about each of the four steps.

WEB SITE
Technology

You can look up vocabulary words online. Click on *Social Studies Library* and select the dictionary at **www.sfsocialstudies.com.**

Matt

What are T-shirts made of?

Ken

Good question! Many T-shirts are made of cotton. Cotton grows on plants. Farmers grow these plants in soil and then harvest the cotton. Long ago, cotton had to be picked by hand. Today, machines do most of the work. 4

Matt

What happens after the cotton is picked?

Ken

The cotton is taken from the farm to a cotton gin. A cotton gin is a big machine that separates the cotton from its seeds. Then the 5 seedless cotton is packed into bales. Some of these bales are sent 6 to our factory.

121

FYI SOCIAL STUDIES Background

Making Yarn

Use the following to supplement what children will read on p. 122.

- A factory where yarn and then cloth is made is called a mill.
- Carding machines, machines with huge rollers and wire teeth, take raw cotton fibers and separate and align them into a thin web. The web is condensed into a ropelike strand.
- Combing machines further clean and straighten the fibers.
- Spinning machines make the cotton rope thinner and twist and wind the cotton into yarn or thread.

2 Teach and Discuss

Page 120

Tell children that the people who make or "produce" the goods in a factory are known as "producers."

1 **What things in your home are made in factories?** Possible answers: Shoes, sofa, stove, toys **Apply Information**

2 **What is a consumer?** Someone who buys things **Make Inferences**

3 **Why would you expect to find consumers in stores?** Consumers buy things. Stores contain things to buy. **Draw Conclusions**

Page 121

4 **Is a farmer a producer, a consumer, or both? Explain.** A farmer is both a producer and a consumer. A farmer produces foods for others to buy at the store. He or she also buys seeds to grow and tools at other stores. **Draw Conclusions**

Ongoing Assessment

If... children do not understand the difference between producers and consumers,	**then...** remind children that a producer is someone who makes or grows something.

5 **What happens just before the cotton is put into bales?** The seeds are separated from the cotton. **Sequence**

6 **What do you predict will happen at the factory?** Possible answer: Workers there will do something to change the cotton into cloth. **Predict**

continued

Page 122

Discuss the differences between natural resources, human resources, and capital resources: Natural resources come from the Earth. Human resources are people who do work. Capital resources are the tools and machines people use. Have children say what resources are used to make T-shirts.

7 **What are three steps to turn cotton fibers into cloth? Tell the steps in order.** Card the fibers, spin the fibers, knit the fibers into cloth **Sequence**

8 **What happens to the yarn?** Workers dye, cut, and sew the cloth. **Sequence**

9 **Are the workers you see producing or consuming? How do you know?** They are producing. They are helping to make something. **If they were shopping for food, would they be producing or consuming?** Consuming; they would be buying something. **Draw Conclusions**

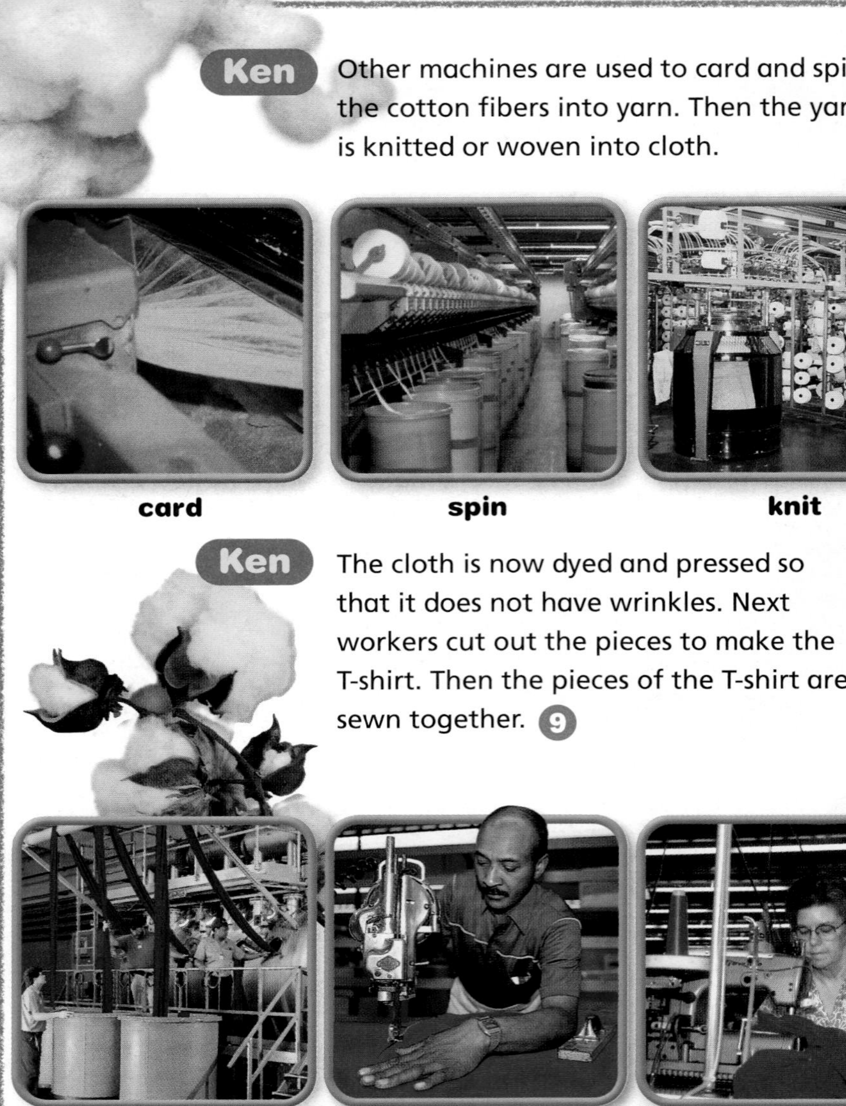

Practice and Extend

ACCESS CONTENT
ESL Support

Charting Cloth Making Mount on squares of oaktag: cotton ball, strand of yarn, cloth swatch. Label them. Tape them to the board. Draw arrows from sample to sample, indicating the sequence. Point to each sample. Describe the sequence of steps. Have children copy the sequence chart.

Beginning Have children respond to these questions by pointing: *Which comes first? What comes after yarn?* (point to yarn)

Intermediate Children use three oral sentences to tell partners about the process.

Advanced Children write three sentences to tell about the process shown.

For additional ESL support, use Every Student Learns Guide, pp. 50–53.

CURRICULUM CONNECTION
Art

Paper T-shirts

- Give children large sheets of white drawing paper. Model how to draw the outline of a T-shirt. Have children follow your model.
- As children draw, have them say what natural resource paper comes from.
- Have children cut out their T-shirts and color them. Ask: *What human resource is helping to make the T-shirts? What capital resources are you using?*

Matt

When can we buy the T-shirts?

Ken

Not yet! First, the T-shirts are placed into boxes. Next, they are loaded onto trucks. Then the trucks deliver them to stores all (10) around the country. Last, the T-shirts are unpacked in the stores. Now consumers like you can buy the T-shirt you like best.

At the end of the tour, we visited the T-shirt shop. I could buy a T-shirt because I had saved the money I earned from walking my neighbor's dog. (11) (12)

What did you learn?

1. What is a factory?
2. Tell how soil, people, and machines are needed to make a T-shirt.
3. **Think and Share** Matt chose to spend the money he earned on a T-shirt. Tell about other choices Matt could have made.

123

Page 123

Talk with children about how producers decide what to produce. Guide them to understand that producers think about people's wants and needs.

(10) **How are the T-shirts sent to stores?** By truck **What are some other ways goods can be sent to stores near and far?** By train, plane, ship **Make Inferences**

(11) **Did Matt produce goods or provide a service to earn his money?** He provided a service—dog walking. **Draw Conclusions**

(12) **Are you and your classmates mostly producers or consumers?** Consumers **Generalize**

3 Close and Assess

Have children retell in their own words the steps for producing T-shirts from cotton plants. **Main Idea and Details**

✓ What did you learn?

1. A factory is a building where people produce goods.

Test Talk

Use Information from the Text

2. Soil is needed to grow the cotton; people care for the cotton plants; people and machines produce cloth and then T-shirts.

   Have children look back at the text to find the right answer.

3. **Think and Share** Matt could have saved the money. He might have spent it on a book or a toy.

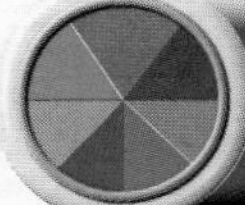

CURRICULUM CONNECTION
Literature

From Start to Finish—More to Read

Children may enjoy learning more about producing goods by reading one of the following:

The Tortilla Factory, by Gary Paulsen (Harcourt Brace, ISBN 0-152-92876-6, 1995)

From Wheat to Pasta, by Robert Egan (Children's Press, ISBN 0-516-20709-1, 1997)

From Tree to Paper, by Wendy Davis (Sundance Pub., ISBN 1-568-01494-5, 1995)

Workbook, p. 29

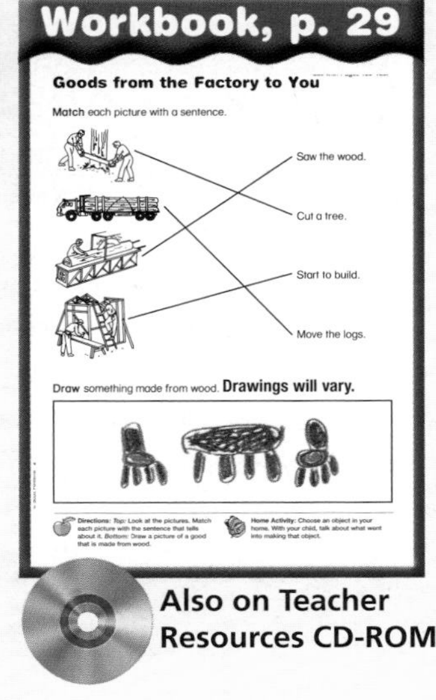
Goods from the Factory to You

Match each picture with a sentence.

Saw the wood.

Cut a tree.

Start to build.

Move the logs.

Draw something made from wood. Drawings will vary.

Also on Teacher Resources CD-ROM.

Use a Compass Rose

Objective

- Use a map to follow a route.

Vocabulary

compass rose Shows directions on a map (p. 124)

route A way to go from one place to another (p. 125)

1 Introduce and Motivate

Preview Read the title of the feature. Point out the compass rose on the map. Ask children what they think the letters *N, S, E, W* stand for. Then read aloud page 124 and have children point in their books to the term *compass rose*. Follow by asking a volunteer to find and read the definition of *route* on p. 125.

Warm Up To activate prior knowledge, ask children how maps are useful to people. Ask how knowing how to find the directions north, south, east, and west on a map can help someone read and follow a map.

Map and Globe Skills

Use a Compass Rose

Find the compass rose on the map. A **compass rose** shows directions on a map. The letters N, S, E, and W stand for north, south, east, and west.

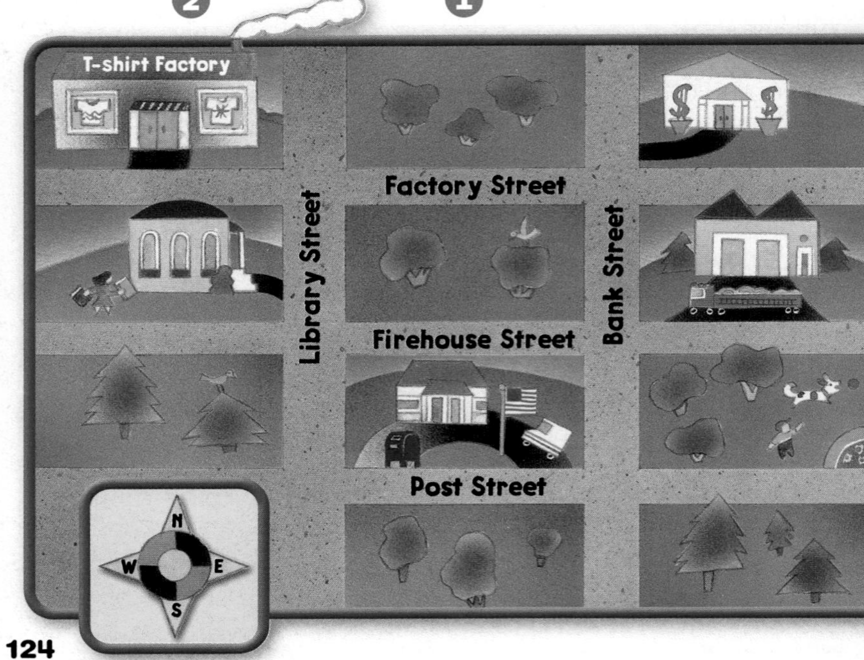

Practice and Extend

SOCIAL STUDIES STRAND
Geography

Where Is It?

- Display a map of the United States. If it doesn't include a compass rose, add one for children's reference.
- Name a direction (north, south) and have children take turns pointing out a state in that direction.
- Continue until all children have had an opportunity to point out a state.

One truck from the T-shirt factory went to the Village Store in Matt's community. The truck followed a route. A **route** is a way to go from one place to another. On the map, trace the truck's route.

- Point to the T-shirt factory.
- Go east on Factory Street.
- Go south on Library Street.
- Go east on Post Street.
- Stop at the Village Store. (3)

1. Is Factory Street north or south of Post Street?
2. Is Library Street east or west of Bank Street?
3. **On Your Own** Write down another route you could take from the T-shirt factory to the Village Store. Ask a classmate to trace your route.

125

2 Teach and Discuss

Pages 124–125

Have children make their own vocabulary cards for the words *compass rose* and *route*. Have them write the definition of each on the flip side of the card.

1. Look at the map with children. Work with them to identify the street names.
2. Use the map symbols and street names to have children locate specific buildings—bank, library, school, village store, factory.
3. Observe children as they trace the route outlined on p. 125 to be certain they understand the task. You may wish to have partners work together to follow the route.

3 Close and Assess

Try it!

1. Factory Street is north of Post Street.
2. Library Street is west of Bank Street.
3. **On Your Own** Possible answer: Travel east on Factory Street, then south on Bank Street, and then east on Post Street.

You may go online to learn more about maps. Click on the *Atlas* at **www.sfsocialstudies.com.**

Workbook, p. 30

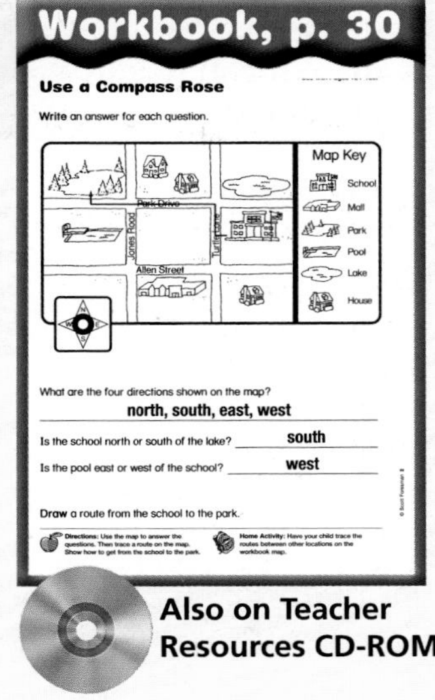

Use a Compass Rose

Write an answer for each question.

What are the four directions shown on the map? **north, south, east, west**

Is the school north or south of the lake? **south**

Is the pool east or west of the school? **west**

Draw a route from the school to the park.

Directions: Use the map to answer the questions. Then trace a route on the map. Show how to get from the school to the park.

Home Activity: Have your child trace the routes between other locations on the workbook map.

Also on Teacher Resources CD-ROM.

Use with pages 120–125

Lesson 3 Wrap-Up

MEETING INDIVIDUAL NEEDS

Leveled Practice

How-to-Do-Its
Children create how-to instructions for others to follow.

Easy Children draw pictures to show how to make or produce something. The product should be simple, requiring four or five steps. Steer children toward doable craft products, such as a paper flower, a paper-plate mask, or a folded paper fan. Each step should be drawn on a separate large index card. **Reteach**

On-Level Children write a sentence on the back of each card, explaining the step in the process. **Extend**

Challenge Children exchange sets of cards with partners. The partners should follow the how-to steps to make the product. Make materials available to children. **Enrich**

Hands-on Activities

CURRICULUM CONNECTION

Reading

What's Inside?

Objective Draw pictures to demonstrate the concept of factory.

Materials paper, crayons

Resources Vocabulary Card: **factory**

Learning Style Kinesthetic/Linguistic

Individual

 **Time** 10–15 minutes

1. Display the Vocabulary Card **factory**. Have children read it with you.

2. Distribute materials. Have children choose a type of factory—ice cream factory, doll factory, sailboat factory.

3. Have children draw the outline of a factory building. Inside the outline they should write what someone would see in that type of factory. Have them label the drawings appropriately.

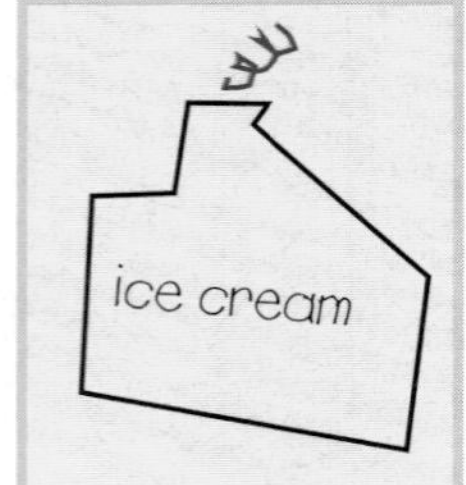

Remind children to add *factory* to their "My Word Book" glossaries.

SOCIAL STUDIES STRAND

Geography

Make a Map

Objective Create a map and write directions for following a route.

Materials drawing paper, pencils, crayons

Learning Style Kinesthetic/Visual

Partners

 **Time** 20–25 minutes

1. Partners make a map. It can show a completely imagined place. The map should show different kinds of buildings. It should include a compass rose.

2. Children should plan a route they want someone to follow. A surprise should await the person at the end of the route (an ice cream factory). Children should write clear directions for following the route, using cardinal directions on the compass rose.

3. Have pairs of children exchange maps and directions with other pairs. They should then trace the prescribed route to find the planned surprise!

Lesson 4 Overview

A Trip to the Bank pages 126–129	Children will learn about how people spend and save their money. They will also learn different ways people can pay for goods and services they buy.	Time 20–30 minutes Resources • Workbook, p. 31 • Transparency 2 • Every Student Learns Guide, pp. 54–57
Read a Pie Chart pages 130–131	Children will learn the meaning of *pie chart*. They will learn to read and make a pie chart.	Time 15–20 minutes Resource • Workbook, p. 32
Linda Alvarado pages 132–133	Children will learn about Linda Alvarado, a community leader and company president.	Time 15–20 minutes

Build Background

Activity

Make Your Own Bank

 **Time** 20–25 minutes

- Have children bring in plastic jars, cans without lids and with smooth rims, or lidded boxes to turn into banks. Have them paint or cover their containers with colorful paper.
- Help children make tops for jars and cans with pieces of cloth stretched across the tops and held with rubber bands. Then help children cut slits in the tops of all their containers.
- Tell children to take home their banks and start saving!

If time is short, help children define a bank as "a safe place to keep money." Encourage children who have banks at home to describe them.

Read Aloud

Money

by Christopher Erickson

Earn it.
Count it.
Spend it.
Lend it.
Save it.
Any way you like, use it.
BUT don't lose it!

A Trip to the Bank

Objective

- Explain the choices people can make about earning, spending, and saving money.

QUICK Teaching Plan

If time is short, have children look at the pictures on pp. 126 and 128. Help them understand that what they see are different ways to pay for goods and services.

- Have children draw a picture of a customer in a bank. They should write a sentence to caption the picture that says what the customer is doing.

1 Introduce and Motivate

Preview Read the lesson title. Have children predict what Matt will do at the bank. Then have children look at pp. 126 and 128 and identify what they see. Ask: *Are all these ways to pay for goods and services?*

Warm Up To activate prior knowledge, talk with children about their experiences with money. Have them describe what money looks like, both paper bills and coins. Ask children to tell how they earn money.

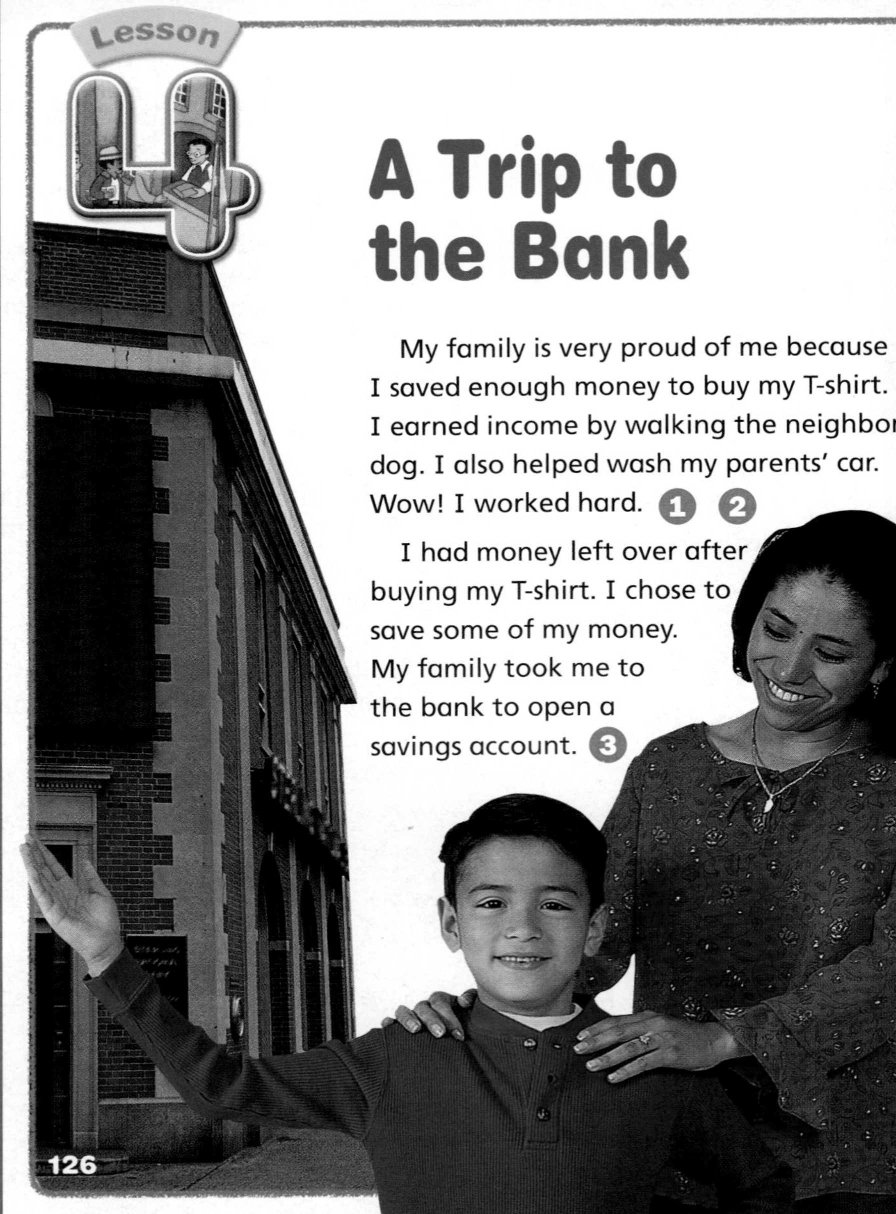

Lesson 4

A Trip to the Bank

My family is very proud of me because I saved enough money to buy my T-shirt. I earned income by walking the neighbor's dog. I also helped wash my parents' car. Wow! I worked hard. 1 2

I had money left over after buying my T-shirt. I chose to save some of my money. My family took me to the bank to open a savings account. 3

126

Practice and Extend

READING SKILL
Main Idea and Details

- Tell children that looking for and understanding the main ideas of a lesson can help them recall what they read. Say that details tell more about main ideas.
- After children have read p. 128 of "A Trip to the Bank," distribute Transparency 5. Display this main idea statement and have children copy it: *People can use checking accounts and credit cards to pay for goods and services.*
- Tell children to look for details on p. 128 that tell more about the main idea. Have them write the details to complete the graphic.

At the bank, we answered questions and signed our names on some papers. When I have income, I will deposit it, or (4) put it into my savings account. Mom or Dad can help me do this at the bank. (5) (6)

127

SOCIAL STUDIES
Background

Banks and Banking

Share some or all of the following with children.

- The word *bank* comes from the Italian *banco* or *banca*, meaning "bench." Early Italian "bankers" did their work from benches in the street.
- The first commercial bank in the United States was established in 1781.
- Banks are truly safe places. They keep cash in fireproof vaults.
- Banks insure customers' money so that it is always available to them.
- Banks pay customers for the privilege of holding and using their money. Banks pay interest on accounts. Money "grows" in a bank.
- Banks also lend money, to customers they are sure can pay it back.

2 Teach and Discuss

Page 126

Discuss with children some of the "jobs" they can do in and around the house to earn money.

(1) **How did Matt earn money?** He walked the neighbor's dog; he washed his parents' car. **Recall and Retell**

(2) **What are some ways adults you know earn money?** Possible answers: They drive a truck; they work in factories; they are teachers. **Draw Conclusions**

(3) **Why do you think Matt chose to save some of his money?** Possible answer: He knew he would need it at another time for something he wanted or for a gift. **Make Inferences**

Page 127

Have children describe what they see in the photo.

(4) **What does the word *deposit* mean? What words help you know?** The words *put it into my savings account* help me understand *deposit*. If you deposit money, you put it in the bank. **Context Clues**

(5) **Why do Matt's parents have to help him?** Answers may include: He is too young to bank on his own. **Draw Conclusions**

(6) **Do you predict that Matt will put all of his income in the bank?** Possible answer: No **What might he do with some of it?** Possible answer: Spend it on clothes or toys **Predict**

continued

Page 128

Tell children that writing a check is like withdrawing, or taking money out of, what someone has in the bank. Say that writing a check for an amount of money greater than what someone has in the bank is against the law.

7 What are some things people spend money on? Think about both goods and services. Possible answers: Food, clothes, movies
Draw Conclusions

8 What are some things Matt's family spends their income on? Groceries, new refrigerator
Recall and Retell

9 Besides paying cash or writing a check, how else may people pay for goods and services? By credit card Recall and Retell

Ongoing Assessment

If... children do not understand the function of a credit card,

then... explain that by using a credit card a person is promising to pay the cost of any purchases.

My parents also have a checking account. They use the money in their checking account to pay for goods and services. 7

My mom writes a check at the grocery store. The grocery store sends the check to the bank. The bank takes the money out of my mom's checking account.

Sometimes my parents use a credit card to pay for goods and services. They bought our refrigerator using a credit card. Then they pay their credit card bill at the end of the month. 8 9

128

Practice and Extend

CURRICULUM CONNECTION
Math

Count the Cash

Have children suppose that they have a coin bank at home that is just for quarters. Now they want to find out how many quarters they have saved and how much that is in dollars.

- Have children pretend to open their banks and shake out coins. Say they have 20 quarters saved up.
- Have children create sets to count the cash.
- Tell children to draw 20 circles to represent the quarters.
- Have them draw a rectangle around each set of four quarters. Then have them count the sets.
- Tell children to pat themselves on the back for saving $5.00! Ask what they would do with the money.

I work to help my family. Every day I make my bed and set the table. I also work to ⑩ ⑪ earn income. Then I can save some of my money and put it into my savings account.

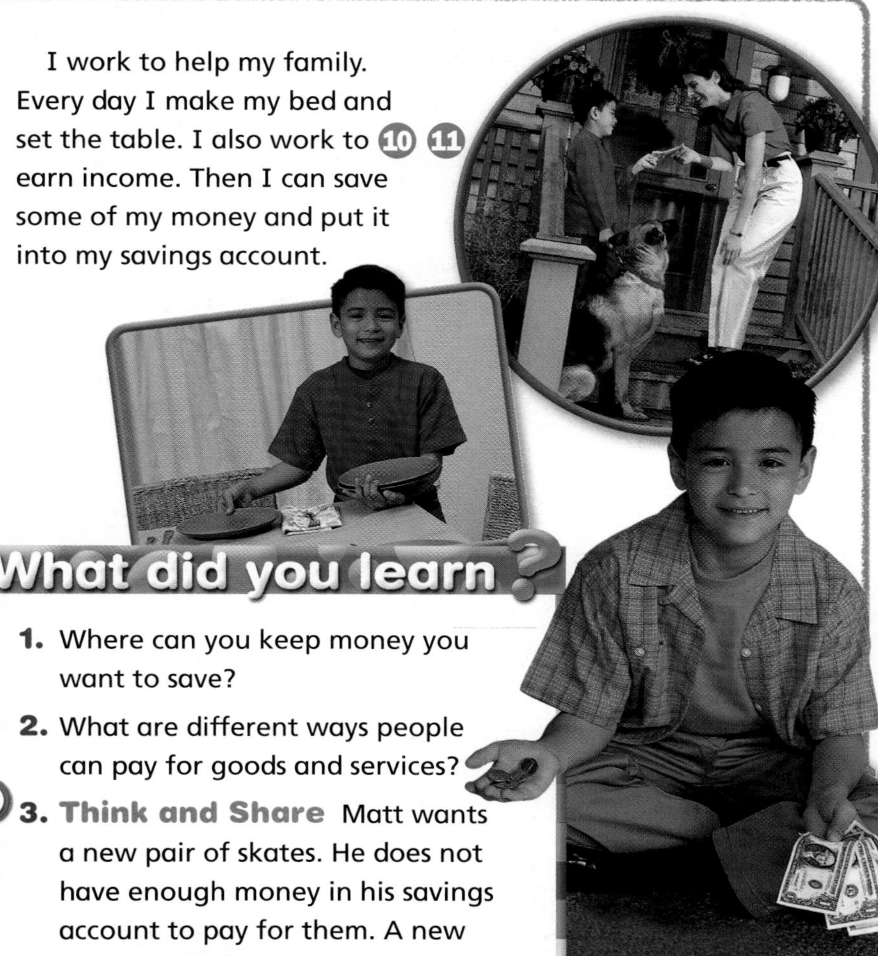

What did you learn?

1. Where can you keep money you want to save?
2. What are different ways people can pay for goods and services?
3. **Think and Share** Matt wants a new pair of skates. He does not have enough money in his savings account to pay for them. A new neighbor with two dogs moves into Matt's neighborhood. **Predict** what you think Matt will do.

Page 129

Talk with children about how work is worthwhile and worthy of respect. Make the point that receiving pay or the amount of pay is not the measure of the value of a job to the family, neighborhood, or community.

⑩ **What work can children your age do at home to help your family?** Possible answers: Help to fold the laundry and empty the dishwasher **How does the work one person does contribute to the good of the family?** Possible answer: It can save others time and energy. Others in the family don't have to do as much work.
Draw Conclusions

⑪ **What work do parents or other adult family members do at home to help their families?** Possible answer: They cook, clean, and shop.
Draw Conclusions

3 Close and Assess

Have children say whether they think most people spend all their income, save all their income, or do a combination of both. Have them explain their answers.

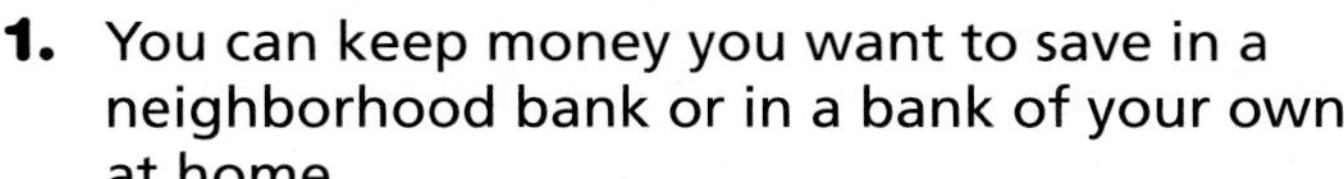

✓ What did you learn?

1. You can keep money you want to save in a neighborhood bank or in a bank of your own at home.
2. People can pay for goods and services by cash, by check, and with a credit card.
3. **Think and Share** A likely prediction is that Matt will probably take the job of walking his neighbor's dogs. He will save the money from his new job to pay for the skates.

SOCIAL STUDIES History

Presidential Money

- Pass around money: penny, nickel, dime, quarter, and dollar bill.
- Ask whether children can identify any of the persons shown on the money. Name those who children don't know.
- Ask what all the men have in common. Encourage children to say what they know about the Presidents.
- Say that the United States honors its Presidents by featuring them on our money.

Workbook, p. 31

A Trip to the Bank

Draw to show a way you might earn money. Drawings will vary.

Write answers to these questions.

What are two kinds of bank accounts? savings account, checking account

How might people pay for goods and services? with money, with a check or credit card

Also on Teacher Resources CD-ROM.

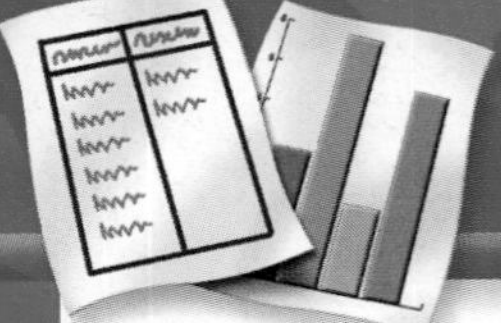

Read a Pie Chart

Objectives

- Obtain information from a pie chart.
- Construct a pie chart.

Vocabulary

pie chart A kind of chart that is drawn in the shape of a circle (p. 130)

1 Introduce and Motivate

Preview Display the term *pie chart* on the board. Then have children locate it in the text of the skills feature. Read the definition with children. Ask a volunteer to read the remaining sentence on the page.

Warm Up To activate prior knowledge, tell children that you are thinking of a food. It is round and has sauce and cheese on top. People cut it into slices to eat it. Many people like it with pepperoni on top. Have children name the food.

Have children draw a round pizza pie. Have them draw lines to slice the pie. Ask different children to say how many slices they made. Say that children will learn about another kind of pie as they read.

Chart and Graph Skills

Read a Pie Chart

A **pie chart** is a kind of chart that is drawn in the shape of a circle. The circle is divided into pieces like slices of a pie. The size of a piece shows the amount it stands for.

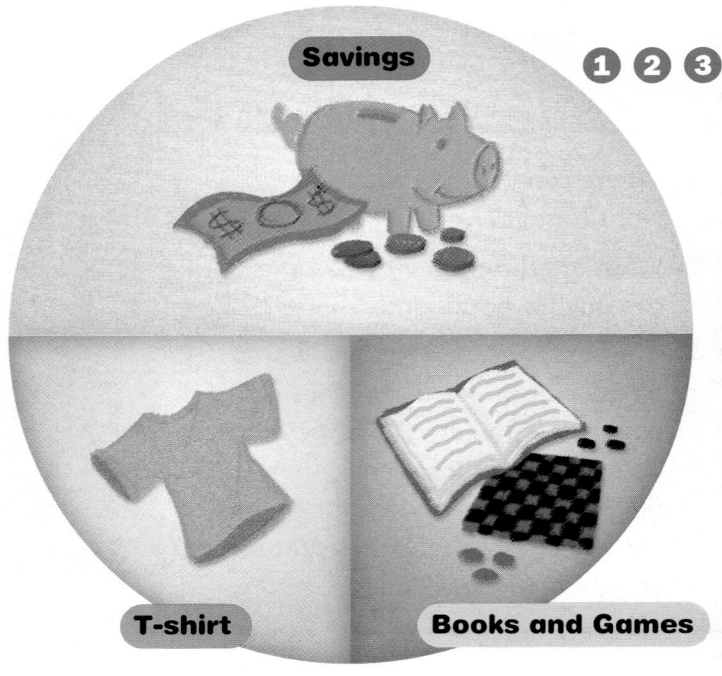

1 2 3

130

Practice and Extend

ACCESS CONTENT ESL Support

Match Game Have children take a closer look at the pie chart on p. 130.

Beginning Direct attention to the pie chart. Ask children to trace with their finger to show you the whole pie. Observe as they trace the circle. Repeat the word *whole*. Then have children trace the lines to show you each part, or slice, of the pie. Repeat the word *part* as each part is traced. Have children repeat the activity, saying the words *whole* and *part* as they do.

Intermediate Point to the top half of the pie chart. Ask children to say how it compares in size with the other two parts. Have children read the label *Savings* with you. Coach them to state: *The Savings part of the pie chart is the largest part.* Have them continue making comparisons among parts of the chart.

Advanced Read the labels on the pie chart with children. Ask them to say what the purpose of the labels is.

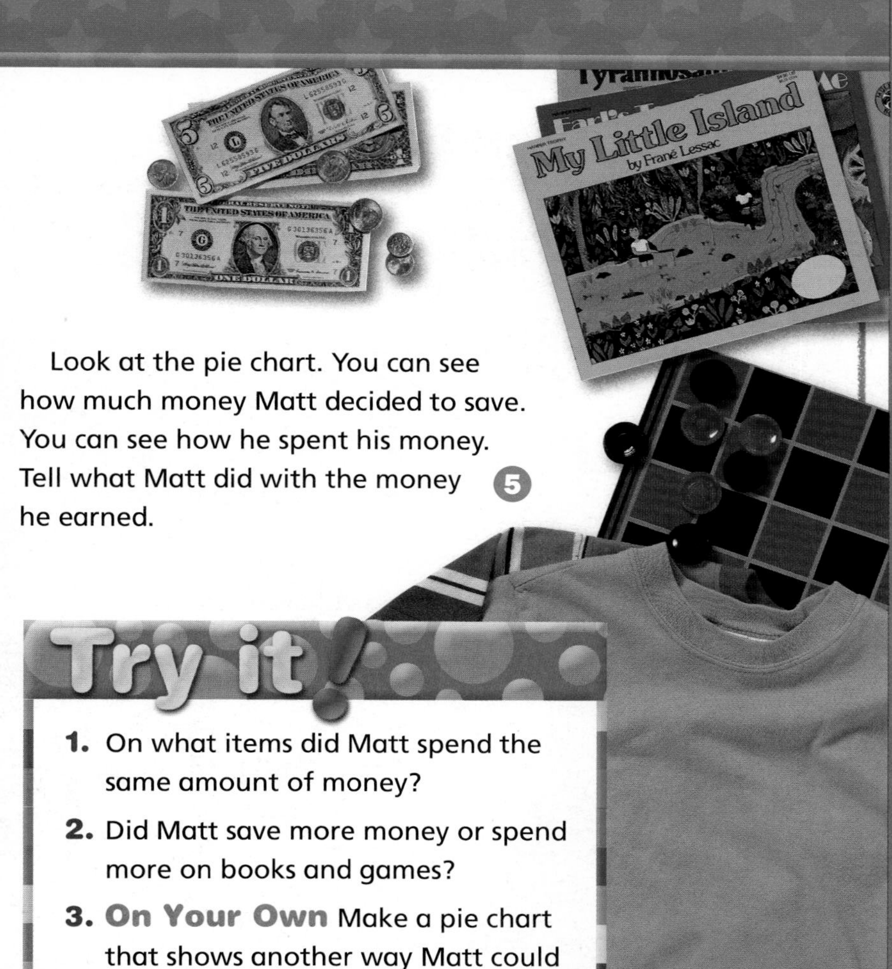

Look at the pie chart. You can see how much money Matt decided to save. You can see how he spent his money. Tell what Matt did with the money ❺ he earned.

Try it!

1. On what items did Matt spend the same amount of money?
2. Did Matt save more money or spend more on books and games?
3. **On Your Own** Make a pie chart that shows another way Matt could spend and save his money.

2 Teach and Discuss

❶ **What information does Matt's pie chart show?** It shows what he did with his money. **Recall and Retell**

❷ **What three things did Matt use his money for?** Savings, a T-shirt, books and games **Interpret Graphs**

❸ **Which things named on the pie chart are goods?** T-shirt, books and games **Categorize**

❹ **Did Matt spend any money on services?** No **How do you know?** No services are shown on the pie chart. **Interpret Graphs**

❺ **Do you think a pie chart like Matt's is a useful tool? Why?** Possible answer: Yes; you can keep track of where your money is with a pie chart like Matt's. **Evaluate**

3 Close and Assess

Try it!

1. Matt spent the same amount of money on the T-shirt and on books and games.
2. He saved more money.
3. **On Your Own** Observe children as they draw their graphs. Offer comments and suggestions at children's request. Help with labeling. Have children share and compare their graphs.

CURRICULUM CONNECTION Math

Another Pie Chart

Tell children they will make another pie chart.

- Say that the class likes four different things for lunch—soup, pizza, salad, and sandwiches. Equal numbers of children like each food.
- Have children draw a large circle. Ask how many parts they should show on the chart.
- Have children "slice" their pies into parts.
- Have children label the parts. Then have them write a title for their pie charts.

Workbook, p. 32

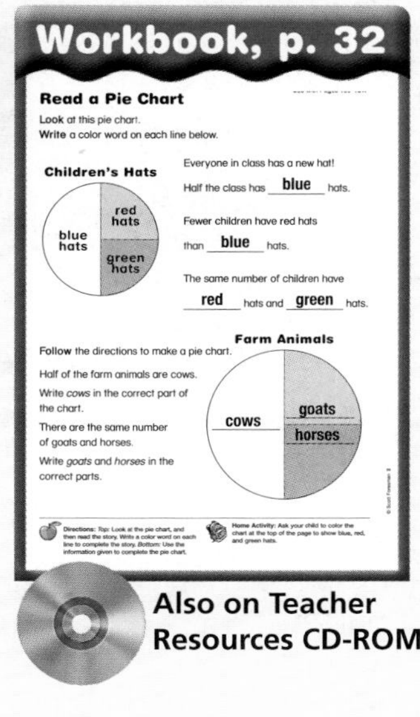

Read a Pie Chart
Look at this pie chart.
Write a color word on each line below.

Children's Hats: red hats, blue hats, green hats

Everyone in class has a new hat!
Half the class has blue hats.
Fewer children have red hats than blue hats.
The same number of children have red hats and green hats.

Follow the directions to make a pie chart.
Half of the farm animals are cows.
Write *cows* in the correct part of the chart.
There are the same number of goats and horses.
Write *goats* and *horses* in the correct parts.

Farm Animals: cows, goats, horses

Also on Teacher Resources CD-ROM.

Linda Alvarado

Objective

- Identify ordinary people who exemplify good citizenship.

1 Introduce and Motivate

Preview Read aloud the title and subtitle of the feature. Have children look at the photos on both pages and say what they know about Linda Alvarado by looking at them. Then read the Think and Share question on p. 133. Have children tell what the question lets them know about Linda Alvarado.

Warm Up To activate prior knowledge, ask children to tell what they think the qualities of a leader are. To start the discussion, offer prompts, such as: *Does a leader set a good example for others? Does a leader solve problems and make decisions?* Have children identify someone in their neighborhood or community who is a leader.

Practice and Extend

SOCIAL STUDIES Background

Linda Alvarado

Share the following information about Linda Alvarado:

- Linda Alvarado is known as a leader in the construction industry. Her company employs about 450 people. Alvarado Construction has worked on such projects as the Colorado Convention Center, the Navy/Marine Training Facility in Aurora, Colorado, and the High Energy Research Laboratory.
- In 1995, she was appointed by then President Clinton to the President's Advisory Commission on Educational Excellence for Hispanic Americans.
- Alvarado is the first Hispanic to be part owner of a U.S. baseball team.

WEB SITE Technology

You may help children find more information about Linda Alvarado by clicking on *Meet the People* at **www.sfsocialstudies.com.**

Linda loved school as a little girl. Her family believed that getting an education was very important. She also played sports with her five brothers. She learned the value of teamwork. Education and teamwork have always been important to Linda Alvarado. 1 2

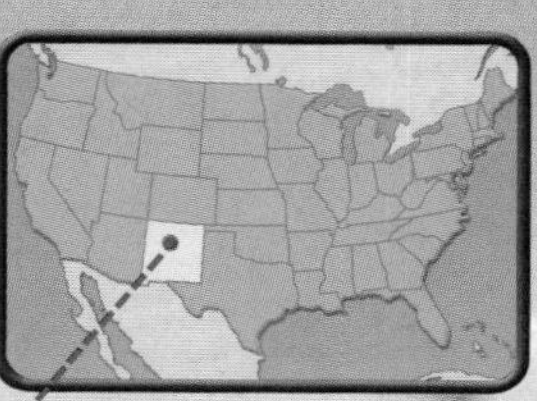

Linda Alvarado was born in Albuquerque, New Mexico.

When Linda Alvarado was older, she was interested in construction. She liked to visit places where buildings were being built. She took many classes in school that taught her about this business. Finally, she started her own construction company.

Today, Linda Alvarado's company is one of the fastest growing businesses of its kind. She is also one of the owners of a major league baseball team.

Linda Alvarado

Linda Alvarado continues to work hard with her company, baseball team, and community. 3

Think and Share

What makes Linda Alvarado a successful member of her community?

For more information, go online to *Meet the People* at **www.sfsocialstudies.com.**

133

2 Teach and Discuss

As a business leader, Linda Alvarado has to think carefully about and plan how to use money. She must decide how much to save and how much to spend. Have children identify some things Linda Alvarado would spend money on. They may suggest: pay for her workers, supplies and equipment, and so on.

1 **How did getting an education help Linda Alvarado?** Possible answer: She developed many kinds of skills in school. She solved problems, read books, and learned to share ideas. **Make Inferences**

2 **What are some characteristics of teamwork?** Possible answers: Working together, cooperating, sharing ideas, putting the good of the group first **Draw Conclusions**

3 **Do you think Linda Alvarado is a good role model for others in her community? Why?** Possible answer: Yes; she has used her skills and talents to become a business owner. She proves that women can be successful. **Evaluate**

3 Close and Assess

Think and Share

Test Talk

Write Your Answer
She started a business that gives many people jobs. She is a good role model for young people who might not want to stay in school. The baseball team she partly owns provides enjoyment for many people.

Ask children to reread their answer to make sure that the answer is correct, complete, and focused.

CURRICULUM CONNECTION
Writing/Drama

Perform an Interview

Have pairs of children work together to create interviewer and interviewee scripts based on the information in the biography.

- Model the process using the fact that Alvarado thinks education is important.
  Interviewer: How do you feel about education?
  Alvarado: I think it is very important, especially if you want to have a good job and good income.
- When the scripts are ready, have pairs of children perform them.
- Encourage children to do a first draft of their scripts. They should proofread and correct their final scripts.

Use with pages 126–133

Lesson 4 Wrap-Up

MEETING INDIVIDUAL NEEDS

Leveled Practice

A Class Bank
Children participate in a banking activity.

Easy Have children make paper one-dollar bills. Show a real bill as a model. Collect the bills and have children help you count them. Then have children choose a place in the room that will be a bank and deposit the money there. **Reteach**

On-Level Model how to make simple deposit slips children can copy. Include the name of your class bank and the day's date. Leave blanks for amount of deposit and name of depositor. Tell children to fill out slips and make deposits with classmate tellers. **Extend**

Challenge Children tellers accept deposits. They match the amount on the deposit slip and the bills turned over. Provide a stamp and pad so the transaction can be "certified." Have the tellers get together to tally and record the day's deposits. **Enrich**

Hands-on Activities

CURRICULUM CONNECTION
Music

Sing a Song

Objective Participate in a song.

Learning Style Auditory/Oral

Group

Time 10–15 minutes

1. Teach children this variation on a counting song. Sing to count up and then count down. The tune is that of "Ten Little Indians."

One little, two little, three little dollars,/(continue with four, five, six; then seven, eight, nine)/
Ten little dollars safe in the bank.

(count down)
Ten little, nine little, eight little dollars,/(continue with seven, six, five)/
Four little, three little, two little dollars—all have been spent/
Only one little dollar left!

2. Encourage children to make up their own variations based on saving and spending.

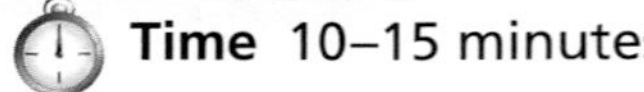

CURRICULUM CONNECTION
Writing

Diagram Leadership

Objective Identify the qualities of leadership.

Materials drawing paper, crayons, pencils

Learning Style Kinesthetic/Visual

Individual

Time 15–20 minutes

1. Have children brainstorm qualities of a leader. Remind them of the Warm Up activity for the biography feature on Linda Alvarado.

2. Draw on the board the outline of a human figure. It can be as simple as the shape of a gingerbread person! Have children copy the shape in the center of a large sheet of drawing paper. Tell them to add eyes, ears, mouth, and heart.

3. Explain that they will connect their list of leadership qualities to different parts of a person. For example, at the board write *Listens to others.* Draw a lead line from the phrase to the figure's ear. Write *Lends a hand to others* and connect it to the figure's hand. Children should get the idea quickly. Have children label their drawings *A Leader.*

4. Encourage children to share and compare their diagrammatic drawings.

Lesson 5 Overview

Countries Trade and Move Goods **pages 134–137**	Children will learn meanings for the words *trade* and *transportation*. They will explore the ways in which countries exchange goods by using different means of transportation.	 Time 20–30 minutes Resources • Workbook, p. 33 • Vocabulary Cards trade transportation • Every Student Learns Guide, pp. 58–61
Bartering Goods and Services **pages 138–139**	Children will learn what it means to barter. They will learn how people in the past got goods and services without using money.	 Time 15–20 minutes

Build Background

Activity

How Are Goods Moved?

 **Time** 15–20 minutes

Help children recall how the apples on Sara's farm (Unit 2) and the T-shirts from the factory were moved to stores. Once children have identified trucks as the means of transportation, have them name other ways goods can be moved from place to place.

Have children draw a picture of each kind of transportation and write sentences to say what kinds of goods might be transported by each.

If time is short, show children pictures of a train, truck, plane, and ship. Have children tell where each moves goods (over land, over water, in the air).

Read Aloud

Moving Goods

by Christopher Erickson

Freight trains
never rest;
transporting goods
from east to west.

Highway trucks
at the speed of light
moving products
day and night.

Boats and planes
with lots of crates
filled with plums,
oranges, and dates!

Lesson 5 Countries Trade and Move Goods

Objective

- Explain how countries are linked by trade and transportation.

Vocabulary

trade to buy, sell, or exchange goods (p. 134)

transportation a way of moving goods or people from place to place (p. 135)

QUICK Teaching Plan

If time is short, have children find the words **trade** and **transportation** in the text and read the definitions. Then have children skim p. 134 to identify some trades the United States makes with other countries. Ask children how they think the goods move between countries.

- Have children name some countries the United States trades with. Tell them to think about the countries that border the United States and about "Made in _____" labels they may have seen on products. Have children locate the countries on a world map or globe.

1 Introduce and Motivate

Preview Display the Vocabulary Cards **trade** and **transportation**. Ask children what they think each word means. Then have them locate the words in the text and read their meanings. Tell children to look at the photos in the lesson to find out some of the things they will learn about.

Warm Up To activate prior knowledge, ask children whether they have ever traded toys, games, or other things with a friend or classmate. Have them describe their experiences. Have pairs of children act out making a trade. Tell them to explain what they are doing as they do it.

Lesson 5 Countries Trade and Move Goods

In my class, we are learning about why countries around the world trade goods. **Trade** means to buy, sell, or exchange goods. Countries need to trade with each other to get goods they do not have.

The United States sells some of the goods we produce, such as wheat and corn, to other countries. We also trade with other countries to get some of the goods we need and want. For example, some companies in the United States buy rubber.

A woman collects a liquid called latex from a rubber tree. The latex is used to make rubber.

134

Practice and Extend

READING SKILL Predict

Target Skill

- Remind children that when someone says what may happen next that is called making a prediction.
- Have children pause after reading p. 136. Tell children the class took a poll to see what children's favorite chocolate products were.
- Have children predict what the most popular chocolate products were. Then have them read p. 137 to check their predictions.

WEB SITE Technology

You can look up the vocabulary words online. Click on *Social Studies Library* and select the dictionary at **www.socialstudies.com.**

Transportation is a way of moving goods or people from place to place. Trains and trucks are two kinds of transportation people can use to send goods over the land. Ships and airplanes are other kinds of transportation people use when they trade goods. 4 5

135

EXTEND LANGUAGE
ESL Support

Draw and Write Children draw pictures, label them, and write sentences about goods and ways to move them.

Beginning Have children draw pictures of a ship, plane, truck, and train using the pictures on p. 135 as models. Ask them to identify each picture in their home language and then with the English equivalent.

Intermediate Children do the above activity. Have them also label the pictures in their home language and English.

Advanced Children do both activities above. They also write sentences using the words.

For additional ESL support, use Every Student Learns Guide, pp. 58–61.

2 Teach and Discuss

Page 134

Make the point that countries depend on one another to obtain goods they need or want. Say that states, communities, and neighborhoods depend on one another too.

1 **Why do countries around the world trade with each other?** To get the goods they need or want **Cause and Effect**

2 **Does trade with another country involve money? What clues do you find in the text?** Yes; the words *sells* and *buy* are clues. Both words mean the use of money. **Draw Conclusions**

3 Tell children that rubber comes from rubber trees. **Do you think that we can grow rubber trees in the United States? Why?** Possible answer: No; the weather conditions are probably not right. If we could, we would not need to trade with other countries to get rubber. **Draw Conclusions**

Page 135

Talk briefly about how the form of transportation to move goods depends on the type of goods and how quickly the goods need to get to their destination.

4 **What kinds of goods do you think are transported by ship?** Possible answers: Large items such as cars or pieces of equipment, large quantities of things such as oil
Analyze Pictures/Make Inferences

5 **If you wanted to move a good quickly from one country to another, which form of transportation would be better—plane or ship?** Plane **Compare and Contrast**

continued

Page 136

Tell children Matt and his friends can enjoy hot chocolate because it is available in their neighborhood stores. The stores get the chocolate from factories in the state or in other states. The factories get the cocoa to make the chocolate from another country. People in each place depend on others in different places. Explain to children that the people who make products, such as the chocolate products mentioned in the lesson, are called *human resources*. The machines that are used to make the product are called *capital resources*.

Begin a list with children to identify other ways people inside and outside the community depend on one another.

GEOGRAPHY Movement

6 Show a map of the United States. Point to Hawaii. **How do you think cocoa beans are transported from Hawaii to other states?** By ship **Draw Conclusions**

Page 137

Remind children of how cotton was used to make T-shirts. Say that cotton and cocoa beans are alike in that both are used to produce different goods.

7 **What happens after the cocoa beans are shipped to factories?** The cocoa beans are made into different chocolate products. **Recall and Retell**

8 **What was the most popular chocolate product shown in the pie chart?** Chocolate milk **Interpret Graphics**

9 **What two chocolate products did children like equally?** Chocolate candy and chocolate cake **Interpret Graphics**

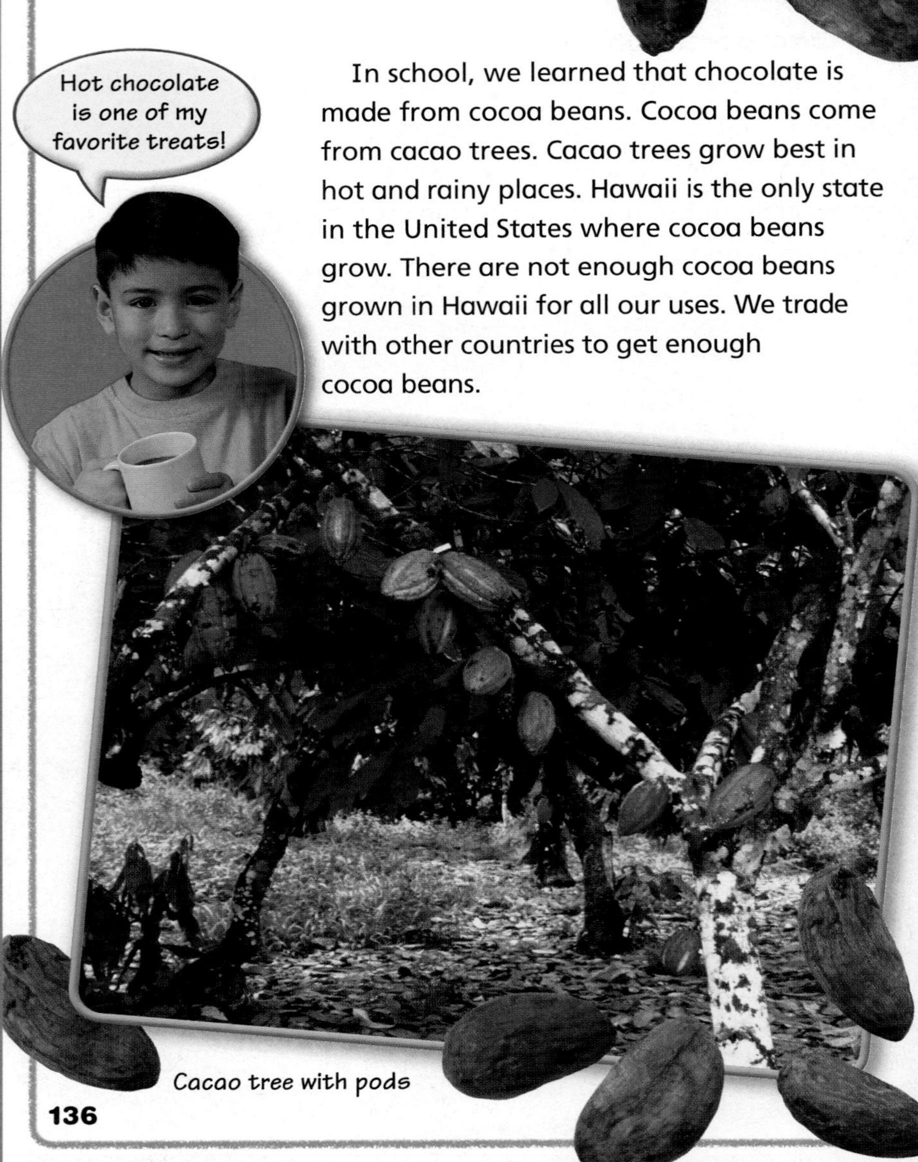

In school, we learned that chocolate is made from cocoa beans. Cocoa beans come from cacao trees. Cacao trees grow best in hot and rainy places. Hawaii is the only state in the United States where cocoa beans grow. There are not enough cocoa beans grown in Hawaii for all our uses. We trade with other countries to get enough cocoa beans.

Cacao tree with pods

136

Practice and Extend

FAST FACTS

Chocolate

- Cocoa beans are really cacao beans. They come from the cacao tree. The term we know, *cocoa*, came from a misspelling!
- Some of the earliest chocolate makers were apothecaries, or early chemists. They were interested in the supposed medicinal benefits of chocolate. They also had the skills and equipment to heat, measure, and blend the ingredients.
- Until early Victorian times chocolate was just for drinking. Then a technique was perfected for making a solid "eating" chocolate.
- The largest chocolate factory in the world is the Hershey factory in Pennsylvania.

The cocoa beans are shipped to factories. Here people and machines make the cocoa beans into different chocolate products. 7

My class made a pie chart of our favorite chocolate products. What product made from chocolate do we like best? 8 9

What did you learn?

1. Tell why countries need to trade with each other.
2. What are some ways that goods could be moved from Europe to the United States?
3. **Think and Share** Look at the label inside a shirt. The label may say where it was made. Tell what kind of transportation might have been used to move the shirt to a store near you.

CURRICULUM CONNECTION Math

Make a Bar Graph

- Tell children to look at the labels of three articles of clothing at home. Tell them to write down the countries in which these pieces of clothing were made. Collect children's findings in a tally chart.
- Review the completed tally chart with children. Then have children use the information from the chart to make a bar graph. Refer children to review what they learned about bar graphs in Unit 2, Lesson 3, pp. 80–81 if they need help.

Workbook, p. 33

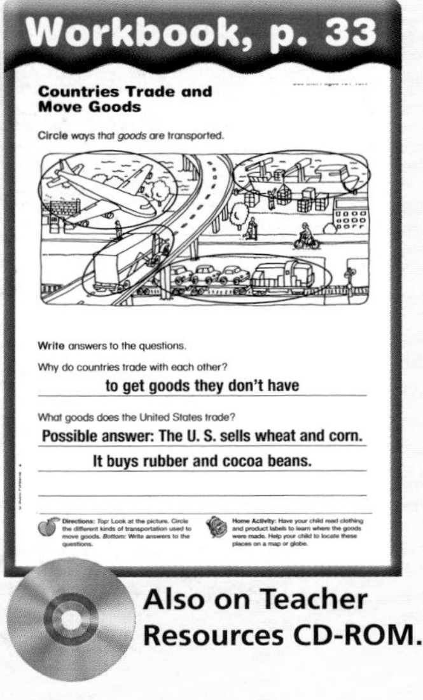

Countries Trade and Move Goods

Circle ways that goods are transported.

Write answers to the questions.

Why do countries trade with each other?

to get goods they don't have

What goods does the United States trade?

Possible answer: The U. S. sells wheat and corn.

It buys rubber and cocoa beans.

Also on Teacher Resources CD-ROM.

3 Close and Assess

Help children recall and retell what they have learned.

Test Talk

Locate Key Words in the Text
Have children locate key words in the text that match key words in the question.

1. Countries need to trade with each other to get the goods they need or want.
2. Possible answer: By plane or by ship
3. **Think and Share** Answers will vary. Help children locate the country from which their shirt or garment came. Then have them say what kind of transportation was most likely used to get it to the store near where they live.

Living History

Bartering Goods and Services

Objective

- Distinguish between the use of barter and money in the exchange of goods and services.

Vocabulary

barter to trade a good or service for another good or service without using money (p. 138)

1 Introduce and Motivate

Preview Talk with children about the illustration on page 138. Then show the word *barter* on the board. Have children read the word with you. Tell children that the word has something to do with the illustration. Have children use what they see in the pictures to try to define *barter*. Then share the definition.

Warm Up To activate prior knowledge, ask children to think about services they could barter for something. Give an example to get children started: *Have you ever offered to do a chore such as folding clothes in exchange for a new book or game, or for permission to go to the movies with friends?*

Living History

Bartering Goods and Services

Long ago, many people did not use coins and paper bills to buy and sell things. They bartered goods to get what they needed. **Barter** means to trade goods or services for other goods or services without using money. 1

138

Practice and Extend

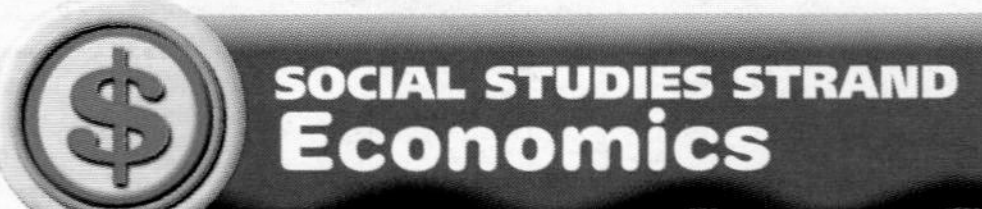

SOCIAL STUDIES STRAND

Economics

Fair Trade

Tell children that when two people trade goods or services and each person feels that he or she has gained something in the trade, the trade is a fair trade.

- List these items on the board: T-shirt, video game, paint set, chocolate bar. Have children copy the list, skipping a line in between items.
- Tell children to write two or three items they would trade for each thing on the list.
- Have children share their ideas.

Today, people still barter. 2 My family sometimes barters services with our neighbors. My dad painted our neighbor's fence. Then our neighbor fixed our car. What other services might people barter?

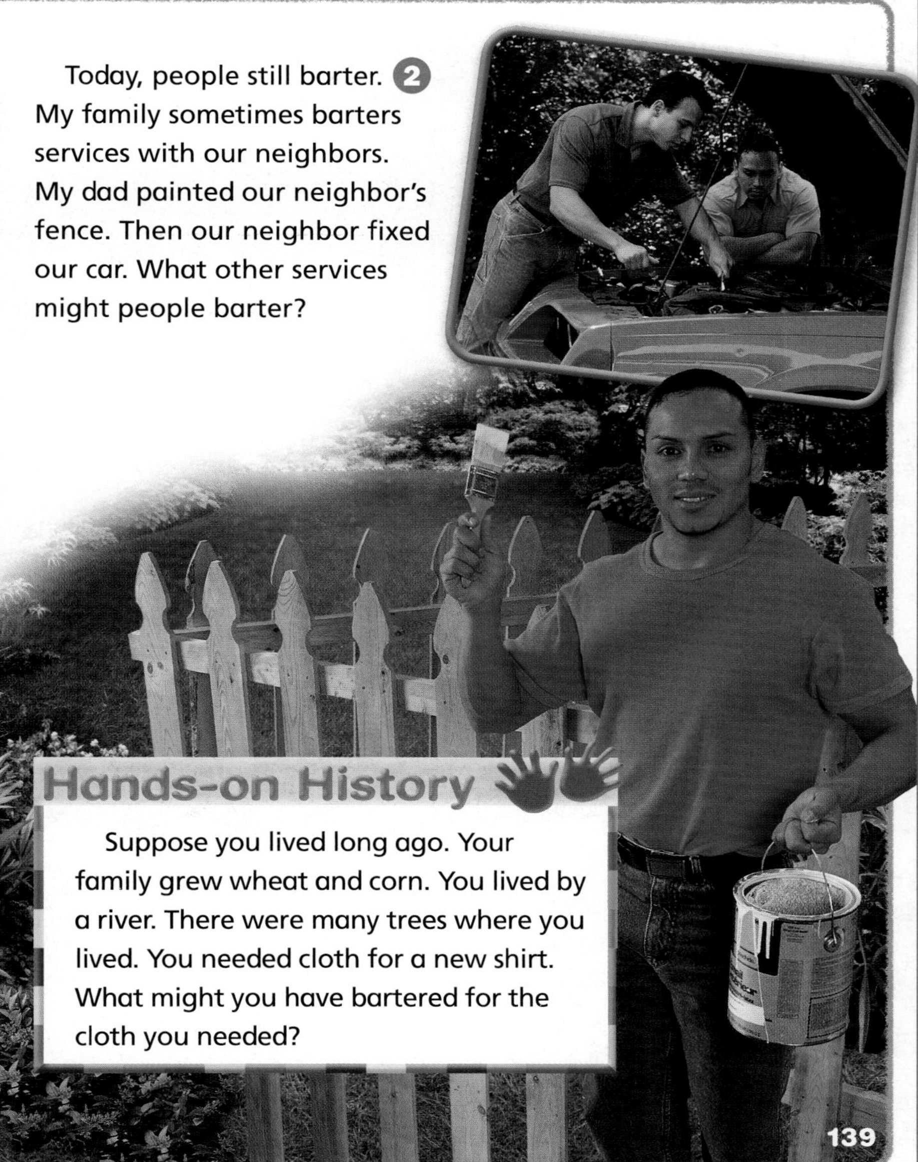

Hands-on History

Suppose you lived long ago. Your family grew wheat and corn. You lived by a river. There were many trees where you lived. You needed cloth for a new shirt. What might you have bartered for the cloth you needed?

139

2 Teach and Discuss

Pages 138–139

Tell children that bartering is a good example of problem solving. Explain that a fisherman who needed cloth but had only fish had a problem. A weaver who had cloth but no fish to eat had a problem. Bartering enabled them both to solve their problems. Note, though, that bartering had its own problems. It wasn't always easy to find someone who had what you needed or wanted what you had.

1 **What kinds of things do you think people mostly bartered for long ago?** Possible answer: Basic needs—food, shelter, clothing
Draw Conclusions

2 **What services that you know how to perform could you use to barter with?** Possible answer: Cleaning and watering a garden **Evaluate**

3 **Do you think the barter Matt's dad made with their neighbor was a good one? Why?** Some children may say that the barter was not good because they think one or the other of the activities is more difficult. **Evaluate**

4 **Which do you think is better—bartering or using money? Why?** Some children may think that bartering is better because it lets people save money.
Compare and Contrast

3 Close and Assess

Hands-on History

Possible answers: Children might say that they would barter some wheat, corn, wood, or fish for cloth.

Use with pages 134–139

Lesson 5 Wrap-Up

MEETING INDIVIDUAL NEEDS Leveled Practice

A Transportation Bulletin Board
Have children use magazine picture cutouts, drawings they make, paints, and small objects to make visual representations of the forms of transportation. Display all levels of children's work in the classroom.

Easy Children choose one form of transportation. They can cut out pictures, draw, or paint to make realistic or abstract collages to represent their choice. They tell about their finished products. **Reteach**

On-Level Children write short captions for their works of art and affix them to the products. **Extend**

Challenge Children create a bulletin board display, including a title. They then write a short paragraph explaining the importance of transportation to the way people live. **Enrich**

Hands-on Activities

CURRICULUM CONNECTION
Writing

Sentence Trade

Objective Demonstrate understanding of new vocabulary words.

Resources Vocabulary Cards: **trade transportation**

Materials paper, pencils

Learning Style Linguistic

Individual

Time 10–15 minutes

1. Display the Vocabulary Cards and show *barter* on the board. Tell children to write completion sentences, one for each word, that give clues to the words' meanings.

2. Have children trade sentences with partners who will complete the sentences.

3. Remind children to add *trade, transportation*, and *barter* to their personal glossaries.

SOCIAL STUDIES STRAND
Economics

Set Up a Trading Post

Objective Demonstrate understanding of trade and trading.

Materials items to trade, large index cards

Learning Style Kinesthetic/Linguistic

Group

Time 20–25 minutes

1. With parents' permission have each child bring in something they would like to trade such as an old toy or storybook. Or, have children draw pictures of something that can be traded. Set up a table to display the goods or pictures.

2. Have each child create a sign on an index card that describes the item they want to trade. Have children place their index cards next to their goods.

3. Set aside class time for children to review the goods that are on display at the trading post. Have children write down on a sheet of paper several possible goods on the table they would like to trade for.

4. Have children take turns proposing their trades. Have possible trading partners work out the details of the trade. Then have children summarize the process of their trade, explaining why they agreed to it.

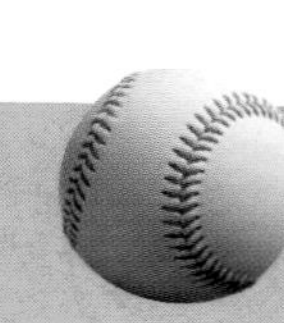

Ending Unit 3

End with Riddles pages 140–141	Children will read and solve riddles about workers who provide community services.	
Unit 3 Review pages 142–145	Children will review unit vocabulary words and the unit skills of making a prediction, following decision-making steps, and using a compass rose. Children will answer questions about what they learned in the unit. Children will learn about several books about work.	Resources • Workbook, p. 34 ✓• Assessment Book pp. 9–12
Unit 3 Project page 146	Children will choose a good or service they would like to sell and develop appropriate business cards to advertise. They will also be directed to a Web site where they can learn more about work. 	Resource • Workbook, p. 35

Wrap-up

Activity

My Unit 3 Flashcards

Tell children they will make a set of flash cards that will help them remember the most important information they learned in Unit 3, *Working Together*.

- Give each child five large index cards.
- Tell children to look back at the five numbered lessons in the unit. Tell them to look for the most important ideas in each lesson.
- Have children number their cards 1–5 and then record the most important ideas of each lesson on the appropriate card. They may use both sides of each card.
- Help children secure their cards as a set with brads.

Performance Assessment

You can use the activity on this page as a performance assessment.

✓ Assessment Scoring Guide

Make Unit 3 Flashcards	
4	Prepares five cards that include the main ideas of the five numbered lessons. Main ideas are accurately and clearly expressed.
3	Prepares five cards. Most record the main ideas of the lessons.
2	Prepares fewer than five cards. Information recorded varies in importance.
1	Prepares fewer than five cards. Information recorded does not reflect main ideas.

Can You Guess These Workers?

Objective

- Obtain information from visual sources such as printed text and pictures.

1 Introduce and Motivate

Preview Read the title of the feature and have children look at the illustrations. Ask why they think these particular workers are shown. Children should realize that the jobs the workers do complete the riddles.

Warm Up Have children share any riddles they know, or have them make up some riddles following a model you provide. Say, for example: *I shine to make the sky bright. I am out in day, not night. What am I?*

2 Teach and Discuss

Have children listen as you read each riddle. Tell them to use the pictures on the page to help them solve the riddles. (p. 140—firefighter, lifeguard; p. 141—nurse, teacher)

1 **What do you notice about the word that completes each riddle? Look at the other words in the riddle.** The answer rhymes with one of the other words. **Details**

2 **Do you think reading and solving riddles about workers is a good way to end the unit? Why?** Some children might say yes because they have been learning about community workers. **Evaluate**

Practice and Extend

Create Riddles

- Help children make a list of the workers they have learned about in the unit. Invite children to name other workers and jobs they know about.
- Have children choose one of the workers from this list and write a riddle about that job on a piece of construction paper. Have them leave space above their riddle for a drawing.
- Display the riddles in class. Have children choose one of their classmate's riddles and solve it by writing the name of the worker/job and drawing a picture. Have the originators of the riddles tell whether or not the riddle was solved correctly.

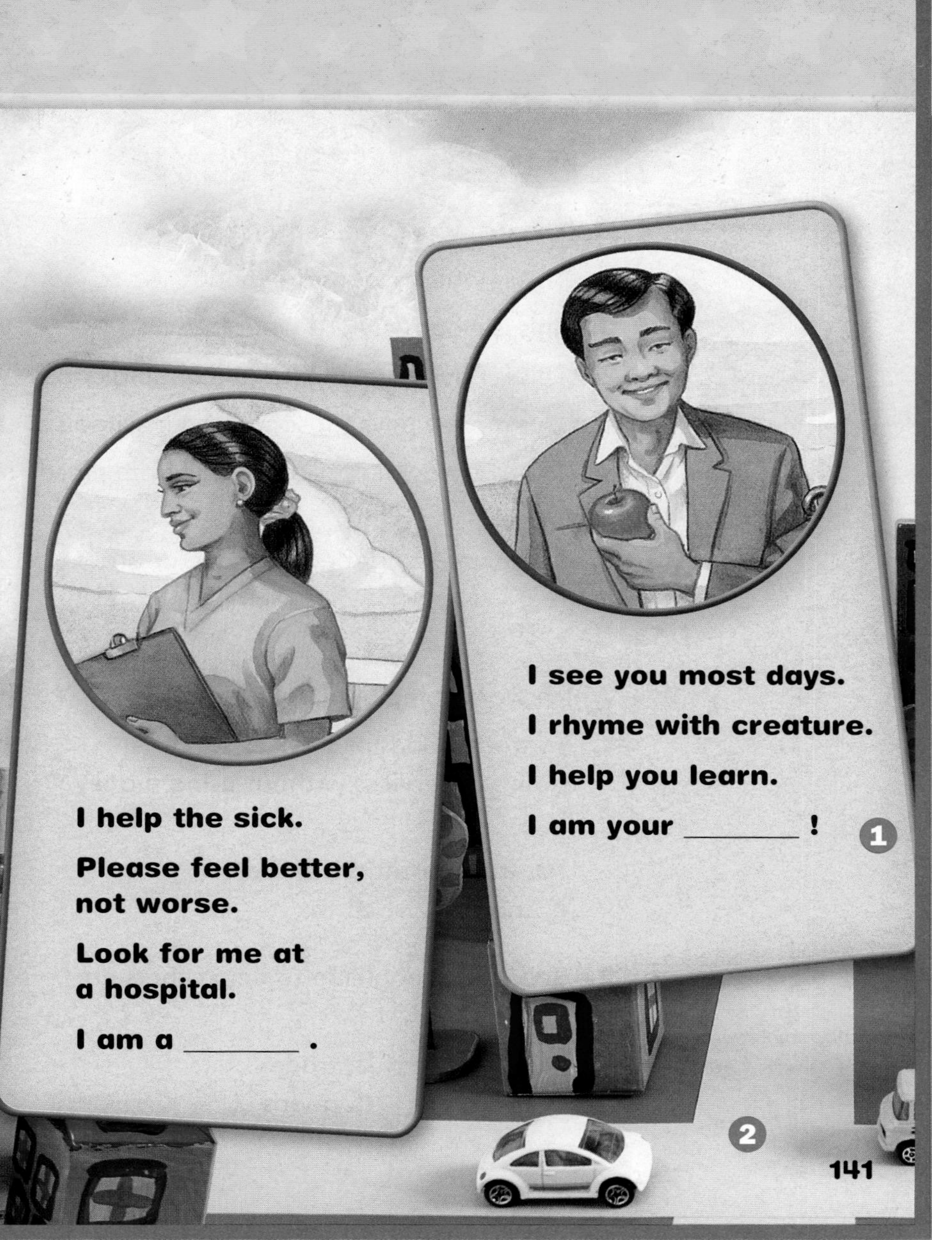

3 Close and Assess

- Ask children if they think riddles are easy or hard to solve. Why?
- Have children say how solving a riddle is like solving a puzzle.
- Encourage children to perform the riddles, adding pantomimed actions.

CURRICULUM CONNECTION
Drama

Play a Variation on a Game

Children may enjoy closing the unit with this variation on the circle game "The Farmer in the Dell." Substitute *mayor* for *farmer*. Have the child who is designated as mayor stand in the center of the circle as children sing or chant: *The mayor of our town/the mayor of our town. Oh, oh, there he (she) goes/the mayor of our town. The mayor gets a* ____(name of a community worker), and so on. The mayor continues to bring into the circle each community worker as he or she is named. Children singing or chanting may not repeat community jobs during the game!

Review

Resources

- Assessment Book, pp. 9–12
- Workbook, p. 34: Vocabulary Review

Vocabulary Review

1. factory
2. income
3. trade
4. tax
5. transportation
6. goods

Answers to Test Prep

1. barter
2. services

Test Talk

Choose the Right Answer
Use Test Prep, Question 2, to model the Test Talk strategy.

Narrow the answer choices.
Tell children to read each answer choice carefully. Children should rule out any choice that they know is wrong.

Choose the best answer.
After children make their answer choice, tell them to recheck their answer.

UNIT 3

Review

Vocabulary Review

tax
factory
transportation
income
trade
goods

Match each word to a sentence.

1. This is where goods are made.
2. This is what we earn when we work.
3. This is buying, selling, or exchanging goods.
4. This money pays for some of our schools.
5. This is a way of moving things from place to place.
6. These are things people make or grow.

★ ★ ★ ★ ★ ★ ★ ★

Which word completes each sentence?

1. To trade goods or services for other goods or services without using money is _______.

   a. transportation **b.** barter
   c. income **d.** tax

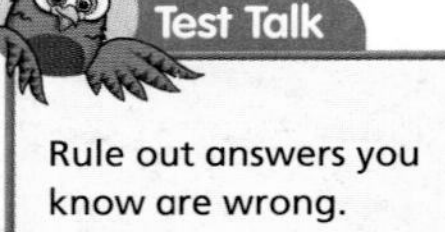

2. Jobs that people do to help others are _______.

   a. services **b.** trade
   c. income **d.** goods

142

Practice and Extend

Assessment Options

✓ Unit 3 Assessment

- Unit 3 Content Test: Use Assessment Book, pp. 9–10
- Unit 3 Skills Test: Use Assessment Book, pp. 11–12

Standardized Test Prep

- Unit 3 tests contain standardized test formats.

✓ Unit 3 Performance Assessment

- See p. 146 for information about using the Unit 3 Project as a means of performance assessment.
- A scoring guide for the Unit 3 Project is provided in the teacher's notes on p. 146.

Test Talk

- Test Talk Practice Book

Skills Review

Predict

A farmer plants cotton. There is no rain. The cotton plants do not grow. The factory cannot get the cotton it needs to make T-shirts. **Predict** what might happen.

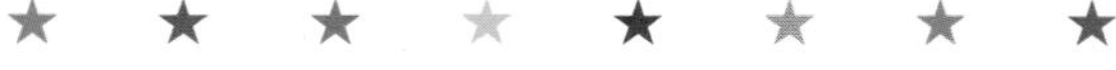

Make a Decision

Think of a decision that you or your classmates might make. Then follow these steps.

1. Tell what decision you need to make.
2. Gather information.
3. List your choices.
4. Tell what might happen with each choice.
5. Make a decision.

143

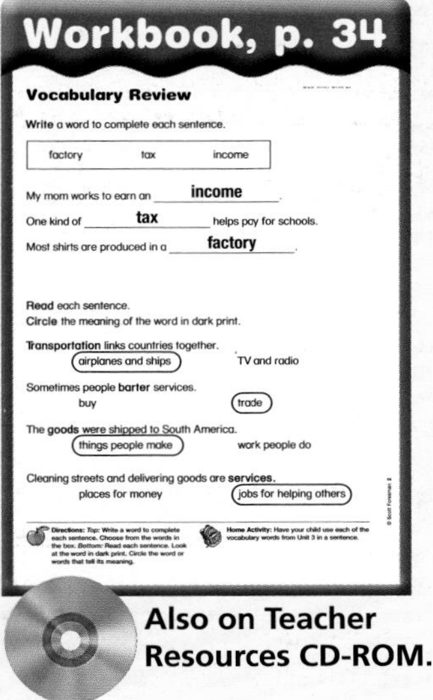

Workbook, p. 34

Vocabulary Review

Write a word to complete each sentence.

factory tax income

My mom works to earn an income.

One kind of tax helps pay for schools.

Most shirts are produced in a factory.

Read each sentence. Circle the meaning of the word in dark print.

Transportation links countries together. (airplanes and ships) TV and radio

Sometimes people **barter** services. buy (trade)

The **goods** were shipped to South America. (things people make) work people do

Cleaning streets and delivering goods are **services**. places for money (jobs for helping others)

Also on Teacher Resources CD-ROM.

Skills Review

Predict

Target Skill

- Children's predictions should indicate that shortages or scarcity of the product would happen.

Use the following scoring guide.

✓ Assessment Scoring Guide

Make a Prediction	
4	Uses all given information to make a plausible prediction.
3	Uses partial information to make an improbable prediction.
2	Disregards most of the given information. Makes an improbable prediction.
1	Shows little understanding of what a prediction is.

Make a Decision

1.–5. Observe children to be certain they include all five steps.

Review

continued

Skills Review

Use a Compass Rose

Observe children as they trace the route. Help them self-orient, as needed, by reminding them to use the compass rose. Note whether they do all five parts of the route.

Skills on Your Own

- Children's maps should be clear and accurate. Children should attend to all three parts of the activity.

Use the following scoring guide.

✓ Assessment Scoring Guide

Make a Map	
4	Shows accurate information and demonstrates understanding of direction.
3	Shows accurate information. Sometimes confuses direction words but self-corrects.
2	Shows little detail on map. Confuses direction words without self-correcting.
1	Vague map. Shows little understanding of directionality.

Review

Skills Review

Use a Compass Rose

This is a map of buildings and streets in Matt's community. Trace this route on the map.

1. Point to Matt's house.
2. Go east on Willow Way.
3. Go north on Robin Road.
4. Go east on School Street.
5. Tell what building you see.

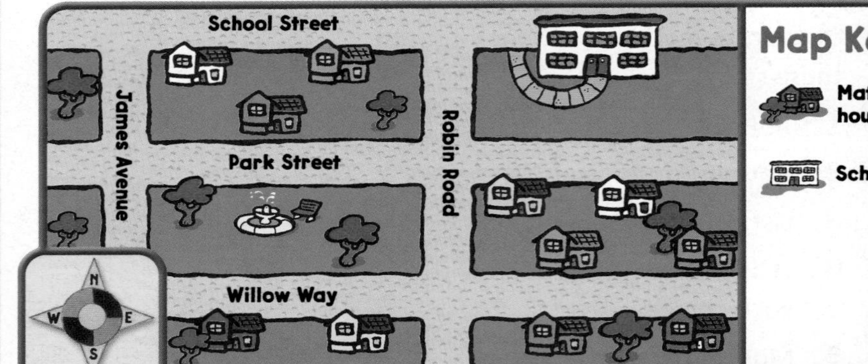

Skills On Your Own

Draw a map of your neighborhood. Put a title and a compass rose on your map. Use the words north, south, east, and west to tell about your map.

Practice and Extend

Revisit the Unit Question

✓ Portfolio Assessment

Have children look back at the list they generated on page 97. It records reasons they think work is important.

- Have children write sentences to say why work is important now that they have read the unit.
- Have children put a check mark next to ideas they got while reading the unit.
- Have children use their sentences to write a short paragraph.
- Suggest children attach their writing to large sheets of drawing paper and label them *People at Work*.
- Have children add their drawings and sentences to their Social Studies portfolio.

What did you learn?

1. What are ways people earn and use their income?
2. How do taxes help a community?
3. Tell how you might barter for goods or services.
4. **Write and Share** Make a list of what a family might choose to buy if they could buy only things that they needed to live.

Read About Work

Look for books like these in the library.

145

What did you learn?

1. Responses may include: People can earn their income by working on a farm or in a factory. People can use their income to buy goods and services. They can save some too.
2. Taxes help a community pay for the services of workers such as firefighters, and police. Taxes help pay for repairs on public buildings and roads.
3. Children's responses should show they understand that barter does not include the exchange of money. Items or services exchanged should be of reasonably equal value.
4. **Write and Share** Children's responses should be restricted to the areas of food, shelter, clothing.

Read About Work

The Gardener, by Sarah Stewart (Farrar, Straus & Giroux, ISBN 0-374-42518-3, 2000) A young girl whose family is facing hard times is sent to live with her uncle. She makes the best of her new situation and also cheers up her uncle's home by joyfully gardening and decorating with flowers. **Easy** ***Caldecott Honor Book***

Once Upon a Company... A True Story, by Wendy Anderson Halperin (Orchard Books, ISBN 0-531-33089-3, 1998) This is the story of three young entrepreneurs who immerse themselves in the wreath-making business. **On-Level**

Uncle Willie and the Soup Kitchen, by DyAnne DiSalvo-Ryan (Mulberry Books, ISBN 0-688-15285-6,1997) A boy visits his uncle who works every day in a soup kitchen, and he makes discoveries about the people who are not just visitors to the soup kitchen but are truly treated as guests. **Challenge** ***Reading Rainbow Book***

Unit 3 Project

Business Basics

Objective
- Make a business card to tell about goods or a service.

Resource
- Workbook, p. 35

Materials
pencils, crayons, index cards or poster board cut into rectangles, sample business cards

Follow This Procedure
- Tell children that they each will choose a business that sells goods or a service.
- They will then advertise, or tell the public about, their goods or service. Tell them that one way a company advertises is by handing out business cards. Show a variety of business card samples.
- Tell children to make their business card for goods or a service of their choice.
- Write the following information on the board:

  Name of your company

  Picture of the goods or service

  Your name
- Have children share their cards with classmates.

✓ Assessment Scoring Guide

	Business Basics
4	Includes the specified information in a clear way that shows understanding of the purpose of a business card.
3	Identifies the goods or service in words or picture but omits some other specified information.
2	Does not identify the goods or service. May include some other specified information.
1	Responds in a way that shows little understanding of the form or purpose of the activity.

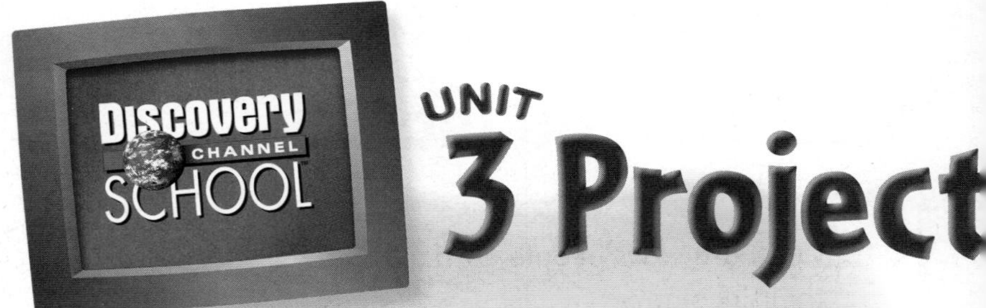

Business Basics

You are going to start a business. A business is a place that sells goods or services. You will advertise its goods or services.

1. **Choose** goods or a service.
2. **Make** a business card for your goods or service.
3. **Give** your goods or service a name. Write your name and the name of your business on the card.
4. **Share** your business cards with your classmates. See how different each one is.

Internet Activity

Go to www.sfsocialstudies.com/activitie to learn more about work.

Practice and Extend

✓ Performance Assessment
- The Unit Project can also be used as a performance assessment activity.
- Use the scoring guide to assess each group's work.

Children can launch the activity by clicking on *Grade 2, Unit 3* at **www.sfsocialstudies.com/activities**.

Workbook, p. 35

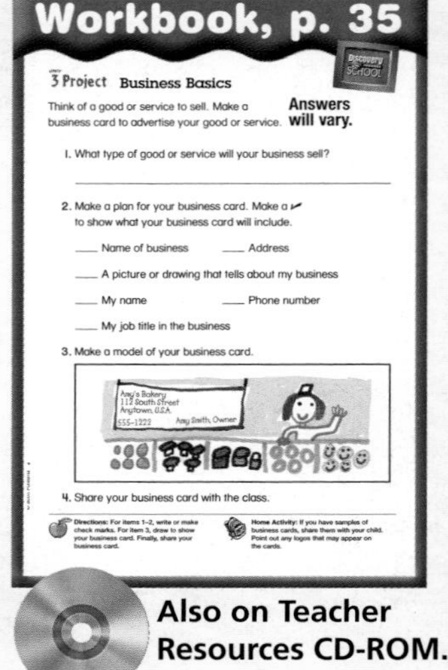
UNIT 3 Project **Business Basics**

Think of a good or service to sell. Make a business card to advertise your good or service. **Answers will vary.**

1. What type of good or service will your business sell?
2. Make a plan for your business card. Make a ✓ to show what your business card will include.

   ___ Name of business ___ Address

   ___ A picture or drawing that tells about my business

   ___ My name ___ Phone number

   ___ My job title in the business
3. Make a model of your business card.
4. Share your business card with the class.

Directions: For items 1–2, write or make check marks. For item 3, draw to show your business card. Finally, share your business card.

Home Activity: If you have samples of business cards, share them with your child. Point out any logos that may appear on the cards.

Also on Teacher Resources CD-ROM.

Our Country Today
UNIT
4

UNIT 4

Unit 4 Planning Guide

Our Country Today

Begin with a Song pp. 148–149 **Vocabulary Preview** pp. 150–151

Reading Social Studies, Main Idea and Details pp. 152–153

Lesson Titles	Pacing	Main Ideas
Lesson 1 **Local Government** pp. 154–157 **Citizen Heroes:** Fairness **Anna Beavers** pp. 158–159	2 days	• Government is a group of people who work together to run a city, state, or country. • Government leaders and citizens work together to make communities better and safer places in which to live. • Anna Beavers helps clothe schoolchildren in her Virginia community. The clothes bring comfort and build confidence levels of the children who receive them.
Lesson 2 **State Government** pp. 160–163 **Chart and Graph Skills: Read a Table** pp. 164–165	2 days	• The state government works to establish order, provide security, and manage conflict by making laws and providing services. • Government collects tax money to pay for services, such as schools, libraries, and parks. • Reading a table is one way to get useful information, such as important facts about each state.
Lesson 3 **Federal Government** pp. 166–169 **Biography: Thurgood Marshall** pp. 170–171	2 days	• Congress is the part of government that writes and votes on laws for all our states. • The president is the leader of a country. • Thurgood Marshall was the first African American justice on the Supreme Court. He fought for the rights of all Americans.
Lesson 4 **Voting for Leaders** pp. 172–175 **Smithsonian Institution: Presidential Treasures** pp. 176–177 **Biography: Susan B. Anthony** pp. 178–179	3 days	• Citizens of the United States must learn about the different candidates running for public office so they can vote for the one best suited for the job. • Everyday belongings of past Presidents tell about them and about our country's history. • Susan B. Anthony helped women get the right to vote.
Lesson 5 **The Land of Freedom** pp. 180–183 **Map and Globe Skills: Use a Map Grid** pp. 184–185 **Here and There: Flags Around the World** pp. 186–187	3 days	• America celebrates its heritage—every citizen's right to make choices—through patriotic songs, symbols, and mottoes. • Using a map grid helps people locate places on a map. • Each country's flag is a special symbol.

✓ **End with a Song** pp. 188–189 ✓ **Unit 4 Review** pp. 190–193 ✓ **Unit 4 Project** p. 194

✓ = Assessment Options

Scott Foresman Social Studies
Indiana Academic Standards

Grade 2 Unit 4 • *Our Country Today*

Lesson Title	Indiana Academic Standards Social Studies
Lesson 1 Local Government pp. 154-157	**IN Academic Standard 2.2.5** Explain the roles people have in making and changing laws. **(Also 2.1.3, 2.2.2, 2.2.3, 2.5.2, 2.5.5)**
Citizen Heroes: Anna Beavers pp. 158-159	**IN Academic Standard 2.2.4** Identify good leaders and good citizens, and explain the qualities that make them admirable. **(Also 2.1.3, 2.2.1, 2.3.3, 2.5.5)**
Lesson 2 State Government pp. 160-163	**IN Academic Standard 2.2.2** Explain why it is necessary to have government. **(Also 2.2.3, 2.2.5, 2.3.3)**
Chart and Graph Skills: Read a Table pp. 164-165	**Reviews IN Academic Standard K.2.3** Identify symbols and traditions associated with being citizens.
Lesson 3 Federal Government, pp. 166-169	**IN Academic Standard 2.2.2** Explain why it is necessary to have government.
Biography: Thurgood Marshall pp. 170-171	**IN Academic Standard 2.2.4** Identify good leaders and good citizens, and explain the qualities that make them admirable.
Lesson 4 Voting for Leaders pp. 172-175	**IN Academic Standard 2.2.5** Explain the roles people have in making and changing laws.
Smithsonian Institution: Presidential Treasures pp. 176-177	**Reviews IN Academic Standard 1.1.2** Compare past and present similarities and differences in daily life.
Biography: Susan B. Anthony pp. 178-179	**IN Academic Standard 2.3.3** Locate the local community and the U.S.
Lesson 5 The Land of Freedom pp. 180-183	**IN Academic Standard 2.1.4** Explain the meaning of community celebrations and traditions. **(Also 2.2.5)**
Map and Globe Skills: Use a Map Grid pp. 184-185	**IN Academic Standard 2.3.2** Identify the absolute and relative location of places.
Here and There: Flags Around the World pp. 186-187	**Previews IN Academic Standard 3.2.5** Explain that the world is divided into countries and identify neighboring countries.

Insert between pages 147b - 147c
For complete standards listing, please see front tab.

Continued on other side →

Scott Foresman Social Studies to the Indiana Academic Standards for English/Language Arts

Grade 2 Unit 4 • *Our Country Today*

Lesson Title	Indiana Academic Standards English/Language Arts
Begin with a Song, pp. 148-149 *Vocabulary Preview, pp. 150-151* *Reading Social Studies, Main Idea and Details, pp. 152-153*	**2.2.5** Restate facts and details in the text to clarify and organize ideas. See also 2.1.2, 2.1.3, 2.1.5, 2.2.2, 2.2.3, 2.2.4, 2.2.7, 2.4.1, 2.4.2, 2.4.4, 2.4.5, 2.4.6, 2.4.7, 2.4.8, 2.5.5, 2.5.6, 2.6.1, 2.6.2, 2.6.3, 2.6.7, 2.6.8, 2.6.9
Lesson 1 Local Government, pp. 154-157	**2.2.5** Restate facts and details in the text to clarify and organize ideas. See also 2.1.2, 2.1.3, 2.1.5, 2.2.2, 2.2.3, 2.2.4, 2.2.6, 2.7.8
Citizen Heroes: Anna Beavers, pp. 158-159	**2.2.5** Restate facts and details in the text to clarify and organize ideas. See also 2.1.2, 2.1.3, 2.1.5, 2.2.2, 2.2.3, 2.2.4, 2.2.7, 2.4.1, 2.4.2, 2.4.4, 2.4.5, 2.4.6, 2.4.7, 2.4.8, 2.5.5, 2.5.6, 2.6.1, 2.6.2, 2.6.3, 2.6.7, 2.6.8, 2.6.9
Lesson 2 State Government, pp. 160-163	**2.2.7** Interpret information from diagrams, charts, and graphs. See also 2.2.2, 2.2.4, 2.4.1, 2.4.2, 2.4.4, 2.4.5, 2.4.6, 2.4.7, 2.4.8, 2.5.5, 2.5.6, 2.6.1, 2.6.2, 2.6.3, 2.6.7, 2.6.8, 2.6.9, 2.7.8
Chart and Graph Skills: Read a Table, pp. 164-165	**2.2.7** Interpret information from diagrams, charts, and graphs. See also 2.2.2, 2.2.4
Lesson 3 Federal Government, pp. 166-169	**2.2.6** Recognize cause-and-effect relationships in a text. See also 2.1.2, 2.1.3, 2.1.5, 2.2.2, 2.2.4, 2.2.5, 2.7.8
Biography: Thurgood Marshall, pp. 170-171	**2.2.6** Recognize cause-and-effect relationships in a text. See also 2.1.2, 2.1.3, 2.1.5, 2.2.2, 2.2.3, 2.2.4, 2.4.1, 2.4.2, 2.4.4, 2.4.5, 2.4.6, 2.4.7, 2.4.8, 2.5.5, 2.5.6, 2.6.1, 2.6.2, 2.6.3, 2.6.7, 2.6.8, 2.6.9
Lesson 4 Voting for Leaders, pp. 172-175	**2.2.5** Restate facts and details in the text to clarify and organize ideas. See also 2.1.2, 2.1.3, 2.1.5, 2.2.2, 2.2.3, 2.2.4, 2.2.7, 2.4.1, 2.4.2, 2.4.4, 2.4.5, 2.4.6, 2.4.7, 2.4.8, 2.5.5, 2.5.6, 2.6.1, 2.6.2, 2.6.3, 2.6.7, 2.6.8, 2.6.9
Smithsonian Institution: Presidential Treasures, pp. 176-177	**2.2.7** Interpret information from diagrams, charts, and graphs. See also 2.2.2, 2.2.4
Biography: Susan B. Anthony, pp. 178-179	**2.2.6** Recognize cause-and-effect relationships in a text. See also 2.1.2, 2.1.3, 2.1.5, 2.2.2, 2.2.3, 2.2.4, 2.4.1, 2.4.2, 2.4.4, 2.4.5, 2.4.6, 2.4.7, 2.4.8, 2.5.5, 2.5.6, 2.6.1, 2.6.2, 2.6.3, 2.6.7, 2.6.8, 2.6.9
Lesson 5 The Land of Freedom, pp. 180-183	**2.2.5** Restate facts and details in the text to clarify and organize ideas. See also 2.1.2, 2.1.3, 2.1.5, 2.2.2, 2.2.3, 2.2.4, 2.2.7, 2.4.1, 2.4.2, 2.4.4, 2.4.5, 2.4.6, 2.4.7, 2.4.8, 2.5.5, 2.5.6, 2.6.1, 2.6.2, 2.6.3, 2.6.7, 2.6.8, 2.6.9, 2.7.8
Map and Globe Skills: Use a Map Grid, pp. 184-185	**2.2.7** Interpret information from diagrams, charts, and graphs. See also 2.2.2, 2.2.4, 2.2.8
Here and There: Flags Around the World, pp. 186-187	**2.2.7** Interpret information from diagrams, charts, and graphs. See also 2.2.2, 2.2.4
End with a Song, pp. 188-189 *Unit 4 Review, pp. 190-193* *Unit 4 Project, p. 194*	**2.2.5** Restate facts and details in the text to clarify and organize ideas. See also 2.1.2, 2.1.3, 2.1.5, 2.2.2, 2.2.3, 2.2.4, 2.2.7, 2.4.1, 2.4.2, 2.4.4, 2.4.5, 2.4.6, 2.4.7, 2.4.8, 2.5.5, 2.5.6, 2.6.1, 2.6.2, 2.6.3, 2.6.7, 2.6.8, 2.6.9, 2.7.8

Vocabulary	Resources	Meeting Individual Needs
government **mayor** **citizen**	• Workbook p. 38 • Transparencies 5, 20 • Vocabulary Cards: government, mayor, citizen • Every Student Learns Guide, pp. 62–65	• ESL Support, TE p. 155 • Leveled Practice, TE p. 159a
governor	• Workbook pp. 39–40 • Transparencies 5, 21, 22 • Vocabulary Card: governor • Every Student Learns Guide, pp. 66–69	• ESL Support, TE p. 161 • Leveled Practice, TE p. 165a
Congress **President**	• Workbook p. 41 • Transparency 5 • Vocabulary Cards: Congress, President • Every Student Learns Guide, pp. 70–73	• ESL Support, TE p. 168 • Leveled Practice, TE p. 171a
	• Workbook pp. 42–43 • Transparency 9 • Every Student Learns Guide, pp. 74–77	• ESL Support, TE p. 173 • Leveled Practice, TE pp. 179a
freedom **motto** **monument**	• Workbook pp. 44–45 • Transparencies 5, 23, 24 • Vocabulary Cards: freedom, motto, monument • Every Student Learns Guide, pp. 78–81	• ESL Support, TE p. 181 • Leveled Practice, TE p. 187a

Providing More Depth

Multimedia Library

- ***Presidents*** **by James Barber**
- ***The Diane Goode's Book of American Folktales and Songs*** **edited by Ann Durrell**
- **Songs and Music**
- **Video Field Trips**
- **Software**

Additional Resources

- Family Activities
- Vocabulary Cards
- Daily Activity Bank
- Social Studies Plus!
- Desk Maps
- Big Book Atlas
- Outline Maps

ADDITIONAL Technology

- AudioText
- The test maker
- Teacher Resources CD-ROM
- Map Resources CD-ROM
- **www.sfsocialstudies.com**

To establish guidelines for children's safe and responsible use of the Internet, use the **Scott Foresman Internet Guide.**

Additional Internet Links
To find out more about:

- our country's government, visit **bensguide.gpo.gov**
- life in the White House, visit **www.whitehouse.gov**

Key Internet Search Terms

- U.S. government
- White House

Unit 4 Objectives

Beginning of Unit 4

- **Use music to learn about a topic.** (pp. 148–149)
- **Use pictures to learn about a topic.** (pp. 150–151)
- **Determine the meanings of words.** (pp. 150–151)
- **Interpret print material by identifying the main idea and details.** (pp. 152–153)

Lesson 1
Local Government
pp. 154–157

- **Identify the functions of government.**
- **Compare the roles of public officials.**
- **Interpret print material by identifying the main idea and details.**
- **Identify characteristics of good citizenship.** (pp. 158–159)

Lesson 2
State Government
pp. 160–163

- **Describe how governments establish order, provide security, and manage conflict.**
- **Use tables to categorize information.** (pp. 164–165)
- **Identify selected symbols such as state birds and flowers.**

Lesson 3
Federal Government
pp. 166–169

- **Identify functions of government.**
- **Identify characteristics of good citizenship such as a belief in justice, truth, equality, and responsibility for the common good.** (pp. 170–171)

Lesson 4
Voting for Leaders
pp. 172–175

- **Identify ways that public officials are selected, including election and appointment to office.**
- **Obtain information from visual sources such as photographs of artifacts.** (pp. 176–177)
- **Identify contributions of historical figures who have influenced the community, state, and nation.** (pp. 178–179)
- **Identify historic figures who have exemplified good citizenship.** (pp. 178–179)

Lesson 5
The Land of Freedom
pp. 180–183

- **Identify patriotic songs, symbols, and mottoes.**
- **Identify people who have worked to improve the lives of American citizens.**
- **Interpret print material by identifying the main idea and details.**
- **Find locations on maps.** (pp. 184–185)
- **Identify flags as national symbols around the world.** (pp. 186–187)

End of Unit 4

- **Identify selected patriotic songs.** (pp. 188–189)

Assessment Options

✓ Formal Assessment

- **What did you learn?** PE/TE pp. 157, 163, 169, 175, 183, 193
- **Unit Review,** PE/TE pp. 190-193
- **Unit 4 Tests, Assessment Book**, pp. 13–16
- **The test maker,** (test-generator software)

✓ Informal Assessment

- **Teacher's Edition Questions,** throughout Lessons and Features
- **Close and Assess,** TE pp. 153, 157, 159, 163, 165, 169, 171, 175, 179, 183, 185, 187, 189
- **Try it!** PE/TE pp. 153, 165, 185
- **Think and Share,** PE/TE pp. 157, 163, 169, 171, 175, 179, 183
- **Fairness in Action,** PE/TE p. 159

Ongoing Assessment

Ongoing Assessment is found throughout the Teacher's Edition lessons using an **If...then** model.

If = students' observable behavior,

then = reteaching and enrichment suggestions

✓ Portfolio Assessment

- **Portfolio Assessment,** TE pp. 147, 192
- **Leveled Practice,** TE pp. 159a, 165a, 171a, 179a, 187a
- **Workbook Pages,** pp. 36–47
- **Unit Review: Skills on Your Own,** PE/TE p. 192
- **Curriculum Connection: Writing,** TE pp. 159, 163, 165a, 171, 179a, 187a

✓ Performance Assessment

- **Hands-on Unit Project (Unit 4 Performance Assessment)** PE/TE pp. 147, 190, 194
- **Internet Activity,** PE p. 194
- **Unit Review: Write and Share,** PE/TE p. 193
- **Scoring Guides,** TE pp. 191, 192, 194

Test Talk

Test-Taking Strategies

Understand the Question

- **Locate Key Words in the Question,** TE p. 159
- **Locate Key Words in the Text,** TE p. 168

Understand the Answer

- **Choose the Right Answer,** Test Talk Practice Book
- **Use Information from the Text,** TE p. 161
- **Use Information from Graphics,** TE p. 187
- **Write Your Answer,** TE p. 179
- *For additional practice, use the Test Talk Practice Book.*

Featured Strategy

Use Information from the Text

Children will:

- Decide where they will look for the answer and make notes about details from the text.
- Use information from the text, then look back at the question and the text to make sure they have the right answer.

PE/TE p. 193, **TE** p. 161

Curriculum Connections

Integrating Your Day

The lessons, skills, and features of Unit 4 provide many opportunities to make connections between social studies and other areas of the elementary curriculum.

Reading

Reading Skill—Main Idea and Details, PE/TE pp. 152–153, TE pp. 154, 166, 180

Reading Skill—Context Clues, TE p. 160

Word Families, TE p. 171a

The Preamble, TE p. 171a

Reading Skill—Put Things in Order, TE p. 172

Writing

What Is Sam Saying?, TE p. 148

Write a Nomination, TE p. 159

Add to "My Word Book," TE p. 159a

Careers, TE p. 163

Question and Answer, TE p. 165a

In the News!, TE p. 171

Why Should I Vote?, TE p. 179a

Puzzles, TE p. 187a

Mottoes, TE p. 187a

Math

Traffic Tallies, TE p. 159a

Count the Votes, TE p. 174

Social Studies

Literature

Our Presidents, TE p. 171a

A Photo Biography, TE p. 179a

Read About Your Country, PE/TE p. 193

Music/Drama

Role Play, TE p. 157

State Songs, TE p. 164

Let's March!, TE p. 187a

"Yankee Doodle Dandy," TE p. 189

Art

Design Your Own Coin!, TE p. 179

Campaign Ad, TE p. 179a

Look for this symbol throughout the Teacher's Edition to find **Curriculum Connections.**

Professional Development

Social Studies in the Early Childhood Classroom

by Sara Miranda Sanchez
Albuquerque Public Schools

Often social studies is viewed as a side subject taught only when there is extra time. Elementary curriculum forms the foundations for a multitude of learning situations and content for students. Invariably, there never seems to be enough time in an elementary school day to cover every issue.

How can social studies have a meaningful place in the primary classroom? As represented in the NCSS Consortium for Interdisciplinary Teaching and Learning position statement (1994), recent calls for educational reform focus on the need for curricula emphasizing conceptual learning that is integrated across traditional subject areas. Eliminating artificial barriers among subject areas gives students a broader context for solving real-life problems.

As a classroom teacher, I, too, struggled with covering language arts, math, science, and social studies in a comprehensive manner while remaining true to early childhood practices. However, I continue to be convinced that integrated curriculum allows for intermingling of content as well as child-centered, interactive learning experiences for students.

The following examples show Scott Foresman's commitment to providing integrated, cross-curricular activities as an important part of teaching social studies.

Count the Votes (Math), *TE p. 174 After learning that people vote on issues and not just for leaders, children take part in a class vote. They work together to tally the votes.*

Design Your Own Coin! (Art), *TE p. 179 After reading about Susan B. Anthony who has been honored with a coin showing her image, children honor someone they know with a coin of their own design.*

ESL Support

ESL

The Role of Students' Identity in Accessing Content

by Jim Cummins, Ph. D.
University of Toronto

Accessing language is not just a matter of language and cognition. Certainly, our instruction should strive to generate maximum cognitive engagement on the part of students if they are to understand the concepts and language of the text. However, equally important in accessing content is the motivation and sense of ownership that students bring to the task. If students feel no sense of ownership or *investment* in the material, they are unlikely to engage cognitively in instruction. If Social Studies is to become more than just a set of inert facts, we need to find ways to make the content relevant to students' lives.

The following examples in the Teacher's Edition suggest ways your ESL students may access content.

Community Government, *p. 155 Children use a simple graphic to discuss how local government works. They make and save their own labeled copies of the graphic for use as a review tool.*

Voting, *p. 173 Children collaborate to analyze a summary statement of the lesson. Together with the teacher, they explore individual words and phrases in the statement, relating those to what they know from their own experiences.*

Read Aloud

O Great America

by Margery Armitage

O great America!
My country fair and free!
Each day is overflowing
with all your gifts to me.
The lofty heights, the fields of grain,
the plains that rivers part,
And, oh! the highest gift of all
your Freedom in my heart!

Build Background

- Read aloud the title. Tell children that the poem they will listen to is also a song.
- Before you share the poem, have children talk about some things they might mention if they wrote a poem about their country.

Read Alouds and Primary Sources

Read Alouds and Primary Sources contains selections to be used with Unit 4.

Bibliography

Ballot Box Battle, The, by Emily Arnold McCully (Dragonfly, ISBN 0-679-89312-1, 1998). **Easy** ***Notable Social Studies Book.***

Hooray for the Fourth of July, by Wendy Watson (Houghton Mifflin, ISBN 0-618-04036-6, 2000). The story of a small town family's celebration of our nation's birthday. **Easy**

Heartland, by Diane Siebert and Wendell Minor (Illustrator) (HarperCollins, ISBN 0-064-43287-4,1992). **On-Level** ***Notable Social Studies Book***

On the Day the Tall Ships Sailed, by Betty Paraskevas and Michael Paraskevas (Illustrator) (Simon & Schuster, ISBN 0-689-82864-0, 2000). A parade of tall ships in New York harbor celebrates American heritage. **On-Level** ***Notable Social Studies Book***

Our Elections, by Richard Steins (Millbrook, ISBN 0-761-30092-9, 1996). **On-Level**

It Happened in the White House: Extraordinary Tales from America's Most Famous Home, by Kathleen Karr and Paul Meisel (Illustrator) (Disney Press, ISBN 0-786-81560-4, 1999). **Challenge**

Purple Mountain Majesties: The Story of Katharine Lee Bates and "America, the Beautiful," by Barbara Younger and Stacey Schuett (Illustrator) (Dutton, ISBN 0-525-45653-8, 1998). **Challenge**

Uncle Sam & Old Glory: Symbols of America, by Delno C. West and Jean M. West with Christopher Manson (Illustrator) (Atheneum, ISBN 0-689-82043-7, 2000). **Challenge**

My America: A Poetry Atlas of the United States, selected by Lee Bennett Hopkins. Illustrated by Stephen Alcorn. (Simon & Schuster, ISBN 0-689-81247-7, 2000). **Teacher reference**

Seeing the Whole Through Social Studies, by Tarry Lindquist (Heinemann, ISBN 0-435-08902-1, 1995). New and exciting ways to present social studies ideas to elementary learners. **Teacher reference**

Discovery Channel School* Videos** ***Heroes of American History. Get to know both early leaders, such as George Washington, and later heroes, such as Martin Luther King, Jr.; 2 videos. 42 minutes.

Look for this symbol throughout the Teacher's Edition to find **Award-Winning Selections**. Additional book references are suggested throughout this unit.

Practice and Extend

✓ **Unit 4 Performance Assessment**

- The Unit 4 Project, *Get Out the Vote!* found on p. 194, is an ongoing performance assessment project to enrich children's learning throughout this unit.
- This project, which has children make a campaign poster and a campaign commercial, may be started now or at any time during this unit of study.
- A performance assessment scoring guide is located on p. 194.

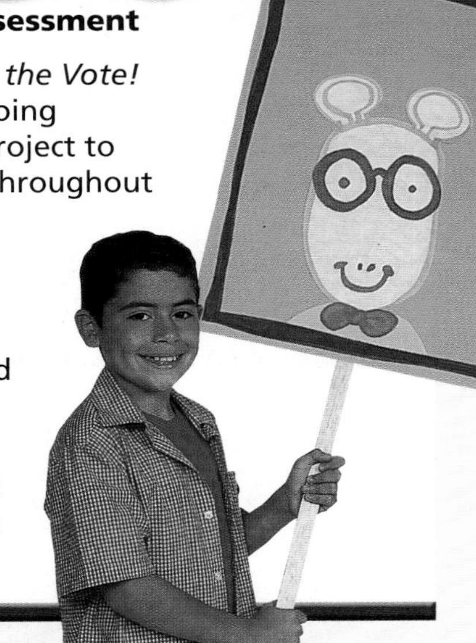

Our Country Today

Unit Overview

This unit introduces children to the concept of government—local, state, and federal—and explores the history of "the land of freedom."

Introduce Sam

Read the unit title and then introduce the featured child for this unit as a second grader named Sam. Talk about what Sam is doing in the photo and why it would be important for him to learn about his country, the United States of America.

Unit Question

- Read aloud the question on the page.
- Initiate a discussion of why people need government.
- To activate prior knowledge, make a list on the board of ideas children have for why people need to work together to run cities, states, and countries.

✓ **Portfolio Assessment** Keep a copy of this list for the Portfolio Assessment at the end of the unit.

Our Country Today

Objective

- Use music to learn about a topic.

Resources

- *Songs and Music* CD, "Our Country Today"
- Poster 7
- Social Studies Plus!

Introduce the Song

Preview Tell children that they will be singing a song about voting. Say that voting is an important right citizens of the United States have.

Warm Up To activate prior knowledge, have children tell why they think people should vote. Relate voting to being a good citizen, someone who cares about what happens to everyone living in the country.

Sing the Song

- Sing the song "Our Country Today" through once as children listen.
- Invite children to join in on a second singing.
- Divide the class into four groups and have each group in turn sing two lines.

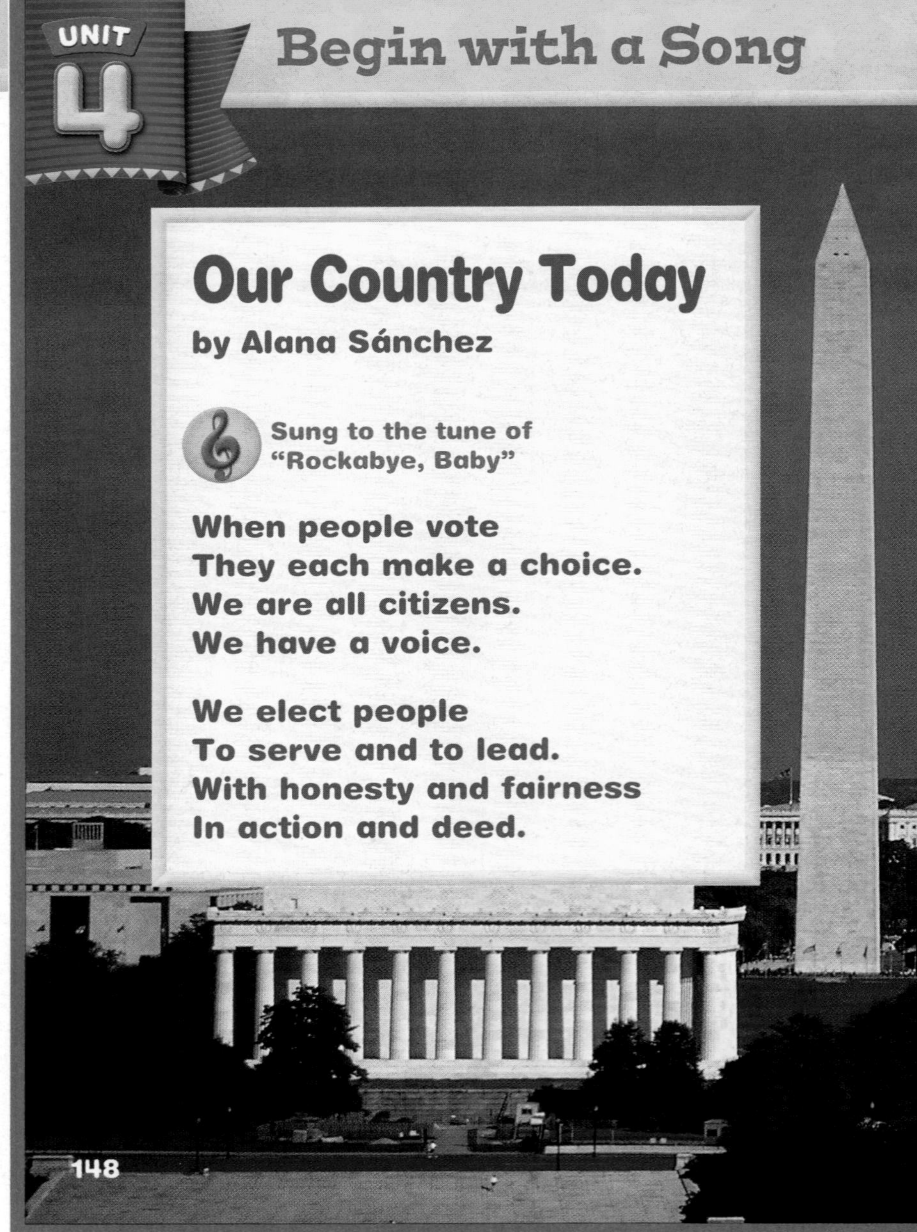

Practice and Extend

What Is Sam Saying?

- Have children notice that the photograph on p. 147 has a speech bubble for Sam. Ask children to think about the photo on pp. 148 and 149 and write a speech bubble.
- What do they think Sam might be saying? Have them think about where he is. Have them think, too, about the words of the song.
- Encourage children to share their ideas.

Technology

Play the CD, *Songs and Music,* to listen to "Our Country Today."

Talk About the Picture

Encourage partners to talk briefly about the picture. Ask them to look for clues in the photo that suggest where Sam is.

1. **Where do you think Sam is?** Most children should recognize some of the monuments in the picture to identify Washington, D.C. **Analyze Pictures**

2. **What clues helped you figure out where Sam is?** Possible answers: The Capitol, the Washington Monument **Analyze Pictures**

3. **Why do you think Sam is holding a flag?** Possible answer: The flag is the symbol of our country. Sam is in the capital city of our country. **Draw Conclusions**

Objectives

- Use pictures to learn about a topic.
- Determine the meanings of words.

Resources

- Workbook, p. 36
- Vocabulary Cards
- Poster 8

Introduce the Vocabulary

Read aloud and point to each vocabulary word and the photograph illustrating it. Have volunteers give the meanings of the words. Then have children find several examples of the vocabulary words in the illustration. Write these examples on the board.

Vocabulary Word	Illustrated Examples
government	Capitol building
mayor	*Citizens for Mayor Jones* sign; man on stage with *Mayor* banner
citizen	Adults in the picture
governor	Man with governor's banner
President	Picture of George Washington
Congress	Capitol building
freedom	Pictures of Martin Luther King, Jr., Susan B. Anthony
monument	George Washington Monument, Jefferson Memorial
motto	*Justice For All* on balloons

SOCIAL STUDIES STRAND
Government

Develop these basic principles of government as you discuss the illustration.

- Governments establish order, provide security, and manage conflict.
- Mayors, governors, and the President lead the government.
- Citizens vote for government leaders.
- Citizens have both rights and responsibilities.
- Freedom is the right to choose what to do.

150

MEETING INDIVIDUAL NEEDS
Leveled Practice

Take a Tour

Invite children to use the illustration to take a tour of Washington, D.C.

Easy Explain that you will be their tour guide. Begin at one end of the illustration and describe in detail all the buildings, people, signs, vehicles, and other things along the way. Have children repeat the vocabulary words as you guide them through Washington, D.C. **Reteach**

On-Level Have children take turns leading a tour through Washington, D.C., using vocabulary words to describe what they see. **Extend**

Challenge Invite children to describe something in Washington, D.C., using some of the vocabulary words. Have others guess what is being described. **Enrich**

WEB SITE Technology

You can look up vocabulary words online. Click on *Social Studies Library* and select the dictionary at **www.sfsocialstudies.com.**

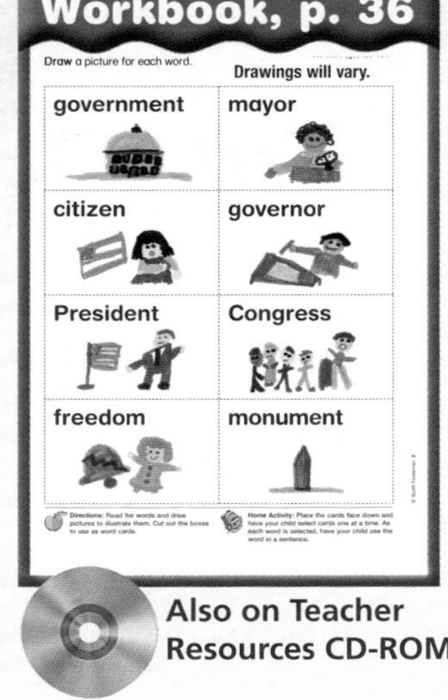

Workbook, p. 36

Draw a picture for each word. Drawings will vary.

government	mayor
citizen	governor
President	Congress
freedom	monument

Also on Teacher Resources CD-ROM.

Talk About the Illustration

Allow children time to study the illustration. Explain that the picture shows a part of Washington, D.C., called the National Mall, where people visit to learn about the history of the United States.

1 **What motto can you find in the illustration?** *Justice For All* **What do you think the motto means?** Possible answer: All people should be treated fairly.

2 **How are the people in the illustration showing that they are good citizens?** Possible answers: They are visiting to learn about their country's history; participating in the government; following the directions of the police.
Analyze Pictures

Look Ahead

Tell children that they will learn more about each of these words as they study Unit 4.

You may want to revisit the picture with children to review the concepts and vocabulary in the unit.

3 **Why do you think monuments are large, important-looking buildings?** Possible answer: They are built to honor people. **Make Inferences**

4 **Who are some leaders of government that people vote for?** Mayor, governor
Analyze Pictures

A Letter to the Editor

Main Idea and Details

Objective

Interpret print material by identifying the main idea and details.

Resource

- Workbook, p. 37

About the Unit Target Skill

- The target reading skill for this unit is Main Idea and Details.
- Children are introduced to the unit target skill here and are given an opportunity to practice it.
- Further opportunities to practice finding the main idea and details are found throughout Unit 4.

1 Introduce and Motivate

Preview To determine if children understand the concept of main idea and details, direct their attention to the photo of Sam on p. 152. Work together to write a sentence that tells what the picture is mostly about—its main idea. (*Sam wrote a letter and made a drawing to go with it.*) Then have children suggest sentences that identify supporting details. (*Sam's drawing shows a car on a hill.*)

Warm Up To activate prior knowledge, write the sentences below on the board. Read the following aloud to have children identify the main idea sentence and then the supporting details:

> Some people live in homes in the suburbs. Others live in crowded big cities. People who live in rural areas have lots of open space. People live in many different places.

Reading Social Studies

A Letter to the Editor

Main Idea and Details

Hi! I'm Sam. I wrote a letter about a traffic problem. I sent the letter to my city's newspaper. What is my letter all about?

February 21, 2003

Dear Editor,

I am writing this letter about a traffic problem. We need a stop sign in my neighborhood. I live at the bottom of a hill. I see many people driving down the hill too fast. Children play in my neighborhood. Drivers need to slow down so nobody gets hurt. A stop sign will slow down the cars. Please print this letter so people will know what we need.

Sincerely,
Sam
Second-Grade Student

Practice and Extend

ESL — BUILD BACKGROUND — ESL Support

Main Idea/Details Transform the sentences in the Warm Up activity into a graphic organizer. Write the main idea sentence in the center circle; write the details in satellite circles. Have children draw a picture to show either the main idea or a detail.

Beginning Have children tell if their picture shows the main idea or a detail. Ask them to label persons or objects in their picture.

Intermediate Have children describe their picture orally and explain why it shows the main idea or a detail. Model the structure: *My picture is a main idea (detail) because* ______.

Advanced Have children write sentences to describe their picture and explain in writing why it is a main idea or a detail.

The **topic** tells what the letter is about. The **main idea** is the most important idea about this topic. **Details** tell more about the main idea.

February 21, 2003

Dear Editor,

I am writing this letter about a traffic problem. We need a stop sign in my neighborhood. I live at the bottom of a hill. I see many people driving down the hill too fast. Children play in my neighborhood. Drivers need to slow down so nobody gets hurt. A stop sign will slow down the cars. Please print this letter so people will know what we need.

Sincerely,
Sam
Second-Grade Student

main idea

detail

detail

detail

Write about something that your neighborhood needs. What is the **topic?** What is the **main idea** about this topic? What are some **details** that tell more about the **main idea?**

153

What's the Limit?

- Help children find out the speed limit in their community, that is, on local streets.
- Help them find the speed limit for major highways nearby. Is there a difference?
- Have children discuss why the speed limit for community streets is usually much lower than that for major highways.

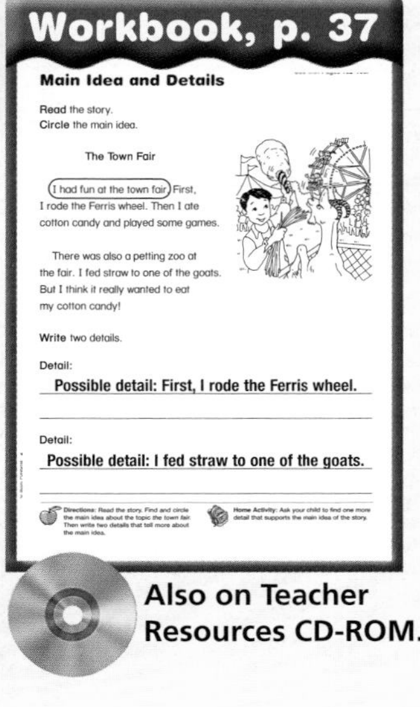

Workbook, p. 37

Main Idea and Details

Read the story.
Circle the main idea.

The Town Fair

I had fun at the town fair. First, I rode the Ferris wheel. Then I ate cotton candy and played some games.

There was also a petting zoo at the fair. I fed straw to one of the goats. But I think it really wanted to eat my cotton candy!

Write two details.

Detail: **Possible detail: First, I rode the Ferris wheel.**

Detail: **Possible detail: I fed straw to one of the goats.**

Directions: Read the story. Find and circle the main idea about the topic *the town fair.* Then write two details that tell more about the main idea.

Home Activity: Ask your child to find one more detail that supports the main idea of the story.

Also on Teacher Resources CD-ROM.

2 Teach and Discuss

Have children read p. 152 to to find out what Sam's letter is about and to whom it is going. Discuss why a newspaper office would be a good place to send a letter about a traffic problem.

Have children read the top of p. 153. Ask children why Sam wrote the topic and the main idea of his letter right at its beginning. (He wanted his reader to know what his letter was about.) Have children tell why Sam added details. (To give more information.)

Ongoing Assessment

If... children do not understand the term *main idea,*

then... suggest they ask themselves this question: *What is the most important idea I want my reader to know?*

3 Close and Assess

Try it!

Brainstorm with children some things their *neighborhood needs* and write the ideas on the board. Then have children choose an idea and write a paragraph. Children's responses should reflect the topic of neighborhood needs, should have a clearly stated main idea as a first sentence, and include at least three supporting details.

Workbook Support

Use the following Workbook pages to support content and skills development as you teach Unit 4. You can also view and print Workbook pages from the Teacher Resources CD-ROM.

Workbook, p. 36

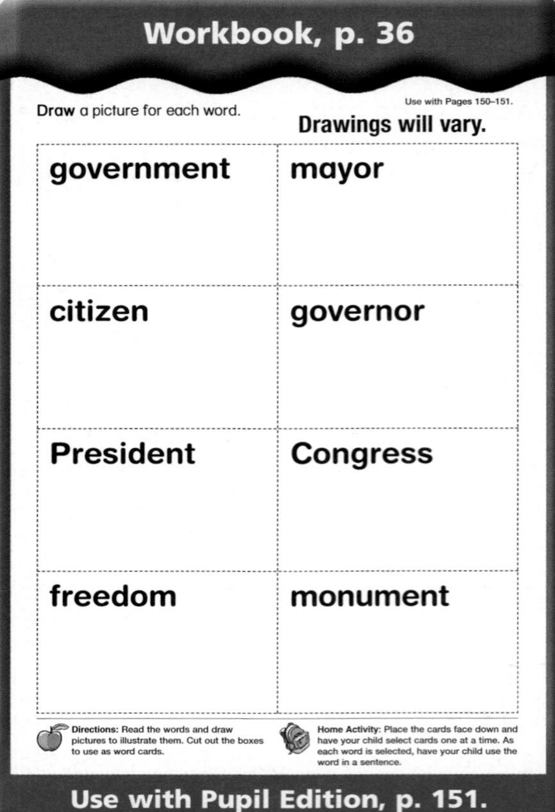

Use with Pages 150–151.

Draw a picture for each word. **Drawings will vary.**

government	mayor
citizen	governor
President	Congress
freedom	monument

Directions: Read the words and draw pictures to illustrate them. Cut out the boxes to use as word cards.

Home Activity: Place the cards face down and have your child select cards one at a time. As each word is selected, have your child use the word in a sentence.

Use with Pupil Edition, p. 151.

Workbook, p. 37

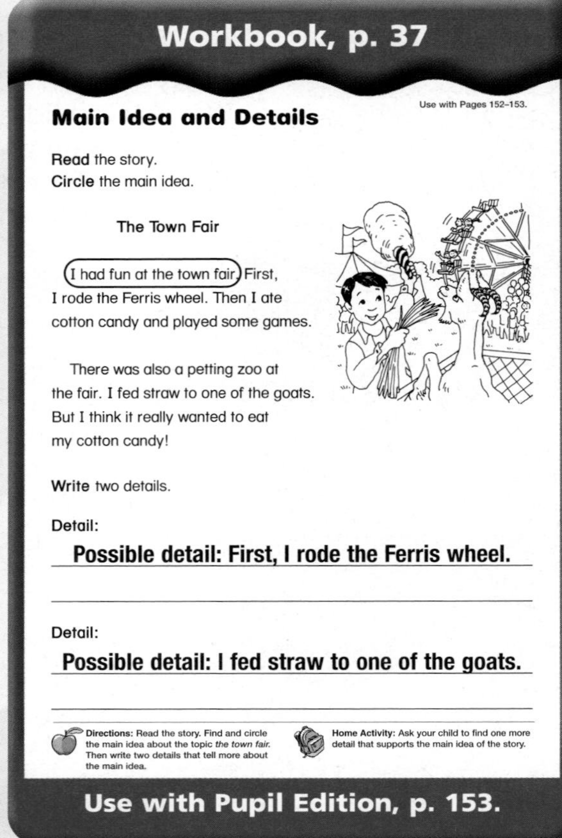

Use with Pages 152–153.

Main Idea and Details

Read the story.
Circle the main idea.

The Town Fair

(I had fun at the town fair.) First, I rode the Ferris wheel. Then I ate cotton candy and played some games.

There was also a petting zoo at the fair. I fed straw to one of the goats. But I think it really wanted to eat my cotton candy!

Write two details.

Detail: **Possible detail: First, I rode the Ferris wheel.**

Detail: **Possible detail: I fed straw to one of the goats.**

Directions: Read the story. Find and circle the main idea about the topic *the town fair*. Then write two details that tell more about the main idea.

Home Activity: Ask your child to find one more detail that supports the main idea of the story.

Use with Pupil Edition, p. 153.

Workbook, p. 38

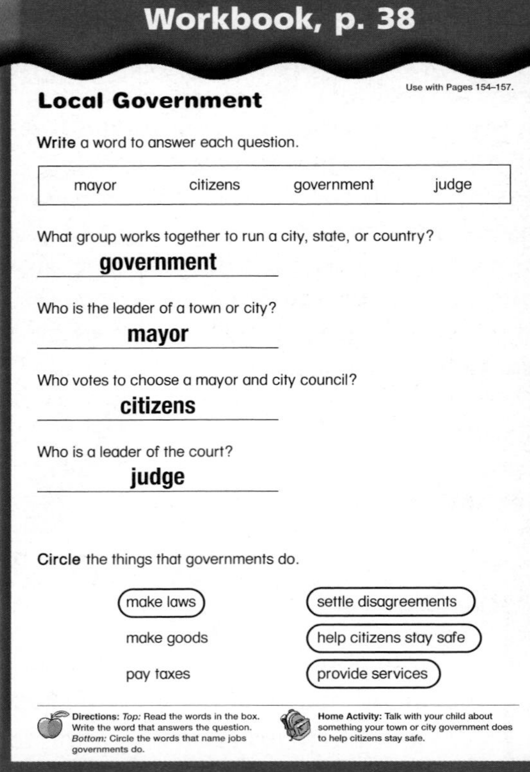

Use with Pages 154–157.

Local Government

Write a word to answer each question.

mayor | citizens | government | judge

What group works together to run a city, state, or country? **government**

Who is the leader of a town or city? **mayor**

Who votes to choose a mayor and city council? **citizens**

Who is a leader of the court? **judge**

Circle the things that governments do.

(make laws) | (settle disagreements)
make goods | (help citizens stay safe)
pay taxes | (provide services)

Directions: *Top:* Read the words in the box. Write the word that answers the question. *Bottom:* Circle the words that name jobs governments do.

Home Activity: Talk with your child about something your town or city government does to help citizens stay safe.

Use with Pupil Edition, p. 157.

Workbook, p. 39

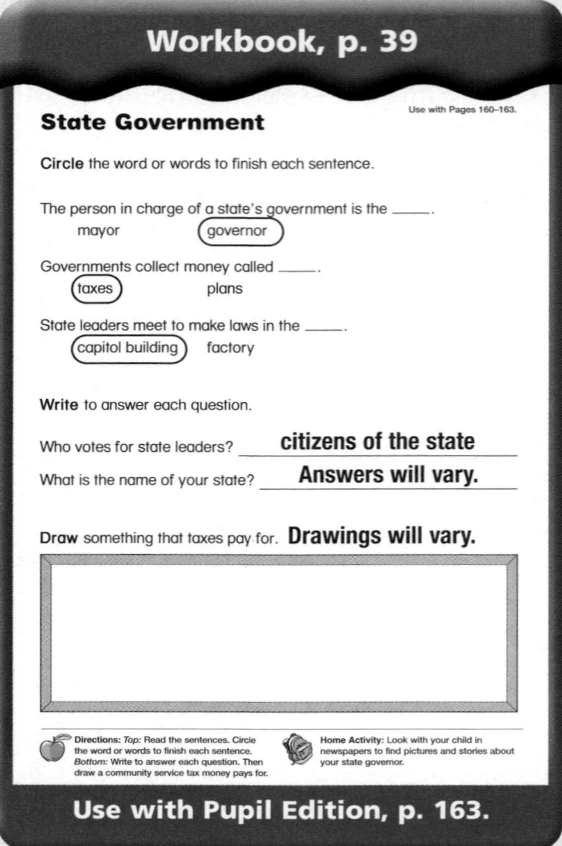

Use with Pages 160–163.

State Government

Circle the word or words to finish each sentence.

The person in charge of a state's government is the _____.
mayor (governor)

Governments collect money called _____.
(taxes) plans

State leaders meet to make laws in the _____.
(capitol building) factory

Write to answer each question.

Who votes for state leaders? **citizens of the state**

What is the name of your state? **Answers will vary.**

Draw something that taxes pay for. **Drawings will vary.**

Directions: *Top:* Read the sentences. Circle the word or words to finish each sentence. *Bottom:* Write to answer each question. Then draw a community service tax money pays for.

Home Activity: Look with your child in newspapers to find pictures and stories about your state governor.

Use with Pupil Edition, p. 163.

Workbook, p. 40

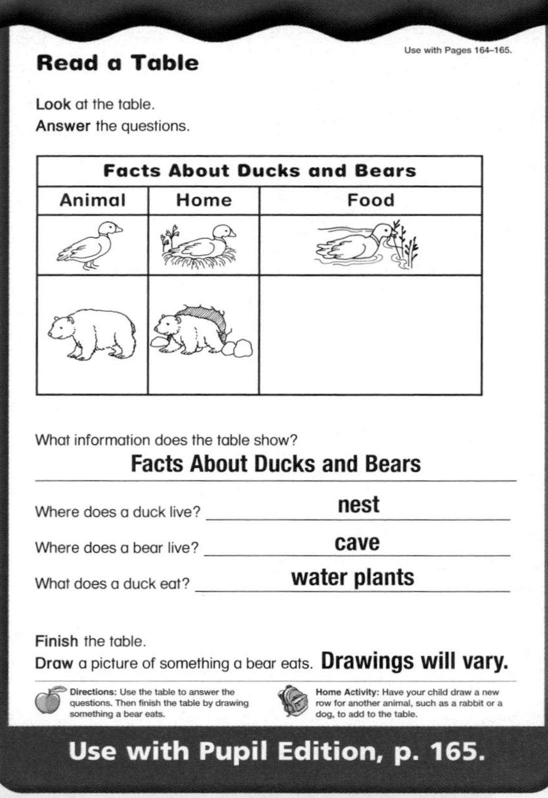

Use with Pages 164–165.

Read a Table

Look at the table.
Answer the questions.

Facts About Ducks and Bears		
Animal	Home	Food

What information does the table show? **Facts About Ducks and Bears**

Where does a duck live? **nest**

Where does a bear live? **cave**

What does a duck eat? **water plants**

Finish the table.
Draw a picture of something a bear eats. **Drawings will vary.**

Directions: Use the table to answer the questions. Then finish the table by drawing something a bear eats.

Home Activity: Have your child draw a new row for another animal, such as a rabbit or a dog, to add to the table.

Use with Pupil Edition, p. 165.

Workbook, p. 41

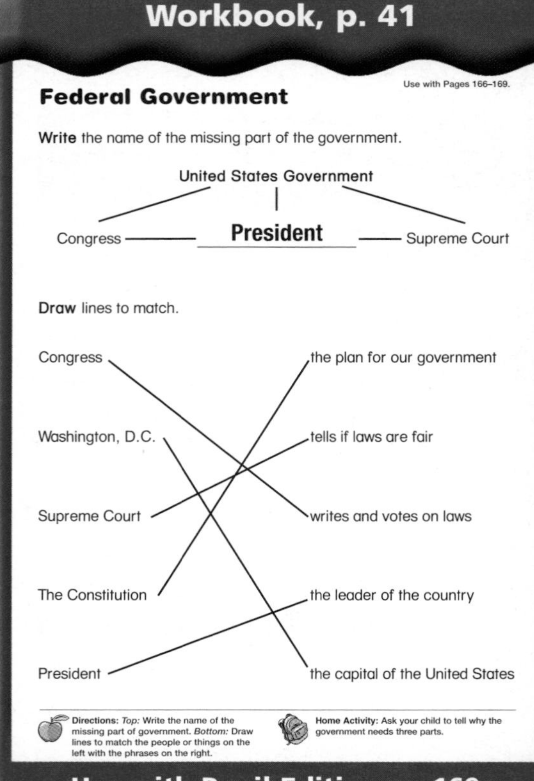

Use with Pages 166–169.

Federal Government

Write the name of the missing part of the government.

United States Government

Congress — **President** — Supreme Court

Draw lines to match.

Congress — writes and votes on laws
Washington, D.C. — the capital of the United States
Supreme Court — tells if laws are fair
The Constitution — the plan for our government
President — the leader of the country

Directions: *Top:* Write the name of the missing part of government. *Bottom:* Draw lines to match the people or things on the left with the phrases on the right.

Home Activity: Ask your child to tell why the government needs three parts.

Use with Pupil Edition, p. 169.

Workbook Support

Workbook, p. 42

Voting for Leaders

Use with Pages 172–175.

Mark a ✓ next to what people do to vote.

- ____ Pay money.
- ✓ Mark a choice on a ballot.
- ✓ Sign up to vote.
- ✓ Get a ballot.
- ____ Visit a capital city.
- ✓ Learn about who is running for office.

Write to answer the questions.

What two things must you be to vote in the United States?

a citizen of the United States; 18 years old

How can you learn about people who are running for office?

Possible answer: by watching TV or reading the newspaper

Directions: *Top:* Read the sentences. Put a check mark next to each sentence that tells something a voter must do. *Bottom:* Write answers for the questions.

Home Activity: Ask your child to tell some ways voters can find out about those who want to be government leaders.

Use with Pupil Edition, p. 175.

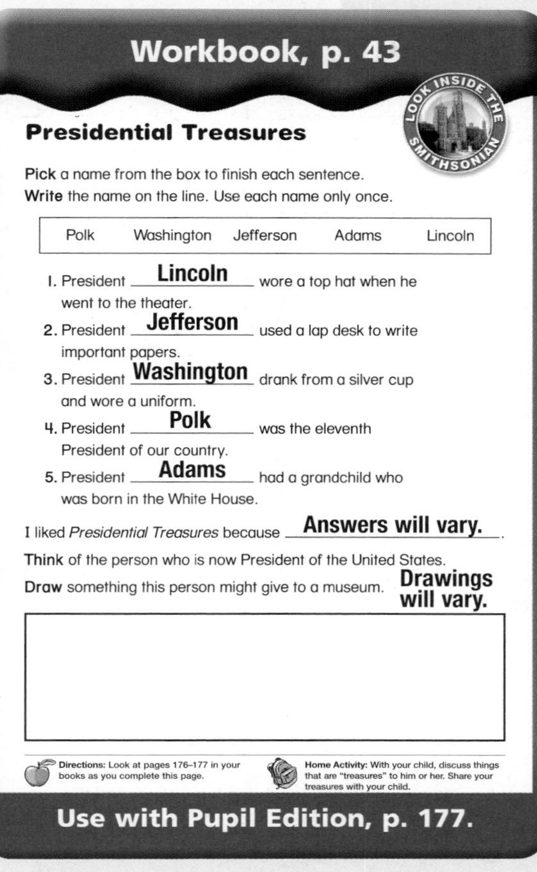

Workbook, p. 43

Presidential Treasures

Pick a name from the box to finish each sentence.
Write the name on the line. Use each name only once.

Polk	Washington	Jefferson	Adams	Lincoln

1. President **Lincoln** wore a top hat when he went to the theater.
2. President **Jefferson** used a lap desk to write important papers.
3. President **Washington** drank from a silver cup and wore a uniform.
4. President **Polk** was the eleventh President of our country.
5. President **Adams** had a grandchild who was born in the White House.

I liked *Presidential Treasures* because **Answers will vary.**

Think of the person who is now President of the United States.
Draw something this person might give to a museum. **Drawings will vary.**

Directions: Look at pages 176–177 in your books as you complete this page.

Home Activity: With your child, discuss things that are "treasures" to him or her. Share your treasures with your child.

Use with Pupil Edition, p. 177.

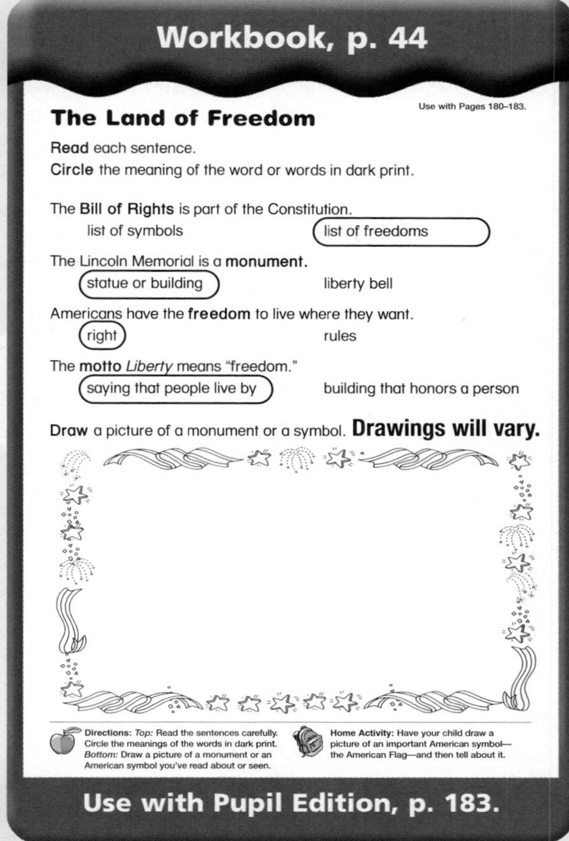

Workbook, p. 44

The Land of Freedom

Use with Pages 180–183.

Read each sentence.
Circle the meaning of the word or words in dark print.

The **Bill of Rights** is part of the Constitution.
list of symbols — (list of freedoms)

The Lincoln Memorial is a **monument.**
(statue or building) — liberty bell

Americans have the **freedom** to live where they want.
(right) — rules

The **motto** *Liberty* means "freedom."
(saying that people live by) — building that honors a person

Draw a picture of a monument or a symbol. **Drawings will vary.**

Directions: *Top:* Read the sentences carefully. Circle the meanings of the words in dark print. *Bottom:* Draw a picture of a monument or an American symbol you've read about or seen.

Home Activity: Have your child draw a picture of an important American symbol—the American Flag—and then tell about it.

Use with Pupil Edition, p. 183.

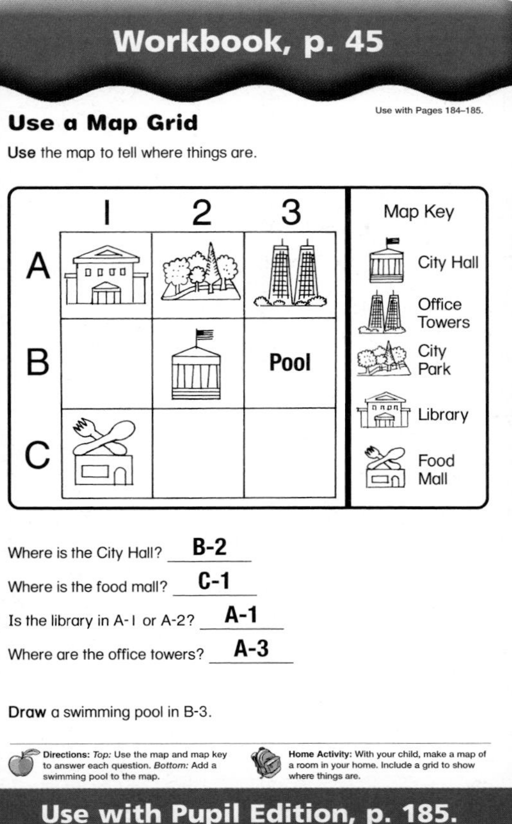

Workbook, p. 45

Use a Map Grid

Use with Pages 184–185.

Use the map to tell where things are.

Where is the City Hall? **B-2**

Where is the food mall? **C-1**

Is the library in A-1 or A-2? **A-1**

Where are the office towers? **A-3**

Draw a swimming pool in B-3.

Directions: *Top:* Use the map and map key to answer each question. *Bottom:* Add a swimming pool to the map.

Home Activity: With your child, make a map of a room in your home. Include a grid to show where things are.

Use with Pupil Edition, p. 185.

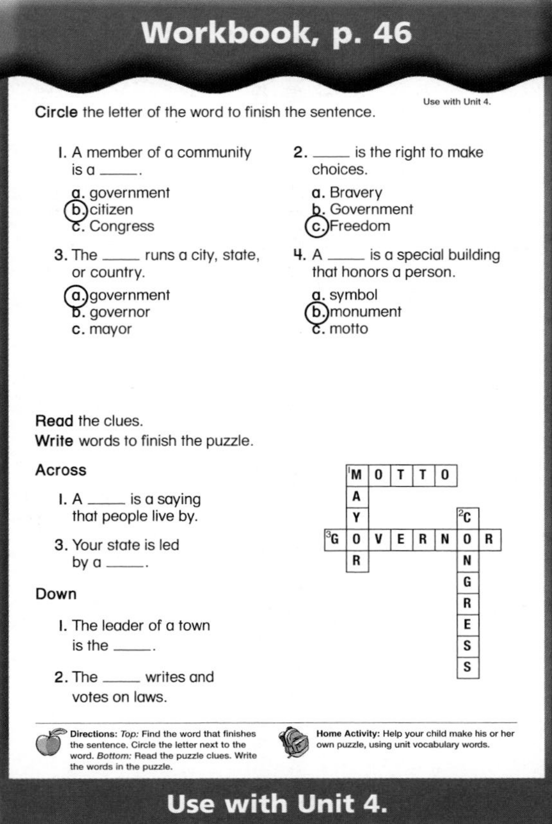

Workbook, p. 46

Use with Unit 4.

Circle the letter of the word to finish the sentence.

1. A member of a community is a ____.
   a. government
   (b.) citizen
   c. Congress
2. ____ is the right to make choices.
   a. Bravery
   b. Government
   (c.) Freedom
3. The ____ runs a city, state, or country.
   (a.) government
   b. governor
   c. mayor
4. A ____ is a special building that honors a person.
   a. symbol
   (b.) monument
   c. motto

Read the clues.
Write words to finish the puzzle.

Across

1. A ____ is a saying that people live by.
3. Your state is led by a ____.

Down

1. The leader of a town is the ____.
2. The ____ writes and votes on laws.

Directions: *Top:* Find the word that finishes the sentence. Circle the letter next to the word. *Bottom:* Read the puzzle clues. Write the words in the puzzle.

Home Activity: Help your child make his or her own puzzle, using unit vocabulary words.

Use with Unit 4.

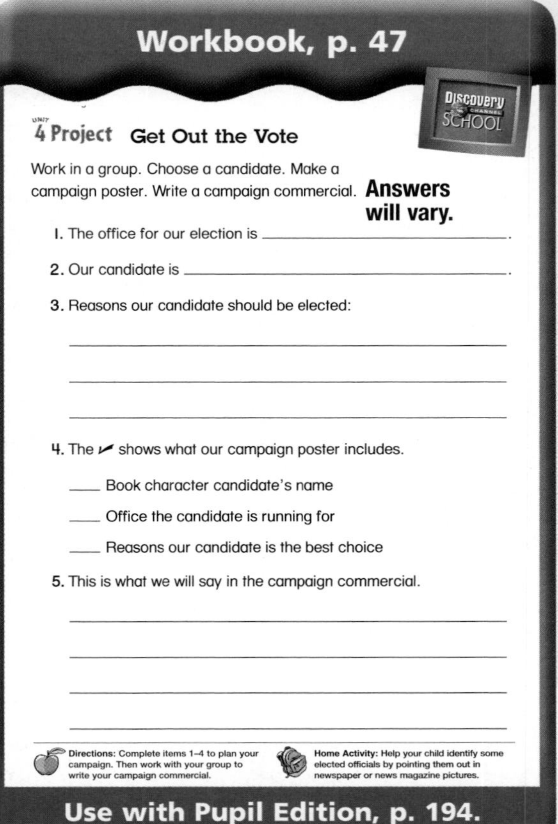

Workbook, p. 47

Unit 4 Project Get Out the Vote

Work in a group. Choose a candidate. Make a campaign poster. Write a campaign commercial. **Answers will vary.**

1. The office for our election is ____.
2. Our candidate is ____.
3. Reasons our candidate should be elected:
4. The ✓ shows what our campaign poster includes.
   - ____ Book character candidate's name
   - ____ Office the candidate is running for
   - ____ Reasons our candidate is the best choice
5. This is what we will say in the campaign commercial.

Directions: Complete items 1–4 to plan your campaign. Then work with your group to write your campaign commercial.

Home Activity: Help your child identify some elected officials by pointing them out in newspaper or news magazine pictures.

Use with Pupil Edition, p. 194.

Assessment Support

Use these Assessment Book pages and the test maker to assess content and skills in Unit 4. You can also view and print Assessment Book pages from the Teacher Resources CD-ROM.

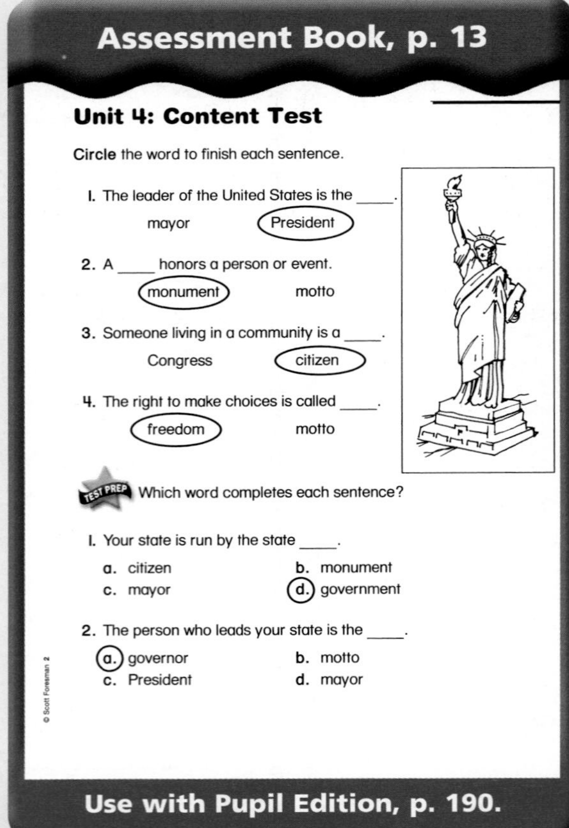

Assessment Book, p. 13

Unit 4: Content Test

Circle the word to finish each sentence.

1. The leader of the United States is the _____.
   mayor (President)
2. A _____ honors a person or event.
   (monument) motto
3. Someone living in a community is a _____.
   Congress (citizen)
4. The right to make choices is called _____.
   (freedom) motto

TEST PREP Which word completes each sentence?

1. Your state is run by the state _____.
   a. citizen b. monument
   c. mayor (d.) government
2. The person who leads your state is the _____.
   (a.) governor b. motto
   c. President d. mayor

© Scott Foresman 2

Use with Pupil Edition, p. 190.

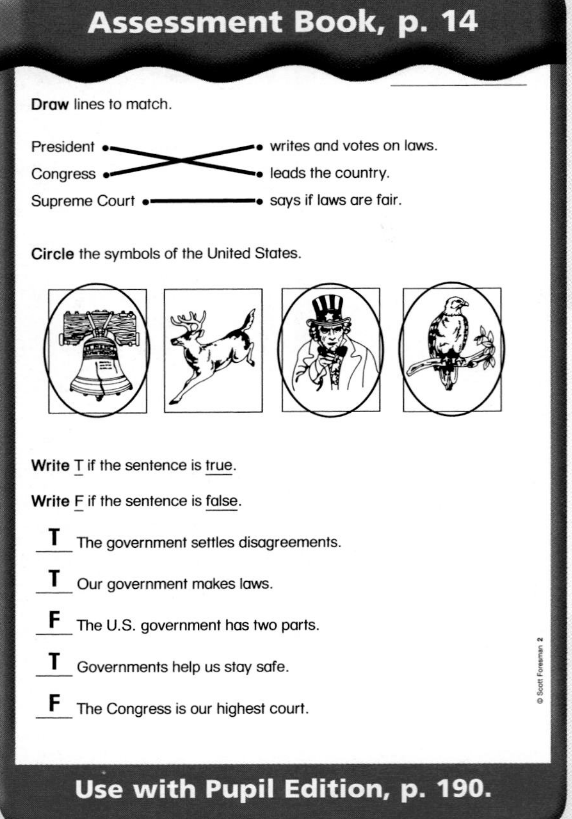

Assessment Book, p. 14

Draw lines to match.

President — leads the country.
Congress — writes and votes on laws.
Supreme Court — says if laws are fair.

Circle the symbols of the United States.

Write T if the sentence is true.

Write F if the sentence is false.

T The government settles disagreements.

T Our government makes laws.

F The U.S. government has two parts.

T Governments help us stay safe.

F The Congress is our highest court.

© Scott Foresman 2

Use with Pupil Edition, p. 190.

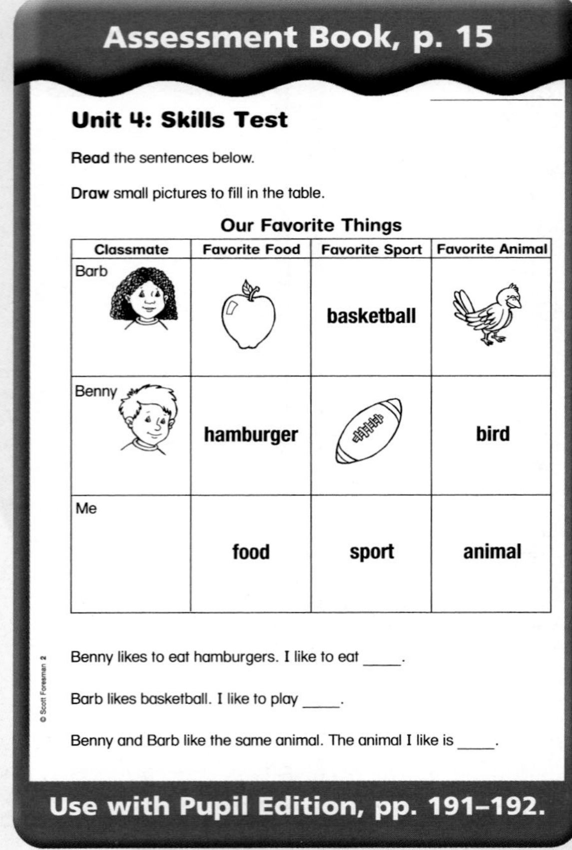

Assessment Book, p. 15

Unit 4: Skills Test

Read the sentences below.

Draw small pictures to fill in the table.

Our Favorite Things

Classmate	Favorite Food	Favorite Sport	Favorite Animal
Barb		basketball	
Benny	hamburger		bird
Me	food	sport	animal

Benny likes to eat hamburgers. I like to eat _____.

Barb likes basketball. I like to play _____.

Benny and Barb like the same animal. The animal I like is _____.

© Scott Foresman 2

Use with Pupil Edition, pp. 191–192.

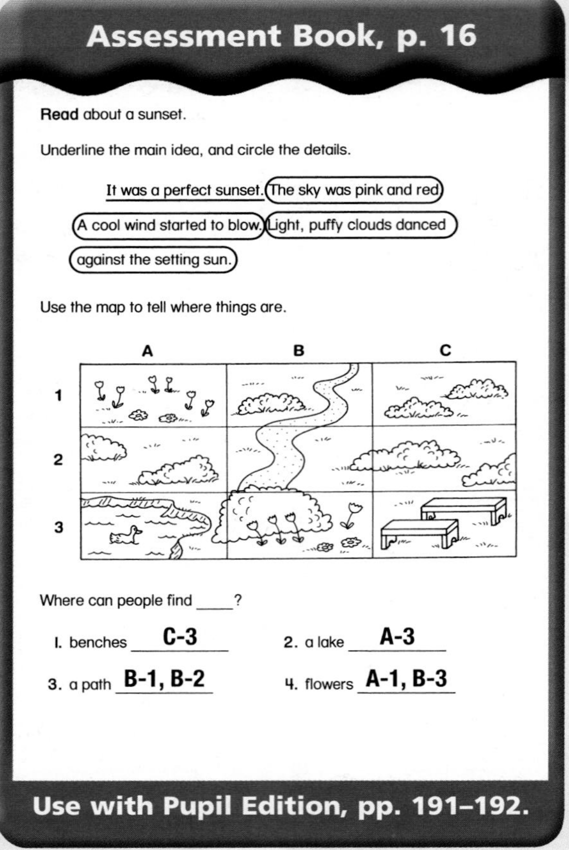

Assessment Book, p. 16

Read about a sunset.

Underline the main idea, and circle the details.

<u>It was a perfect sunset.</u> (The sky was pink and red.) (A cool wind started to blow.) (Light, puffy clouds danced against the setting sun.)

Use the map to tell where things are.

Where can people find _____?

1. benches C-3
2. a lake A-3
3. a path B-1, B-2
4. flowers A-1, B-3

Use with Pupil Edition, pp. 191–192.

Lesson 1 Overview

Local Government **pages 154–157**	Children will learn the meanings of the words *government, mayor*, and *citizen* and explore how local government works to make communities better and safer places to live.	 Time 20–30 minutes Resources • Workbook, p. 38 • Vocabulary Cards government mayor citizen • Every Student Learns Guide, pp. 62-65
Anna Beavers **pages 158–159**	Children will learn how Anna Beavers helps the children in her Virginia community to look good and feel better about themselves.	 Time 15–20 minutes

Build Background

Activity

In the Mayor's Chair

 **Time** 20–25 minutes

Talk briefly with children about what they think a mayor of a city or town does. If possible, have newspaper clippings showing your mayor in action. Then have children fold a sheet of drawing paper in half. Tell them to draw themselves in the role of the mayor in each part of the paper. Their pictures should show two different mayoral activities. Encourage children to write captions for their pictures.

Collect and display the pictures so children can compare their ideas.

If time is short, have children work together to create a short list of interview questions they would like to ask their mayor.

Read Aloud

Citizens One and All

by Mimi Latham

In each and every city and town,
Local government's all around.
A mayor is elected there,
And laws are made for all to share.

We're citizens of a community,
And we're proud as we can be.
People joining all together,
We make our cities and towns
Better and BETTER!

Local Government

Objectives

- Identify functions of government.
- Compare the roles of public officials.
- Interpret print material by identifying the main idea and supporting details.

Vocabulary

government a group of people who work together to run a city, state, or country (p. 154)

mayor the leader of a town or city (p. 155)

citizen a member of a community, state, and country (p. 155)

If time is short, write the following on the board: *mayor + city council + each citizen = good city government.*

- Talk with children about the meanings of the terms and how each member of the equation interacts with the others to achieve good local government.

1 Introduce and Motivate

Preview Display the Vocabulary Cards **government**, **mayor**, and **citizen**. Ask children what they think each word means. Share the meaning of each word. Have children locate the terms as they preview the lesson.

Warm Up To activate prior knowledge, discuss some of the local laws in your community. Focus on laws children may be familiar with, such as traffic and street safety laws, sanitation laws, and so on. Ask children to name some laws they know about. Ask who makes the laws in the community and who enforces or makes sure people obey the laws.

Local Governmen

I want to solve the traffic problem in my neighborhood. My mom and I called our
1 local government for help. A **government** is a group of people who work together to run a city, state, or country. A government provic services, makes laws, helps us stay safe, and settles disagreements. 2

154

Practice and Extend

Review the definitions of topic, main idea, and details.

- After children read pp. 154–157, assign partners to work together.
- Write on the board: *Main Idea: Citizens who are in government work together with other citizens.*
- Have partners record two details that support the main idea. (Possible details: *The city council makes laws to help the citizens. The police make sure citizens are safe.*)

WEB SITE Technology

You can look up vocabulary words online. Click on *Social Studies Library* and select the dictionary at **www.sfsocialstudies.com.**

A **mayor** is the leader of a town or city. The mayor works with a group of people called the city council. The mayor and city council make laws and provide services to their citizens. A **citizen** is a member of a community, state, and country. ③

The citizens in my community vote to elect our mayor and city council. These leaders, like all citizens, are responsible for doing their jobs and obeying laws. The mayor and city council will help decide if a stop sign is needed in my neighborhood. ④ ⑤

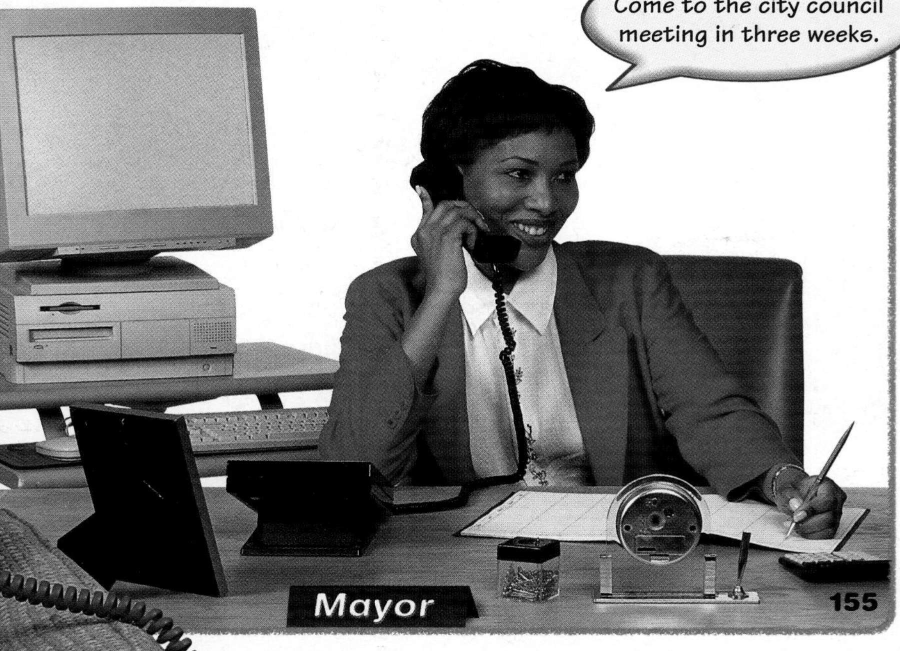

Mayor

155

2 Teach and Discuss

Page 154

Help children identify Sam, his mom, and the mayor in the photograph on pp. 154 and 155. As children read the pages, be certain they read Sam's speech bubble to know what solution he is thinking about.

① **What is the purpose of a stop sign? How would it help solve the problem?** It makes drivers stop for a short time to look around before moving along a busy street; it slows down traffic. A stop sign makes drivers more aware of what is around them so people are safer. **Solve Problems**

② **Name three things government does.** Government makes laws, helps us stay safe, and settles disagreements. **Main Idea and Details**

Page 155

③ **What person in the school is in charge of the whole school, just as a mayor is in charge of the whole city?** Children should recognize that the principal is the school leader. The teachers work with the principal to make rules and decisions for the school. **Compare and Contrast**

④ **The mayor and the city council members are elected. What does it mean to "elect" someone?** It means to vote to give someone a job. **Context Clues**

⑤ **Why is it important for citizens to vote?** Every person's vote or opinion counts; whoever gets the most votes will represent the whole community. **Make Inferences**

ESL ACCESS CONTENT

ESL Support

Community Government Draw the graphic shown below on the board and label it.

Beginning As you read brief definitions, have children point to the correct label on the graphic: (*mayor*) leader of the city or town, (*city council*) helps make laws, (*citizens*) people in the community.

Intermediate Have children copy and label their own graphics. Ask volunteers to point to the labels and define orally the role of the person or persons.

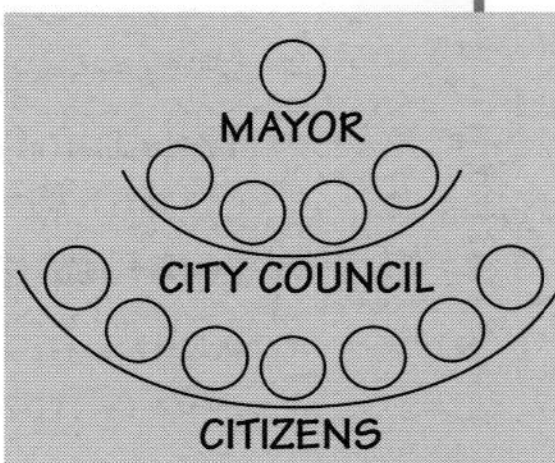

Advanced Have children use their graphics and discussion to write sentences to tell how people in the community work together for good government.

For additional ESL support, use Every Student Learns Guide, pp. 62-65.

continued

Page 156

6 Why did Sam's mom set up a neighborhood meeting? Possible answers: She wanted to discuss the neighborhood traffic problem. She wanted to get their support for a new stop sign. She wanted to hear ideas others might have had about how to solve the problem. **Cause and Effect**

7 Compare and contrast the jobs of the mayor and city council members to the jobs of police officers. The mayor and city council work to make laws. Police officers make sure people obey the laws. **Compare and Contrast**

8 Why is the county courthouse an important place in the community? Judges who work there decide if people have broken any laws. **Recall and Retell**

Page 157

If in Unit 1, Lesson 1 you and children began a list of ways children act responsibly in their community, revisit that list now. Ask children to add ideas they learn in this lesson to the list.

9 Why did a police officer give a report? To give the people at the meeting more information about the traffic problem so they could make a good decision about what to do **Make Inferences**

Problem Solving

10 What problem-solving steps did Sam and the others follow? Sam identified the problem. People in the neighborhood got more information by sharing what they knew about the problem and by listening to the police officer's report. The mayor and city council discussed what to do. They voted. The problem was solved with the new stop sign. **Recall and Retell**

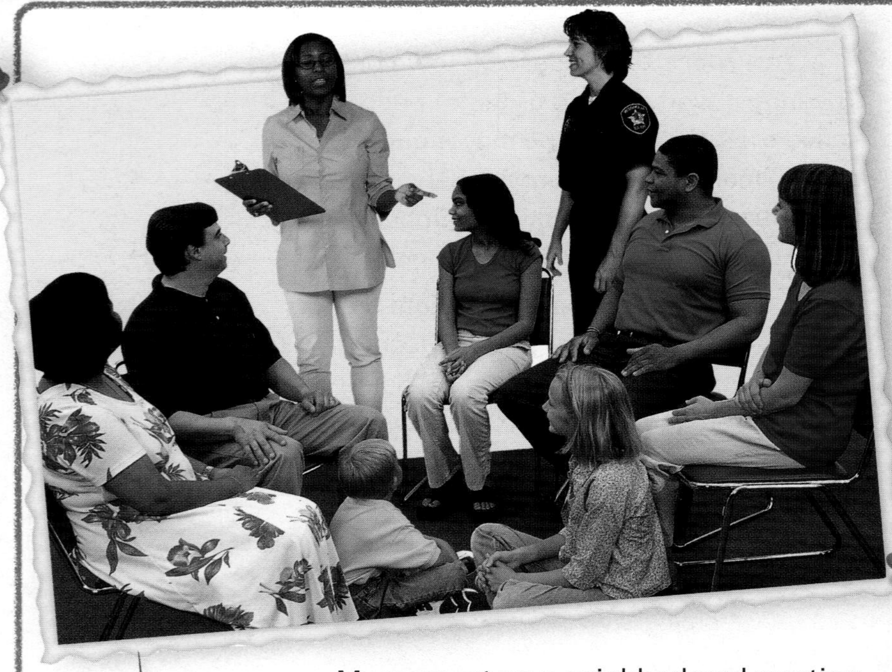

My mom set up a neighborhood meeting.
We will work together to make our 6
neighborhood a safer place to live.

The local police will help by checking the
speed of the cars on our street. If the police
catch someone speeding, the person gets a 7
ticket. The person may go to the county
courthouse. Here, a judge, or leader of the
court, will decide if a law has been broken. 8

Some government offices are in the county courthouse.

156

Practice and Extend

SOCIAL STUDIES Economics

Money Fines

- Write *fine* on the board and ask children what the word means. Then have children use a dictionary to find a definition for *fine* that relates to money.
- Explain that many times people pay money fines when they get a ticket from a police officer.
- Tell children that the money that is collected by the court goes back into the community to help pay for community services.
- Help children recall some of the community services and community workers they learned about in Unit 3.

We went to the city council meeting. A police officer gave a report about the speed of the cars on our 9 street. The mayor and city council thanked us for our hard work. They talked about the problem. Then they voted to put a stop sign in my neighborhood. My neighborhood is now a safer place to live! 10

11

What did you learn?

1. How did the local government help Sam?
2. Tell what a mayor and city council do for their town or city.
3. **Think and Share** Write about how the problem in Sam's neighborhood was solved. Include the **topic** and the **main idea.** Include **details** that tell more about the **main idea** in other sentences.

11 **What are some ways we can work together in our school community to make it a better place?** Possible answers: We can follow the school rules; we can treat each other with respect; we can think about what is good for everyone, not just some people. **Generalize**

3 Close and Assess

Have children say why they think Sam and the people in his neighborhood were successful in getting the new stop sign.

✓ What did you learn?

1. The local government helped Sam by listening to his ideas, checking the speed of the cars on the street, inviting him to a city council meeting, and voting to put a stop sign in his neighborhood.
2. The mayor is the leader of a town or city. The city council works with the mayor to make laws and provide services to the citizens.
3. **Think and Share** Children's responses should include a clearly-stated topic (traffic problem), a main idea that identifies the specific problem (cars moving too fast through the neighborhood), and details (such as Sam's letter to the newspaper, contacting the local government, attending the meeting, hearing the vote, and finally getting the new stop sign).

CURRICULUM CONNECTION Drama

Role Play

- Have children work in small groups to dramatize the city council meeting, using the details on p. 157 as a guide.
- Children should work together to list the characters, assign roles, and act out the meeting for the rest of the class.

Workbook, p. 38

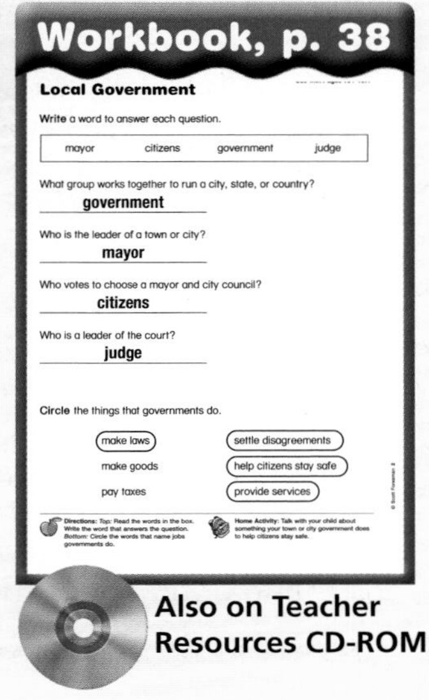

Local Government

Write a word to answer each question.

mayor citizens government judge

What group works together to run a city, state, or country? **government**

Who is the leader of a town or city? **mayor**

Who votes to choose a mayor and city council? **citizens**

Who is a leader of the court? **judge**

Circle the things that governments do.

(make laws) (settle disagreements)
make goods (help citizens stay safe)
pay taxes (provide services)

Also on Teacher Resources CD-ROM.

CITIZEN HEROES

Anna Beavers

Objective

- Identify characteristics of good citizenship.

1 Introduce and Motivate

Preview Read aloud the title of the feature and then the first paragraph. Have children say what they know about Anna Beavers so far. Have them predict what else they may find out about her as they read.

Warm Up To activate prior knowledge, write the word *fair* on the board. Read it with children and ask them to give examples of what it means to be fair when dealing with others. As needed, offer prompts to get children talking. Ask, for example: *What happens when you and your friends play games? What are some ways you play fairly?* Then write *unfair* on the board and discuss its meaning. Have children tell how it feels to be treated unfairly.

2 Teach and Discuss

As you read with children, discuss the pictures. Ask children if they get additional information from the pictures.

1 **What unfair problem did Mrs. Beavers see happening among the children?** She saw that children with dirty or torn clothing were being teased. **Main Idea and Details**

CITIZEN HEROES

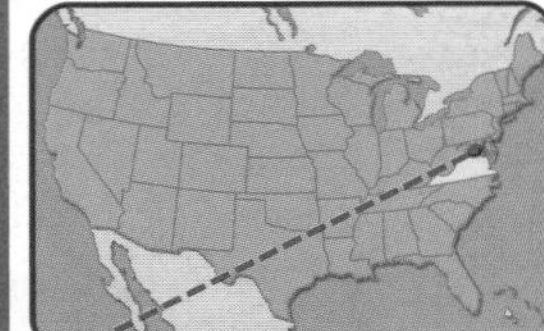

Anna Beavers lives in Loudoun County, Virginia.

Anna Beavers

Almost 50 years ago, a teacher named Anna Beavers decided to solve a problem in 1 her community. Some children needed better clothes to wear to school.

Mrs. Beavers saw children come to school in clothes that were dirty or torn. Children judged unfairly and made fun of these children because of the clothes they wore.

158

Practice and Extend

SOCIAL STUDIES
Background

Possible Misconceptions

- Some children may assume that the message of the feature is that if someone dresses differently in any way from most others he or she will have problems or be treated unfairly.
- Make the point that Mrs. Beavers' goal was to make sure children were dressed neatly and appropriately for school. She wanted all the children to feel comfortable and good about themselves.

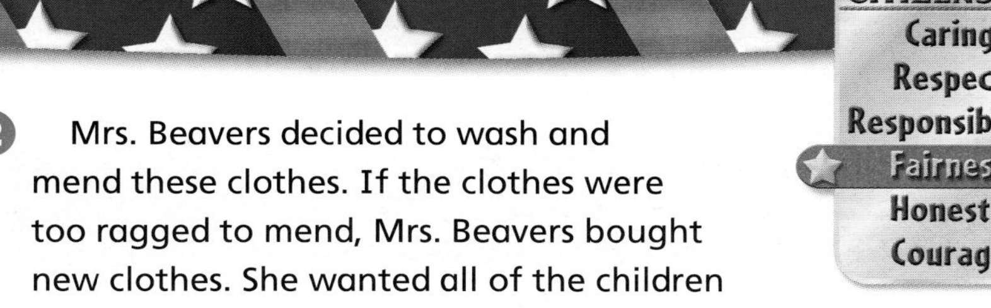

2 Mrs. Beavers decided to wash and mend these clothes. If the clothes were too ragged to mend, Mrs. Beavers bought new clothes. She wanted all of the children to have nice clothes. Today, Mrs. Beavers is still helping children look good and feel good about themselves.

Although Mrs. Beavers is retired, she continues helping children in her Virginia community. She mends clothes. She teaches children who are sick or behind in school. Anna Beavers respects people, including children, and is very caring. She does good deeds for others and believes in fairness for all. 3 4

What can you do to treat others fairly?

159

CURRICULUM CONNECTION Writing

Write a Nomination

- Have children write a paragraph nominating Anna Beavers for a *Citizen of the Year* award.
- Tell children to begin their paragraphs with: *I think Anna Beavers should become Citizen of the Year because ....* Remind children to include specific details that tell why Anna Beavers is a good candidate for the award.
- Encourage children to review their writing to check for and correct mistakes in spelling and grammar.
- Invite volunteers to share their paragraphs with the class.

Locate Key Words in the Question
Make sure that children understand the question. Have children find the key words.

2 How did Anna Beavers help solve the problem? She washed and mended old clothes for children, or she bought new ones. The clothes made the children look like everyone else in school, so the teasing probably stopped. **Solve Problems**

3 Why do you think Mrs. Beavers continues to help people in her community even though she is retired from her job? Possible answer: She enjoys helping people. She sees that there are still many people who need help. **Make Inferences**

4 Do you think Anna Beavers deserves to be called a Citizen Hero? Why? Possible answers: Yes; she works hard to be a good citizen—someone who treats others fairly, someone who is caring and thinks about the common good. **Evaluate**

3 Close and Assess

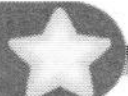

Fairness in Action

Read the question with children. Answers will vary. Possible answers: Not tease others; get to know people before making up my mind about them.

Use with pages 154–159

Lesson 1 Wrap-Up

MEETING INDIVIDUAL NEEDS

Leveled Practice

Describe a Neighborhood Problem

Have children draw pictures that illustrate a problem—real or imaginary—they'd like to solve in their own neighborhood to make it a better or safer place to live.

Easy Have children add note-like labels or callouts to their drawings to help a viewer better understand the problem and what might be done to resolve it. **Reteach**

On-Level Have children use their callouts to write sentences about the problem and possible solutions. They should start with a main idea sentence that states the problem, following up with detail sentences. **Extend**

Challenge Suggest that children rewrite their sentences as *persuasive* letters that they might send to the mayor's office. Explain that a persuasive letter tries to convince the reader to agree with what is said by offering reasons why something should be done. **Enrich**

Hands-on Activities

CURRICULUM CONNECTION

Writing

Add to "My Word Book"

Objective Define and illustrate the words *government, mayor,* and *citizen.*

Resources Vocabulary Cards: **government mayor citizen**

Materials crayons, pencils

Learning Style Visual

Individual

Time 10–15 minutes

1. Display the Vocabulary Cards. Direct children to find the "G" "M" and "C" pages in their word book and write *government, mayor*, and *citizen* in a word space on the appropriate page.

2. Have children draw pictures to illustrate the words and write a sentence using the words.

SOCIAL STUDIES STRAND

Government

Our Town

Objective Make a plan for governing a new city/town.

Materials paper, pencils, art supplies

Learning Style Verbal/Linguistic

Group

Time 35–45 minutes

1. Tell the class that it will create its own new city/town.

2. Help children come up with a name for their town, elect a mayor and a city council, write some laws, and provide a list of services they will provide to their citizens.

3. Suggest that children also design and make a banner to announce their new city/town.

4. Allow time for sharing.

CURRICULUM CONNECTION

Math

Traffic Tallies

Objective Count and record the number of vehicles that pass through an intersection.

Materials paper, pencil

Learning Style Visual

Partners

Time 20 minutes

1. Have children find out how much traffic passes through a street outside your school.

2. Have partners make a four-column chart and label the columns: *Cars, Trucks, Bikes, Other*.

3. Look out a classroom window, or other window that affords a traffic view, and have partners record the number of each kind of vehicle that passes by.

4. Work with children to compare their results.

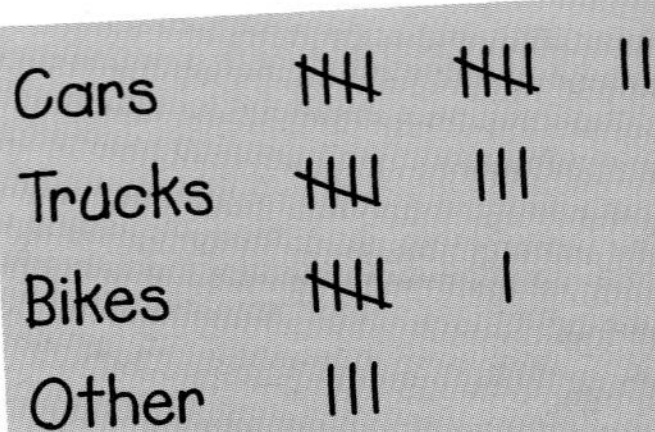

Lesson 2 Overview

State Government **pages 160–163**	Children will learn the meaning of the word *governor* and explore how their state government works to make the laws and provide services. 	Time 20 minutes Resources • Workbook, p. 39 • Vocabulary Card governor • Every Student Learns Guide, pp. 66-69
Read a Table **pages 164–165**	Children will learn how to read a table to find out important facts about our states.	 Time 15–20 minutes Resource • Workbook, p. 40

Build Background

Activity

How Many States?

 **Time** 15–20 minutes

- Duplicate a simple outline of a U.S. map for each child, including state boundaries but excluding state names. Then use an overhead transparency to display a U.S. map, including state names.
- Challenge children to write the state names in the appropriate spaces. Have children color their own state and write the name of the state capital. (Show them approximate location.)
- End by naming your governor. Have children write the name in the margin around the map, drawing a lead line to your state.

If time is short, have children name as many states as they know. List the responses and have children add to the list throughout the unit as they learn more state names.

Read Aloud

Fifty Nifty States

by Nina Evans

Our country's formed of 50 states,
Each with a government to make it great!
Whether Springfield, Boston, or Sante Fe,
Each state has a capital where leaders stay.
The capitol building's where leaders pause,
All joining together to make state laws.

State Government

Objective

- Describe how governments establish order, provide security, and manage conflict.

Vocabulary

governor the leader of a state's government (p. 160)

If time is short, read the text on p. 160. Help children compare and contrast city and state government in terms of the functions of mayor and governor and their status as elected officials.

- Have children read the information on the two posters on p. 163 to further compare city and state government.

1 Introduce and Motivate

Preview Display the Vocabulary Card **governor**. Cover the *or* at the end of the word to reveal *govern*. Say that a governor is someone who governs. Ask children if they know what a governor governs. Have children locate the term as they preview the lesson.

Warm Up To activate prior knowledge, write *We live in the state of* _______ and have children complete the sentence. Then invite a volunteer to locate the state on a classroom map. Discuss the surrounding states, bodies of water, and so on. Encourage children to share what they may know about the state—state symbols, state attractions, famous residents, and so forth.

State Governmen

I live in the state of California. Every state has
1 own government. The **governor** is the leader o
2 state's government. The governor works with oth
state leaders. The citizens of each state vote to el
their leaders. 3

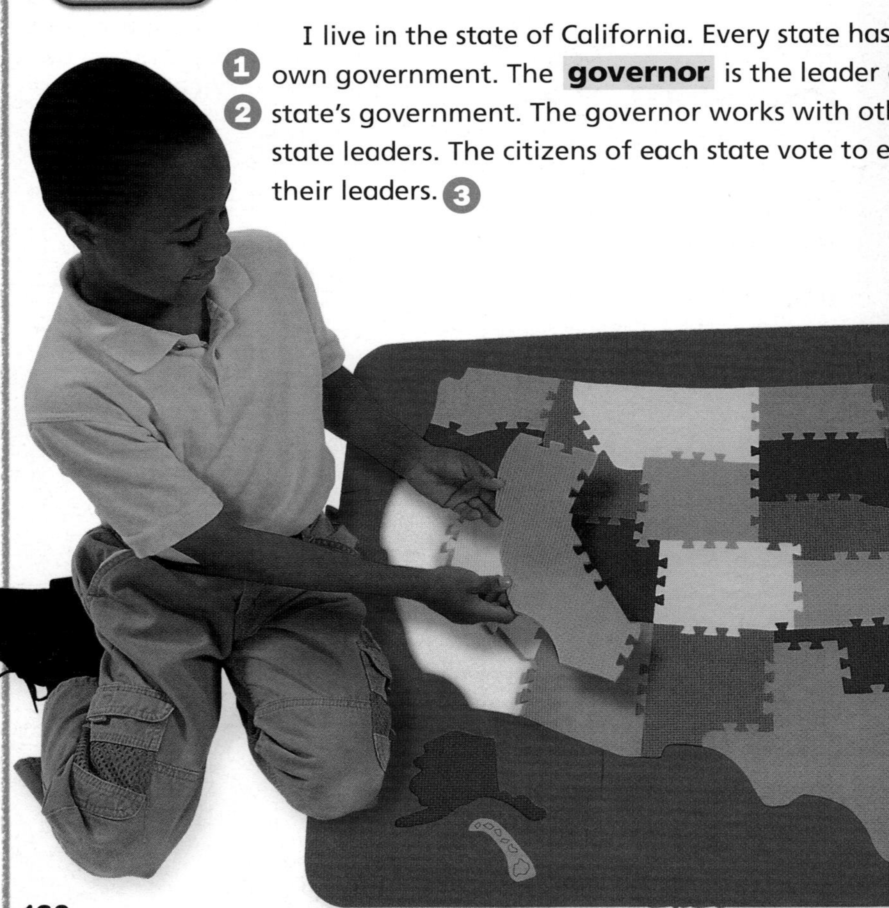

160

Practice and Extend

READING SKILL Context Clues

- Remind children that they can often figure out the meaning of an unfamiliar word by looking at surrounding words and sentences.
- After children have read pp. 160–163, have them write the words *budget* and *run* on a sheet of paper.
- Instruct children to look back at the text on pp. 162–163 to find words that help them understand the meanings of *budget* and *run*. Ask children to copy the words that they identify as context clues.

WEB SITE Technology

You can look up vocabulary words online. Click on *Social Studies Library* and select the dictionary at **www.sfsocialstudies.com.**

Every state also has its own capital. The capital of California is Sacramento. This is the city where many leaders of our state live and work. The capitol building is where leaders 4 meet to make the laws for our state. Find the capital of California on the map. It is marked with a star.

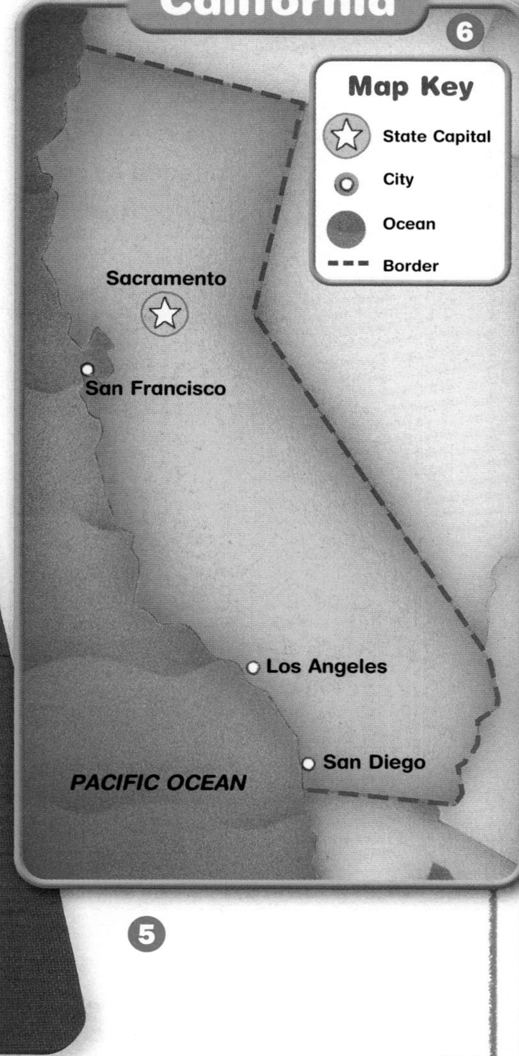

5

EXTEND LANGUAGE ESL Support

Familiar Leaders Have children brainstorm a list of people who are leaders—in the community, school, or country. Record their ideas and have each child choose a person to draw.

Beginning Have children label their pictures and complete: ______ *is a leader in our* ______.

Intermediate Have children label their pictures and write a more elaborate description: ______ *is a leader in our* ______. *He/She is* ______ *(courageous, helpful, etc.).*

Advanced Have children label their pictures and write a description using this structure: ______ *is a leader in our* ______ *because he/she* ______.

For additional ESL support, use Every Student Learns Guide, pp. 66-69.

2 Teach and Discuss

Page 160

Have children describe what Sam is doing in the photograph on p. 160. Help them identify the puzzle as a map of the United States.

1 **Who is the leader of a state's government?** The governor **Main Idea and Details**

2 **How many state governments are there altogether?** 50 **How do you know?** There are 50 states. Each state has its own government. **Draw Conclusions**

Test Talk

Use Information from the Text

3 **What is one important role citizens play in the state government?** Citizens vote for/elect the governor and other leaders. **Make Inferences**

Children should look back at the text to make sure they have the right answer.

Page 161

4 **Where do state leaders meet to make laws?** They meet in the capital city in the capitol building. **Recall and Retell**

5 **Why do you think the cities of Los Angeles, San Diego, and San Francisco are shown on the California map?** Possible answer: They are important cities in the state. **Interpret Maps**

6 **What symbol on the map key indicates a major, or important, city?** A circle **Interpret Maps**

continued

Page 162

7 Why does the government collect taxes? To help pay for community services **Cause and Effect**

8 What are some community services taxes pay for? Look at the picture. Taxes pay for parks, libraries, schools. **Analyze Pictures**

9 In what ways are schools, parks, and libraries important to communities? Possible answers: Schools and libraries are places where people can learn. Parks are areas where people can relax and enjoy the outdoors. Parks give people safe places to go in their free time. **Make Inferences**

Ongoing Assessment

If... children don't understand the importance of schools, libraries, and parks,	**then...** review the function of each. Ask children where people could go as alternatives for places to learn or relax.

7 Government collects tax money to pay for services in our communities. Then the governor and other leaders make a budget to decide how to use the tax money. They want to spend the money they have for community services needed by citizens. We drew pictures of some things taxes help pay for in our community.

Schools, libraries, and parks make o communities better places to live.

162

Practice and Extend

FYI SOCIAL STUDIES Background

Who Makes the Laws in Your State?

- Legislators are our lawmakers. They write and help pass laws.
- Every state but Nebraska has a two-house legislature.
- Nineteen states call their legislative body the *General Assembly*; North Dakota and Oregon call it the *Legislative Assembly*; Massachusetts and New Hampshire call it the *General Court.*
- Every upper house is called the *Senate.* Most states call their lower house the *House of Representatives.*

My class made posters about our local and state governments. Who makes laws for my state? (10)

I want to be a great leader!

Someday, I'd like to be a government leader. Maybe I'll be mayor. I can help run my city. Maybe I'll be governor. Then I can help run my state! (11)

What did you learn?

1. How are the jobs of a mayor and governor alike? How are they different?
2. Name some services the government provides for your community.
3. **Think and Share** Tell why it is important for governments to make laws and see that these laws are followed.

CURRICULUM CONNECTION Writing

Careers

- Recall with children that Sam says, "Someday I'd like to be a government leader."
- Have children think about a job they'd like to do when they grow up. Provide books they can look through for ideas.
- Have children write about their ambitions. Have them begin with: *Someday, I'd like to be a* ______. Encourage them to give reasons for their choices.

Workbook, p. 39

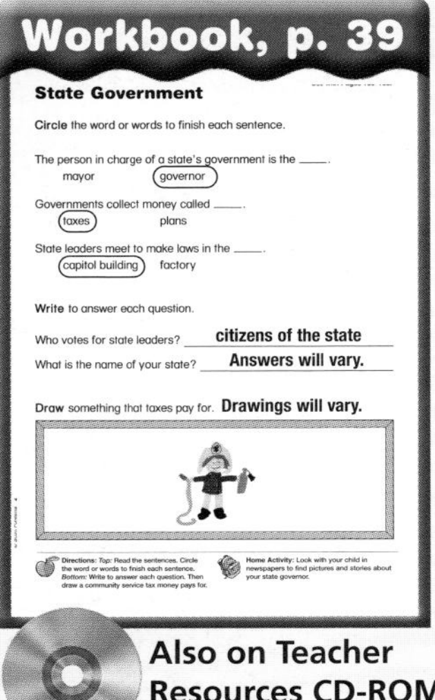

State Government

Circle the word or words to finish each sentence.

The person in charge of a state's government is the ____.
mayor (governor)

Governments collect money called ____.
(taxes) plans

State leaders meet to make laws in the ____.
(capitol building) factory

Write to answer each question.

Who votes for state leaders? citizens of the state

What is the name of your state? Answers will vary.

Draw something that taxes pay for. Drawings will vary.

Also on Teacher Resources CD-ROM.

Page 163

Read the posters with children. Make the point that both mayors and governors are elected offficals. Help children understand that governments have laws to establish order, police forces to provide security, and courts to manage conflict.

(10) **Officials in the city and in the state have three main duties. What are they?** To make laws, to carry out laws, and to decide if laws have been broken **Generalize**

(11) **What do you think are some qualities of a great leader?** Possible answers: Fairness, intelligence, caring, and honesty **Express Ideas**

3 Close and Assess

Have children explain what they have learned about state government.

✓ What did you learn?

1. **Alike:** A mayor and a governor are both government leaders; both work with others to make laws; both are elected by citizens. **Different:** A mayor is the leader of a town or city; a governor is the leader of a state.
2. Possible answers: Police and fire protection, schools, libraries, parks
3. **Think and Share** Children should be aware that laws help keep order among large numbers of people. Without laws, each person would do what he or she wanted. That would be confusing and dangerous. It is important that people know police will make others obey the laws. People need to know there is someone they can go to if there are problems or conflicts.

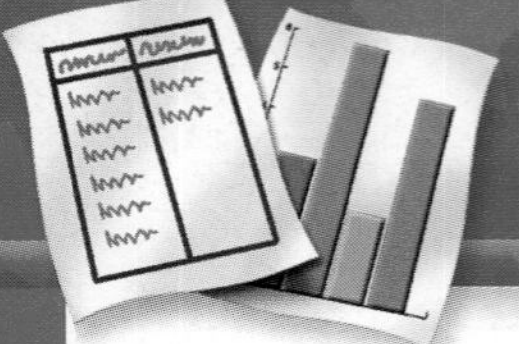

Read a Table

Objectives

- Use tables to categorize information.
- Identify selected symbols such as state birds and flowers.

1 Introduce and Motivate

Preview Read the title of the feature with children. Then ask a volunteer to read the first sentence on p. 164. Read the column headings with children.

Warm Up To activate prior knowledge, talk about the lists you and children make in class—lists of who will do class chores, what supplies are needed for a project, and so on. Tell children that lists are a handy way of recording information. Tell them that they will learn about a special kind of list called a table in this lesson.

2 Teach and Discuss

Begin by demonstrating how to read the table, showing children how to read across and down. Help children locate New Jersey's state bird.

1 **What is the title of the table?** *Learn About States* **Interpret Tables**

2 **How many states are shown on the table?** Three **What are they?** Florida, New Jersey, Pennsylvania **Interpret Tables**

Chart and Graph Skills

Read a Table

Look at the table. A **table** is a kind of list. A table gives information that people can use.

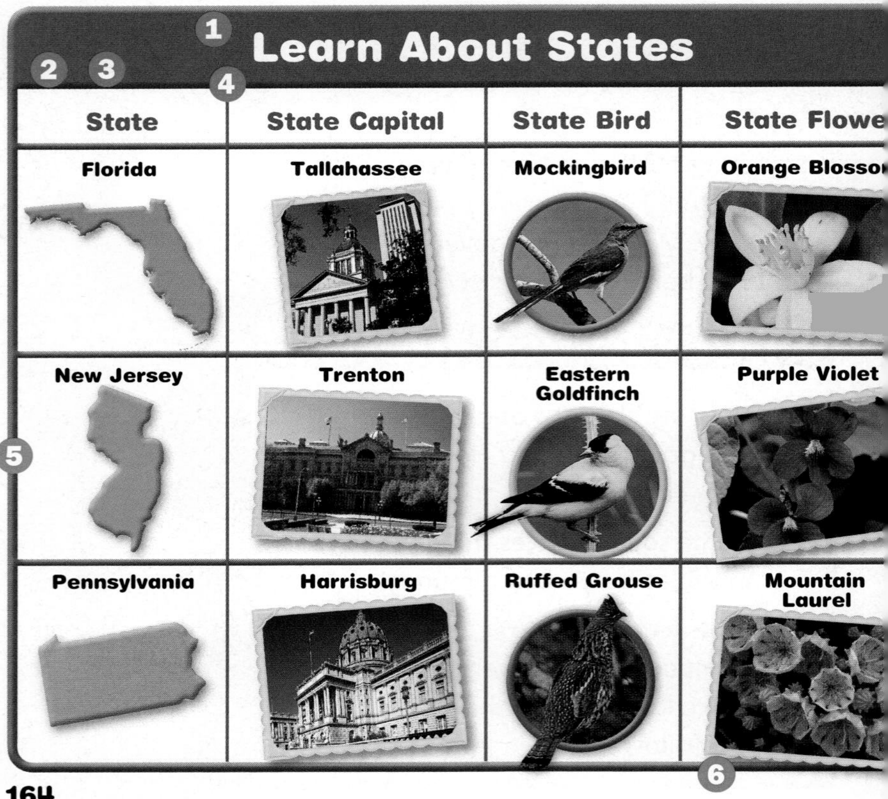

Learn About States

State	State Capital	State Bird	State Flowe
Florida	Tallahassee	Mockingbird	Orange Blosso
New Jersey	Trenton	Eastern Goldfinch	Purple Violet
Pennsylvania	Harrisburg	Ruffed Grouse	Mountain Laurel

164

Practice and Extend

Share these excerpts from state songs:

- "Swanee River" (Florida/official) by Stephen C. Foster
  Way down upon the Swanee River,
  Far, far away,
  There's where my heart is turning ever,
  There's where the old folks stay.
- "Ode to New Jersey" (unofficial) Author unknown
  The rolling wave is on thy shore, Jerseyland,
  My Jerseyland!
- "Pennsylvania" (official) by Eddie Khoury and Ronnie Bonner
  Pennsylvania, Pennsylvania
  Mighty is your name,
  Steeped in glory and tradition,
  Object of acclaim...

This table lists important facts about some of our states. Each state has a capital city. Each capital city has a capitol building where the state law makers meet.

States also have symbols. These symbols help us understand what makes each state special. The state bird and the state flower are two symbols of our states.

1. What is the capital of Pennsylvania?
2. What is Florida's state flower?
3. **On Your Own** Learn about the capital, state bird, and state flower of your state. Make a table showing this information. Include a drawing of your state's capitol building.

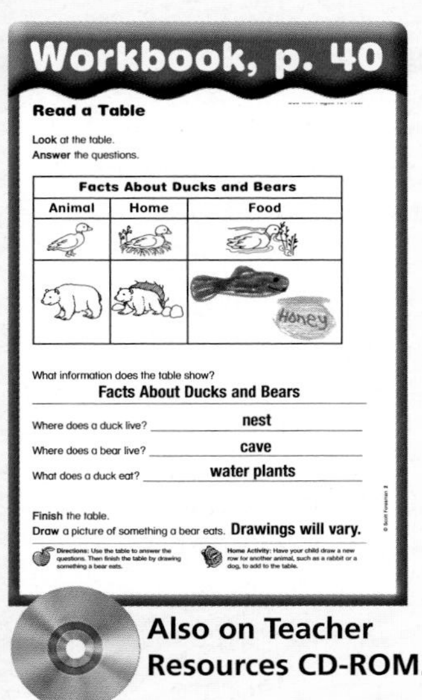

Workbook, p. 40

Read a Table

Look at the table.
Answer the questions.

Facts About Ducks and Bears		
Animal	Home	Food
		Honey

What information does the table show? **Facts About Ducks and Bears**

Where does a duck live? **nest**

Where does a bear live? **cave**

What does a duck eat? **water plants**

Finish the table.
Draw a picture of something a bear eats. **Drawings will vary.**

Directions: Use the table to answer the questions. Then finish the table by drawing something a bear eats.

Home Activity: Have your child draw a new row for another animal, such as a rabbit or a dog, to add to the table.

Also on Teacher Resources CD-ROM.

3 What information does the table show? The state capital, state bird, and state flower for three different states **Interpret Tables**

4 What do the three state capitol buildings have in common? They are large, look important or official, and look similar to one another. **Analyze Pictures**

5 What is the state capital of New Jersey? Trenton **The state flower?** Violet **Interpret Tables**

6 How do you think each state chooses its symbols? Possible answers: People make suggestions. They name birds and flowers they see all the time in their state. People vote to make the best choice. **Make Inferences**

3 Close and Assess

To increase awareness of tables and their uses, have children go on a table hunt! Encourage them to keep track of the numbers of tables they see in books, newspapers, and classroom or school displays, and the information they deliver.

Try it!

1. Harrisburg
2. Orange Blossom
3. **On Your Own** Check to see that the format of children's tables is similar to the one in the lesson. Look for headings that are properly and clearly labeled. Check the accuracy of children's information.

Use with pages 160–165

Lesson 2 Wrap-Up

MEETING INDIVIDUAL NEEDS
Leveled Practice

Learn About the State Capitol

Have children draw pictures of their state capitol building based on pictures you show.

Easy Have children write captions for their drawings. The caption should include identification of the building in the drawing, the city where it is located, and information about what happens in the building. **Reteach**

On-Level Have children write a caption that names the current governor. Then show children the state flag and tell them what the state motto is. Have them add a picture of the flag and the motto to their drawings. **Extend**

Challenge Show a simple map of the area around your capitol building. Identify three or four nearby government buildings and cross streets. On the flip side of their drawings, have children make simple area maps with labels. They can use their drawings and new maps in oral presentations. **Enrich**

Hands-on Activities

CURRICULUM CONNECTION
Writing

Question and Answer

Objective Demonstrate understanding of new and reviewed vocabulary words.

Resources Vocabulary Cards
governor government citizen mayor

Materials pencils, paper

Learning Style Visual/Linguistic

Individual

Time 10–15 minutes

1. Display the Vocabulary Cards for children's reference.

2. Have children write questions to which the vocabulary words are answers.

3. Provide a model: *Who is the leader of a state?* Have children add the new word *governor* to their "My Word Book" glossaries.

Question:
Who is the leader of a state?

SOCIAL STUDIES STRAND
Geography

State Capitals

Objective Name state capitals.

Materials U.S. map, paper, pencil

Learning Style Visual/Verbal

Partner 

Time 30–45 minutes

1. Display a U.S. map. Briefly review the map symbol for a state capital and help children find the capital of their own state.

2. Then distribute a list of the 50 states to pairs of children.

3. Have partners work together to explore the map and write the names of the capital next to each state.

4. Challenge children to learn the names and capitals of neighboring states.

SOCIAL STUDIES STRAND
History

Statehood Day!

Objective Express ideas about celebrating a statehood day.

Materials paper, pencils

Learning Style Verbal

Group 

Time 20–30 minutes

1. Use an almanac to help children find out the month, day, and year your state joined the country. If time is short, tell them the date.

2. Have children form small groups to talk about ways your school might celebrate statehood day. Tell children to think about activities, presentations, songs, decorations, and so on. Group members should jot down notes.

3. A spokesperson for each group should share the group's ideas.

4. If possible, plan to celebrate statehood day in your classroom.

Lesson 3 Overview

Federal Government **pages 166–169**	Children will learn the meanings of the words *Congress* and *President.* They will learn how the President, Congress, and the Supreme Court work together to govern the United States.	 Time 20 minutes Resources • Workbook, p. 41 • Vocabulary Cards Congress President • Every Student Learns Guide, pp. 70-73
Thurgood Marshall **pages 170–171**	Children will read about how Thurgood Marshall—the first African American justice on the U.S. Supreme Court—worked for equal treatment for all people.	 Time 15–20 minutes

Build Background

Activity

The President's Job

 **Time** 15–20 minutes

- On chart paper, write the following headings *What I Know, What I Want to Know, What I Learned.*
- Tell children they will learn about the job of the President of the United States. Say that you will fill in the first two columns on the chart now. The third column will be filled in after the lesson has been read.
- Call on volunteers to tell what they know about the job of President. Ask others to identify things they would like to know or find out as they read. Record children's ideas.
- Plan to revisit the K-W-L chart after reading.

If time is short, have children identify one or two things they would like to learn about the President's job.

Read Aloud

In Washington, D.C.

by Eric Meyer

In Washington, D.C.
The President is busy
Leading the country
For you and for me.

The Congress writes laws
To address each good cause.
Members work long days
To help in many ways.

When citizens disagree
On a law that is key,
The Supreme Court can say
"This is a law you
must obey!"

Federal Government

Objective

- Identify functions of government.

Vocabulary

Congress the part of the government that writes and votes on laws for all of our states (p. 167)

President the leader of our country (p. 168)

QUICK Teaching Plan

If time is short, guide children in skimming the pages of the lesson to learn the functions of the Congress, the President, and the Supreme Court.

- Have children use background knowledge to try to answer the first question at the end of the lesson.

1 Introduce and Motivate

Preview Read aloud the title of the lesson. If children are curious, explain that the word *federal* means "having agreed to join together." Say that our government is federal in the sense that it serves fifty states that have agreed to join together. Display the Vocabulary Cards **Congress** and **President**. Have children find the words in the lesson and read their definitions.

Warm Up To activate prior knowledge, have children tell how they think the President's job may be similar to that of a governor or mayor.

Federal Government

The government in our country works for all of the people in the country. The government follows a plan that was written long ago. This plan for government is called the United States Constitution. ❶

166

Practice and Extend

READING SKILL Main Idea and Details

- In this lesson, there are opportunities for children to identify main ideas and supporting details.
- After children read p. 167, have them go back to the second paragraph. On a sheet of paper, have them write the main idea of the paragraph and two supporting details.

WEB SITE Technology

You can look up vocabulary words online. Click on *Social Studies Library* and select the dictionary at **www.sfsocialstudies.com.**

The center of our government is in ❷ ❸ Washington, D.C., our country's capital. The United States government has three parts. Our country needs all of the parts to make government work fairly.

One part of government is Congress. The **Congress** writes and votes on laws for all of our states. Citizens from each ❹ state elect leaders to be in Congress. These leaders are called lawmakers because they make laws. ❺

Congress works in the United States Capitol.

United States Capitol

167

2 Teach and Discuss

Help children identify the document pictured on p. 166 as the United States Constitution.

Page 166

❶ **Why is having a written plan for government important?** A written plan is a lasting record of what people wanted our government to be and how it actually runs. A written plan also lets people in the future know how the government works and should continue to work. **Make Inferences**

Page 167

❷ **What is the capital city of the United States?** Washington, D.C. **Recall and Retell**

❸ **What states are around Washington, D.C.? Look at a map.** Virginia, Maryland **Interpret Maps**

✓ Ongoing Assessment

If... children are having difficulty understanding that Washington, D.C., is a capital city even though it is not in any one state,

then... show that it is between two states, Virginia and Maryland. Say that both states gave land when President Washington wanted to build a capital city.

❹ **How are members of Congress selected?** They are elected by the people in their home states. **Recall and Retell**

❺ **Why are leaders in Congress called lawmakers?** They write and vote on laws. **Cause and Effect**

SOCIAL STUDIES Background

About Congress

- Congress consists of two bodies: the Senate and the House of Representatives.
- The 100-member Senate consists of 2 senators from each of the 50 states. The House of Representatives has 435 members. The number of representatives depends on a state's population.
- The Constitution gives Congress "all legislative powers" of the federal government, including control over government taxing and spending.
- The Senate must approve the President's choices for Supreme Court justices.

continued

Page 168

After children read the page, have them answer the question at the end.

6 **How is the President selected?** He is elected by all the citizens of the country who choose to vote in the election. **Recall and Retell**

Test Talk

Locate Key Words in the Text

7 **What are two things the President does?** He signs laws. He works with leaders from other countries.

Ask children if the answer is *right there* or if they have to *think and search* for it.
Main Idea and Details

8 **Why does the President work with leaders from other countries?** Possible answer: The President shares ideas with other leaders. He works with them to keep peace in the world. **Do you think this is an important part of the President's job?** Possible answer: Yes, the safety and well-being of many people depend on how the President works with other world leaders.
Cause and Effect/Evaluate

9 **Does the President work in the United States Capitol building? How do you know?** No; the words under the picture say that he works in the White House. **Analyze Pictures**

The President heads another part of government. The **President** is the leader of our country. Citizens from 6 every state vote for our President. The President signs laws. The President works with leaders from other 7 countries. Who is our President? 8

9 The President lives and works in the White Hous

168

Practice and Extend

ACCESS CONTENT
ESL Support

Three-Part Government Display: *Congress, President, Supreme Court*. Have children fold a sheet of paper into three panels. Have them copy a term onto each panel.

Beginning Read the names of the parts of government. Explain that all three parts work together to form the government of our country, the federal government. Have children write a plus sign (+) between the parts to show how they are related. Write *Our Federal Government*. Have children copy it as a headline.

Intermediate Have children do the above and then write the function of each part of the government. Provide help, as needed.

Advanced Have children use their charts to explain orally how our federal government works.

For additional ESL support, use Every Student Learns Guide, pp. 70-73.

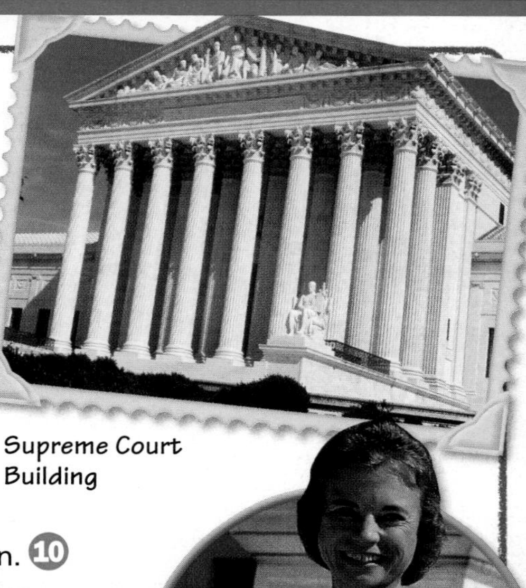

Supreme Court Building

Another part of government is the Supreme Court. There are nine judges called Supreme Court justices. The President chooses the justices, but one part of Congress must approve the President's choices. 11

The Supreme Court tells us if laws are fair. They also decide if laws have been broken. 10 The justices use the United States Constitution as their guide.

Sandra Day O'Connor was the first woman Supreme Court Justice, 1981

What did you learn?

1. Compare the jobs of a mayor, a governor, and the President. How are these jobs alike? How are they different?
2. How does a person become a Supreme Court justice?
3. **Think and Share** If you could work in one of the three parts of government, tell which you would choose and why.

169

Page 169

10 **What are two things the Supreme Court does?** The Supreme Court decides if laws are fair; it decides if laws have been broken.
Main Idea and Details

11 **Find on p. 169 an example of how different parts of the government work to be fair.** Possible answer: Even though the President can name judges to the Supreme Court, one part of Congress must approve them. This prevents the President from just picking people he may like.
Apply Information

3 Close and Assess

Guide children in summarizing the lesson.

What did you learn?

1. **Alike:** All three are elected leaders who work with others to make laws.
   Different: A mayor leads a city government; a governor leads a state government; the President leads the country's government. The President meets with leaders of other countries.
2. A Supreme Court justice is chosen by the President and approved by members of one part of Congress.
3. **Think and Share** Children's responses will vary. Check for their understanding of the differing functions of the parts of the government. Look for the reasons they want to work for a particular government branch.

G SOCIAL STUDIES STRAND Government

The President's Job

- Revisit the K-W-L chart you and children began in Build Background.
- Review the information already in the chart.
- Have children add new information they learned in the lesson. Help them correct ideas found to be erroneous.

Workbook, p. 41

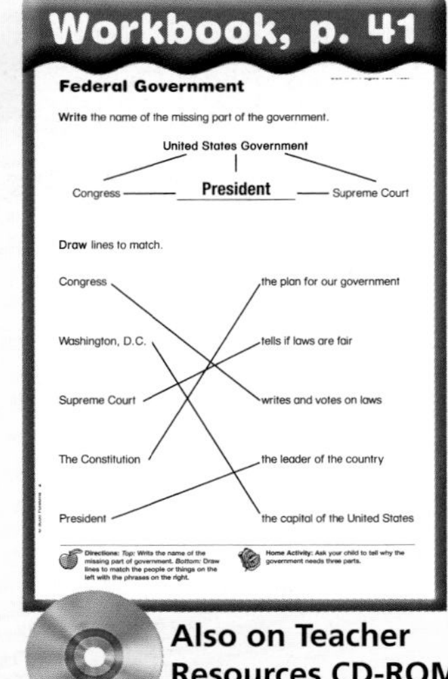

Federal Government

Write the name of the missing part of the government.

United States Government

Congress — President — Supreme Court

Draw lines to match.

Congress	the plan for our government
Washington, D.C.	tells if laws are fair
Supreme Court	writes and votes on laws
The Constitution	the leader of the country
President	the capital of the United States

Also on Teacher Resources CD-ROM.

Thurgood Marshall

Objectives

- Identify characteristics of good citizenship such as a belief in justice, truth, equality, and responsibility for the common good.
- Identify contributions of historical figures such as Thurgood Marshall.

1 Introduce and Motivate

Preview Have children read the Think and Share question at the bottom of p. 171. Help them change the question into a statement. Say that the statement tells the main idea of the biographical feature they will read.

Warm Up To activate prior knowledge, write *equal rights* on the board. Ask children what they think this term means. Then make the connection between equal rights and being treated fairly.

Practice and Extend

SOCIAL STUDIES Background

About Thurgood Marshall

- In 1954, as an attorney, Marshall successfully argued the case of *Brown* v. *Board of Education of Topeka* (the case referenced on page 171) before the U.S. Supreme Court. In this case, racial segregation in American public schools was declared unconstitutional.
- Marshall was appointed to the U.S. Supreme Court by President Lyndon B. Johnson in 1967.
- Marshall retired in 1991 and died in 1993.

WEB SITE Technology

You may help children find out more about Thurgood Marshall by clicking on *Meet the People* at **www.sfsocialstudies.com/biography.**

As a young boy, Thurgood's father would take him to the courthouse to watch trials. Thurgood and his brother attended 1 college in Pennsylvania. Then Thurgood applied to law school but was turned down because he was an African American. 2 This event led him to spend the rest of his life working for equal rights. He was accepted at another law school, where he graduated at 3 the top of his class. 4

hurgood Marshall was born in Baltimore, Maryland.

As a lawyer, Thurgood Marshall brought many cases before the Supreme Court. In one case, black children could not go to school with white children. This case was about segregation. Segregation means that people are kept apart because of the color of their skin. Thurgood Marshall won this case.

Supreme Court justices, 1967

Thurgood Marshall was chosen to become a Supreme Court justice. He continued to work for fair and equal treatment for all people.

Thurgood Marshall

Think and Share

How did Thurgood Marshall help all Americans to be treated equally and fairly?

For more information, go online to *Meet the People* at **www.sfsocialstudies.com.**

171

2 Teach and Discuss

Read the biography with children. Explain what it means to graduate "at the top of your class."

1 **How did Thurgood Marshall become interested in studying law?** His father took him to the courthouse to watch trials. **Recall and Retell**

2 **Why did Thurgood Marshall spend his life working for equal rights?** He knew what it felt like to be treated unfairly. He was not allowed to go to a law school because he was African American. **Cause and Effect**

Decision Making

3 **When Thurgood Marshall was turned down by one law school, he had a decision to make. What might he have done instead of trying to get into another school?** Possible answers: He might have given up on learning the law. He might have looked for a different kind of job. **Make Inferences**

4 **What does Thurgood Marshall's decision show about him?** Possible answer: He was a determined person who had confidence in himself. **Draw Conclusions**

3 Close and Assess

Think and Share

Children's responses should include: As a lawyer, Thurgood Marshall brought many cases of unfair treatment for some citizens before the Supreme Court. He won some of those cases.

CURRICULUM CONNECTION Writing

In the News!

- Have children write newspaper headlines to tell about the outcome of the school segration case Thurgood Marshall argued as a lawyer.
- Tell children that newspaper headlines are worded to catch people's attention and to make them want to read the story that follows.
- Show examples to get children thinking: *Thurgood Does Good—Equality for All! Schools Must Obey!*
- Give children the option of working with partners. Have children share their headlines.

Use with pages 166–171

Lesson 3 Wrap-Up

MEETING INDIVIDUAL NEEDS Leveled Practice

Read Aloud Again!
Revisit the Read Aloud poem "In Washington, D.C." See p. 166a. Write the poem on chart paper. Read the poem aloud.

Easy Cover the name of each government part in the text of the poem. Read the poem. Pause for children to supply the name of the government part. **Reteach**

On-Level Have children select a stanza of the poem and copy it. Have them use the text of the stanza and what they know from the lesson to create a riddle about that particular part of our government. **Extend**

Challenge Have children use the poem as a model for writing their own poem about our three-part system of federal government. **Enrich**

Hands-on Activities

CURRICULUM CONNECTION
Reading

Word Families

Objective Demonstrate understanding of new vocabulary; identify words in the same family.

Materials crayons, pencils, paper

Learning Style Visual/Verbal

Individual

Time 10–15 minutes

1. Write *President* and *Congress* on the board. Below, write these related words: *Presidency, Presidential; Congressional, Congressperson*. Help children notice that words are related. Use each word in an oral sentence.

2. You may wish to point out the adjective ending *-al* in *Presidential* and *Congressional*. Note that *Congressperson* is a compound word.

Remind children to add *President* and *Congress* to their word books.

SOCIAL STUDIES STRAND
History

The Preamble

Objective Listen to understand the Preamble.

Materials Video: *Schoolhouse Rock: America Rock!* (ASIN 156994088, 1997), a copy of the Preamble

Learning Style Auditory

Group

Time 20 minutes

1. Show the video. It uses cartoons and music to introduce the Preamble.

2. Have children share their responses to the video.

3. Read aloud the Preamble, pausing to explain difficult vocabulary and concepts.

4. Have children jot down one important idea they learned from their viewing and listening experiences.

CURRICULUM CONNECTION
Literature

Our Presidents

Objective Locate information about the U.S. Presidents.

Materials *So You Want to Be President?* by Judith St. George (Philomel/Putnam, ISBN 0-399-23407-1, 2000).

Learning Style Auditory/Visual

Group/Individual

Time 20 minutes

1. Read excerpts from the book to get children interested.

2. Encourage children to explore *So You Want to Be President?* on their own. Some may find the text challenging. Suggest that those children browse with the help of partners.

3. After they have spent time with the book, ask children if it is a storybook or a book that gives them information. Tell them that books that give information are nonfiction books.

Lesson 4 Overview

Voting for Leaders **pages 172–175**	Children will learn how citizens of the United States vote for leaders. They also learn some of the ways in which people find out about the candidates. 	 Time 20–30 minutes Resources • Workbook, p. 42 • Every Student Learns Guide, pp. 74–77
Smithsonian Institution: Presidential Treasures **pages 176–177**	Children will view everyday belongings of past Presidents to learn about them and about our country's past.	 Time 15–20 minutes Resource • Workbook, p. 43
Susan B. Anthony **pages 178–179**	Children will learn about Susan B. Anthony and how she helped women win the right to vote.	Time 15–20 minutes

Build Background

Activity

Let's Vote On It

 **Time** 10–15 minutes

Have children participate in the voting process. Write the names of two cartoon characters: Mickey Mouse and Bugs Bunny. Tell children to pretend that the two characters want to receive the title *Most-Liked Animal Character*. Explain that children will take part in a vote.

Take a "raised hand" count to see how many children vote for each character. Record the number of votes beside the characters' names.

Review the outcome with children. Verify the accuracy of the vote by comparing the total number of votes to the number of children in the class. Declare a winner!

If time is short, ask children to explain what it means to vote. Have children describe some of the times they have voted for something or someone.

Read Aloud

Voting Day

by Eric Meyer

On a Tuesday in November,
On a day we should remember,
Many citizens make a note
To mark a ballot and cast their vote.

Lesson 4 Voting for Leaders

Objective

- Identify ways that public officials are selected, including election and appointment to office.

QUICK Teaching Plan

If time is short, read the first sentence in the second paragraph on p. 172 with children. Then have them use the pictures in the lesson and what they may know from their own experiences to talk about the steps in the voting process.

1 Introduce and Motivate

Preview Write the word *vote* on the board. Have volunteers explain what the word means. Then have children look back at Lesson 1 in Unit 1 to find the definition. Read the title of the lesson and tell children that *Voting for Leaders* is the topic of this lesson.

Warm Up To activate prior knowledge, ask children to identify some offices citizens vote for.

2 Teach and Discuss

Page 172

Tell children that citizens 18 years and older were given the right to vote in 1971. An amendment, or change, was made to the Constitution. Previously, citizens had to be 21 years old to vote.

1 Can any man or woman over 18 years old vote? No; he or she must be a citizen.
Main Idea/Details

Lesson 4 Voting for Leaders

KEEP AMERICA STRONG

Our class is learning about how we choose leaders. Next week, we will vote for a class leader. What makes a good leader? What do you know about voting?

1 Every American citizen who is at least 18 years old has the right to vote. 2 First a citizen must sign up to vote. 3 Then citizens learn about the people who are running for office.

VOTE NOW

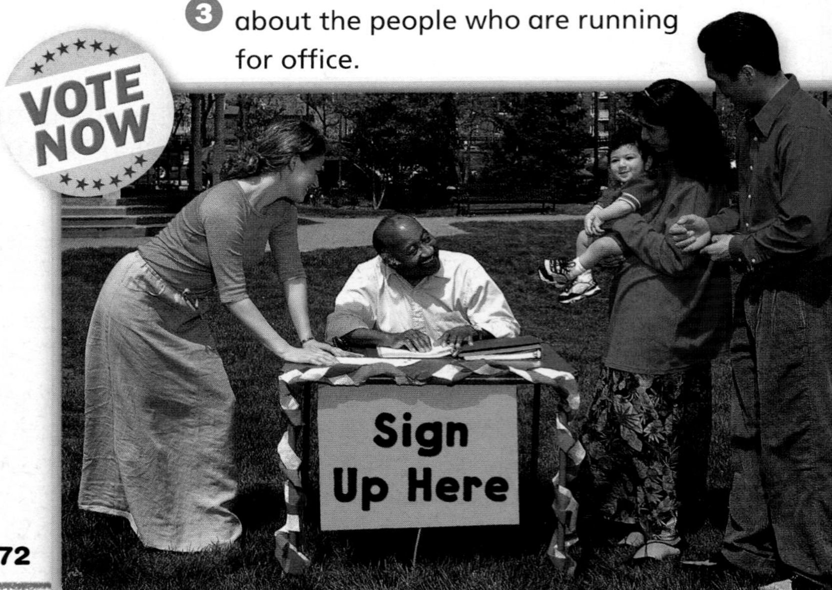

172

Practice and Extend

READING SKILL
Put Things in Order

Sequence

- As children read Lesson 4, encourage them to notice the steps in the voting process.
- After children have read pp. 172–175, have them make a numbered list of the steps.
- Have children share and compare their lists with partners.

Citizens make decisions about who they want as their leaders. They ask themselves many questions. Who will do the best job? Can I trust the person? Will this person work hard to make our country a better place to live and work? You may have talked with your family about how to choose a leader. 4

Vote For Governor

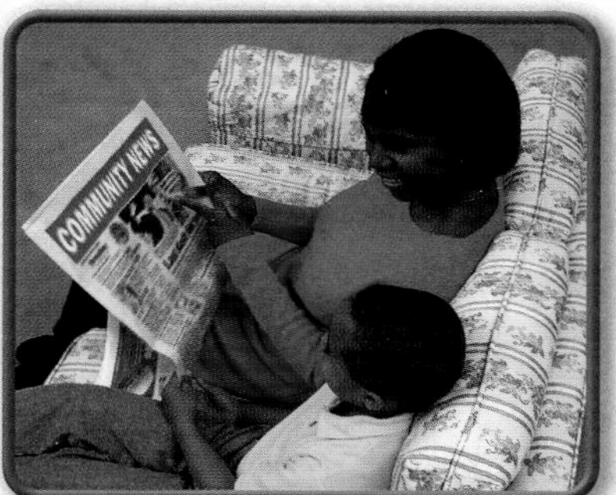

My parents read the newspaper to get information. 5

They watch television programs about the people running for office.

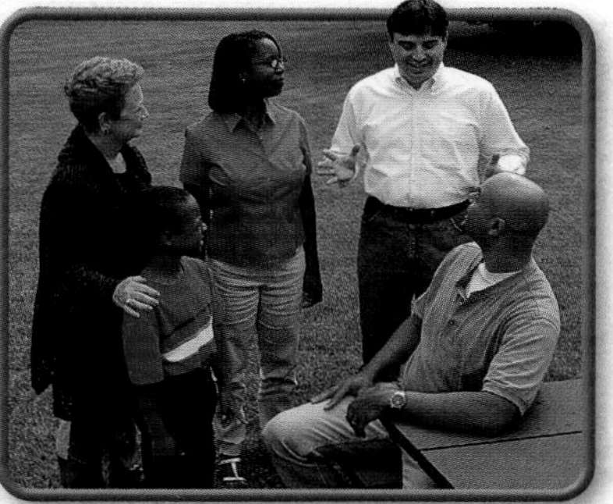
They talk to friends and neighbors about important issues.

6

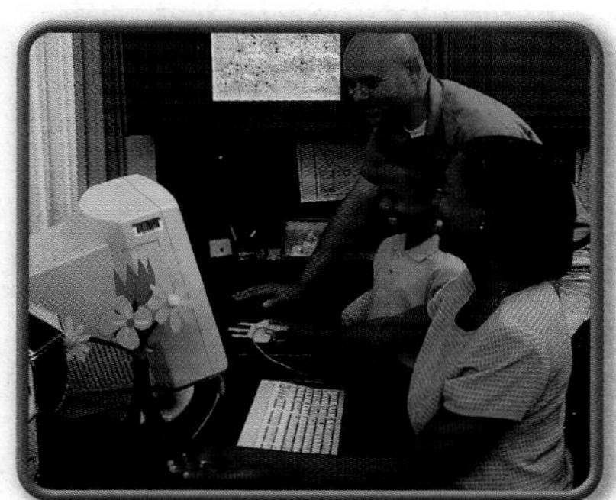
They use the computer to learn more about these issues.

173

ACCESS CONTENT

ESL Support

Voting On the board, write: *Citizens vote for leaders who run for office.* Draw a T chart with the vertical line closer to the left. In the left part of the chart, list: *citizens, vote for, leaders, run for, office*. Brainstorm with children the meanings.

Beginning As children volunteer meanings, write them on the chart. Ask children to copy the completed chart on paper.

Intermediate After children copy the chart, have them check the meanings of the terms in their pupil book.

Advanced Have children explore the verb phrases *vote for* and *run for*, using dictionaries or other sources.

For additional ESL support, use Every Student Learns Guide, pp. 74–77.

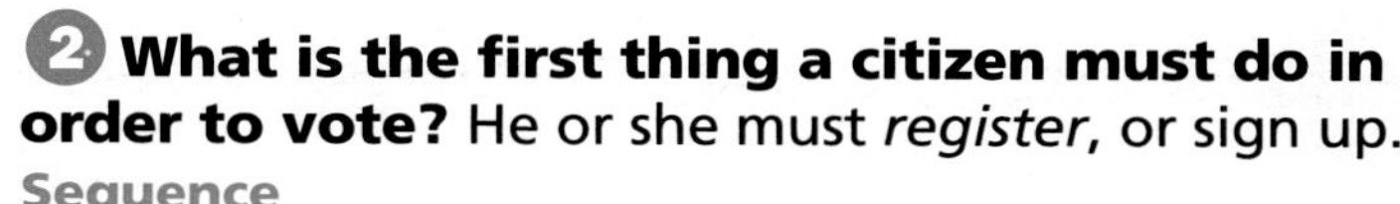

2 **What is the first thing a citizen must do in order to vote?** He or she must *register*, or sign up. **Sequence**

3 **Why do you think 18 years old was chosen as an appropriate age for voting?** Possible answer: People at age 18 are old enough to understand the voting process, find out about candidates, and make thoughtful decisions. **Make Inferences**

Page 173

After children have read the page, ask them which information source they would use to find out about people running for office. Have them say why.

4 **What kinds of questions do people ask themselves when choosing a leader?** Who will do the best job? Are they trustworthy? Will they work hard to make the country a better place to live and work? **Recall and Retell**

5 **How can people learn more about a citizen who wants to be a leader?** They can read the newspaper, watch programs on television, talk with neighbors about issues, or find information using their computers. **Main Idea and Details**

6 **What are some qualities voters should look for in a leader?** Possible answers: Intelligence, honesty, responsibility, interest in the common good, ability to solve problems and make decisions **Make Inferences**

continued

Page 174

Mention that how someone votes depends on where that person lives. Some people use paper ballots. Others use either manual or electronic voting machines.

7 **What is a ballot?** A list of the names of people running for office **Context Clues**

8 **Why is it important to read a ballot carefully before voting?** Possible answer: To be sure a voter understands who is running for office, how the ballot is set up, and how to mark the ballot **Make Inferences**

9 **Why do you think voting is both a privilege and a responsibility?** Possible answer: Voting is a right guaranteed in the United States Constitution. It allows people to have a say in what will happen in their country and in their lives. Voting is a responsibility because people should care about what happens in their country. **Draw Conclusions**

When it's time for the election, citizens vote. First, they get a ballot. A ballot lists the 7 names of people running for different offices. 8 Next, each citizen marks his or her choices on the ballot. Last, each vote gets counted. 9

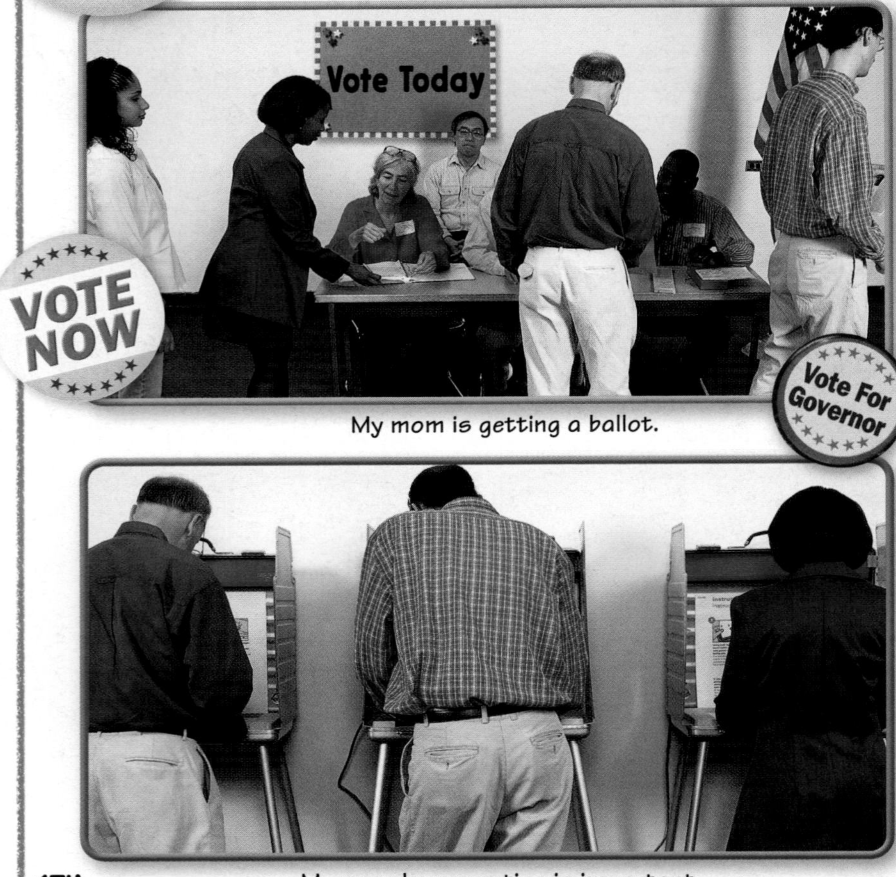

My mom is getting a ballot.

My mom knows voting is important.

174

Practice and Extend

SOCIAL STUDIES Background

Possible Misconceptions

- Tell children that some people in government jobs are appointed; that is, they are given their jobs. Citizens do not vote for them in an election.
- Tell children that the President appoints the members of his Cabinet with the advice and consent of the Senate. Those people hold very important jobs in the federal government—for example, the Secretary of State, the Secretary of Defense.
- Explain, too, that federal judges, some state judges, and ambassadors (people who represent the United States in other countries) are also appointed, not elected.

CURRICULUM CONNECTION Math

Count the Votes

- Tell children that in addition to voting for leaders, people also vote on important issues, such as whether to build a new school or housing for senior citizens.
- Tell children they are going to hold an in-class vote on where to go on an upcoming class outing.
- Begin by brainstorming possible places to visit such as a park, nature center, or museum. List the choices.
- Have children vote by writing the place name on a slip of paper. Have official counters tally the votes.
- Have children use the tallies to create and present a bar graph.

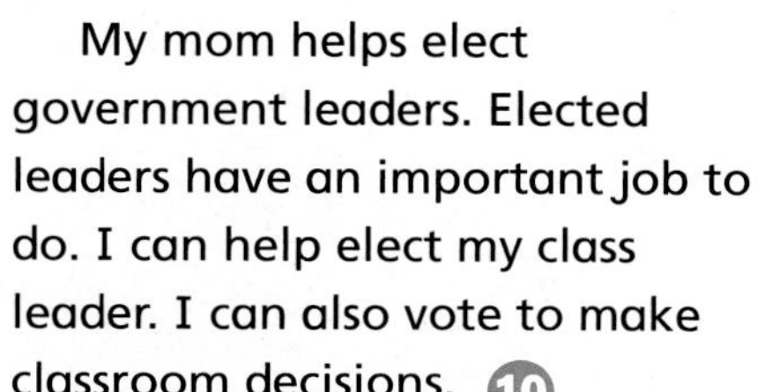

My mom helps elect government leaders. Elected leaders have an important job to do. I can help elect my class leader. I can also vote to make classroom decisions. (10)

What did you learn?

1. How can a citizen of our country who is at least 18 years old help elect a leader?
2. Name three ways you could learn more about a candidate running for office.
3. **Think and Share** Think of reasons why a person is a good leader. Write a story about a leader.

175

Page 175

Have children name some of the elected leaders they should know about—the current President, Vice-President, state governor, state lieutenant governor.

(10) **What would a class leader do in your class?** Possible answers: Greet visitors and tell them about the class, represent the class at assemblies, run class meetings, and help conflicts to get resolved peacefully. **Express Ideas**

3 Close and Assess

Have children recall and retell the steps in the voting process.

✓ What did you learn?

1. By voting
2. Possible answers: Newspapers, radio or television, Web sites, magazines, talking with friends and family
3. **Think and Share** Children's stories describe someone who shows one or more of these traits: smart, caring, a good problem solver, honest, fair. The stories should include specific actions that reflect the traits.

FAST FACTS

Our Presidents

- Franklin D. Roosevelt served 12 years, the longest of any President.
- John F. Kennedy was the youngest person elected President.
- Presidents Washington and Madison signed the Constitution.
- There have been two father-son sets of Presidents—John Adams and John Quincy Adams; George Bush and George W. Bush.

Workbook p. 42

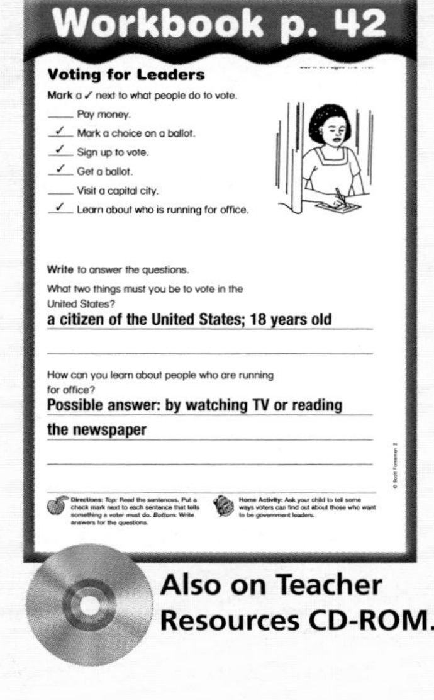

Voting for Leaders

Mark a ✓ next to what people do to vote.

___ Pay money.
✓ Mark a choice on a ballot.
✓ Sign up to vote.
✓ Get a ballot.
___ Visit a capital city.
✓ Learn about who is running for office.

Write to answer the questions.

What two things must you be to vote in the United States?

a citizen of the United States; 18 years old

How can you learn about people who are running for office?

Possible answer: by watching TV or reading the newspaper

Directions: *Top:* Read the sentences. Put a check mark next to each sentence that tells something a voter must do. *Bottom:* Write answers for the questions.

Home Activity: Ask your child to tell some ways voters can find out about those who want to be government leaders.

Also on Teacher Resources CD-ROM.

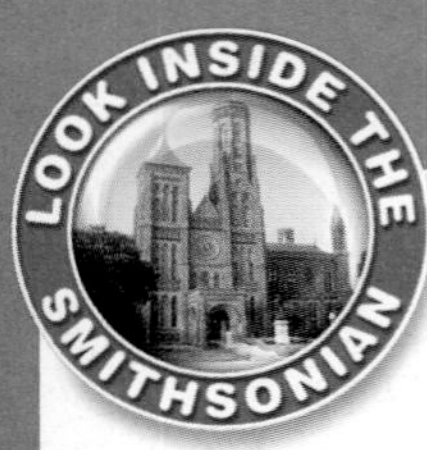

Presidential Treasures

Objective

- Obtain information from visual sources such as photographs of artifacts.

Resource

- Workbook, p. 43

1 Introduce and Motivate

Preview Read aloud the title, introduction, and text in the speech bubble. Then identify each object. Focus children's attention on the hat, uniform, and eyeglasses. Ask volunteers to describe what they see. Encourage children to compare and contrast the objects with their present-day counterparts. Have children then think and talk about the materials that were used to make the cup, the doll, and the lap desk. Share the background information that appears on this page.

Warm Up To activate prior knowledge, have children identify people who wear different kinds of uniforms. Discuss why certain jobs—nurse, firefighter, military person, police officer—require people to wear uniforms.

2 Teach and Discuss

Have children follow along as you read the captions.

1 Describe the symbol on Washington's Camp Cup. Possible answer: It looks like a fierce dragon with wings. The dragon is sitting on a crown. **Symbols can mean different things to different people. What do you think the symbol on this cup says about Washington's family?** Possible answer: The animal may mean that they were strong and powerful; the crown may mean that they were important people. Analyze Pictures/Make Inferences

Practice and Extend

SOCIAL STUDIES Background

About Some Presidential Treasures

- **Jefferson's Writing Desk** Jefferson designed the lap desk himself. It has a hinged writing board and a drawer for paper and pens. It also has an inkwell.
- **Sally, the White House Doll** It has a completely cloth body and a head made of bisque, a white unglazed porcelain.
- **Washington's Uniform** Legend has it that Washington wore the uniform seen here when he resigned his commission as Commander-in-Chief.

2 Look closely at Sally, the White House Doll. Why does it appear that the doll has been well cared for? Possible answer: Her clothing is neat and clean, not torn. Her face is not cracked. No parts are missing. **Analyze Pictures**

3 Why do you think a lap desk was so important to Thomas Jefferson? Possible answer: He was able to carry all of his writing supplies with him. **Make Inferences**

3 Close and Assess

Have children revisit each of the objects. Then ask them to discuss:

- why Washington's cup was made from the metal silver
- why is it interesting for us to know about the doll
- why Jefferson's writing desk is an especially important object for a museum to keep and display

Close by asking children to identify the object they find most interesting. Have them explain why.

WEB SITE Technology

You can visit the Smithsonian Institution online. Click on Smithsonian at **www.sfsocialstudies.com** or go to **www.si.edu**.

Workbook, p. 43

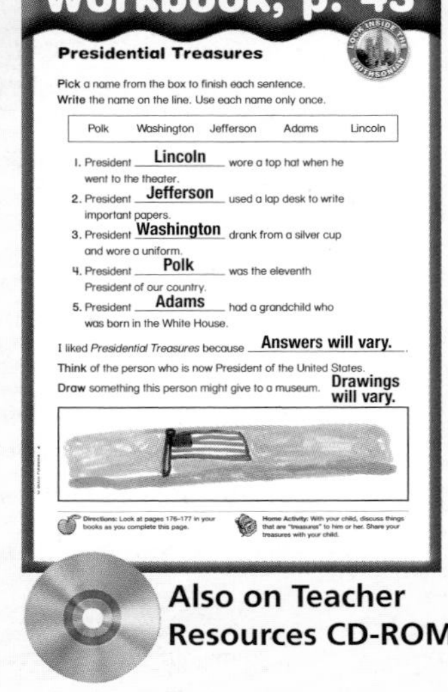
Presidential Treasures

Pick a name from the box to finish each sentence. Write the name on the line. Use each name only once.

Polk Washington Jefferson Adams Lincoln

1. President **Lincoln** wore a top hat when he went to the theater.
2. President **Jefferson** used a lap desk to write important papers.
3. President **Washington** drank from a silver cup and wore a uniform.
4. President **Polk** was the eleventh President of our country.
5. President **Adams** had a grandchild who was born in the White House.

I liked *Presidential Treasures* because **Answers will vary.**

Think of the person who is now President of the United States. Draw something this person might give to a museum. **Drawings will vary.**

Also on Teacher Resources CD-ROM.

Susan B. Anthony

Objectives

- Identify contributions of historical figures who have influenced the community, state, and nation.
- Identify historic figures who have exemplified good citizenship.

1 Introduce and Motivate

Preview Read the title of the feature. Tell children that Susan B. Anthony was a leader for equal rights. Have children look at the illustration to predict what they will read about.

Warm Up To activate prior knowledge, ask children why they think people sometimes have to disagree with, or complain about, an unfair situation to get the results they want. Encourage several responses.

2 Teach and Discuss

Help children realize that having your likeness on coins or paper money is a great honor. Traditionally, in this country, it had been reserved for Presidents, who were all men. Pass around a Susan B. Anthony coin for children to see.

1 **Why do you think Susan B. Anthony voted in the election even though she knew it was not allowed?** Possible answers: She knew that doing so would get people's attention. People would notice her and maybe listen to her complaint that women were being treated unfairly.
Make Inferences

Meet Susan B. Anthony

1820–1906
Equal Rights Leader

Susan B. Anthony helped women get the right to vote. She was the first woman to be pictured on United States money.

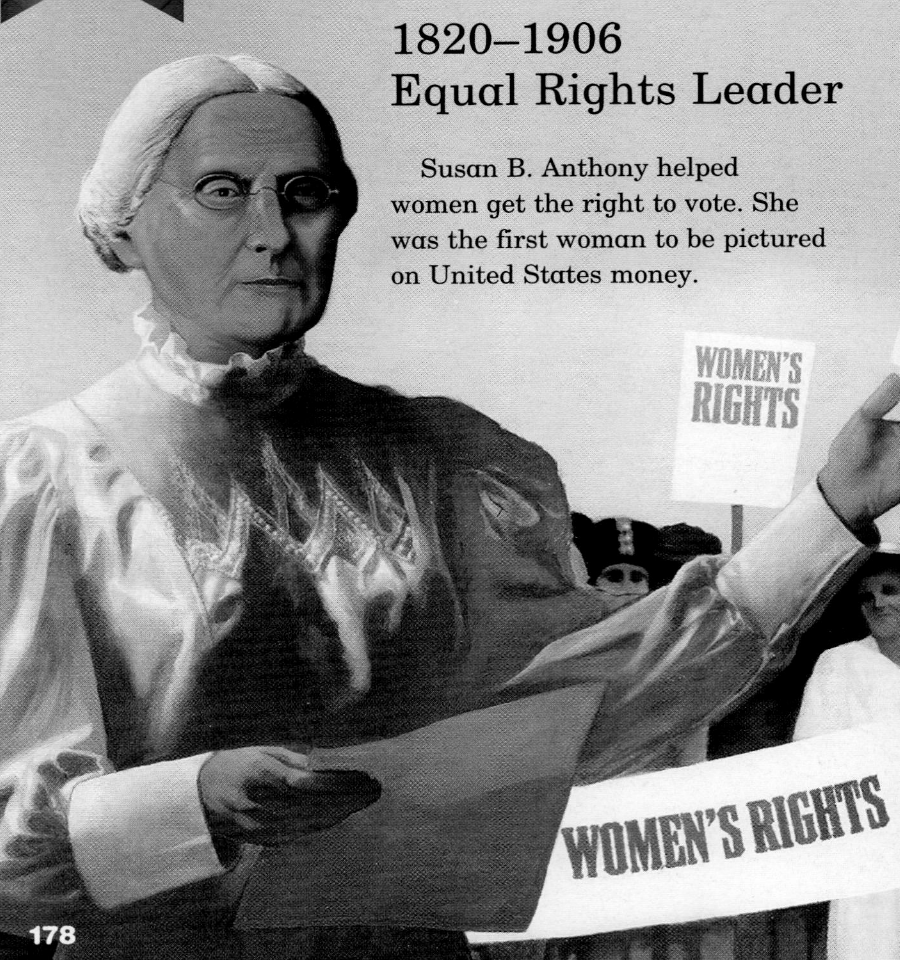

178

Practice and Extend

SOCIAL STUDIES
Background

Susan B. Anthony—The Early Years

- Susan B. Anthony was raised as a Quaker. Quakers were very serious in their religious beliefs and traditions.
- Susan B. Anthony's father, Daniel, did not allow music, toys, or games to be played in the house because he wanted his children to concentrate on more important things such as education.

WEB SITE
Technology

You may help children find out more about Susan B. Anthony by clicking on *Meet the People* at **www.sfsocialstudies.com.**

Susan B. Anthony lived during a time when men and women were not treated equally. Women were not allowed to vote. Many women did not go to school.

Susan B. Anthony was born in Adams, Massachusetts.

Susan's family was interested in her education. Susan learned to read and write at the age of three. When she was older, her family found a college that allowed women to attend. Susan became a teacher.

Susan B. Anthony believed that women should have the same rights as men. She believed that women should have the right to vote. She voted in the 1872 presidential election. She was arrested and fined. She refused to pay the fine. (1)

Susan B. Anthony seated at her desk

Susan B. Anthony traveled around the country, talking about women's rights. She spoke at meetings and wrote books. Her hard work led to amending, or changing, the United States Constitution. (2) In 1920, women were allowed to vote for the first time. (3)

Susan B. Anthony dollar coin

Think and Share

How did Susan B. Anthony work to improve the lives of American citizens?

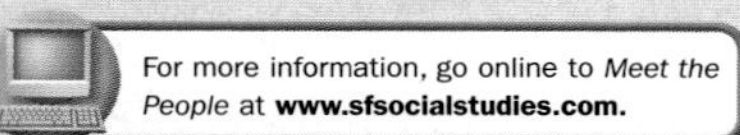

For more information, go online to *Meet the People* at **www.sfsocialstudies.com.**

CURRICULUM CONNECTION
Art

Design Your Own Coin!

- If possible, show children examples of coins from around the world. Note that most countries honor people by putting their pictures on coins or on paper money.
- Have children select a leader or an average citizen to honor with a coin.
- Using a construction paper circle, have them design a coin that bears the person's likeness.
- Encourage children to create a two-sided coin that includes words and other symbols that would reflect the life and work of their honoree.
- Plan a display!

(2) What happened as a result of Susan B. Anthony's talking to people and writing books? She, along with many other people, helped make a change in the Constitution, and women were allowed to vote. **Cause and Effect**

(3) What are some leadership qualities Susan B. Anthony showed? Possible answer: She was smart, confident, and took action to solve a problem. **Draw Conclusions**

3 Close and Assess

Have children write their responses to the Think and Share question.

Think and Share

Write Your Answer

Children should ask themselves, "Is the information in my written answer correct?"

Answers should reflect: Susan B. Anthony wanted everyone to be treated fairly and equally. Her work helped make a change in the Constitution in 1920. Now, women can vote, just as men. Women now can help make decisions about what will happen in cities, states, and our country.

Use with pages 172–179

Lesson 4 Wrap-Up

MEETING INDIVIDUAL NEEDS

Leveled Practice

Presidential Who's Who

Have children look through magazines and newspapers to find and cut out pictures of the current President and Vice-President.

Easy Have children label their pictures, indicating in a general way what the person is doing—working in his office, talking with the press, greeting visitors from another country, and so on. Provide help with labeling as needed. **Reteach**

On-Level After children do the activity suggested for Easy, have them find one or two biographical facts about the President and Vice-President. **Extend**

Challenge Have children turn the facts they gathered into a short paragraph. **Enrich**

Hands-on Activities

CURRICULUM CONNECTION
Art

Campaign Ad

Objective Express ideas visually.

Materials art paper, crayons, pencils

Learning Style Linguistic/Kinesthetic

Individual

Time 20–30 minutes

1. Tell children to make believe that they are running for President.
2. Have them create an ad for a magazine that announces their candidacy.
3. Have children tell about themselves in the ad and mention at least three things they would like to do for people if they were elected President.

CURRICULUM CONNECTION
Literature

A Photo Biography

Objective Obtain more information about a historical figure.

Materials *Susan B. Anthony: A Photo-Illustrated Biography*, by Lucille Davis (Bridgestone Books, ISBN 1-560-65750-2, 1998)

Learning Style Verbal/Visual

Group

Time 15–20 minutes

1. Read the title and author of the book. Then take children on a brief picture walk. Have children identify some things they would like to learn about Susan B. Anthony.
2. After reading, have children make personal responses.
3. Have children write two interesting new facts they learned. Encourage them to check their punctuation and spelling before finalizing their ideas.

CURRICULUM CONNECTION
Writing

Why Should I Vote?

Objective Explain the importance of voting.

Materials paper, pencil

Learning Style Linguistic

Individual

Time 15–20 minutes

1. Have each child write a paragraph about why it is important for people to vote.
2. Then have each child make a button to wear that reminds people to vote.
3. Have children take turns reading their paragraphs to the class as they wear their "Vote!" buttons.

Lesson 5 Overview

The Land of Freedom **pages 180–183**	Children will learn the vocabulary words *freedom, monument,* and *motto*. They will also learn about some of this country's symbols and the way in which we honor citizens such as past Presidents and Dr. Martin Luther King, Jr. 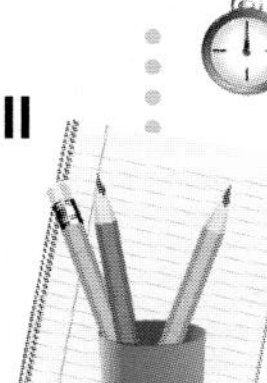	Time 20–30 minutes Resources • Workbook, p. 44 • Vocabulary Cards **freedom** **monument** **motto** • Every Student Learns Guide, p. 78–81
Use a Map Grid **pages 184–185**	Children will learn how to use a map grid.	 Time 15–20 minutes Resource • Workbook, p. 45
Flags Around the World **pages 186–187**	Children will learn about the flags of countries around the world.	 Time 15–20 minutes

Build Background

Activity

Make a "Me" Flag!

 **Time** 20–30 minutes

Have children make personal flags with symbols that show what they "are all about."

Display the flags and have children try to guess which flag belongs to whom.

If time is short, have children describe what a personal flag would look like. Encourage them to talk about both colors and images.

Read Aloud

Freedom!

by Christopher Erickson

In the United States
citizens have rights
To sing, have fun,
and look at the sights.
Flags wave in the wind
and statues stand tall.
They remind us of the freedoms
That exist for one and all.

The Land of Freedom

Objectives

- Identify patriotic songs, symbols, and mottoes.
- Identify people who have worked to improve the lives of American citizens.
- Interpret print materials by identifying the main idea and details.

Vocabulary

freedom every citizen's right to make choices (p. 180)

motto a word or saying that people try to live by (p. 181)

monument a building or statue that honors a person or an event (p. 182)

If time is short, have children look at the illustrations in the lesson and discuss the meaning of the American symbols.

- Have children read and try to answer the first question at the bottom of p. 183.

1 Introduce and Motivate

Preview Display the Vocabulary Cards **freedom**, **motto**, and **monument**. Ask children what they think each word means. Then have children locate each word in the lesson and read its meaning. Ask volunteers to use the words in oral sentences.

Warm Up To activate prior knowledge, point to the U.S. flag in your classroom and have children talk about what the colors, stars, and stripes represent. The color white stands for liberty, red for courage, and blue for loyalty. The thirteen stripes represent the original colonies. And the 50 stars stand for the current 50 states. Discuss how the flag represents freedom.

The Land of Freedom

Many people in our country have fought for freedom.

Freedom is every citizen's right to make choices. The Bill of Rights is a list of freedoms for all Americans. It is an important part of our Constitution. 1

Our country's national anthem, or song, is called "The Star-Spangled Banner." The last part says that we live in ". . . the land of the free and the home of the brave."

180

Practice and Extend

READING SKILL
Main Idea and Details

Target Skill

- Remind children that the main idea is the most important thing that a writer wants a reader to understand.
- After children read p. 182, have them write the main idea of the second paragraph. Then have children identify details that support that main idea.
- Have children exchange papers with partners to compare main ideas.

WEB SITE
Technology

You can look up vocabulary words online. Click on *Social Studies Library* and select the dictionary at **www.sfsocialstudies.com.**

A **motto** is a word or saying that people try to live by. The motto *Liberty* means ④ "freedom." The motto *E Pluribus Unum* means "out of many, one." Americans are many people who live in one country.

We have symbols that stand for our country too. The rose is our national flower. Here are other symbols I have made.

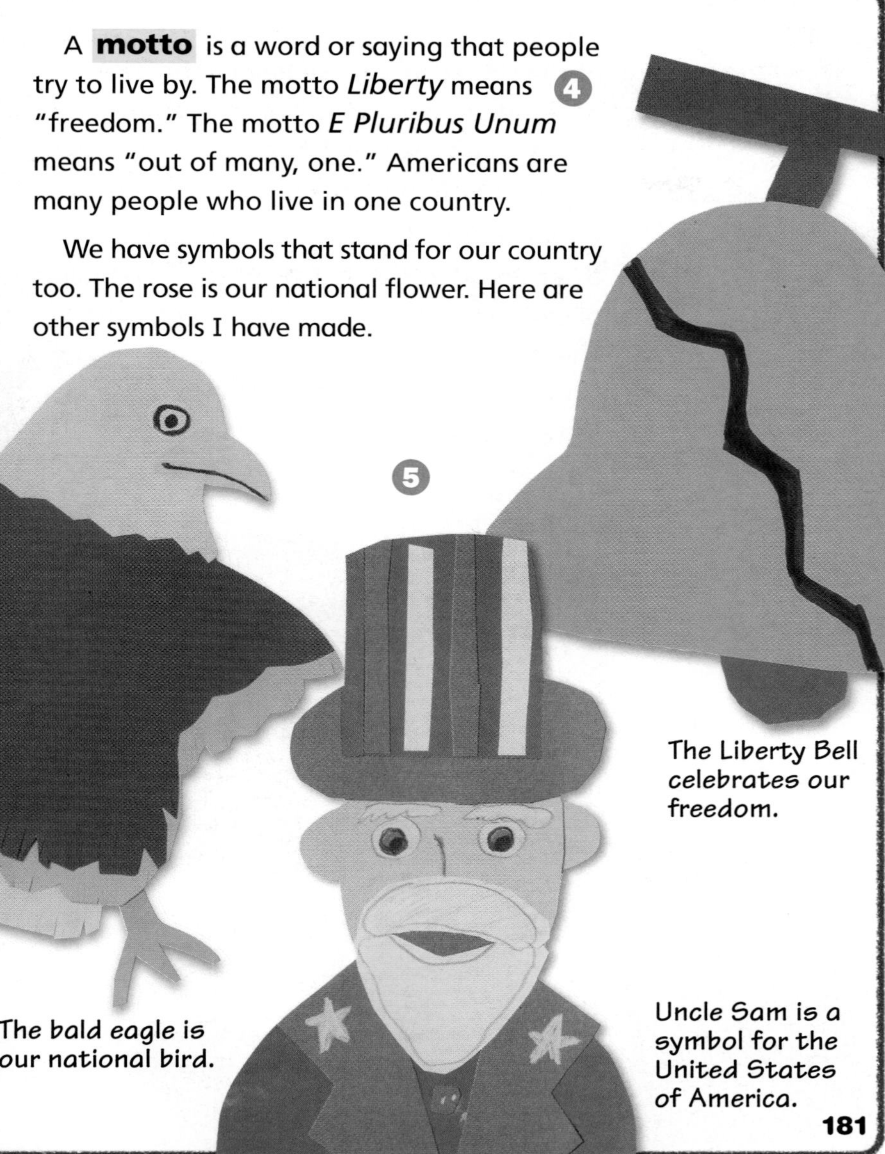

⑤

The Liberty Bell celebrates our freedom.

The bald eagle is our national bird.

Uncle Sam is a symbol for the United States of America.

181

2 Teach and Discuss

Page 180

Share with children some of the rights guaranteed in the Bill of Rights—such as freedom of religion, freedom of the press, and freedom of speech.

① **What is the Bill of Rights?** A list of freedoms Americans have **Recall and Retell**

② **Why do you think we have a national song that celebrates our freedom?** Possible answer: Americans are proud of the fact that we have so many freedoms. **Make Inferences**

③ **What are some occasions when the "The Star-Spangled Banner" is played and sung?** Baseball games, the Olympics, other athletic competitions, school assemblies **Recall and Retell**

Page 181

Help children with the pronunciation of *E pluribus unum*. Supplement the definition given by adding that the motto means Americans believe in the same things.

④ **Why is *Liberty* a good motto for our country?** Possible answer: *Liberty* is another word for *freedom*. Americans are proud of all the freedoms they have. **Evaluate**

⑤ **What are three symbols of our country?** The bald eagle, the Liberty Bell, and Uncle Sam **Where are some places you see these symbols?** Possible answers: Public buildings, the White House, on souvenir clothing and other articles **Analyze Pictures**

ESL — EXTEND LANGUAGE: ESL Support

National Symbols Have children draw a symbol they associate with their country of origin.

Beginning Have children write simple captions in their first language for their drawings. Then help them recite the English equivalent.

Intermediate Have children write a sentence or two in English to explain the significance of the symbol they drew.

Advanced Have children write a short paragraph comparing and contrasting the symbol they drew with one of the American symbols mentioned/shown in the lesson.

For additional ESL support, use Every Student Learns Guide, pp. 78–81.

continued

Page 182

Tell children that George Washington is often referred to as the "Father of our Country." Have them say why they think this is so.

Encourage children who have visited Washington, D.C., to tell about their experiences.

6 **Why do we build monuments in the United States?** To honor past Presidents and others who have contributed to our history **Cause and Effect**

7 **Which Presidents are honored with monuments in Washington, D.C.?** Washington, Jefferson, Lincoln **Main Idea and Details**

8 **Look at the pictures of the three monuments. How are they alike? How are they different?** Possible answer: They are alike because they are all important-looking buildings. They honor Presidents. They are different in that they represent different Presidents and show different symbols. **Compare and Contrast**

GEOGRAPHY
Movement

9 **If we as a class were planning to visit Washington, D.C., how might we travel there?** Possible answers: Bus, train, plane **Draw Conclusions**

10 **Besides having a picture on coins, paper money, and monuments, what are some other ways we honor important people?** Possible answers: Likenesses on stamps, streets named after the person, statues, public buildings named after the person, national holidays **Draw Conclusions**

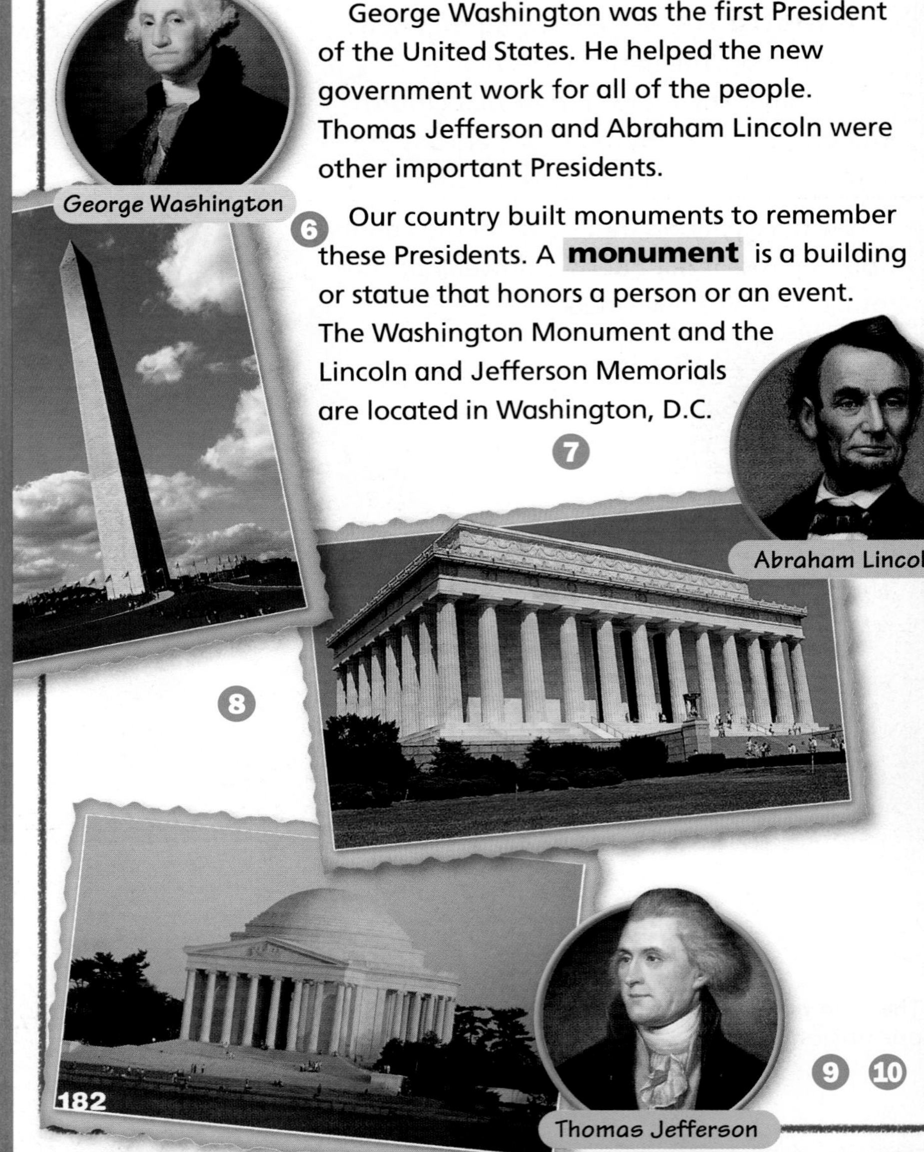

Practice and Extend

SOCIAL STUDIES
History

Fact Finding

- Have children work in teams of three.
- Each team should find and write three interesting facts about Presidents Washington, Jefferson, and Lincoln.
- After each team has done its research, have it report to the group.
- Collect children's facts in a *Presidents' Fact File.*

SOCIAL STUDIES
Background

- Washington, D.C., also is home to the Franklin Delano Roosevelt Memorial.
- It consists of four outdoor galleries, or rooms, one for each year of FDR's terms in office.

Dr. Martin Luther King, Jr., wanted all people to be treated fairly. For a long time (11) African Americans were treated unfairly because of the color of their skin. Dr. King made speeches and led peaceful marches. He is remembered on Martin Luther King, Jr., Day in January each year. (12)

What did you learn?

1. Tell what you think it would be like to live in a country that did not have our freedoms.
2. Name two symbols and one motto that stand for our country.
3. **Think and Share** Write about the **topic** of a famous American. Begin with your **main idea.** Add **details** that tell more about your **main idea.**

183

Page 183

Mention to children that Dr. Martin Luther King, Jr., was also a Baptist minister.

(11) **What did Martin Luther King, Jr., have in common with Susan B. Anthony and Thurgood Marshall?** All three fought for fair treatment of all citizens. **Compare and Contrast**

(12) **What are some ways we can work together in our school community to make it a better place?** Possible answers: We can follow the school rules; we can treat each other fairly; we can think about what is good for everyone, not just some people. We can resolve conflicts peacefully. **Cause and Effect**

3 Close and Assess

Have children explain two ways Americans honor their first President, George Washington.

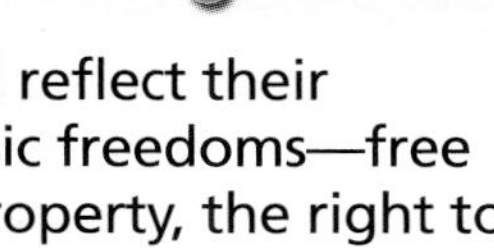

✓ What did you learn?

1. Children's responses should reflect their understanding of some basic freedoms—free speech, the right to own property, the right to an education, freedom to live and work anywhere in the country.
2. Symbols might include the Liberty Bell, Uncle Sam, and the bald eagle. Mottoes might include "*liberty* means freedom" and *E pluribus unum*," Latin for "Out of Many, One."

Think and Share Check children's writing for a clearly-stated main idea and several supporting details. Children's choices for a subject to write about should reflect prominent Americans.

SOCIAL STUDIES STRAND Citizenship

Dr. Martin Luther King, Jr.

- Tell children that Martin Luther King, Jr., led a big march to make people aware of the need for fair treatment for all people.
- Explain that he gave a famous speech that told how he dreamed of a future when people would accept each other as fellow Americans and not judge each other by the color of their skin.
- Ask children to "dream" about their futures. What could they do as citizens to make sure people were treated fairly?

Workbook, p. 44

The Land of Freedom

Read each sentence.
Circle the meaning of the word or words in dark print.

The **Bill of Rights** is part of the Constitution.
list of symbols — (list of freedoms)

The Lincoln Memorial is a **monument.**
(statue or building) — liberty bell

Americans have the **freedom** to live where they want.
(right) — rules

The **motto** *Liberty* means "freedom."
(saying that people live by) — building that honors a person

Draw a picture of a monument or a symbol. **Drawings will vary.**

Also on Teacher Resources CD-ROM.

Use a Map Grid

Objective

- Find locations on maps.

Vocabulary

grid a pattern of lines that form squares (p. 185)

1 Introduce and Motivate

Preview Have children identify the graphic as a map. Ask them how this map is different from others they have seen and used. Introduce the term *grid,* giving its definition. Have children trace the lines that form one square of the map grid.

Warm Up To activate prior knowledge, ask children to name some important places in Washington, D.C., that they have already learned about. Make a quick list on the board. As children work with the map and grid, check off any places on the list that correspond to those shown on the map.

Map and Globe Skills

Use a Map Grid

Look at this map of Washington, D.C. Many of the buildings and monuments you are learning about can be found on this map.

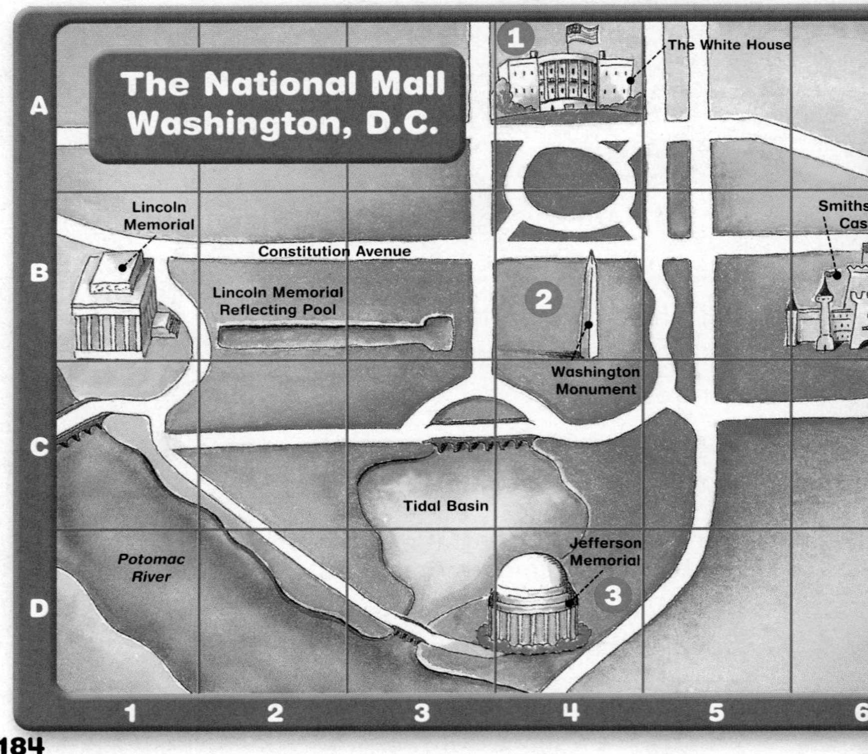

184

Practice and Extend

SOCIAL STUDIES STRAND
Geography

Use a Compass Rose

Take this opportunity to have children review how to use a compass rose.

- Refer children to the compass rose shown on the map grid.
- Have children use what they know about cardinal and intermediate directions to answer a short list of questions such as:

  Is the White House north or south of the Jefferson Memorial?

  Is the Lincoln Memorial east or west of the Washington Monument?

  Would a vistor walk southeast or northeast to get from the White House to the Capitol?

This map has a grid. A **grid** is a pattern of lines that form squares. The squares have numbers and letters. You can use a grid to find places on the map. Point to the Lincoln Memorial. It is in square B-1. Point to the Smithsonian Castle. Name this square's letter and number.

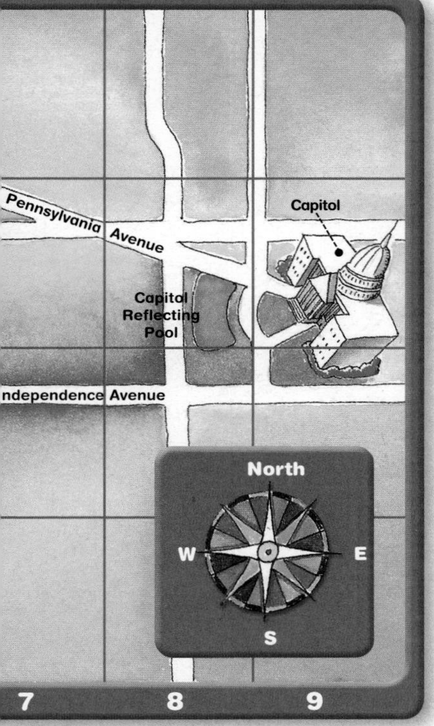

Try it!

1. Find the White House on the map. Tell the square's letter and number.
2. What is found in square B-4?
3. **On Your Own** Point to the White House. Move south three squares. What is the name of the building in this square? What is its letter and number?

185

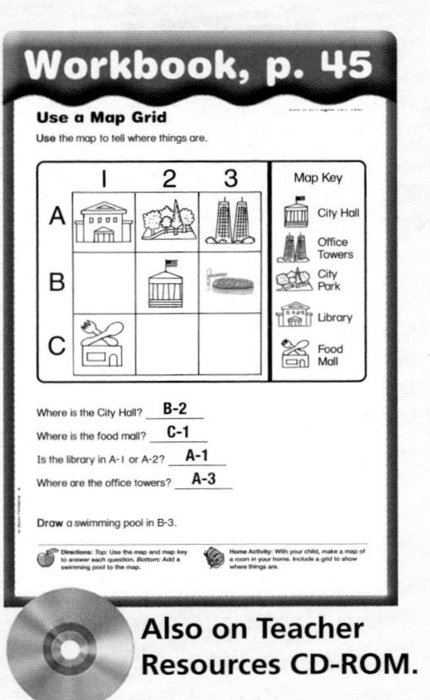
Workbook, p. 45

Use a Map Grid

Use the map to tell where things are.

	1	2	3
A			
B			
C			

Map Key: City Hall, Office Towers, City Park, Library, Food Mall

Where is the City Hall? B-2

Where is the food mall? C-1

Is the library in A-1 or A-2? A-1

Where are the office towers? A-3

Draw a swimming pool in B-3.

Also on Teacher Resources CD-ROM.

2 Teach and Discuss

Note that this lesson is an introductory activity to familiarize children with coordinates. A true use of a grid map would include an index with given coordinates so the map reader could find a location on the map.

Read through the text with children. Then have them go back to answer the questions in the text of p. 185.

Call out coordinates on the map and ask different children if anything is shown in that square. If the answer is yes, have the child identify what is shown. If children have difficulty reading the place names, have them point to the correct square and help them read the name. **Interpret Maps**

Have children find the Capitol on the map. Ask what they notice. Help them see that it occupies two squares. Have children name those squares B-8 and B-9. **Interpret Maps**

3 Close and Assess

Have children tell why a visitor to Washington, D.C., would find the map useful.

Try it!

1. A-4
2. Washington Monument
3. **On Your Own** Jefferson Memorial, D-4

Flags Around the World

Objective

- Identify flags as national symbols throughout the world.

1 Introduce and Motivate

Preview Have children look at flags shown on the two pages and compare and contrast them.

Warm Up To activate prior knowledge, have children describe the American flag and where they can see it displayed.

2 Teach and Discuss

Make the point that no two countries' flags are exactly alike, although countries sometimes do use the same mix of colors, patterns, and/or symbols.

As needed, help children read the captions that tell about the flags.

① **Why do you think the Canadian flag has a maple leaf on it?** Possible answer: There are many maple trees in Canada. Canada also produces various maple products and sells them throughout the world. Draw Conclusions

Flags Around the World

Sam and his class are learning about flags from other countries. Each flag has different colors and designs that represent its country.

① Canada: This country has many maple trees. Find the red maple leaf on the flag.

② Brazil: Find the globe in the center. The stars are arranged to look like the night sky over Brazil.

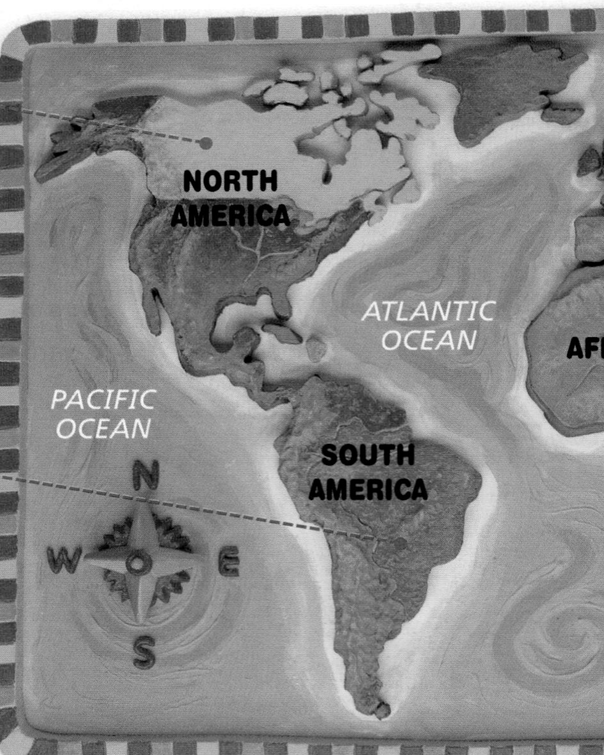

186

Practice and Extend

FYI SOCIAL STUDIES Background

About Betsy Ross

- Betsy Ross was a seamstress at the time of the American Revolution.
- She lived in Philadelphia, Pennsylvania, with her husband, John Ross, whose uncle was a signer of the Declaration of Independence.
- It is thought that Betsy Ross sewed the very first stars and stripes flag. It has been reported that George Washington headed up the committee that approached Betsy Ross about making the flag. The committee provided her with a rough design from which to work.
- The stars and stripes flag was officially adopted in 1777.

The American flag is red, white, and blue. The stars stand for each of our 50 states. The stripes stand for the first 13 states in the United States.

For more information, go online to the *Atlas* at **www.sfsocialstudies.com.**

ARCTIC OCEAN

EUROPE

ASIA

INDIAN OCEAN

AUSTRALIA

India: There are three stripes of orange-yellow, white, and green. The symbol in the center is a *Dharma chakra,* or wheel. 3

Kenya: This flag has three wide stripes. Find the warrior's shield and spears at the center of the flag. 4

187

CURRICULUM CONNECTION
Art

Flags from Around the World

- Have children work in small groups.
- Give them picture books and reference books that show some of the different flags from around the world. Assign each group one of the following continents: North America, South America, Africa, Asia, and Europe. Have children from the groups copy different flags representing countries on their continent. Each flag should be labeled.
- Display the flags grouped by continent. Encourage children to talk about the different symbols they see and what they may represent.

Test Talk

Use Information from Graphics
Tell children to use details in the picture of the flag to support their answer.

2 Do you think the people of Brazil are proud of their country? What clues do you see in the flag? Possible answer: Yes; the flag shows a beautiful starry sky. The people of Brazil want others to think Brazil is a beautiful place to live. **Analyze Pictures**

3 On which continent is India located? Look at your map. Asia **Interpret Maps**

4 What symbols on the flag of Kenya let you know the country honors its people and their history? The shield and spears **Analyze Pictures**

3 Close and Assess

Encourage children to tell something new they learned by reading and looking at the illustrations in the feature.

Use with pages 180–187

Lesson 5 Wrap-Up

MEETING INDIVIDUAL NEEDS
Leveled Practice

The Value of Freedom

Discuss with children what they learned about freedom in Lesson 5.

Easy Have children write two sentences to say what *freedom* means to them. **Reteach**

On-Level Have children do the Easy activity and then list some of the freedoms that they and their families have in the United States. **Extend**

Challenge Have children do both the Easy and On-level activities. Then have them write to say which freedom they and their family now enjoy they would miss the most if it were taken away. **Enrich**

Hands-on Activities

CURRICULUM CONNECTION
Writing

Puzzles

Objective Demonstrate an understanding of new vocabulary.

Resources Vocabulary Cards: **freedom monument motto**

Materials large-celled graph paper or ordinary line paper, pencils

Learning Style Linguistic

Group/Partner

Time 15–20 minutes

1. Display the Vocabulary Cards. Review the meanings of the words.
2. Have children make crossword puzzles that contain the three words. Have them figure out how to make the words fit together. Then have them write clues.
3. When the puzzles are ready, have pairs of children exchange them and solve them.

Remind children to add *freedom, motto,* and *monument* to their word books.

CURRICULUM CONNECTION
Music

Let's March!

Objective Listen and respond to patriotic songs/marches.

Materials tapes of John Phillip Sousa marches, tape player

Learning Style Auditory/Kinesthetic

Group

Time 15–20 minutes

1. Play one or more of the Sousa march songs.
2. Encourage children to talk about the songs—their energetic rhythms, the instruments used to play them. Have children compare the marches to some of the patriotic songs they have discussed in class.
3. Choose a march to replay and invite children to "step lively and proudly" around the classroom. Ask them if they feel patriotic as they march.

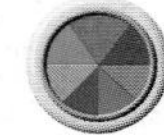

CURRICULUM CONNECTION
Writing

Mottoes

Objective Express ideas in writing.

Materials construction paper, pencils, crayons

Learning Style Verbal/Linguistic

Group

Time 20–25 minutes

1. Recall with children what a motto is.
2. Tell children they will work together in groups to create a motto for the class. Say that each motto will be the class motto for a week at a time.
3. Before children begin, model creating one or two mottoes: *A smile makes friends. Sharing is caring.*
4. Have each group create a banner with its motto. Each week display a new motto, and encourage children to live up to its words.

Ending Unit 4

End with a Song **pages 188–189**	Children will listen to, sing, and talk about the patriotic song "You're a Grand Old Flag" by George M. Cohan. 	Resource • *Songs and Music* CD
Unit 4 Review **pages 190–193**	Children will review unit vocabulary words and the unit skills of finding main idea and details and reading a table and a map grid. Children will answer questions about what they learned in the unit. Children will learn about several books about our country.	Resources ✓ • Assessment Book, pp. 13–16 • Workbook, p. 46
Unit 4 Project **page 194**	Children will learn how to make a campaign poster and commercial. They will also be directed to a Web site where they can learn more about campaigns and voting.	Resource • Workbook, p. 47

Wrap-up

Activity

A "My Country 'Tis of Thee" Poster

Tell children they will make a poster to show and tell why our country is a great place to live.

- Tell children they should think about how our country's three-part government works, how leaders are elected, and the rights and freedoms people have. They should use pictures and short sentences to express their ideas.
- Have children share their posters, supplementing what they drew and wrote.

Performance Assessment
You can use the activity on this page as a performance assessment.

✓ Assessment Scoring Guide

Make a Poster	
4	Includes important information about how our federal government works and people's freedoms and rights in a logical and clear presentation.
3	Focuses mainly on one of the above, but does so logically and clearly.
2	Unfocused presentation; random sequence of ideas so poster is neither clear nor persuasive.
1	Lacks understanding of the purpose of the assignment.

You're a Grand Old Flag

Objective

- Identify selected patriotic songs.

1 Introduce and Motivate

Preview Have children read the song title with you. Ask them to look at the illustration to say what holiday they think is being celebrated and why. Discuss why the flag is just the right symbol for celebrating the Fourth of July.

Warm Up To activate prior knowledge, have children who have marched in or attended parades tell about their experiences. Ask them especially to comment on the music—was it quiet and slow or loud and lively?

2 Teach and Discuss

Read the lyrics of the song twice as children listen. Have them identify any unfamiliar words so you can explain them. Then reread the lyrics and invite children to chime in as much as they can.

1 **What words at the very beginning of the song let you know the songwriter was proud of his flag?** He calls the flag *grand* and *high flying.* **Draw Conclusions**

2 **Why do you think he mentions that Americans are brave?** Possible answer: Americans fought a war to get freedom from Great Britain and other wars to remain free. **Make Inferences**

Practice and Extend

About George M. Cohan

- George M. Cohan (1878–1942) was a popular musical theatre performer.
- He wrote more than 40 musicals.
- His shows are not often performed any longer, but some of Cohan's songs continue to be very popular. One example is "Yankee Doodle Dandy."
- Cohan also wrote the most popular patriotic song of World War I, "Over There."

You're a Grand Old Flag

by George M. Cohan

You're a grand old flag,
You're a high flying flag ❶
And forever in peace may you wave.
You're the emblem of the land I love.
The home of the free and the brave. ❷

Ev'ry heart beats true
'Neath the red, white, and blue,
Where there's never a boast or brag.
Should auld acquaintance be forgot, ❸
Keep your eye on the grand old flag.

189

CURRICULUM CONNECTION
Music

"Yankee Doodle Dandy"

- Teach children the words to the song.
- Explain references they will not know.
- Have children listen for words in the song that name symbols of the United States (Uncle Sam, Fourth of July).
- Tell children that the same man who wrote "You're a Grand Old Flag" wrote "Yankee Doodle Dandy."

AUDIO CD
Technology

Play the CD, *Songs and Music,* to listen to "You're a Grand Old Flag."

❸ **Many people salute the flag by placing a hand over the heart as the flag passes by in a parade or other ceremony. Why do people salute their flag?** Possible answer: To show respect and love for their country **Draw Conclusions**

3 Close and Assess

- Listen to the audio CD "You're a Grand Old Flag" with children. Encourage them to sing along and clap out the beat.
- Ask children if they like the song and why or why not.
- Encourage children to make up a name for a song that would help everyone celebrate the Fourth of July.
- End by reinforcing the idea that Americans are respectful of symbols of and practices in their country. Remind children that as citizens they should be quiet, attentive, and respectful during the recitation of the Pledge of Allegiance, the passing of the flag, and the singing of the national anthem.

Review

Resources

- Assessment Book, pp. 13–16
- Workbook, p. 46: Vocabulary Review

Vocabulary Review

1. freedom
2. motto
3. President
4. monument
5. citizen

Answers to Test Prep

1. government
2. Congress

UNIT 4

Review

Vocabulary Review

motto
freedom
monument
citizen
President

Tell which word completes each sentence.

1. Every citizen's right to make choices is a _____.
2. A word or saying that people try to live by is a _____.
3. The leader of our country is the _____.
4. A statue that honors a person is a _____.
5. A member of a community, state, or country is a _____.

★ ★ ★ ★ ★ ★ ★ ★

Which word completes each sentence?

1. A group of people who work together to run a city, state, or country is a _____.
   a. government **b.** Congress
   c. President **d.** mayor
2. The _____ writes and votes on laws for our country.
   a. mayor **b.** governor
   c. President **d.** Congress

190

Practice and Extend

Assessment Options

✓ Unit 4 Assessment

- Unit 4 Content Test: Use Assessment Book, pp. 13–14
- Unit 4 Skills Test: Use Assessment Book, pp. 15–16

Standardized Test Prep

- Unit 4 tests contain standardized test formats.

✓ Unit 4 Performance Assessment

- See p. 194 for information about using the Unit 4 Project as a means of performance assessment.
- A scoring guide for the Unit 4 Project is provided in the teacher's notes on p. 194.

Test Talk

- Test Talk Practice Book.

Skills Review

Main Idea and Details

Write about a symbol that stands for our country. Put your **main idea** in the first sentence. Put **details** that support your **main idea** in other sentences.

Read a Table

Look at the table to answer these questions.

1. Which flag shows a grizzly bear?

2. Which state is called the Lone Star State?

State	Flag	About the Flag
Texas		This is called the Lone Star Flag.
California	CALIFORNIA REPUBLIC	The grizzly bear stands for courage.
North Carolina		The colors are the same as the American flag.
Virginia		The state seal is in the center of this flag.
Indiana		The flaming torch stands for liberty.

WEB SITE Technology

For more information, you can select the dictionary or encyclopedia from *Social Studies Library* at **www.sfsocialstudies.com.**

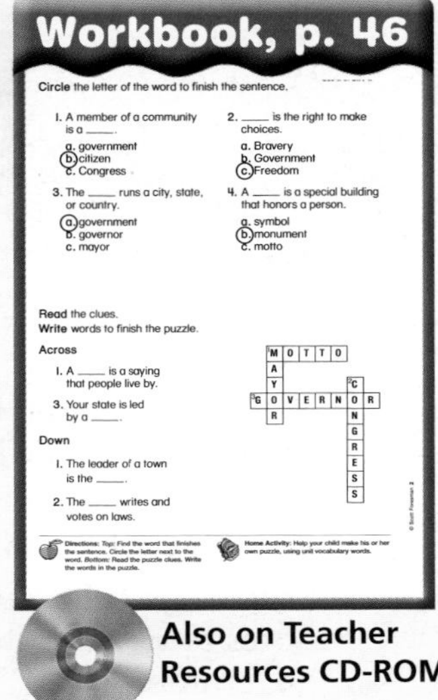

Workbook, p. 46

Circle the letter of the word to finish the sentence.

1. A member of a community is a ____.
   a. government
   (b.) citizen
   c. Congress
2. ____ is the right to make choices.
   a. Bravery
   b. Government
   (c.) Freedom
3. The ____ runs a city, state, or country.
   (a.) government
   b. governor
   c. mayor
4. A ____ is a special building that honors a person.
   a. symbol
   (b.) monument
   c. motto

Read the clues.
Write words to finish the puzzle.

Across
1. A ____ is a saying that people live by.
3. Your state is led by a ____.

Down
1. The leader of a town is the ____.
2. The ____ writes and votes on laws.

Directions: Top: Find the word that finishes the sentence. Circle the letter next to the word. Bottom: Read the puzzle clues. Write the words in the puzzle.

Home Activity: Help your child make his or her own puzzle, using unit vocabulary words.

Also on Teacher Resources CD-ROM.

Skills Review

Main Idea and Details

Target Skill

- Children's paragraphs should demonstrate ability to distinguish between main idea and details.

Use the following scoring guide.

✓ Assessment Scoring Guide

	Main Idea
4	Includes a clearly stated main idea related to the topic. Supports the main idea with multiple relevant details.
3	Includes a clearly stated main idea but some details are irrelevant.
2	No clearly stated main idea; a random reiteration of information from the lesson.
1	Identifies a symbol but does not supply details.

Read a Table

1. California

2. Texas

Review

continued

Skills Review

Use a Map Grid

1. B-2
2. Sports Center

Skills on Your Own

- Children's maps should be clear and accurate. Children should demonstrate understanding of how to use a map grid.

Use the following scoring guide.

✓ Assessment Scoring Guide

Make and Read a Map with a Grid	
4	Shows accurate information and demonstrates how to use a map grid.
3	Shows accurate information. Misreads the chosen item on the map grid but understands the function of the grid.
2	Spatially inaccurate map. Shows little understanding of the function the grid.
1	Little detail in map. Cannot use map grid to locate.

Review

Skills Review

Use a Map Grid

Read the grid map to answer these questions.

1. In which square is the State Capitol?
2. What is in square C-3?

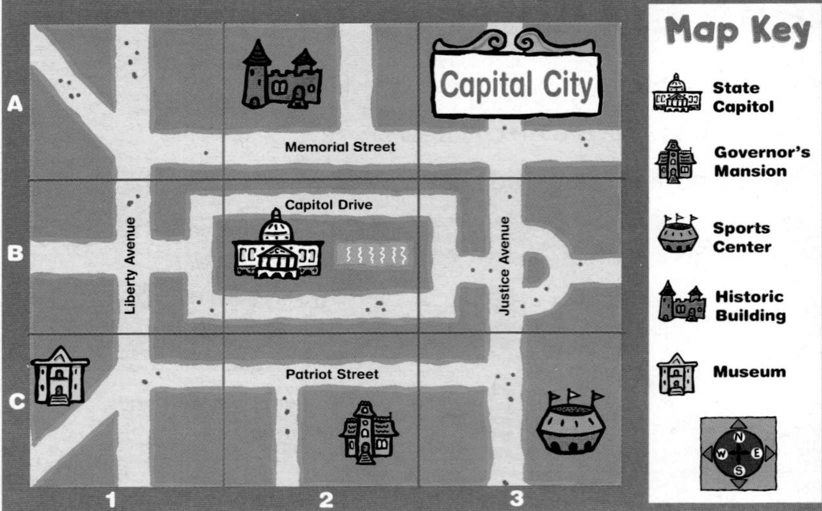

Skills On Your Own

Make a map of your classroom. Put a grid on your map. Use the grid to tell the location of something on your map.

192

Practice and Extend

Revisit the Unit Question

✓ Portfolio Assessment

Have children look back at the list they generated on p. 147. It records why they think people need government.

- Now that children have read the unit, have them write sentences to tell why people need government.
- Have children put a check mark next to reasons they learned while reading the unit.
- Encourage children to use their original list and their notes to write sentences about local, state, and federal government.
- Suggest children add their sentences to their Social Studies portfolio.

What did you learn?

1. Why do we need government?
2. Explain why libraries, schools, and parks are important to a community.
3. Why do you think it is important for citizens to vote?
4. **Write and Share** Write about the following **topic:** What people in government do. Put your **main idea** in the first sentence. Write other sentences that give **details** about the **main idea.**

Look for details to support your answer.

Read About Your Country

Look for books like these in the library.

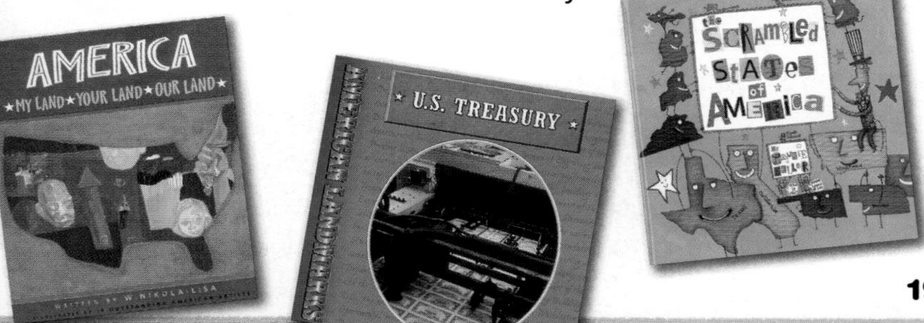

What did you learn?

1. Government establishes order, maintains security, and manages conflict.
2. Libraries, schools, and parks provide places to learn and relax.
3. Children's responses should mention that voting is a way for everyone's opinion to be counted. It is a way for people to help choose leaders and make decisions about some laws.
4. **Write and Share** Check children's responses for a clearly stated main idea in the first sentence followed by relevant details. Responses should reflect that government protects people's rights and freedoms and enforces laws.

Use Information from the Text
Use What did you learn? Question 3, to model the Test Talk strategy.

Decide where you will look for the answer.
Have children make notes about details from the text that answer the question.

Use information from the text.
Have children look at the question and the text to make sure they have the right answer.

For additional practice, see the Test Talk Practice Book.

Read About Your Country

America: My Land, Your Land, Our Land, by W. Nicola-Lisa (Lee & Low Books, ISBN 1-880-00037-7, 1997) Fourteen spreads introduce "land" opposites—rough/smooth, wet/dry. **Easy**

U.S. Treasury, by Jason Cooper (The Rourke Corporation, ISBN 0-865-93550-5, 1999) **On-Level**

Scrambled States of America, by Laurie Keller (Henry Holt, ISBN 0-805-05802-8,1998) Bored and restless, the fifty states, the protagonists of this story, have a party. **Challenge**

Unit 4 Project

Get Out the Vote

Objective

- Identify and present the qualities of a leader in a campaign poster and commercial.

Resource

- Workbook, p. 47

Materials

paper, pencils, crayons, large sheets of paper, sample political posters, shoebox or other small box

Follow This Procedure

- Explain that the class is going to hold an election. Children will choose an elected office for a character from a favorite book.
- Share samples of campaign posters. Discuss how posters let voters know about candidates.
- Suggest offices the candidates may run for, such as president, governor, or mayor.
- Have children work in groups of three or four. Help each group choose a candidate.
- Invite children to draw a poster to tell about their candidate. They should also write a short commercial. Both the poster and the commercial should focus on leadership qualities.
- Make a ballot box and voting ballots that include the candidates' names. Count the ballots and announce the results.

✓ Assessment Scoring Guide

Get Out the Vote	
4	Poster and commercial have a clear focus—the qualities that make a candidate a good leader—and a logical presentation.
3	Poster and commercial focus on leadership qualities, but the presentation is disorganized.
2	Poster and commercial stray from the topic. The presentation of ideas is random.
1	Poster and commercial show little understanding of the project.

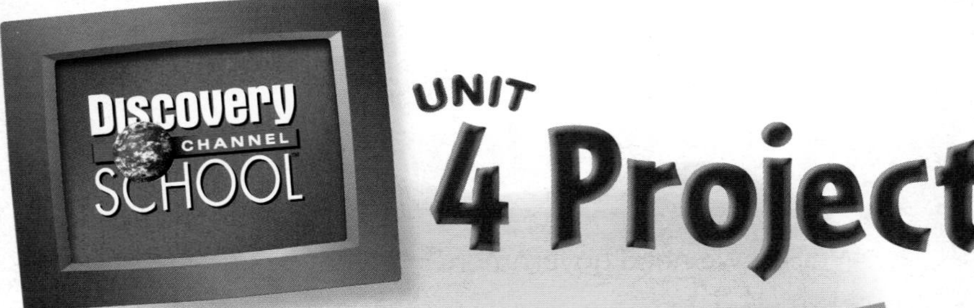

Get Out the Vote

Elections are important. Now is your chance to campaign for your own candidate.

Arthur for President

1 **Work** as a class and choose an office for your election.

2 **Divide** into groups. In your group, choose a character from a book to run for the office.

3 **Draw** a campaign poster for your candidate. Write a campaign commercial for your candidate. Explain to the class why your candidate is the best choice.

4 **Vote** for the best candidate.

Internet Activity

Go to www.sfsocialstudies.com/activities to learn more about our country today.

194

Practice and Extend

Hands-on Unit Project

✓ Performance Assessment

- The Unit Project can also be used as a performance assessment activity.
- Use the scoring guide to assess each group's work.

WEB SITE Technology

Children can launch the activity by clicking on *Grade 2, Unit 4* at **www.sfsocialstudies.com/activities**.

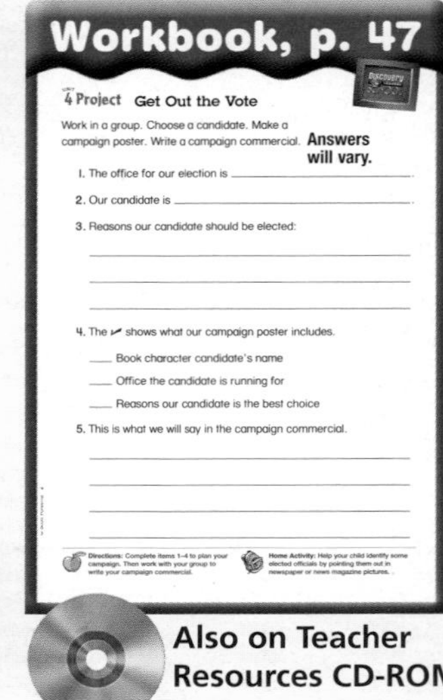

Workbook, p. 47

Unit 4 Project **Get Out the Vote**

Work in a group. Choose a candidate. Make a campaign poster. Write a campaign commercial. **Answers will vary.**

1. The office for our election is ______.
2. Our candidate is ______.
3. Reasons our candidate should be elected:
4. The ✓ shows what our campaign poster includes.
   - ___ Book character candidate's name
   - ___ Office the candidate is running for
   - ___ Reasons our candidate is the best choice
5. This is what we will say in the campaign commercial.

Directions: Complete items 1–4 to plan your campaign. Then work with your group to write your campaign commercial.

Home Activity: Help your child identify some elected officials by pointing them out in newspaper or news magazine pictures.

Also on Teacher Resources CD-ROM.

Our Country Long Ago

UNIT 5

Unit 5 Planning Guide

Our Country Long Ago

Begin with a Song pp. 196–197 **Vocabulary Preview** pp. 198–199

Reading Social Studies, Put Things in Order (Sequence) pp. 200–201

Lesson Titles	Pacing	Main Ideas
Lesson 1 **The First Americans** pp. 202–205 **Citizen Heroes: Honesty Ella Cara Deloria** pp. 206–207 **Smithsonian Institution: Native American Clothing** pp. 208–209	3 days	• Native American groups inhabit diverse regions of our country and have lifestyles reflective of where they live. • Ella Cara Deloria, a Sioux, researched and wrote many books about the Sioux language and culture. • Native American clothing is shown to be both practical for everyday life and highly decorative.
Lesson 2 **Colonies** pp. 210–213 **Map and Globe Skills: Read a History Map** pp. 214–215	2 days	• St. Augustine, Jamestown, and Plymouth were among the first European settlements in North America. Americans celebrate Thanksgiving to commemorate the feast shared by the Pilgrims and Native Americans. • A history map is one way to learn about early settlements.
Lesson 3 **Thirteen Colonies, One Country** pp. 216–219 **Biography: Paul Revere** pp. 220–221	2 days	• More people came to America to form 13 colonies. The colonists fought a war for independence. • Paul Revere warned people that British troops were arriving.
Lesson 4 **Our Country Grows** pp. 222–225 **Chart and Graph Skills: Read a Time Line** pp. 226–227 **Then and Now: Westward Ho!** pp. 228–229	3 days	• Lewis and Clark explored the American West. • A time line shows the events of the Lewis and Clark expedition. • During the 1860s, a railroad was built to join the East and West Coasts of America.
Lesson 5 **We Remember Americans** pp. 230–233 **Biography: Sojourner Truth** pp. 234–235	2 days	• Americans began to traffic in African slaves. Harriet Tubman and Frederick Douglass, who had been slaves themselves, helped other slaves find freedom. • Sojourner Truth spoke out for the rights of African Americans.

✓ **End with a Song** pp. 236–237 ✓ **Unit 5 Review** pp. 238–241 ✓ **Unit 5 Project** p. 242

 = Assessment Options

Scott Foresman Social Studies
Indiana Academic Standards

Grade 2 Unit 5 • *Our Country Long Ago*

Lesson Title	Indiana Academic Standards Social Studies
Lesson 1 The First Americans pp. 202-205	**IN Academic Standard 2.3.7** Identify ways that the physical environment influences human activities. **(Also 2.1.1)**
Citizen Heroes: Ella Cara Deloria pp. 206-207	**IN Academic Standard 2.1.3** Identify individuals who had an impact on communities. **(Also 2.1.4, 2.2.4, 2.5.3, 2.5.5)**
Smithsonian Institution: Native American Clothing pp. 208-209	**IN Academic Standard 2.1.1** Listen to historical stories and compare life in the past and present. **(Also 2.5.3)**
Lesson 2 Colonies pp. 210-213	**IN Academic Standard 2.1.4** Explain the meaning of community celebrations and traditions. **(Also 2.1.1)**
Map and Globe Skills: Read a History Map pp. 214-215	**IN Academic Standard 2.3.6** Identify map symbols of cultural or human features. **(Also 2.3.1)**
Lesson 3 Thirteen Colonies, One Country pp. 216-219	**IN Academic Standard 2.1.4** Explain the meaning of community celebrations and traditions.
Biography: Paul Revere pp. 220-221	**IN Academic Standard 2.2.4** Identify good leaders and good citizens, and explain the qualities that make them admirable. **(Also 2.3.3)**
Lesson 4 Our Country Grows pp. 222-225	**IN Academic Standard 2.1.1** Listen to historical stories and compare life in the past and present. **(Also 2.3.2, 2.4.5)**
Chart and Graph Skills: Read a Time Line pp. 226-227	**IN Academic Standard 2.1.5** Develop a simple timeline of important events.
Then and Now: Westward Ho! pp. 228-229	**IN Academic Standard 2.1.2** Identify changes that have occurred in the community. **(Also 2.1.1, 2.3.1, 2.3.6)**
Lesson 5 We Remember Americans pp. 230-233	**Reviews IN Academic Standard K.1.3** Listen to and retell stories about people who showed honesty, courage, and responsibility.
Biography: Sojourner Truth pp. 234-235	**IN Academic Standard 2.2.4** Identify good leaders and good citizens, and explain the qualities that make them admirable. **(Also 2.3.3)**

Insert between pages 195b - 195c
For complete standards listing, please see front tab.

Continued on other side →

Scott Foresman Social Studies to the Indiana Academic Standards for English/Language Arts

Grade 2 Unit 5 • *Our Country Long Ago*

Lesson Title	Indiana Academic Standards English/Language Arts
Begin with a Song, pp. 196-197 *Vocabulary Preview, pp. 198-199* *Reading Social Studies, Put Things in Order (Sequence), pp. 200-201*	**2.5.6** Write for different purposes and to a specific audience or person. See also 2.1.2, 2.1.3, 2.1.5, 2.2.2, 2.2.3, 2.2.4, 2.2.7, 2.4.1, 2.4.2, 2.4.4, 2.4.5, 2.4.6, 2.4.7, 2.4.8, 2.5.5, 2.5.6, 2.6.1, 2.6.2, 2.6.3, 2.6.7, 2.6.8, 2.6.9, 2.7.8
Lesson 1 The First Americans, pp. 202-205	**2.2.7** Interpret information from diagrams, charts, and graphs. See also 2.2.2, 2.2.4, 2.2.6, 2.7.8
Citizen Heroes: Ella Cara Deloria, pp. 206-207	**2.2.5** Restate facts and details in the text to clarify and organize ideas. See also 2.1.2, 2.1.3, 2.1.5, 2.2.2, 2.2.3, 2.2.4, 2.2.7, 2.4.1, 2.4.2, 2.4.4, 2.4.5, 2.4.6, 2.4.7, 2.4.8, 2.5.5, 2.5.6, 2.6.1, 2.6.2, 2.6.3, 2.6.7, 2.6.8, 2.6.9, 2.7.8
Smithsonian Institution: Native American Clothing, pp. 208-209	**2.2.7** Interpret information from diagrams, charts, and graphs. See also 2.2.2, 2.2.4
Lesson 2 Colonies, pp. 210-213	**2.2.6** Recognize cause-and-effect relationships in a text. See also 2.1.2, 2.1.3, 2.1.5, 2.2.2, 2.2.3, 2.2.4, 2.4.1, 2.4.2, 2.4.4, 2.4.5, 2.4.6, 2.4.7, 2.4.8, 2.5.5, 2.5.6, 2.6.1, 2.6.2, 2.6.3, 2.6.7, 2.6.8, 2.6.9, 2.7.8
Map and Globe Skills: Read a History Map, pp. 214-215	**2.2.7** Interpret information from diagrams, charts, and graphs. See also 2.2.2, 2.2.4
Lesson 3 Thirteen Colonies, One Country, pp. 216-219	**2.2.6** Recognize cause-and-effect relationships in a text. See also 2.1.2, 2.1.3, 2.1.5, 2.2.2, 2.2.3, 2.2.4, 2.4.1, 2.4.2, 2.4.4, 2.4.5, 2.4.6, 2.4.7, 2.4.8, 2.5.5, 2.5.6, 2.6.1, 2.6.2, 2.6.3, 2.6.7, 2.6.8, 2.6.9
Biography: Paul Revere, pp. 220-221	**2.2.6** Recognize cause-and-effect relationships in a text. See also 2.1.2, 2.1.3, 2.1.5, 2.2.2, 2.2.3, 2.2.4
Lesson 4 Our Country Grows, pp. 222-225	**2.2.6** Restate facts and details in the text to clarify and organize ideas. See also 2.1.2, 2.1.3, 2.1.5, 2.2.2, 2.2.3, 2.2.4, 2.2.7, 2.7.8
Chart and Graph Skills: Read a Time Line, pp. 226-227	**2.2.7** Interpret information from diagrams, charts, and graphs. See also 2.2.2, 2.2.4
Then and Now: Westward Ho! pp. 228-229	**2.2.7** Interpret information from diagrams, charts, and graphs. See also 2.2.2, 2.2.4, 2.4.1, 2.4.2, 2.4.4, 2.4.5, 2.4.6, 2.4.7, 2.4.8, 2.5.5, 2.5.6, 2.6.1, 2.6.2, 2.6.3, 2.6.7, 2.6.8, 2.6.9
Lesson 5 We Remember Americans, pp. 230-233	**2.2.5** Restate facts and details in the text to clarify and organize ideas. See also 2.1.2, 2.1.3, 2.1.5, 2.2.2, 2.2.3, 2.2.4, 2.2.7, 2.7.8
Biography: Sojourner Truth, pp. 234-235	**2.2.5** Restate facts and details in the text to clarify and organize ideas. See also 2.1.2, 2.1.3, 2.1.5, 2.2.2, 2.2.3, 2.2.4, 2.2.7, 2.5.6, 2.7.8
End with a Song, pp. 236-237 *Unit 5 Review, pp. 238-241* *Unit 5 Project, p. 242*	**2.2.7** Interpret information from diagrams, charts, and graphs. See also 2.2.2, 2.2.4, 2.4.1, 2.4.2, 2.4.4, 2.4.5, 2.4.6, 2.4.7, 2.4.8, 2.5.5, 2.5.6, 2.6.1, 2.6.2, 2.6.3, 2.6.7, 2.6.8, 2.6.9, 2.7.8

Vocabulary	Resources	Meeting Individual Needs
shelter **tradition**	• Workbook, pp. 50–51 • Transparencies 9, 25, 26 • Vocabulary Cards: shelter, tradition • Every Student Learns Guide, pp. 82–85	• ESL Support, TE p. 204 • Leveled Practice, TE p. 209a
explorer **colony** **colonist**	• Workbook, pp. 52–53 • Transparencies 5, 27 • Vocabulary Cards: explorer, colony, colonist • Every Student Learns Guide, pp. 86–89	• ESL Support, TE p. 212 • Leveled Practice, TE p. 215a
independence	• Workbook, p. 54 • Transparencies 2, 28, 29 • Vocabulary Card: independence • Every Student Learns Guide, pp. 90–93	• ESL Support, TE p. 217 • Leveled Practice, TE p. 221a
pioneer	• Workbook, pp. 55–56 • Transparencies 5, 30, 31, 32, 33 • Vocabulary Card: pioneer • Every Student Learns Guide, pp. 94–97	• ESL Support, TE p. 224 • Learning Styles, TE p. 229a
	• Workbook, p. 57 • Transparency 9 • Every Student Learns Guide, pp. 98–101	• ESL Support, TE p. 232 • Leveled Practice, TE p. 235a

Providing More Depth

Multimedia Library

- ***Explorers* by Rupert Matthews**
- ***I Am Rosa Parks* by Rosa Parks**
- **Songs and Music**
- **Video Field Trips**
- **Software**

Additional Resources

- Family Activities
- Vocabulary Cards
- Daily Activity Bank
- Social Studies Plus!
- Big Book Atlas
- Outline Maps
- Desk Maps

ADDITIONAL Technology

- AudioText
- The test maker
- Teacher Resources CD-ROM
- Map Resources CD-ROM
- **www.sfsocialstudies.com**

To establish guidelines for children's safe and responsible use of the Internet, use the **Scott Foresman Internet Guide.**

Additional Internet Links
To find out more about:

- Lewis and Clark, visit **www.pbs.org**
- colonial life, visit **www.history.org**

Key Internet Search Terms

- U.S. explorers
- American colonial life

Unit 5 Objectives

Beginning of Unit 5

- **Obtain information about a topic using oral sources, such as songs.** (pp. 196–197)
- **Obtain information about a topic by using visual sources, such as pictures.** (pp. 198–199)
- **Determine the meanings of words.** (pp. 198–199)
- **Sequence information.** (pp. 200–201)

Lesson 1
The First Americans
pp. 202–205

- **Compare the lives and contributions of various Native American groups.**
- **Locate the regions of the Powhatan, the Sioux, and the Pueblo Indians on United States maps.**
- **Explain how people have influenced local community history.** (pp. 206–207)
- **Obtain information from visual sources such as photographs of artifacts.** (pp. 208–209)

Lesson 2
Colonies pp. 210–213

- **Describe how weather patterns, natural resources, seasonal patterns, and natural hazards affect activities and settlement patterns.**
- **Explain the significance of national celebrations, such as Thanksgiving.**
- **Obtain information from a variety of visual sources, including maps.** (pp. 214–215)

Lesson 3
Thirteen Colonies, One Country
pp. 216–219

- **Explain the significance of national celebrations, such as Independence Day.**
- **Explain how selected customs and celebrations reflect an American love of individualism and freedom.**
- **Identify historic figures, such as Paul Revere, who have exemplified good citizenship.** (pp. 220–221)

Lesson 4
Our Country Grows pp. 222–225

- **Name several sources of information about a given period or event.**
- **Create and interpret a time line.** (pp. 226–227)
- **Describe how science and technology have changed transportation.** (pp. 228–229)

Lesson 5
We Remember Americans
pp. 230–233

- **Identify contributions of historical figures who have influenced the nation.**
- **Compare various interpretations of the same time period using evidence such as photographs.**
- **Identify historic figures, such as Sojourner Truth, who have exemplified good citizenship.** (pp. 234–235)

End of Unit 5

- **Obtain information about a topic using oral sources, such as music.** (pp. 236–237)
- **Explain how selected symbols reflect an American love of freedom.** (pp. 236–237)

Assessment Options

✓ Formal Assessment

- **What did you learn?** PE/TE pp. 205, 213, 215, 219, 225, 233, 241
- **Unit Review,** PE/TE pp. 238–241
- **Unit 5 Tests, Assessment Book,** pp. 17–20
- **The test maker,** (test generator software)

✓ Informal Assessment

- **Teacher's Edition Questions,** throughout Lessons and Features
- **Close and Assess,** TE pp. 201, 205, 207, 209, 213, 215, 219, 221, 225, 227, 229, 233, 235, 237
- **Try it!** PE/TE pp. 201, 227
- **Think and Share,** PE/TE pp. 205, 213, 219, 221, 225, 233, 235
- **Honesty in Action,** PE/TE p. 207
- **Hands–on History,** PE/TE p. 229

Ongoing Assessment

Ongoing Assessment is found throughout the Teacher's Edition lessons using an **If...then** model.

If = students' observable behavior, **then =** reteaching and enrichment suggestions

✓ Portfolio Assessment

- **Portfolio Assessment,** TE pp. 195, 240
- **Leveled Practice,** TE pp. 198, 209a, 215a, 221a, 235a
- **Learning Styles,** p. 229a
- **Workbook,** pp. 48–59
- **Unit Review: Skills On Your Own,** PE/TE p. 240
- **Curriculum Connection: Writing,** TE pp. 197, 207, 212, 229a, 233, 234, 235a

✓ Performance Assessment

- **Hands–on Unit Project** (Unit 5 Performance Assessment), PE/TE pp. 195, 242
- **Internet Activity,** PE p. 242
- **Unit Review: Write and Share,** PE/TE p. 241
- **Scoring Guides,** TE pp. 236a, 239, 240

Test Talk

Test-Taking Strategies

Understand the Question

- **Locate Key Words in the Question,** TE p. 207
- **Locate Key Words in the Text,** TE p. 219

Understand the Answer

- **Choose the Right Answer,** Test Talk Practice Book
- **Use Information from the Text,** TE p. 225
- **Use Information from Graphics,** TE pp. 215, 239
- **Write Your Answer,** TE p. 235

For additional practice, use the Test Talk Practice Book.

Featured Strategy

Use Information from the Graphics

Children will:

– Understand the question and form a statement that begins "I need to find out..."

– Skim the graphics to find the right information to support their answer.

PE/TE p. 239, **TE** pp. 215, 239

Curriculum Connections

Integrating Your Day

The lessons, skills, and features of Unit 5 provide many opportunities to make connections between social studies and other areas of the elementary curriculum.

Social Studies

Reading

Reading Skill—Put Things in Order, **PE/TE pp. 200–201,** TE pp. 202, 230

Reading Skill—Main Idea and Details, TE pp. 210, 222

Word Families, TE p. 215a

Reading Skill—Cause and Effect, TE p. 216

Many Words from One, TE pp. 209a, 221a

Writing

Write a Diary Entry, TE p. 197

Write About a Family Tradition, TE p. 207

Important Americans, TE p. 221a

Other Pioneers, TE p. 229a

New Information, TE p. 233

Choose a Name, TE p. 234

Words to Keep, TE p. 235a

Math

Solve a Word Problem, TE p. 201

Keeping Time, TE p. 226

How Long Did the War Last? TE p. 232

Literature

Paul Revere's Ride, TE p. 221

The Best of the West, TE p. 229a

Read About America's History, PE/TE p. 241

Science

Steam Power, TE p. 229

The Big Dipper, TE p. 236

Music/Drama

Improvised Skits, TE p. 235a

Art

Build a Native American Shelter, TE p. 209a

Thanksgiving Place Mats, TE p. 215a

Create a Time Capsule, TE p. 218

Join the Parade, TE p. 221a

Wagons Ho! TE p. 229a

A Mural, TE p. 235a

Look for this symbol throughout the Teacher's Edition to find **Curriculum Connections.**

Professional Development

Improving History Instruction in the Social Studies Classroom

by Rita I. Geiger
Norman Oklahoma Public Schools

Elementary children relate primarily to the present, and the effective elementary social studies teacher should focus mainly on present experiences in the immediate environment. However, the teacher can help children begin to understand the past or "history" through a variety of strategies and activities.

The use of music, art, and literature related to certain historical time periods immerse the children in the culture of the era. Reading primary sources such as letters and diaries, examining clothing, and manipulating artifacts aid in making predictions and reflecting about the lives of the people who wrote, wore, and used the items. Historical persons who are the subject of research projects might be impersonated throughout the school day by children in period clothing who model some of their characters' behaviors.

For young learners, an important goal of history instruction is to make the past seem real and to help them gain an insight into how their own lives and also current events have been shaped by the events and people of the past. Studying the past can help explain the present.

The following Teacher's Edition examples reflect Rita Geiger's strategies.

- ***Smithsonian Feature—Native American Clothing,*** *TE pp. 208–209: Children have an opportunity to study examples of authentic clothing from the past.*
- ***Paul Revere's Ride,*** *TE p. 221: The teacher shares a beautifully illustrated version of Longfellow's famous narrative poem.*
- ***Improvised Skit,*** *TE p. 235a: Children assume the roles of historical figures they have just learned about.*

ESL Support

Activate Prior Knowledge/Build Background

by Jim Cummins, Ph. D.
University of Toronto

In a classroom with second language learners from diverse backgrounds, prior knowledge about a particular topic may vary widely. Finding out what children know about a particular topic allows the teacher to supply relevant concepts or vocabulary that some or all children may be lacking but which will be important for understanding the upcoming text or lesson. Building this context permits children to understand more complex language and to pursue more cognitively demanding activities. It lessens the cognitive load of the text and frees up brain power.

Teachers can use a variety of strategies to activate children's prior knowledge. Discussion, visual stimuli, direct experience, writing, and dramatization can all be highly effective.

The following examples from the Teacher's Edition demonstrate strategies for activating prior knowledge and then building on it.

- ***Picture It,*** *TE p. 204: Children draw pictures and then write to tell what they know about ways in which people in the past obtained their food.*
- ***Meeting Needs,*** *TE p. 224: Children take the roles of pioneers and pantomime doing chores the pioneers would have had to do to survive.*

Read Aloud

Covered Wagon Days

by Fifth Grade Children/Pasadena City Schools

Across the plains roll our wagon trains,
On the way to the gold field far,
Where the cattle prowl and the
coyotes howl
And the herds of buffalo are.
Roll along, roll along,
Roll along across the plains.

Build Background

- Read aloud the title and tell children this verse is a song written by fifth graders. Have children share what they may know about covered wagons and their use in the past.
- Before you share the poem, have children describe what it may have been like to travel across country.

Read Alouds and Primary Sources

Read Alouds and Primary Sources contains additional selections to be used with Unit 5.

Bibliography

I Have Heard of a Land, by Joyce Carol Thomas and Floyd Cooper (Illustrator) (HarperTrophy, ISBN 0-064-43617-9, 2000) **Easy** ***Coretta Scott King Honor Book***

Minty: A Story of Young Harriet Tubman, by Alan Schroeder and Jerry Pinkney (Illustrator) (Puffin, ISBN 0-140-56196-X, 2000) **Easy** ***Coretta Scott King Honor Book***

New Hope, by Henri Sorensen (Econo-Clad Books, ISBN 0-613-08432-2, 1999) **Easy** ***Notable Social Studies Book***

Freedom River, A, by Doreen Rappaport and Bryan Collier (Illustrator) (Jump at the Sun, ISBN 0-786-80350-9, 2000) **On-Level** ***Coretta Scott King Honor Book***

Gift of the Sacred Dog, The, by Paul Goble (Aladdin Paperbacks, ISBN 0-020-43280-1, 1984) **On-Level**

Pueblo Storyteller, by Diane Hoyt-Goldsmith and Lawrence Migdale (Illustrator) (Holiday House, ISBN 0-823-41080-3, 1994) **On-Level**

Tapenum's Day: A Wampanoag Indian Boy in Pilgrim Times, by Kate Waters and Russ Kendall (Photographer) (Scholastic Trade, ISBN 0-590-20237-5, 1996) **On-Level** ***Notable Social Studies Book***

Seaman: The Dog Who Explored the West With Lewis and Clark, by Gail Langer Karwoski and James Watling (Illustrator) (Peachtree Publishers; ISBN 1-561-45190-8, 1999) **Challenge**

Ten Mile Day and the Building of the Transcontinental Railroad, by Mary Ann Fraser (Henry Holt, ISBN 0-805-04703-4, 1996) **Challenge**

Thunder from the Clear Sky, by Marcia Sewall (Aladdin Paperbacks, ISBN 0-689-82176-X, 1998) Alternating narratives between a Pilgrim and a Wampanoag of their people's first encounters make for an informative book. **Challenge** ***Notable Social Studies Book***

Kids' America, by Steven Caney (Workman Publishing, ISBN 0-911-10480-1, 1978) **Teacher Reference**

***Discovery Channel School* Videos**

Native Americans. Find out what happened to three Native American groups after European settlers came to North America; 52 minutes.

Look for this symbol throughout the Teacher's Edition to find **Award-Winning Selections**. Additional book references are suggested throughout this unit.

Practice and Extend

✓ **Unit 5 Performance Assessment**

- The Unit 5 Project, *Do an Interview*, found on p. 242, is an ongoing performance assessment project to enrich children's learning throughout the unit.
- This project, which has children prepare for and conduct an interview, may be started now or at any time during this unit of study.
- A performance assessment scoring guide is located on p. 242.

Our Country Long Ago

Unit Overview

In this unit, children will learn about the beginnings and growth of our country. They will be introduced to Native American groups, early settlers who came from Europe, and explorers who led the way for westward expansion.

Introduce Mara

Read the unit title and introduce the featured child for this unit as a second-grader named Mara. Have children say why they think Mara is dressed the way she is.

Unit Question

- Read the question on this page.
- Help children name some important events in the history of our country—the arrival of the first settlers from Europe, the fight for independence from England. Have them tell why each event is important.
- To activate prior knowledge, make a list on chart paper of children's responses to the unit question: Why is it important to learn about our country's history?

✓ **Portfolio Assessment** Keep a copy of this list for the Portfolio Assessment at the end of the unit.

Objective

- Obtain information about a topic using oral sources, such as songs.

Resources

- *Songs and Music* CD "Living in America"
- Social Studies Plus!
- Poster 9

Introduce the Song

Preview Tell children that they will be singing a song about settlers who came to this country. Focus attention on the picture of Mara.

Warm Up To activate prior knowledge, ask if Mara and the other children in the photo are dressed in the way that children today dress for school every day. Have volunteers name articles of clothing they see that are different from those children usually wear today.

Explain that Mara and her classmates are dressed in a way similar to that of the settlers who first came to this country.

Sing the Song

- Read aloud the title of the song and then the lyrics.
- Have children raise their hands any time they hear a word or phrase that is unfamiliar to them. Provide clarification.
- Model how to sing the song. Then have children sing it with you.
- Be certain children understand that the second verse of the song refers to the fight for independence from England.

Practice and Extend

SOCIAL STUDIES Background

Possible Misconceptions

- The word *Soon* at the beginning of the second verse of the song may mislead children to believe that the colonists began thinking about independence from England shortly after their arrival.
- Make the point that the first permanent settlers came to this country in 1607. The Revolutionary War—the fight for independence—did not begin until 1775!
- Tell children it took over 150 years of settlement and growth before the colonists were ready to fight for their independence.

Talk About the Picture

Begin by having children talk about the scene generally. Have children speculate on where Mara and her classmates are. Then help children focus on the details of the picture. Have them talk about what each child is doing, how each may be feeling, what the purpose of their dressing up may be.

Help children realize that Mara and the others probably are learning about all the different chores the settlers had to do to meet their needs.

1 **We use light bulbs to light our homes. What did the settlers use to light their homes?** Candles **We buy our clothing ready-made at the store. How did the settlers get clothing?** They made it. **Compare and Contrast**

2 **Think about other chores settlers would have to do. Do you think the settlers had much free time? Explain your thinking.** Possible answer: No; they had many chores of all kinds to do. Beside making candles and clothing and churning butter, they had to wash clothes by hand. They had to grow food too. **Make Inferences**

CURRICULUM CONNECTION
Writing

Write a Diary Entry

- Tell children that often people who came to this country kept diaries or journals to record their experiences. Tell them that they will write their own diary entries.
- Have children imagine that they are traveling by ship along with settlers coming to our country. Tell them to write how they feel as they approach the land. What are their hopes and dreams?
- Write *Dear Diary* on the board. Have children copy the words to begin their diary entries.

AUDIO CD
Technology

Play the CD, *Songs and Music,* to listen to "Living in America."

Vocabulary Preview

Objectives

- Obtain information about a topic by using visual sources, such as pictures.
- Determine the meanings of words.

Resources

- Workbook, p. 48
- Vocabulary Cards
- Poster 10

Introduce the Vocabulary

Read aloud and point to each vocabulary word and the photograph illustrating it. Have volunteers give the meanings of the words, as they are able. Then have children find examples of the vocabulary words in the illustration. Write these examples on the board.

Vocabulary Word	Illustrated Examples
shelter	tepee, longhouse, log cabin
tradition	weaver using a hand loom, Thanksgiving feast, Native American pottery, blanket
explorer	pictures of Columbus, Lewis and Clark
colony	models of Plymouth and Jamestown colonies
colonist	people shown in each colony
independence	Declaration of Independence exhibit, fireworks display
pioneer	wagon train

SOCIAL STUDIES STRAND
History

Listed below are some basic principles of government. Develop these ideas as you discuss the illustration.

- Groups, individuals, and events can have an important effect on the history of a community, state, or nation.
- Native Americans, explorers, colonists, and pioneers helped settle our country.
- Customs, celebrations, and symbols represent American beliefs and principles.
- The love of independence has been important throughout our history.

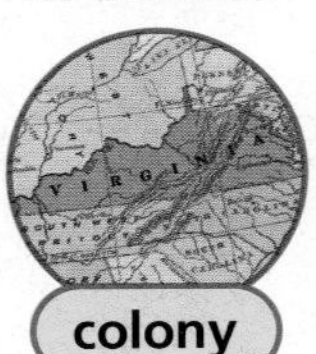

198

Practice and Extend

MEETING INDIVIDUAL NEEDS
Leveled Practice

Take a Tour

Invite children to use the illustration to take a tour of the museum exhibits.

Easy Walk children through the various exhibits, stopping to talk about what is shown. Incorporate the vocabulary words in your tour talk, asking children to repeat each word as you proceed. **Reteach**

On-Level Have volunteers take the role of tour guide. Encourage them to use the new vocabulary words as they talk about the exhibits. **Extend**

Challenge Have children give clues that include the new vocabulary so others can find a particular exhibit. Model giving clues such as: *Shelters can be made in different shapes.* **Enrich**

colonist

independence

pioneer

199

Talk About the Illustration

Allow children time to study the illustration. Tell them that the illustration shows many different exhibits that tell about our country's history. Help children notice that the exhibits represent the very first settlers, the Native Americans, as well as later settlers who came from across the ocean.

1 **Find the tepee, the longhouse, and the log cabin. What are they examples of?** Shelters **Generalize**

2 **What are two things you see at the top of p. 198 that show crafts that are part of Native American traditions?** Pottery, loom and blanket **Analyze Pictures/Make Inferences**

Look Ahead

Tell children that they will learn more about each of these words as they study Unit 5.

You may want to revisit the picture with children to review the concepts and vocabulary in the unit.

3 **How do you know the four people in the pictures at the top of p. 199 are explorers?** Possible answers: They are looking out over unsettled land. There are no other people shown. **Make Inferences**

4 **Why are fireworks shown near the Declaration of Independence exhibit?** Possible answer: People often celebrate Independence Day with fireworks. **Draw Conclusions**

5 **What are some things you can learn by looking at the two colonies shown at the bottom of p. 199?** Possible answers: What the colonists wore, how they farmed the land, what their homes looked like. **Analyze Pictures**

WEB SITE Technology

You can look up vocabulary words online. Click on *Social Studies Library* and select the dictionary at **www.sfsocialstudies.com.**

Workbook, p. 48

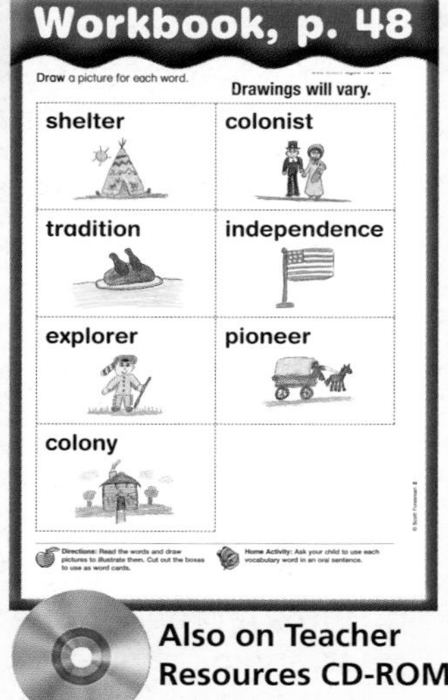

Also on Teacher Resources CD-ROM.

Mara's Project

Put Things in Order

Objective

Sequence information.

Resource

- Workbook, p. 49

About the Unit Target Skill

- The target reading skill for this unit is Put Things in Order.
- Children are introduced to the unit target skill here and are given an opportunity to practice it.
- Further opportunities to put things in order are found throughout Unit 5.

1 Introduce and Motivate

Preview To determine if children understand the concept of order and of ordering steps in a process, have them name some things they must do in order to accomplish a task. Children may suggest steps for: getting dressed, making a sandwich, playing a game, and so on.

Warm Up To activate prior knowledge, have children listen carefully as you describe three steps. Say that the steps are not in the correct order. Repeat the steps before asking children to say which step should be first, which should be next, and which should be last. Give these steps in this order: cook the egg in a pan, eat the egg, take the egg out of the refrigerator.

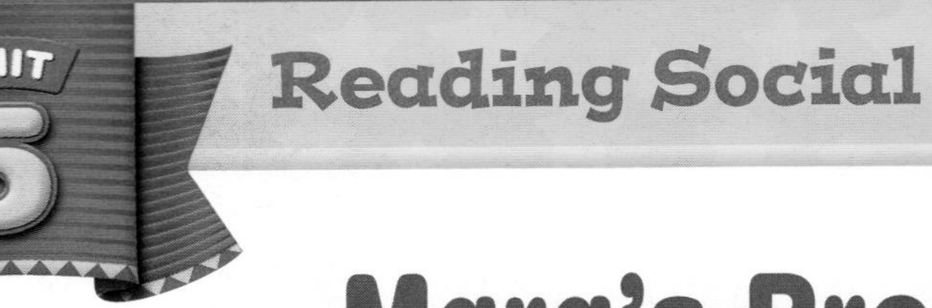

Reading Social Studies

Mara's Project

Put Things in Order

Hi, my name is Mara. I am working on a project about the Pueblo people. As you read about my project, look for clue words that tell the order in which things happen. **First, next,** and **last** are clue words.

First, I went to the library and looked for books. I checked out books to help with my project.

Next, I read the books and drew pictures to show how the Pueblo people live.

Last, I told my class about what I learned. I showed them my pictures.

200

Practice and Extend

ESL — ACTIVATE PRIOR KNOWLEDGE
ESL Support

Sequence Have three volunteers join you in the front of the room. Explain that you will arrange the volunteers in a certain order. Use the words *first, next,* and *last* to describe the order you arrange.

Beginning Reorder the three volunteers. Ask: *Who is first? Who is next? Who is last?* Children should name the volunteers as their positions are called out.

Intermediate Encourage children who are seated to take turns reordering the volunteers. The child who does the arranging should ask: *Who is first? (next, last)* Others respond with complete sentences: Tina is *first*.

Advanced Have children write sentences to describe the order of the volunteers: *Neil is last.*

Now look at these pictures. Tell what I did. Use the clue words **first, next,** and **last.**

First

Next

Last

Try it!

Tell about how you get ready for school. Use the clue words **first, next,** and **last.** Draw pictures to show the order in which things happen.

201

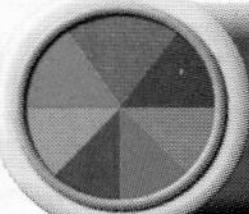

CURRICULUM CONNECTION

Math

Solve a Word Problem

- Ask children to think about the order of the steps they would use to solve the problem. Say: *Jan made two pink candles in art class. Reid made six red candles. How many candles did the two children make?*
- Repeat the word problem at least twice.
- Remind children to use the words *first, next,* and *last* as they talk about their problem-solving steps.

Workbook, p. 49

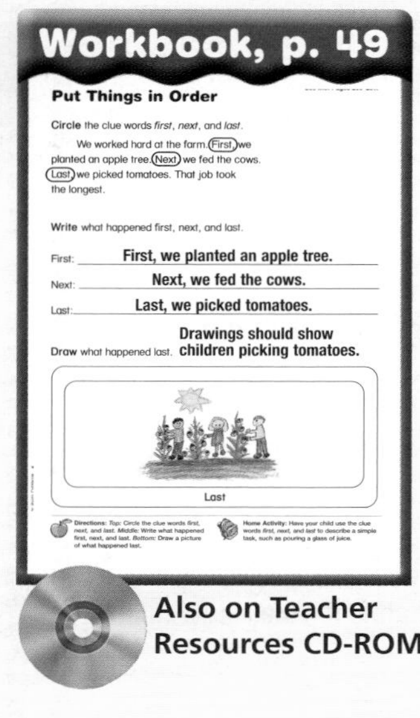

Put Things in Order

Circle the clue words *first, next,* and *last.*

We worked hard at the farm. First, we planted an apple tree. Next, we fed the cows. Last, we picked tomatoes. That job took the longest.

Write what happened first, next, and last.

First: **First, we planted an apple tree.**

Next: **Next, we fed the cows.**

Last: **Last, we picked tomatoes.**

Draw what happened last. **Drawings should show children picking tomatoes.**

Last

Directions: *Top:* Circle the clue words first, next, and last. *Middle:* Write what happened first, next, and last. *Bottom:* Draw a picture of what happened last.

Home Activity: Have your child use the clue words *first, next,* and *last* to describe a simple task, such as pouring a glass of juice.

Also on Teacher Resources CD-ROM.

2 Teach and Discuss

Read pages 200–201 with children. Have children think about the order in which Mara did things.

- Ask children if the order in which Mara did things was important for her to get the results she wanted—an interesting report with information about the Pueblo people. Have them say why or why not. (Mara could not have done her report if she had not first gone to the library and then read the books and drawn her pictures.) **Sequence**

Ongoing Assessment

If... children are confused by the concept of order,

then... remind them that the letters of the alphabet are in order. Have children tell which letter is first, next, and last.

- Have children tell how the labels for the photos on p. 201 help someone know in which direction to "read" the photos. (The labels let a reader know the order in which to look at the photos. A reader should begin at the left and continue across the page, toward the right.) **Analyze Information**
- Ask children how else might someone label the photos to show their correct order. Possible answer: Use the numbers 1, 2, and 3. **Apply Information**

3 Close and Assess

Try it!

Children's responses will vary. Listen as children talk to be certain they include the clue words *first, next, last* and that the words are used accurately. Look at their pictures to check for correct ordering of events.

Workbook Support

Use the following Workbook pages to support content and skills development as you teach Unit 5. You can also view and print Workbook pages from the Teacher Resources CD-ROM.

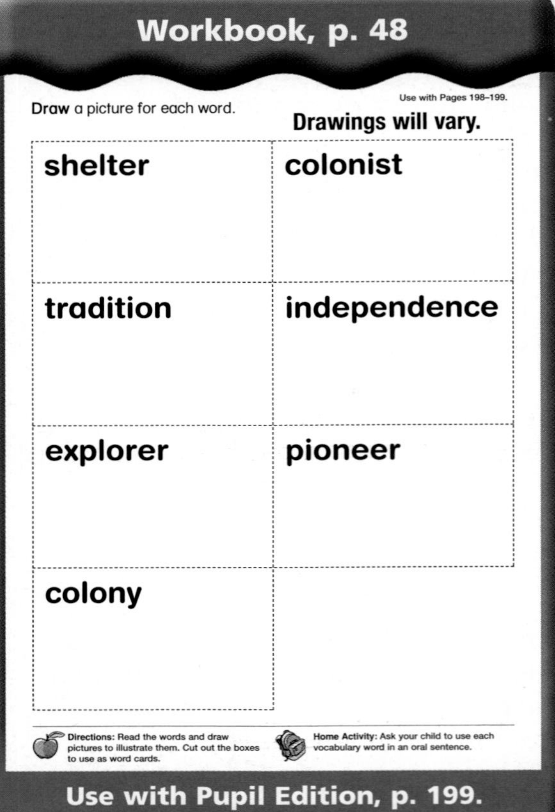

Workbook, p. 48

Use with Pages 198–199.

Draw a picture for each word. **Drawings will vary.**

shelter	colonist
tradition	independence
explorer	pioneer
colony	

Directions: Read the words and draw pictures to illustrate them. Cut out the boxes to use as word cards.

Home Activity: Ask your child to use each vocabulary word in an oral sentence.

Use with Pupil Edition, p. 199.

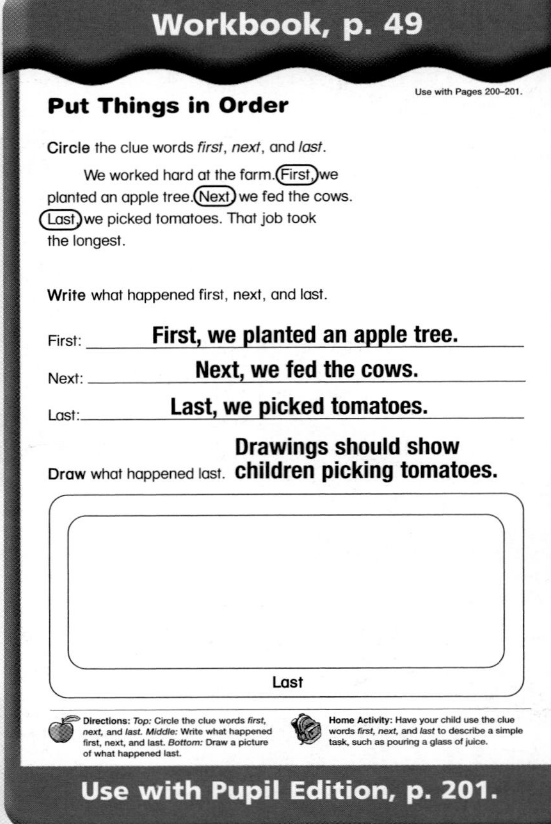

Workbook, p. 49

Use with Pages 200–201.

Put Things in Order

Circle the clue words *first*, *next*, and *last*.

We worked hard at the farm. First, we planted an apple tree. Next, we fed the cows. Last, we picked tomatoes. That job took the longest.

Write what happened first, next, and last.

First: **First, we planted an apple tree.**

Next: **Next, we fed the cows.**

Last: **Last, we picked tomatoes.**

Draw what happened last. **Drawings should show children picking tomatoes.**

Last

Directions: *Top:* Circle the clue words *first*, *next*, and *last*. *Middle:* Write what happened first, next, and last. *Bottom:* Draw a picture of what happened last.

Home Activity: Have your child use the clue words *first*, *next*, and *last* to describe a simple task, such as pouring a glass of juice.

Use with Pupil Edition, p. 201.

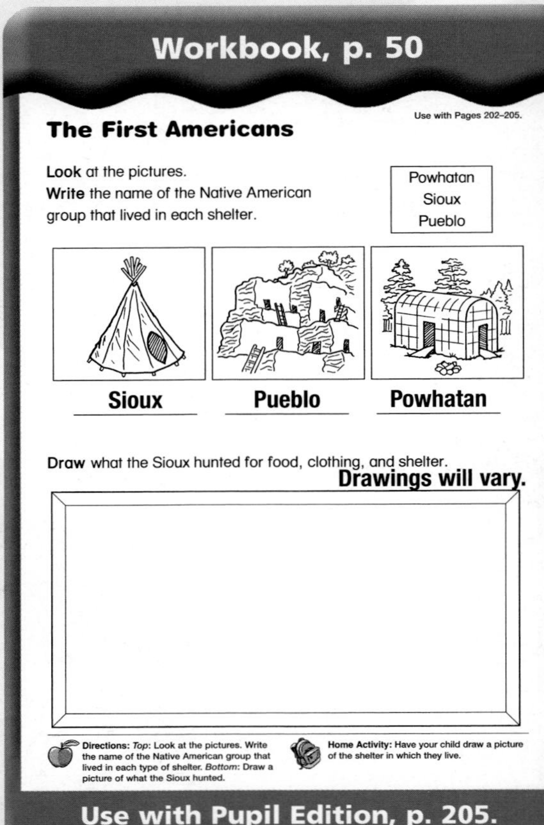

Workbook, p. 50

Use with Pages 202–205.

The First Americans

Look at the pictures.
Write the name of the Native American group that lived in each shelter.

Powhatan
Sioux
Pueblo

Sioux | **Pueblo** | **Powhatan**

Draw what the Sioux hunted for food, clothing, and shelter. **Drawings will vary.**

Directions: *Top*: Look at the pictures. Write the name of the Native American group that lived in each type of shelter. *Bottom*: Draw a picture of what the Sioux hunted.

Home Activity: Have your child draw a picture of the shelter in which they live.

Use with Pupil Edition, p. 205.

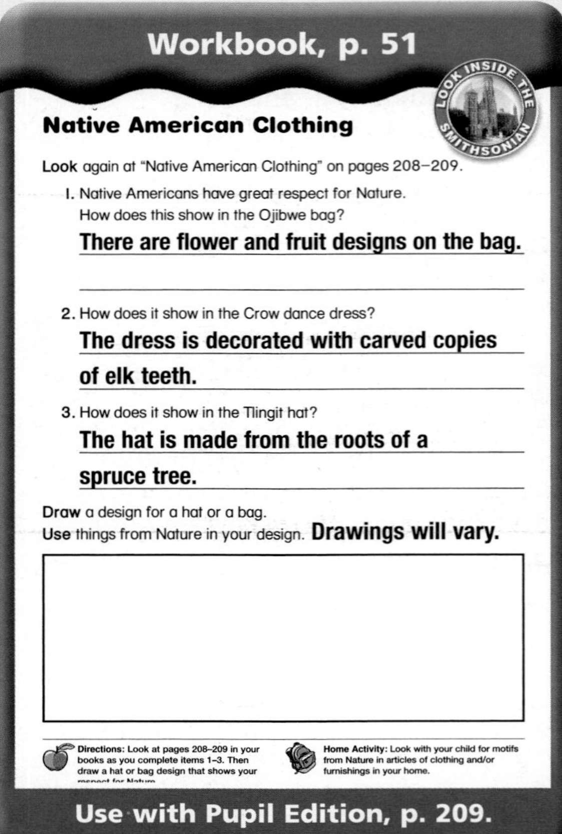

Workbook, p. 51

LOOK INSIDE THE SMITHSONIAN

Native American Clothing

Look again at "Native American Clothing" on pages 208–209.

1. Native Americans have great respect for Nature. How does this show in the Ojibwe bag?
   There are flower and fruit designs on the bag.
2. How does it show in the Crow dance dress?
   The dress is decorated with carved copies of elk teeth.
3. How does it show in the Tlingit hat?
   The hat is made from the roots of a spruce tree.

Draw a design for a hat or a bag.
Use things from Nature in your design. **Drawings will vary.**

Directions: Look at pages 208–209 in your books as you complete items 1–3. Then draw a hat or bag design that shows your respect for Nature.

Home Activity: Look with your child for motifs from Nature in articles of clothing and/or furnishings in your home.

Use with Pupil Edition, p. 209.

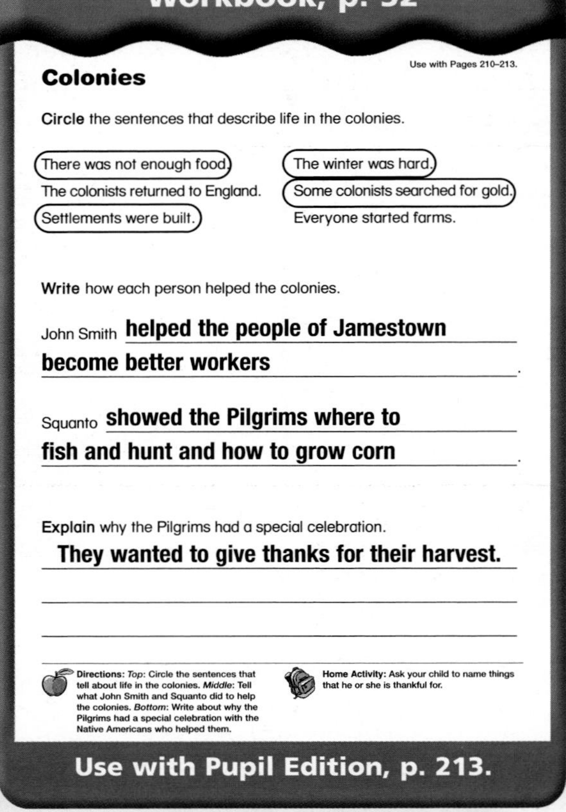

Workbook, p. 52

Use with Pages 210–213.

Colonies

Circle the sentences that describe life in the colonies.

There was not enough food. | The winter was hard.
The colonists returned to England. | Some colonists searched for gold.
Settlements were built. | Everyone started farms.

Write how each person helped the colonies.

John Smith **helped the people of Jamestown become better workers**.

Squanto **showed the Pilgrims where to fish and hunt and how to grow corn**.

Explain why the Pilgrims had a special celebration.

They wanted to give thanks for their harvest.

Directions: *Top*: Circle the sentences that tell about life in the colonies. *Middle*: Tell what John Smith and Squanto did to help the colonies. *Bottom*: Write about why the Pilgrims had a special celebration with the Native Americans who helped them.

Home Activity: Ask your child to name things that he or she is thankful for.

Use with Pupil Edition, p. 213.

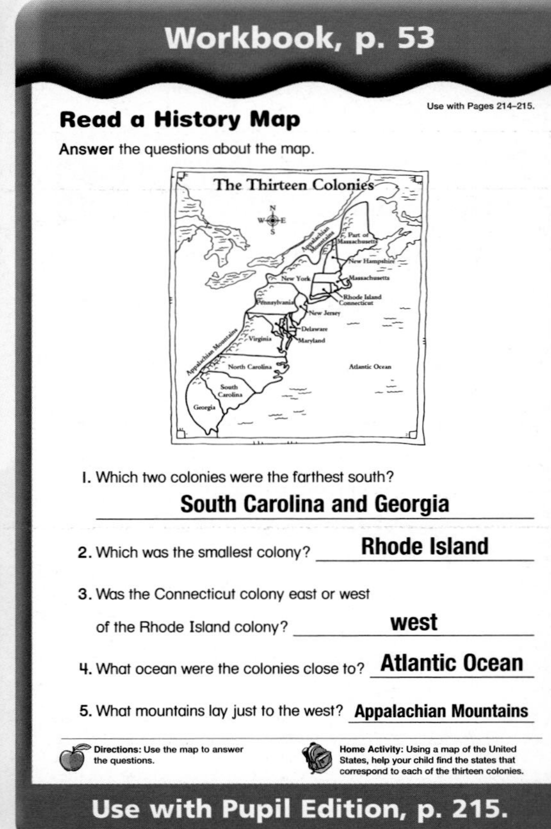

Workbook, p. 53

Use with Pages 214–215.

Read a History Map

Answer the questions about the map.

The Thirteen Colonies

1. Which two colonies were the farthest south?
   South Carolina and Georgia
2. Which was the smallest colony? **Rhode Island**
3. Was the Connecticut colony east or west of the Rhode Island colony? **west**
4. What ocean were the colonies close to? **Atlantic Ocean**
5. What mountains lay just to the west? **Appalachian Mountains**

Directions: Use the map to answer the questions.

Home Activity: Using a map of the United States, help your child find the states that correspond to each of the thirteen colonies.

Use with Pupil Edition, p. 215.

Workbook Support

Workbook, p. 54

Use with Pages 216–219.

Thirteen Colonies, One Country

Circle the correct answers.

1. What did the colonists think was unfair?
   working as farmers — (taxes)
2. What did most of the colonists want?
   (to be free from England) — to move back to England
3. What did Thomas Jefferson write?
   the Constitution — (the Declaration of Independence)
4. Who led the American army during the war with England?
   (George Washington) — Patrick Henry

Answer the question.

Why do Americans celebrate Independence Day?
Independence Day honors our country's birthday. On this holiday, we celebrate our country's freedom.

Directions: *Top:* Circle the correct answer to each question. *Bottom:* Write about why Americans celebrate Independence Day on July 4th.

Home Activity: Ask your child to name some other holidays that Americans like to celebrate.

Use with Pupil Edition, p. 219.

Workbook, p. 55

Use with Pages 222–225.

Our Country Grows

Look at the information in the boxes.
Write answers to the questions below.

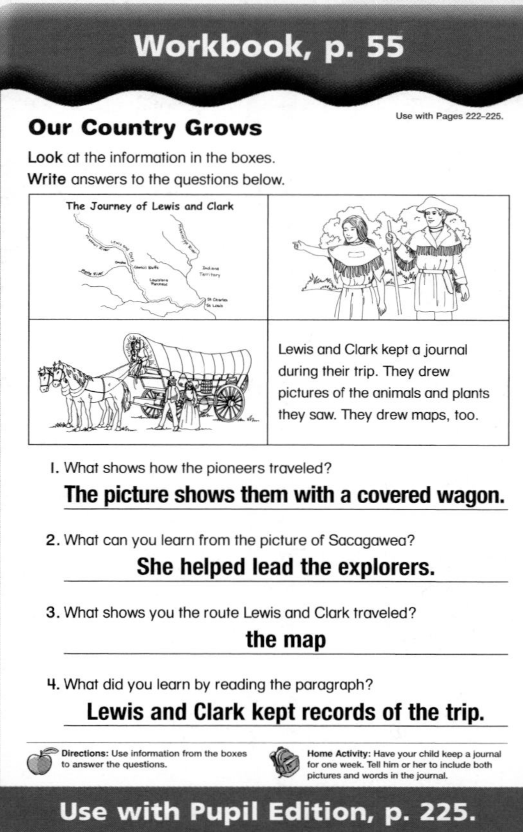

Lewis and Clark kept a journal during their trip. They drew pictures of the animals and plants they saw. They drew maps, too.

1. What shows how the pioneers traveled?
   The picture shows them with a covered wagon.
2. What can you learn from the picture of Sacagawea?
   She helped lead the explorers.
3. What shows you the route Lewis and Clark traveled?
   the map
4. What did you learn by reading the paragraph?
   Lewis and Clark kept records of the trip.

Directions: Use information from the boxes to answer the questions.

Home Activity: Have your child keep a journal for one week. Tell him or her to include both pictures and words in the journal.

Use with Pupil Edition, p. 225.

Workbook, p. 56

Use with Pages 226–227.

Read a Time Line

Add this fact to complete the time line.
- William Penn settles Philadelphia in 1682.

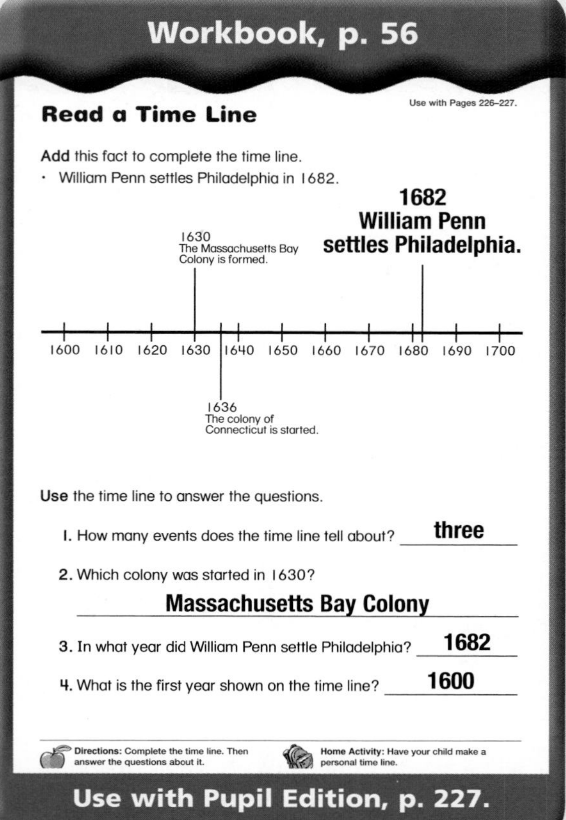

Use the time line to answer the questions.

1. How many events does the time line tell about? **three**
2. Which colony was started in 1630?
   Massachusetts Bay Colony
3. In what year did William Penn settle Philadelphia? **1682**
4. What is the first year shown on the time line? **1600**

Directions: Complete the time line. Then answer the questions about it.

Home Activity: Have your child make a personal time line.

Use with Pupil Edition, p. 227.

Workbook, p. 57

Name ______

Lesson 5 Review

Use with Pages 230–233.

We Remember Americans

Write *T* by the sentences that are true.

T Slaves were not free.
T Africans were sold into slavery.
____ Slaves chose their own jobs
T Slaves were not paid for their work.

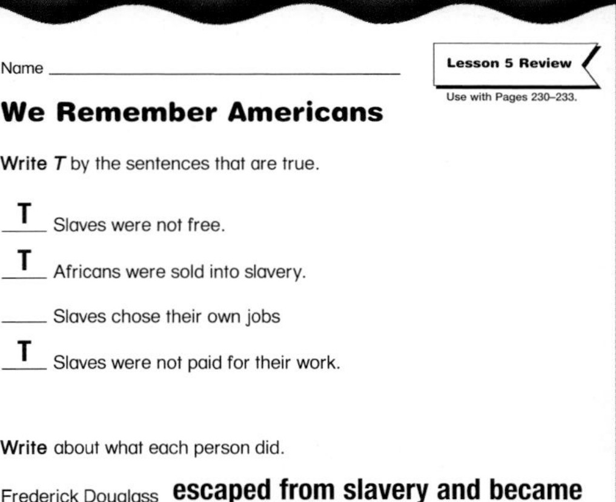

Write about what each person did.

Frederick Douglass **escaped from slavery and became a great speaker and writer**.

Abraham Lincoln **helped to end slavery in the United States**.

Harriet Tubman **helped people escape slavery**.

Jackie Robinson **was the first black baseball player to play on an all-white team**.

Use with Pupil Edition, p. 233.

Workbook, p. 58

Use with Unit 5.

Write the word that goes with the meaning.

tradition	colony	independence	colonist

1. a place settled by people from another country **colony**
2. to be free from other people or places **independence**
3. something that is done in a certain way **tradition**
4. a person who lives in a new place **colonist**

Draw lines to match.

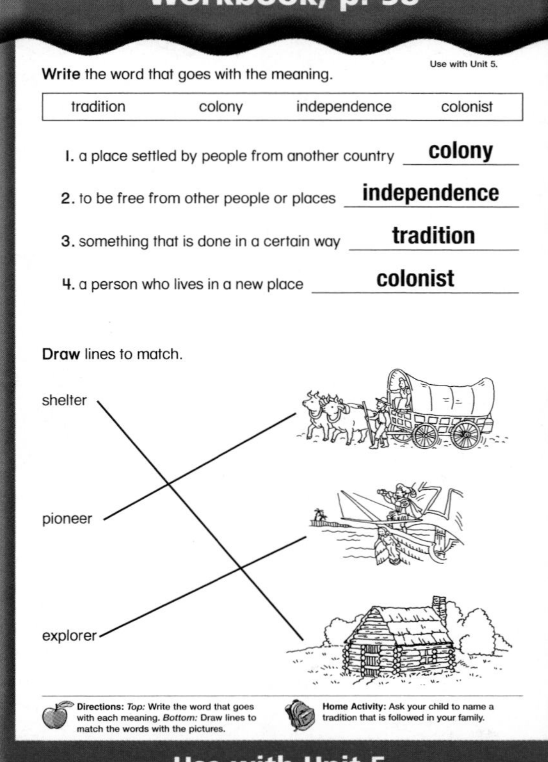

Directions: *Top:* Write the word that goes with each meaning. *Bottom:* Draw lines to match the words with the pictures.

Home Activity: Ask your child to name a tradition that is followed in your family.

Use with Unit 5.

Workbook, p. 59

Discovery Channel School

Unit 5 Project **Do an Interview**

Choose a person from the past to talk with. Write and draw to let others know about the person. **Answers will vary.**

1. The name of the person is ______.
2. I chose this person because ______.
3. Draw a picture of the person as he or she looked in the past.
   Drawings will vary.
4. Write questions you would like to ask the person. Then find information about the person to answer each question.

Question 1 ______
Answer 1 ______
Question 2 ______
Answer 2 ______
Question 3 ______
Answer 3 ______

Directions: Complete items 1–3 about the person you have chosen to interview. For item 4 write questions and answers for your interview presentation.

Home Activity: Practice doing an interview with your child. Take turns asking each other questions.

Use with Pupil Edition, p. 242.

Assessment Support

Use these Assessment Book pages and the test maker to assess content and skills in Unit 5. You can also view and print Assessment Book pages from the Teacher Resources CD-ROM.

Assessment Book, p. 17

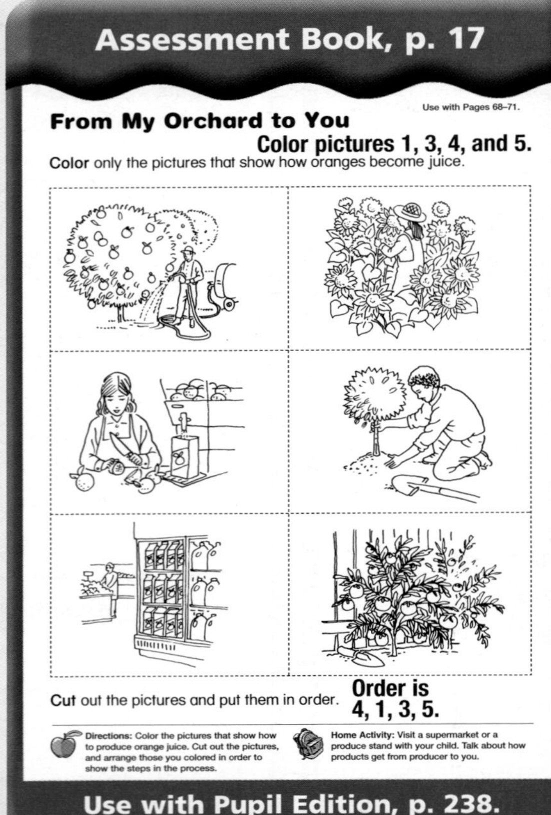

Use with Pages 68–71.

From My Orchard to You

Color pictures 1, 3, 4, and 5.

Color only the pictures that show how oranges become juice.

Cut out the pictures and put them in order. Order is 4, 1, 3, 5.

Directions: Color the pictures that show how to produce orange juice. Cut out the pictures, and arrange those you colored in order to show the steps in the process.

Home Activity: Visit a supermarket or a produce stand with your child. Talk about how products get from producer to you.

Use with Pupil Edition, p. 238.

Assessment Book, p. 18

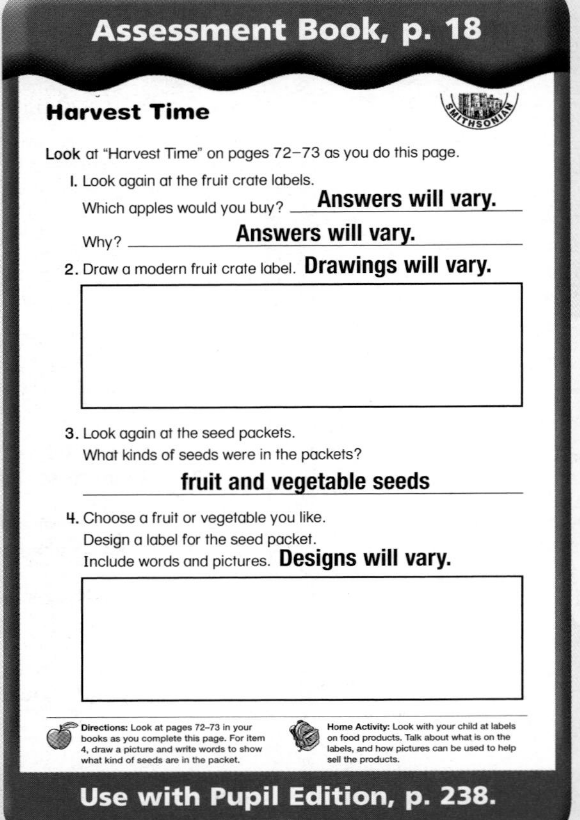

Harvest Time

Look at "Harvest Time" on pages 72–73 as you do this page.

1. Look again at the fruit crate labels.
   Which apples would you buy? Answers will vary.
   Why? Answers will vary.
2. Draw a modern fruit crate label. Drawings will vary.
3. Look again at the seed packets.
   What kinds of seeds were in the packets?
   fruit and vegetable seeds
4. Choose a fruit or vegetable you like.
   Design a label for the seed packet.
   Include words and pictures. Designs will vary.

Directions: Look at pages 72–73 in your books as you complete this page. For item 4, draw a picture and write words to show what kind of seeds are in the packet.

Home Activity: Look with your child at labels on food products. Talk about what is on the labels, and how pictures can be used to help sell the products.

Use with Pupil Edition, p. 238.

Assessment Book, p. 19

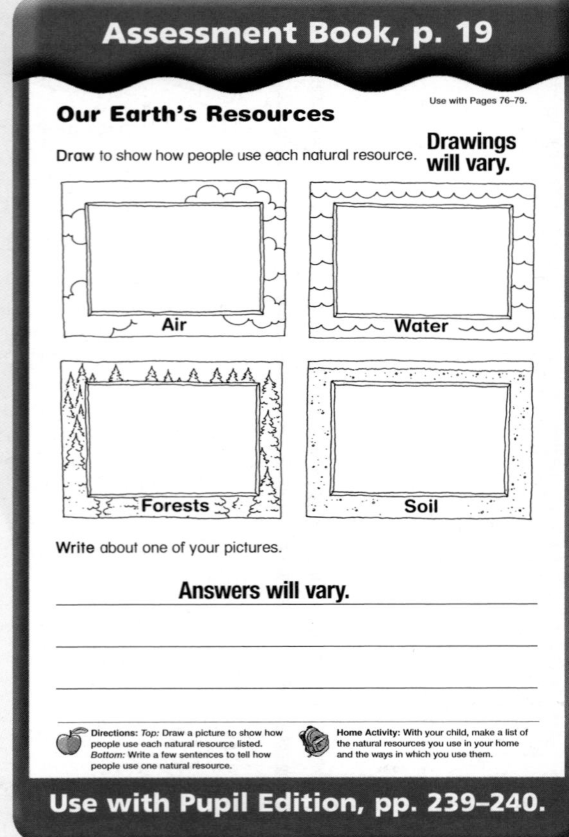

Use with Pages 76–79.

Our Earth's Resources

Draw to show how people use each natural resource. Drawings will vary.

Air | Water | Forests | Soil

Write about one of your pictures.

Answers will vary.

Directions: *Top:* Draw a picture to show how people use each natural resource listed. *Bottom:* Write a few sentences to tell how people use one natural resource.

Home Activity: With your child, make a list of the natural resources you use in your home and the ways in which you use them.

Use with Pupil Edition, pp. 239–240.

Assessment Book, p. 20

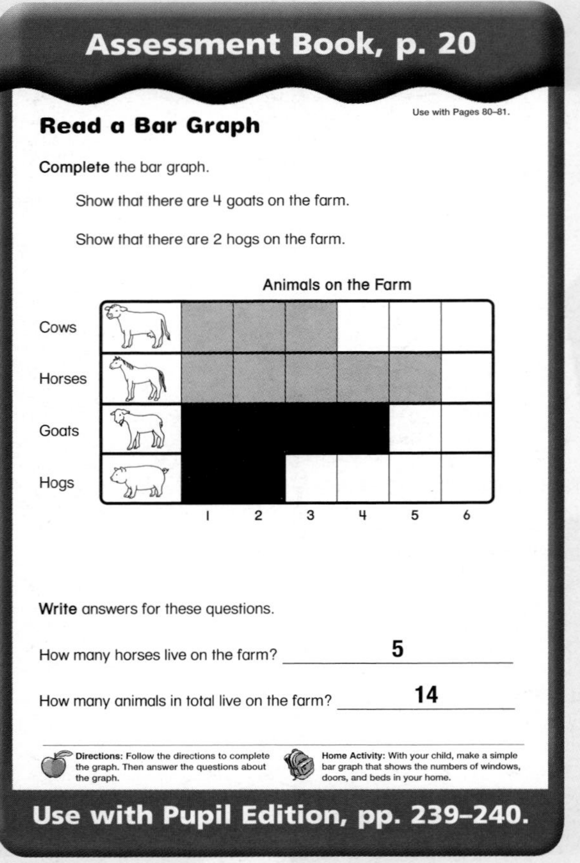

Use with Pages 80–81.

Read a Bar Graph

Complete the bar graph.

Show that there are 4 goats on the farm.

Show that there are 2 hogs on the farm.

Write answers for these questions.

How many horses live on the farm? 5

How many animals in total live on the farm? 14

Directions: Follow the directions to complete the graph. Then answer the questions about the graph.

Home Activity: With your child, make a simple bar graph that shows the numbers of windows, doors, and beds in your home.

Use with Pupil Edition, pp. 239–240.

Lesson 1 Overview

The First Americans

pages 202–205

Children will learn the vocabulary word *shelter*. They will also learn about the ways of life of three Native American groups: the Powhatan, the Sioux, and the Pueblo.

 Time 20–30 minutes

Resources

- Workbook, p. 50
- Vocabulary Card **shelter**
- Every Student Learns Guide, pp. 82–85

Ella Cara Deloria

pages 206–207

Children will learn the vocabulary word *tradition*. They will also learn how Ella Cara Deloria wrote about the traditions of the Sioux.

Time 15–20 minutes

Resource

- Vocabulary Card **tradition**

Smithsonian Institution: Native American Clothing

pages 208–209

Children will view and learn about examples of Native American clothing.

Time 15–20 minutes

Resource

- Workbook, p. 51

Build Background

Activity

Home Sweet Home

 **Time** 20–30 minutes

- Tell children they will draw pictures of homes they might have built if they lived long ago.
- Say that the only material they can use for their homes is what is available in nature—wood from trees, stones, grasses, leaves, earth, and so on.
- Tell children to think about the climate they now live in. Ask them what materials they would use and what building design would give them the best shelter.

If time is short, have children discuss the kinds of homes they would build.

Read Aloud

Who?

by Bonnie Flynn

Who are these people?
The Earth is their friend.
Rain and rainbows,
Desert sands and forest trees,
Great lakes and fast rivers,
And all the Earth's
animals
Are loved by these.
These people are . . .
Native Americans.

The First Americans

Objectives

- Compare the lives and contributions of various Native American groups.
- Locate the regions of the Powhatan, the Sioux, and the Pueblo Indians on United States maps.

Vocabulary

shelter a place where people live (p. 203)

QUICK Teaching Plan

If time is short, have children look at the map on p. 202 and identify the region of the United States in which each Native American group lives. Then have children review the table on p. 203.

- Use the map and the table to discuss with children ways in which climate—temperature and rainfall—and the available natural resources influenced the choices each Native American group made in terms of their clothing, housing, transportation, and foods.

1 Introduce and Motivate

Preview Display the Vocabulary Card **shelter** and define it as "a place where people live." Then have children preview the lesson. Encourage volunteers to describe the different sources of information they see that tell about the Native American homes.

Warm Up To activate prior knowledge, ask children to describe the different kinds of shelters they think Native Americans built.

Practice and Extend

READING SKILL Put Things in Order

Sequence Have children read Lesson 1 and identify the activity that is sequenced in steps.

- Have children illustrate and write the steps for making a tepee.
- Tell them to use the words *First*, *Next*, and *Last* to label their steps and drawings.

WEB SITE Technology

You can look up vocabulary words online. Click on *Social Studies Library* and select the dictionary at **www.sfsocialstudies.com.**

We made a table that tells about Native American culture, or way of life. Each group used the resources around them to make their food, clothing, and shelter. A **shelter** is a place where people live.

Native American Groups

	Food	Clothing	Shelter	Transportation
Powhatan	deer, fish, nuts, berries, corn	made from hides of animals	longhouse	walked, used canoes
Sioux	buffalo	made of buffalo hides	tepee	walked, rode horses
Pueblo	corn, beans, squash	made of cotton fibers	adobe buildings	walked

3

SOCIAL STUDIES Background

About Native Americans

- Tell children that Native American groups who shared the same culture had the same way of finding food and building shelters. They used the natural resources around them to meet their basic needs.
- Make the point that the Native American group names *Powhatan, Sioux,* and *Pueblo* are not necessarily what members of the groups referred to themselves as. For example, Spanish explorers referred to Native Americans they encountered in the Southwest as "Pueblo" because these people lived in villages. The Spanish word for *village* is *pueblo.*

2 Teach and Discuss

Page 202

Model how to pronounce the names of the Native American groups. Have a current map of the U.S. available. After children read p. 202 and answer the map questions, share: There are still members of Native American groups living in the same geographic areas today; for example, the Cheyenne River Sioux Reservation is in north-central South Dakota.

1 **Which Native American group lives in the southwestern part of the country?** the Pueblo **Look at the map. What states are in the area where the Pueblo live?** New Mexico, Arizona, Texas **Interpret Maps**

2 **In what part of the country did the Powhatan live?** East Coast **What state or states are in that area today?** Virginia, Delaware, Maryland **Interpret Maps**

Page 203

As you discuss the table, have children think about how weather and seasonal patterns affected where different groups settled.

Explain that the Sioux did not have horses until after the Europeans came to North America.

3 **Look at the table. Identify ways in which the Pueblo depended on the physical environment and its natural resources to satisfy their basic needs.** The Pueblo used the clay soil of the area to build homes and make pottery. They also used stone for their buildings. They used the land and water to grow crops such as corn, beans, and squash. Because of the warm weather in the area, they needed only light clothes, which they made from cotton. **Analyze Information**

Lesson 1 continued

Page 204

Help children read the page, as needed. Discuss the illustrations.

4 Who among the Powhatan built homes? The women **Why do you think women did this job?** Possible answer: The men had to fish and hunt for food. The women were at the village site taking care of the children, so they were there to work on building homes.
Recall and Retell/Draw Conclusions

5 Why did the Sioux build homes they could carry with them? They hunted buffalo. They needed to be able to follow the herds as they moved. **Cause and Effect**

Ongoing Assessment

If... children do not understand why the Sioux needed portable homes,	**then...** explain that buffalo herds traveled great distances to feed and find water. The Sioux had to travel far, too, so they needed to be able to set up and take down campsites easily and quickly.

The Powhatan

Many Powhatan lived along the Atlantic coast. The winters were mild and the summers were hot. The men fished and hunted. They made canoes out of trees. The women gathered and grew the food. The women also built the homes and cared for their children. 4

Powhatan children listened to legends and stories and played games. One game was played to see who could count sticks fastest.

Powha bowl

The Sioux

Many Sioux lived on the grassy plains. The winters were very cold and the summers were hot. The Sioux hunted buffalo for making food, clothing, and homes.

The Sioux who hunted needed homes that they could take down quickly. They moved often to hunt for buffalo. They made tepees. 5 First, they tied long poles together. Next, the bottoms of the poles were spread out to make a circle. Last, they covered the poles with buffalo hides.

Sioux painted buffalo robe

204

Practice and Extend

ACTIVATE PRIOR KNOWLEDGE
ESL Support

Picture It Talk about how people in the past got their food. With children's help, identify and write on the board: *fishing, hunting, gathering plants,* and *growing new plants.*

Beginning Have children choose one animal-related and one "green" way of getting food. Have them draw a picture to show each. Encourage children to use the words on the board to label their pictures.

Intermediate Have children do the above. Then have them write a sentence for each picture, telling in more detail what it shows.

Advanced After children do both activities above, have them write to tell why people often used more than just one way to get food.

For additional ESL support, use Every Student Learns Guide, pp. 82–85.

The Pueblo

Many Pueblo people lived in the dry desert of the Southwest. There were few wild plants to gather or animals to hunt for food. Some Pueblo farmed.

The Pueblo lived in villages in stone or adobe homes. Clay bricks that are baked in the sun are called adobe. 6

The Pueblo made clay pots to store food and water. Clay pots are still made by some Pueblo people.

Pueblo farmers watching their crops

7 8

Painted pottery bowl

What did you learn?

1. Look at the map on page 202. Which Native American group is closest to the Atlantic Ocean?
2. Look at the table on page 203. Explain how each group used the resources around them to meet their needs.
3. Tell how the Sioux people made tepees. Use the clue words **first, next,** and **last** to tell the order in which things happen.

205

Page 205

6 How did the weather of the Southwest affect the way the Pueblo built their settlements and gathered food? Possible answer: The hot and dry weather was good for baking clay into bricks to make adobe shelters. There were few plants in the region so the Pueblo had to plant food crops. They became farmers. **Draw Conclusions**

GEOGRAPHY
Region

7 How is the region or area the Pueblo lived in—the Southwest—different from the region the Powhatan lived in? The southwest region is hot and dry. Few plants grow there and there are few large animals. The Powhatan lived on the East Coast, an area of forests, mountains, rivers, many different plants, and wildlife. **Compare and Contrast**

8 What sources did you use in this lesson to obtain information about Native Americans? Map, table, reports, pictures **What are some other sources you predict you may learn more from?** Possible answers: Library books, encyclopedia, web sites **Recall and Retell/Predict**

3 Close and Assess

✓ What did you learn?

1. The Powhatan lived close to the Atlantic Ocean.
2. The Powhatan hunted animals for food and clothing; they gathered fruits and nuts; they used wood to build longhouses and canoes. The Sioux used buffalo for food, clothing, and shelter. The Pueblo made adobe bricks out of clay to build shelters.
3. **Think and Share** *First*, they tied long poles together. *Next*, the bottoms of the poles were spread out to make a circle. *Last*, they covered the poles with buffalo hides.

C SOCIAL STUDIES STRAND Culture

Powhatan Dugouts

The canoes, or dugouts, the Powhatan made were invaluable to their way of life.

- Dugouts were made from whole trees. Their size depended on the size of the tree.
- To hollow the cut tree, or log, a fire was set in it. The burned areas were cut away with sharp tools.
- The finished canoe was long with a flat or V-shaped bottom.

Ask children how a dugout differed from the boats most settlers arrived in.

Workbook, p. 50

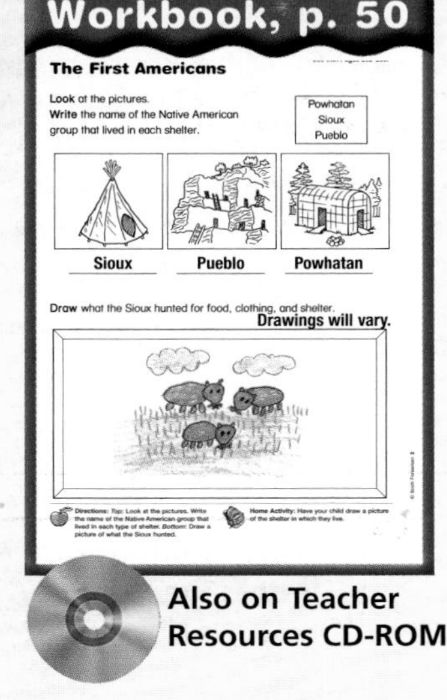

The First Americans

Look at the pictures. Write the name of the Native American group that lived in each shelter.

Powhatan
Sioux
Pueblo

Sioux | Pueblo | Powhatan

Draw what the Sioux hunted for food, clothing, and shelter.

Drawings will vary.

Also on Teacher Resources CD-ROM.

CITIZEN HEROES

Ella Cara Deloria

Objective

- Explain how local people have influenced local community history.

Vocabulary

tradition something that is done a certain way for many years (p. 207)

1 Introduce and Motivate

Preview Read aloud the title of the biographical feature and the first paragraph as children look at the picture on p. 206. Ask children to tell what they know about Ella Cara Deloria from what they heard and saw. Then, display the Vocabulary Card **tradition**. Have children locate the word on p. 207 and listen as you read its definition. Say that children will read about a woman who felt strongly about preserving Native American traditions. You may wish to share with children that Ella Cara Deloria was born in 1889 and died in 1971.

Warm Up To activate prior knowledge, ask volunteers to name some of the traditions, such as celebrating a birthday with a special meal or visiting a special place on a holiday, they and their families follow.

CITIZEN HEROES

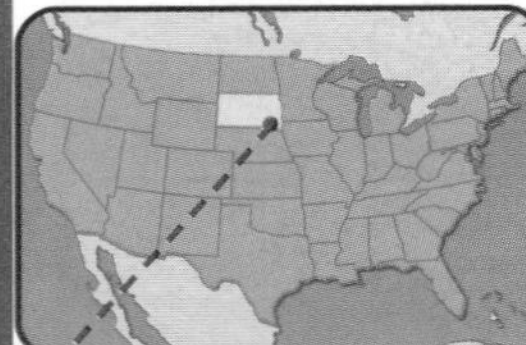

Ella Cara Deloria was born on the Yankton Sioux reservation in South Dakota.

Ella Cara Deloria

Ella was born on a Sioux reservation in South Dakota. The people on her reservation were also called Dakota. She was given the Dakota name Anpetu Waste. In English, this name means Beautiful Day.

Ella spoke Sioux before she learned English. Her parents wanted her to have a good education. She went away to school. Later, she went to college to become a teacher.

206

Practice and Extend

SOCIAL STUDIES STRAND
Culture

Borrowed Language

- Tell children that in the United States many state names, such as *Kentucky, Idaho*, and *Minnesota*, are borrowed from the languages of Native Americans.
- Give some examples of other words that came from Native American languages— *moccasin, raccoon, moose, chipmunk,* and *pecan.*
- Have children discuss why they think these particular words were carried into English by settlers who lived near Native American groups.

BUILDING CITIZENSHIP
Caring
Respect
Responsibility
Fairness
Honesty
Courage

Ella Cara Deloria studied the culture, or way of life, of the Sioux people. Because she was an honest person and spoke the language, the Sioux trusted her. They spoke with her about their families and their ceremonies. Storytellers shared stories of their ancestors. (1)

Ella Cara Deloria

Ella Cara Deloria wrote many books about the Sioux language and culture. In *Waterlily,* she tells the story of a young Dakota woman. She also wrote about Sioux traditions. A **tradition** is something that is done a certain way for many years. She wanted to keep the Sioux traditions alive. (2)

Ella Cara Deloria is remembered as a person who wrote truthful accounts of the history of her community. She helped others understand the culture of the Sioux people.

Honesty in Action

Why do you think it was important for Ella Cara Deloria to be honest in what she said and wrote? How can you practice honesty?

CURRICULUM CONNECTION
Writing

Write About a Family Tradition

- Help children recall their discussion in the Warm Up in which they talked about their family traditions.
- Have them draw and write to describe a favorite tradition.
- Set aside a time for children to share their work. You may wish to help children collect their traditions in a book they can browse when they have free time.

WEB SITE
Technology

You can look up vocabulary words online. Click on *Social Studies Library* and select the dictionary at **www.sfsocialstudies.com.**

2 Teach and Discuss

The term *Sioux* refers to all of the Sioux groups (Dakota, Lakota, and Nakota) in general. Note that Native American groups prefer to be called by their specific names.

Ella Cora Deloria published her research of the Sioux peoples and their culture and traditions between 1932 and 1948. Her first book, *Dakota Texts,* is a collection of traditional stories.

The pronunciation of *Anpetu Waste* is (ən•pe´•tü wəs´• te).

Test Talk

Locate Key Words in the Question
Have children ask themselves, " What is this question about?"

(1) **What did the Sioux share with Ella Cara Deloria?** They shared accounts of their family life, religious ceremonies, and handed-down stories. **Main Idea and Details**

(2) **How did Ella Cara Deloria influence the history of her community?** Possible answer: She wrote books about the Sioux culture and traditions. **Draw Conclusions**

3 Close and Assess

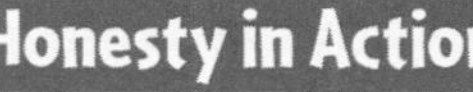

Honesty in Action

Possible answer: Ella Cara Deloria had to be honest in her intentions when she met with the Sioux to convince them to share their culture. She had to write a correct account of what the Sioux told her for it to be a "history" of the people. Children's responses to the second question will vary but may include keeping promises or telling the truth.

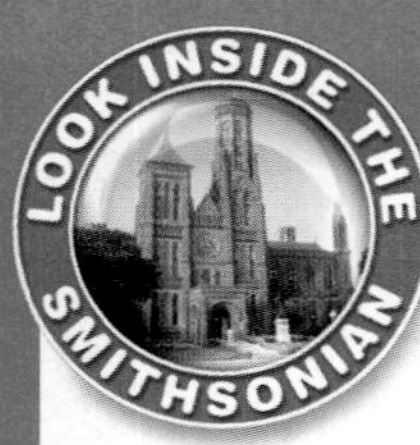

Native American Clothing

Objective

- Obtain information from visual sources such as photographs of artifacts.

Resource

- Workbook, p. 51

1 Introduce and Motivate

Preview Read the title of the feature while children look at the photographs. Have children try to identify the objects before you read the labels and captions. Talk about the designs in each object. Point out, for example, the scroll or vine-like patterns on the moccasins, the flowers and fruits on the beaded bag, the arrangement of the copies of the elk teeth in horizontal rows, the squares, triangles, and stripes on the boy's shirt. Tell children that Native Americans had and still have great respect for nature. Their designs reflect the patterns and colors observable in nature. Invite children to talk about the designs they see in the Tlinglit hat. Note, too, that Native Americans used materials they could find around them—the spruce roots for the hat, for example.

Warm Up To activate prior knowledge, have children talk about any crafts they may have participated in—weaving potholders, braiding colorful lengths of cord to make long necklaces or keychains, patchworking. Have children describe the process, mentioning the amount of time and concentration it took.

Practice and Extend

SOCIAL STUDIES Background

About the Native American Clothing

- Moccasins—Most of the moccasin beadwork was made by women. The first thing Apache did upon waking was to put on their moccasins so they were ready to move quickly should an enemy be nearby.
- Beaded bag—The flower and fruit motifs represent a Woodland culture.
- Dress—The Crow used only the two upper canines from elk for decorative purposes. Acquiring a large number meant a man had to be a very good hunter. That is why the Crow made replicas of the elk teeth.

Crow Dance Dress
This child's dress is made of red and blue wool and decorated with carved copies of elk teeth. Elk teeth represented love and long life.

Ojibwe Beaded Bag
Most of these bags were made by women and worn by men. Each bag took as long as a year to make!

Tlingit Hat
Many Tlingit people gathered spruce roots from nearby forests. This hat was woven from spruce roots and decorated with a painted design.

Seminole Boy's Shirt
Women and girls sewed these big shirts for the men and boys in their families. Great care was taken in making the patchwork designs.

Artifacts are from the Smithsonian Institution. 209

2 Teach and Discuss

Have children follow along as you read the names of the articles of clothing and the captions.

1 **Why do you think it was important that the moccasins Native Americans wore were strong and long-lasting?** Possible answers: Native Americans walked to get from place to place for the most part. They did not walk on streets or even roads. They walked over rough ground. Their moccasins had to protect their feet from being hurt. It probably took a long time and much work to make moccasins, so they had to last a long time. **Make Inferences**

2 **How is the Crow dress like and different from dresses you see today?** Possible answer: It is shaped like dresses of the present. It has a pretty pattern and colors. It is different because it has objects on it that look like animal teeth. **Compare and Contrast**

3 **Describe the Seminole boy's shirt you see at the bottom of page 209. It has patchwork designs on it. What do you think the word *patchwork* means?** Possible answer: Small pieces of cloth in different colors and shapes made into a design **Analyze Pictures**

3 Close and Assess

Revisit each of the articles of clothing, inviting children to comment on their colors, designs, and the materials from which they are made. Encourage children to discuss:

- why the Ojibwe people often decorated beaded bags with flower and fruit designs;
- why hats were an important article of clothing for some Native American groups;
- which articles of clothing shown probably took the longest to make and why;
- which article of clothing they think is most interesting and why.

WEB SITE Technology

You can visit the Smithsonian Institution online. Click on Smithsonian at **www.sfsocialstudies.com.** or go to **www.si.edu.**

Workbook, p. 51

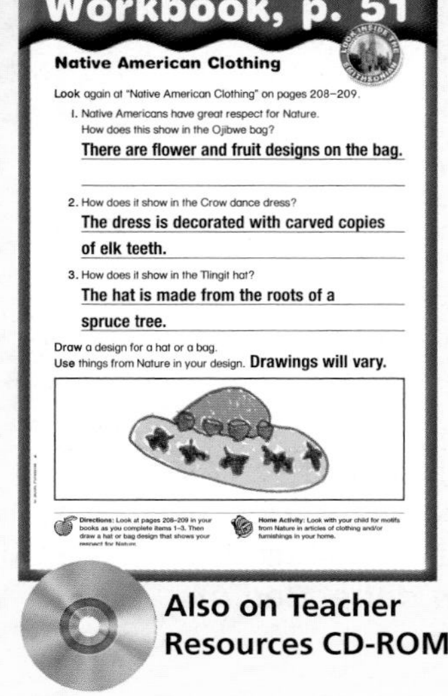

Native American Clothing

Look again at "Native American Clothing" on pages 208–209.

1. Native Americans have great respect for Nature. How does this show in the Ojibwe bag? There are flower and fruit designs on the bag.
2. How does it show in the Crow dance dress? The dress is decorated with carved copies of elk teeth.
3. How does it show in the Tlingit hat? The hat is made from the roots of a spruce tree.

Draw a design for a hat or a bag. Use things from Nature in your design. Drawings will vary.

Also on Teacher Resources CD-ROM.

Use with pages 202–209

Lesson 1 Wrap-Up

MEETING INDIVIDUAL NEEDS Leveled Practice

Native American Life

Have children choose which Native American group they would like to represent in the following activities.

Easy Have each child introduce him- or herself as a member of the selected Native American group. Have children state one fact about the way members of the group live. **Reteach**

On-Level Have children elaborate on life in their group by telling about the region in which they live and the weather and natural resources there. **Extend**

Challenge Have children further elaborate by finding out about a tradition, custom, or artifact associated with their group and then telling about it. **Enrich**

Hands-on Activities

CURRICULUM CONNECTION **Reading**

Many Words from One

Objective Demonstrate understanding of new vocabulary; make new words.

Resource Vocabulary Cards: **shelter, tradition**

Materials pencils, paper

Learning Style Verbal/Linguistic

Individual 

Time 10–15 minutes

1. Display the Vocabulary Cards and have children give the meaning for each word. Call on volunteers to use the words in oral sentences.

2. Tell children they will use the letters in each vocabulary word to make smaller words. Give examples: *shelter/he, let, sheet.*

3. Have children make as many words as possible.

Remind children to add *shelter* and *tradition* to their personal glossaries.

CURRICULUM CONNECTION **Art**

Build a Native American Shelter

Objective Demonstrate understanding by creating visuals.

Materials construction paper, straws, craft sticks, pipe cleaners, clay, crayons

Learning Style Kinesthetic/Social

Partner 

Time 25–30 minutes

1. Have partners work together to build either a tepee, long house, or adobe dwelling.

2. Display the completed dwellings in class. Use them to review the ways in which the Native Americans depended on natural resources.

SOCIAL STUDIES STRAND **Culture**

A Native American Story

Objective Listen and respond to a story.

Materials *The Gift of the Sacred Dog*, by Paul Goble (Aladdin Paperbacks, ISBN 0-020-43280-1, 1984)

Learning Style Auditory/Kinesthetic

Group 

Time 15–20 minutes

1. Read aloud the story and show the illustrations as you read.

2. Talk about the character, setting, and story events.

3. Have children respond to the story by drawing pictures of their favorite parts and labeling them.

Lesson 2 Overview

Colonies **pages 210–213**	Children will learn the vocabulary words *explorer, colony*, and *colonist*. They will learn about the first European settlements in North America: St. Augustine, Jamestown, and Plymouth. Children will also learn about the origins of the Thanksgiving holiday.	 Time 20–30 minutes Resources • Workbook, p. 52 • Vocabulary Cards explorer colony colonist • Every Student Learns Guide, pp. 86–89
Read a History Map **pages 214–215**	Children will learn more about Jamestown and Plymouth by reading a history map.	 Time 15–20 minutes Resource • Workbook, p. 53

Build Background

Activity

Living in a New Land

Time 20–30 minutes

- Tell children to suppose that they will move deep into the forest, far away from any city or town.
- Have them each decide on six things that they need to begin a new life in the wilderness. They may draw or cut out pictures of those objects.
- Have children use envelopes with the flaps cut off to make "suitcases" they can pack with their objects. They can add paper handles, if they wish.
- Partners can share and compare the objects they packed, explaining why each would be important.

If time is short, just have children identify their six objects and say why they chose to include each for their move into the wilderness.

Read Aloud

Brave Explorers Sailed

by Eric Meyer

Brave explorers sailed
in search of lands to claim.
In large ships they traveled
through wind and rain.

Many families would
follow
and start colonies
near the sea.
They planted crops,
built new homes,
and gave thanks
on bended knee.

Colonies

Objectives

- Describe how weather patterns, natural resources, seasonal patterns, and natural hazards affect activities and settlement patterns.
- Explain the significance of national celebrations, such as Thanksgiving.

Vocabulary

explorer a person who travels to a new place to learn about it (p. 210)

colony a place that is settled by people from another country (p. 210)

colonist a person who lives in a colony (p. 211)

QUICK Teaching Plan

If time is short, guide children in making a three-column chart with the column headings *St. Augustine, Jamestown,* and *Plymouth.* Then have children scan the lesson for one or two facts about each colony. Then complete the chart.

Lesson

Colonies

Explorers from Europe sailed across the Atlantic Ocean and landed on the shores of North America. An **explorer** is a person who travels to a new place to learn about it. Christopher Columbus was an explorer. He sailed to the Americas.

Explorers from Spain reached Florida while searching for gold. They built a 1 Spanish colony there called St. Augustine. A **colony** is a place that is settled by people from another country. Soon more people from Spain came to live in North America.

Spanish gold coin 3

2 St. Augustine is the ol… European community i… United States.

210

1 Introduce and Motivate

Preview Display the Vocabulary Cards **explorer**, **colony**, and **colonist**. Have children find each word in the lesson text and read the definition aloud with you. Use each word in a sentence.

Warm Up To activate prior knowledge, ask children to tell what they know about the Pilgrims and Thanksgiving. Have them tell why Americans still celebrate Thanksgiving today.

Practice and Extend

READING SKILL
Main Idea and Details

- Remind children that the main idea of a paragraph is the most important idea the writer wants readers to know. Details tell more about the main idea.
- After children read p. 211, read aloud these details from the second paragraph: *Many of them (colonists) became ill. They did not have enough food.*
- Have children identify the main idea of the paragraph. Then have them identify one additional supporting detail.

WEB SITE
Technology

You can look up vocabulary words online. Click on *Social Studies Library* and select the dictionary at **www.sfsocialstudies.com.**

Later, English colonists settled Jamestown. A **colonist** is a person who lives in a colony. England ruled the Jamestown colonists.

The Jamestown colonists had hard times. Many of them became ill. They did not have enough food. They did not know how to farm the new land. Some colonists spent their time looking for gold instead of food. 4

A leader named John Smith helped the Jamestown colonists become better workers. The colonists cleared land, built homes, planted crops, and hunted for food. They 5 traded with the Powhatan people for corn.

Other people wanted to live in our country too.

Jamestown Fort

211

SOCIAL STUDIES STRAND
Citizenship

John Smith

- Tell children that John Smith was a leader who ensured the success of Jamestown.
- Explain that besides guiding the people of Jamestown through periods of illness and starvation, he also established trade with the Powhatan and completed a map of Virginia.
- Ask children to think about why it is important to have leaders in a community—especially if it is a brand-new community.
- Have children identify the characteristics of good citizenship exemplified by John Smith.

2 Teach and Discuss

Page 210

Tell children that the name *America* comes from the name of an Italian explorer, Amerigo Vespucci.

After children read, have them find on a map: Europe, Spain, North America, and Florida.

1 **What are some reasons explorers traveled to new places?** They wanted to learn about new lands; some hoped to find gold to take back to their countries. **Main Idea and Details**

2 **Why is St. Augustine important in U.S. history?** It is the oldest European community in the United States. **Recall and Retell**

3 **What sources of information did you use to learn about St. Augustine?** The facts in the lesson, the pictures of St. Augustine and the objects used and found there **Analyze Information**

Page 211

4 **Why didn't the colonists have enough food?** They didn't know how to farm the land to grow food; some colonists spent their time looking for gold instead of trying to find or grow food. **Cause and Effect**

5 **How did John Smith help the colonists adapt to their new environment?** He helped them clear the land to build homes; he taught them how to plant crops and hunt for food. **Recall and Retell**

Lesson 2 continued

Page 212

Tell children that the Pilgrims were a group of people from England who came to North America seeking religious freedom. Say, too, that the Wampanoag (wäm′•pə•nō′•ag) were Native Americans who lived in the coastal regions of present-day Rhode Island and Massachusetts.

6 How were the experiences of the Jamestown colonists and the Pilgrims alike? Both groups faced problems. Many colonists in Jamestown were sick. Both the settlers in Jamestown and the Pilgrims did not have enough food. Both groups survived thanks to help from others. John Smith helped the Jamestown colonists. Squanto helped the Pilgrims. **Compare and Contrast**

7 What natural resources did the Jamestown colonists and the Pilgrims depend on to help them survive? The water for drinking and fishing; the trees for wood to make fires and build homes; the land to plant crops **Draw Conclusions**

The Pilgrims sailed to America on the *Mayflower*. The Pilgrims wanted a better life in a new land.

When the Pilgrims landed, they built a settlement called Plymouth. Their first winter was very cold. They did not have enough food to eat.

Then the Pilgrims met a member of the Wampanoag tribe. The Pilgrims called him Squanto. Squanto helped the Pilgrims survive. He showed them where to fish and hunt. He taught them how to plant corn. 6 7

In the fall, the Pilgrims harvested their crops. Pilgrim leaders decided to have a special celebration. They wanted to give thanks to God for their food.

Winter in Plymouth Colony

212

Practice and Extend

EXTEND LANGUAGE ESL Support

Colonial Life Children extend their understanding of what life was like for the colonists.

Beginning Have each child draw a picture of a colonist doing something to survive. Below the picture, have children write the name of the colony in which their colonist lived.

Intermediate Have children write a sentence to say what resource(s)—natural or man-made—the colonist is using.

Advanced Have children work in a group and use their pictures, labels, and sentences to explain how the colonists learned to survive.

For additional ESL support, use Every Student Learns Guide, pp. 86–89.

SOCIAL STUDIES STRAND Economics

Trade/Barter

- Help children recall what barter is.
- Explain that the colonists traded or bartered things they owned for food, such as corn, which the Native Americans had. The colonists bartered things they had brought with them from Europe.
- Have children talk about the kinds of things the colonists may have traded with the Native Americans. Tell children to think about what the Native Americans would have thought were most useful or appealing to them.

The Pilgrims invited the Wampanoag to their celebration. They probably ate foods like **8** cornbread, fish, deer, and turkey. They danced and played games. Later, this celebration was called Thanksgiving.

Thanksgiving celebration

Today, Thanksgiving is a national holiday. Thanksgiving is celebrated on the fourth **9** Thursday in November. It is a time when we give thanks for our family and friends. Some people show thanks by helping others in their community. How do you celebrate Thanksgiving?

What did you learn?

1. How was life hard for the Jamestown colonists?
2. Why is Thanksgiving an important holiday?
3. **Think and Share** Tell or write about how Squanto helped the Pilgrims.

213

Workbook, p. 52

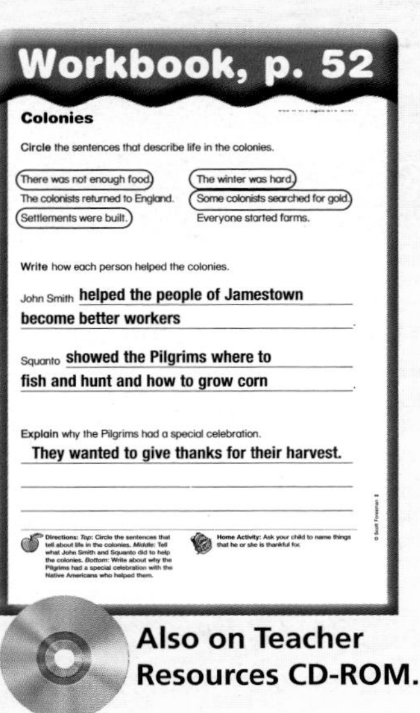

Colonies

Circle the sentences that describe life in the colonies.

(There was not enough food.) (The winter was hard.)
The colonists returned to England. (Some colonists searched for gold.)
(Settlements were built.) Everyone started farms.

Write how each person helped the colonies.

John Smith helped the people of Jamestown become better workers

Squanto showed the Pilgrims where to fish and hunt and how to grow corn

Explain why the Pilgrims had a special celebration.

They wanted to give thanks for their harvest.

Also on Teacher Resources CD-ROM.

Page 213

Tell children that prior to the harvest/ Thanksgiving celebration they shared with the Pilgrims, Native American groups had been having harvest celebrations for many years.

8 Why do you think the Pilgrims invited the Wampanoag to their thanksgiving celebration? Possible answers: They wanted to show friendship toward the Native Americans; they wanted to express their thanks. **Draw Conclusions**

9 What is a *national* holiday? A national holiday is one celebrated in the whole country. **Why do you think Thanksgiving is a national holiday?** Thanksgiving reminds people of their history. It also gives Americans a day in which to think about all they have to be thankful for. **Draw Conclusions**

3 Close and Assess

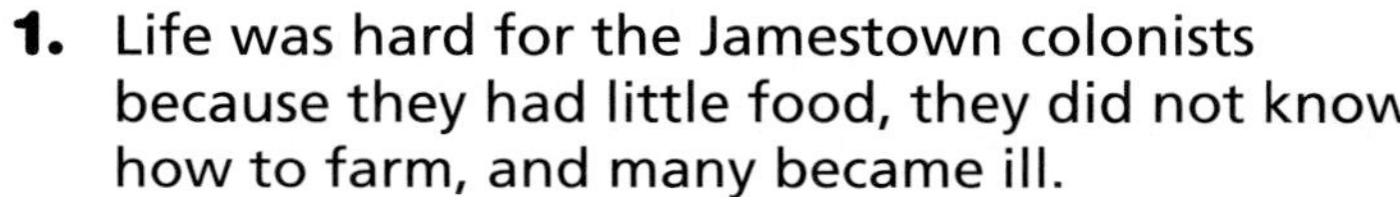

✓ What did you learn?

1. Life was hard for the Jamestown colonists because they had little food, they did not know how to farm, and many became ill.
2. Thanksgiving is an important holiday because it reminds people of our country's past and how hard the colonists worked to survive. It is a time for people to give thanks for their country, homes, clothing, and food.
3. **Think and Share** Squanto helped the Pilgrims by showing them where to hunt and fish. He also taught them how to plant corn.

Read a History Map

Objective

- Obtain information from a variety of visual sources, including maps.

1 Introduce and Motivate

Preview Read the title of the feature. Then have children read p. 214 with you to find out what they will learn about. Have children describe how the map is like and different from maps they have seen.

Warm Up To activate prior knowledge, have children tell what they can find out by looking at maps. Guide them to talk about how they use maps to identify landforms and bodies of water; to tell what a place is near or far from (relative location); and to tell exactly where a place is (absolute location).

2 Teach and Discuss

1 What is alike about the way both groups of colonists named their settlements? The names reminded them of home—the colonists at Jamestown named their settlement for their king; the Pilgrims named their settlement, Plymouth, after the place they left. **Compare and Contrast**

Map and Globe Skills

Read a History Map

History maps can show where places were located a long time ago. This history map shows the settlements of Jamestown and Plymouth.

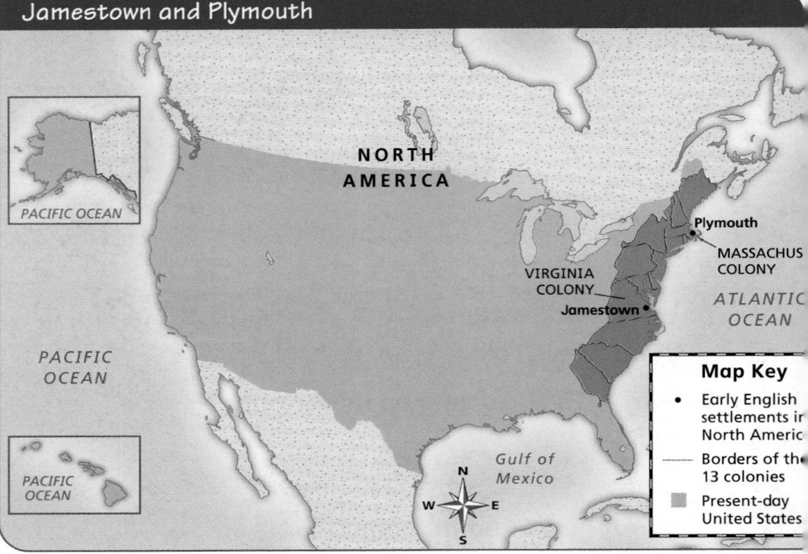

214

Practice and Extend

FYI SOCIAL STUDIES **Background**

The *Mayflower* Crossing

- The *Mayflower*, the ship on which the Pilgrims came to America, was originally intended to carry cargo. And, it did. It was 12 years old when it brought the Pilgrims to America.
- Passengers stayed in a five-foot-high area meant for cargo. Each had a living space about the size of a twin-sized mattress.
- There were 102 passengers, including 34 children.
- Passengers could not bathe or wash their clothing in fresh water.
- The crossing took 66 days.

In 1607, three English ships sailed up a river. They named the river James after their king. They named the place they settled Jamestown. Jamestown became part of the Virginia colony.

Village of Jamestown, 1615

In 1620, the Pilgrims landed on a rocky coast. They named the place they settled Plymouth after the town they sailed from in England. Plymouth became part of the ❶ Massachusetts colony. ❷ ❸

What did you learn?

1. Jamestown and Plymouth are located near what ocean?
2. Is Plymouth north or south of Jamestown?
3. **On Your Own** Draw a map that shows where the Pilgrims and the Wampanoag celebrated Thanksgiving. Put a title on your map.

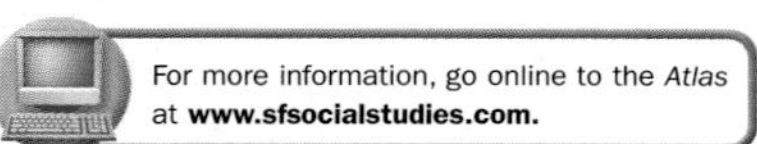

For more information, go online to the *Atlas* at **www.sfsocialstudies.com.**

Workbook, p. 53

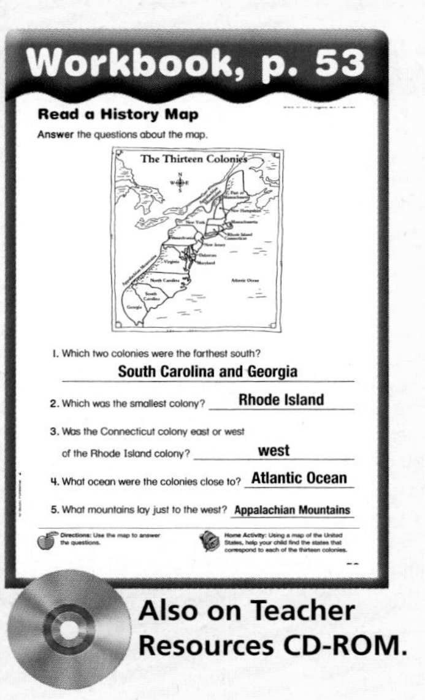

Read a History Map

Answer the questions about the map.

The Thirteen Colonies

1. Which two colonies were the farthest south? **South Carolina and Georgia**
2. Which was the smallest colony? **Rhode Island**
3. Was the Connecticut colony east or west of the Rhode Island colony? **west**
4. What ocean were the colonies close to? **Atlantic Ocean**
5. What mountains lay just to the west? **Appalachian Mountains**

Also on Teacher Resources CD-ROM.

❷ **What country did both groups of colonists come from?** Both groups came from England. **How do you know?** The lesson tells us that three ships sailed from England to what would be Jamestown. The Pilgrims named their settlement after the place they left in England. **Context Clues**

❸ **Today, what are *Virginia* and *Massachusetts* the names of?** States in the United States **Draw Conclusions**

3 Close and Assess

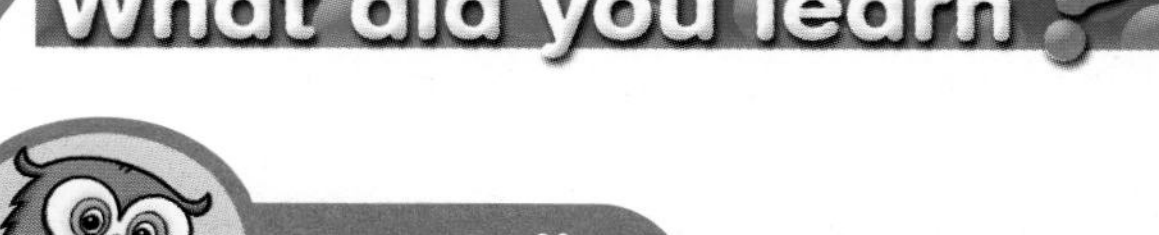

✓ What did you learn?

Test Talk

Use Information from Graphics
Tell children to look back at the map to find the right answer.

1. Jamestown and Plymouth are located near the Atlantic Ocean.
2. Plymouth is north of Jamestown.
3. **On Your Own** Check children's maps for the relative location of Plymouth, to see that Plymouth is labeled, and to note that the map has a title.

Lesson 2 Wrap-Up

MEETING INDIVIDUAL NEEDS

Leveled Practice

Mapping History

Children use maps they make to demonstrate their understanding of the first colonies. Provide children with large outline maps of North America.

Easy Have children use labels to indicate the relative locations of the settlements of St. Augustine, Jamestown, and Plymouth. Have them indicate the Atlantic Ocean. They should add a compass rose to help them talk about the location of each settlement relative to the others. **Reteach**

On-Level On the flip side of their maps, children should write two sentences about problems the colonists faced in each of the three settlements: St. Augustine, Jamestown, Plymouth. **Extend**

Challenge Have children write three map questions based on the maps they drew. Then partners should exchange their maps and questions for responses. **Enrich**

Hands-on Activities

CURRICULUM CONNECTION

Reading

Word Families

Objective Demonstrate understanding of new vocabulary; identify related words.

Learning Style Visual/Verbal

Group

Time 10–15 minutes

1. Write *explorer, colony*, and *colonist* on the board. Review their meanings with children.

2. Then write these related words on the board: *exploration, colonial,* and *colonize*. Have children notice that they are related to the vocabulary words.

3. Give the meaning of each new word and then use it in a sentence.

Remind children to add *explorer, colony*, and *colonist* to their "My Word Book" glossaries.

CURRICULUM CONNECTION

Art

Thanksgiving Place Mats

Objective Create visual materials to express ideas about Thanksgiving.

Materials construction paper, crayons, markers, plastic wrap, tape

Learning Style Kinesthetic/Visual

Individual

Time 15–20 minutes

1. Tell children they will make Thanksgiving-related place mats.

2. Have children draw pictures that represent the Thanksgiving celebration held by the Pilgrims and the Wampanoag. Suggestions include pictures of the foods eaten, the attendees, the setting, and so on.

3. Have children wrap their mats with clear plastic wrap that can be taped at the back of the mats.

Use the placemats to discuss the significance of the first, as well as present-day, Thanksgiving celebrations.

Lesson 3 Overview

Thirteen Colonies, One Country pages 216–219	Children will learn the vocabulary word *independence*. They will also learn about the causes and effects of the American Revolution.	Time 20–30 minutes Resources • Workbook, p. 54 • Vocabulary Card independence • Every Student Learns Guide, pp. 90–93
Paul Revere pages 220–221	Children will learn about Paul Revere's patriotism.	Time 15–20 minutes

Build Background

Activity

Freedom Banners

Time 20–30 minutes

- Remind children that freedom is one of the basic ideas on which the United States is based.
- Discuss the definition of *freedom* (a person's right to make choices). Talk about some ways people in the United States exercise their freedom every day—choosing where they will live, voting for government officials, choosing what work they will do.
- Have children make their own freedom banners—colorful strips of paper with a saying that relates to freedom in daily practice.

If time is short, have children participate in the discussion portion of the activity above.

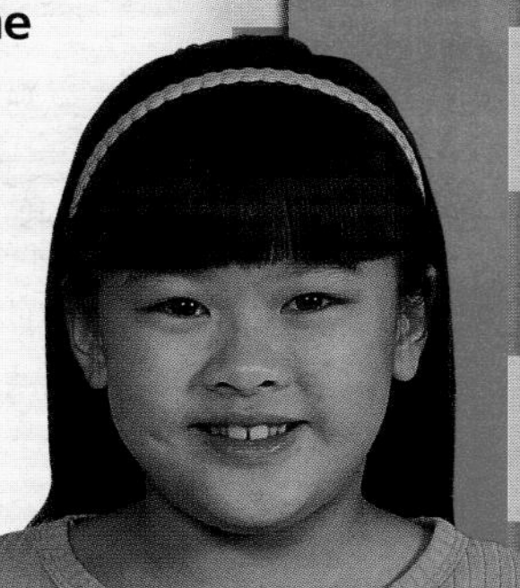

Read Aloud

Independence

by Eric Meyer

The people
who lived in the colonies
thought independence
was the only way.
So they organized
and fought for their freedom
to create the country
we live in today.

Lesson 3 Thirteen Colonies, One Country

Objectives

- Explain the significance of national celebrations, such as Independence Day.
- Explain how selected customs and celebrations reflect an American love of individualism and freedom.

Vocabulary

independence to be free from other people or places (p. 217)

QUICK Teaching Plan

If time is short, have children talk about the significance of our Independence Day holiday. Identify the main causes of the American Revolution as part of the discussion.

1 Introduce and Motivate

Preview Display the Vocabulary Card **independence**. Have children look through the lesson to find and read its definition. Point out that *independence* is similar in meaning to *freedom*. Note that people who are free have the right to make choices.

Warm Up To activate prior knowledge, ask children if they know the name of the document our founding fathers signed to say that the 13 original colonies would no longer be ruled by England; the document that said the colonists wanted to be free. (Declaration of Independence)

Lesson 3 Thirteen Colonies, One Country

Here is a map of the 13 colonies.

Many more people from England and other countries came to live in America after the colonists in Jamestown and the Pilgrims in Plymouth. Soon there were 13 colonies.

The colonies were still ruled by England. There were laws that many of the colonists did not like. The colonists had to pay taxes that they thought were unfair.

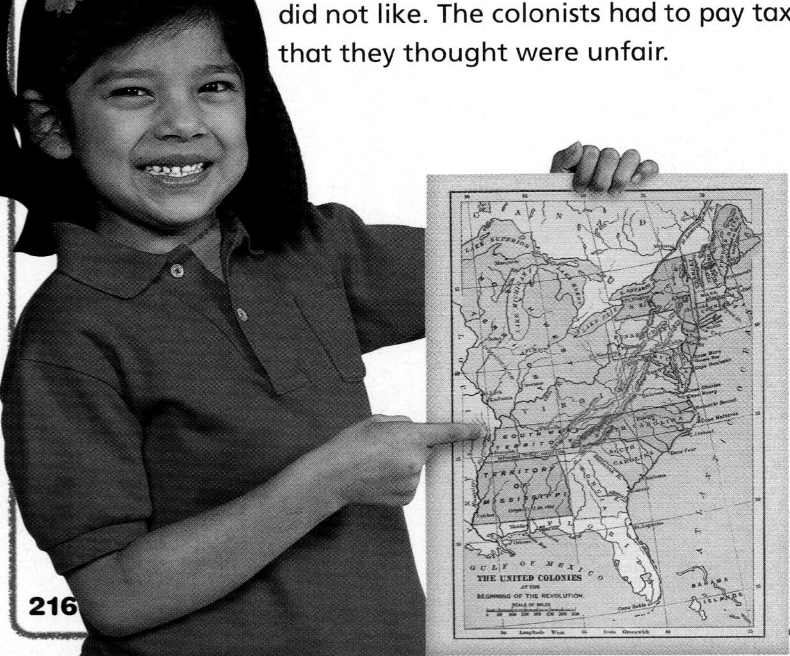

English Colonies, 1775

216

Practice and Extend

READING SKILL
Cause and Effect

- Remind children that as they read they should look for reasons why things happen. They should think about cause-and-effect relationships.
- After children read p. 217, ask them to write down the cause, or reason why, Thomas Jefferson wrote the Declaration of Independence.
- Have partners compare their "causes."

WEB SITE
Technology

You can look up vocabulary words online. Click on *Social Studies Library* and select the dictionary at **www.sfsocialstudies.com.**

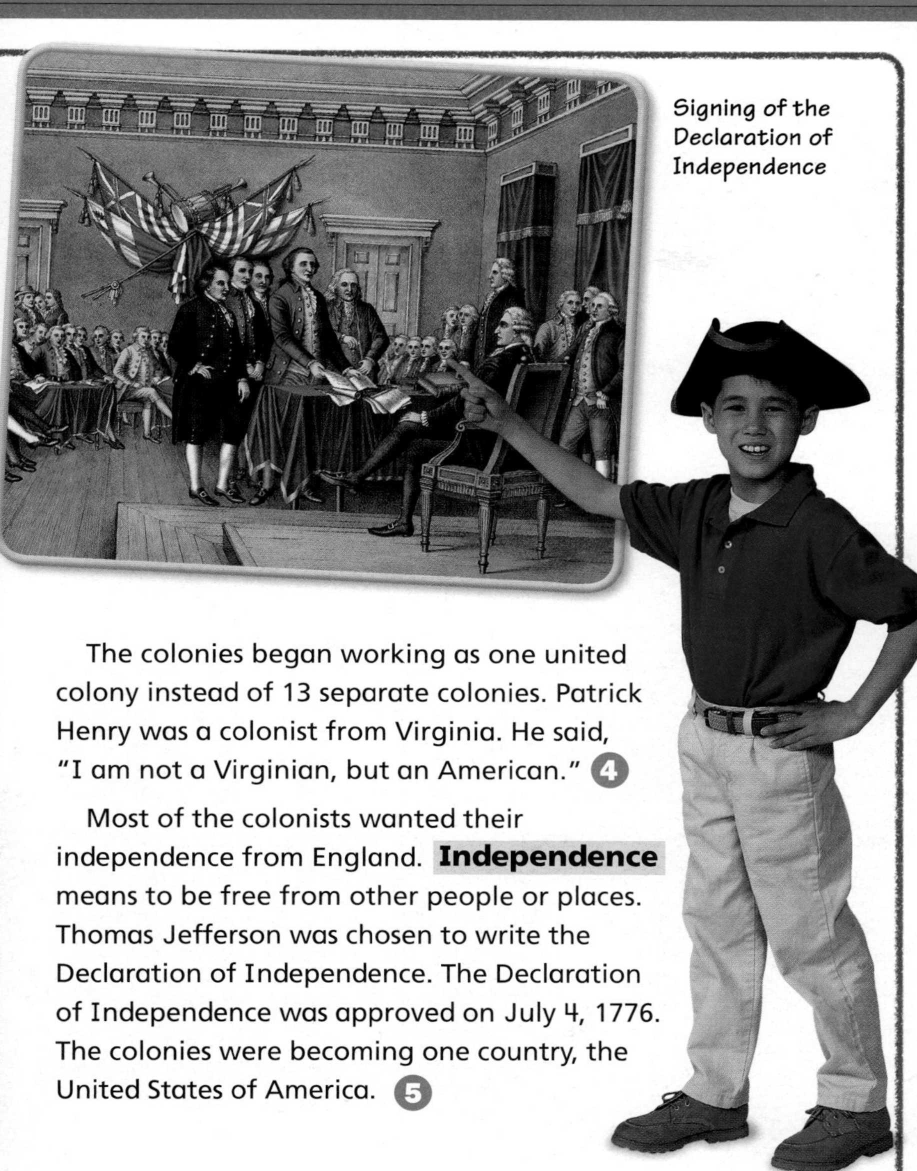

Signing of the Declaration of Independence

The colonies began working as one united colony instead of 13 separate colonies. Patrick Henry was a colonist from Virginia. He said, "I am not a Virginian, but an American." 4

Most of the colonists wanted their independence from England. **Independence** means to be free from other people or places. Thomas Jefferson was chosen to write the Declaration of Independence. The Declaration of Independence was approved on July 4, 1776. The colonies were becoming one country, the United States of America. 5

BUILD BACKGROUND

ESL Support

What Is a Country? Have children draw 13 small circles on sheets of drawing paper. Have them label the drawing *13 colonies.*

Beginning Have children draw a large circle around the 13 small circles, which represent the colonies. Have them add the label *A New Country*. Talk about how the 13 colonies joined together to become a new country.

Intermediate Have children write a sentence to tell how the colonies worked together to become a new country.

Advanced Have children write sentences to tell what the colonies had to do to gain their independence.

For additional ESL support, use Every Student Learns Guide, pp. 90–93.

2 Teach and Discuss

Page 216

Have children read the speech bubble and the map caption to identify the map.

1 **What country ruled the colonies?** England
Recall and Retell

2 **If a government puts a tax on goods people need or want to buy, are the goods more expensive or less expensive?** More expensive **How do you know?** A tax is money a government collects. People would have to pay more money for the goods they buy. **Draw Conclusions**

3 **Why do you think the colonists thought it was unfair that England taxed items they needed?** Possible answer: The colonists were not living in England, and they felt they should not have to pay money to that government. **Make Inferences**

Page 217

Discuss Patrick Henry's quote with children.

4 **Why do you think the colonists started to work together?** Possible answer: It is easier to get a large task done if many people work together.
Make Inferences

5 **What are some ideas you think were written in the Declaration of Independence?** Children may say that the document said the colonists wanted to be free; that they would not pay taxes to England; that they wanted to make their own rules and laws. **Draw Conclusions**

continued

Page 218

Point out Lexington and Concord in Massachusetts on a map. Say that they were the sites of the first battles in the Revolutionary War.

6 **What did the colonists do to win their independence?** They fought England. **Main Idea and Details**

7 **Why did the colonists need the help of Spain and France?** Possible answer: The colonists had just joined together. They formed a brand-new country that didn't have much power. England had been a country for a long time. **Make Inferences**

8 **What role did George Washington play after the war?** After the war, George Washington became the first President of the United States of America. **Analyze Pictures**

George Washington became our country's first President. 8

England did not want to give the colonies independence. Many colonists were willing to fight England to be free. Some colonists, however, chose to be loyal to England. 6

The American Revolution began. George Washington was chosen to be the leader of the army. France and Spain agreed to help the United States. The war was long and 7 hard. In the end, the Americans won their independence.

218

George Washington at Valley Forge

Practice and Extend

FAST FACTS

The Colonial Army

- The colonies entered the war without an army or a navy. England had a well-trained army and was well-known for its navy.
- Some colonists did not take sides in the war. They were unconcerned about the outcome.
- Though more experienced in warfare, British leaders did not take risks in fighting the colonists. American leaders were more willing to take chances in building their strategies.
- Colonial soldiers often went without pay, food, and good clothing. There was little money available.
- About 7,200 Americans were killed during the war. More than 8,000 were wounded.

CURRICULUM CONNECTION Art

Create a Time Capsule

- Have children draw pictures and write sentences that tell why they enjoy living in a country that is free and independent.
- Explain that you will collect their work to place in a time capsule—a container that will be closed and put away in a safe place until a date in the future.
- Tell children that July 4, 2076, will be the three hundredth birthday of the United States. Say that people in that year can open the time capsule.
- Seal children's work in a large envelope or box. See if a local library or government office is willing to hold the class time capsule until the tricentennial date!

My family and I celebrate Independence Day on July 4 each year. It is the holiday that honors our country's birthday. On ⑨ Independence Day, we celebrate our country's freedom. It is a tradition in my family to go to a parade, have a picnic, and watch fireworks. How do you celebrate Independence Day? ⑩

What did you learn?

1. Why did many Americans want their independence from England?
2. What did George Washington do during the American Revolution?
3. **Think and Share** Write about why it is important for Americans to remember July 4, 1776.

219

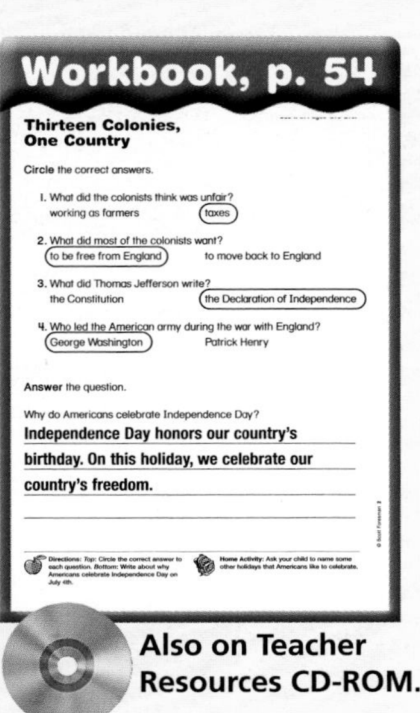

Workbook, p. 54

Thirteen Colonies, One Country

Circle the correct answers.

1. What did the colonists think was unfair?
   working as farmers — (taxes)
2. What did most of the colonists want?
   (to be free from England) — to move back to England
3. What did Thomas Jefferson write?
   the Constitution — (the Declaration of Independence)
4. Who led the American army during the war with England?
   (George Washington) — Patrick Henry

Answer the question.

Why do Americans celebrate Independence Day?

Independence Day honors our country's birthday. On this holiday, we celebrate our country's freedom.

Directions: *Top:* Circle the correct answer to each question. *Bottom:* Write about why Americans celebrate Independence Day on July 4th.

Home Activity: Ask your child to name some other holidays that Americans like to celebrate.

Also on Teacher Resources CD-ROM.

Page 219

Tell children that July 4, 1976, was the United States bicentennial—the two hundredth birthday of the United States. Tell them that a special quarter was minted that year to celebrate the special occasion. If possible, circulate a bicentennial quarter in class.

⑨ **Why do Americans celebrate Independence Day?** Independence Day is the birthday of our country. **Main Idea and Details**

⑩ **What are some things people do on Independence Day that show their love of freedom?** Sing patriotic songs; wave flags; listen to speeches about freedom; wear red, white, and blue

3 Close and Assess

✓ What did you learn?

Test Talk

Locate Key Words in the Text

1. The colonists wanted to make their own laws, and they didn't want to pay unfair taxes to England.

Have children look back at the text. Ask, "Is the answer right there, or do you have to think and search? Does the answer depend on the text and you?"

2. He was the commander of America's army.
3. **Think and Share** Children's responses should show an understanding that July 4th is the date that the colonists declared that the colonies were free and independent of England. The date marks the birthday of our country.

Paul Revere

Objective

- Identify historic figures, such as Paul Revere, who have exemplified good citizenship.

1 Introduce and Motivate

Preview Have children read the title with you. As children look at the illustrations for the feature, tell the meaning of *patriot* and *silversmith*. Say that a patriot is a person who loves his or her country. In this lesson, a patriot is a colonist who wanted independence from England. A silversmith was and still is someone who makes silver objects, such as cups, serving trays, and candlesticks.

Warm Up To activate prior knowledge, have children share what they know about Paul Revere's famous ride.

Practice and Extend

SOCIAL STUDIES Background

About Paul Revere

- Like many people of his time, Paul Revere was also trained in other skills, including dentistry, engraving, and printing.
- Paul Revere was one of the men who threw British tea into Boston Harbor during a protest known as the Boston Tea Party.
- Revere was captured by the British the night of his famous ride before reaching Concord, his planned destination.

WEB SITE Technology

You may help children find out more about Paul Revere by clicking on *Meet the People* at **www.sfsocialstudies.com.**

Paul Revere was a patriot. Patriot was the name given to a colonist who wanted independence from England. In 1775, Paul Revere learned that the English troops in Boston were going to march through the countryside. He and his friends made a secret signal to let Americans know. Two lanterns **1** would be placed in Boston's North Church steeple. One lantern would be lit if the English left Boston by land. Two lanterns would be lit if the English left Boston by sea. **2**

Two lanterns were seen on the night of April 18, 1775. Paul Revere rode from Boston to a town called Lexington. He and another rider reached Lexington in time to warn others so they could escape before the English troops arrived. **3**

Paul Revere is remembered as a patriot and a craftsman. He is also remembered in a poem called "Paul Revere's Ride." **4**

Paul Revere was born in Boston, Massachusetts.

North Church

Paul Revere made beautiful silverware.

Think and Share

How did Paul Revere show that he felt responsible for the safety of the colonists?

For more information, go online to *Meet the People* at **www.sfsocialstudies.com.**

CURRICULUM CONNECTION
Literature

Paul Revere's Ride

Share with children a version of Henry Wadsworth Longfellow's famous narrative poem, "The Midnight Ride of Paul Revere." A wonderful choice is the picture book version, *Paul Revere's Ride,* illustrated by Ted Rand. (Puffin, ISBN 0-140-55612-5, 1996).

2 Teach and Discuss

Tell children that the house in which Paul Revere lived and the North Church—both in Boston—still stand and are popular tourist destinations. As needed, explain the meaning of *steeple*.

1 **Why did Paul Revere want the Americans to know that the British troops were on the move?** Possible answer: He thought the troops may have had plans to attack the colonists. **Cause and Effect**

2 **Why was a high church steeple a good choice as a place to show a signal?** The lanterns could be seen for a great distance. **Draw Conclusions**

3 **What are some character traits that made Paul Revere a good citizen?** Possible answers: Brave, caring, unselfish, clever **Make Inferences**

4 **Compare and contrast Paul Revere and George Washington.** Possible response: Both men were patriots; both wanted the colonies to be free; both were brave and thought about the good of all the people. Washington led the army and later became President. Paul Revere worked as a silversmith. **Compare and Contrast**

3 Close and Assess

Think and Share

Paul Revere put himself in danger to warn the other colonists. He probably prevented an attack by the British on unsuspecting colonists. His actions probably saved lives.

Use with pages 216–221

Lesson 3 Wrap-Up

MEETING INDIVIDUAL NEEDS Leveled Practice

Show How We Celebrate!

Have children draw pictures to show some of the ways Americans celebrate Independence Day.

Easy Have children write captions for their pictures that include the date of Independence Day. **Reteach**

On-Level On the flip side of their drawings, have children write two or three sentences to tell about their pictures and why they included what they did. Encourage them to mention any national symbols they've included. **Extend**

Challenge Have children use their captioned pictures and sentences as the basis for a short speech about why all Americans should participate in some way in Independence Day celebrations. **Enrich**

Hands-on Activities

CURRICULUM CONNECTION **Reading**

Many Words from One

Objective Demonstrate understanding of new vocabulary; complete a word search.

Materials paper, pencils

Learning Style Visual/Verbal

Group

Time 10–15 minutes

1. Display *independence* and review its meaning with the group.

2. Then have children work independently to search for and write all the little words within *independence. (in, pen, end, den)*

3. Challenge children to use all the little words they find in a single written sentence.

Remind children to add *independence* to their "My Word Book" glossaries.

CURRICULUM CONNECTION **Writing**

Important Americans

Objective Learn more about historical figures.

Materials children's encyclopedias, nonfiction books, paper, pencils

Learning Style Linguistic/Social

Partners

Time 25–30 minutes

1. Have each pair of children choose one of the important Americans they learned about in Lesson 3.

2. Have children work together to find and read additional information on their person.

3. As a group, have children compare the experiences of their subjects.

CURRICULUM CONNECTION **Art**

Join the Parade

Objective Create props appropriate for celebrating Independence Day.

Learning Style Social/Kinesthetic

Group

Time 20–25 minutes

1. Tell children to imagine that it is July 3, 1776, and that tomorrow is the very first Independence Day.

2. Have each child create a prop to wear or display in the first Independence Day parade. Children can make small American flags, banners, colonial hats, buttons, pompoms, and so on.

3. After children have completed their objects, have them line up for a parade.

Play a marching song to inspire them as they march around the classroom in celebration of their country's birthday.

Lesson 4 Overview

Our Country Grows **pages 222–225**	Children will learn about the expedition of Lewis and Clark. They will also learn the vocabulary word *pioneer* and how the pioneers settled the West by traveling the Oregon Trail. 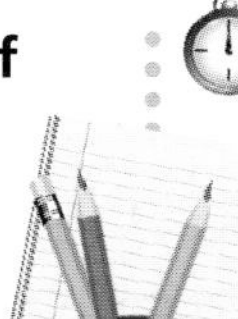	 Time 20–30 minutes Resources • Workbook, p. 55 • Vocabulary Card **pioneer** • Every Student Learns Guide, pp. 94–97
Read a Time Line **pages 226–227**	Children will learn how to create a time line.	 Time 15–20 minutes Resource • Workbook, p. 56
Westward Ho! **pages 228–229**	Children will learn about the railroad that was built to link the East Coast to the West Coast.	Time 15–20 minutes

Build Background

Activity

From Sea to Sea

 **Time** 20–30 minutes

- Display a physical map of North America to familiarize children with significant landforms and bodies of water. Begin in the east and move westward across the map, noting such features as oceans, mountains, lakes, and rivers.
- Encourage children to talk about how explorers may have felt seeing these great North American features for the first time.
- Have children draw a picture of one place you have talked about and create a one-or two-sentence caption.

If time is short, ask children how explorers traveled cross-country. Have them identify some of the hardships explorers would have faced.

Read Aloud

The Pioneers

by Christopher Erickson

The pioneers moved west.
They were brave and bold.
Along rocky trails
their wagons rolled and rolled.

They led their families
through blizzards and rains,
with high hopes and dreams,
they went 'cross deserts and plains.

Our Country Grows

Objective

- Name several sources of information about a given period or event.

Vocabulary

pioneer a person who goes first and prepares the way for others (p. 224)

QUICK Teaching Plan

If time is short, read aloud the exploration sequence Lewis and Clark followed (pp. 222–223) as children study the illustrations, especially the map, in the lesson.

1 Introduce and Motivate

Preview Display the Vocabulary Card **pioneer**. Encourage children to say what they know about pioneers and their role in settling the western part of our country. Then have children locate the meaning of *pioneer* on p. 224 and read it with you. Encourage children to browse the remaining pages in the lesson.

Warm Up To activate prior knowledge, read aloud the first sentence on p. 222. Ask children why they think President Thomas Jefferson wanted to explore the West. Ask what kinds of character traits explorers needed to successfully explore new lands.

Lesson

Our Country Grows

Thomas Jefferson, the third President of the United States, wanted to explore the West. The United States bought a huge area of land in the West from the French. President Jefferson sent a group of people to find a way to the Pacific Ocean. 1

First, the explorers set out from St. Louis, Missouri. Meriwether Lewis and William Clark led the explorers. They traveled up the Missouri River. 2

Next, Lewis and Clark met a Shoshone woman named Sacagawea. She helped the explorers find food. Sacagawea also helped the explorers talk to other Native Americans they met along the way. 3

Last, Lewis and Clark led the explorers across the Rocky Mountains. They continued on until they saw the Pacific Ocean.

222

Practice and Extend

READING SKILL Main Idea and Details

- Have children define the terms *main idea* and *details.*
- After children read p. 224, have them write the main idea of the second paragraph. Have them also list two details that support the main idea.
- Have partners compare their main ideas and details.

WEB SITE Technology

You can look up vocabulary words online. Click on *Social Studies Library* and select the dictionary at **www.sfsocialstudies.com.**

Lewis and Clark returned to St. Louis. The trip had lasted about two and a half years. Lewis and Clark drew maps and wrote journals about their trip. 4 5

William Clark's diary

SOCIAL STUDIES STRAND
History

In Her Honor

- Pass around the newly-minted Sacagawea dollar coin.
- Ask children to identify some of the details on the coin.
- Explain that Sacagawea actually did bring her infant son on the expedition.
- Discuss why Sacagawea has been honored with a coin bearing her likeness.

2 Teach and Discuss

Pages 222–223

Tell children that President Thomas Jefferson paid $15 million for the lands between the Mississippi River and the Pacific Ocean. Note, too, that the Lewis and Clark expedition included about 40 people—each chosen for a special skill or ability such as carpentry, Native American languages, and plant science.

1 **What did President Jefferson want his explorers to find?** A way to the Pacific Ocean
Main Idea and Details

2 **What was the starting point of Lewis and Clark's trip?** St. Louis, Missouri **What means of transportation did they use at first?** Boat
Make Inferences

3 **Why was it important to have someone who could help the explorers communicate with the Native Americans?** Possible answer: The explorers could explain their purpose as a friendly one. They could ask for help moving from place to place since the Native Americans knew the areas they lived in. **Make Inferences**

4 **Look at the map. Are the Rocky Mountains east or west of the Pacific Ocean?** East
Interpret Maps

5 **What contribution did Lewis and Clark make to our country's history?** Possible answer: They helped map out the western part of the country. They made it possible for pioneers to move west to build homes and communities.
Draw Conclusions

continued

Page 224

Tell children that as more people came to the United States, land in the East became scarce and more expensive.

6 Why did many pioneers want to move to the West? They wanted to get land so they could build homes. **Cause and Effect**

Ongoing Assessment

If... children don't understand why people would want to leave the East to make such long and hard trips west,

then... explain that people were offered free land in the West if they agreed to farm it.

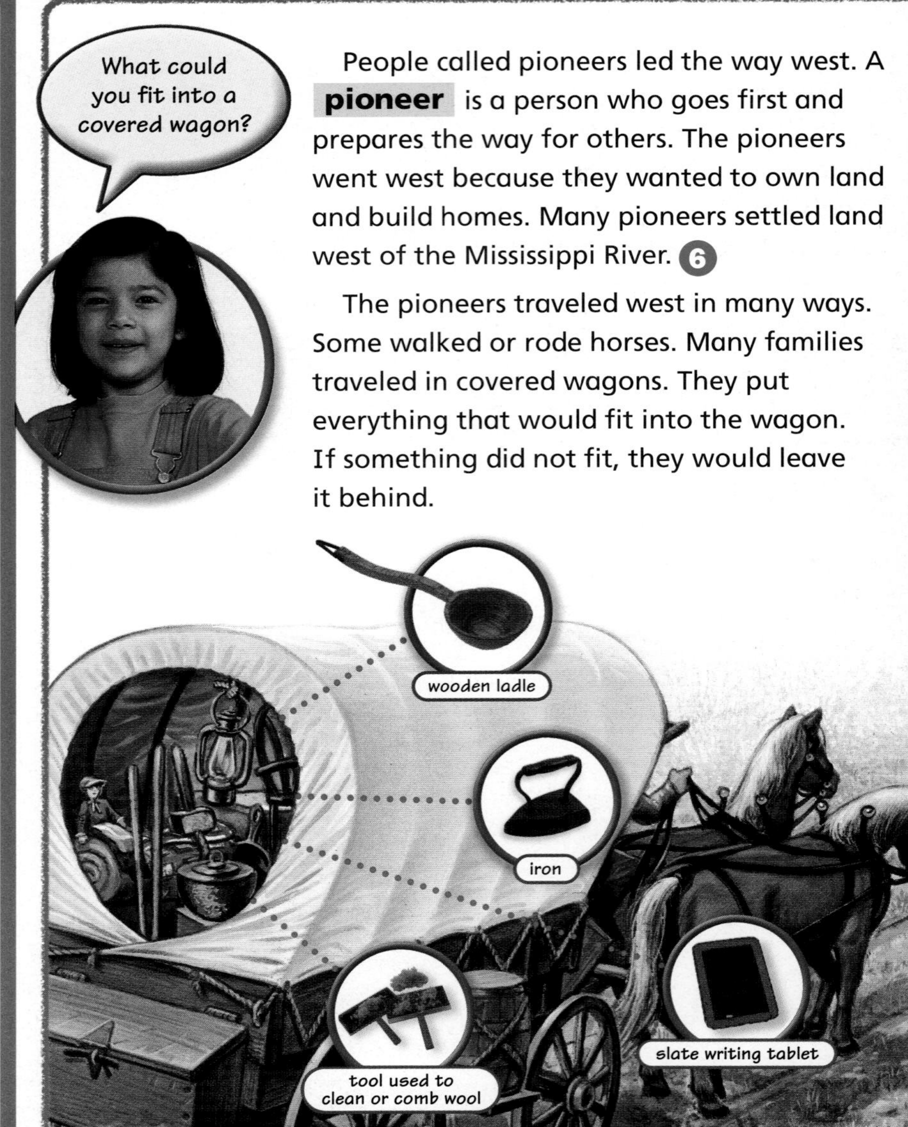

People called pioneers led the way west. A **pioneer** is a person who goes first and prepares the way for others. The pioneers went west because they wanted to own land and build homes. Many pioneers settled land west of the Mississippi River. 6

The pioneers traveled west in many ways. Some walked or rode horses. Many families traveled in covered wagons. They put everything that would fit into the wagon. If something did not fit, they would leave it behind.

Practice and Extend

ACTIVATE PRIOR KNOWLEDGE

ESL Support

Meeting Needs Talk briefly with children about some of the chores they think the pioneers had to do along their journey westward. Tell children to think about how the pioneers would have met their needs.

Beginning Have children be pioneers and pantomime doing one or more necessary chores.

Intermediate Have children describe what they are doing and why as they pantomime.

Advanced Have children write sentences to tell about the chores the pioneers had to do and why they were important to their survival.

For additional support, use Every Student Learns Guide, pp. 94–97.

SOCIAL STUDIES STRAND

Economics

Scarcity and Opportunity Cost

- Explain the concept of *opportunity cost.* Say that an opportunity is a chance to do something. People must make choices about giving things up in order to do something they want. What they give up is the opportunity cost.
- Ask children what was scarce, or in short supply, in the wagons in which pioneers traveled. (space)
- Help children understand that the belongings the pioneers left behind were the opportunity cost for lightening the load of their wagons.
- Have children give specific examples of what the pioneers may have left behind.

Many pioneers followed the Oregon Trail to the West. The trail was long and hard. The pioneers faced bad weather. The rain and wind ruined many wagons. The pioneers traveled during snowstorms. They crossed deserts. They even had to cross the Rocky Mountains. 7 8

What did you learn?

1. Tell three ways that you learned about Lewis and Clark.
2. Find the Mississippi River on the map. Now find the Rocky Mountains. Which is farther west?
3. **Think and Share** Suppose you were a pioneer following the Oregon Trail to the West. Tell what happened **first**, **next**, and **last** on your long trip.

225

SOCIAL STUDIES STRAND Geography

The Mighty Mississippi

- Trace the Mississippi River on a classroom map.
- Tell children that the river is over 2,000 miles long and acts as a natural boundary between the eastern and western United States.
- Ask children what they think the pioneers did when they reached the Mississippi River. Discuss the difficulties in crossing such a large river.

Workbook, p. 55

Our Country Grows

Look at the information in the boxes. Write answers to the questions below.

The Journey of Lewis and Clark

Lewis and Clark kept a journal during their trip. They drew pictures of the animals and plants they saw. They drew maps, too.

1. What shows how the pioneers traveled? **The picture shows them with a covered wagon.**
2. What can you learn from the picture of Sacagawea? **She helped lead the explorers.**
3. What shows you the route Lewis and Clark traveled? **the map**
4. What did you learn by reading the paragraph? **Lewis and Clark kept records of the trip.**

Also on Teacher Resources CD-ROM.

Page 225

Tell children that pioneers also traveled on other trails such as the Santa Fe Trail and the California Trail on their journeys westward.

7 **How did pioneers solve the problem of possibly getting lost on their way west?** They followed the Oregon Trail. **Solve Problems**

Test Talk

Use Information from the Text

8 **What were some of the hardships the pioneers faced?** Storms, crossing deserts and mountains, loss of their wagons **Recall and Retell**

Children should look back at the text to make sure they have all of the right information.

3 Close and Assess

What did you learn?

1. Pictures, map, and lesson text
2. The Rocky Mountains are farther west.
3. **Think and Share** Answers will vary. The events children tell about should reflect an understanding of details given in the lesson text. Listen for inclusion of the time order words *first, next,* and *last*.

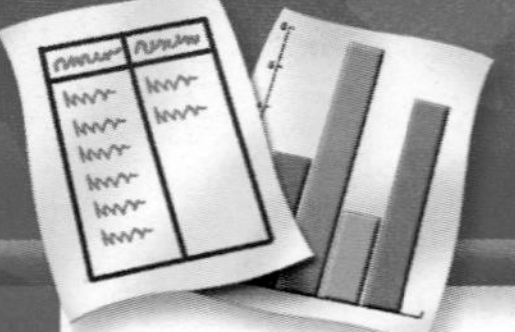

Read a Time Line

Objective

- Create and interpret a time line.

Vocabulary

time line shows the order in which things happened (p. 226)

1 Introduce and Motivate

Preview Have children find and read the definition of *time line* on p. 226. Then have them look at the time line and identify its topic.

Warm Up To activate prior knowledge, tell children to suppose that they will make a time line about special events or celebrations that happen in class during the months of the school year. Have them say which month would be shown first on their time line and which month would be shown last.

2 Teach and Discuss

Pages 226–227

Read the time line with children.

1 How are the events of the time line arranged? In the order in which they happen
Sequence

2 In which month of the year did Lewis and Clark see many new animals? September
Interpret Time Lines

Chart and Graph Skills

Read a Time Line

I've learned a lot about how our country grew. I made a time line to show some things that happened on the trip Lewis and Clark made. A **time line** shows the order in which things happened. 1

226

Practice and Extend

Keeping Time

- Talk with children about ways people measure time.
- Have children generate a list of time units—second, minute, hour, day, month, year. Have them say how much time each unit represents. Record their responses.
- Challenge children to tell or find out what "ten years of time" is called and what "100 years of time" is called.

1. What month did Lewis and Clark begin their trip?
2. What happened in November?
3. **On Your Own** Make a time line that shows how you have grown. Draw pictures of you as a baby, a toddler, and a second grader.

227

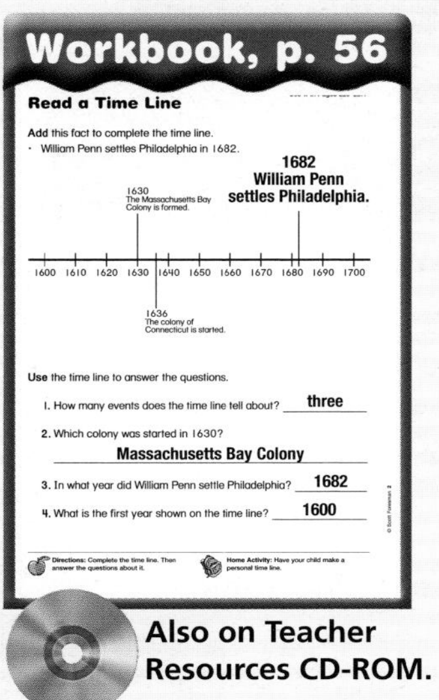

Workbook, p. 56

Read a Time Line

Add this fact to complete the time line.
- William Penn settles Philadelphia in 1682.

1630 The Massachusetts Bay Colony is formed.
1682 William Penn settles Philadelphia.
1636 The colony of Connecticut is started.

1600 1610 1620 1630 1640 1650 1660 1670 1680 1690 1700

Use the time line to answer the questions.

1. How many events does the time line tell about? three
2. Which colony was started in 1630? Massachusetts Bay Colony
3. In what year did William Penn settle Philadelphia? 1682
4. What is the first year shown on the time line? 1600

Also on Teacher Resources CD-ROM.

③ **How is a time line like a graph?** Possible answer: Both a time line and a graph give information in an easy-to-read form. They are both like pictures that help someone understand information quickly. **Compare and Contrast**

3 Close and Assess

Try it!

1. Lewis and Clark began their trip in May.
2. Lewis and Clark met Sacagawea in November.
3. **On Your Own** Children's time lines will vary greatly. Be sure children indicate the entries on their time lines in the correct time sequence.

Westward Ho!

Living History

Objective

- Describe how science and technology have changed transportation.

1 Introduce and Motivate

Preview Read aloud the title of the lesson and have children look at and talk about the pictures. Have children use the pictures to tell what they think is the main idea of the feature.

Warm Up To activate prior knowledge, have children name different kinds of transportation the explorers and pioneers of the past used to travel westward. Then have children identify some ways people in the present can travel from the East Coast to the West Coast.

2 Teach and Discuss

Pages 228–229

1 **How did people solve the problem of getting supplies to communities in the West?** They built a railroad that would connect the East Coast with people living in the West. **Solve Problems**

2 **Why do you think the United States government asked two railroad companies to work together?** The job was a very big one. It would have taken too long for just one company and its workers to build the whole new railroad. **Make Inferences**

Westward Ho!

Living History

Many more people wanted to come to the West. Trains were a faster way to travel than covered wagons. Trains were needed so that communities in the West could get supplies they needed. 1

There were many railroads in the East, but few in the West. The country needed a railroad that could link the East Coast to the West Coast.

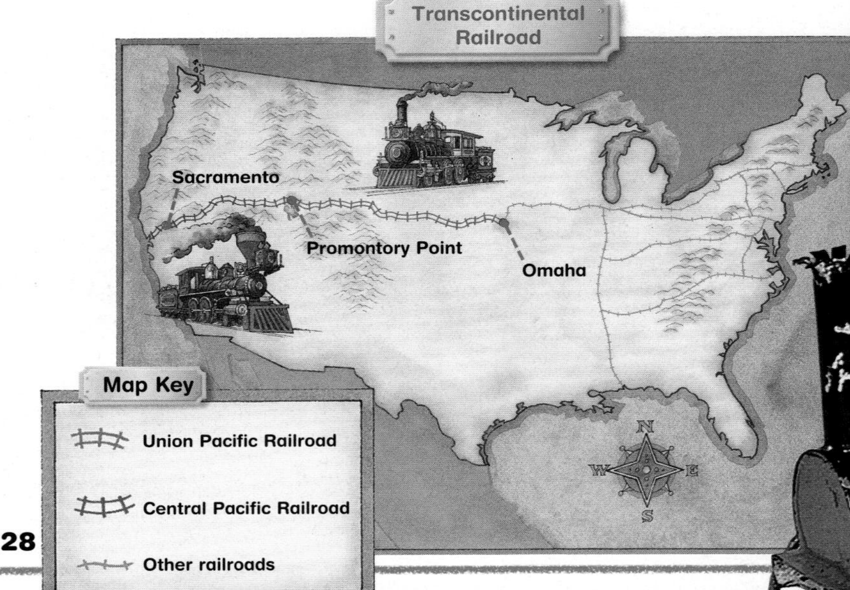

228

Practice and Extend

FYI SOCIAL STUDIES Background

About the Transcontinental Railroad

- Congress passed the Pacific Railway Act in 1862. As a result, two companies—Union Pacific Railroad and Central Pacific Railroad—were given the responsibility of laying tracks for the cross-country railroad.
- Part of the task involved laying track aross the Rocky Mountains.
- Labor was supplied by thousands of Chinese and European immigrants.
- In return for building the railroad, the two companies involved were awarded government monies in the form of loans and substantial land grants.

Two groups built the western part of the railroad. One group started near Omaha, Nebraska. The other group started in Sacramento, California. The two groups met and joined the railroad tracks at Promontory Point in present-day Utah. It took seven years to build this railroad. 2

Then

4

Today, high-speed trains link some cities. These trains have a rounded shape and weigh less than older trains. They run with help from computers. High-speed 3 trains can move people very quickly from one city to another. 5

Now

Hands-on History

Write about how transportation has changed since the pioneers traveled out west. Draw two pictures that show transportation in the past and in the present.

229

CURRICULUM CONNECTION
Science•Technology

Steam Power

- Tell children that the early trains were called steam locomotives. Steam was their source of power.
- Explain that coal, a black rock that can be burned for heat, was burned in a firebox. The heat from the burning coal turned water in the locomotive's engine into steam.
- Tell children that large quantities of coal had to be mined, or dug out of the earth, to supply the trains.
- Have children discuss how mining so much coal might have affected the physical environment.

3 **What helps today's high-speed trains move people and goods quickly?** Their design; the trains are shaped differently and are not as heavy as older trains. **Recall and Retell**

4 **How do the pictures on p. 229 help someone better understand how trains have changed since the past?** Possible answer: By looking at the pictures, someone can see more details of how the trains are different. **Analyze Pictures**

5 **How do high-speed trains help people live better today?** Possible answer: People can move from place to place more quickly. **Draw Conclusions**

3 Close and Assess

Hands-on History

Children's responses should show an understanding that science and technology have made train travel better. Their drawings should include transportation modes from the past—horse, wagon, small boats—and today's transportation modes—plane, high speed trains, cars.

Use with pages 222–229

Lesson 4 Wrap-Up

MEETING INDIVIDUAL NEEDS
Learning Styles

Who's Who

Discuss briefly the contributions made by Thomas Jefferson, Lewis and Clark, and Sacagawea to the expansion of our country.

Kinesthetic Learning Have children make simple finger puppets of one or more of the characters they discussed, using strips of paper they tape to fit around their fingers. Children can draw facial features and add appropriate clothing. They can use the puppets to share what they know about the person.

Verbal Learning Have children work in groups. They should choose a person and take part with the others in the group to improvise a dialogue among the characters.

Linguistic Learning Have children write skits involving two or more of the characters.

Hands-on Activities

CURRICULUM CONNECTION
Writing

Other Pioneers

Objective Demonstrate understanding of new vocabulary.

Materials paper, pencils

Learning Style Linguistic

Individual

Time 10–15 minutes

1. Display *pioneer* and review its meaning.
2. Ask children if they think there are pioneers today.
3. After a brief discussion, have children write about some modern-day pioneers, telling why they have chosen them.

Remind children to add *pioneer* to their "My Word Book" glossaries.

CURRICULUM CONNECTION
Literature

The Best of the West

Objective Share books related to the lesson topics.

Materials Picture books (see below)

Learning Style Visual/Verbal

Group 

Time 20–25 minutes

1. Share one or both books.

   Lewis and Clark: Explorers of the American West, by Steven Kroll (Holiday House, ISBN 0-823-41273-3, 1994)

   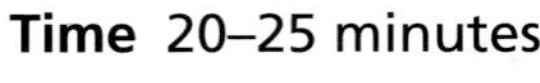

   Aurora Means Dawn, by Scott Russell Sanders (Bradbury, ISBN 0-027-78270-0, 1989) This book tells of the experiences of a westward-bound family.

2. Read to children and discuss the people, places, and events in the stories.

CURRICULUM CONNECTION
Art

Wagons Ho!

Objective Respond to factual information by creating visual materials.

Materials paper, cardboard, crayons, tape, paste, scissors

Learning Style Kinesthetic/Social

Partners

Time 25–30 minutes

1. Have children work with partners to make a simple wagon using construction paper and cardboard. Wagons should include the "cart" and wheels.
2. Have children draw pictures or make 3-D representations of things the pioneers would have brought with them. Tell children to place the objects in their wagons.
3. Have children join their wagons in a wagon train. Set aside time for children to review the objects in the wagons.

Lesson 5 Overview

We Remember Americans **pages 230–233**	Children will learn how people were taken from Africa and forced into slavery in North America. They will also learn how people such as Harriet Tubman and Frederick Douglass, who had been slaves themselves, helped other slaves escape to freedom.	Time 20–30 minutes Resources • Workbook, p. 57 • Every Student Learns Guide, pp. 98–101
Sojourner Truth **pages 234–235**	Children will learn about Sojourner Truth, who spoke out for the rights of African Americans.	Time 15–20 minutes

Build Background

Activity

What Do You Know?

Time 15–20 minutes

- Begin a K–W–L chart with children built around the topic of slavery. Head three columns: *What I Know, What I Want to Know,* and *What I Learned.*
- Focus on the first two columns. Ask children to define slavery. Combine and rephrase children's ideas to form a working definition. Then ask volunteers to tell what they know about slavery. List their responses in the first column. Review the list. Then have children identify some questions they have about slavery. List those in the second column.
- Tell children that after reading the lesson, they will fill in the third column of the chart.

If time is short, have children think of one thing they would say to convince others that slavery is wrong.

Read Aloud

The Struggle for Equality!

by Eric Meyer

Many Africans were brought
so far across the sea
to live in America
and lead lives that were not free.

For over two hundred years,
they worked for no pay
doing farm work and housework
each and every day.

Finally slavery ended,
the struggle was done.
But the fight for equality
has yet to be won.

Lesson 5 We Remember Americans

Objectives

- Identify contributions of historical figures who have influenced the nation.
- Compare various interpretations of the same time period using evidence such as photographs.

QUICK Teaching Plan

If time is short, begin to discuss the concept of slavery by reading its definition on p. 230. Have children add what they know. Use the pictures and captions on p. 231 to introduce two former slaves who went on to become prominent in the fight against slavery—Harriet Tubman and Frederick Douglass.

1 Introduce and Motivate

Preview Read the title of the lesson. Have children look at the pictures thoughout the lesson to predict what they will read about.

Warm Up To activate prior knowledge, ask children to tell how they think President Abraham Lincoln helped African Americans who were slaves in our country.

Lesson 5 We Remember Americans

As the country grew, not all people were free. Some people were taken from their homes in Africa. They were made to come to America in ships and sold into slavery. Slavery is being owned and having to work for someone else. 1

Some slaves worked in factories or as servants in homes. Many worked outdoors on small farms or plantations. They raised crops like cotton and sugar. Slaves did not get paid for their hard work. 2 3

Slaves workin a Virgi planta

230

Practice and Extend

READING SKILL Put Things in Order

Sequence

- Remind children that events in history happen in a certain order.
- After children read pp. 230–233, write these events on the board in this jumbled order:

  Slaves had to work at jobs for no pay.

  Slaves were made to come from Africa to America.

  President Lincoln helped to end slavery.
- Tell children to write the events in the correct order on a sheet of paper.

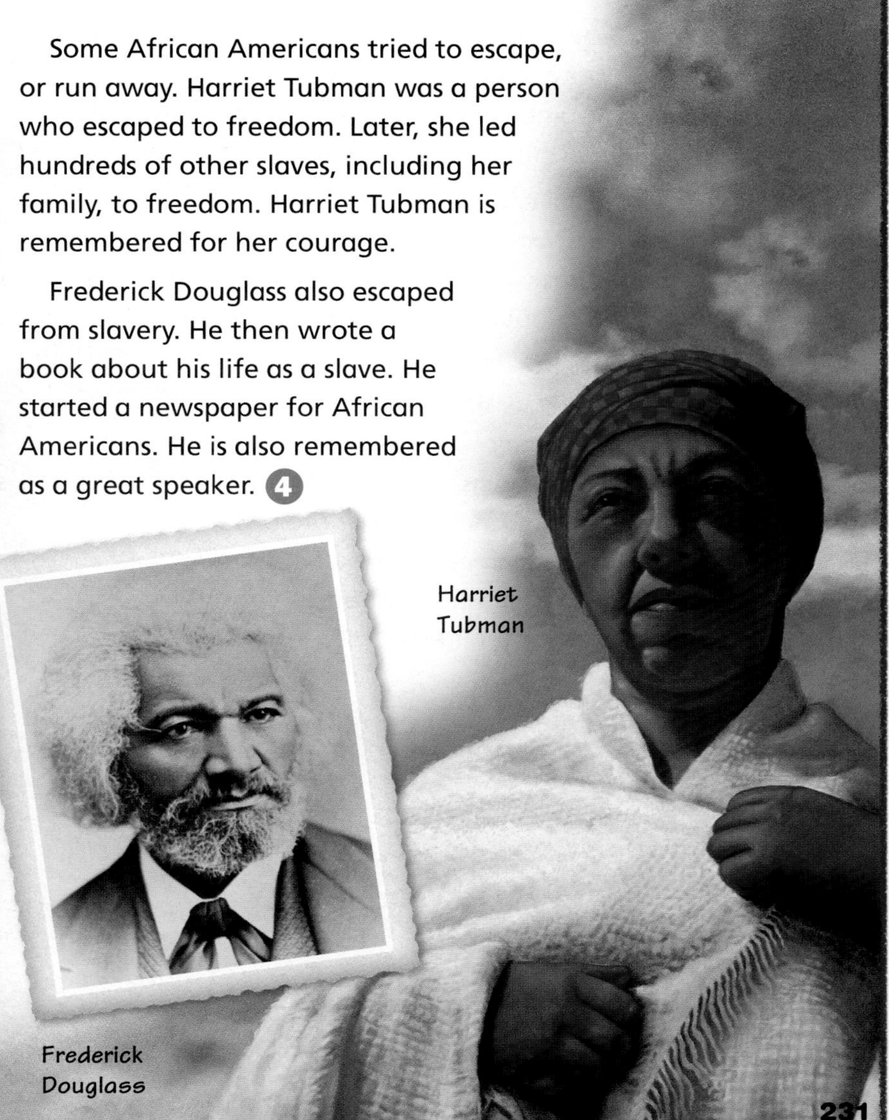

Some African Americans tried to escape, or run away. Harriet Tubman was a person who escaped to freedom. Later, she led hundreds of other slaves, including her family, to freedom. Harriet Tubman is remembered for her courage.

Frederick Douglass also escaped from slavery. He then wrote a book about his life as a slave. He started a newspaper for African Americans. He is also remembered as a great speaker. 4

Harriet Tubman

Frederick Douglass

231

SOCIAL STUDIES Background

About the Underground Railroad

- Escaping slaves used the Underground Railroad.
- It was not a railroad, nor was it under the ground.
- It was a network, or chain, of people willing to help runaway slaves by offering them food, clothing, and a safe place to hide during the day.
- The people who helped slaves were called "conductors" after real railroad workers.
- It was extremely dangerous for people to help slaves because slave catchers followed runaway slaves. "Conductors" were often putting their lives at risk.

2 Teach and Discuss

Page 230

Explain that slaves could not go to school, own personal property, or vote.

1 **Who were the slaves?** People taken by force from their homes in Africa to work in America **Recall and Retell**

2 **How were slaves treated differently than other workers?** Slaves could not decide what jobs they would do; they had to do whatever their owners told them to do; they did not get paid for their work. **Main Idea and Details**

3 **Why do you think some people brought slaves to work in our country?** Possible answer: They didn't want to work hard themselves; they didn't want to pay workers. **Make Inferences**

Ongoing Assessment

If... children don't understand why some people wanted slaves,	**then...** make the point that the plantations on which many slaves worked were very large and needed many workers. It would have been very expensive to hire so many workers.

Page 231

4 **What qualities of a leader did Harriet Tubman and Frederick Douglass show?** Possible answer: They both were determined to be free; both had courage to help themselves and then to help others; both were caring and wanted people to be treated fairly. **Draw Conclusions**

Lesson 5 continued

Page 232

Tell children that the Civil War was fought between Americans living in the northern states and those living in the southern states. Use a map to identify some states that fought as the North (NY, PA, IA) and some that fought as the South (TX, FL, NC).

5 **Why do you think some Americans did not agree that slavery was wrong?** Possible answer: They were owners of slaves; they would have lost many workers if there were no more slaves. **Make Inferences**

6 **What are two freedoms some African Americans still did not have after the end of slavery?** Some could not vote or work in the government. **Recall and Retell**

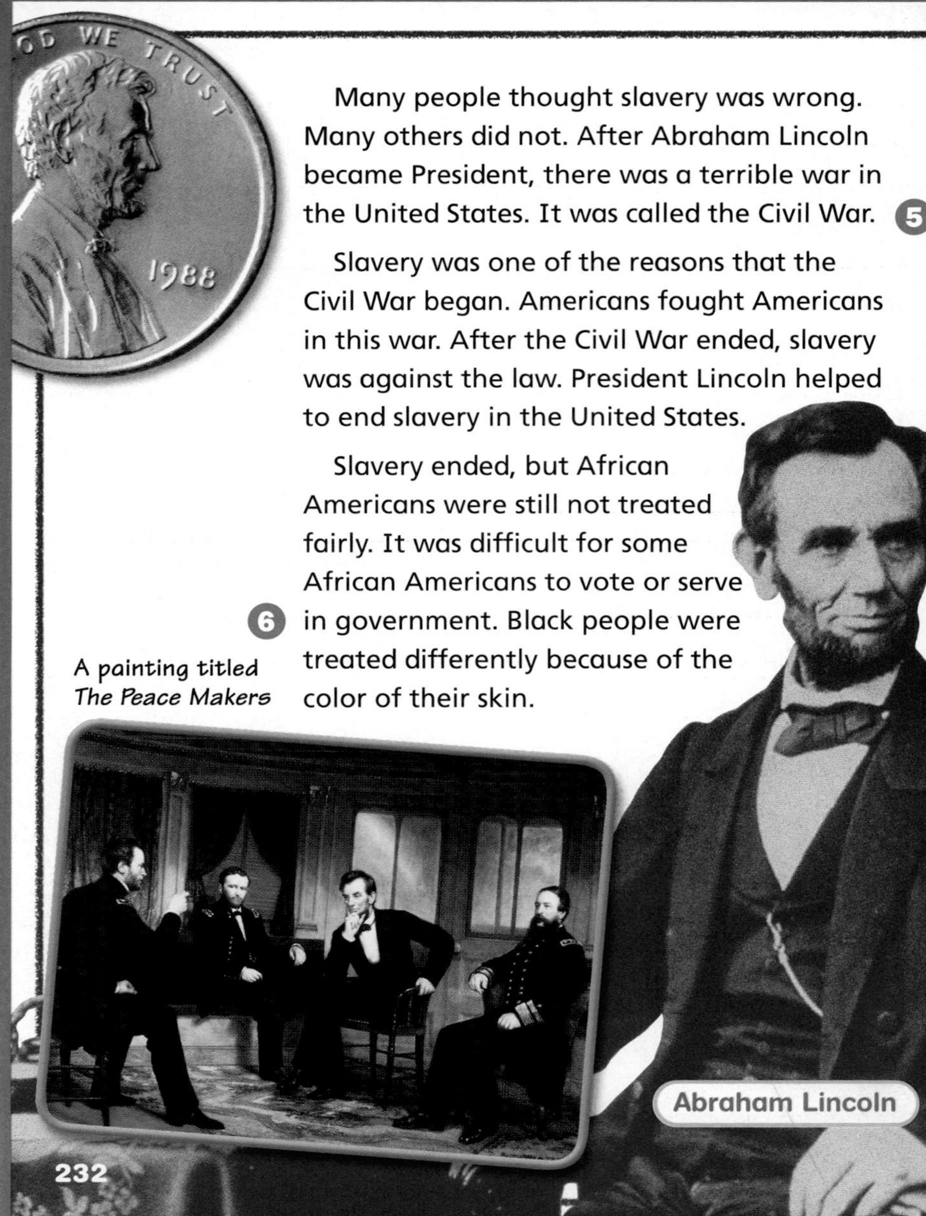

Many people thought slavery was wrong. Many others did not. After Abraham Lincoln became President, there was a terrible war in the United States. It was called the Civil War. 5

Slavery was one of the reasons that the Civil War began. Americans fought Americans in this war. After the Civil War ended, slavery was against the law. President Lincoln helped to end slavery in the United States.

Slavery ended, but African Americans were still not treated fairly. It was difficult for some African Americans to vote or serve
6 in government. Black people were treated differently because of the color of their skin.

A painting titled *The Peace Makers*

Abraham Lincoln

232

Practice and Extend

EXTEND LANGUAGE
ESL Support

A Closer Look Write this sentence on the board: *It was difficult for some African Americans to vote or serve in government.* Have children read the sentence with you. Then create a T chart. In the left part of the chart, write *difficult, vote,* and *serve in government.*

Beginning Have children work together to give a meaning for each word or phrase. Record the responses in the chart.

Intermediate Have children use each word or phrase in an oral sentence.

Advanced Have children use dictionaries to look up the meaning of *serve* as it is used in the example sentence. Have them also find other meanings for *serve.*

For additional support, use Every Student Learns Guide, pp. 98–101.

CURRICULUM CONNECTION
Math

How Long Did the War Last?

- Tell children that the Civil War began in 1861 and that it ended in 1865. Have children subtract to find out how long the war lasted.
- You may wish to have them cover the tens, hundreds, and thousands columns before they do their subtraction, since the numbers are identical. Confirm that the war lasted four years.
- Tell children that in those four years over 600,000 soldiers died.

More than 50 years ago, black people were not allowed to play professional sports with white people. Jackie Robinson was the first black player in modern major league baseball. He became a member of the Brooklyn Dodgers. Jackie Robinson said, "The right of every American to first-class citizenship is the most important issue of our time."

Jackie Robinson

Brooklyn Dodgers, 1947

What did you learn?

1. How did Harriet Tubman show courage?
2. What was the name of the war in which Americans fought Americans?
3. **Think and Share** Make a poster showing why Abraham Lincoln was an important leader.

233

Page 233

Explain that *first-class citizenship* refers to having all the rights and freedoms of every other citizen, not just having some rights or freedoms.

7 **How do you think Jackie Robinson is feeling in the photo?** Possible answer: He is feeling proud and excited about being on the team. **Analyze Pictures**

8 **What sources did you have throughout the lesson to help you learn about life for African Americans in the United States?** Text in the lesson, pictures and their captions, the photograph of Jackie Robinson and his team **Analyze Primary Sources**

Close and Assess

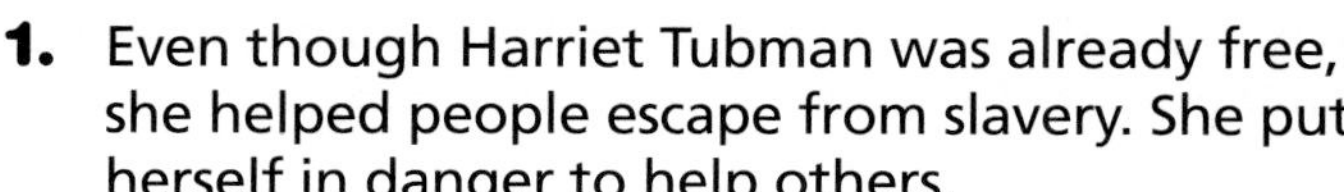

1. Even though Harriet Tubman was already free, she helped people escape from slavery. She put herself in danger to help others.
2. In the Civil War, Americans fought Americans.
3. **Think and Share** Children's posters should reflect Abraham Lincoln's role in bringing the Civil War and slavery to an end.

CURRICULUM CONNECTION Writing

New Information

- Revisit the K–W–L chart begun before reading the lesson. Read through the entries in the second column—questions about slavery children wanted answered.
- Have children write new information they learned by reading the lesson. Ask if what they learned corresponds to any of the questions on the chart.
- If questions remain unanswered, help children find the answers in other resources.

Workbook, p. 57

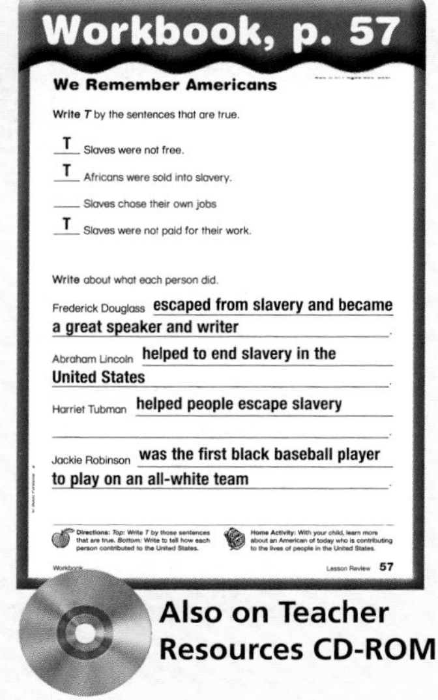

We Remember Americans

Write *T* by the sentences that are true.

T Slaves were not free.

T Africans were sold into slavery.

___ Slaves chose their own jobs.

T Slaves were not paid for their work.

Write about what each person did.

Frederick Douglass escaped from slavery and became a great speaker and writer

Abraham Lincoln helped to end slavery in the United States

Harriet Tubman helped people escape slavery

Jackie Robinson was the first black baseball player to play on an all-white team

Workbook Lesson Review 57

Also on Teacher Resources CD-ROM.

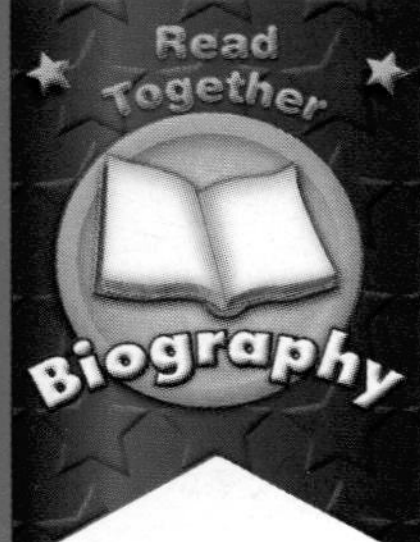

Sojourner Truth

Objective

- Identify historic figures, such as Sojourner Truth, who have exemplified good citizenship.

1 Introduce and Motivate

Preview Read aloud the title and subtitle of the feature. Explain the meanings of *abolitionist* (someone who wants to end slavery) and *suffragist* (someone who wants women to be able to vote). Ask children if they think the name *Sojourner Truth* is the pictured woman's real name. Have them read to find out.

Warm Up To activate prior knowledge, have children say what they think the word *truth* means. Have them then identify other traits someone who is always truthful would probably have.

Practice and Extend

Choose a Name

- Have children choose names that reflect the kind of person they are, just as Sojourner Truth did.
- Tell children to change just one part of their name, either the first name or the last name.
- Give some examples to get children's thinking started: Honesty Smith, Corrine Caring.
- Have children write their new names on small index cards or name tags that they can wear for the day.

When Sojourner Truth was born, she was named Isabella Baumfree. She was a slave until she was about 30 years old. She then changed her name to Sojourner Truth. *Sojourner* means "traveler." She traveled (1) around the country speaking out for the rights of African Americans. She spoke out against slavery. Although she had not learned to read or write, she was a good speaker. (2) President Abraham Lincoln knew of her speeches and invited her to the White House.

Sojourner Truth wanted people to have better lives. When people were freed from slavery, she helped them find new places to live. She gathered supplies for African American soldiers during the Civil War.

Sojourner Truth also spoke out for women's rights. She believed that women should have the right to vote. She spoke at (3) many meetings that supported the women's (4) rights movement.

Sojourner Truth was born in Ulster County, New York.

Sojourner Truth and Abraham Lincoln

Think and Share

Do you think Sojourner Truth chose a good name for herself? Why or why not?

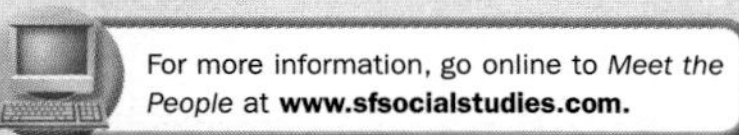

For more information, go online to *Meet the People* at **www.sfsocialstudies.com.**

WEB SITE Technology

You may help children find out more about Sojourner Truth by clicking on *Meet the People* at **www.sfsocialstudies.com.**

2 Teach and Discuss

Have children follow along as you read. After reading, help children compare Sojourner Truth with Frederick Douglass and Harriet Tubman.

(1) **Why do you think Isabella Van Wagener changed her name to Sojourner Truth?** Possible answer: She wanted a name that let people know who she was—that she was a person who traveled from place to place and spoke the truth. **Make Inferences**

(2) **Why didn't Sojourner Truth know how to read and write?** Possible answer: Slaves were not allowed to go to school, so few learned to read and write. **Recall and Retell**

(3) **What did Sojourner Truth speak out against?** Slavery **What did she speak out for?** The right of women to vote **Main Idea and Details**

(4) **How did Sojourner Truth show that she was a good citizen?** Possible answer: She wanted all people to be treated fairly. She was caring and truthful. **Draw Conclusions**

3 Close and Assess

Think and Share

Have children write a response to the question.

Write Your Answer

Possible answer: Yes; her new name let people know about her—that she traveled to get her messages across to people, that she spoke the truth.

Ask children to reread their answer to make sure it answers the question.

Use with pages 230–235

Lesson 5 Wrap-Up

MEETING INDIVIDUAL NEEDS
Leveled Practice

A News Story

Recall with children the main points of the lesson. Have them work together to decide on an event they would like to help make a newspaper story about.

Easy Have children draw a picture to show the event. **Reteach**

On-Level Have children write a headline to get people interested in reading more about the event. Give some examples, such as: *Slaves Freed!* or *Harriet Tubman Speaks Out!* **Extend**

Challenge Have children write a short news article about the event. Have them answer the questions *Who? What? Where? When?* and *Why?* in their articles. **Enrich**

Hands-on Activities

CURRICULUM CONNECTION
Writing

Words to Keep

Objective Build vocabulary.

Materials drawing paper, crayons

Learning Style Linguistic

Individual

Time 15–20 minutes

1. Have children go back through the lesson and the biographical feature to find five words they would like to save for later use.

My Special Words

2. Have children write each word and use it in a sentence. They may wish to add a picture as well.
3. Have children add the words in a separate section of "My Word Book" glossary.

CURRICULUM CONNECTION
Drama

Improvised Skits

Objective Respond dramatically to factual information.

Materials paper, pencils

Learning Style Verbal/Kinesthetic

Partners

Time 20–25 minutes

1. Have children work with partners to develop short skits that involve two characters—an escaping slave and either Harriet Tubman or Frederick Douglass.
2. After talking through their ideas, have partners improvise dialogue and actions to perform their skit.

CURRICULUM CONNECTION
Art

A Mural

Objective Respond artistically to factual information.

Materials drawing paper, crayons, markers, paper suitable for a mural display

Learning Style Social/Kinesthetic

Group

Time 20–25 minutes

1. Have small groups decide on an event to depict—slaves are brought to our country, slaves work on plantations, or slaves are freed.
2. Members of each group should draw individual pictures of the event.
3. Collect and group pictures by time frame of the event. Mount them in a three-sectioned mural, labeled *first, next, last.*
4. Help children label the parts of the mural.

Ending Unit 5

End with a Song pages 236–237	Children will talk about and then listen to the song "Follow the Drinkin' Gourd."	Resource • *Songs and Music* CD
Unit 5 Review pages 238–241	Children will review unit vocabulary words and the unit skills of sequence, reading a history map, and reading a time line. Children will answer questions about what they learned in the unit. Children will learn about several books about America's history.	Resources • Workbook, p. 58 ✓• Assessment Book, pp. 17–20
Unit 5 Project page 242	Children will learn how to prepare questions for and conduct an interview. They will also be directed to a Web site where they can learn more about people in history.	Resource • Workbook, p. 59

Wrap-up

Activity

An American History Scrapbook

Tell children they will make scrapbooks to show what they learned in the unit.

- Have children draw pictures they can later cut out of people, places, or things in the unit they especially want to remember.
- Have them mount their cut-out pictures on colorful construction paper. Encourage children to write labels or short captions for their scrapbook pages.
- Have children write *My American History* on a cover sheet. Then help children staple their pages together.

Performance Assessment

You can use the activity on this page as a performance assessment.

✓ Assessment Scoring Guide

Make an American History Scrapbook	
4	Scrapbook pages accurately represent information from the unit and follow the chronology of the lessons.
3	Pages represent several key ideas from the lessons accurately.
2	Pages focus on only one or two historical time periods but do so accurately.
1	Pages show random ideas sometimes represented carelessly.

Follow the Drinkin' Gourd

Objectives

- Obtain information about a topic using oral sources, such as music.
- Explain how selected symbols reflect an American love of freedom.

1 Introduce and Motivate

Preview Read the title of the song and have children look at the illustration. Have children think about what they mainly read about in Lesson 5. Ask them what they think the song tells about.

Warm Up To activate prior knowledge, ask children if they have ever looked up at the night sky to see the stars. Encourage children to tell how the stars looked to them. Ask if they were able to see any patterns the stars may have formed. Could they see any familiar shapes in the night sky?

Practice and Extend

The Big Dipper

- Use an encyclopedia or other reference source to show children a picture of the Big Dipper.
- Identify it as a constellation, or a group of stars that form a pattern or picture.
- Point out the individual stars that form the shape of the dipper. Then point to the North Star.
- Tell children that slaves headed north because in many northern states slavery was against the law.
- Ask children how they think the Big Dipper got its name.

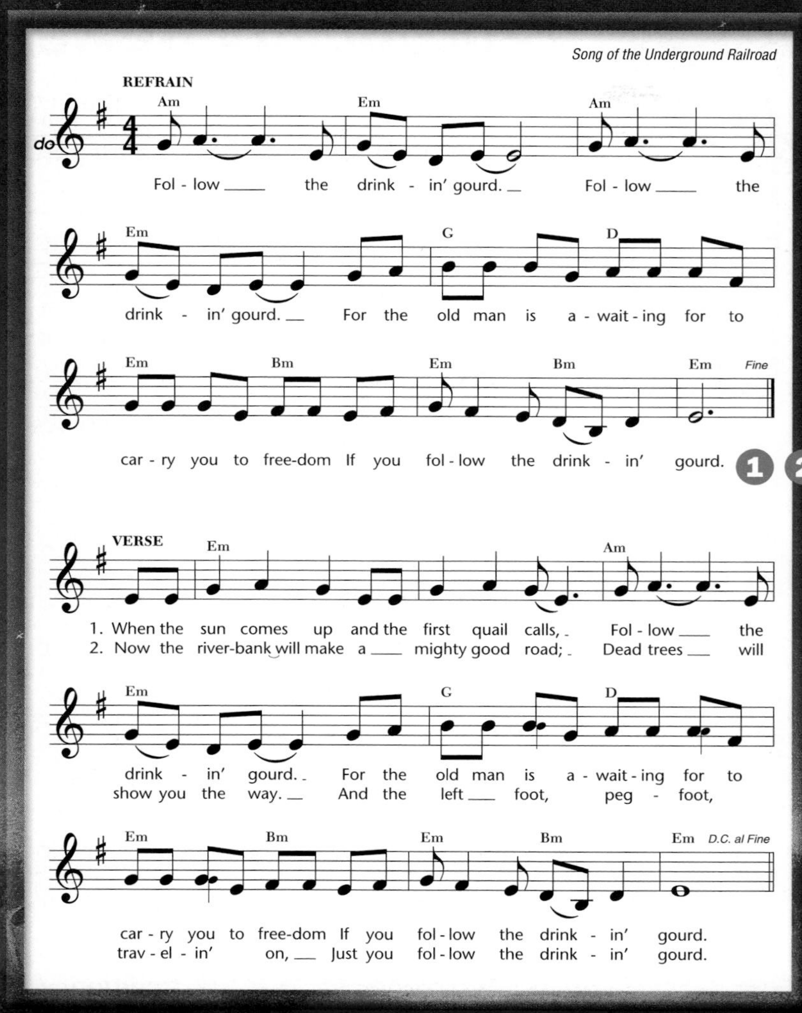

2 Teach and Discuss

Pages 236–237

Read the paragraph and the song lyrics aloud as children follow along. On a second reading, have children join in on the words "Follow the drinkin' gourd."

To help children better understand the song lyrics, you may wish to do the Science activity suggested at the bottom of p. 236.

1 What did the "drinkin' gourd" lead the slaves to? Freedom **Recall and Retell**

2 The "drinkin' gourd" was a symbol to the slaves. It is still a symbol today to many people. What is it a symbol of? Freedom; how much the slaves had to go through to get their freedom **Draw Conclusions**

3 Close and Assess

- Have children do a choral reading of the song lyrics.
- After several practice readings, tape children.
- Play the musical version available on CD and then replay the children's tape.
- Have children compare and contrast the two renditions.

SOCIAL STUDIES Background

About "The Drinkin' Gourd"

- The words to the song were a secret message to the slaves. They were a set of directions for getting from one place to another.
- Slaves knew that quails, a type of bird, spent their winters in the South. The reference to the quails narrowed the best time for running away to the North to the winter season.
- The "old man" is a guide who will meet the slaves to help them as they travel farther north.
- Other verses of the song give other directions the slaves would understand.

AUDIO CD Technology

Play the CD, *Songs and Music*, to listen to "Follow the Drinkin' Gourd."

UNIT 5 Review

Resources

- Assessment Book, pp. 17–20
- Workbook, p. 58: Vocabulary Review

Vocabulary Review

1. pioneer
2. shelter
3. colonist
4. tradition
5. explorer

Answers to Test Prep

1. colony
2. independence

UNIT 5 Review

Vocabulary Review

explorer
pioneer
colonist
shelter
tradition

Choose a word to go with each clue.

1. a person who goes first and prepares the way for others
2. a place where people live
3. a person who lives in a colony
4. something that is done a certain way for many years
5. a person who travels to a new place to learn about it

★ ★ ★ ★ ★ ★ ★ ★

Which word completes each sentence?

1. A place that is settled by people from another country is a _______.
   - **a.** independence **b.** shelter
   - **c.** colony **d.** tradition
2. To be free from other people or places is _______.
   - **a.** independence **b.** pioneer
   - **c.** colony **d.** tradition

238

Practice and Extend

Assessment Options

✓ Unit 5 Assessment

- Unit 5 Content Test: Use Assessment Book, pp. 17–18
- Unit 5 Skills Test: Use Assessment Book, pp. 19–20

Standardized Test Prep

- Unit 5 tests contain standardized test formats.

✓ Unit 5 Performance Assessment

- See p. 242 for information about using the Unit 5 Project as a means of performance assessment.
- A scoring guide for the Unit 5 Project is provided in the teacher's notes on p. 242.

Test Talk

- Test Talk Practice Book

Skills Review

Put Things in Order

Tell what you did today. Use the words **first, next,** and **last** to tell the order in which things happened.

★ ★ ★ ★ ★ ★ ★ ★

Map and Globe Skills

Read a History Map

Test Talk

Use the map to help you find the answers.

Look at the map.

1. What does the color orange on this map show?
2. What ocean is a border for many of the 13 colonies?

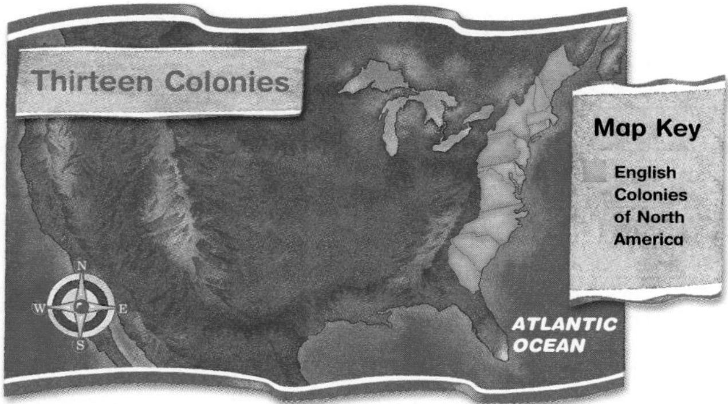

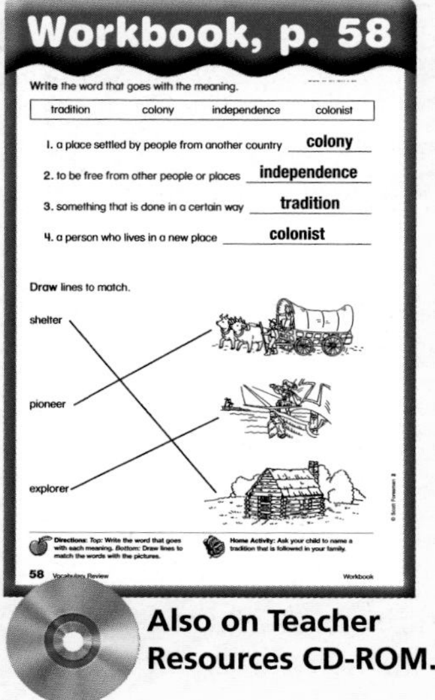
Workbook, p. 58

Write the word that goes with the meaning.

tradition	colony	independence	colonist

1. a place settled by people from another country colony
2. to be free from other people or places independence
3. something that is done in a certain way tradition
4. a person who lives in a new place colonist

Draw lines to match.

shelter

pioneer

explorer

Also on Teacher Resources CD-ROM.

Skills Review

Put Things in Order

Target Skill

- Children's responses should show an understanding of logical order and include the sequence words.

Use the following scoring guide.

✓ Assessment Scoring Guide

Sequence	
4	Responds logically and includes the time clue words.
3	Responds logically but omits some time clue words.
2	Responds illogically; uses time clue words inappropriately.
1	Shows little understanding of sequence.

Map and Globe Skills

Read a History Map

Use Information from Graphics
Use Read a History Map, Question 1, to model the Test Talk strategy.

Understand the question.
Have children identify places in the question. Children should finish the statement "I need to find out...."

Use information from graphics.
Ask children to skim the map to find the correct information.

1. It shows which of the 13 colonies were English.

For additional practice, use the Test Talk Practice Book.

2. The Atlantic Ocean is a border for the colonies.

Review

continued

Skills Review

Read a Time Line

1. June

2. Memorial Day

3. Independence Day

Skills On Your Own

- Children's time lines should be clear and accurate. Children should demonstrate understanding of sequence.

Use the following scoring guide.

✓ Assessment Scoring Guide

Make a Time Line	
4	Shows accurate information and demonstrates understanding of sequence.
3	Shows accurate information. Labeling is inconsistent.
2	Includes only birthday information. Incomplete response.
1	Shows little understanding of sequencing in a time line.

Review

Skills Review

Read a Time Line

This is a time line that shows some holidays Americans celebrate. Look at the time line to answer these questions.

1. What month do we celebrate Flag Day?

2. What holiday is celebrated in May?

3. What holiday is last on this time line?

Skills on Your Own

Make a celebration time line of your own. Fill in other holidays that you celebrate. Fill in your birthday. Draw pictures above your time line to show each special day.

Practice and Extend

Revisit the Unit Question

✓ Portfolio Assessment

Have children look back at their list they generated on p. 195. It records why they think it is important to learn about our country's history.

- Have children write sentences to say why Americans should know about their country's history.
- Have them put a check mark next to a new idea they learned while reading the unit.
- Encourage children to use their original list and their sentences to write a paragraph about why knowing our history is important.
- Suggest children add their paragraphs to their Social Studies portfolio.

What did you learn?

1. What resources did the Native Americans use to make their food, clothing, and shelters?
2. Why were many of the colonists willing to fight England?
3. Why did the pioneers move west?
4. **Write and Share** Tell what you would do if you were a pioneer packing your covered wagon for your trip out west. Use the words **first, next,** and **last** to tell the order in which things would happen.

Read About America's History

Look for books like these in the library.

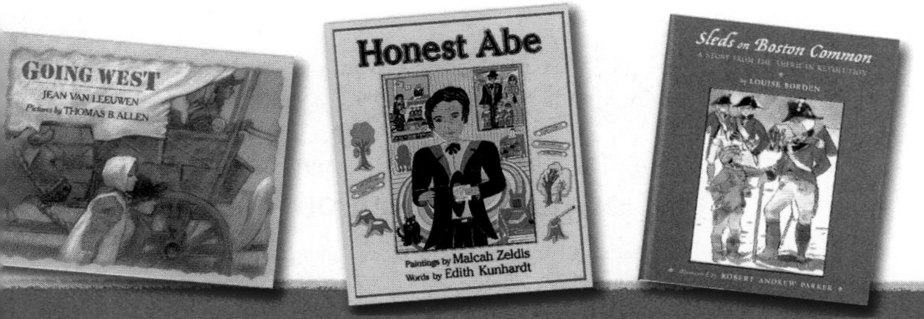

241

What did you learn?

1. Possible answers: Soil to plant crops; trees to make shelters; buffalo for food, shelter, and clothing. other animals for clothing.
2. They wanted their freedom from England.
3. Pioneers wanted land to build homes on.
4. **Write and Share** Children's responses should reflect their understanding of goods that would help meet their basic needs and should include the sequence words as specified.

Read About America's History

You may wish to have these books or similar ones available for children to read.

Going West, by Jean Van Leeuwen (HarperCollins, ISBN 0-064-40693-8, 1997). Told from the viewpoint of Hannah, a seven-year-old girl, this is the story of a family heading out West in a covered wagon. **Easy**

Honest Abe, by Edith Kunhardt (Mulberry Books, ISBN 0-688-15838-2, 1998). This is a fine picture book biography of Lincoln, following him from log cabin to White House. **On-Level**

Sleds on the Boston Common, by Louise Borden (Margaret McElderry, ISBN 0-689-82812-8, 2000). Young brothers want to run their sleds on the hills of the Boston Common, but there is a problem. British soldiers are camped in their way. The boys muster courage to ask that the soldiers move and they do. Based on folklore. **Challenge**

Unit 5 Project

Do an Interview

Objective

- Research and present information about a historic American in an interview format.

Resource

- Workbook, p. 59

Materials

paper, pencils, children's encyclopedia, appropriate nonfiction books, newspaper or magazine interviews

Follow This Procedure

- Tell children they will interview a person from the past.
- Model writing some typical interview questions on the board.
- Pair children. Have them together choose someone to interview, write three interview questions, and research the answers.
- When the interview questions and answers are ready, have one child take the role of the interviewer, the other the role of the interviewee. Each pair of children should perform an interview for the class.

✓ Assessment Scoring Guide

	Do an Interview
4	Prepares three questions and accurate answers appropriate to the chosen figure. Shows an understanding of the interview process.
3	Prepares three questions, at least one of which is inappropriate or incorrectly answered. Shows an understanding of the interview process.
2	Prepares fewer than three questions and answers. Shows some understanding of the interview process.
1	Prepares vague questions and/or answers. Shows minimal understanding of the interview process.

Do an Interview

Here's your chance to talk to a person from the past.

1. **Choose** a person, such as an explorer, a leader, or pioneer.
2. **Prepare** a list of questions to ask and the answers.
3. **Choose** who will play this person and who will play a news reporter.
4. **Present** the interview to your class.

Internet Activity

Go to www.sfsocialstudies.com/activities to learn more about our country long ago.

242

Practice and Extend

✓ Performance Assessment

- The Unit Project can also be used as a performance assessment activity.
- Use the scoring guide to assess each group's work.

Children can launch the activity by clicking on *Grade 2, Unit 5* at **www.sfsocialstudies.com/activities**.

Workbook, p. 59

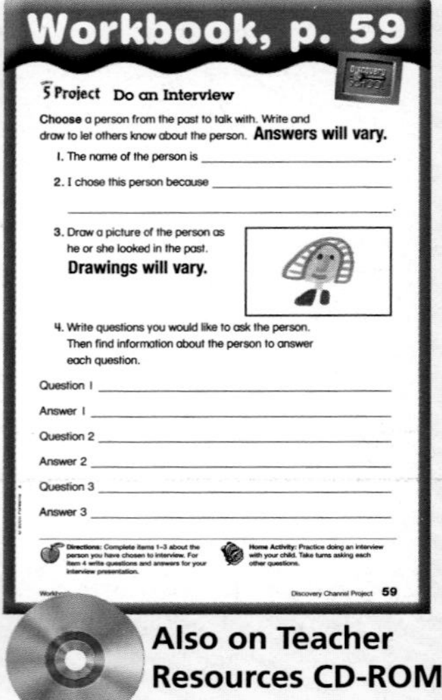
5 Project Do an Interview

Choose a person from the past to talk with. Write and draw to let others know about the person. **Answers will vary.**

1. The name of the person is ______
2. I chose this person because ______
3. Draw a picture of the person as he or she looked in the past. **Drawings will vary.**
4. Write questions you would like to ask the person. Then find information about the person to answer each question.

Question 1 ______
Answer 1 ______
Question 2 ______
Answer 2 ______
Question 3 ______
Answer 3 ______

Discovery Channel Project 59

Also on Teacher Resources CD-ROM.

People and Places in History

UNIT 6

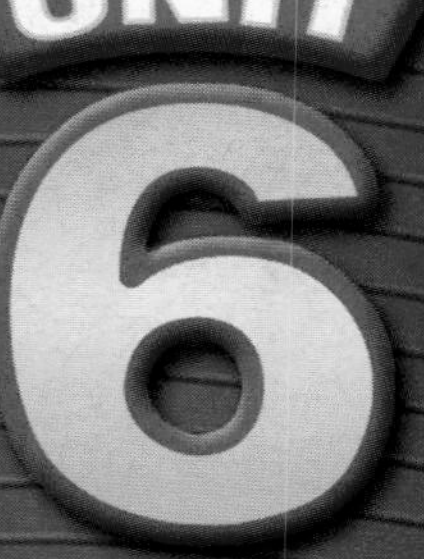

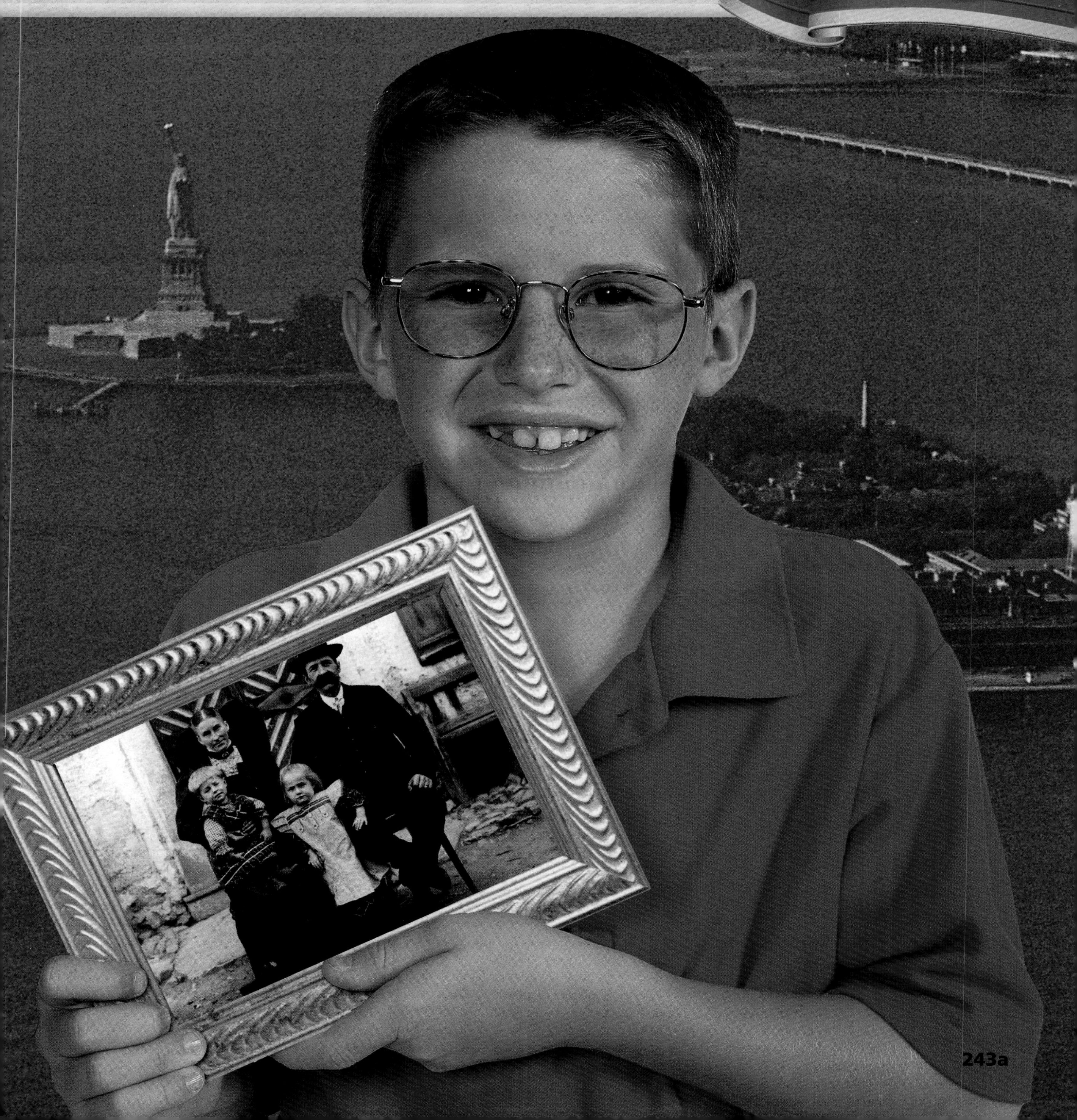

UNIT 6

Unit 6 Planning Guide

People and Places in History

Begin with a Song pp. 244–245 **Vocabulary Preview** pp. 246–247

Target Skill **Reading Social Studies, Recall and Retell** pp. 248–249

Lesson Titles	Pacing	Main Ideas
Lesson 1 **Family History** pp. 250–253 **Citizen Heroes: Courage Ellen Ochoa** pp. 254–255	2 days	• Many immigrants, hoping for a better way of life, entered the United States through Ellis Island and Angel Island. • Ellen Ochoa, the first Hispanic woman in space, exemplifies courage in action.
Lesson 2 **People Celebrate** pp. 256–259 DK **Spring** pp. 260–261 **Chart and Graph Skills: Read a Calendar** pp. 262–263	3 days	• Holidays mark important events from the past; customs people follow link generations within a family. • People all around the world celebrate spring. • Calendars help people mark time.
Lesson 3 **Landmarks in Our Country** pp. 264–267 **Biography: Ieoh Ming Pei** pp. 268–269 **Here and There: Landmarks Around the World** pp. 270–271	3 days	• Important local and national landmarks tell about our country's past. • I. M. Pei, a Chinese-American architect, creates new landmarks. • Landmarks in ancient China and Egypt tell about their past.
Lesson 4 **A Step Back in Time** pp. 272–275 **Chart and Graph Skills: Read a Diagram** pp. 276–277	2 days	• Artifacts give important clues as to how people lived their daily lives in the past. Inventions make life easier and more comfortable for people. • Diagrams are pictures that give information in a succinct way.
Lesson 5 **Linking Our World** pp. 278–281 **Biography: Robert Fulton** pp. 282–283	2 days	• Science and technology change ways people communicate and ways they travel and move goods. • Robert Fulton's steamboat enabled people, as well as goods, to move more quickly along waterways.

✓ **End with a Folktale** pp. 284–285 ✓ **Unit 6 Review** pp. 286–289 ✓ **Unit 6 Project** p. 290

✓ = Assessment Options

Scott Foresman Social Studies Indiana Academic Standards

Grade 2 Unit 6 • *People and Places in History*

Lesson Title	Indiana Academic Standards Social Studies
Lesson 1 Family History pp. 250-253	**IN Academic Standard 2.5.5** Identify people of different backgrounds and explain how they contribute to the community. **(Also 2.1.1, 2.1.2)**
Citizen Heroes: Ellen Ochoa pp. 254-255	**Reviews IN Academic Standard K.1.3** Listen to and retell stories about people who showed honesty, courage, and responsibility.
Lesson 2 People Celebrate pp. 256-259	**IN Academic Standard 2.1.4** Explain the meaning of community celebrations and traditions. **(Also 2.1.5, 2.5.3, 2.5.5)**
Spring pp. 260-261	**IN Academic Standard 2.1.4** Explain the meaning of community celebrations and traditions. **(Also 2.5.3)**
Chart and Graph Skills: Read a Calendar pp. 262-263	**Reviews IN Academic Standard K.1.2** Identify celebrations and holidays remembering and honoring events and people.
Lesson 3 Landmarks in Our Country pp. 264-267	**IN Academic Standard 2.3.4** Identify places that are nearby or related to the local community. **(Also 2.3.2)**
Biography: Ieoh M. Pei pp. 268-269	**IN Academic Standard 2.5.5** Identify people of different backgrounds and explain how they contribute to the community.
Here and There: Landmarks Around the World pp. 270-271	**Previews IN Academic Standard 3.5.5** Use resources to gather cultural information.
Lesson 4 A Step Back in Time pp. 272-275	**IN Academic Standard 2.3.7** Identify ways that the physical environment influences human activities.
Chart and Graph Skills: Read a Diagram pp. 276-277	**IN Academic Standard 2.4.5** Explain that people must make choices and incur opportunity costs.
Lesson 5 Linking Our World pp. 278-281	**IN Academic Standard 2.5.4** Explain how changes in technology have influenced traditions. **(Also 2.1.1)**
Biography: Robert Fulton pp. 282-283	**IN Academic Standard 2.3.3** Locate the local community and the U.S.

Insert between pages 243b - 243c
For complete standards listing, please see front tab.

Continued on other side →

Scott Foresman Social Studies to the Indiana Academic Standards for English/Language Arts

Grade 2 Unit 6 • *People and Places in History*

Lesson Title	Indiana Academic Standards English/Language Arts
Begin with a Song, pp. 244-245 *Vocabulary Preview, pp. 246-247* *Reading Social Studies, Recall and Retell, pp. 248-249*	**2.7.8** Retell stories, including characters, setting, and plot. See also 2.1.2, 2.1.3, 2.1.5, 2.2.2, 2.2.4, 2.2.7
Lesson 1 Family History, pp. 250-253	**2.7.8** Retell stories, including characters, setting, and plot. See also 2.1.2, 2.1.3, 2.1.5, 2.2.2, 2.2.4, 2.2.7
Citizen Heroes: Ellen Ochoa, pp. 254-255	**2.2.5** Restate facts and details in the text to clarify and organize ideas. See also 2.1.2, 2.1.3, 2.1.5, 2.2.2, 2.2.3, 2.2.4, 2.2.7, 2.5.6, 2.7.8
Lesson 2 People Celebrate, pp. 256-259	**2.2.7** Interpret information from diagrams, charts, and graphs. See also 2.2.2, 2.2.4, 2.7.8
DK Spring, pp. 260-261	**2.7.8** Retell stories, including characters, setting, and plot. See also 2.1.2, 2.1.3, 2.1.5, 2.2.2, 2.2.4
Chart and Graph Skills: Read a Calendar, pp. 262-263	**2.2.7** Interpret information from diagrams, charts, and graphs. See also 2.2.2, 2.2.4, 2.7.8
Lesson 3 Landmarks in Our Country, pp. 264-267	**2.2.7** Interpret information from diagrams, charts, and graphs. See also 2.1.2, 2.1.3, 2.1.5, 2.2.2, 2.2.4, 2.2.8, 2.7.8
Biography: I. M. Pei, pp. 268-269	**2.2.7** Interpret information from diagrams, charts, and graphs. See also 2.1.2, 2.1.3, 2.1.5, 2.2.2, 2.2.4
Here and There: Landmarks Around the World, pp. 270-271	**2.7.8** Retell stories, including characters, setting, and plot. See also 2.1.2, 2.1.3, 2.1.5, 2.2.2, 2.2.4, 2.2.7
Lesson 4 A Step Back in Time, pp. 272-275	**2.7.8** Retell stories, including characters, setting, and plot. See also 2.1.2, 2.1.3, 2.1.5, 2.2.2, 2.2.4, 2.2.7
Chart and Graph Skills: Read a Diagram, pp. 276-277	**2.2.7** Interpret information from diagrams, charts, and graphs. See also 2.1.2, 2.1.3, 2.1.5, 2.2.2, 2.2.4
Lesson 5 Linking Our World, pp. 278-281	**2.2.5** Restate facts and details in the text to clarify and organize ideas. See also 2.1.2, 2.1.3, 2.1.5, 2.2.2, 2.2.3, 2.2.4, 2.5.6, 2.7.8
Biography: Robert Fulton, pp. 282-283	**2.7.8** Retell stories, including characters, setting, and plot. See also 2.1.2, 2.1.3, 2.1.5, 2.2.2, 2.2.4, 2.5.6
End with a Folktale, pp. 284-285 *Unit 6 Review, pp. 286-289* *Unit 6 Project, p. 290*	**2.3.2** Create different endings to stories and identify the reason and the impact of the different ending. See also 2.1.2, 2.1.3, 2.2.7, 2.7.8

Vocabulary	Resources	Meeting Individual Needs
immigrant	• Workbook, p. 62 • Transparency 8 • Vocabulary Card: immigrant • Every Student Learns Guide, pp. 102–105	• ESL Support, TE p. 252 • Leveled Practice, TE p. 255a
holiday **custom**	• Workbook, pp. 63–64 • Transparencies 9, 34, 35 • Vocabulary Cards: holiday, custom • Every Student Learns Guide, pp. 106–109	• ESL Support, TE pp. 258 • Learning Styles, TE p. 263a
landmark	• Workbook, p. 65 • Vocabulary Card: landmark • Every Student Learns Guide, pp. 110–113	• ESL Support, TE p. 266 • Leveled Practice, TE p. 271a
artifact **invention**	• Workbook, pp. 66–67 • Transparencies 8, 36 • Vocabulary Cards: artifact, invention • Every Student Learns Guide, pp. 114–117	• ESL Support, TE p. 274 • Leveled Practice, TE p. 277a
communication	• Workbook, p. 68 • Vocabulary Card: communication • Every Student Learns Guide, pp. 118–121	• ESL Support, TE p. 279 • Leveled Practice, TE p. 283a

Providing More Depth

Multimedia Library

- ***Technology* by Roger Bridgman**
- ***Watch the Stars Come Out* by Diane Goode**
- **Songs and Music**
- **Video Field Trips**
- **Software**

Additional Resources

- Family Activities
- Vocabulary Cards
- Daily Activity Bank
- Social Studies Plus!
- Big Book Atlas
- Outline Maps
- Desk Maps

ADDITIONAL Technology

- AudioText
- The test maker
- Teacher Resources CD-ROM
- Map Resources CD-ROM
- **www.sfsocialstudies.com**

To establish guidelines for children's safe and responsible use of the Internet, use the **Scott Foresman Internet Guide.**

Additional Internet Links
To find out more about:

- Ellis Island, visit **www.ellisisland.org**
- The Great Wall of China, visit **www.pbs.org**

Key Internet Search Terms

- immigration
- ancient civilizations

Unit 6 Objectives

Beginning of Unit 6

(pp. 244–245)

- **Obtain information about a topic by using oral sources, such as songs.** (pp. 244–245)
- **Obtain information about a topic by using visual sources, such as pictures.** (pp. 246–247)
- **Determine the meanings of words.** (pp. 246–247)
- **Summarize by recalling and retelling information in a logical sequence.** (pp. 248–249)

Lesson 1
Family History pp. 250–253

- **Explain that the United States is a land of poeple who have diverse ethnic origins.**
- **Name several sources of information about a given period or event.**
- **Identify characteristics of good citizenship.** (pp. 254–255)

Lesson 2
People Celebrate pp. 256–259

- **Explain how selected customs and celebrations reflect an Ameican love of individualism, inventiveness, and freedom.**
- **Obtain information about a topic using visual sources such as photographs.** (pp. 260–261)
- **Identify examples of the local cultural heritage.** (pp. 260–261)
- **Describe and measure calendar time.** (pp. 262–263)

Lesson 3
Landmarks in Our Country
pp. 264–267

- **Identify and explain the significance of various community, state, and national landmarks.**
- **Explain how people influence communities.** (pp. 268–269)
- **Use designations of time periods such as ancient times and modern times.** (pp. 270–271)
- **Locate Egypt and China on a world map.** (pp. 270–271)

Lesson 4
A Step Back in Time pp. 272–275

- **Explain how the contributions of China and Egypt have influenced the present world in terms of architecture, inventions, the calendar, and written language.**
- **Obtain information about a topic using a diagram.** (pp. 276–277)

Lesson 5
Linking Our World pp. 278–281

- **Use vocabulary related to chronology, including *past, present,* and *future*.**
- **Describe how science and technology have changed communication and transportation.**
- **Identify historic figures who have exhibited a love of individualism and inventiveness.**
- **Identify how Robert Fulton exhibited a love of inventiveness.** (pp. 282–283)

End of Unit 6

- **Explain the significance of selected stories of the local cultural heritage.** (pp. 284–285)

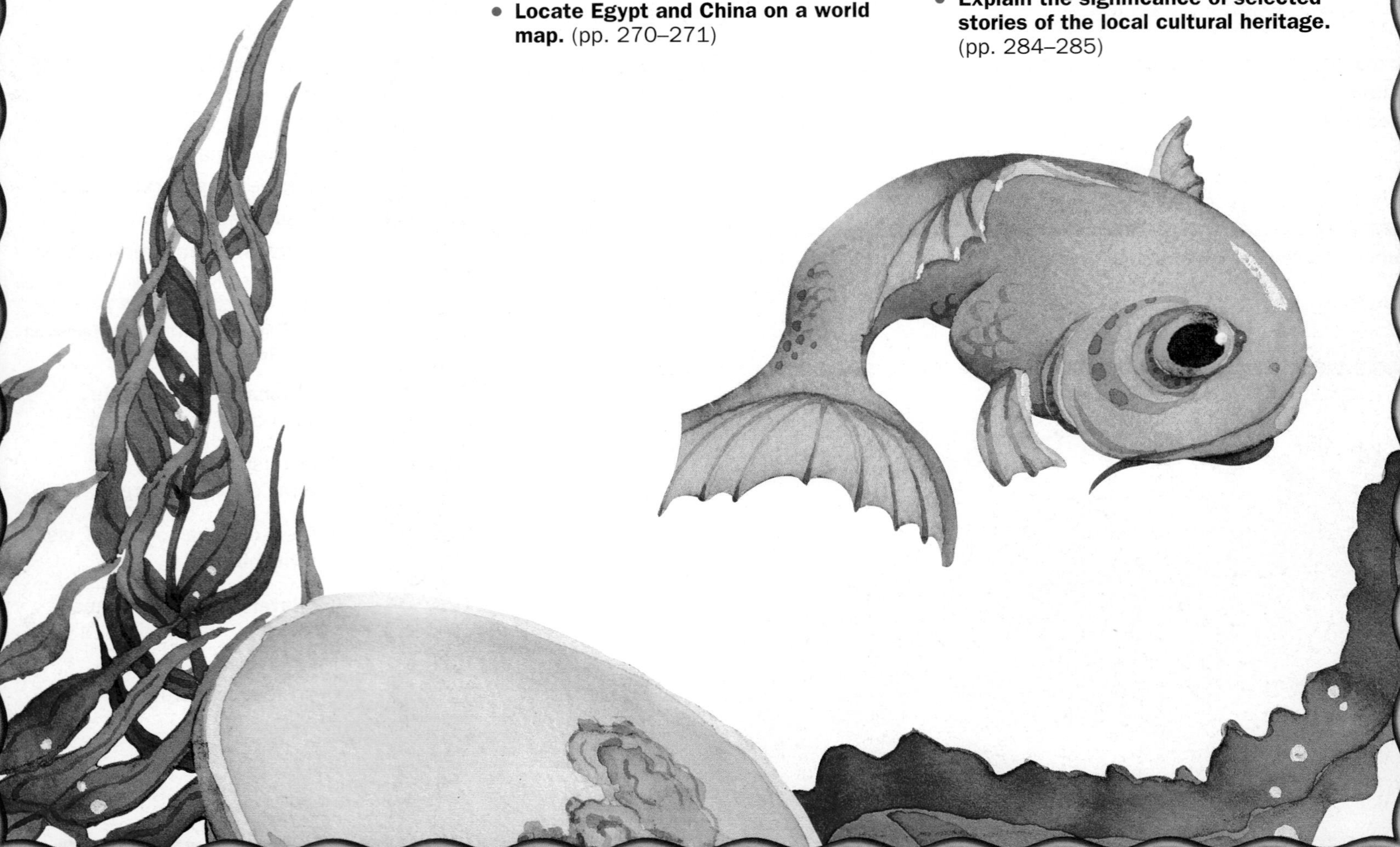

Assessment Options

✓ Formal Assessment

- **What did you learn?** PE/TE pp. 253, 259, 267, 275, 281
- **Unit Review,** PE/TE pp. 286-289
- **Unit 6 Tests, Assessment Book,** pp. 17–20
- **The test maker,** (test generator software)

✓ Informal Assessment

- **Teacher's Edition Questions,** throughout Lessons and Features
- **Close and Assess,** TE pp. 249, 253, 255, 259, 263, 267, 269, 271, 275, 277, 281, 283, 285
- **Try it!** PE/TE pp. 249, 263, 277
- **Think and Share,** PE/TE pp. 253, 259, 267, 269, 275, 281, 283, 289
- **Courage in Action,** PE/TE p. 255
- **Hands-on History,** PE/TE p. 271

Ongoing Assessment

Ongoing Assessment is found throughout the Teacher's Edition lessons using an **If...then** model.

If = students' observable behavior,	**then =** reteaching and enrichment suggestions

✓ Portfolio Assessment

- **Portfolio Assessment,** TE pp. 243, 288
- **Leveled Practice,** TE pp. 246, 255a, 271a, 277a, 283a
- **Learning Styles,** TE p. 263a
- **Workbook,** pp. 60–70
- **Unit Review: Skills on Your Own,** PE/TE p. 288
- **Curriculum Connection: Writing,** TE pp. 245, 253, 262, 271a, 277a, 283, 283a, 285

✓ Performance Assessment

- **Hands-on Unit Project** (Unit 6 Performance Assessment), PE/TE pp. 243, 290
- **Internet Activity,** PE p. 290
- **Unit Review: Think and Share,** PE/TE p. 289
- **Scoring Guides,** TE pp. 287, 288

Test Talk

Test-Taking Strategies

Understand the Question

- **Locate Key Words in the Question,** TE p. 258
- **Locate Key Words in the Text,** TE p. 279

Understand the Answer

- **Choose the Right Answer,** Test Talk Practice Book
- **Use Information from the Text,** TE p. 255
- **Use Information from Graphics,** TE p. 271
- **Write Your Answer,** TE p. 275

For additional practice, use the Test Talk Practice Book.

Featured Strategy

Write Your Answer

Children will:

– Make sure their answer is correct.

– Make sure their answer is complete.

PE/TE p. 288, **TE** p. 275

Curriculum Connections

Integrating Your Day

The lessons, skills, and features of Unit 6 provide many opportunities to make connections between social studies and other areas of the elementary curriculum.

Reading

Reading Skill—Recall and Retell, PE/TE pp. 248-249, TE p. 250

Word Families, p. 255a

Reading Skill—Put Things in Order (Sequence), TE p. 256

Word Accordions, p. 263a

Reading Skill—Classify/Categorize, TE p. 264

About Being an Architect, TE p. 269

Two Words in One, TE p. 271a

Hieroglyph Messages, TE p. 273

Word Search, TE p. 277a

Reading Skill—Compare and Contrast, TE p. 278

Extend Vocabulary, TE p. 283a

The Ups and Downs of Flight, TE p. 283a

Math

Time Lines, TE p. 259

A New Calendar, TE p. 277a

Writing

Write a Poem, TE p. 245

Welcome Signs, TE p. 253

Play a Game, TE p. 262

Ode to a Landmark, TE p. 271a

Let's Find Out!, TE p. 277a

Name a Steamboat, TE p. 283

Communicate in Code, TE p. 283a

A New Story Ending, TE p. 285

Social Studies

Literature

More to Read, TE p. 275

Read About People and Places in History, PE/TE p. 289

Science

Seasons of the Year, TE p. 263

Make a Diagram, TE p. 276

Music/Drama

Sing a Song, TE p. 249

On Stage! TE p. 255a

Perform a Skit, TE p. 284

Art

Liberty on Parade, TE p. 255a

Picturing Spring Celebrations, TE p. 261

Holiday Greeting Cards, TE p. 263a

Design the Perfect School, TE p. 268

Inside a Pyramid, TE p. 271

Be a Builder, TE p. 271a

Draw a Steamboat, TE p. 282

Look for this symbol throughout the Teacher's Edition to find **Curriculum Connections.**

Professional Development

Real-World Knowledge and Authentic Assessment

by Dr. James B. Kracht
Texas A & M University

New state and national standards demand the use of authentic assessment techniques to determine how well students master complex real-world tasks. Alternative assessment techniques should be used along with traditional assessment techniques for effective and efficient assessment of student learning. Although the design of authentic assessment tools requires some special knowledge and skills, classroom teachers can develop this expertise through reading, professional development, and practice.

Assessing Knowledge and Skills Through a Performance Task

A performance task is a scenario that provides students with an opportunity to demonstrate what they know and are able to do based on key ideas of the unit.

End-of-unit performance assessments appear on pp. 48, 96, 146, 194, 242, and 290 of this Teacher's Edition. Take a look at the performance assessment for this unit on p. 290.

My Hero *Children use what they have learned about people they have read about in the unit—Robert Fulton (inventor), I.M. Pei (contemporary architect), Ellen Ochoa (astronaut), and the many immigrants who came to this country—and their prior knowledge to define what a hero is. With that base, they then choose a personal hero, talk about him or her, and create a tangible tribute.*

ESL Support

Extend Language: The Nature of Academic Language

by Jim Cummins, Ph. D.
University of Toronto

In order to understand how to extend students' grasp of academic language and how to use language powerfully, it is important to distinguish the following three very different aspects proficiency in language:

- *Conversational fluency*
- *Discreet language skill*
- *Academic language proficiency*

The development of academic language proficiency, for both ESL and non-ESL students, requires specific instructional strategies designed to enable students to harvest the language they encounter in the content areas.

The following examples from the Teacher's Edition demonstrate strategies for exploring and extending language.

Courage, *TE p. 258 Children relate the key word* courage *to the more familiar word* brave. *They also are introduced to the related word* courageous.

Inventions, *TE p. 274 The key concept word* inventions *is explored through examples familiar to children. They demonstrate by writing their understanding of how inventions benefit people and how inventions can be improved.*

Read Aloud

Our History

by Catherine Cate Coblentz

Our history sings of centuries
Such varying songs it sings!
It starts with winds, slow moving sails,
It ends with skies and wings.

Build Background

- Talk with children about how people from other countries came in the past to America. Encourage children to describe those sailing ships and to comment on how long it took to make the journey.
- Talk with children about how people travel today to go long distances.

Read Alouds and Primary Sources

Read Alouds and Primary Sources contains additional selections to be used with Unit 6.

Bibliography

Grandfather's Journey, by Allen Say (Houghton Mifflin, ISBN 0-395-57035-2, 1993) Both the narrator and the grandfather want to return to Japan, but when they do they feel out of place. **Easy** ***Caldecott Medal Winner***

Peppe the Lamplighter, by Elisa Bartone and Ted Lewin (Illustrator) (Mulberry Books, ISBN 0-688-15469-7, 1997) Times are hard for Peppe and his family who live in Little Italy in New York City. Peppe is grateful to take the place of the street lamp lighter. **Easy** ***Caldecott Honor Book***

Dreaming of America: An Ellis Island Story, by Eve Bunting and Ben F. Stahl (Illustrator) (Troll, ISBN 0-816-76521-9, 2001) IRA Teachers' Choice. **On-Level**

Real McCoy, The: The Life of an African American Inventor, by Wendy Towle and Wil Clay (Illustrator) (Scholastic Paperbacks, ISBN 0-590-48102-9, 1995) **On-Level**

Rushmore, by Lynn Curlee (Scholastic, ISBN 0-590-22573-1, 1999) **On-Level** ***Notable Social Studies Book***

Freedom's Gifts: A Juneteenth Story, by Valerie Wilson Wesley and Sharon Wilson (Illustrator) (Simon & Schuster, ISBN 0-689-80269-2, 1997) Cousins learn to appreciate the meaning of the Texas Juneteenth holiday. **Challenge** ***Notable Social Studies Book***

Through the Eyes of Your Ancestors, by Maureen Taylor (Houghton Mifflin, ISBN 0-395-86982-X, 1999) This book can help children get to know their ancestors. **Challenge**

Keepsakes: Using Family Stories in Elementary Classrooms, by Linda Winston (Heinemann, ISBN 0-435-07235-8, 1997) This book demonstrates how elementary teachers can draw on family stories. **Teacher Reference**

Discovery Channel School* Videos *Landmarks of Civilization. Visit the landmarks built by people on three continents—the Great Wall of China, Pueblo Bonito, and castles on the Rhine; 26 minutes.

Look for this symbol throughout the Teacher's Edition to find **Award-Winning Selections**. Additional book references are suggested throughout this unit.

Practice and Extend

✓ **Unit 6 Performance Assessment**

- The Unit 6 Project, *My Hero* on p. 290, is a performance assessment project to enrich children's learning throughout the unit.
- This project, which has children describe the qualities and accomplishments of a hero, may be started now or at any time during this unit of study.
- A performance assessment scoring guide is on p. 290.

People and Places in History

Unit Overview

In this unit, children will learn about immigrants and how they contribute to the United States. Children will begin to understand how holidays, landmarks, and artifacts tell about the past. Finally, children will read about how communication and transportation link people.

Introduce Michael

Read the unit title and introduce the featured child for this unit as a second grader named Michael. Focus children's attention on the photographs on the page. Have children say who they think the people in the photos are.

Unit Question

- Ask children the question on this page.
- Encourage children to express their ideas about the importance of learning about the past.
- Have children suggest some things other than photos that can help them learn about the past.

✓ **Portfolio Assessment** As children discuss the unit question, jot down their responses on chart paper. Keep a copy of the list for the Portfolio Assessment at the end of the unit.

We Share History

Objective

- Obtain information about a topic using oral sources, such as music.

Resources

- Poster 11
- Social Studies Plus!
- *Songs and Music* CD "We Share History"

Introduce the Song

Preview Tell children they will sing a song about ways in which people can learn about history, or things that happened in the past.

Warm Up To activate prior knowledge, ask children to identify some things their families may have in their homes that tell about the past. Help children mention photos, paintings, old books, furniture that may have been passed down within the family, keepsake letters, and legal documents such as birth certificates.

Sing the Song

- Sing the song once and then have children sing "We Share History."
- Have children tell about an event from their past—their first day of school, games they played as three- or four-year-olds, or a special time spent with a grandparent.

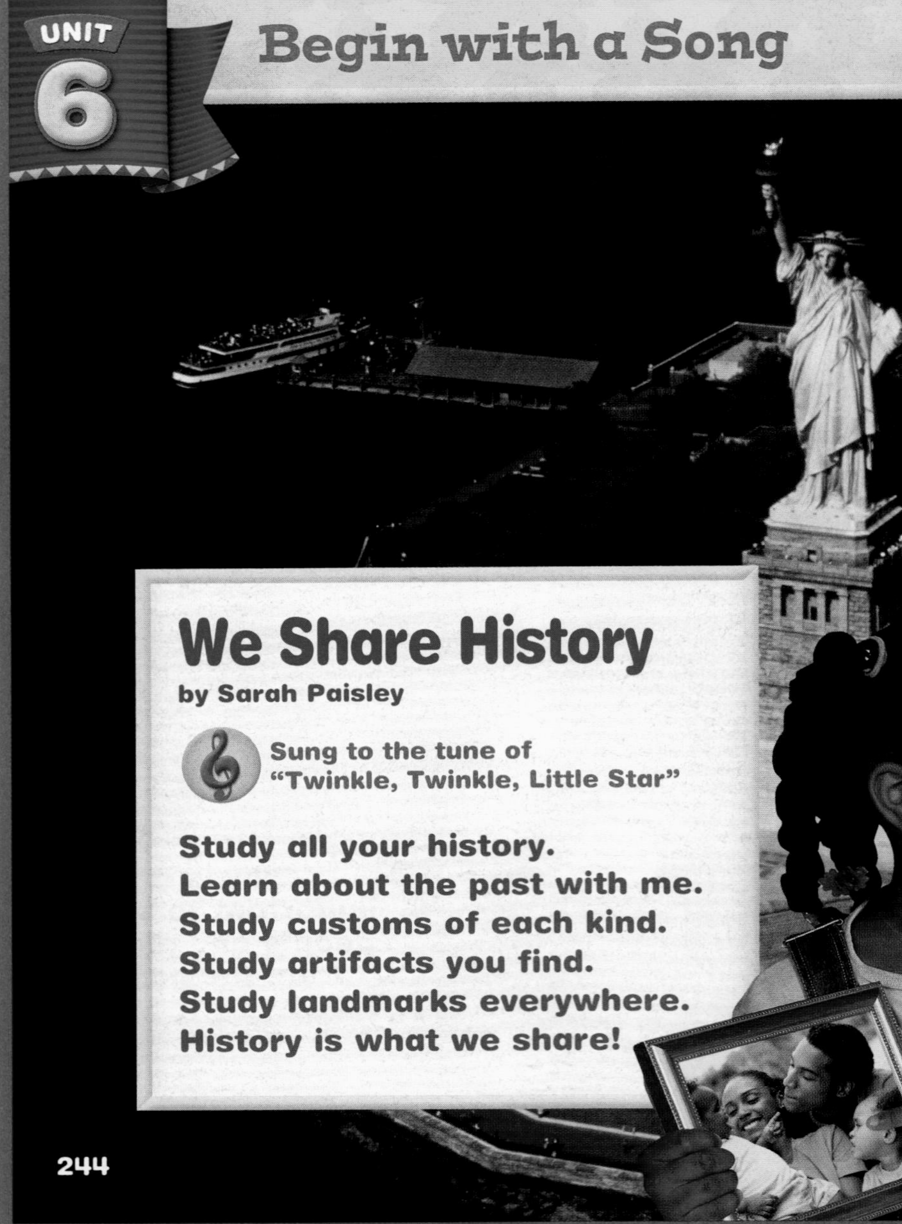

Practice and Extend

SOCIAL STUDIES STRAND
Geography

Where Our Families Came From

- Call on volunteers from among children who are recent arrivals in this country to identify their country of origin. Make a list.
- Recall the meaning of *ancestor* and then invite others in the class to say where they think their ancestors came from. Add those country names to the list.
- Use colorful stick pins to help children locate the countries from the list on a world map.
- Help children name the continents on which the countries are located.

Talk About the Pictures

Talk briefly with children about the photographs the youngsters in the picture are holding. Ask if they think the photos show the present or the past, and why.

1 **Why do you think photographs are good sources of information about the past?** Possible answer: Photos show many different things at once—how people dressed, what kind of transportation they used, how the streets and buildings looked. Some photos look modern while others may look old-fashioned or historic. **Evaluate**

2 **Besides old photos that people have at home, where else can you look at photos showing the past?** Possible answers: In old newspapers and books in the library; at the museum **Draw Conclusions**

CURRICULUM CONNECTION
Writing

Write a Poem

- Reread the lyrics to "We Share History."
- Have children write two- or four-line poems telling what history is to them.
- Plan a time for children to share their poems orally.

AUDIO CD
Technology

Play the CD, *Songs and Music,* to listen to "We Share History."

Vocabulary Preview

Objectives

- Use pictures to learn about a topic.
- Determine the meanings of words.

Resources

- Workbook, p. 60
- Vocabulary Cards
- Poster 12

Introduce the Vocabulary

Read aloud and point to each vocabulary word and the photograph illustrating it. Have volunteers give the meanings of the words, as they are able. Then have children find examples of the vocabulary words in the illustration. Write these examples on the board.

Vocabulary Word	Illustrated Examples
immigrant	Each person shown leaving the ship in America
holiday	Signs for Heritage Festival and July 4th parade
custom	People of different cultures performing
landmark	Statue of Liberty, Ellis Island
artifact	Pottery, moccasins
invention	Watch, book
communication	Cell phone, microphone, loudspeaker

SOCIAL STUDIES STRAND
Culture

Listed below are some basic ideas about culture. Develop these ideas as you discuss the illustration.

- The United States is a country of people from diverse cultures.
- People of different cultures and traditions contribute to the community, state, and nation.
- American customs and symbols, such as July 4th parades and the Statue of Liberty, contribute to our country's national identity.

Practice and Extend

Join the Festivities

Invite children to use the illustration to join in on the Heritage Festival.

Easy Lead children through the festival, moving across the top of the pages, then the middle of the pages, and lastly the bottom of the pages. Use the new vocabulary words as you talk about things shown. **Reteach**

On-Level Have volunteers choose one center of activity in the illustration to talk about. Have them use appropriate new vocabulary words. **Extend**

Challenge Give children individual new vocabulary words. Have them locate and talk about the portion of the illustration that relates to each word. **Enrich**

Talk About the Picture

Allow children time to study the picture. Read the signs with them, explaining the meaning of *heritage* (something that is handed down from earlier generations or the past). Talk briefly about the different kinds of clothing children see people wearing in the illustration.

1 A festival is a happy event, a celebration. What are people doing that lets you know they are happy? Possible answers: Dancing, singing, parading **Draw Conclusions**

2 What invention do you see in the exhibit booth that helps people tell time? Watch **What artifact is a kind of covering for the foot?** Moccasin **Analyze Pictures**

Look Ahead

Tell children that they will learn more about each of these words as they study Unit 6.

You may want to revisit the picture with children to review the concepts and vocabulary in the unit.

3 Why do you think some people are painting a picture of immigrants coming to America? Possible answer: Immigrants bring their customs and traditions **Make Inferences**

4 What holiday parade is the man in the ticket booth selling tickets for? July 4th parade **Analyze Pictures**

You can look up vocabulary words online. Click on *Social Studies Library* and select the dictionary at **www.sfsocialstudies.com.**

Workbook, p. 60

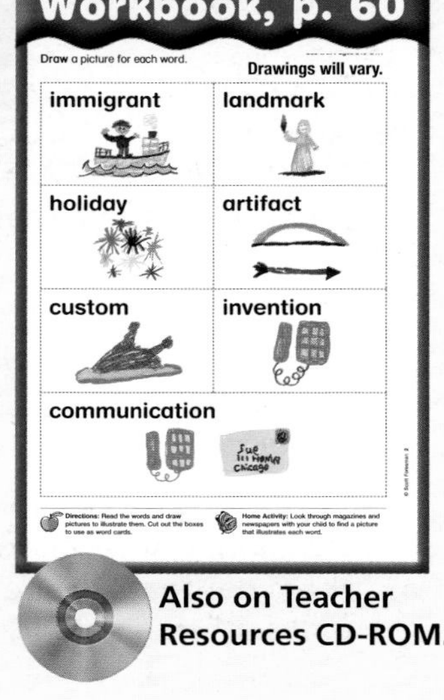

Draw a picture for each word.

Drawings will vary.

immigrant	landmark
holiday	artifact
custom	invention
communication	

Also on Teacher Resources CD-ROM.

Michael's Family History

Recall and Retell

Objective

Summarize by recalling and retelling information in a logical sequence.

Resource

- Workbook, p. 61

About the Unit Target Skill

- The target reading skill for this unit is Recall and Retell. Children are introduced to the unit target skill here and are given an opportunity to practice it.
- Further opportunities to recall and retell are found throughout Unit 6.

1 Introduce and Motivate

Preview To determine if children understand the concept of recalling and retelling, call on several children to recall and retell a story the class shared or a familiar folktale. Have children listen to and compare each other's versions.

Warm Up To activate prior knowledge, ask children to tell what they do when they tell a friend about a story they have read or a television show they have seen. Do children try to repeat every word from the book or show, or do they just tell the most important ideas? Ask them why. Children should be aware that it would take too long to repeat exactly what happened.

UNIT 6 Reading Social Studies

Michael's Family History

Recall and Retell

Target Skill

I wrote a story about my family. Read my story to find out what it is about.

Hi! I'm Michael.

My Family History

My family has a history, or story of the past. I was born in the United States. My parents and grandparents were born here too. My great-grandparents were born in a small town in Germany.

My great-grandparents came to America in 1920, more than 80 years ago! They went to live in Detroit, Michigan. My great-grandpa bought his own bakery. My grandpa and dad now run the bakery. Someday I hope to run the bakery too.

Practice and Extend

ESL EXTEND LANGUAGE

ESL Support

Focus on *Recall* Make a drawing on the board to link *recall* and *remember* with the phrase *think back.*

think back
recall ⟷ remember

Beginning Ask children to think back in order to remember or recall something they did yesterday. Have them pantomime the action. Help children complete an oral sentence such as: *I recall that I played ball.*

Intermediate Have children draw a picture of something they did yesterday and write a sentence, including the word *recall,* below the picture as a caption.

Advanced Have children recall two other things they did yesterday and write to tell about them. Encourage the use of *recall* and *remember* in their sentences.

Recalling is thinking about something you have read or heard. **Retelling** is putting it into your own words. Think about Michael's family history. Tell the story in your own words.

This is a picture of my grandpa, my dad, and me.

Try it!

Fold a piece of paper in half from side to side. Now fold it from side to side again. Open your paper and draw four things that happened in "My Family History." Draw them in the order they happened. Use your pictures to **retell** the story of Michael's family.

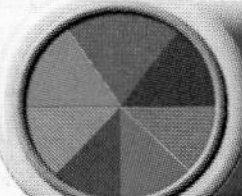

CURRICULUM CONNECTION
Music

Sing a Song

- Ask children to think back to recall how to sing a favorite song, such as "If You're Happy and You Know It" or "Row, Row, Row Your Boat."
- Have children collaborate to get the words in correct sequence for you to write.
- Have children sing the song with you.

Workbook, p. 61

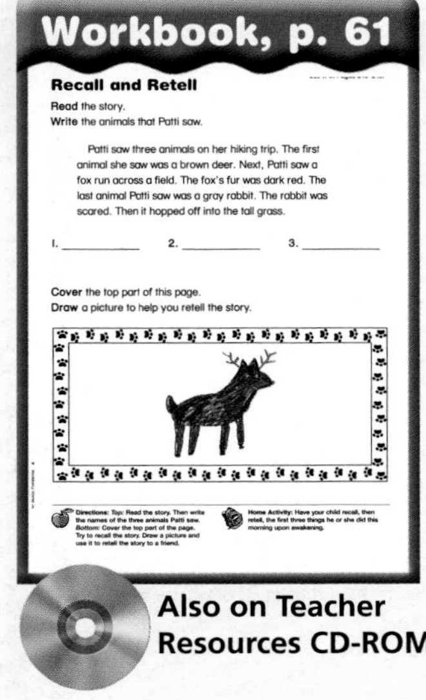

Recall and Retell

Read the story.
Write the animals that Patti saw.

Patti saw three animals on her hiking trip. The first animal she saw was a brown deer. Next, Patti saw a fox run across a field. The fox's fur was dark red. The last animal Patti saw was a gray rabbit. The rabbit was scared. Then it hopped off into the tall grass.

1. ________ 2. ________ 3. ________

Cover the top part of this page.
Draw a picture to help you retell the story.

Directions: *Top:* Read the story. Then write the names of the three animals Patti saw. *Bottom:* Cover the top part of the page. Try to recall the story. Draw a picture and use it to retell the story to a friend.

Home Activity: Have your child recall, then retell, the first three things he or she did this morning upon awakening.

Also on Teacher Resources CD-ROM.

2 Teach and Discuss

Read pp. 248 and 249 with children. Help them notice that Michael tells his family history in the order in which it happened. Point out clues such as "more than 80 years ago," "now," "Someday."

Tell children it is easier to recall what happened and then retell the information if they think about order.

Help children associate the term *retelling* with events that have already happened, or events from the past.

3 Close and Assess

Try it!

Observe children as they make their four-part pictures. Offer assistance with folding as needed. Guide children who need help to put their events in a logical sequence.

Suggest that children repeat the activity at home. They can retell events from their family's history.

Workbook Support

Use the following Workbook pages to support content and skills development as you teach Unit 6. You can also view and print Workbook pages from the Teacher Resources CD-ROM.

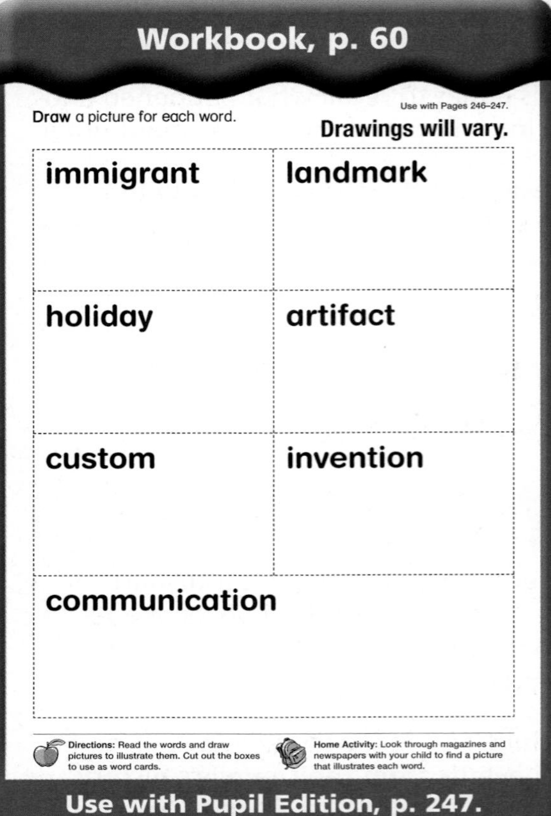

Workbook, p. 60

Use with Pages 246–247.

Draw a picture for each word. **Drawings will vary.**

immigrant	landmark
holiday	artifact
custom	invention
communication	

Directions: Read the words and draw pictures to illustrate them. Cut out the boxes to use as word cards.

Home Activity: Look through magazines and newspapers with your child to find a picture that illustrates each word.

Use with Pupil Edition, p. 247.

Workbook, p. 61

Use with Pages 248–249.

Recall and Retell

Read the story.
Write the animals that Patti saw.

Patti saw three animals on her hiking trip. The first animal she saw was a brown deer. Next, Patti saw a fox run across a field. The fox's fur was dark red. The last animal Patti saw was a gray rabbit. The rabbit was scared. Then it hopped off into the tall grass.

1. deer 2. fox 3. rabbit

Cover the top part of this page.
Draw a picture to help you retell the story. **Drawings will vary.**

Directions: *Top:* Read the story. Then write the names of the three animals Patti saw. *Bottom:* Cover the top part of the page. Try to recall the story. Draw a picture and use it to retell the story to a friend.

Home Activity: Have your child recall, then retell, the first three things he or she did this morning upon awakening.

Use with Pupil Edition, p. 249.

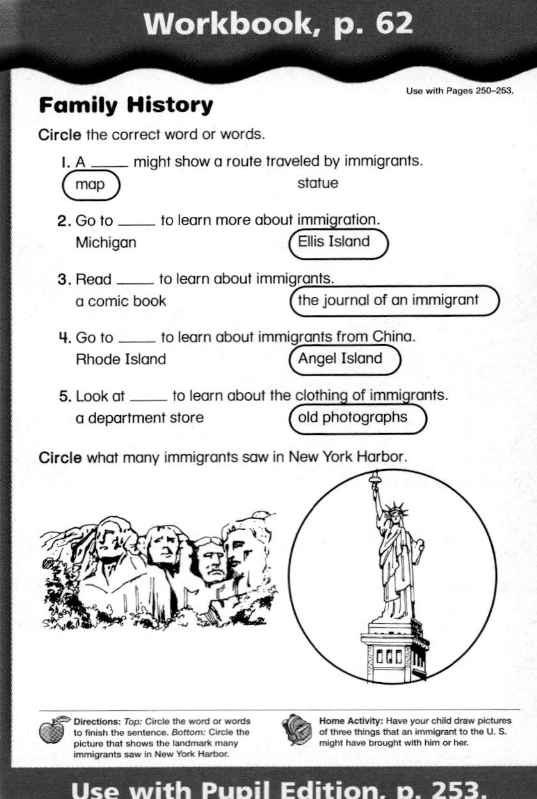

Workbook, p. 62

Use with Pages 250–253.

Family History

Circle the correct word or words.

1. A ____ might show a route traveled by immigrants.
   (map) statue
2. Go to ____ to learn more about immigration.
   Michigan (Ellis Island)
3. Read ____ to learn about immigrants.
   a comic book (the journal of an immigrant)
4. Go to ____ to learn about immigrants from China.
   Rhode Island (Angel Island)
5. Look at ____ to learn about the clothing of immigrants.
   a department store (old photographs)

Circle what many immigrants saw in New York Harbor.

Directions: *Top:* Circle the word or words to finish the sentence. *Bottom:* Circle the picture that shows the landmark many immigrants saw in New York Harbor.

Home Activity: Have your child draw pictures of three things that an immigrant to the U. S. might have brought with him or her.

Use with Pupil Edition, p. 253.

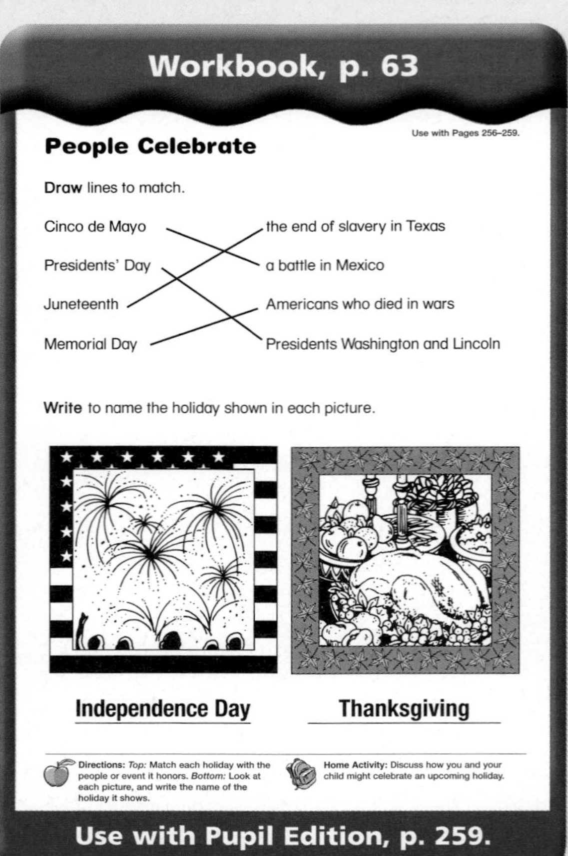

Workbook, p. 63

Use with Pages 256–259.

People Celebrate

Draw lines to match.

Cinco de Mayo	the end of slavery in Texas
Presidents' Day	a battle in Mexico
Juneteenth	Americans who died in wars
Memorial Day	Presidents Washington and Lincoln

Write to name the holiday shown in each picture.

Independence Day — Thanksgiving

Directions: *Top:* Match each holiday with the people or event it honors. *Bottom:* Look at each picture, and write the name of the holiday it shows.

Home Activity: Discuss how you and your child might celebrate an upcoming holiday.

Use with Pupil Edition, p. 259.

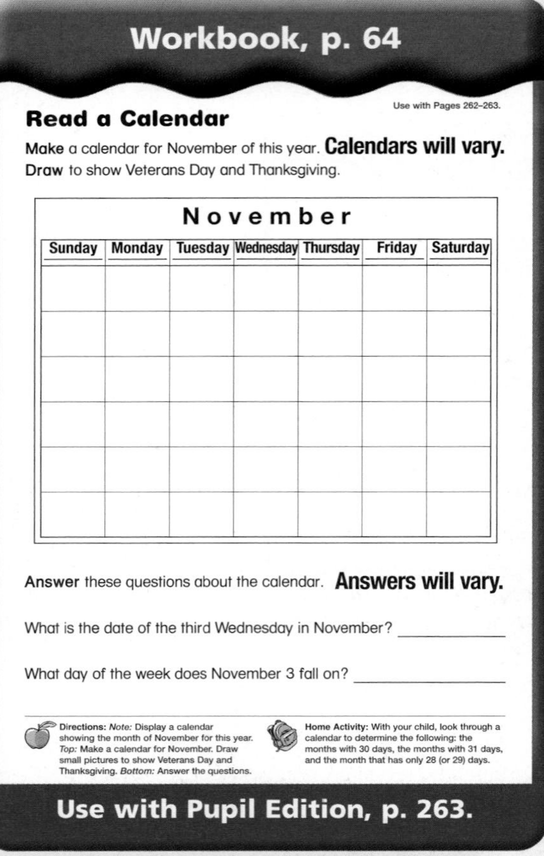

Workbook, p. 64

Use with Pages 262–263.

Read a Calendar

Make a calendar for November of this year. **Calendars will vary.**
Draw to show Veterans Day and Thanksgiving.

November

Sunday	Monday	Tuesday	Wednesday	Thursday	Friday	Saturday

Answer these questions about the calendar. **Answers will vary.**

What is the date of the third Wednesday in November? ________

What day of the week does November 3 fall on? ________

Directions: *Note:* Display a calendar showing the month of November for this year. *Top:* Make a calendar for November. Draw small pictures to show Veterans Day and Thanksgiving. *Bottom:* Answer the questions.

Home Activity: With your child, look through a calendar to determine the following: the months with 30 days, the months with 31 days, and the month that has only 28 (or 29) days.

Use with Pupil Edition, p. 263.

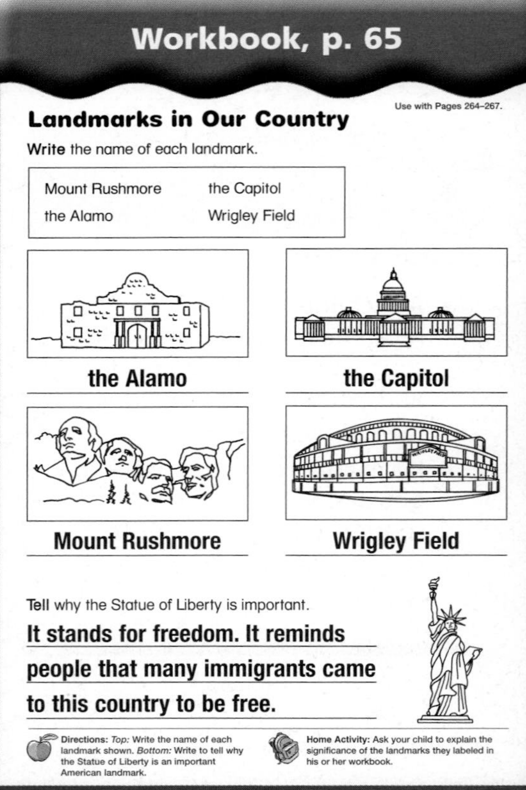

Workbook, p. 65

Use with Pages 264–267.

Landmarks in Our Country

Write the name of each landmark.

Mount Rushmore	the Capitol
the Alamo	Wrigley Field

the Alamo — the Capitol

Mount Rushmore — Wrigley Field

Tell why the Statue of Liberty is important.

It stands for freedom. It reminds people that many immigrants came to this country to be free.

Directions: *Top:* Write the name of each landmark shown. *Bottom:* Write to tell why the Statue of Liberty is an important American landmark.

Home Activity: Ask your child to explain the significance of the landmarks they labeled in his or her workbook.

Use with Pupil Edition, p. 267.

Workbook Support

Workbook, p. 66

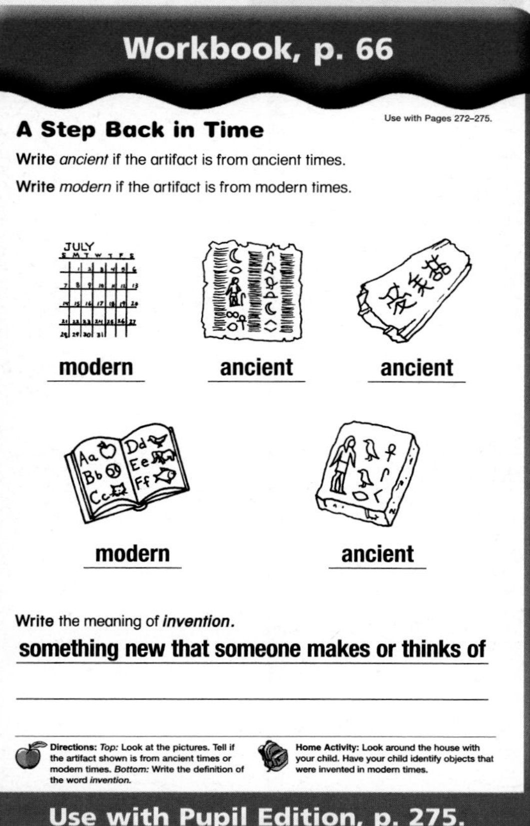

A Step Back in Time

Use with Pages 272–275.

Write *ancient* if the artifact is from ancient times.

Write *modern* if the artifact is from modern times.

modern — ancient — ancient

modern — ancient

Write the meaning of ***invention***.

something new that someone makes or thinks of

Directions: *Top:* Look at the pictures. Tell if the artifact shown is from ancient times or modern times. *Bottom:* Write the definition of the word *invention*.

Home Activity: Look around the house with your child. Have your child identify objects that were invented in modern times.

Use with Pupil Edition, p. 275.

Workbook, p. 67

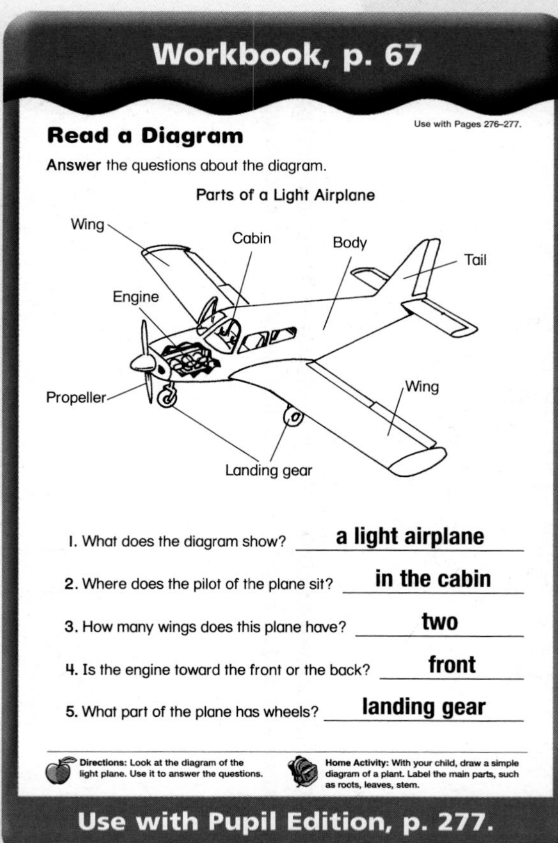

Read a Diagram

Use with Pages 276–277.

Answer the questions about the diagram.

Parts of a Light Airplane

1. What does the diagram show? **a light airplane**
2. Where does the pilot of the plane sit? **in the cabin**
3. How many wings does this plane have? **two**
4. Is the engine toward the front or the back? **front**
5. What part of the plane has wheels? **landing gear**

Directions: Look at the diagram of the light plane. Use it to answer the questions.

Home Activity: With your child, draw a simple diagram of a plant. Label the main parts, such as roots, leaves, stem.

Use with Pupil Edition, p. 277.

Workbook, p. 68

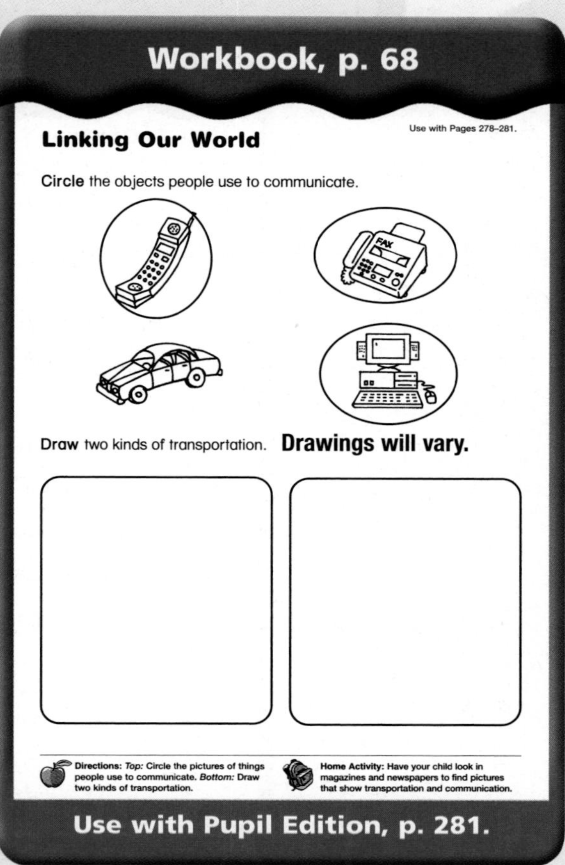

Linking Our World

Use with Pages 278–281.

Circle the objects people use to communicate.

Draw two kinds of transportation. **Drawings will vary.**

Directions: *Top:* Circle the pictures of things people use to communicate. *Bottom:* Draw two kinds of transportation.

Home Activity: Have your child look in magazines and newspapers to find pictures that show transportation and communication.

Use with Pupil Edition, p. 281.

Workbook, p. 69

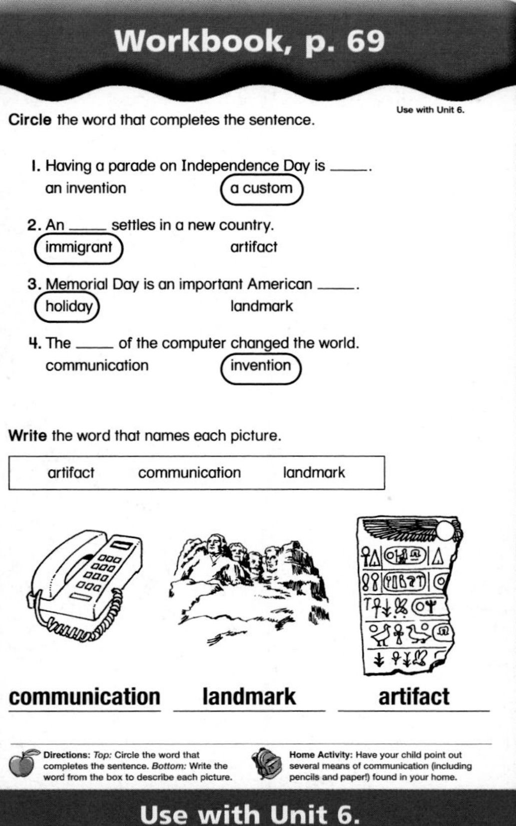

Use with Unit 6.

Circle the word that completes the sentence.

1. Having a parade on Independence Day is ____.
   an invention — (a custom)
2. An ____ settles in a new country.
   (immigrant) — artifact
3. Memorial Day is an important American ____.
   (holiday) — landmark
4. The ____ of the computer changed the world.
   communication — (invention)

Write the word that names each picture.

artifact	communication	landmark

communication — landmark — artifact

Directions: *Top:* Circle the word that completes the sentence. *Bottom:* Write the word from the box to describe each picture.

Home Activity: Have your child point out several means of communication (including pencils and paper!) found in your home.

Use with Unit 6.

Workbook, p. 70

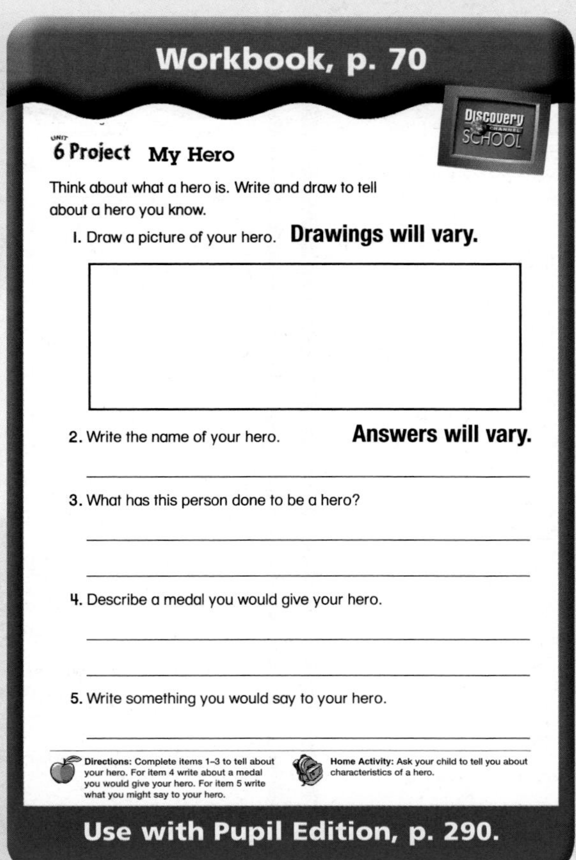

Unit 6 Project My Hero

Think about what a hero is. Write and draw to tell about a hero you know.

1. Draw a picture of your hero. **Drawings will vary.**
2. Write the name of your hero. **Answers will vary.**
3. What has this person done to be a hero?
4. Describe a medal you would give your hero.
5. Write something you would say to your hero.

Directions: Complete items 1–3 to tell about your hero. For item 4 write about a medal you would give your hero. For item 5 write what you might say to your hero.

Home Activity: Ask your child to tell you about characteristics of a hero.

Use with Pupil Edition, p. 290.

Assessment Support

Use these Assessment Book pages and the test maker to assess content and skills in Unit 6. You can also view and print Assessment Book pages from the Teacher Resources CD-ROM.

Assessment Book, p. 21

Unit 6: Content Test

Write the word that goes with each definition.

landmark	immigrant	custom
communication	artifact	holiday

1. a person who settles in another country **immigrant**
2. sharing ideas with others **communication**
3. a special day **holiday**
4. an object made and used by people **artifact**
5. a building that is important or interesting **landmark**
6. a special way that a group does something **custom**

TEST PREP Which word completes each sentence?

1. The wheelbarrow was an ____ of the Chinese.
   a. custom
   (b.) invention
   c. holiday
   d. immigrant

2. The Alamo is an example of a ____.
   (a.) landmark
   b. custom
   c. pyramid
   d. holiday

Use with Pupil Edition, p. 286.

Assessment Book, p. 22

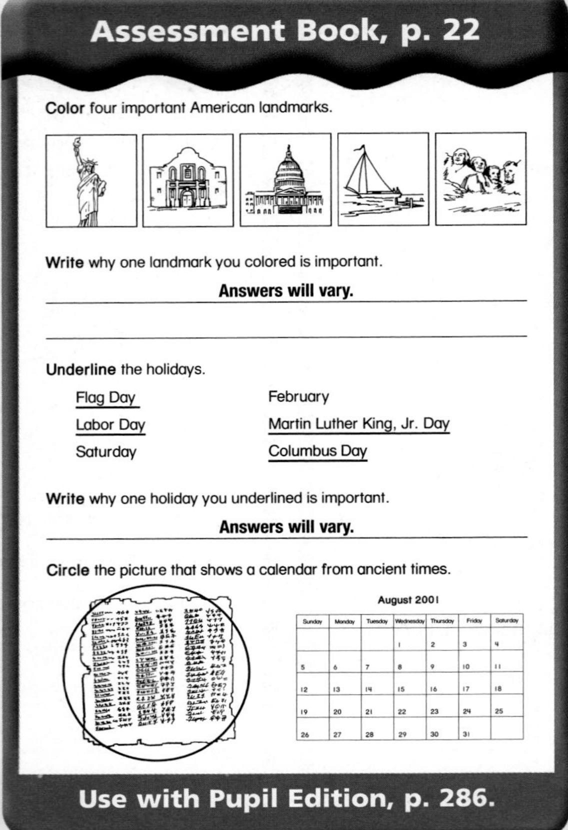

Color four important American landmarks.

Write why one landmark you colored is important.

Answers will vary.

Underline the holidays.

Flag Day
February
Labor Day
Martin Luther King, Jr. Day
Saturday
Columbus Day

Write why one holiday you underlined is important.

Answers will vary.

Circle the picture that shows a calendar from ancient times.

Use with Pupil Edition, p. 286.

Assessment Book, p. 23

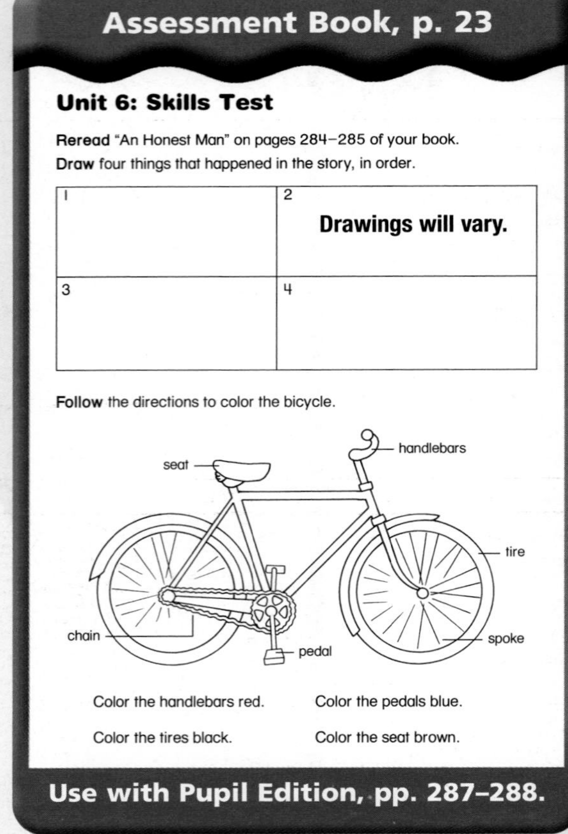

Unit 6: Skills Test

Reread "An Honest Man" on pages 284–285 of your book.
Draw four things that happened in the story, in order.

1	2 **Drawings will vary.**
3	4

Follow the directions to color the bicycle.

Color the handlebars red. Color the pedals blue.

Color the tires black. Color the seat brown.

Use with Pupil Edition, pp. 287–288.

Assessment Book, p. 24

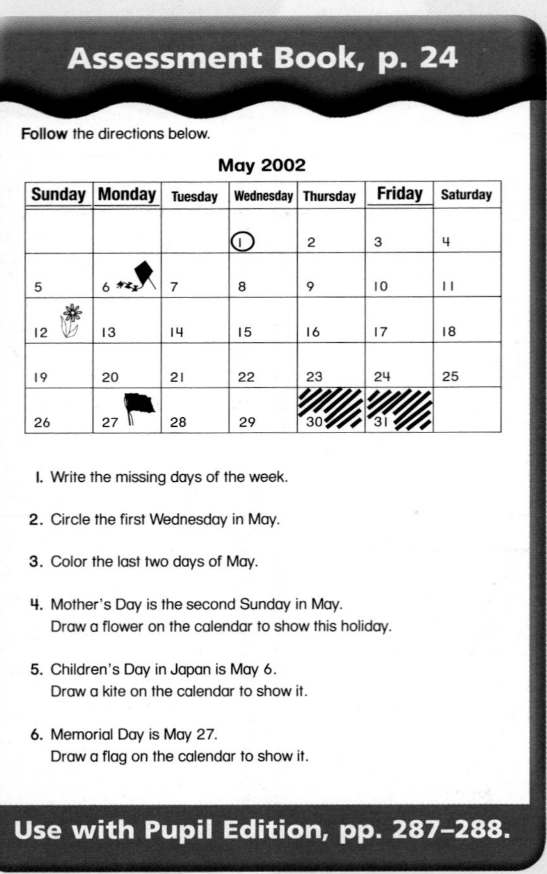

Follow the directions below.

May 2002

Sunday	Monday	Tuesday	Wednesday	Thursday	Friday	Saturday
			(1)	2	3	4
5	6	7	8	9	10	11
12	13	14	15	16	17	18
19	20	21	22	23	24	25
26	27	28	29	30	31	

1. Write the missing days of the week.
2. Circle the first Wednesday in May.
3. Color the last two days of May.
4. Mother's Day is the second Sunday in May. Draw a flower on the calendar to show this holiday.
5. Children's Day in Japan is May 6. Draw a kite on the calendar to show it.
6. Memorial Day is May 27. Draw a flag on the calendar to show it.

Use with Pupil Edition, pp. 287–288.

Lesson 1 Overview

Family History **pages 250–253**	Children will learn the meaning of *immigrant*. They will also learn about how many immigrants entered the United States through Ellis Island and Angel Island. 	 Time 20–30 minutes Resources • Workbook, p. 62 • Vocabulary Card **immigrant** • Every Student Learns Guide, pp. 102–105
Ellen Ochoa **pages 254–255**	Children will learn about Ellen Ochoa, the first Hispanic female in NASA's Space Program.	Time 15–20 minutes

Build Background

Activity

A Symbol of America

 **Time** 15–20 minutes

Show children a photo or illustration of the Statue of Liberty. Note that many people who came to this country long ago saw the Statue of Liberty as they arrived here. Say that the Statue of Liberty means many different things to different people.

Have children draw their own pictures of the Statue of Liberty and write one word below the picture to say what the statue means to them. (Hope, Dreams, Freedom, and so on)

If time is short, have children look at the photo or illustration and say in one word what the Statue of Liberty means to them. List their responses.

Read Aloud

We Remember Them with Pride!

by Christopher Erickson

Our ancestors said good-bye
to places they knew so well.
They journeyed to America.
Their story is important to tell!

These immigrants continued
to come
and the cities grew tall
and wide.
The newcomers inspired
our nation.
We remember them
with pride!

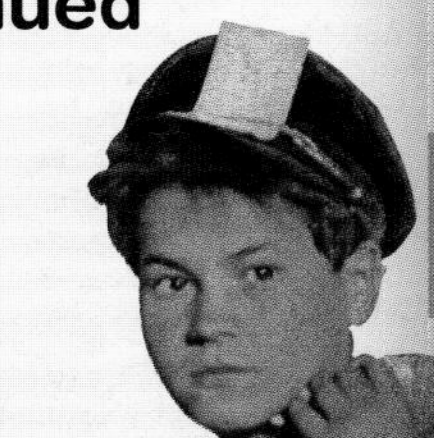

Family History

Objectives

- Explain that the United States is a land of people who have diverse ethnic origins.
- Name several sources of information about a given period or event.

Vocabulary

immigrant a person who settles in a new country (p. 250)

QUICK Teaching Plan

If time is short, have children look at the photographs of Ellis Island and Angel Island on pp. 251 and 252 to compare what they see in each picture.

1 Introduce and Motivate

Preview Display the Vocabulary Card **immigrant** and define the word as "a person who settles in a new country." Read aloud the first page of the lesson. Then have children predict what the remainder of the lesson will be about.

Warm Up To activate prior knowledge, ask children to identify some of the reasons they think people want to come and live in this country.

Family History

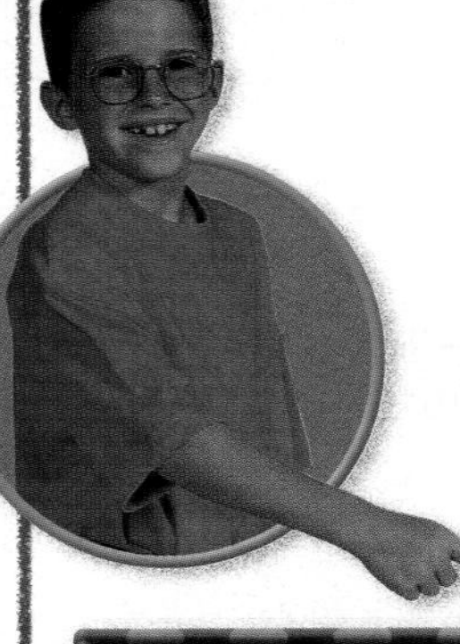

My great-grandparents came to America on a ship. The arrow on the map shows the route they took. Their long journey took them across the Atlantic Ocean. 1

The first thing they saw when they came into New York Harbor was the Statue of Liberty. To them, it stood for hope and freedom. Many immigrants, like my great-grandparents, came to America in search of a better life. An **immigrant** is a person who settles in a new country. 2

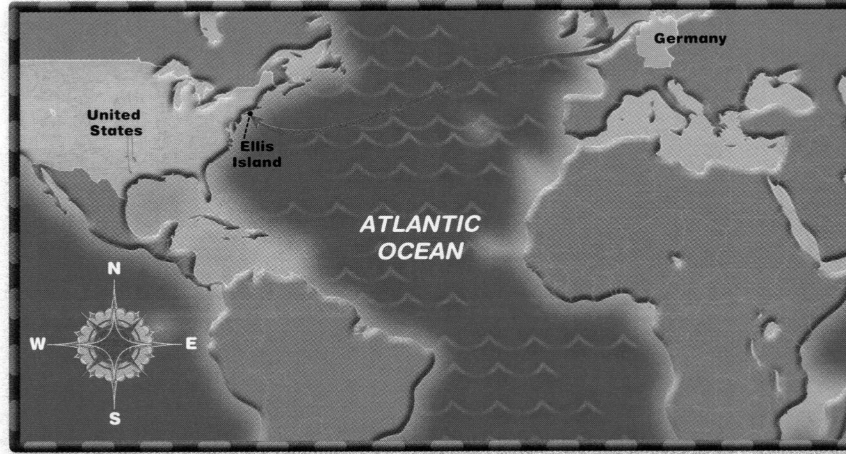

250

Practice and Extend

READING SKILL Recall and Retell

Target Skill

- Review the meanings of *recall* and *retell*. As needed, refer children to p. 249.
- After children read p. 253, have them pause to recall the visit Michael and his family made to Ellis Island. Have partners retell what they learned from the lesson.
- Move around the room to monitor children's retellings. Help them think of the order of the ideas as they present them.

WEB SITE Technology

You can look up vocabulary words online. Click on *Social Studies Library* and select the dictionary at **www.sfsocialstudies.com.**

My great-grandparents arrived at Ellis Island, located in New York Harbor. They were checked by a doctor. They had to prove they were healthy and able to work hard.

Immigrants on Ellis Island were asked many questions. *Why do you want to live here? Is someone waiting for you?*

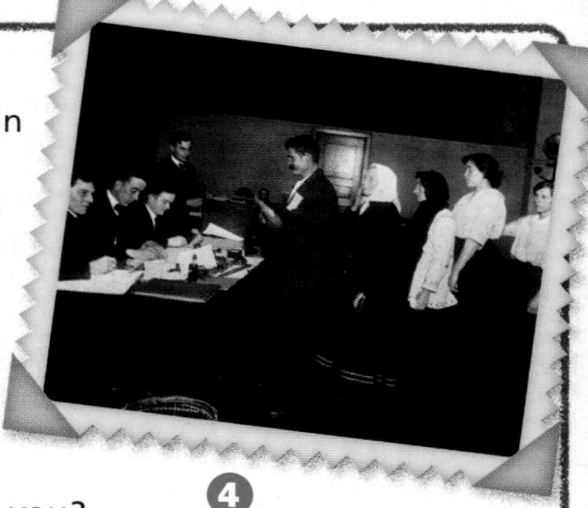

4 Immigrants stand in line at Ellis Island.

My great-grandmother had a brother living in Detroit, Michigan. When my great-grandparents left Ellis Island, they traveled by train from New York City to Detroit. 3

Ellis Island

251

SOCIAL STUDIES
Background

About Ellis Island

- The first immigrants arrived at Ellis Island on Jan. 1, 1892.
- Between 1892 and 1924 over 12 million immigrants entered the United States through Ellis Island.
- At one time, many thousands of immigrants were processed each day.
- Ellis Island opened as a museum in 1990.

2 Teach and Discuss

Page 250

Tell children that most of the immigrants who came to this country at the same time as Michael's great-grandparents came from Europe. Have children locate Europe on a world map. Remind them that Europe is a continent.

1 **Why did immigrants travel from Europe to this country by ship?** Possible answers: They couldn't travel by train or bus because they had to cross an ocean. Planes were not used much back then. Ships were their only choice. **Draw Conclusions**

2 **What kinds of things do people mean when they say they want "a better life"?** Possible answers: Freedom; a chance to own a home or start a business **Make Inferences**

Page 251

Have children talk briefly about what they see in the photos of Ellis Island.

3 **Why was it important for immigrants to know someone already living here?** Possible answer: The people who already lived in this country could help the immigrants find a place to live or help them find a job. **Make Inferences**

4 **How is the clothing the people in the photo are wearing like and different from clothing people wear today?** Possible answers: Like: Women wore skirts and blouses just as they do today. Men wore trousers and vests or jackets. Different: The clothing of the immigrants looks heavier than clothing people wear today. There wasn't much variety in what people wore. **Analyze Pictures**

continued

Page 252

Have children point to China on their map. Say that China is a very large country on the continent of Asia.

5 **What two sources of information, other than the words on the page, do you have to learn about Angel Island?** Photographs and map **Draw Conclusions**

6 **What are some things Michael's and Amy's ancestors may have had to give up to come to America?** Possible answer: Their homes in Europe and Asia, their friends, and other family members **Make Inferences**

Page 253

Tell children that today people from all over the world come to the United States. They don't pass through Ellis Island or Angel Island anymore. They arrive at airports and docks in cities such as Los Angeles, Miami, and New York City.

Before children read, review the meaning of *museum*—a place where objects relating to history are kept and displayed.

7 **Why do Ellis Island and Angel Island have museums?** Possible answers: To tell the story of immigration; the buildings there are important places in history **Draw Conclusions**

Chinese immigrants 5

My friend, Amy, had ancestors who were immigrants too. They came to America from China. They traveled from China to San Francisco, California. What ocean did they travel across?

Many immigrants from Asia stopped at Angel Island. Angel Island is an island in the San Francisco Bay. Some immigrants had to live on Angel Island before they could enter the United States. 6

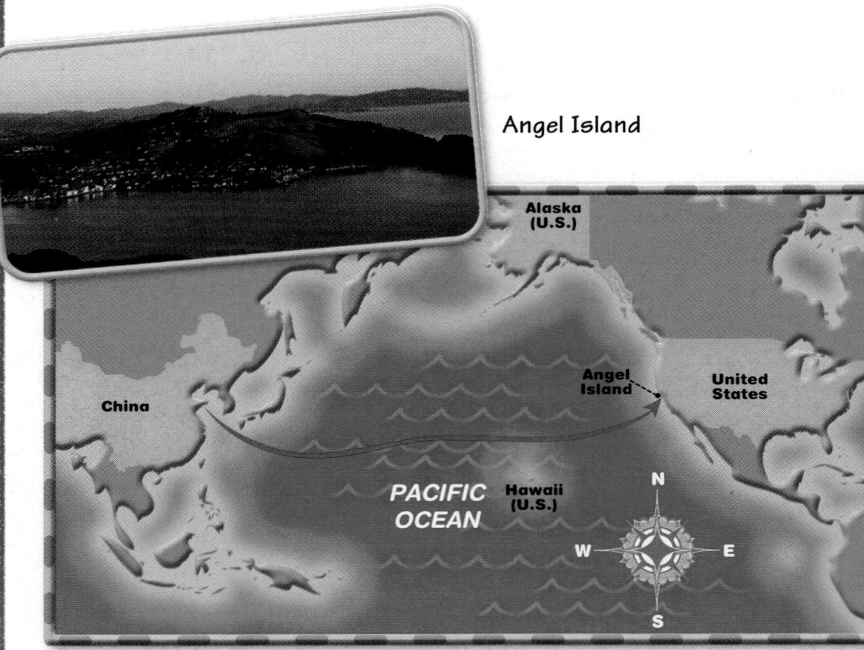

Angel Island

252

ESL

EXTEND LANGUAGE
ESL Support

Ways of Travel Write on the board these ways that people travel today: *car, bus, train, plane, ship, bicycle*. Read the list as you point to each word.

Beginning Have children name their favorite way of travel and tell why they prefer it.

Intermediate Have children choose two ways people travel from the list and write a sentence to compare their speeds—*A plane moves faster than a car.*

Advanced Have children write sentences to tell how people traveled in the past.

For additional ESL support, use Every Student Learns Guide, pp. 102–105.

Today, Ellis Island and Angel Island have museums. You can visit the places where many people stopped before beginning their new lives in America. 7 8

My family visited Ellis Island last summer. We saw my great-grandparents' names on the American Immigrant Wall of Honor. This wall honors immigrants who have come to America from around the world. There are many names on the wall.

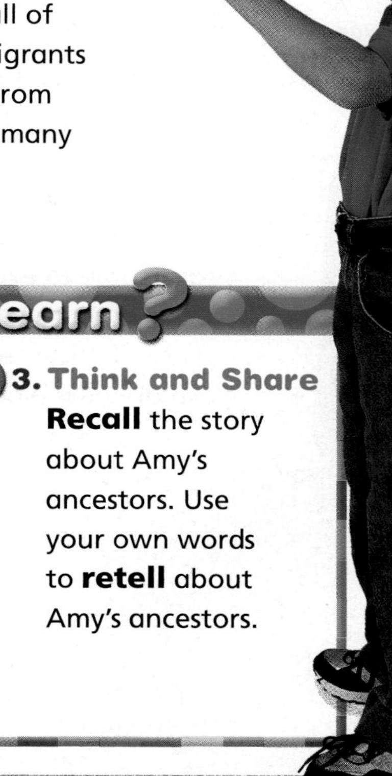

What did you learn?

1. Use the pictures in the lesson to compare Ellis Island and Angel Island. Tell how they are alike and different.
2. What does the Statue of Liberty stand for?
3. **Think and Share** **Recall** the story about Amy's ancestors. Use your own words to **retell** about Amy's ancestors.

253

8 **What kinds of things would you expect to see in those museums?** Photos, maps, names and arrival dates of the immigrants **Make Inferences**

3 Close and Assess

Have children tell something special they learned about immigrants by reading the lesson text and by looking at the maps and photos.

✓ What did you learn?

1. Both islands are surrouded by water and have buildings. Ellis Island is covered in concrete. Angel Island is hilly and green.
2. Most children will probably answer—freedom and hope. Accept other reasonable responses.
3. **Think and Share** Children's retelling should include: Amy's ancestors were immigrants from China to San Francisco, California. They traveled across the Pacific Ocean.

CURRICULUM CONNECTION
Writing

Welcome Signs

Have children make signs with words and art that would welcome newcomers to the United States.

Workbook, p. 62

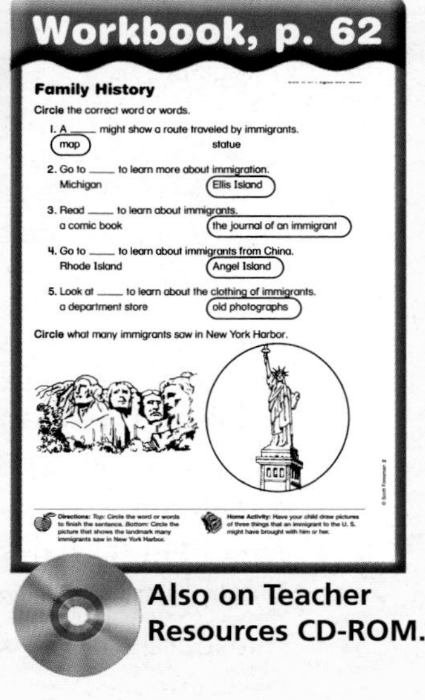

Family History

Circle the correct word or words.

1. A ____ might show a route traveled by immigrants. (map) statue
2. Go to ____ to learn more about immigration. Michigan (Ellis Island)
3. Read ____ to learn about immigrants. a comic book (the journal of an immigrant)
4. Go to ____ to learn about immigrants from China. Rhode Island (Angel Island)
5. Look at ____ to learn about the clothing of immigrants. a department store (old photographs)

Circle what many immigrants saw in New York Harbor.

Also on Teacher Resources CD-ROM.

CITIZEN HEROES

Ellen Ochoa

Objective

- Identify characteristics of good citizenship.

1 Introduce and Motivate

Preview Read aloud the title of the feature as children look at the illustrations. Have them tell what kind of job Ellen Ochoa (ō • chō´ • ə) needs courage to do.

Warm Up To activate prior knowledge, ask children to identify some of the things an astronaut does.

2 Teach and Discuss

Tell children what NASA stands for—the National Aeronautics and Space Administration. Then read aloud the feature as children follow along.

1 **What has Ellen Ochoa done that is unusual for any American?** She became an astronaut; she has gone on several space flights. Recall and Retell

2 **What are some character traits Ellen Ochoa has in common with other explorers?** Possible answers: She is curious about places she has never been. She is brave because she knows the dangers of going into space but chooses to go anyway. She is cooperative because each member of the crew must do his or her job well for the success of the whole mission. Make Inferences

CITIZEN HEROES

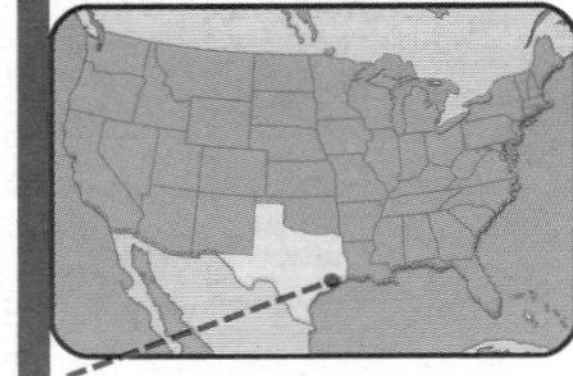

Ellen Ochoa trained at the Johnson Space Center in Houston, Texas.

Ellen Ochoa

It took courage for immigrants to come to America. Many didn't speak English or know anyone in this country. For Ellen Ochoa, it takes a different kind of courage to do her job!

Ellen Ochoa became the first Hispanic female astronaut in NASA's Space Program. She has been on three space flights and is looking forward to more. 1 She thinks it is very important for people to explore space. It takes courage and a sense of adventure to explore new places. 2

254

Practice and Extend

SOCIAL STUDIES Background

About the International Space Station

Share the following:

- The space station is a joint project of 16 different countries, including the United States, Russia, Japan, Brazil, and Germany.
- The space station circles the Earth and is only partially completed.
- When finished, the space station will be about the size of the largest passenger plane.
- The space station will include living space for up to seven astronauts.
- Future research projects include studying how plants grow in space and how spending long periods of time in space affects people.

As a student, Ellen Ochoa always liked school. As an astronaut, she learns new things every day just as she did in school. She thinks that being an astronaut is very exciting!

Ellen Ochoa helped develop computer systems to explore space. She also helped invent better ways for people to look closely at objects in space. She was a (3) crew member on a space flight that delivered supplies to the International Space Station. Ellen Ochoa dreams of helping build a space station. She has received many awards from NASA for her service. (4)

Dr. Ochoa aboard Discovery Space Shuttle

Courage in Action

Why does it take courage to explore new places?

Test Talk

Use Information from the Text

(3) **What two things has Ellen Ochoa done that let you know she is good in science and math?** She helped invent computer systems used to explore space. She helped invent ways for people to look closely at objects in space. **Draw Conclusions**

Children should look back at the text to make sure they have the right information.

(4) **Why do you think Ellen Ochoa was chosen to be a Citizen Hero?** Possible answer: She is exploring space and inventing things for the good of all people in the United States. **Evaluate**

3 Close and Assess

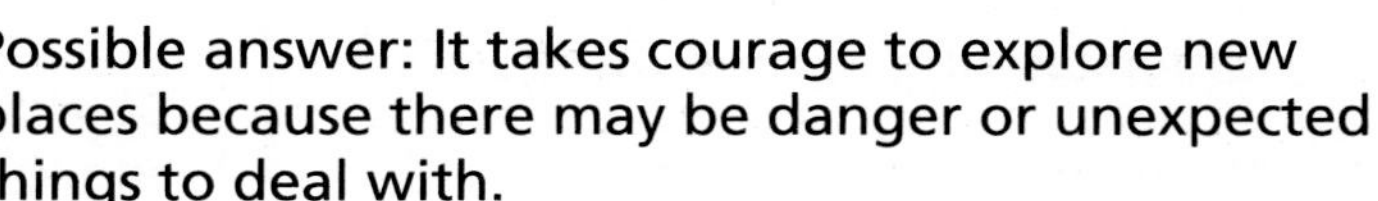

Courage in Action

Possible answer: It takes courage to explore new places because there may be danger or unexpected things to deal with.

FYI SOCIAL STUDIES Background

Possible Misconceptions

Children may assume that Ellen Ochoa was the first woman in space. Share the following:

- Cosmonaut Valentina Tereshkova of the former Soviet Union was the first woman in space (1963).
- Astronaut Sally Ride was the first American woman in space (1983).
- Astronaut Mae Jemison was the first African American woman in space (1992).

Use with pages 250–255

Lesson 1 Wrap-Up

MEETING INDIVIDUAL NEEDS

Leveled Practice

Coming to America

Talk briefly with children about what it must have been like for immigrants coming to America.

Easy Tell children that most immigrants had few things with them when they reached Ellis Island or Angel Island. Tell children to draw pictures of five things that they as adult immigrants coming to the United States would have brought with them. **Reteach**

On-Level After doing the Easy activity, have children carry their five belongings with them as they wait to be asked the question, "Why do you want to live in America?" Have partners take turns asking and then responding to the question. **Extend**

Challenge After doing both the Easy and On-Level activities, have children who have passed the questioning phase, sign the official "register." Children should sign their name, say in what state they will live, and what job they will do. **Enrich**

Hands-on Activities

CURRICULUM CONNECTION

Reading

Word Families

Objective Demonstrate understanding of new vocabulary.

Materials paper, pencils

Learning Style Visual/Kinesthetic

Individual

Time 10–15 minutes

1. Display the word *immigrant* and have children say its meaning. Call on children to use the word in oral sentences.

2. Display the related words *migrate, immigrate* and *migration, immigration* and define each.

3. Have children write the new words in sentences.

Remind children to add *immigrant* to their "My Word Book" glossaries.

migrate
immigrate
migration
immigration

CURRICULUM CONNECTION

Art

Liberty on Parade

Objective Construct props for and engage in a liberty parade.

Materials scissors, construction paper, crayons, markers, pictures of the Statue of Liberty

Learning Style Kinesthetic

Individual

Time 20–30 minutes

1. Help children prepare props to carry in a liberty parade. Possibilities include torches and tablets and paper "musical" instruments.

2. Children who choose to make tablets should write *July 4, 1776* on them.

3. Children who want to carry musical instruments may choose to make flutes or drums.

4. A lively patriotic song to march to will encourage participation.

CURRICULUM CONNECTION

Drama

On Stage!

Objective Prepare a skit that dramatizes the immigrant experience.

Materials paper, pencils

Learning Style Social/Linguistic

Group

Time 25–30 minutes

1. Have each group prepare a skit that illustrates one portion of an immigrant family's journey to the United States. Dramas can include such characters as an immigrant family, a ship captain, and officials at Ellis or Angel Island.

2. Set aside class time for each group to perform a dramatic reading of their play. Then ask children what they learned about immigrants from the skits.

Lesson 2 Overview

People Celebrate **pages 256–259**	Children will learn the meaning of the vocabulary words *holiday* and *custom*. They will also learn that some holidays mark or remember important events from the past as well as certain customs people follow during holidays.	 Time 20–30 minutes Resources • Workbook, p. 63 • Vocabulary Cards holiday custom • Every Student Learns Guide, pp. 106–109
DK Spring **pages 260–261**	Children will learn that people around the world welcome spring in different ways	
Read a Calendar **pages 262–263**	Children will learn how to read a calendar.	 Time 15–20 minutes Resource • Workbook p. 64

Build Background

Activity

Special Days

 **Time** 15–20 minutes

Ask children to name some of the special days that they and their families celebrate. List their responses on the board.

Have each child draw a picture that relates to one of the special days on the list.

Display the pictures in class. Have children take turns guessing the special day that each picture illustrates.

If time is short, build the list suggested above. Ask children what they do on those days. Then discuss what person or event is celebrated on this day.

Read Aloud

Holidays

by Eric Meyer

The stores are closed
and so is school.
We have the day off.
That is the rule!

There might be a party
or a parade to see.
Enjoy the holiday.
It's for you and
for me!

People Celebrate

Objective

- Explain how selected customs and celebrations reflect an American love of individualism, inventiveness, and freedom.

Vocabulary

holiday a special day (p. 256)

custom a special way that a group does something (p. 257)

QUICK Teaching Plan

If time is short, have children review the time line on pages 256–257. Then have children write one sentence about a holiday of their choice. Have volunteers share their sentences with the class.

1 Introduce and Motivate

Preview Display the Vocabulary Cards **holiday** and **custom**. Have children locate the words in the lesson text and read the definitions. Then have children look at the pictures in the lesson to see some ways people celebrate holidays.

Warm Up To activate prior knowledge, have children talk about some ways many Americans celebrate July 4th.

Lesson 2

People Celebrate

My family and I celebrate many holidays. A **holiday** is a special day. Many people do not work on holidays. Some holidays are national holidays, or days that are important
1 to all Americans. Look at the time line. How do you celebrate these national holidays?

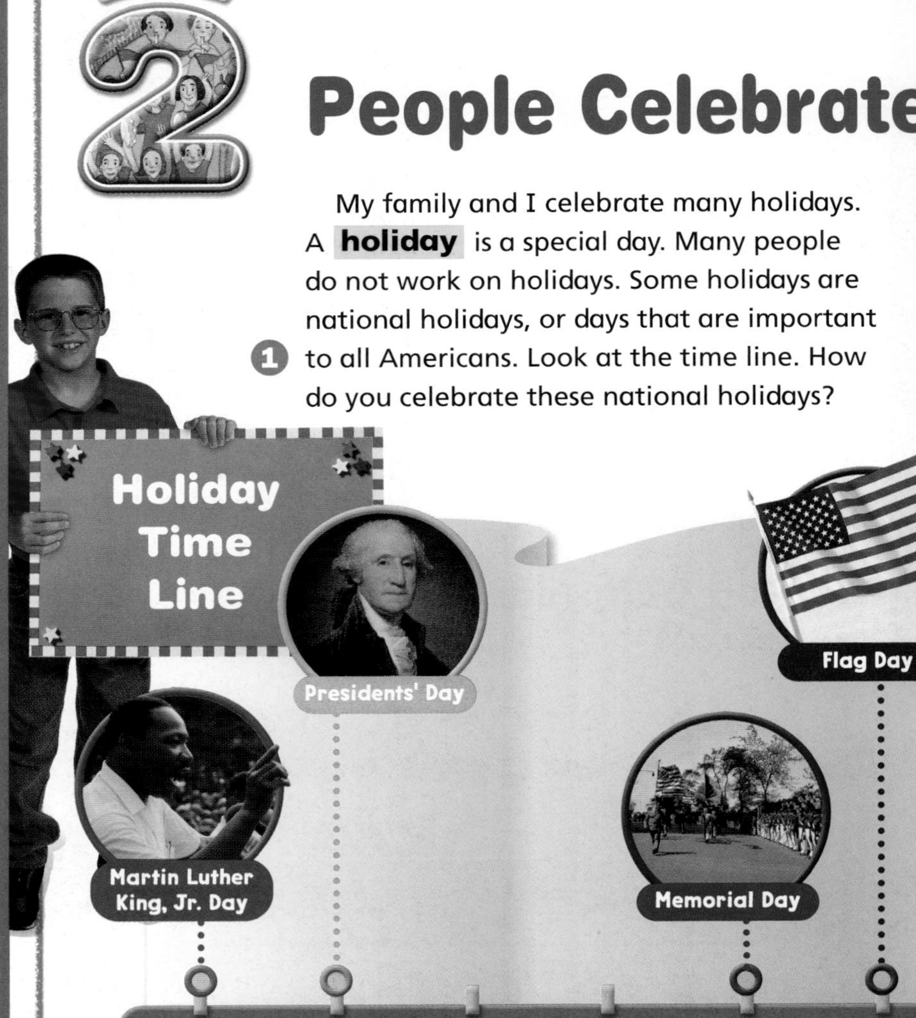

2

256

Practice and Extend

READING SKILL Put Things in Order

Sequence

- Remind children that holidays are events that happen during a year. They occur in the same sequence, or order, each year.
- Ask children to look at the holidays that occur on the time line between January and March (Martin Luther King, Jr. Day and Presidents' Day). Continue by quarters through the end of the year.
- Write the holidays on the board out of sequence. Let children volunteer to number them in the order in which they occur.
- Have children tell which holiday comes *first, next*, and *last* in the year.

Two holidays, Memorial Day and Veterans Day, remember people who fought in wars for our country. Memorial Day honors all United States citizens who have died in war. On Veterans Day, we remember all of the men and women who have fought to keep our country free. In which months are these holidays celebrated? 3

In many communities, it is a custom to march in parades on these holidays. A **custom** is a special way that a group does something. It is also a custom to give speeches on these holidays.

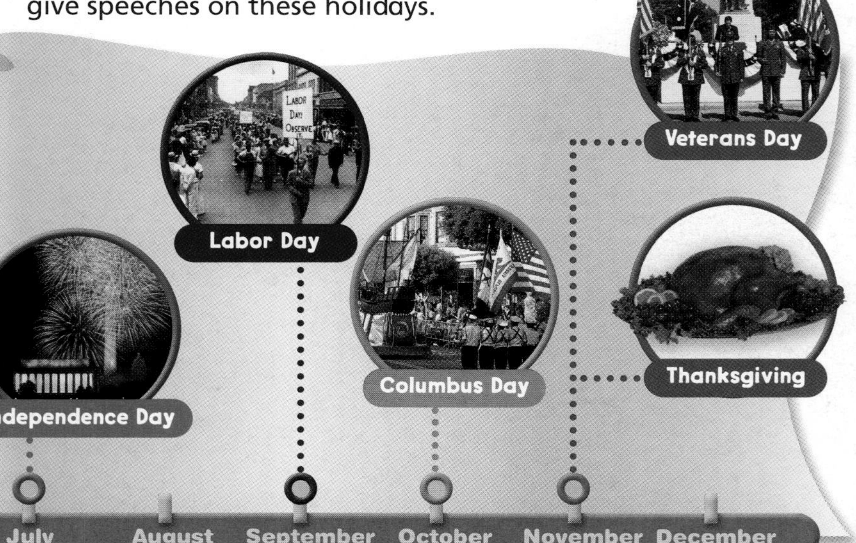

2 Teach and Discuss

Page 256

Read the time line with children. Talk briefly about what each holiday celebrates. Note that holidays are not the only way to remember important people and events. Explain that the cultural heritage of the nation, state, or community is often remembered with celebrations. Talk about how in addition to holidays, paintings, statues, poems, and stories also help celebrate or remember people, events, or cultural heritage. Identify some famous national and local examples.

1 **What is a national holiday?** A national holiday is one that is important to all Americans. Many people do not have to work on national holidays. **Recall and Retell**

2 **How are Presidents' Day and Martin Luther King, Jr. Day alike? How are they different?** Possible answer: They are alike because both holidays celebrate men who worked for the good of all citizens in this country. They are different because Martin Luther King, Jr. was not a President, but King worked to see that all people were treated fairly. **Compare and Contrast**

Page 257

Tell children that in some places on Memorial Day and Veterans Day people put small flags on the graves of soldiers who fought in wars.

3 **How does honoring those who went to war show Americans' love of freedom?** Possible answer: It shows that Americans are thankful for their freedom and understand the sacrifices men and women make to keep our country free. **Make Inferences**

SOCIAL STUDIES Background

About Labor Day

- Children may know less about the history of Labor Day as a holiday than some other holidays on the time line.
- Write the word *labor* on the board. Define *labor* as "work people do." Explain that a laborer is a worker.
- Labor Day was made a national holiday by the United States Congress in 1894. It had been an unofficial holiday for 12 years before then.

WEB SITE Technology

You can look up vocabulary words online. Click on *Social Studies Library* and select the dictionary at **www.sfsocialstudies.com.**

continued

Page 258

After children have read the page, have them talk about the holidays they celebrate with their families that reflect their cultural heritage, such as Chinese New Year, Kwanzaa, Children's Day, Christmas, or Hanukkah.

Test Talk

Locate Key Words in the Question
Ask children to look for key words in the question.

4 What event does Cinco de Mayo celebrate?
It celebrates the winning of a battle by Mexicans against France. **Recall and Retell**

5 Do you think Cinco de Mayo is a national holiday in Mexico? Explain your thinking.
Possible answer: Yes; it is a holiday that is important to all the people in that country; it celebrates freedom from another country, France.
Make Inferences

SOCIAL STUDIES STRAND
Culture

Piñatas

- Tell children that many Mexican children and Mexican American children also have piñatas for other celebrations, such as birthday parties. Children are blindfolded, then each has a chance to hit the piñata with a stick to break it open.
- Explain that piñatas are made from very thin, colored paper and paste and are often formed in the shape of an animal.
- If possible, bring in a piñata to show the class.

Breaking a piñata

Many communities celebrate other holidays. Cinco de Mayo, or May 5, is an important holiday for Mexican Americans. It celebrates the courage of the Mexican people. On this day, in 1862, there was a battle in Mexico. A small Mexican Army won a battle against a much larger French Army. 4 5

Today, people celebrate this holiday in many ways. It is a custom to have fiestas, or feasts. Foods like warm tortillas, tamales, and rice are served. Children break piñatas filled with toys and candies.

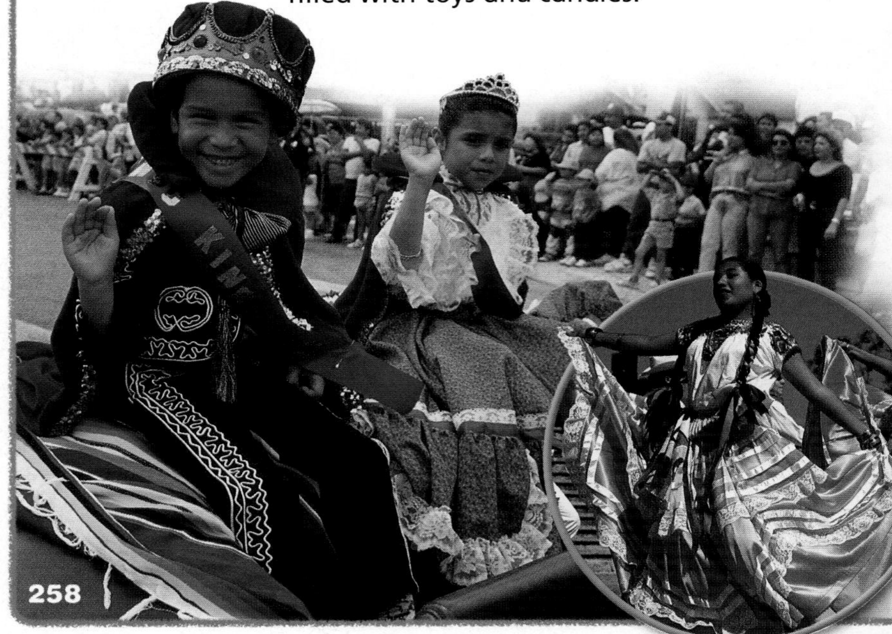

258

Practice and Extend

EXTEND LANGUAGE
ESL Support

Courage Write *courage* on the board. Say that someone who has courage is brave, or courageous. Talk about some people who must have courage to do their jobs.

Beginning Have individual children name someone whom they think has courage. It can be one of the workers they've talked about. Help them complete these oral sentences: ___ *is brave. He/She has courage.*

Intermediate Have children write two sentences about a person they feel has courage.

Advanced Have children make lists of ways people can honor others who are courageous.

For additional ESL support, use Every Student Learns Guide, pp. 106–109.

Some African Americans celebrate June 19 each year. It is called Juneteenth. In 1865, this day marked the end of slavery (6) in Texas.

On Juneteenth, it is a custom that families get together. They may tell stories about their ancestors. Some families have picnics and play baseball. Other people celebrate in churches. They sing joyful songs and give thanks for freedom. (7)

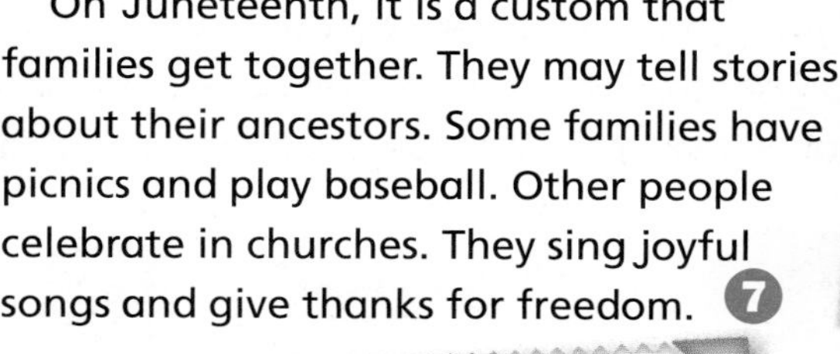

Celebrating Juneteenth then and now

What did you learn?

1. What are three national holidays that Americans celebrate?
2. How do you celebrate Memorial Day in your state or community?
3. **Think and Share** Draw a picture of a holiday custom that you share with your family. Write a poem about your picture.

Page 259

Tell children that Juneteenth is a state holiday in Texas. Juneteenth celebrates the day in 1865 when General Gordon Granger arrived in Galveston, Texas and announced the signing of the Emancipation Proclamation, which freed slaves.

(6) **How does Juneteenth reflect an American love of freedom?** Possible answer: It marks the day when slavery ended in Texas and slaves became free. **Draw Conclusions**

(7) **What "freedom day" do all Americans celebrate in the summertime?** July 4th, our country's Independence Day **Draw Conclusions**

3 Close and Assess

Have children tell why national holidays are important. (They give Americans an opportunity to stop and think about important people and events in our history.)

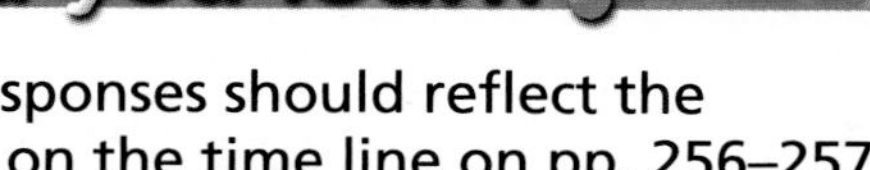

✓ What did you learn?

1. Children's responses should reflect the information on the time line on pp. 256–257 and in the lesson text.
2. Possible answers: Go to a parade; have a party; put a wreath on a statue that honors American soldiers; visit a cemetery where loved ones are buried
3. **Think and Share** Display children's completed drawings in class. Group pictures that illustrate the same holiday. Use the visuals to discuss each of the holidays. Encourage volunteers to share their poems.

CURRICULUM CONNECTION Math

Time Lines

- Make available several calendars for children to use.
- Have each child choose a month to represent on a time line. Tell them to think about a month when there are several celebrations in their own family.
- Have children plot and label the events on a time line. Remind them to put their events in the correct order.

Workbook, p. 63

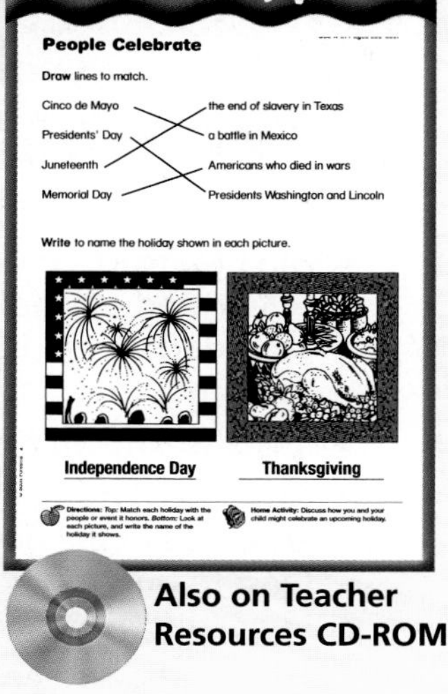

People Celebrate

Draw lines to match.

Cinco de Mayo — the end of slavery in Texas
Presidents' Day — a battle in Mexico
Juneteenth — Americans who died in wars
Memorial Day — Presidents Washington and Lincoln

Write to name the holiday shown in each picture.

Independence Day

Thanksgiving

Directions: *Top:* Match each holiday with the people or event it honors. *Bottom:* Look at each picture, and write the name of the holiday it shows.

Home Activity: Discuss how you and your child might celebrate an upcoming holiday.

Also on Teacher Resources CD-ROM.

Spring

Objectives

- Obtain information about a topic using visual sources such as photographs.
- Identify examples of the local cultural heritage.

1 Introduce and Motivate

Preview Have children read aloud the title of the feature. Then have them listen as you read the introductory text. Talk briefly with children about what they see in the photographs.

Warm Up To activate prior knowledge, have children name some things they associate with spring. Encourage children to name any special celebrations or holidays they may know about that occur in springtime.

2 Teach and Discuss

Read aloud the text about each celebration. As needed, review the meaning of *harvest*.

1 **What are some things springtime festivals have in common?** They usually have flowers, music, and dancing. **Recall and Retell**

2 **Why do you think people in Zambia celebrate the harvest?** Possible answers: To show that they are grateful for the crops they grew and that there is plenty of food **Make Inferences**

Spring

1 Springtime festivals celebrate new life, energy and growth. For many children, these are happy, colorful festivals with flowers, music, and dancin

Chinese New Year starts on the first day of the Chinese calendar and lasts for 15 days. Man Po and her family feast, visit friends, and watch colorful street parades.

The N'cwala ceremony is held each February to celebrate the harvest. Groups of dancers perform their warrior dance. M'sangombe is the youngest dancer in his group.

Fête des Mères is celebrated on the last Sunday in May. Matilde calls this day Mommy's Festival. Matilde brings her mother breakfast in bed and recites the poem she has learned.

Hina Matsuri is celebrated March 3. This is a day dedicated to dolls. During the festival, Sayo displays her dolls in the best room of the house.

2 3

Man Po from Hong Kong

M'sangombe from Zambia

Matilde from France

Sayo from Japan

260

Practice and Extend

FYI SOCIAL STUDIES Background

About Hina Matsuri

- Hina Matsuri, or Girls' Festival, originally was celebrated on the third day of the third month (lunar calendar). It still is celebrated on the third day of the third month.
- It is also known as the Dolls' Festival.
- An elegant display of stylized Japanese court dolls is arranged in the girls' homes. A girl may serve a miniature feast to guests who come to admire her dolls.
- The dolls are often inheritances, passed from generation to generation.

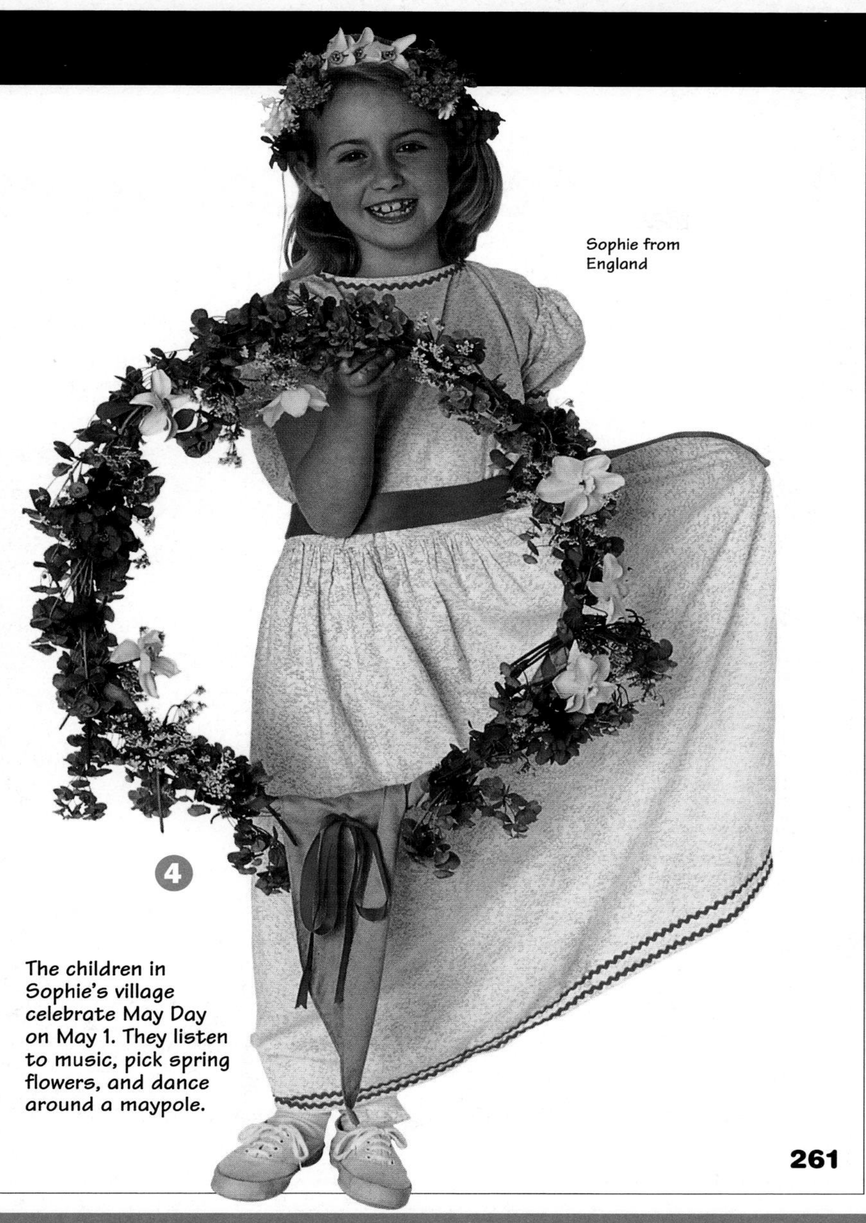

Sophie from England

4

The children in Sophie's village celebrate May Day on May 1. They listen to music, pick spring flowers, and dance around a maypole.

261

CURRICULUM CONNECTION
Art

Picturing Spring Celebrations

- Have children select a celebration they have read about. Have them use the text to draw a picture of what people do to celebrate.
- Ask children to caption their pictures with the name of the celebration and the name of its country of origin.

3 What holiday in the United States is similar to Fête des Mères? Mother's Day **How do you know?** Matilde calls it Mommy's Festival. Both days honor mothers. **Compare and Contrast**

4 How do some girls in England dress on May Day? They wear fancy, long springtime dresses and wreaths of flowers in their hair. **Analyze Pictures**

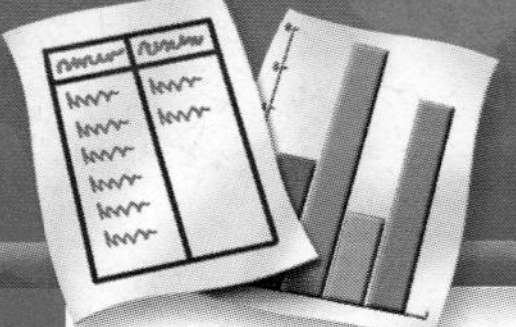

Read a Calendar

Objective

- Describe and measure calendar time.

1 Introduce and Motivate

Preview Have children look at the illustration on pp. 262–263. Ask if they know what it shows. Then read aloud the title of the feature. Have children identify places where they see calendars.

Warm Up To activate prior knowledge, have children take turns saying the names of the days of the week beginning with Monday. Continue by having children take turns saying the names of the months of the year. Repeat the activity several times so children have the opportunity to say the names of different days and different months. Then have children measure calendar time by days, by weeks, by months, and by years.

Chart and Graph Skills

Read a Calendar

A **calendar** is a kind of chart that shows days, weeks, months, and years. A calendar helps us tell about and measure time. It also helps us remember important days. 1

May

Sunday	Monday	Tuesday	Wednesday	Thursda
				1
4	5	6	7	8
11 Mother's Day	12	13	14	15
18	19	20	21	22
25	26 Memorial Day	27	28	29

262

Practice and Extend

Play a Game

- Distribute an index card to each child. Have children write a question using the calendar shown on pp. 262–263. Model with questions such as: *What is the date of the third Tuesday in May?* and *On what day of the week does the last day of May fall? How much time is there between May 14 and May 21?*
- When children have finished their questions, have them exchange index cards and write the answers to the questions on the flip side of the index card.

Look at Michael's calendar for May. How many days are in this month? Find the day Michael celebrates his birthday. On which day of the week is Mother's Day? 2

1. What national holiday do we celebrate in May?
2. On what four days does Michael have soccer games?
3. **On Your Own** Draw your own calendar for this month. Put important dates on it.

263

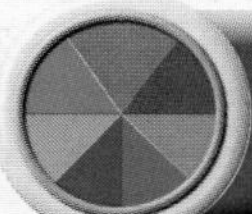

CURRICULUM CONNECTION
Science

Seasons of the Year

- Use a large wall calendar to have children help you group the months of the year by season.
- Once groups have been established, talk about the local weather during different seasons.
- Have children choose a season to draw and write about. They should include what the weather conditions are and show people dressed appropriately.

Workbook, p. 64

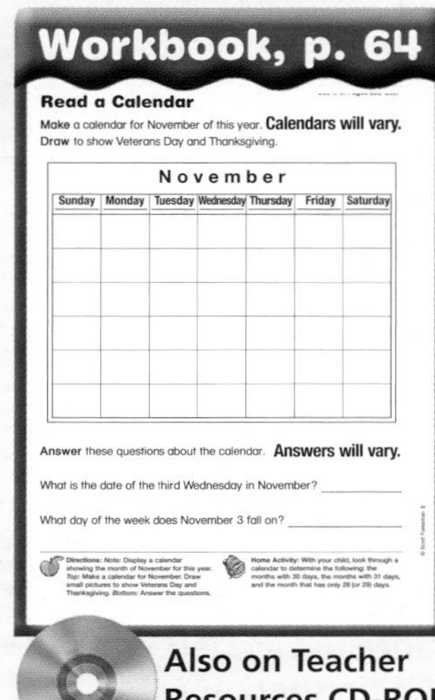

Also on Teacher Resources CD-ROM.

2 Teach and Discuss

Pages 262–263

After they read the pages, have children answer the questions posed in the text.

1 **How is a calendar useful?** Possible answers: It measures time. It helps people remember important dates and holidays. **Recall and Retell**

2 **How are a calendar and a time line alike? How are they different?** Possible answer: Alike—Both show important dates; Different—Calendars are charts that indicate every day of a year; time lines show only dates on which important events occurred. **Compare and Contrast**

Ongoing Assessment

If... children are confused about how to read a calendar,	**then...** choose a month on a large wall calendar and show children how to read each row across from left to right and then to sweep back to read the next row.

3 Close and Assess

Try it!

1. Memorial Day
2. Michael has soccer games on May 5, May 10, May 17, and May 24.
3. **On Your Own** Check children's calendars for the name of the month, correct placement of the names of the days of the week, and the numbering of days.

Use with pages 256–263

Lesson 2 Wrap-Up

MEETING INDIVIDUAL NEEDS
Learning Styles

Holidays

Have children recall the definition of *holiday*. Talk briefly about the holidays they have learned about in the lesson.

Verbal Learning Have children describe their favorite holiday in detail, talking about special activities, foods, and so on. Children should feel free to name holidays other than those in the lesson.

Musical Learning Have children make up a new holiday song, writing words to a familiar tune such as "Row, Row, Row Your Boat" or "Twinkle, Twinkle Little Star."

Kinesthetic Learning Have children cut out or draw pictures that represent a favorite holiday. They can use the cutouts or drawings to make a holiday collage.

Hands-on Activities

CURRICULUM CONNECTION
Art

Holiday Greeting Cards

Objective Make a holiday card.

Materials construction paper, crayons, and colored pencils

Learning Style
Kinesthetic/Linguistic

Partners

Time 15–20 minutes

1. Have partners choose a holiday that they learned about or that they celebrate with their families.

2. Have children fold a sheet of construction paper in half.

3. On the front of the card, have one child draw a picture or several pictures that illustrate the holiday. On the inside of the card, have the partner write an appropriate holiday greeting.

CURRICULUM CONNECTION
Reading

Word Accordions

Objective Practice spelling the vocabulary words.

Materials 8" by 1" construction paper strips, pencils

Learning Style
Linguistic/Kinesthetic

Individual

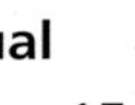

Time 15–20 minutes

1. Give each child two strips. Show them how to fold the paper strips accordion style. Have children fold the first strip six times in order to make seven "spaces" and the second strip five times to make six "spaces."

2. Have children spell out *holiday* on the strip with seven spaces. Tell them to write one letter in each space. Offer assistance as needed. When children have finished, have them point to and say each letter as they spell the word aloud.

3. Then have children spell out *custom* on the strip with six spaces, following the same procedure. Observe children as they work.

4. Encourage children to save the strips to use as spelling tools.

Remind children to add *holiday* and *custom* to their "My Word Book" glossaries.

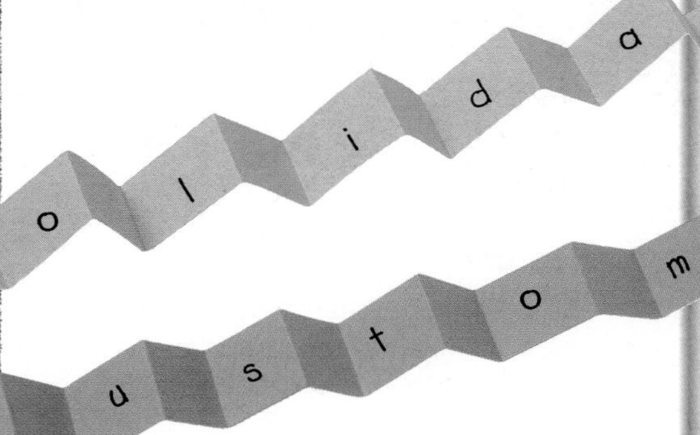

Lesson 3 Overview

Landmarks in Our Country **pages 264–267**	Children will learn the meaning of the vocabulary word *landmark*. They will also learn about some of the important landmarks of the United States.	 Time 20–30 minutes Resources • Workbook, p. 65 • Vocabulary Card **landmark** • Every Student Learns Guide, pp. 110–113
I. M. Pei **pages 268–269**	Children will learn about I. M. Pei, the Chinese American architect who has designed landmark buildings around the world.	 Time 15–20 minutes
Landmarks Around the World **pages 270–271**	Children will learn about some of the important landmarks located around the world.	 Time 15–20 minutes

Build Background

Activity

Community Landmarks

 **Time** 15–20 minutes

- Tell children to think about important places in their community or state that they have visited. Examples might include a museum, a special monument or statue, a historical park, or a well-known sports stadium.
- Then have children choose one of these places, draw a picture of it, and explain why it is important.

If time is short, omit the drawing part of the activity described above.

Read Aloud

Landmarks

by Christopher Erickson

A statue in the harbor
standing tall and proud;
The Alamo in Texas;
we honor them aloud.

An arch near the river
shines brightly in the sun.
Landmarks in America;
remain when day is done!

Landmarks in Our Country

Objective

- Identify and explain the significance of various community, state, and national landmarks.

Vocabulary

landmark a building or place that is important or interesting (p. 264)

QUICK Teaching Plan

If time is short, name the landmarks in the lesson as children look at the pictures. Ask if children can name landmarks in their state.

1 Introduce and Motivate

Preview Display the Vocabulary Card **landmark** and share the definition as "a building or place that is important or interesting." Then have children look through the lesson to find two landmarks they think most people would recognize and be able to name.

Warm Up To activate prior knowledge, remind children that in earlier lessons they have talked about different landmarks, among them: the United States Capitol, the Washington Monument, and the Statue of Liberty. Ask why each is considered a landmark.

Landmarks in Our Country

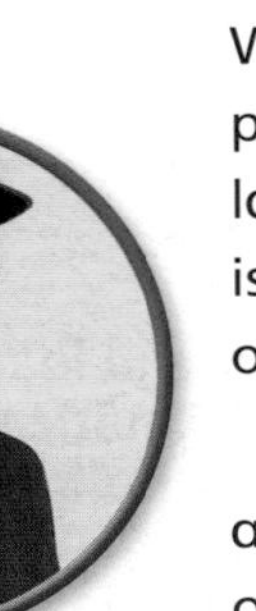

My dad is taking me on a trip to Chicago. We will see the Cubs play baseball! The Cubs play at Wrigley Field. This ballpark is a landmark in the community. A **landmark** is a building or place that is important or interesting.

Wrigley Field was built more than 85 years ago. It is one of the oldest ballparks in our country. Look at these pictures. How has Wrigley Field changed over time?

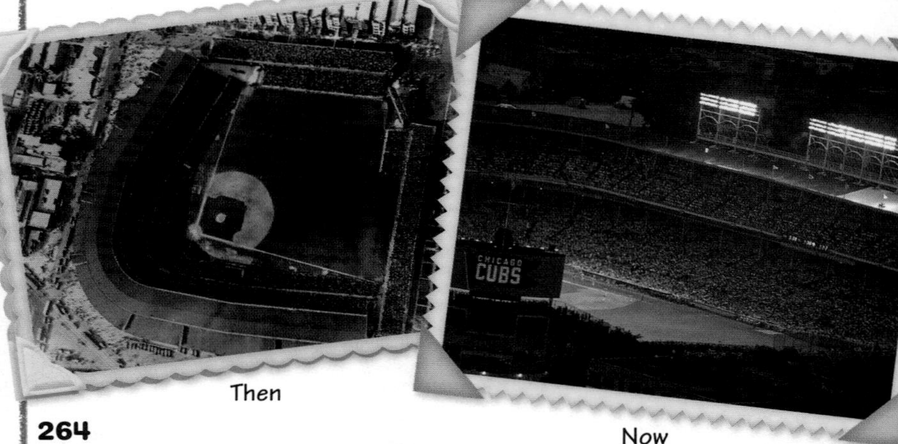

Then

Now

Practice and Extend

READING SKILL Classify/Categorize

- After children have read the lesson, note that landmarks are grouped in a special way. Talk about how the landmarks are grouped.
- Say that there is another way to group the same landmarks.
- Copy the chart below on the board. Then tell children to copy it.
- Have children look back through the lesson to categorize, or group, the landmarks as *Important Buildings* and *Other Important Places.*

Important Buildings	Other Important Places
1. ________	1. ________
2. ________	2. ________
3. ________	3. ________
	4. ________

Every state has important landmarks. What are some landmarks in your state?

The Gateway Arch is at the edge of the Mississippi River in Missouri. It reminds people that America grew much larger when pioneers moved out west.

4

e Atchison County Courthouse in nsas is built of stone. The clock the tower is easy to see from far ay. For more than 100 years, this ilding has been used for county vernment business.

3

In 1836, Texas was fighting to be free from Mexico's rule. For 13 days, a small group of Texans defended the Alamo against thousands of Mexican soldiers. The Alamo is a famous landmark to Texans.

265

SOCIAL STUDIES

Background

About the Alamo

- It was built as a Roman Catholic mission called San Antonio de Valero.
- The mission consisted of a monastery and a church surrounded by high walls—like a fort.
- David "Davy" Crockett and Jim Bowie, famous frontiersmen, helped defend the Alamo.
- Some people think Crockett survived the Mexican attack and later was shot; others do not.

WEB SITE

Technology

You can look up vocabulary words online. Click on *Social Studies Library* and select the dictionary at **www.sfsocialstudies.com.**

2 Teach and Discuss

Page 264

Reinforce the fact that a landmark does not need to be related to government or government officials. It can be anything that is important to the people of an area or a country and tells something about history.

1 **Why do you think a ballpark can be a landmark?** Possible answers: Because it tells about the sports that people enjoy; if it is very old, it shows how buildings used to look **Make Inferences**

2 **Which photo shows Wrigley Field in the present?** The photo on the right **What does it show that enables people to enjoy baseball games at nighttime?** Electric lights that can shine on the playing field **Analyze Pictures**

Page 265

Show a map of the United States. Have children use their map skills to locate St. Louis, Missouri; San Antonio, Texas; and Atchison, Kansas.

Help children answer the question at the top of the page.

3 **Which landmark looks like a small fort?** The Alamo **Analyze Pictures**

4 **Which landmark on this page is a government building?** Atchison County Courthouse **Analyze Pictures**

continued

Page 266

After children read, explain that in the United States there are many important Native American landmarks. One example is the large, pyramid-like earth mounds in Cahokia, a Native American site in Illinois. Another is Pueblo Bonito (Pretty Village) in New Mexico, the ancient Anasazi town made from adobe. This site is considered one of the greatest architectural achievements of the northern Native Americans.

5 **Why do you think the four Presidents you see were chosen to be on Mount Rushmore?** Possible answers: They did great things for the country—George Washington fought in the war to free the country; Abraham Lincoln ended slavery; Thomas Jefferson wrote the Declaration of Independence; Theodore Roosevelt gave us our National Parks System. They are the Presidents people felt most strongly about at the time the memorial was sculpted. **Make Inferences**

6 **What country gave the Statue of Liberty to the United States as a gift?** France **Recall and Retell**

SOCIAL STUDIES STRAND
Geography

Crazy Horse Memorial

- South Dakota is home to more than just Mount Rushmore. It is home to a project that has been going on since 1948—the carving of an enormous statue of Crazy Horse, the great leader of the Oglala Sioux.
- When finished, the Crazy Horse Memorial will be the largest statue in the world.

Ask children why it is important for the people who live in the United States today to remember and honor Native Americans with important monuments, statues, and paintings. Encourage children to talk about any of these they may have seen.

Our country has national landmarks too. National landmarks are important because they help us learn about the history of our country.

5 Mount Rushmore is a landmark in the Black Hills of South Dakota. The faces of Presidents George Washington, Thomas Jefferson, Theodore Roosevelt, and Abraham Lincoln are carved into the side of a mountain.

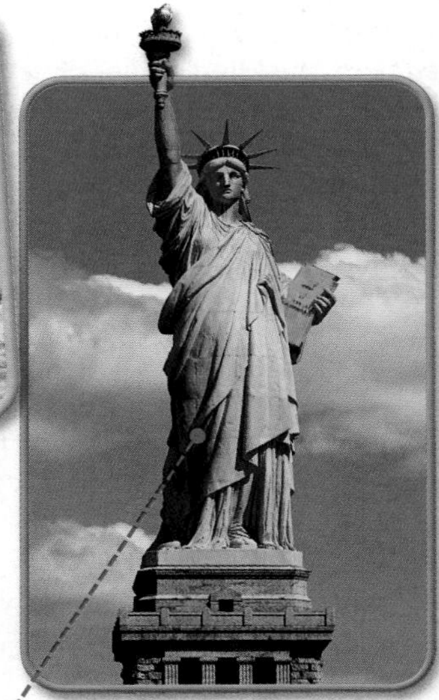

The Statue of Liberty stands for liberty, or freedom. The Statue of Liberty was a gift from the people of France to the people of the United States. 6

The United States Capitol is located in Washington, D.C. Congress works in the Capitol building.

266

Practice and Extend

ESL
EXTEND LANGUAGE
ESL Support

Exploring Landmarks Note that there are three kinds of landmarks on the page: building, statue, and sculpture, or carving. Write the terms on the board.

Beginning Have children choose one type of landmark to draw, using the photo as a model. Ask them to say if they drew a building, statue, or carving.

Intermediate Have children write a one sentence caption for their picture that includes its name and type of landmark.

Advanced Have children use their drawings and captions to explain why they chose to draw that particular landmark.

For additional ESL support, use Every Student Learns Guide, pp. 110–113.

United States Landmarks

CANADA
Mt. Rushmore
SOUTH DAKOTA
Wrigley Field
NEW YORK
The Statue of Liberty
7
The Atchison County Courthouse
ILLINOIS
8
KANSAS
MISSOURI
WASHINGTON, D.C.
The Gateway Arch
United States Capitol
PACIFIC OCEAN
TEXAS
The Alamo
Gulf of Mexico
N W E S
ATLANTIC OCEAN
MEXICO
9

What did you learn?

1. Why is the United States Capitol an important landmark?
2. Look at the map. Tell where the United States Capitol is located.
3. **Think and Share** Draw a picture of a statue or other landmark in your community. Explain why it is important.

267

Follow the Clues

- Have partners each write directions to a landmark shown on the map on p. 267.
- The directions should have three clues. For example: *Begin at the United States Capitol. Travel north until you reach the nearest landmark. Then go west to a large statue carved into the side of a mountain.*
- Have partners follow each other's clues.

Workbook, p. 65

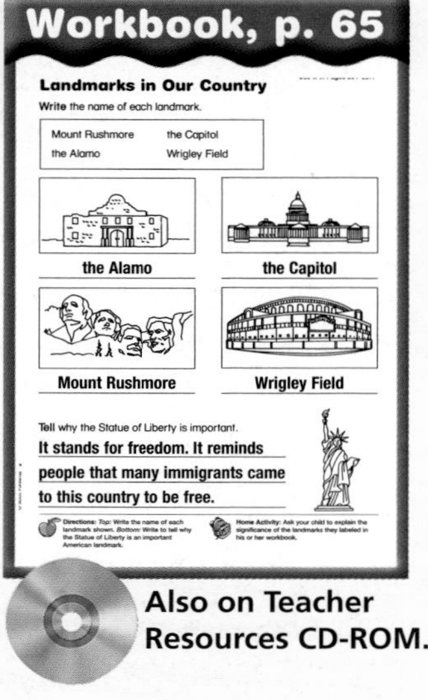

Landmarks in Our Country

Write the name of each landmark.

Mount Rushmore, the Capitol, the Alamo, Wrigley Field

the Alamo | the Capitol | Mount Rushmore | Wrigley Field

Tell why the Statue of Liberty is important.

It stands for freedom. It reminds people that many immigrants came to this country to be free.

Also on Teacher Resources CD-ROM.

Page 267

Have children use the map to find each of the landmarks they've learned about. Before children answer the questions that follow, differentiate between cardinal (north, south, east, west) and intermediate (northwest, southeast) directions. Model using intermediate directions by noting that to get from the Gateway Arch to the Alamo someone would have to travel south and west. Say that the Alamo is southwest of the Gateway Arch.

7 **Is the Statue of Liberty northeast or southwest of the Gateway Arch?** Northeast
Interpret Maps

8 **Which two landmarks are along the east coast?** United States Capitol and Statue of Liberty
Interpret Maps

9 **Which landmark is farthest south?** The Alamo **Interpret Maps**

3 Close and Assess

Have children tell which landmark they would like to visit and why.

✓ What did you learn?

1. The United States Capitol was in the past and still is today the place where Congress works.
2. Washington, D.C.
3. **Think and Share** Observe children as they draw. Have them talk about their pictures-in-progress. Remind them to write a sentence saying why their landmark is important.

Ieoh Ming Pei

Objective

- Explain how people influence communities.

1 Introduce and Motivate

Preview Read aloud the title of the feature. The pronunciation of Pei is (pā). Then have children find the definition of *architect* on p. 269. Encourage them to look at the map and its caption to find out where I. M. Pei was born.

Warm Up To activate prior knowledge, ask children if all buildings look the same. Have them think about why buildings look different. Help them understand that the purpose of a building often affects its design, or the way it looks.

2 Teach and Discuss

Tell children that the story of I. M. Pei is an example of how immigrants have contributed greatly to the United States.

1 **What did I. M. Pei do after becoming a citizen of the United States?** He started a business; he traveled around the world to design buildings. Sequence

2 **Do you think the schools he has designed would look like the airline terminals he has designed? Why?** Possible answer: No; they probably look different because they have different purposes. Make Inferences

Practice and Extend

CURRICULUM CONNECTION
Art

Design the Perfect School

- Invite children to be architects.
- Have them draw sketches of what they think the perfect school would look like.
- Have them think about shape, size, number of windows and doors, what the area surrounding the building would look like, and so on.
- Encourage children to share their building designs.

WEB SITE
Technology

You may help children find out more about I. M. Pei by clicking on *Meet the People* at **www.sfsocialstudies.com.**

Ieoh Ming Pei was born in Canton (now Guangzhou), China.

I. M. Pei was born in China. When he was a teenager, he was fascinated by the tall modern buildings he saw. When he was 18 years old, he came to the United States. He wanted to become an architect. An architect is a person who designs buildings.

After he finished school, I. M. Pei worked for other architects. He also taught students about how to design buildings. During this time, he became a citizen of the United States. Then he started his own architecture business. 1 He designed projects in the United States and around the world.

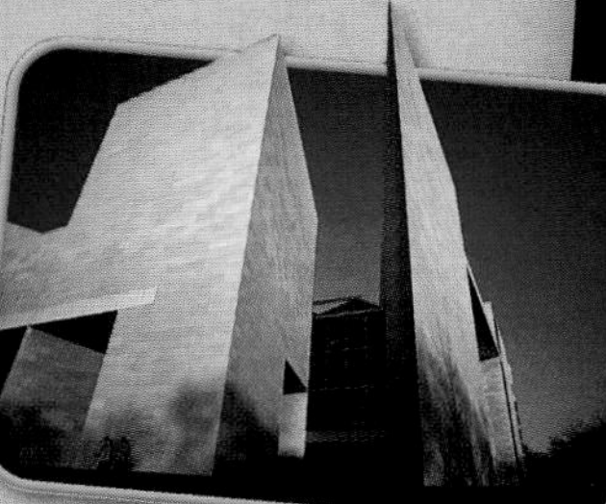

East Wing, National Gallery of Art, Washington, D.C.

I. M. Pei has designed libraries, office buildings, airline terminals, hotels, and schools, but his favorite 2 work is designing museums. He enjoys learning about places and people so he can design buildings that fit the special needs of each. He likes to design buildings that people enjoy visiting. 3 4

Think and Share

How has I. M. Pei made the world a more beautiful place to live?

For more information, go online to *Meet the People* at **www.sfsocialstudies.com.**

269

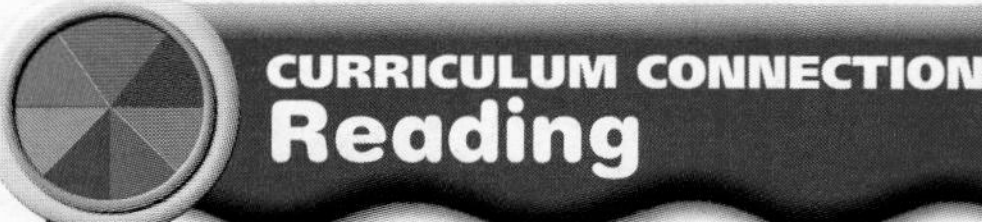

CURRICULUM CONNECTION
Reading

About Being an Architect

Children may enjoy reading the following book to find out what architects do.

Day in the Life of an Architect, by Mary Bowman-Kruhm (Rosen Publishing Group, ISBN 0-823-95297-5, 1999).

3 Why do you think some of the buildings designed by I. M. Pei have become landmarks? Possible answers: Because they are interesting to look at; because important things happen in them; because in the future they will let people know how today's architects thought about buildings. **Make Inferences**

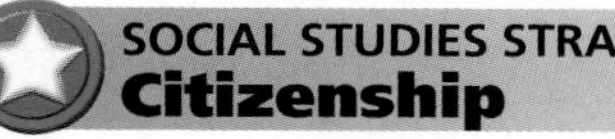

SOCIAL STUDIES STRAND
Citizenship

4 How has I. M. Pei shown that he is a good citizen? Possible answer: He designs buildings for many different purposes and many different people. He works to make his community, the country, and the world a more beautiful place. **Draw Conclusions**

3 Close and Assess

Think and Share

I. M. Pei's buildings are beautiful. They have special designs. The buildings meet the needs of people who visit or work in them.

Landmarks Around the World

Objectives

- Use designations of time periods such as ancient times and modern times.
- Locate Egypt and China on a world map.

1 Introduce and Motivate

Preview Write the words *ancient* and *modern* on the board and read them aloud. Ask children to give examples of some things they think are ancient and modern. Help them recognize that *ancient* means "very old" and *modern* means "present-day" or "recent."

Warm Up To activate prior knowledge, encourage children to tell what they know about Egypt and China. Then display a world map. Have volunteers locate Egypt and China. Ask children to name the continents on which the countries are located.

2 Teach and Discuss

Page 270

Tell children that some of the workers who built pyramids were slaves. Help children recall that a slave is someone who is owned by another person.

❶ **Why do you think the pyramids are considered to be landmarks?** Possible answer: Because they were built long ago and let people know about life in ancient Egypt **Draw Conclusions**

Landmarks Around the World

Take a look at two countries that have important landmarks. Our first stop is the country of Egypt on the continent of Africa. Find Egypt on the globe.

In ancient Egypt, kings and queens were buried inside stone pyramids. A pyramid has four triangular sides that come to a point at the top.

It took thousands of people to build one pyramid. Each block of stone weighed more than your family's car! Some pyramids are so large that they could cover several football fields.

Today, we still wonder how the Egyptians built the pyramids without using modern machines. How do you think they built them?

❶ ❷ ❸

270

Practice and Extend

FAST FACTS

Egypt

- The Nile River, which flows through Egypt, runs from south to north.
- Some of the stones used to build the pyramids were transported on the Nile River from southern Egypt. Pyramids were built near the river.
- There are about 80 ancient pyramids in Egypt today.
- "Mer" is the ancient Egyptian word for *pyramid*.
- Jewelry, clothing, weaponry, chariots, and many other things kings and queens used in their daily lives were buried with them for use in the afterlife.

Our next stop is the country of China. Look at the globe. On which continent is China located?

4 The Great Wall of China was built more than 2,000 years ago. It took about 1 million people to build it! Ancient Chinese states first built walls for protection. Later these walls were joined together and called the Great Wall.

If you put the Great Wall across the United States, from east to west, it would be much longer than our country!

5

Hands-on History

The pyramids in Egypt and the Great Wall in China are ancient landmarks still standing today. Draw a modern landmark that you think will still be standing thousands of years from now.

271

CURRICULUM CONNECTION
Art

Inside a Pyramid

- Tell children that they will draw what they think a pyramid looked like inside.
- Have children think about how ancient Egyptians would have gotten from the bottom to the top of the pyramid; what a typical room might have looked like, and what everyday items would have been placed in a room for the comfort of the king or queen in the afterlife.
- Have children label parts of their drawings. Ask volunteers to share their work.

2 Why were the pyramids built of stone? Possible answers: Stone was available. Stone also lasts a very long time, and it was important that these tombs last a long time. **Make Inferences**

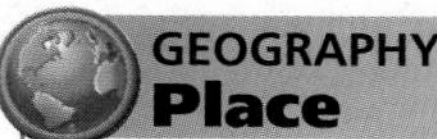

GEOGRAPHY
Place

3 How is Egypt different from the place you live? Possible answers: Egypt has great pyramids; it appears that much of the land is covered with sand. **Compare and Contrast**

Page 271

Tell children that the Great Wall of China was a work in progress and was built, rebuilt, and added on to for several thousand years; much of the wall as it looks today was built between 1368–1644.

4 Was the Great Wall of China built in ancient times or modern times? Ancient times **Draw Conclusions**

Test Talk

Use Information from Graphics
Have children use details from the photo of the Great Wall to support their answer.

5 What natural resources do you think Chinese people used to build the Great Wall? Possible answers: Stone, earth, clay **Analyze Pictures**

3 Close and Assess

Hands-on History

Children's answers will vary. Drawings most probably will reflect landmarks they have read about, such as the United States Capitol, the Statue of Liberty, or Mount Rushmore.

Use with pages 264–271

Lesson 3 Wrap-Up

MEETING INDIVIDUAL NEEDS Leveled Practice

A Special Monument

Have children think about what a landmark that honors schoolchildren would look like. Brainstorm a list of ideas in preparation for the activities.

Easy Have children write a name for their landmark. **Reteach**

On-Level Have children write two or three sentences to explain the significance of their landmark. **Extend**

Challenge Have children say where their landmark is located and why. **Enrich**

Hands-on Activities

CURRICULUM CONNECTION
Reading

Two Words in One

Objective Demonstrate understanding of new vocabulary; identify compound words.

Materials paper, pencils

Learning Style Verbal/Linguistic

Individual

Time 10–15 minutes

1. Display the word *landmark*, noting that it is a compound word. Have children tell how each part of *landmark* contributes to its meaning.

2. Have children make a list of as many compound words as they can in three minutes.

3. Have children share their lists.

Remind children to add *landmark* to their "My Word Book" glossaries.

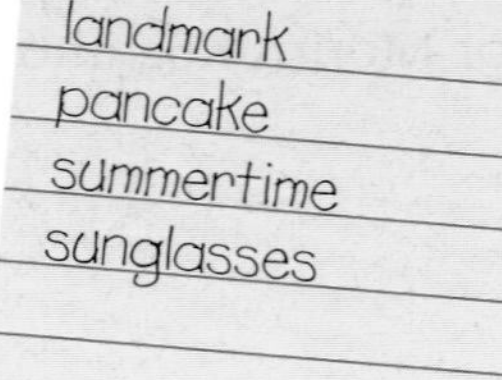

CURRICULUM CONNECTION
Writing

Ode to a Landmark

Objective Write a poem.

Materials paper, pencils

Learning Style Linguistic

Individual

Time 15–20 minutes

1. Tell children they will write *odes*, which are poems that praise someone or something. Say that each child will write a four-line ode to a landmark.

2. Begin a list on the board of words children might use: *glorious, awesome, mighty, magnificent*. Encourage their additions. Suggest that children look up the words in a dictionary.

3. Share an example: *Hurray for the Wall!/It is so great and long,/ Mighty and strong!/ It will never ever fall.*

4. Ask volunteers to share their odes.

CURRICULUM CONNECTION
Art

Be a Builder

Objective Create visual materials based on factual information.

Materials construction paper, cardboard, small boxes, clay, sticks, pencils, paint, crayons, pipe cleaners

Learning Style Kinesthetic/Verbal

Group

Time 25–30 minutes

1. Have each group choose a landmark from Lesson 3 to construct using whatever art supplies are available.

2. Have children write an exhibit-type label that tells about the landmark and the materials used in its construction.

Lesson 4 Overview

A Step Back in Time

pages 272–275

Children will learn the meaning of the vocabulary words *artifact* and *invention*. They will also learn about how artifacts provide people with useful information about the past and how people still use some of the things that were made by others long ago.

 Time 20–30 minutes

Resources

- Workbook, p. 66
- Vocabulary Cards **artifact** **invention**
- Every Student Learns Guide, pp. 114–117

Read a Diagram

pages 276–277

Children will learn how to read a diagram and see how diagrams are useful.

 Time 15–20 minutes

Resource

- Workbook p. 67

Build Background

Activity

Show and Tell

 **Time** 15–20 minutes

- Have children name some things they use on a daily basis—things that make life better, easier, or more enjoyable. Suggest a toothbrush, markers, stapler, and backpack to get children thinking.
- Have each child bring in one of the discussed items from home.
- Set aside class time for children to take turns showing the class their object. Have them describe its purpose and explain what it might tell people in the future about how we live.

If time is short, select an item for the whole class to talk about.

Read Aloud

Artifacts and Treasures

by Eric Meyer

Dig deep underground
in many different lands
for artifacts and treasures
buried beneath the sands.

Ancient toys and pottery, and
jewels that shine so bright
are valuable clues from long ago
and quite an amazing sight!

A Step Back in Time

Objective

- Explain how the contributions of ancient China and Egypt have influenced the present world in terms of architecture, inventions, the calendar, and written language.

Vocabulary

artifact an object made and used by people (p. 272)

invention something new that someone makes or thinks of (p. 275)

QUICK Teaching Plan

If time is short, help children transform the second question in *What Did You Learn?* (p. 275) into a statement: Ancient China and Egypt developed items we still use in modern times.

1 Introduce and Motivate

Preview Display the Vocabulary Cards **artifact** and **invention**. Read aloud the definition for each word. Explain that when an item or tool is brand new, or just thought of, it is an *invention.* After it has been in use by people for a long time, the item or tool is an *artifact.*

Warm Up To activate prior knowledge, give children clues that will help them identify these inventions: clock, ballpoint pen, airplane, computer.

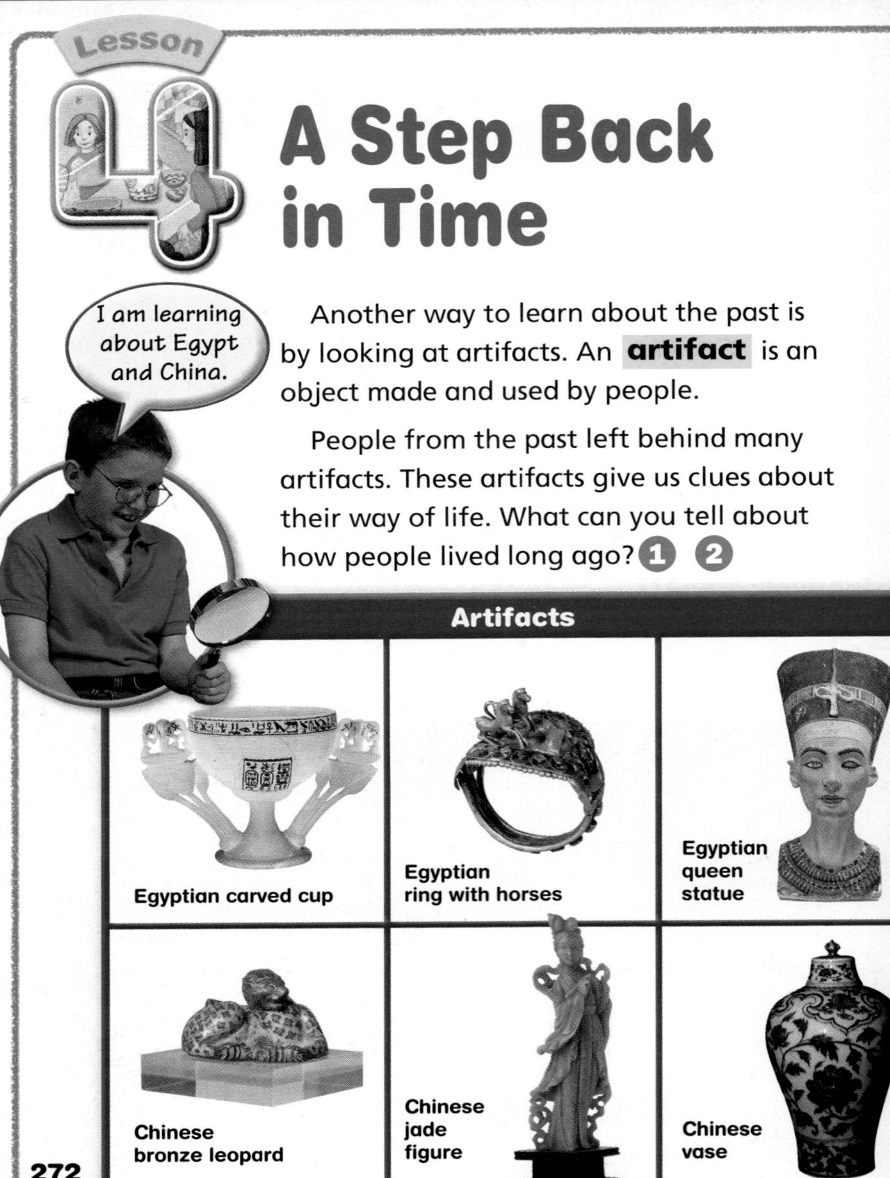
Lesson 4

A Step Back in Time

Another way to learn about the past is by looking at artifacts. An **artifact** is an object made and used by people.

People from the past left behind many artifacts. These artifacts give us clues about their way of life. What can you tell about how people lived long ago? 1 2

Artifacts

Egyptian carved cup

Egyptian ring with horses

Egyptian queen statue

Chinese bronze leopard

Chinese jade figure

Chinese vase

272

Practice and Extend

READING SKILL
Recall and Retell

Target Skill

- Tell children that when they recall something, they think back to remember it. When they retell, they use their own words to give someone information about what they recall.
- After children have read p. 275, have them close their books. Tell them to recall two things they read about. Then have them write to retell the information in their own words.
- Have partners share their retellings.

WEB SITE
Technology

You can look up vocabulary words online. Click on *Social Studies Library* and select the dictionary at **www.sfsocialstudies.com.**

Egypt

Egyptian hieroglyphics

The Egyptians had a system of writing called hieroglyphics. They drew pictures and symbols on walls. They also wrote on stone and clay tablets.

Later, the Egyptians made ink and pens. They wrote on papyrus, a thin paper-like material made from tall grass. Our word *paper* comes from the word *papyrus*. ③

China

Chinese characters

The Chinese had a system of writing too. They wrote symbols called characters on bones, shells, and strips of bamboo. These characters stood for objects and ideas. Today, the Chinese still use characters as their system of writing. ④

273

CURRICULUM CONNECTION
Reading

Hieroglyph Messages

- Tell children that the inside walls of the pyramids were filled with hieroglyphics that often told the life story of the king or queen who was buried there.
- Have children create their own hieroglyphics to communicate information about themselves in the same way that the ancient Egyptians used hieroglyphics to tell about their way of life.
- Tell children their messages should include at least five little pictures that form a sentence or sentences.
- Display the pictures in class and have volunteers attempt to "read" their classmates' pictures.

2 Teach and Discuss

Page 272

Tell children that people who look for artifacts from the past are called *archaeologists*. Explain that archaeologists dig at or near the sites where cities or communities once existed, in the hope of finding artifacts from these ancient places.

① **What are some things, other than artifacts, that let people know about the past?** Possible answers: old photographs, old newspapers, landmarks, historic statues, and paintings
Recall and Retell

② **What does the Egyptian queen statue tell you about the ancient Egyptians?** Possible answer: They respected and thought highly of their rulers. **Make Inferences**

Page 273

Help children with the pronunciation of *hieroglyphics* (hī′•ər•ə•glif′•iks) and *papyrus* (pə•pī′•rəs).

③ **What tool made by ancient Egyptians is still in use in our modern world?** Pens
Draw Conclusions

④ **What Chinese-made material used for writing and keeping ideas is still in use today?** Paper **Why do you think paper was an important invention?** Possible answer: It is easier to write on than bones or shells. **Express Ideas**

continued

Page 274

Tell children that the Egyptians were largely a farming people. They used the water from the Nile River to irrigate and grow crops.

5 **What do all calendars do?** They measure the passage of time in some way. **Draw Conclusions**

6 **Why do you think measuring the seasons was important to the Egyptians?** Possible answers: So they would know when to plant and harvest their crops; so they would know when the Nile River was going to rise and fall **Main Idea and Details**

7 **How are the Egyptian calendar and the calendar we use today alike?** Both calendars are based on 12 months. **Compare and Contrast**

Nile River

5 6 The Egyptians and the Chinese used calendars. An Egyptian calendar measured the seasons. It also measured the rise and fall of the Nile River. The Egyptian calendar had 12 months in one year. Each month had 30 days that added up to 360 days. The Egyptians then added 5 days at the end of the year to make 365 days. How many days do we have in one year? 7

The Chinese use a calendar based on the phases of the moon. It is called the Chinese Lunar Calendar. *Lunar* means "like the moon." Each lunar year is named after an animal.

Egyptian stone calendar

Chinese calendar

274

Practice and Extend

SOCIAL STUDIES
Background

About World Regions

Help children compare and contrast Egypt and China. Note that farming is important in both countries.

- Egypt is a hot, dry desert country. Only a narrow band of "green land" exists thanks to the Nile River. Egyptian farmers grow wheat and barley. They irrigate the land.
- China is a vast country that includes different climates. Different crops are grown in the different climate regions—rainy, hot southern China: rice and sugarcane; drier, cooler north: wheat and barley. The Chinese irrigate the land.

Ask children what important crops Egypt and China have in common.

EXTEND LANGUAGE
ESL Support

Inventions Review the meaning of *invention*. Write the following on the board in random order: *television, pen, car, cat, leaf, light bulb.* Read the words aloud as you point to them.

Beginning Reread the words, one at a time, asking each time if the word names an invention. Have children choose an invention to draw and label.

Intermediate Have children explain how their selected invention helps people.

Advanced Have children think of a way to make that invention even better. Encourage them to share their ideas in writing and drawings.

For additional ESL support, use Every Student Learns Guide, pp. 114–117.

An **invention** is something new that someone makes or thinks of. The Chinese (8) made many inventions. Many of these inventions, such as the wheelbarrow and kite, are still used today. (9)

Luxor obelisk, Egypt

The ancient Egyptians built obelisks. An obelisk is a huge monument that points toward the sky. The Washington Monument in Washington, D.C., (10) is built in the shape of an obelisk.

What did you learn?

1. What do we learn by looking at artifacts?
2. What have ancient China and Egypt given us that we still use in modern times?
3. **Think and Share** Draw a picture of something that you use today that may someday be an artifact. Write about why you think it might become an artifact.

275

Page 275

(8) **Why do people invent things?** Possible answer: They want to find a better, easier, or faster way to do something. **Make Inferences**

(9) **What is the purpose of a wheelbarrow?** Possible answer: To move things that are too heavy to carry by hand **Analyze Pictures**

(10) **What do Egyptian obelisks and the Washington Monument have in common?** Possible answer: They are all monuments that point toward the sky. **Recall and Retell**

3 Close and Assess

Have children identify two things they learned in the lesson that they would like to share with someone else. Have them explain why they chose the information they did.

✓ What did you learn?

Test Talk

Write Your Answer
Children should ask themselves, "Is the information in my written answer correct?"

1. Artifacts show how people did everyday tasks, what materials they had to make things, and what things were important to their daily lives.
2. Ink, pens, kites, and wheelbarrows
3. **Think and Share** Observe children as they work. Remind them that artifacts are usually very useful things people needed to make their lives easier and more comfortable.

CURRICULUM CONNECTION Literature

More to Read

Children may enjoy browsing or reading the following books about China and Egypt.

- ***Favorite Children's Stories from China and Tibet,*** by Lotta Carswell Hume (Tuttle Publishing, ISBN 0-804-83303-6, 2001)
- ***The Legend of Mu Lan: A Heroine of Ancient China,*** by Wei Jiang and Cheng An Jiang (Victory Press, ISBN 1-878-21714-3, 1997)
- ***Vinnie in Egypt,*** by Elizabeth Bott, (Pageturner Books, ISBN 0-970-46780-X, 2000)

Workbook, p. 66

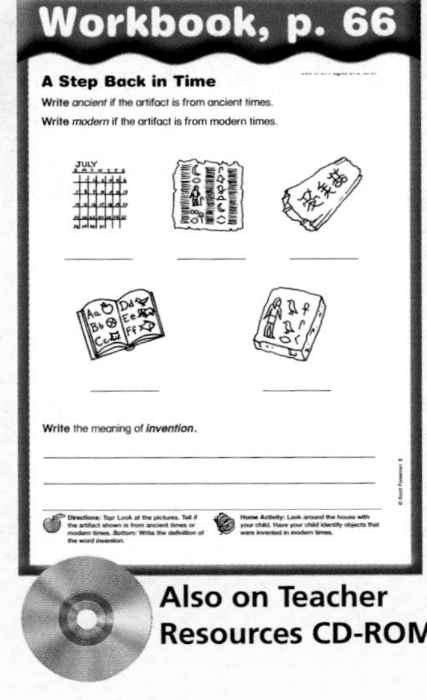

A Step Back in Time

Write *ancient* if the artifact is from ancient times.
Write *modern* if the artifact is from modern times.

Write the meaning of *invention*.

Also on Teacher Resources CD-ROM.

Read a Diagram

Objective

- Obtain information about a topic using a diagram.

Vocabulary

diagram a drawing that shows parts of something (p. 277)

1 Introduce and Motivate

Preview Read aloud the title of the feature and share the meaning of **diagram.** Then read the first sentence. Ask children to tell what they think the diagram on pp. 276–277 shows.

Warm Up To activate prior knowledge, ask children who may have put together a toy or model of some kind to tell about their experiences. Have them tell if they read written directions or if they also used a picture with labels to help them.

2 Teach and Discuss

Pages 276–277

Read the feature aloud as children follow along. After reading, have children answer the question posed in the last sentence on p. 277. (yoke)

1 If you didn't read the sentences on p. 276, how could you tell that a chariot was used for transportation? Possible answer: It looks like a cart that someone could ride in. **Interpret Diagrams**

2 Did people sit down to ride in a chariot? How do you know? No; there were no seats. **Interpret Diagrams**

Read a Diagram

Some people in ancient Egypt traveled in a kind of wheeled cart called a chariot. Chariots were pulled by horses. Chariots were used as transportation for the king and other important people. Chariots were also used for fighting and racing.

Practice and Extend

Make a Diagram

- Have children draw a simple diagram of a plant or an animal of their choice.
- Remind them to give their diagram a title and to include clear labels for the most important parts of the plant or animal.

Below is a diagram of a chariot. A **diagram** is a drawing that shows the parts of something. A diagram gives information in a chart or picture instead of sentences.

Look at this diagram. What part of the chariot fits across the back of the horse?

Try it!

1. What was a chariot driver called?
2. How many spokes do you see in one wheel?
3. **On Your Own** Make a diagram of your favorite toy. Label the parts.

Scarcity

- Explain that chariots were made from wood.
- Ask children if they think there were many trees in Egypt from which to get wood. Have children look back at the pictures in Lesson 4, as needed.
- Remind children that when something is scarce, or there is not enough for everyone who wants it, it becomes more expensive. Only wealthy Egyptians could afford wooden chariots.

Workbook, p. 67

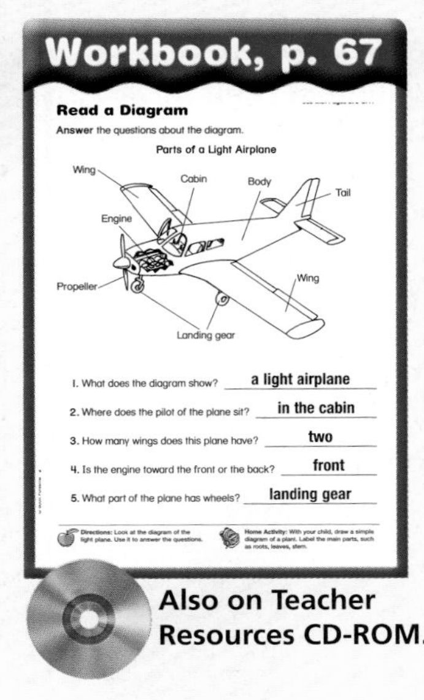
Read a Diagram

Answer the questions about the diagram.

Parts of a Light Airplane

Wing, Cabin, Body, Tail, Engine, Propeller, Wing, Landing gear

1. What does the diagram show? **a light airplane**
2. Where does the pilot of the plane sit? **in the cabin**
3. How many wings does this plane have? **two**
4. Is the engine toward the front or the back? **front**
5. What part of the plane has wheels? **landing gear**

Also on Teacher Resources CD-ROM.

❸ **How is a diagram like a bar graph?** Possible answer: They both give information in a form that is like a picture, that is quicker to read than words. **Compare and Contrast**

❹ **Why do you think that things that need to be put together, such as a table or a bike, come with a diagram?** Possible answer: A diagram lets people see how the parts of something fit together and what the finished product should look like. **Make Inferences**

3 Close and Assess

Try it!

1. Charioteer
2. Six
3. **On Your Own** Tell children to choose a toy that has at least three different parts. Check that children's labels are accurately placed. Display children's diagrams on a bulletin board or collect them into a booklet that children can review after they have completed the lesson.

Use with pages 272–277

Lesson 4 Wrap-Up

MEETING INDIVIDUAL NEEDS

Leveled Practice

News About Artifacts

Have children pretend to be part of an archaeological dig in either Egypt or China. Show encyclopedia pictures of some typical artifacts from ancient times. Show examples of jewelry, pottery, and so on.

Easy Have children select an artifact that they think the world should know about. Have them draw a sketch and label it with the name of the artifact. **Reteach**

On-Level Have children write a newspaper headline that tells about finding the artifact. **Extend**

Challenge Have children turn their sketch into a diagram by adding labels of important parts of the artifact. Have them write a sentence that explains how it was used or why it was valued. **Enrich**

Hands-on Activities

CURRICULUM CONNECTION

Reading

Word Search

Objective Demonstrate understanding of new vocabulary.

Resources Vocabulary Cards **artifact, invention**

Materials paper, pencils

Learning Style Visual/Linguistic

Individual

Time 10–15 minutes

1. Display the words *artifact* and *invention*. Review the meaning of each.

2. Send children on a word search. Have them find as many little words in each of the vocabulary words as they can. (*art, fact, act, a, in, vent, invent, on*) You may wish to set a time limit.

Remind children to add *artifact* and *invention* to their "My Word Book" glossaries.

CURRICULUM CONNECTION

Math

A New Calendar

Objective Create calendars.

Materials construction paper, markers, crayons, calendars

Learning Style Verbal/Social

Group

Time 20–25 minutes

1. Have children think about how many days there will be in their calendar week, whether or not there would be weekends, and so on. Encourage children to discuss their rationales.

2. Have each group create a calendar, counting out days and weeks for one month, and creating new names for days and whatever else they wish.

3. Have children compare their calendars.

CURRICULUM CONNECTION

Writing

Let's Find Out!

Objective Write to express interest in a topic.

Materials chart paper, pencils, nonfiction resources about ancient Egypt and China

Learning Style Social/Linguistic

Group

Time 15–20 minutes

1. Work with the whole class to develop a list of topics relating to Egypt and China that children would like to find out more about. Record the list on chart paper.

2. When children have independent learning time, have small groups do light research to satisfy an interest in one of the listed topics.

3. Plan times when groups can report orally from notes they take on their findings.

Lesson 5 Overview

Linking Our World **pages 278–281**	Children will learn the meaning of the vocabulary word *communication*. They will also learn about different devices that people use to communicate with one another. In addition, children will explore how people travel over great distances.	 Time 20–30 minutes Resources • Workbook, p. 68 • Vocabulary Card **communication** • Every Student Learns Guide, pp. 118–121
Meet Robert Fulton **pages 282–283**	Children will learn about Robert Fulton and his work as an inventor.	 Time 15–20 minutes

Build Background

Activity

Keeping in Touch

 **Time** 15–20 minutes

Talk about ways in which people stay in touch—writing letters, face-to-face conversation, using a computer (e-mail), or talking on the telephone.

Have children look in newspapers and magazines for pictures that show people staying in touch. Tell each child to cut out one picture and mount it on construction paper.

Display the pictures and list on the board the different ways that people "talk" with their friends and family members.

If time is short, have children brainstorm lists of past and present ways of communicating.

Read Aloud

Communication

by Larson James

Write a letter;
talk on the phone.
Read the paper
when you're all alone.

Send a fax
or go online.
Communication
is mighty fine!

Lesson 5 Linking Our World

Objectives

- Use vocabulary related to chronology, including *past, present*, and *future*.
- Describe how science and technology have changed communication and transportation.
- Identify historic figures who have exhibited a love of individualism and inventiveness.

Vocabulary

communication the sharing of ideas and information with others (p. 278)

QUICK Teaching Plan

If time is short, help children change the first question at the end of p. 281 to a statement: Inventions have changed communication and transportation. Then have children look at the pictures in the lesson to identify some inventions.

1 Introduce and Motivate

Preview Display the Vocabulary Card **communication**. Ask children to read the first paragraph on p. 278 to find its definition. Then have them skim p. 278 to name some important means of communication.

Warm Up To activate prior knowledge, have children think about ways people communicated in the past and ways they communicate today, in the present. Ask if there are fewer or more ways to communicate in the present. Have children explain their thinking.

Lesson 5 Linking Our World

People share ideas in many ways. Sharing ideas and information with others is **communication.** Communication links people in our world together.

1 Long ago, people wrote on walls and stone. Today, people use inventions such as the telephone, computer, and fax machine to 2 communicate. What would happen if we didn't have these inventions? How would we communicate with someone in another country?

In class, we learn how important it is to communicate and work together. How are these people communicating?

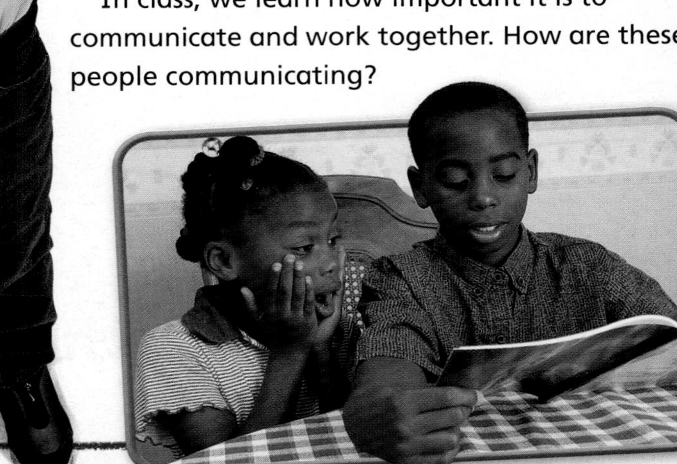

278

Practice and Extend

READING SKILL Compare and Contrast

- Remind children that when they compare and contrast, they look for ways things are alike and different.
- After children read pp. 280 and 281, have them copy the heading *Transportation* from the board. Below it have them write *Past* and *Present* as column headings.
- Tell children to make a chart by filling in ways of transportation from the past and the present. Explain that they can use what they know from their own experience as well as information they have read.

WEB SITE Technology

You can look up vocabulary words online. Click on *Social Studies Library* and select the dictionary at **www.sfsocialstudies.com.**

Some people communicate in other ways. Helen Keller was someone who could not hear or see. She communicated by using a form of sign language. She also learned Braille. Braille is a special way to read and write. Helen Keller helped others who couldn't hear or see. She wrote books about her life. 3 4

Reading Braille

Anne Sullivan reading to Helen Keller

279

ESL — ACCESS CONTENT
ESL Support

Ways We Communicate Make a list on the board of feelings people have: happy, sad, angry, frightened. Read the list and have each child select a feeling he or she will communicate in some way.

Beginning Have children use facial expressions and gestures to communicate their selected feeling. Have observers identify the feeling.

Intermediate Have children use only words to communicate their selected feeling. Discourage use of facial expression or body language.

Advanced Have children write to describe their selected feeling.

For additional ESL support, use Every Student Learns Guide, pp. 118–121.

2 Teach and Discuss

Page 278

After reading, have children answer the questions posed in the last two paragraphs.

1 **Besides writing on walls and stones, how do you think people communicated in the past?** Possible answers: By talking to one another, by writing letters, by sending a message through another person **Make Inferences**

Test Talk

Locate Key Words in the Text
Tell children to go back and look at the text to find the right answer.

2 **What has changed the way people communicate?** Inventions, such as the telephone, computer, fax machine **Main Idea and Details**

Page 279

After reading, explain that banking machines and elevators have Braille letters and numbers so people who are unable to see can use them.

Decision Making

3 **Helen Keller had important choices to make in dealing with her lack of sight and hearing. She decided to do her best to overcome it. What other choice could she have made?** Possible answer: She could have just felt sorry for herself and relied on others to do things for her. **Express Ideas**

4 **In what way was Helen Keller a good citizen?** Possible answer: She was caring. She tried to help others who had problems. **Draw Conclusions**

continued

Page 280

Make the point that people are able to keep making new inventions because of scientific knowledge and technology. Explain that *technology* means "the ways and materials through which scientific knowledge is applied."

5 Which means of transportation used in the past are still used in the present? Trains, ships
Recall and Retell

Ongoing Assessment

If... children are having difficulty distinguishing between transportation and communication, **then...** tell them that transportation is the movement of people and goods and communication is the exchange of information and ideas.

6 What is one contribution Henry Ford made to life in America? Possible answers: He built some of the first cars in America. The cars enabled people to get from place to place more quickly, which in turn helped the country grow.
Main Idea and Details

7 Ford's Model T is a symbol of inventiveness. Can you think of some things that show that people continue to be good at thinking of new and helpful inventions? Possible answers: Juice boxes, microwave popcorn, CDs and CD players **Apply Information**

8 What do you predict transportation will be like in the future? Possible answer: People will travel in cars that drive themselves. **Predict**

Henry Ford sitting in his first car

Transportation also links people in our world. In the past, most people traveled by using horses, wagons, and trains. 5

In 1893, Henry Ford built an engine that used gasoline. A few years later, he built what was called a "horseless carriage." It had a motor on a frame with bicycle wheels. These first cars were very expensive because they were built one by one.

Soon, Henry Ford and his company started building many cars at the same time. They built a less expensive car that more people could buy. It was called the Model T. 6 7

Cars today are much different from the Model T. They are safer and more comfortable. Computers help cars of the present run better.

280

Practice and Extend

SOCIAL STUDIES STRAND
Economics

The Assembly Line

Tell children that Henry Ford was able to reduce the cost of his automobile by reducing the cost of producing the car. One way was through use of the assembly line.

- A moving belt brought auto parts to a line of workers. Each worker performed a specific task in putting together a car. As each task was done, the car-in-progress moved on.
- This method reduced assembly time from $12\frac{1}{2}$ hours to about $1\frac{1}{2}$ hours.
- Ford hired more workers, and they did not need to be as skilled. Job opportunities grew.

Ask children how they think Ford's methods benefited the communities in which he had car plants. How did Ford's methods benefit consumers?

For hundreds of years, inventors experimented with flying machines. Then, in 1903, the Wright brothers made the first successful powered airplane flight. 9

Amelia Earhart was the first woman to fly alone across the Atlantic Ocean. She continued to make long flights and encouraged other women to fly. In 1937, Amelia Earhart began a flight around the world. Her plane disappeared. Amelia Earhart and the Wright brothers are remembered each year on National Aviation Day. 10

Today, many people travel to different parts of the world by jets. What kind of transportation might link communities in the future?

What did you learn?

1. How have inventions changed communication and transportation?
2. Why is Amelia Earhart an important person in our country's history?
3. **Think and Share** Make a poster. Show transportation in the past, the present, and the future. Tell about your poster.

281

Workbook, p. 68

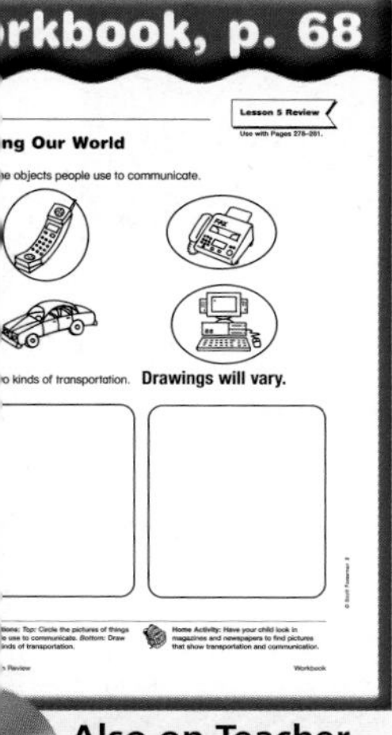
Lesson 5 Review

ng Our World

Drawings will vary.

Also on Teacher Resources CD-ROM.

Page 281

Talk briefly with children about the differences between early airplanes, such as the Wright brothers' plane, and modern jets. Show pictures for comparison, if possible.

After reading, have children answer the question posed at the end of the page.

9 **How did the invention of the airplane change transportation?** Possible answer: Airplanes gave people another choice for traveling long distances across oceans and land. Airplane travel was much faster. **Draw Conclusions**

10 **What special day celebrates the inventiveness of the Wright Brothers and the courage of Amelia Earhart?** National Aviation Day **Recall and Retell**

3 Close and Assess

✓ What did you learn?

1. Inventions have made it much easier and a lot quicker for people to keep in touch and travel from place to place.
2. Amelia Earhart was the first woman to fly alone across the Atlantic Ocean. She encouraged other women to fly too. She tried to make a flight around the world.
3. **Think and Share** Encourage children to group their drawings by time period, using the labels *Past, Present*, and *Future*. Suggest, too, that they add picture-specific labels to their drawings.

Robert Fulton

Objective

- Identify how Robert Fulton exhibited a love of inventiveness.

1 Introduce and Motivate

Preview Read aloud the title and subtitle of the feature. Have children tell what an artist does. Ask if they think it is unusual for a person to be both an inventor and an artist. Have volunteers explain their thinking.

Warm Up To activate prior knowledge, remind children that they have read about many different people who have contributed to the American way of life, people who valued freedom, individualism, and inventiveness.

Have children turn to the Table of Contents in their books to help them remember some of the people and their accomplishments. Tell them that as they read, they should think about how Robert Fulton is like and different from those people.

Have children use the Table of Contents to locate the page on which they will begin reading.

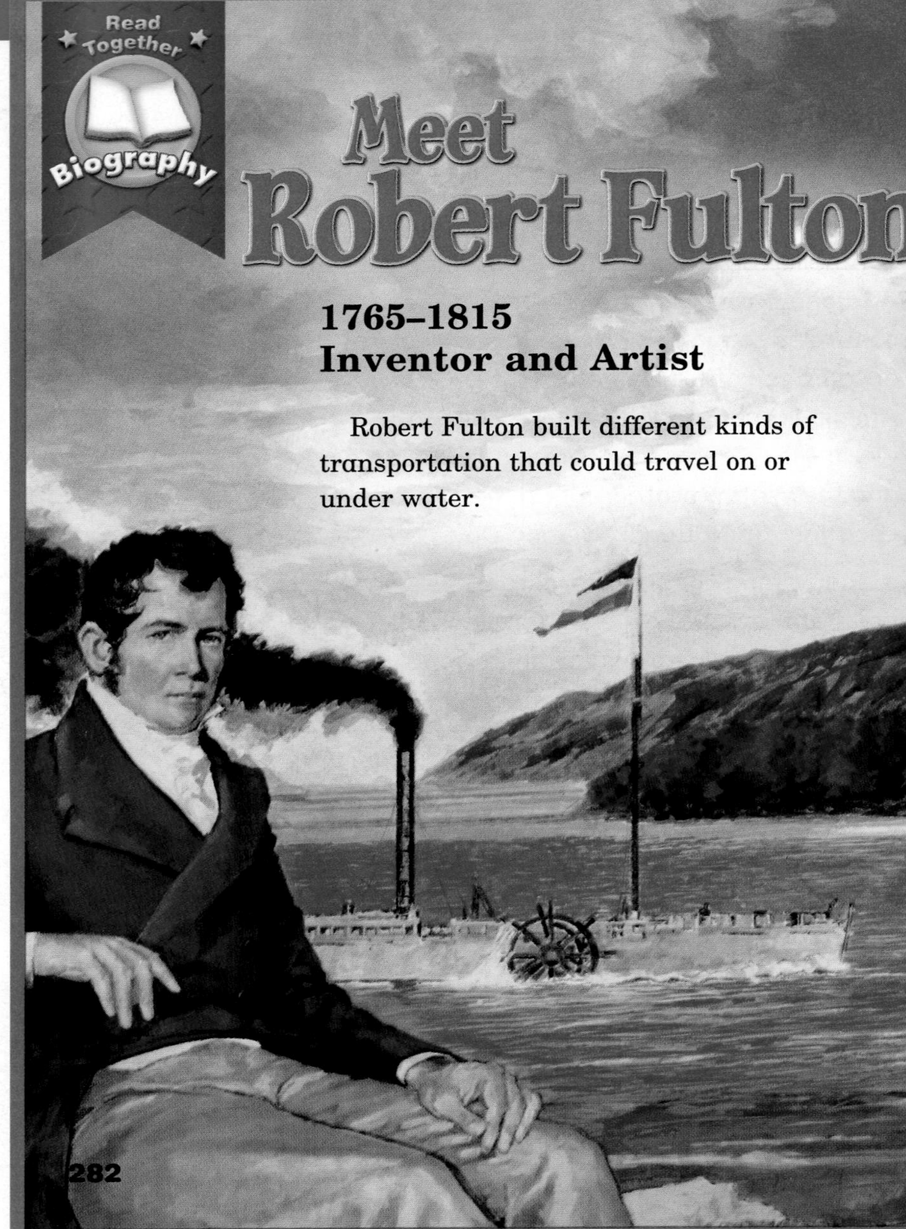

Practice and Extend

CURRICULUM CONNECTION Art

Draw a Steamboat

- Have children use the picture of the steamboat on p. 282 and other sources to draw their own steamboats.
- Then have children refer to a map of the United States and find a coastal or river city on which their steamboat might travel.

WEB SITE Technology

You may help children find out more about Robert Fulton by clicking on *Meet the People* at **www.sfsocialstudies.com.**

As a young man, Robert was interested in painting. He was also interested in new inventions.

Robert Fulton moved from the United States to France. While in France, he had an idea for a new use for submarines. He built the *Nautilus*. It was a submarine, or boat that could travel underwater. It could even travel under ships! Robert Fulton also planned the building of a steamboat. 1

Robert Fulton moved back to the United States and began work building a steamboat. He made many improvements to the steamboat over the next few years. 2 In 1807, his boat, called the *Clermont*, was tested on the Hudson River. It was the first steamboat service that moved both people and goods. The *Clermont* traveled from New York City to Albany. 3

Fulton Street in New York City is named after this famous inventor. A statue in Statuary Hall, Washington, D.C., also honors Robert Fulton.

Robert Fulton was born in Lancaster County, Pennsylvania.

the Nautilus

Fulton Street, New York City

Think and Share

How have Americans remembered Robert Fulton?

For more information, go online to *Meet the People* at **www.sfsocialstudies.com.**

283

CURRICULUM CONNECTION
Writing

Name a Steamboat

- Share with children that Robert Fulton's steamboat was usually called the *Clermont*, after the home of the U.S. minister to France, Robert Livingston. It was Livingston who got Fulton interested in steamboats. The registered name of the steamboat was the *North River Steamboat*.
- Have children write names for steamboats. Suggest that they choose names that have some special significance to them.
- If children drew a steamboat for the activity on p. 282, have them add the name to their drawing.

2 Teach and Discuss

Tell children that one way Americans honor the inventiveness of people is to name streets or public buildings, such as schools, after them. Give as examples the Robert Fulton School in North Bergen, New Jersey, and the Thomas A. Edison School in Morton Grove, Illinois.

1 **In what way do you think a steamboat might be better than a sailboat?** A sailboat depends on wind to move; it can be slow even when it does move. A steamboat has an engine that moves it in any weather. **Make Inferences**

2 **Why did it take years before Robert Fulton had a steamboat he could test?** He was working to improve, or make it better. **Recall and Retell**

3 **Why was it important that the *Clermont* transport people as well as goods?** Possible answer: The new steamboat service gave people another choice for traveling from place to place. **Draw Conclusions**

3 Close and Assess

Think and Share

A street in New York City is named after Robert Fulton. A statue honors him in Washington, D.C.

Use with pages 278–283

Lesson 5 Wrap-Up

MEETING INDIVIDUAL NEEDS

Leveled Practice

Travel and Learn

Refer children to a map of the world. Tell children to locate a city, country, or region indicated on the map that they would like to visit.

Easy Have children draw pictures of the kinds of transportation they would like to use to reach their destination. **Reteach**

On-Level Have children tell about two of the communication tools they might use to learn about their destination and its inhabitants before traveling there. **Extend**

Challenge Have children learn about the landforms of their destination on a landform map, through reference sources, or on the Internet. Tell children to write a brief description of these landforms. **Enrich**

Hands-on Activities

CURRICULUM CONNECTION
Reading

Extend Vocabulary

Objective Demonstrate understanding of vocabulary.

Materials chart paper, marker

Learning Style Verbal

Group

Time 10–15 minutes

1. Remind children that people can communicate without saying a word. People can use facial expressions and gestures.

2. Have children help you build a list of ways people communicate silently. Start off the list with *wink, wave, shrug*.

3. Have children suggest as many entries for the list as possible.

4. End by having children demonstrate each word on the list. Remind children to add *communication* to their "My Word Book" glossaries.

CURRICULUM CONNECTION
Reading

The Ups and Downs of Flight

Objective Share a story about the inventiveness of the Wright brothers.

Materials *Wright vs. Wrong!: The True and Not-So-True Story of the Airplane* by Gigi Tegge (Greene Bark Press, ISBN 1-880-85126-1, 1997)

Learning Style Auditory/Visual

Group

Time 20–25 minutes

1. Read the book aloud and share the illustrations.

2. Have children give personal responses to the story.

3. Ask children to say what new information they learned from listening to the book.

CURRICULUM CONNECTION
Writing

Communicate in Code

Objective Express ideas in writing.

Materials paper, pencils

Learning Style Linguistic

Partners

Time 20 minutes

1. Tell children that one fun way to communicate is by secret code.

2. Have partners work together to make up a code. Say that the code can be complex, such as creating a new symbol for each letter in the alphabet, or the code can be simple, such as replacing each message letter with the letter that follows it in the alphabet.

A = *
B = #
C = △
D = •>

3. Have partners practice writing and decoding messages.

Ending Unit 6

End with a Folktale **pages 284–285**	Children will listen to and then talk about a Chinese folktale called "An Honest Man," as told by Li Hongling.	
Unit 6 Review **pages 286–289**	Children will review unit vocabulary words and the unit skills of recall and retell, reading a calendar, and reading a diagram. Children will answer questions about what they learned in the unit. Children will learn about several people and places in history through reading books.	Resources • Workbook, p. 69 ✓• Assessment Book, pp. 17–20
Unit 6 Project **page 290**	Children will learn how to describe the qualities and accomplishments of a hero.	Resource • Workbook, p. 70

Wrap-up

Activity

A History Scroll

Tell children they will make scrolls that contain important information for children of the future.

- Have children draft a list of three things they learned in the unit that they want children in the future to know and not forget. They should say why each piece of information is important.
- When the drafts are completed, have children copy neatly what they wrote on plain white paper.
- Show children how to roll their documents into a scroll and secure them with string, ribbon, or yarn.

Performance Assessment
You can use the activity on this page as a performance assessment.

✓ Assessment Scoring Guide

Make a History Scroll	
4	List includes three items and clear reasons why they are important historically.
3	Fewer than three items but clear reasons for inclusion are given.
2	Three list items included; only partial or no reasons for their inclusion are given.
1	No real list; incomplete or unclear thoughts expressed.

An Honest Man

Objective

- Identify selected stories and explain their significance as examples of cultural heritage.

1 Introduce and Motivate

Preview Read the title and subtitle of the feature. Ask children if they know what a folktale is. Explain that folktales are stories that are passed down from one generation to another. They generally reflect the customs and often the traditions of a group of people. Say that in many folktales animals can speak and act like people. Events and characters in folktales often appear in "threes." (*Three Little Pigs, Goldilocks and the Three Bears, Three Billy Goats Gruff*)

Warm Up To activate prior knowledge, ask children to tell some ways people show that they are honest. Guide the discussion to include: People tell the truth; they return things they borrow or find, and so on.

UNIT 6

End with a Folktale

An Honest Man

A Chinese Folktale as told by Li Hongling

It is a custom for the Chinese to create stories about their world. Sharing these stories is another way to communicate.

1 Long ago, there was a valley where ten poor families lived. In the valley was a pool of water. One day many guests came to visit one of the families. It was rare for visitors to come to the valley, so the head of the family welcomed them and decided to have a feast. Because he was a poor man, he did not have enough plates for all of his guests, so he borrowed some from a neighbor. 2

After the meal, he went to the pool to clean the plates. Suddenly one of the plates slid into the water, and, though he searched and searched, he could not find it. He was very much disturbed by this and sat by the pool feeling very unhappy, trying to figure out what to do.

284

Practice and Extend

CURRICULUM CONNECTION
Drama

Perform a Skit

- After children have listened to and read the story, invite them to do a special retelling of it.
- Have children take the roles of the poor man and the goldfish, and the man's neighbors and his guests at the feast.
- Have groups of children improvise dialogue and add appropriate actions. Tell them to speak as the characters might speak.
- Encourage as many children as possible to participate in the performance.

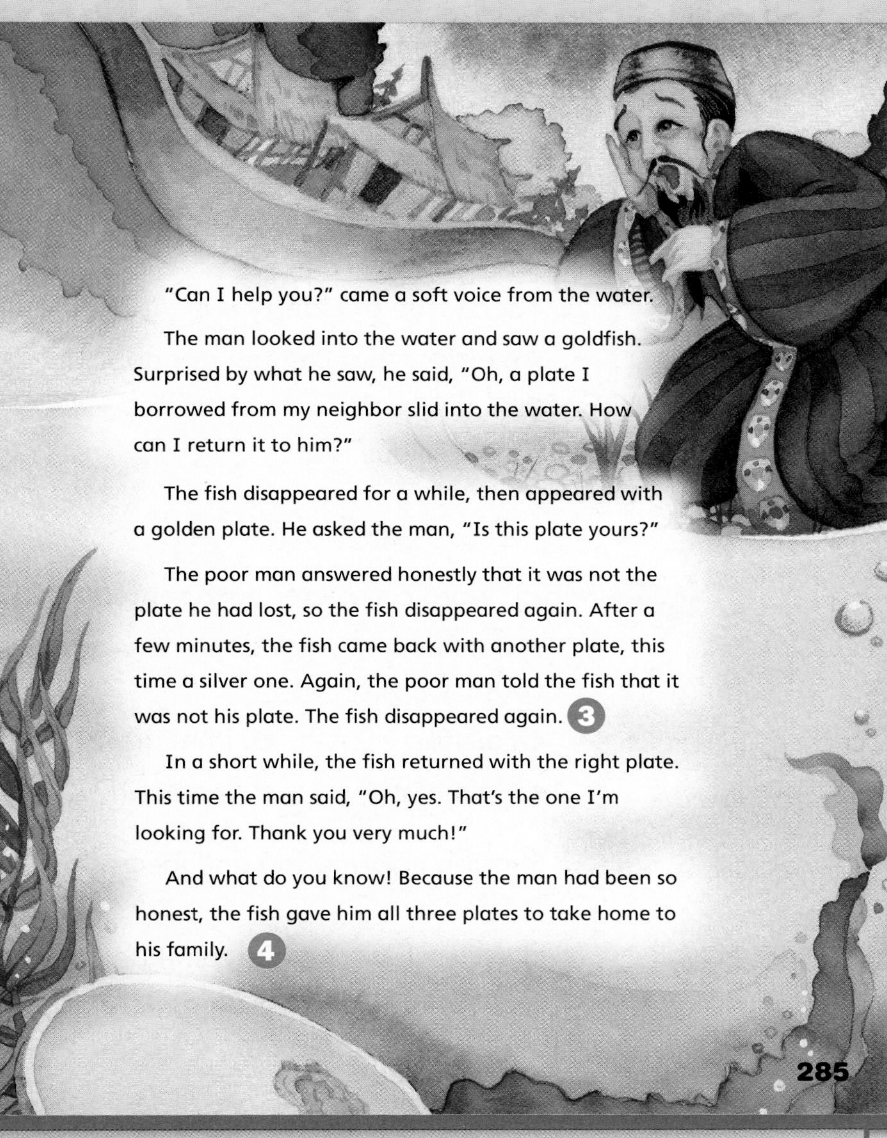

"Can I help you?" came a soft voice from the water.

The man looked into the water and saw a goldfish. Surprised by what he saw, he said, "Oh, a plate I borrowed from my neighbor slid into the water. How can I return it to him?"

The fish disappeared for a while, then appeared with a golden plate. He asked the man, "Is this plate yours?"

The poor man answered honestly that it was not the plate he had lost, so the fish disappeared again. After a few minutes, the fish came back with another plate, this time a silver one. Again, the poor man told the fish that it was not his plate. The fish disappeared again. 3

In a short while, the fish returned with the right plate. This time the man said, "Oh, yes. That's the one I'm looking for. Thank you very much!"

And what do you know! Because the man had been so honest, the fish gave him all three plates to take home to his family. 4

285

2 Teach and Discuss

Pages 284–285

Read aloud the introductory paragraph. Then read the story aloud once. Reread the story and ask children to raise their hands when they hear a word or phrase they don't understand. Pause to explain or clarify.

1 **When did the events of the story take place—in the past or the present? How do you know?** Past; the words *long ago* are clues. **Draw Conclusions**

2 **How did the poor man solve the problem of not having enough plates?** He borrowed some from a neighbor. **Recall and Retell**

3 **Why did the goldfish bring a gold plate and then a silver plate to the man?** Possible answer: To test his honesty **Make Inferences**

SOCIAL STUDIES STRAND
Economics

The Value of Metals

4 **Why might the man have wanted a gold or silver plate?** Possible answer: He was poor; gold and silver plates were probably worth a lot of money. **Draw Conclusions**

3 Close and Assess

- Encourage children to recall and retell the story or parts of the story in their own words.
- Have volunteers say which part of the story they liked best and why.
- Ask children what another good title for this story might be.

CURRICULUM CONNECTION
Writing

A New Story Ending

- After children have recalled and retold the story in their own words, ask them to think about how the story ending would have been different if the man had taken the gold or silver plates.
- Have children work with partners to write new endings for the story.
- Encourage pairs of children to share and compare their new story endings.

UNIT 6

Review

Resources

- Assessment Book, pp. 17–20
- Workbook, p. 69: Vocabulary Review

Vocabulary Review

1. custom
2. landmark
3. artifact
4. holiday

Answers to Test Prep

1. (b) immigrant
2. (c) communication

UNIT 6

Review

Vocabulary Review

landmark
holiday
artifact
custom
invention

Choose a word from the box to complete each sentence.

1. Giving speeches on Memorial Day is a _______.
2. The Statue of Liberty is a _______.
3. An object that can tell us about the past is an _______.
4. A special day is a _______.

★ ★ ★ ★ ★ ★ ★ ★

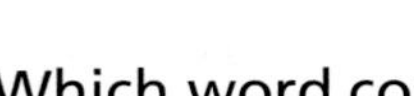

Which word completes each sentence?

1. A person who settles in a new country is an _______.
   a. artifact **b.** immigrant
   c. invention **d.** landmark
2. Sharing information and ideas is _______.
   a. invention **c.** communication
   b. custom **d.** landmark

286

Practice and Extend

Assessment Options

✓ Unit 6 Assessment

- Unit 6 Content Test: Use Assessment Book, pp. 17–18
- Unit 6 Skills Test: Use Assessment Book, pp. 19–20

Standardized Test Prep

- Unit 6 tests contain standardized test formats.

✓ Unit 6 Performance Assessment

- See p. 290 for information about using the Unit 6 Project as a means of performance assessment.
- A scoring guide for the Unit 6 Project is provided in the teacher's notes on p. 290.

Test Talk

- Test Talk Practice Book

Skills Review

Recall and Retell

Recall what you read about Helen Keller or another important person. **Retell** the story of that person in your own words.

★ ★ ★ ★ ★ ★ ★ ★

Study Skills

Read a Calendar

Use this calendar to answer the questions.

1. How many days are there in one week?
2. What holiday is celebrated on the fourth Thursday of November?
3. Is Veterans Day before or after Election Day?

November

Sunday	Monday	Tuesday	Wednesday	Thursday	Friday	Saturday
						1
2	3	4 VOTE NOW Election Day	5	6	7	8
9	10	11 Veterans Day	12	13	14	15
16	17	18	19	20	21	22
23	24	25	26	27 Thanksgiving	28	29
30						

287

WEB SITE
Technology

For more information, you can select the dictionary or encyclopedia from *Social Studies Library* at **www.sfsocialstudies.com.**

Workbook, p. 69

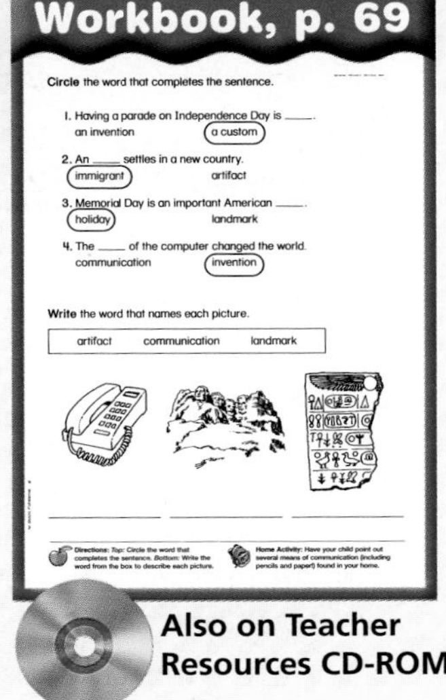

Circle the word that completes the sentence.

1. Having a parade on Independence Day is ____.
an invention / (a custom)
2. An ____ settles in a new country.
(immigrant) / artifact
3. Memorial Day is an important American ____.
(holiday) / landmark
4. The ____ of the computer changed the world.
communication / (invention)

Write the word that names each picture.

artifact communication landmark

Also on Teacher Resources CD-ROM.

Answers to Skills Review

Recall and Retell

Target Skill

- Children's responses should demonstrate understanding of the terms *recall* and *retell*; important events should be retold in logical order.

Use the following scoring guide.

✓ Assessment Scoring Guide

Recall and Retell	
4	Recalls important ideas and retells them in logical order.
3	Recalls important ideas but retells them randomly.
2	Recalls insignificant details in random order.
1	Attempts but cannot complete the task.

Study Skills

Read a Calendar

1. 7
2. Thanksgiving
3. After

Review

continued

Skills Review

Read a Diagram

1. Two
2. Pedal
3. Seat

Skills on Your Own

- Children's diagrams should show the major parts of a car—wheels, body, windshield, headlights, steering wheel. Most parts should be labeled. Children's descriptions should be clear and accurately reflect information on the diagram.

Use the following scoring guide.

✓ Assessment Scoring Guide

Draw a Diagram	
4	Outline of car with 4 or more major parts accurately labeled.
3	Outline of car with 3 or more major parts correctly labeled.
2	Outline of car with fewer than 3 major parts correctly labeled.
1	Outline of car with fewer than 3 major parts, no label.

Test Talk

Write Your Answer
Use Skills on Your Own to model the Test Talk Strategy.

Make sure the answer is correct.
Children should make sure their written answer has the correct details.

Make sure the answer is complete.
Children should make sure their written answer has only relevant details.

For additional practice, use the Test Talk Practice Book.

Review

Skills Review

Read a Diagram

Look at the diagram of a bicycle.

1. How many tires are on a bicycle?
2. What does your foot push to make the bicycle move?
3. Where do you sit on the bicycle?

Test Talk

Is your answer complete and correct?

Skills on Your Own

Draw a diagram of a car. Label some of the parts. Write a description of a car.

Practice and Extend

Revisit the Unit Question

✓ Portfolio Assessment

- Have children look back at the list they generated on page 243. It records reasons why they think it is important to learn about people and places from the past.
- Now that children have read the unit, ask them to suggest additional reasons they have learned and talked about.
- Add them to the original list and put a check mark next to them.
- Have children draw a picture and write a paragraph to tell more about a reason on their revised list.
- Suggest children add their paragraphs to their Social Studies portfolio.

What did you learn?

1. Why do immigrants come to the United States?
2. Explain why many Mexican Americans celebrate Cinco de Mayo.
3. Explain why national landmarks are important?
4. **Think and Share** Think of a new holiday you could add to the calendar. Name your holiday. Tell how you would celebrate this holiday.

Read About People and Places in History

Look for books like these in the library.

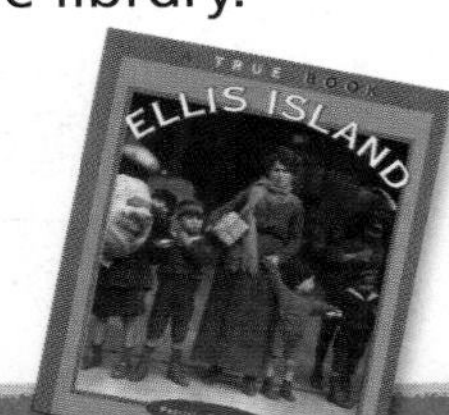

What did you learn?

1. They come to find a better way of life.
2. They celebrate the bravery of their Mexican ancestors in their fight for freedom.
3. National landmarks honor important people in our country or represent events or ideas that are part of our country's history.
4. **Think and Share** Answers will vary. Some children may suggest holidays that reflect important family events such as moving to a new home; other children may suggest days such as Ice Cream Day or No Homework Day.

Read About People and Places in History

Look for books such as these in the library.

Halmoni and the Picnic, by Sook Nyul Choi (Houghton Mifflin, ISBN 0-395-61626-3, 1993). Yunmi, a third grader worries when her grandmother who is new to this country decides to bring Korean food to a class picnic. **Easy**

My Name Is Maria Isabel, by Alma Flor Ada (Aladdin Paperbacks, ISBN 0-689-80217-X, 1995). There are three girls named Maria in the class, so the teacher decides to call the newest one Mary. This upsets Maria Isabel Lopez, but all ends well when her teacher agrees to call her Maria Isabel. **On-Level**

Ellis Island: A True Book, by Patricia Ryon Quiri (Children's Press, ISBN 0-516-20622-2, 1998). Easy to read text and numerous photos make this a good research tool for students. **Challenge**

Big Book/Pupil Book p. 290

Unit 6 Project

My Hero

Objective

- Describe the qualities and accomplishments of a hero.

Resource

- Workbook, p. 70

Materials

paper, pencils, crayons or other coloring materials

Follow This Procedure

- Tell children they will describe someone they think is a hero. Talk with children about what makes a person a hero.
- Have children choose someone they have read about in the unit or a friend, family member, or someone in the community.
- Children should write the names of their heroes and give three reasons why they chose this person as their hero.
- Encourage children to draw a picture of their hero or design a medal, plaque, ribbon, or other award for their hero.
- Have volunteers use their writing to present their hero "testimonials" to the class.

✓ Assessment Scoring Guide

	My Hero
4	Gives three reasons why the selected person is a hero. Language is clear.
3	Gives fewer than three reasons why the selected person is a hero. Language is clear but limited.
2	Gives random information about the selected person. Language is unclear, vague.
1	Shows little understanding of what makes a hero. Does not complete the activity.

My Hero

Talk about your own hero.

1 **Choose** a person you think is a hero.

2 **Write** why the person is a hero to you.

3 **Draw** a picture of your hero. Draw or make a medal or a ribbon for your hero.

4 **Tell** the class about your hero.

Internet Activity

Go to www.sfsocialstudies.com/activities to learn more about places in history.

290

Practice and Extend

✓ Performance Assessment

- The Unit Project can also be used as a performance assessment activity.
- Use the scoring guide to assess each group's work.

Children can launch the activity by clicking on *Grade 2, Unit 6* at **www.sfsocialstudies.com/activities**.

Workbook, p. 70

6 Project My Hero

Think about what a hero is. Write and draw to tell about a hero you know.

1. Draw a picture of your hero.
2. Write the name of your hero.
3. What has this person done to be a hero?
4. Describe a medal you would give your hero.
5. Write something you would say to your hero.

Also on Teacher Resources CD-ROM.

Reference Guide

Table of Contents

Atlas

Photograph of the Earth

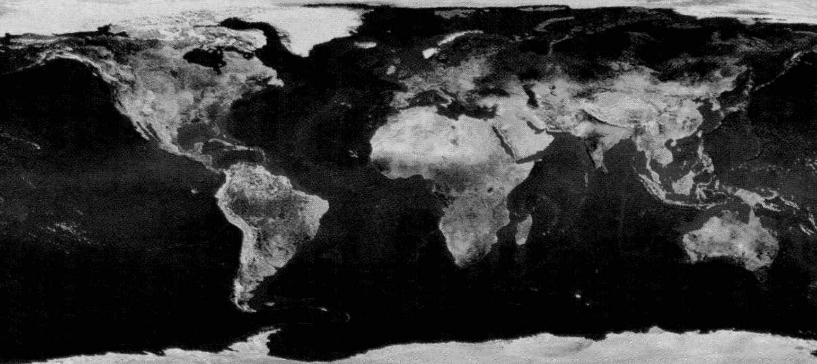

Atlas

Photograph of North America

Atlas

Map of the World

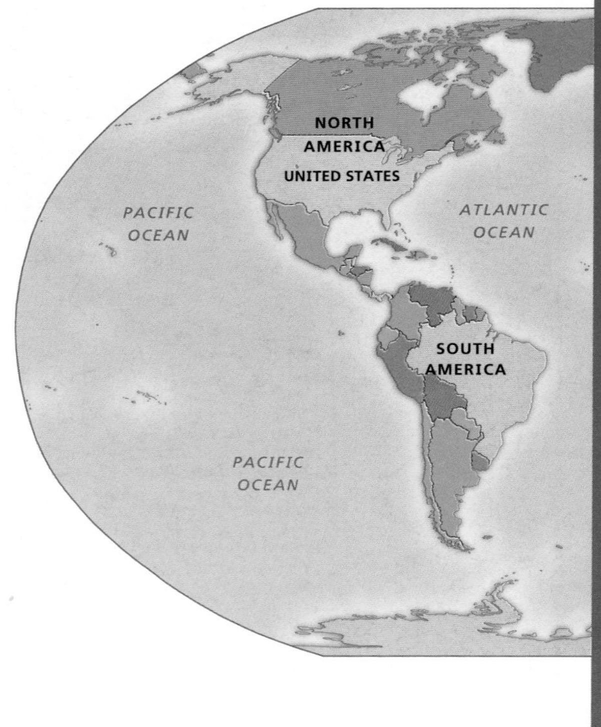

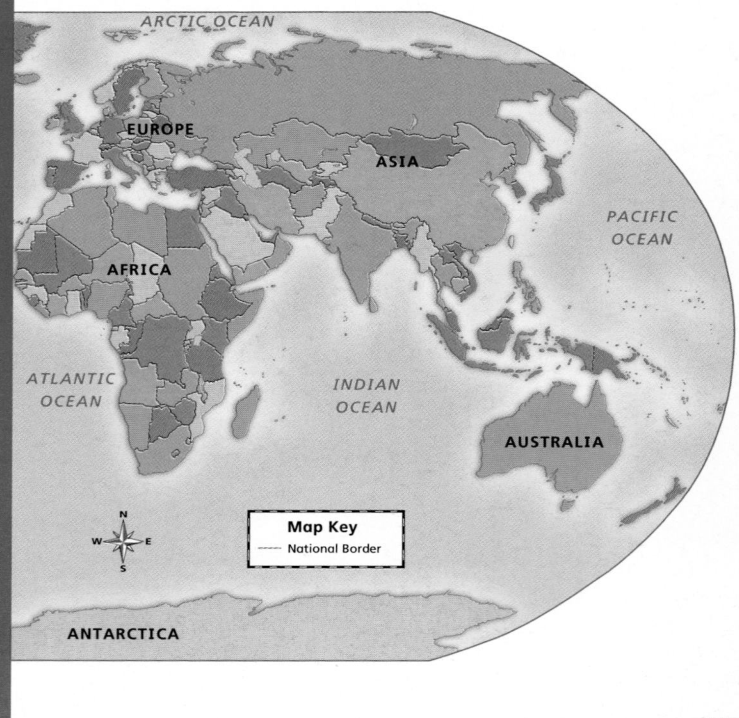

Atlas

Map of the United States of America

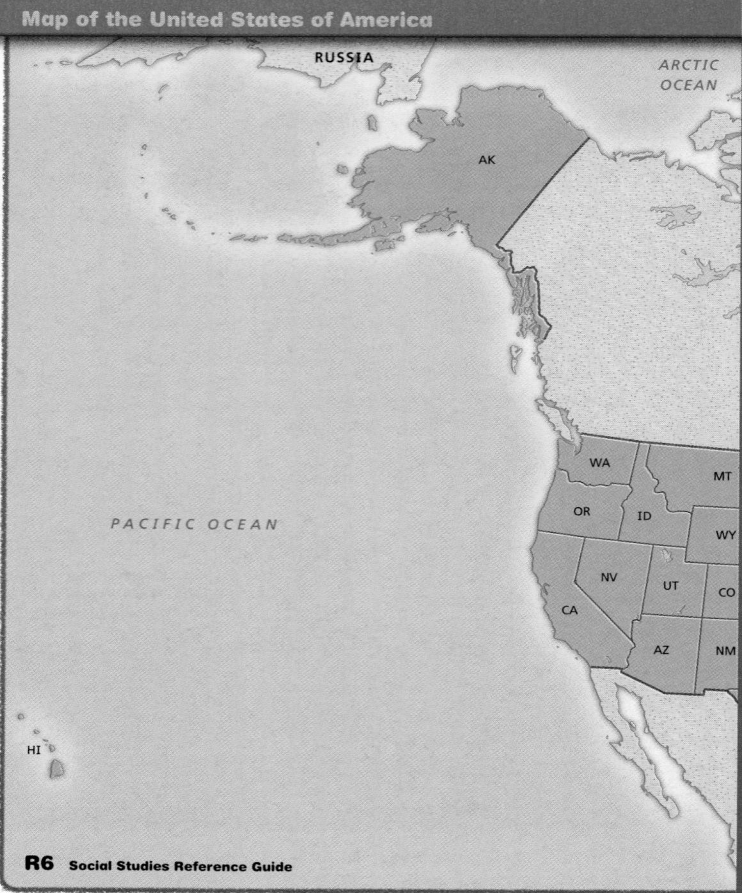

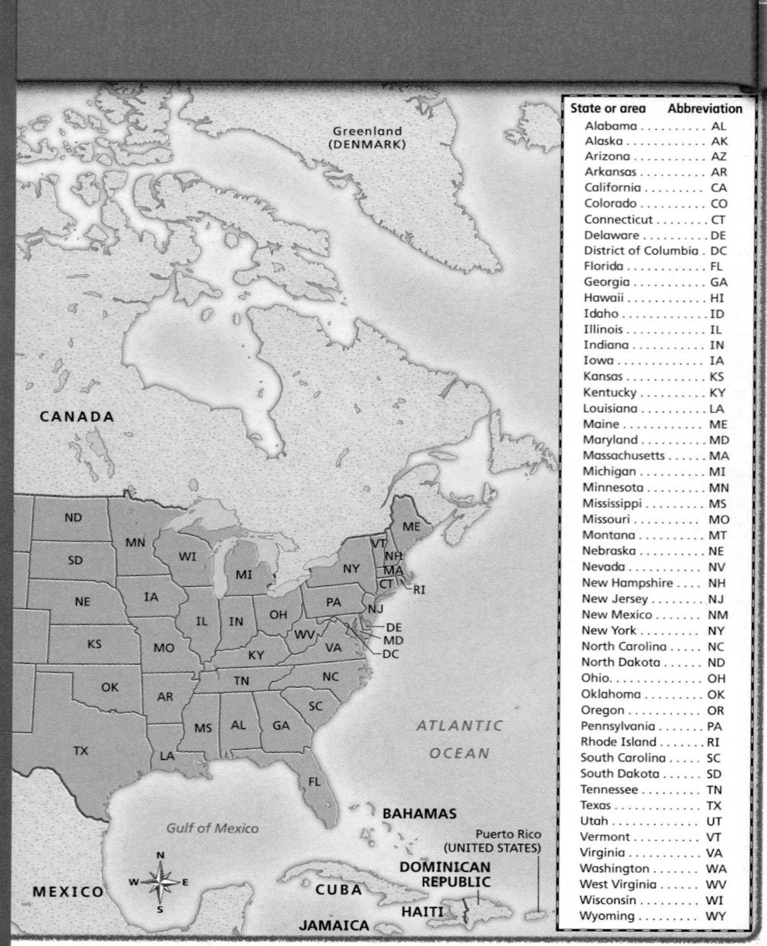

State or area	Abbreviation
Alabama	AL
Alaska	AK
Arizona	AZ
Arkansas	AR
California	CA
Colorado	CO
Connecticut	CT
Delaware	DE
District of Columbia	DC
Florida	FL
Georgia	GA
Hawaii	HI
Idaho	ID
Illinois	IL
Indiana	IN
Iowa	IA
Kansas	KS
Kentucky	KY
Louisiana	LA
Maine	ME
Maryland	MD
Massachusetts	MA
Michigan	MI
Minnesota	MN
Mississippi	MS
Missouri	MO
Montana	MT
Nebraska	NE
Nevada	NV
New Hampshire	NH
New Jersey	NJ
New Mexico	NM
New York	NY
North Carolina	NC
North Dakota	ND
Ohio	OH
Oklahoma	OK
Oregon	OR
Pennsylvania	PA
Rhode Island	RI
South Carolina	SC
South Dakota	SD
Tennessee	TN
Texas	TX
Utah	UT
Vermont	VT
Virginia	VA
Washington	WA
West Virginia	WV
Wisconsin	WI
Wyoming	WY

Atlas

Map of Our Fifty States

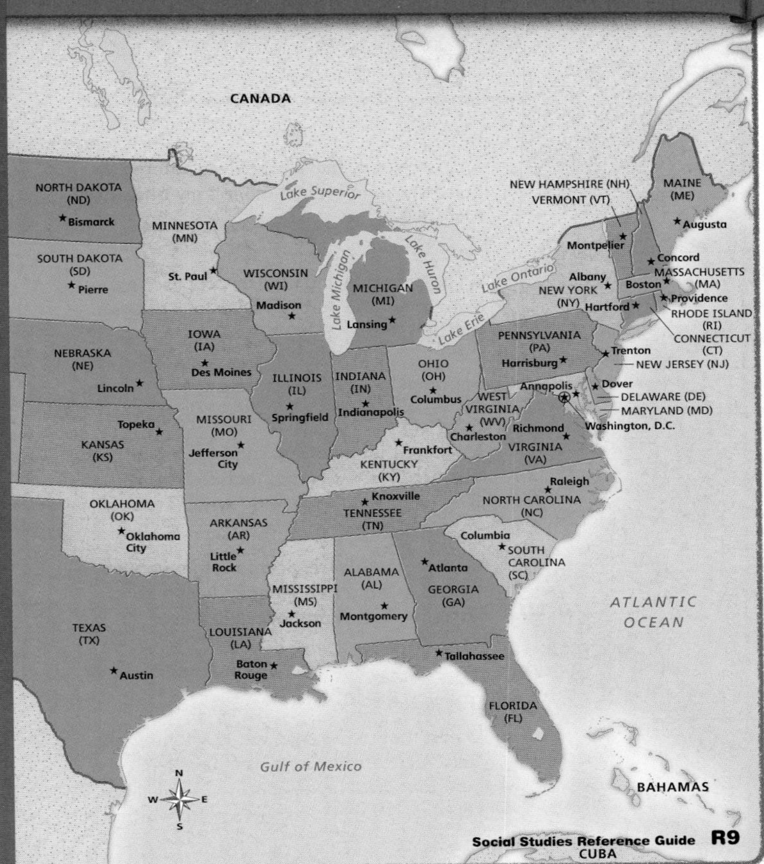

Geography Terms

forest
large area of land where many trees grow

hill
rounded land higher than the land around it

island
land with water all around it

lake
large body of water with land all or nearly all around it

mountain
highest land on Earth

ocean
a huge body of salt water

peninsula
land that is almost surrounded by water

plain
large, mostly flat, area of land

river
large stream of water leading to a lake, other river, or ocean

valley
low land between mountains or hills

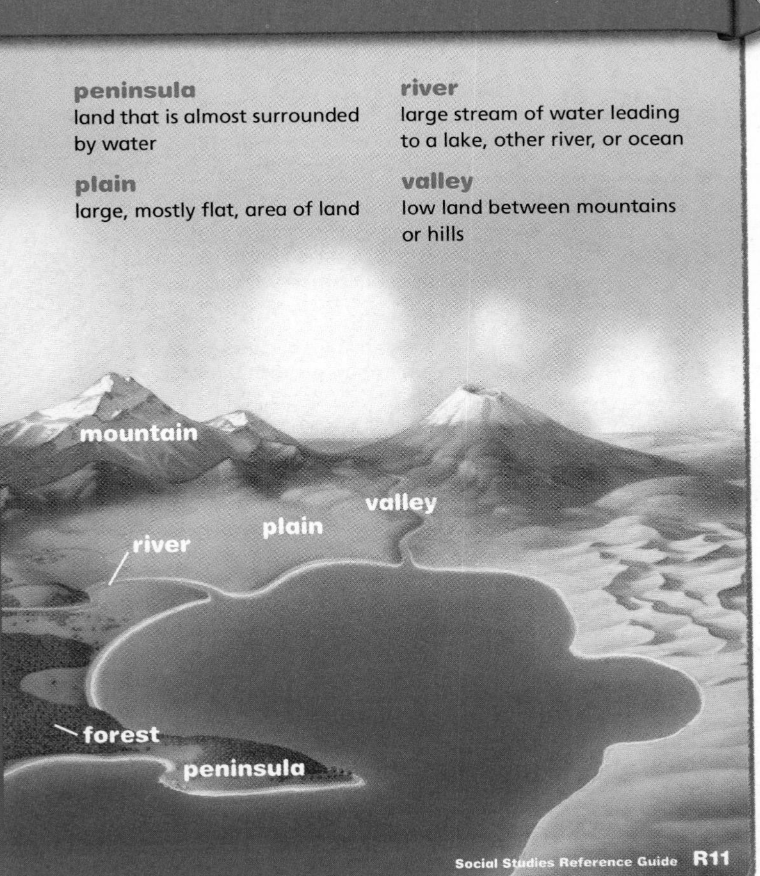

Picture Glossary

A

ancestor
A person in my family who lived before I was born. My great-grandmother is my **ancestor.** (page 68)

artifact
An object made and used by people. We can learn about the past when we look at an **artifact.** (page 272)

B

bar graph
A picture that helps you compare groups. This **bar graph** shows foods that Josh's class likes. (page 80)

barter
To trade goods or services for other goods or services without using money. People can **barter** to get what they need. (page 138)

C

calendar
A chart that shows days, weeks, months, and years. A **calendar** helps us remember important days. (page 262)

capital
The city where the leaders of a state or country work. Washington, D.C., is the **capital** of the United States. (page 33)

citizen
A member of a community, state and country. I am a **citizen** of the United States of America. (page 155)

colonist
A person who lives in a colony. A **colonist** in Jamestown had to work hard. (page 211)

colony
A place that is settled by people from another country. Virginia was an English **colony.** (page 210)

communication
Sharing ideas and information with others. The telephone is used for **communication.** (page 278)

community
A place that is made up of many neighborhoods. There are many stores in my **community.** (page 16)

compass rose
Shows directions on a map. He saw the directions on the **compass rose.** (page 124)

Congress
The part of government that writes and votes on laws for all of our states. I hope to be elected to **Congress** someday. (page 167)

conservation
The care and protection of land, water, plants, and animals. Park rangers teach people about **conservation.** (page 82)

consumer
Someone who buys and uses goods. A **consumer** buys goods at the store. (page 71)

crop
A kind of plant that people grow and use. Corn is a **crop** that provides food. (page 78)

custom
A special way that a group does something. It is a **custom** to celebrate some holidays by having a parade. (page 257)

D

diagram
A drawing that shows the parts of something and gives information. We look at the **diagram** to learn more about a chariot. (page 277)

E

explorer
A person who travels to a new place to learn about it. Meriwether Lewis was an **explorer.** (page 210)

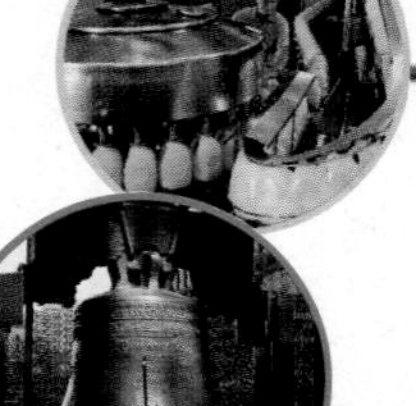

F

factory
A building where people produce or process goods. Juice is bottled in this **factory.** (page 120)

freedom
Every citizen's right to make choices. The Liberty Bell is a symbol of **freedom.** (page 180)

G

geography
The study of the Earth and the ways people use it. The globe helps me learn about **geography.** (page 56)

goods
Things that people make or grow. Many kinds of **goods** are sold in stores. (page 104)

government
A group of people who work together to run a city, state, or country. Our **government** makes laws to help keep us safe. (page 154)

governor
The leader of a state's government. The **governor** came to our city. (page 160)

grid
A pattern of lines that form squares. The **grid** helps me find places on the map. (page 185)

H

history
Tells the story of people and places from the past. Pictures of people can tell you about **history.** (page 22)

history map
Shows where places were located a long time ago. This **history map** shows the English colonies. (page 214)

holiday
A special day. Our favorite **holiday** is Thanksgiving Day. (page 256)

I

immigrant
A person who settles in a new country. My grandfather was an **immigrant** to our country. (page 250)

income
Money that someone earns. Some of my family's **income** is used to buy shoes. (page 104)

independence
To be free from other people or places. The colonists wanted **independence** from England. (page 217)

invention
Something new that someone makes or thinks of. The wheelbarrow is an **invention** many people use. (page 275)

L

landform
Different shapes on the surface of the earth. A mountain is a kind of **landform.** (page 56)

landmark
A building or place that is important or interesting. Mount Rushmore is a **landmark.** (page 264)

law
A rule that everyone must follow. Police officers help make sure the **law** is followed. (page 9)

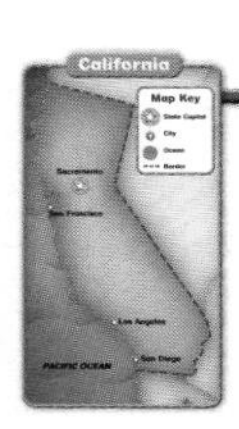

M

map
A drawing that shows where places are located. We found our state on the **map.** (page 20)

map key
Tells what the symbols on a map stand for. The **map key** helps us read the map. (page 20)

mayor
The leader of a town or city. The **mayor** spoke at the town meeting. (page 155)

monument
A building or statue that honors a person or event. The Lincoln Memorial is a famous **monument.** (page 182)

motto
A word or saying that people try to live by. A **motto** is written on this symbol. (page 181)

N

natural resource
A useful material that comes from the earth. Soil is a **natural resource.** (page 76)

P

pie chart
A kind of chart that is drawn in the shape of a pie. Matt made a **pie chart** to show how he used his income. (page 130)

pioneer
A person who goes first and prepares the way for others. A **pioneer** needed to work very hard. (page 224)

President
The leader of our country. The **President** gave a speech. (page 168)

producer
Someone who makes or grows something. A farmer is a **producer.** (page 68)

R

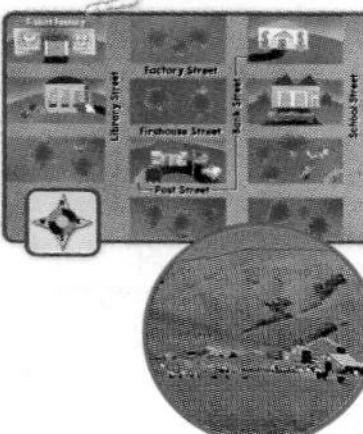

route
A way to go from one place to another. This map shows the **route** from the post office to the bank. (page 125)

rural
An area with small communities and open space. The farm is in a **rural** area. (page 26)

S

services
Job that people do to help others. A restaurant worker provides **services.** (page 105)

shelter
A place where people live. People need **shelter.** (page 203)

suburb
A type of community that is located near a city. The **suburb** I live in is close to New York City. (page 25)

symbol
A picture that stands for something. She found the **symbol** for a tree on the map. (page 20)

T

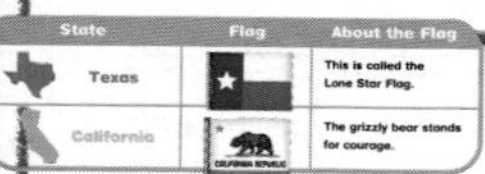

State	Flag	About the Flag
Texas		This is called the Lone Star Flag.
California		The grizzly bear stands for courage.

table
A kind of list. The **table** showed important information. (page 164)

tax
Money that is collected by a government. Some of our **tax** money will be used to build a new school. (page 113)

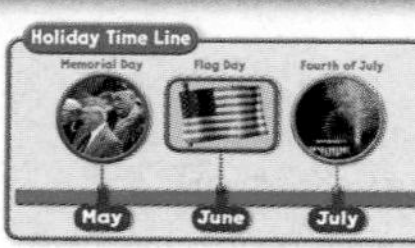

time line
Shows the order in which things happen. We made a **time line** about holidays. (page 226)

trade
To buy, sell, or exchange goods. People can **trade** goods at a market. (page 134)

tradition
Something that is done a certain way for many years. Celebrating Independence Day is a family **tradition.** (page 207)

transportation
A way of moving goods or people from place to place. An airplane is one kind of **transportation.** (page 135)

U

urban
An area that has a city. We just moved to an **urban** area. (page 24)

V

vote
A choice that gets counted. We **vote** for class president. (page 11)

Index

Index

Credits

Illustrations

20 Robert Krugle ; 28, 132 Meryl Treatner ; 34 Marc Scott ; 42 Susan Tolonen ; 46, 144, 192 David Brion ; 60, 124, 161 Diane Teske Harris ; 74 Stacey Schuett ; 86 Ann Barrow ; 90 Claudia Hammer ; 90 Shelly Bartek ; 100 Martha Aviles ; 116 Bill & Debbie Farnsworth ; 140 Darryl Ligason ; 140 Lauren E. Simeone ; 170 Keaf Holliday ; 178 Tony Wade ; 184 Steven Mach ; 186 Amy Vangsgard ; 202 Derek Grinnell ; 222, 228 Tony Morse ; 239, 240 Bill Reynolds ; 252 Mark Stein ; 271 Doug Knutson

Photographs

Unit 1: 2 (C) Joseph Sohm/Corbis; 4 (CL) Joseph Sohm/Corbis; 5 (TR)Joseph Sohm/Corbis, (CR) Thomas Hallstein; 8 (BC) Michael S. Yamashita/Corbis-Bettmann, (C) Gail Moody/Corbis-Bettmann; 9 (B) Coco McCoy/Rainbow, (TR) PhotoDisc, (CR) Chris Rogers/Rainbow, (CL) Corbis; 12 Kids Care Clubs; 13 Kids Care Clubs; 17 (TR) Max Alexander/© Dorling Kindersley, (CR) Ann Stratton/FoodPix; 18 (CL) Rich LaSalle/Stone; 19 (TR) Gail Mooney/Corbis, (CR) Evan Agostini/Liaison Agency; 22 (B) SuperStock; 24 (BL) Michael S. Yamashita/Corbis-Bettmann; 25 Robert Shafer/Stone; 26 (B) Bob Daemmrich/Image Works, (CR) Paul Redman/Stone; 27 (C) Peter Pearson/Stone, (TR) Bill Bachmann/PhotoEdit, (CL) Joseph A. Rosen; 29 King Ranch Archives; 33 (TR) J. Pickerell/Image Works, (B) Bob Rowan; Progressive Image/Corbis; 35 The Granger Collection, New York; 38 (BL) Elsa Peterson/D. Donne Bryant Stock Photography, (BR) D Palais/ Ait Directors & TRIP Photo Library, (CL) James P. Rowan Stock Photography ; 39 (CR) Keren Su/Stone, (BL) SuperStock, (BR) D. Clegg/Art Directors & TRIP Photo Library; 40 Barnabas and Anabel Kindersley/© Dorling Kindersley; 41 Barnabas and Anabel Kindersley/© Dorling Kindersley; Unit 2: 49 (Bkgrd) Frederick D. Atwood Frederick D. Atwood ; 50 (Bkgrd) Frederick D. Atwood Frederick D. Atwood ; 52 (TL) Joel W. Rogers/Corbis, (BL) Kunio Owaki/Corbis Stock Market; 53 (CR) Craig Aurness/Corbis; 55 (BL) Ryan McVay/PhotoDisc; 57 (BL) Gary Braasch/Woodfin Camp & Associates; 58 (TR) Charles Feil/Views from Above, (CR) Dean Abramson/ Stock, Boston Inc/PictureQuest, (BR) Catherine Karnow/Woodfin Camp & Associates; 59 (TR) Myrleen Ferguson/PhotoEdit, (CR) Dan Budnik/Woodfin Camp & Associates; 62 (CL) RubberBall Productions/PictureQuest, (CR) David Muench/Corbis; 63 (TC) Heather Titus/Stone; 64 (TL) Sondra Dawes/Image Works, (BC) Yann Arthus-Bertrand/Corbis; 66 (BC) Corbis/Corbis-Bettmann, (TL) Marilyn "Angel" Wynn/Native Stock; 67 (CR) PhotoDisc ; 68 (BC) Courtesy Stark Brothers Nurseries; 69 (TL) Courtesy Washington Apple Commission, (CR) John Heseltine/Corbis ; 70 (TL) Vincent Dewitt/Stock Boston ; 72 Smithsonian Institution; 73 Smithsonian Institution; 75 (CR) Justin Sullivan/AP/Wide World, (BR) AP/Wide World; 77 (TR) Dan McCoy/Rainbow; 78 (TL) Robert Glusic/PhotoDisc, ; 82 National Park Service; 83 (TR) National Park Service, (B) George Lepp/Corbis; 84 (C) National Park Service, (TR) NPS Photo/United States Department of the Interior; 87 (CR) George Rinhart/Corbis-Bettmann ; 88 (BR) Rebecca Shelby/Earth Angels/Courtesy Guardian Angel Settlement Association, (BC) Gary W. Carter/Corbis ; 89 (BC) Corbis; Unit 3: 100 (TL) Jeff Greenberg/Photo Researchers, Inc., (TC) Jeffry Myers/Stock Boston, (BC) T. del Amo/H. Armstrong Roberts; 101 (TR) Corbis, (TC) Lester Lefkowitz/Corbis Stock Market ; 103 (TR) Paul A. Souders/Corbis ; 114 (CL) Jimmy Dorantes/Latin Focus, (BR) B. Mahoney/Image Works, (TR) Greg Kuchik/Volume Series 43: Business & Occupations/PhotoDisc; 115 (TR) R. Lord/Image Works, (CL) SuperStock; 118 (B, CL) Aberdeen Fire Department, Maryland/© Dorling Kindersley; 119 (TC) Aberdeen Fire Department, Maryland/© Dorling Kindersley; 120 (CL) Amy C. Etra/PhotoEdit; 121 (CL) PhotoDisc, (TL) Richard Hamilton Smith/Corbis, (BL) Inga Spence/Index Stock Imagery; 122 (TC, TL, TR) Courtesy of National Cotton Council of America, (BL) Courtesy Gaston County Dyeing Machine, (BR) Amy C. Etra/PhotoEdit ; 127 (L) Richard Lord/PhotoEdit; 133 (BR, CR) Courtesy of Linda Alvarado/Alvarado Construction Inc.; 134 (BR) Michael S. Yamashita/Corbis; 135 (TC) Lester Lefkowitz/Corbis Stock Market, (BC) Gallo Images/Corbis ; 136 (BC) Charles O. Cecil/ Words & Pictures/PictureQuest; 138 (BC) F.S. Church/North Wind Picture Archives; Unit 4: 147 (Bkgd) John Neubauer/PhotoEdit; 148 (Bkgd) Jeff Greenberg/PhotoEdit ; 150 (TL) Phillip Gould/Corbis, (TC) Grasser/Mauritius/H. Armstrong Roberts, (BC) Daemmrich Photography ; 151 (TR) Vivian Ronay, (BR) R. Kord/H. Armstrong Roberts; 156 (CL) W.J. Scott/H. Armstrong Roberts ; 164 (TC) Mary Ann McDonald/Visuals Unlimited, (CR) William J. Weber/Visuals Unlimited, (CL) Andre Jenny/ Focus Group/PictureQuest, (C) Maslowski/Photo Researchers, Inc., (CR) Pat O'Hara/Corbis, (BL) H. Abernathy/H. Armstrong Roberts, (BC) Arthur C. Smith III/Grant Heilman Photography, (BR) Hal Horwitz/Corbis; 167 (TR) Mark Wilson/Newsmakers/Liaison; 168 (BC) Dennis O'Clair/Stone; 169 (CR) Fred Ward/Black Star; 171 (BR) Bettman Archives/Corbis-Bettmann, (CR) Corbis-Bettmann; 176 Smithsonian Institution; 177 Smithsonian Institution ; 179 (CR) Corbis-Bettmann, (BR) TimePix; 182 (CL) Hisham F. Ibrahim/PhotoDisc, (TL) Museum of the City of New York/Corbis, (BL) D. Gaudette/Stone, (BC) Corbis-Bettmann, (C) David Jennings/Image Works, (CR) The Granger Collection, New York; 183 (Bkgd) Archive Photos; 191 (C) Runk/Schoenberger/Grant Heilman Photography, (B) Joseph Sohm; Visions of America/Corbis; Unit 5: 195 (Bkgd) Robert Glusic/PhotoDisc; 196 (TC) The Newark Museum/Art Resource, NY, (BC) The Purcell Team/Corbis; 198 (TL) John Elk III/Stock Boston, (TL) Bill Ross/Corbis; 199 (TR) North Wind Picture Archives, (CR) N. Carter/North Wind Picture Archives, (BR) The Granger Collection, New York ; 203 (TL) Phyllis Picardi/Stock Boston, (C,TCC) Marilyn "Angel" Wynn, (CL) Momatiuk/Eastcott/Woodfin Camp & Associates, (CC) Corbis, (CR) North Wind Picture Archives, (BL) Reinhard Brucker/Westwind Enterprises, (BC) Werner Forman Archive/Arizona State Museum/Art Resource, NY, (BCC) David Weintraub/Stock Boston; 204 (TR) Marilyn "Angel" Wynn ; 208 Smithsonian Institution; 209 Smithsonian Institution ; 210 (BL) North Wind Picture Archives, (BR) N. Carter/North Wind Picture Archives ; 212 (TR) The Granger Collection, New York, (BR)North Wind Picture Archives; 213 Tom McCarthy/PhotoEdit ; 217 Stock Montage Inc.; 218 (B)Stock Montage Inc., (TL)Museum of the City of New York/Corbis; 221 The Granger Collection, New York; 222 The Granger Collection, New York ; 223 North Wind Picture Archives ; 229 (TR) Corbis-Bettmann, (CR) David Ulmer/Stock Boston, (B) Art Resource, NY; 230 The Granger Collection, New York ; 232 The Granger Collection, New York ; 233 (C)The Granger Collection, New York, (BR)Corbis-Bettmann ; 240 (C) Joseph Nettis/Stock Boston, (L) Kevin Fleming/Corbis, (R) AP/Wide World; Unit 6: 243 (BL) M. Lee/Art Directors & TRIP Photo Library, (Bkgrd)Austrian Archives/Corbis; 245 (CL) Eyewire, Inc., (CR) Bob Krist/Corbis, (BR) Horace Bristol/Corbis; 246 (BC) Archive Photos; 247 (CR) Gemma Giannini/Grant Heilman Photography ; 251 (TR) Corbis-Bettmann, (B) Catherine Ursillo/Photo Researchers, Inc.; 252 (T) The Granger Collection, New York, (B) PictureQuest; 253 Jeff Greenberg/PhotoEdit ; 254 NASA/Photo Researchers, Inc.; 256 Corbis-Bettmann ; 257 (BC) S. Grant/Art Directors & TRIP Photo Library, (TC) Corbis-Bettmann ; 258 © Bob Daemmrich/Stock Boston; 259 Daemmrich Photography; 267 (BR) Ellis Herwig/Stock Boston, (CR) Owen Franken/Corbis; 268 Charles Preitner/Visuals Unlimited; 269 Peter Menzel/Stock Boston; 270 (TR) H. Rogers/Art Directors & TRIP Photo Library, (BR) The Granger Collection, New York; 271 (TR) Rudi von Briel/PhotoEdit, (BR) Jack Fields/Corbis; 272 Lloyd Cluff/Corbis; 273 (C) John Lei/Stock Boston, (CL) Gemma Giannini/Grant Heilman Photography, (TR) Bill Gallery/Stock Boston, (CR) Farrell Grehan/Photo Researchers, Inc.; 274 Charles Preitner/Visuals Unlimited; 277 (TR) Michael Newman/PhotoEdit, (R) Lloyd Cluff/Corbis, (BL) Will & Deni McIntyre/Photo Researchers, Inc. ; 278 (TL) Ewing Galloway/Index Stock Imagery, (B) Bettmann/Corbis; 279 (B) Corbis-Bettmann, (TR) PictureQuest; 280 Barnabas Kindersley/© Dorling Kindersley; 281 Mark E. Gibson/Visuals Unlimited

Front and End Matter

H4 (BC) Eyewire, Inc., (TC) Jim Cummins/FPG International LLC, (TR) Jim Arbogast/PhotoDisc, (TL) Britt J. Erlanson-Messens/Image Bank, (BL) Stephen Simpson/FPG International LLC; H5 (TR) Don Klumpp/Image Bank; H8 (C) Richard Cummins/Corbis, (BC) Patrick Bennett/Corbis, (BR) Kelly/Mooney Photography/Corbis; H9 (BR) Ron Thomas (1994)/FPG International LLC ; H12 (CC) Douglas Slone/Corbis

"Our History" by Catherine Cate Coblentz, published in *Child Life Magazine,* October 1945. Reprinted by permission.

Notes

Facing Fear: Helping Students Cope with Tragic Events

Together, we can save a life

As much as we would like to protect our children, we cannot shield them from personal or community tragedies. We can, however, help them to be prepared for unforeseen dangerous events and to learn about facing and moving beyond their fears, sadness, and related concerns.

Common Responses to Trauma and Disaster

Children experience many common reactions after a trauma. These include reexperiencing the event (for example, flashbacks), avoidance and numbing of feelings, increased agitation, and changes in functioning. These reactions may be manifested in clingy behaviors, mood changes, increased anxieties, increased startle responses (for example, more jumpy with noises), physical complaints, and regressive behavior. Increased aggressive behaviors may also be seen. When the trauma or disaster is human-made, such as a terrorist event, children may react with hurtful talk, behaviors, or play. All of these reactions are normal responses and will, in general, dissipate with time. However, should these persist or increase over time, a referral to a mental health professional might be considered. Similarly, should these reactions result in a danger to self or others, immediate action is warranted.

Issues of Safety, Security, and Trust

In the aftermath of terrorism or other tragic events, very young children can feel overwhelmed with concerns of safety, security, and trust. They are often unsure where to turn for help. When the safety of their world is threatened, they may feel insecure and fearful. As a result, they may be more anxious and frightened. Children may be more clingy with teachers as well as with parents. This may be due to worry about their own safety as well as the safety of those important to them. Abandonment is a major childhood fear, so children need frequent reassurance they will be cared for and will not be left behind. This message may need to be repeated many times each day. By returning to a regular classroom routine, teachers can help to reinforce a sense of security in young children.

Children's increased fear may also encompass a worry that the trauma will reoccur. Because children this age have not developed a complete sense of time, exposure to replays of the trauma or disaster via television may lead them to believe that the event is happening again and again. This reexposure can result in increasing worry and fear. Limiting this exposure, as well as exposure to adult conversations about the event, may reduce the stress in children.

Expressing Thoughts and Feelings

Young children may have difficulty putting their thoughts and feelings into words. In order to express these, they may act out ideas through play. Teachers may see play that attempts to recreate the event. Children may repeatedly erect buildings with blocks only to knock them down. Children may pretend to be rescue workers or to be rescued. Children may also become more aggressive or destructive in their play as they act out feelings of anger about what has happened. Teachers may see a direct link to the event (for example, buildings being destroyed) or behaviors seemingly unrelated to the event (such as a game of tag on the playground). Children this age may talk incessantly about the event. To these repetitions, children may gradually add new bits of knowledge that they gain from others. At times, as young children try to make the story "fit" into their concept of the world around them, the repetitions may come to include misinformation or misperceptions of the event. Questions related to the trauma may be equally repetitive. Teachers may answer a child's question only to have the same question repeated within a few minutes. Having the same answer will increase the child's sense of security and help the child process the trauma.

Children this age may have difficulty understanding the results of the event. For example, very young children have magical thinking as well as the belief in the reversibility of loss. Therefore, they may believe that those killed in a disaster will return or that buildings can be easily rebuilt. Children may have many questions and discussions about death and dying. They do not have a mature grasp of the irreversibility of death.

Identifying Factors to Predict Children at Greatest Risk

Changes in behavior are likely after young children experience a trauma or disaster. One indicator of increased distress may be more whining and irritable behaviors. Young children may have more angry outbursts or temper tantrums, even over seemingly minor events. They may also be more defiant in their behaviors. The opposite may also be seen; some children will become more withdrawn and less engaged in classroom activities.

Children may show a change in functioning. They may have toileting accidents. A return to baby talk is not unusual. Sleep may be disrupted after a trauma, so children may be less rested, which can also produce more irritability. Children may want more help with schoolwork. Not only does this demonstrate increased stress, it also addresses the need for an increased sense of safety and security by having the teacher provide one-on-one attention. At times, children may have problems with attention and concentration on new work presented, which may require multiple presentations of the material.

(continued on the following page)

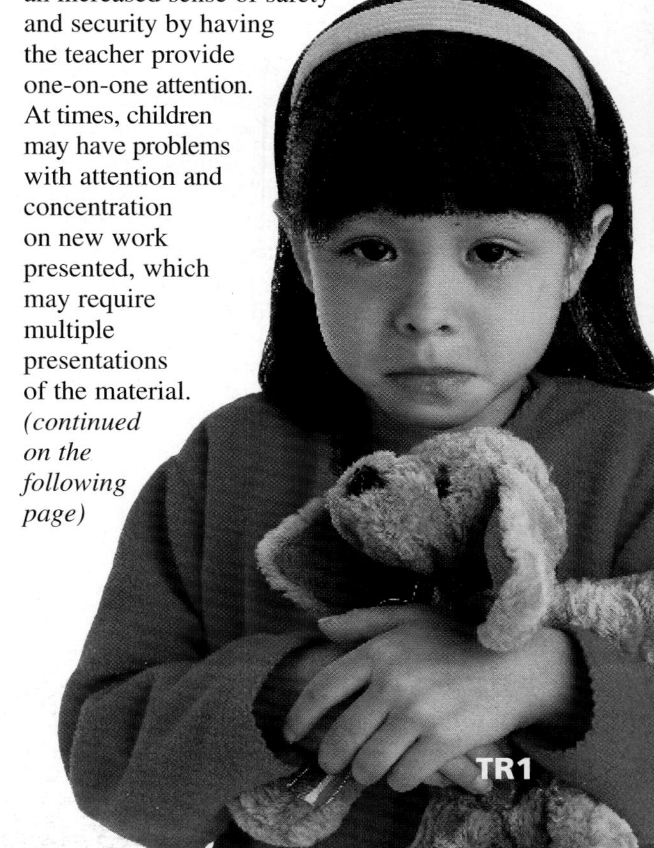

(continued from p. TR1)

Moving Forward in Spite of Life-Affecting Events

Frightening events, such as the terrorist attacks in the United States on September 11, 2001, the Oklahoma City bombing in 1995, earthquakes, tornadoes, and hurricanes here and in other countries, massive transportation accidents, and war or armed conflict or other military action, impact us all. Events that are caused by human beings can be particularly frightening and raise unique concerns. Terrorist actions and other violent acts are designed to instill fear in individuals and communities, if not countries. Because they happen without warning, there is no time to prepare. This unpredictability leaves us witha heightened sense of vulnerability and anxieties that the event could be repeated again, anywhere. With increased media coverage, even those not directly impacted can be significantly affected by an event. Images make us feel closer to the victims, and we may perceive ourselves as victims of the actions as well. The questions that arise from disasters of human design are difficult, if not impossible, to answer. We want answers to "why" and "how could they" and are often left frustrated by the lack of satisfying responses. This frustration also gives rise to intense feelings of anger. The anger toward the perpetrators may be uncomfortable and difficult to express in productive ways. As adults struggle with reactions and feelings in the aftermath of a terrorist action or tragic event, children are similarly searching for how to best handle their feelings. At all ages, they take cues from adults around them (parents, teachers, and community and national leaders).

Children need to know that their reactions and feelings to such events are normal. They need to recognize that others feel very similarly. Most important, children need to know that they will begin to feel better with time and that it is acceptable to enjoy friends, family, and activities. They need to know that there are things they can do to help themselves move forward in a positive way.

Activities to Help Children Address Fears

The following activities are designed to help you help your students address their fears and move beyond them.

- **What Happened**—Divide a piece of poster board into five areas. In each area, draw a symbol for one of the senses. As you discuss a trauma/disaster, record what children saw with their eyes, felt inside, heard with their ears, smelled with their nose, and tasted in their mouth.
- **Searching for a Sense of Safety**—Help children list people they can count on and places they can go for safety in an emergency. Remind children that it is important for them to know their own address, phone number, name (first and last), and parents' names (first and last) to give to helpers in order to reunite them with their families.
- **Naming Feelings**—Help children share ideas and feelings with each other by having them draw a picture of a feeling they or other children may have had after a trauma or disaster. Remind them that feelings may vary and that there are no rights and wrongs.
- **Dealing with Feelings**—Distribute strips of paper and ask children to write down or draw some feelings they would like to get rid of. Then tape each strip to the string of a balloon and release the balloon outdoors. Discuss with children how letting go of the balloon might help them let go of bad feelings.
- **Finding Hidden Treasures**—On yellow or gold paper, duplicate coins to serve as "treasure coins." Distribute to children and have them write or draw a good thing, feeling, activity, or person they have in their life. Remind children to use both sides of the coin and to use as many treasure coins as they would like. Invite children to share their treasures. You may also wish to make a treasure chest to store the coins.

Books for Young Readers

Smoky Night Bunting, Eve. Illus. by David Diaz. Harcourt Brace, 1999. Children who witness the Los Angeles riots experience dangerous times.

A Terrible Thing Happened: A story for children who have witnessed violence or trauma Holmes, Margaret, and Sasha J. Mudloff. Illus. by Cary Pillo and Thomas Payne. American Psychological Association, 2000. Children explore conscious and subconscious feelings they might have after a traumatic event.

Thunder Cake Polacco, Patricia. Paper Star, 1997. A young girl overcomes her fear of thunderstorms as she helps her grandmother make a cake.

Pip's Magic Stoll, Ellen. Voyager Picture Book, 1999. A young salamander tries to find the wizard who will help him overcome his fear of the dark.

My Many Colored Days Dr. Seuss. Illus. by Lou Fancher and Steve Johnson. Knopf, 1996. Children explore a colorful book about feelings and emotions.

American Red Cross

Information on American Red Cross *Facing Fear: Helping Young People Deal with Terrorism and Tragic Events*

The American Red Cross *Facing Fear* curriculum contains lesson plans for teachers and includes hands-on or interactive activities for the classroom that will help students and their families prepare for disastrous situations and equip them with tools to sort out their feelings and fears.

For further information or to obtain copies of the *Facing Fear* curriculum materials, or the curriculum materials that focus on natural disaster preparedness, called *Masters of Disaster*™, contact your local American Red Cross chapter. Visit **http://www.redcross.org** to find your nearest Red Cross chapter, and visit **www.redcross.org/disaster/masters** for specific information on the curriculum. American Red Cross products are available exclusively from local Red Cross chapters in the United States.

With permission, parts above were adapted from Healing After Trauma Skills, *Robin H. Gurwitch and Anne K. Messenbaugh, University of Oklahoma Health Sciences Center.*

Cause and Effect

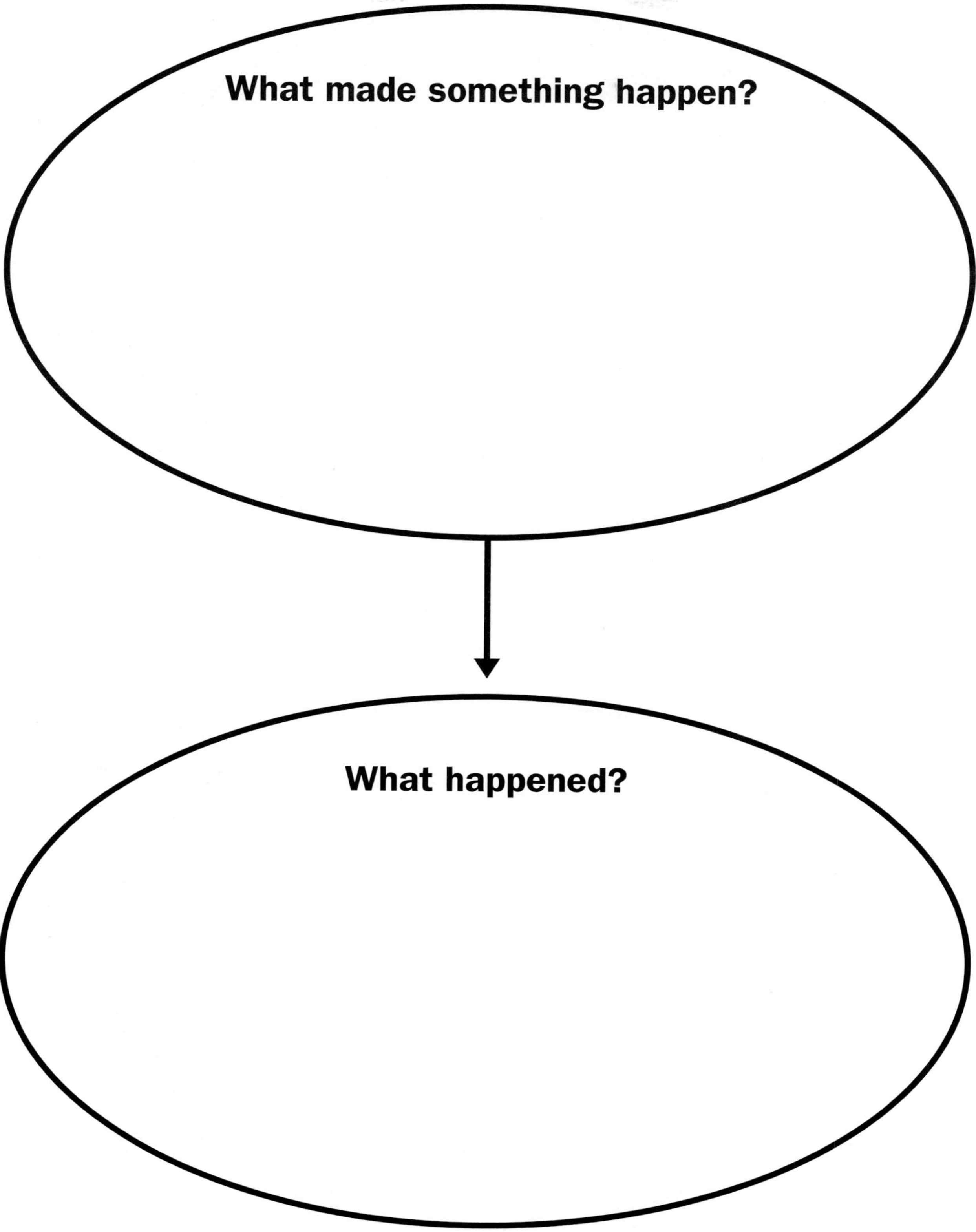

Cause and Effect

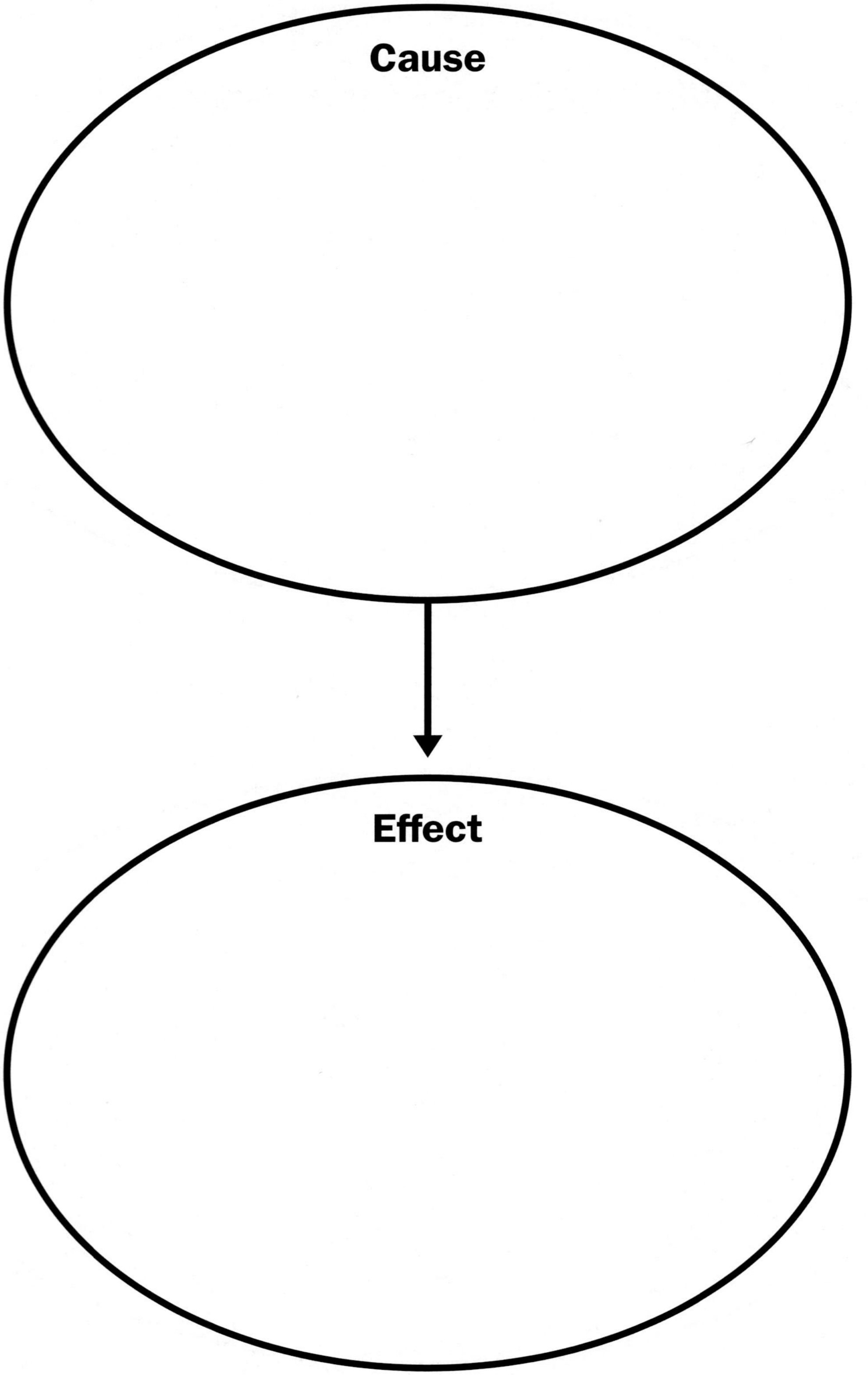

Compare and Contrast (Venn Diagram)

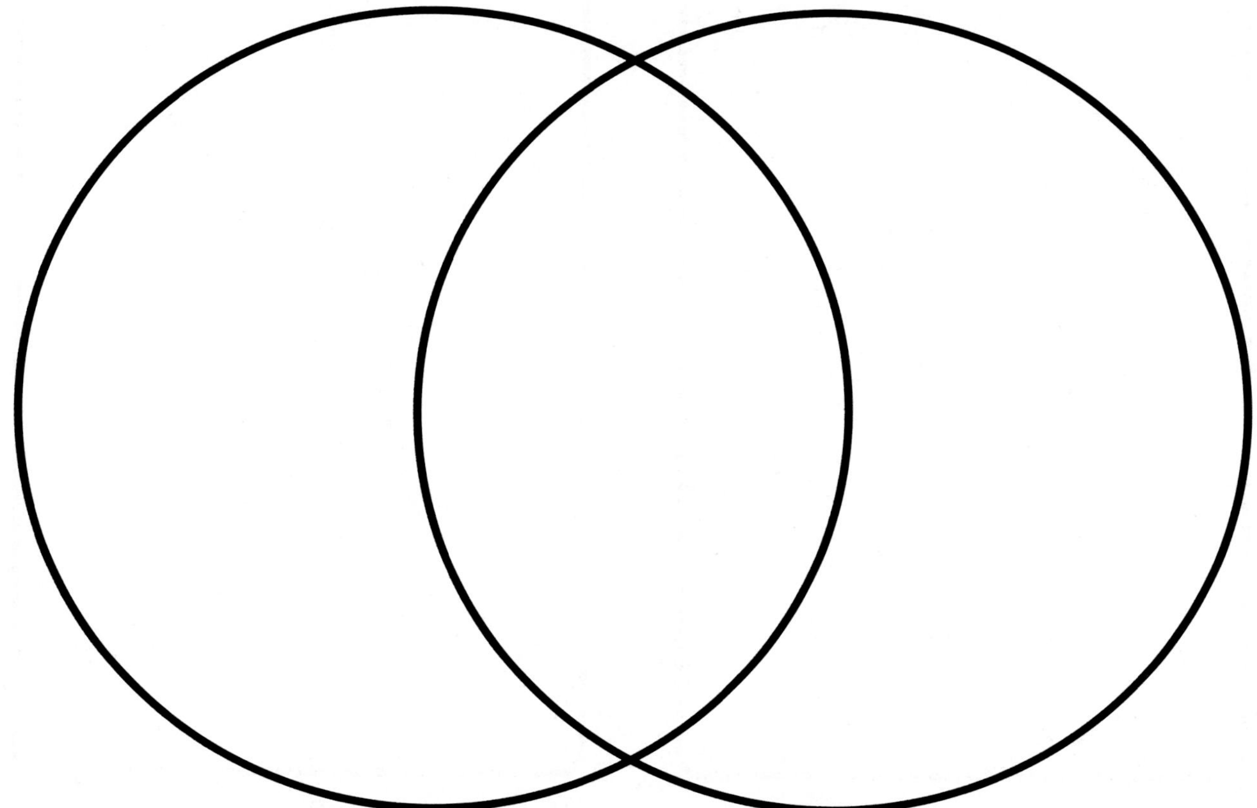

Compare and Contrast

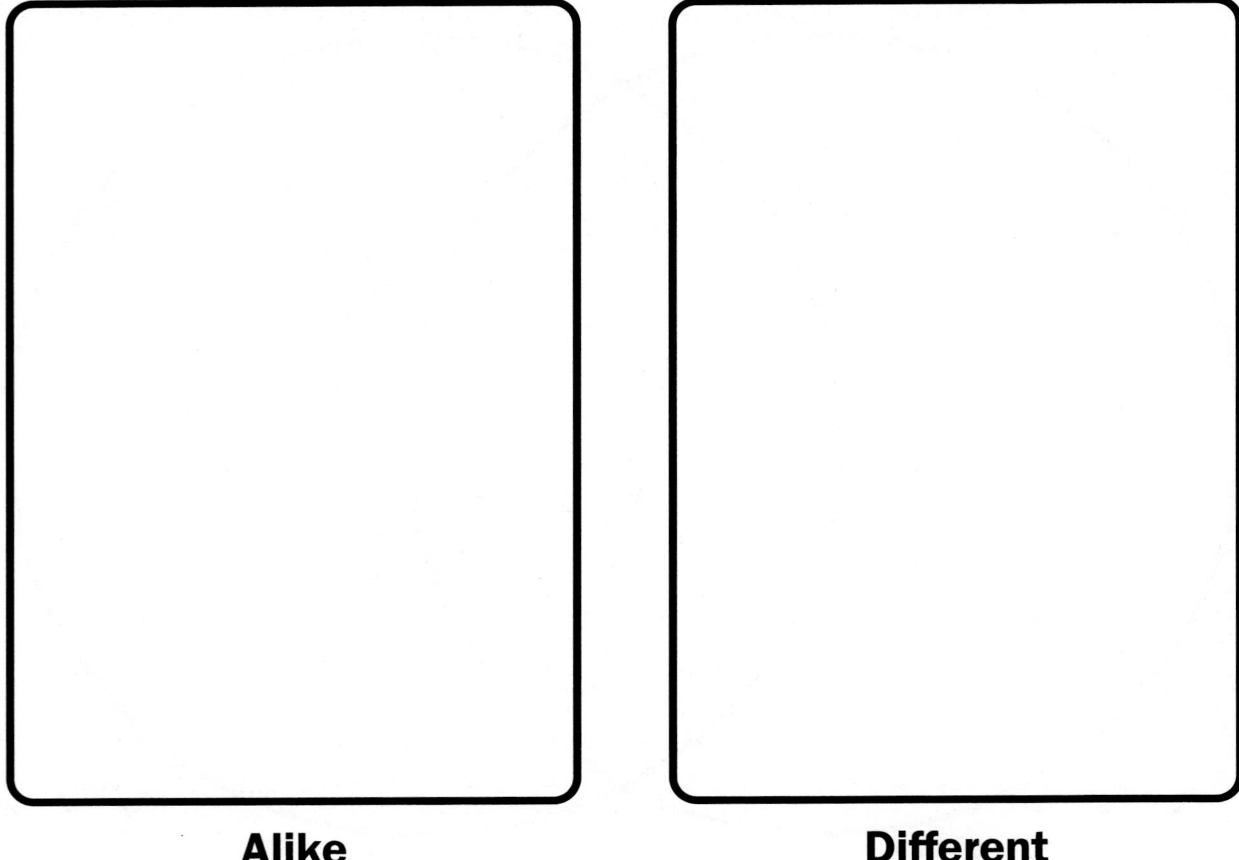

Main Idea and Details

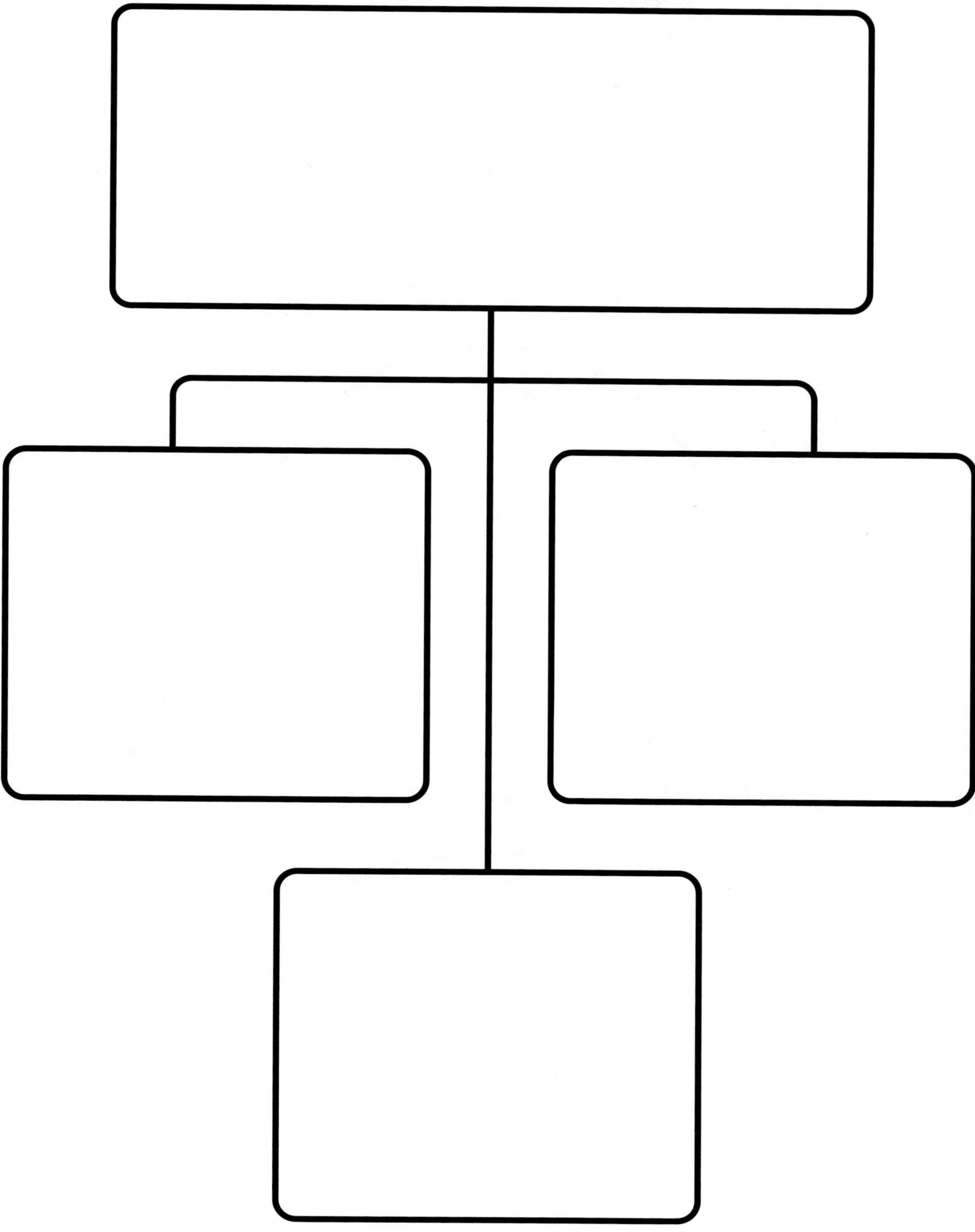

Predict

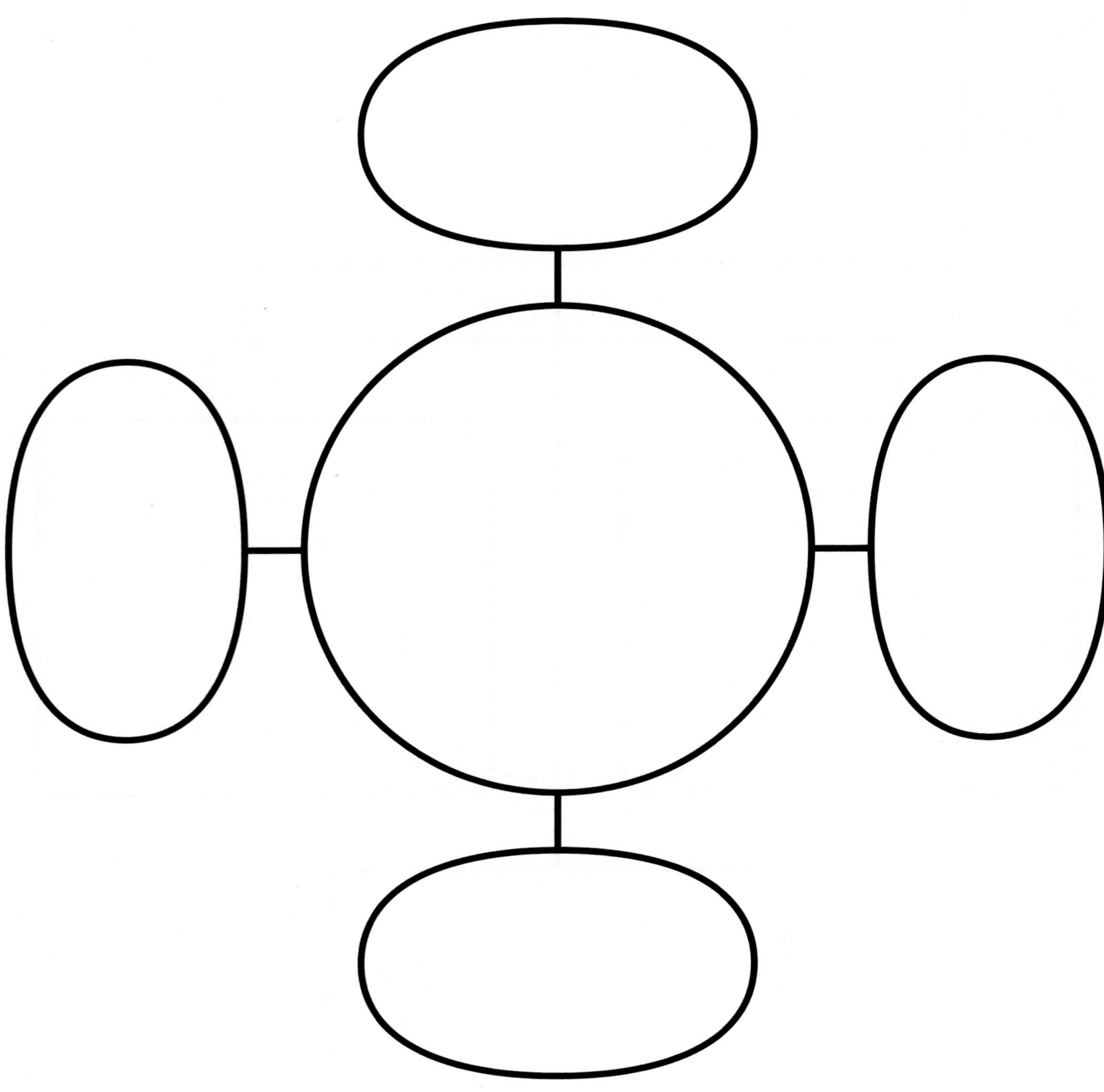

Predict

Recall and Retell

Sequence

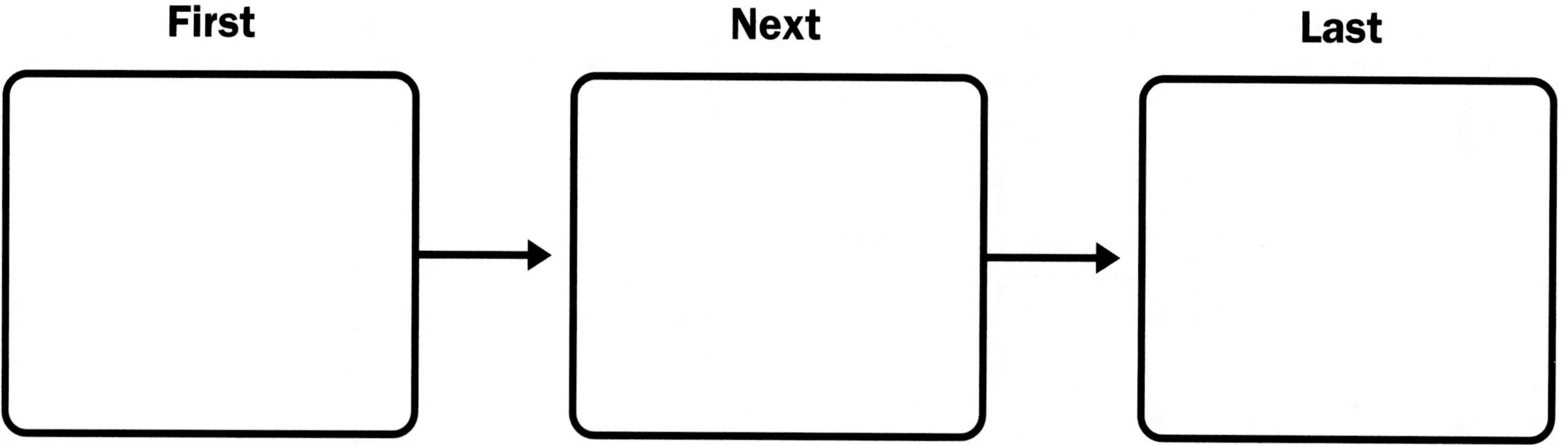

Use a Decision-Making Process

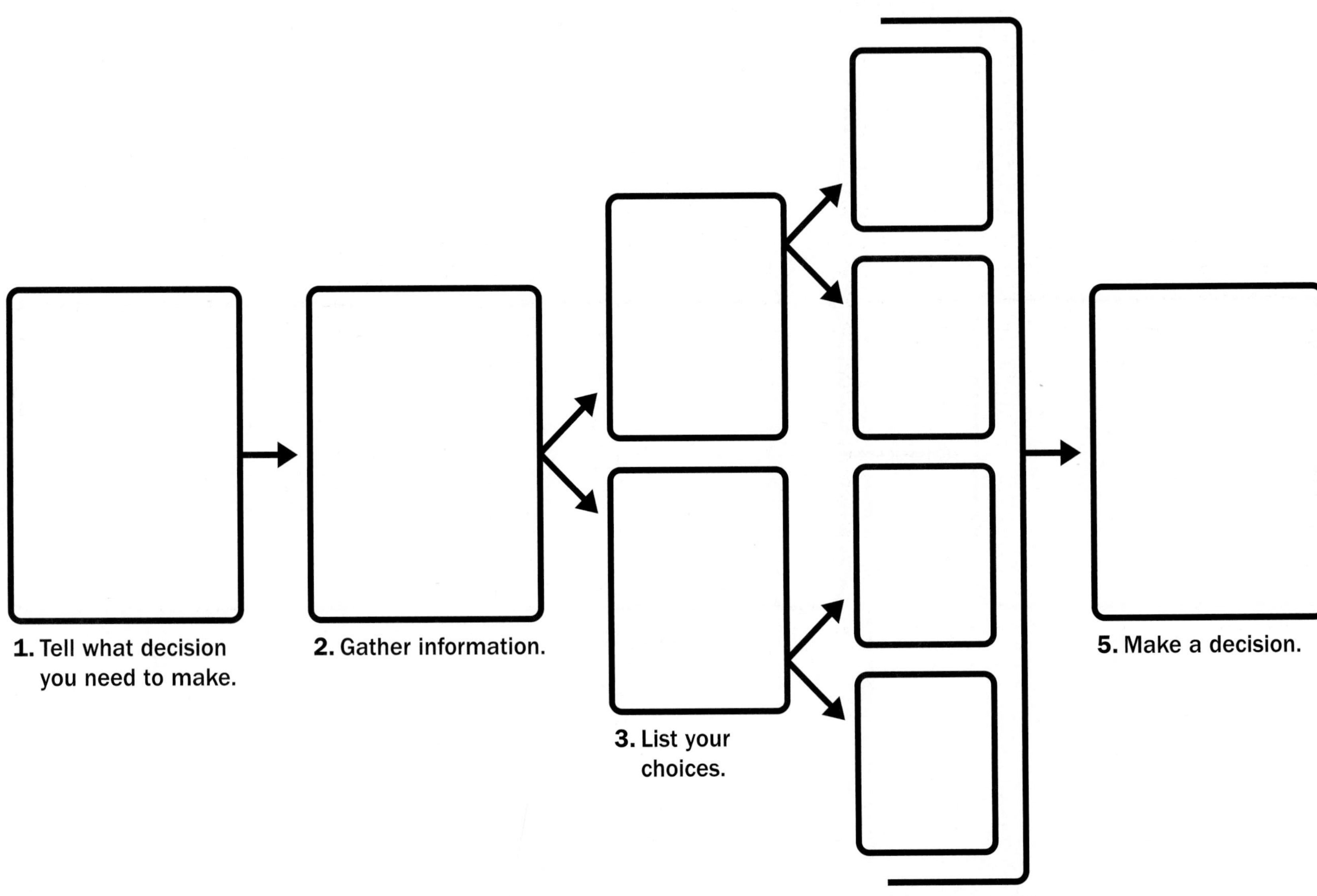

Use a Problem-Solving Process

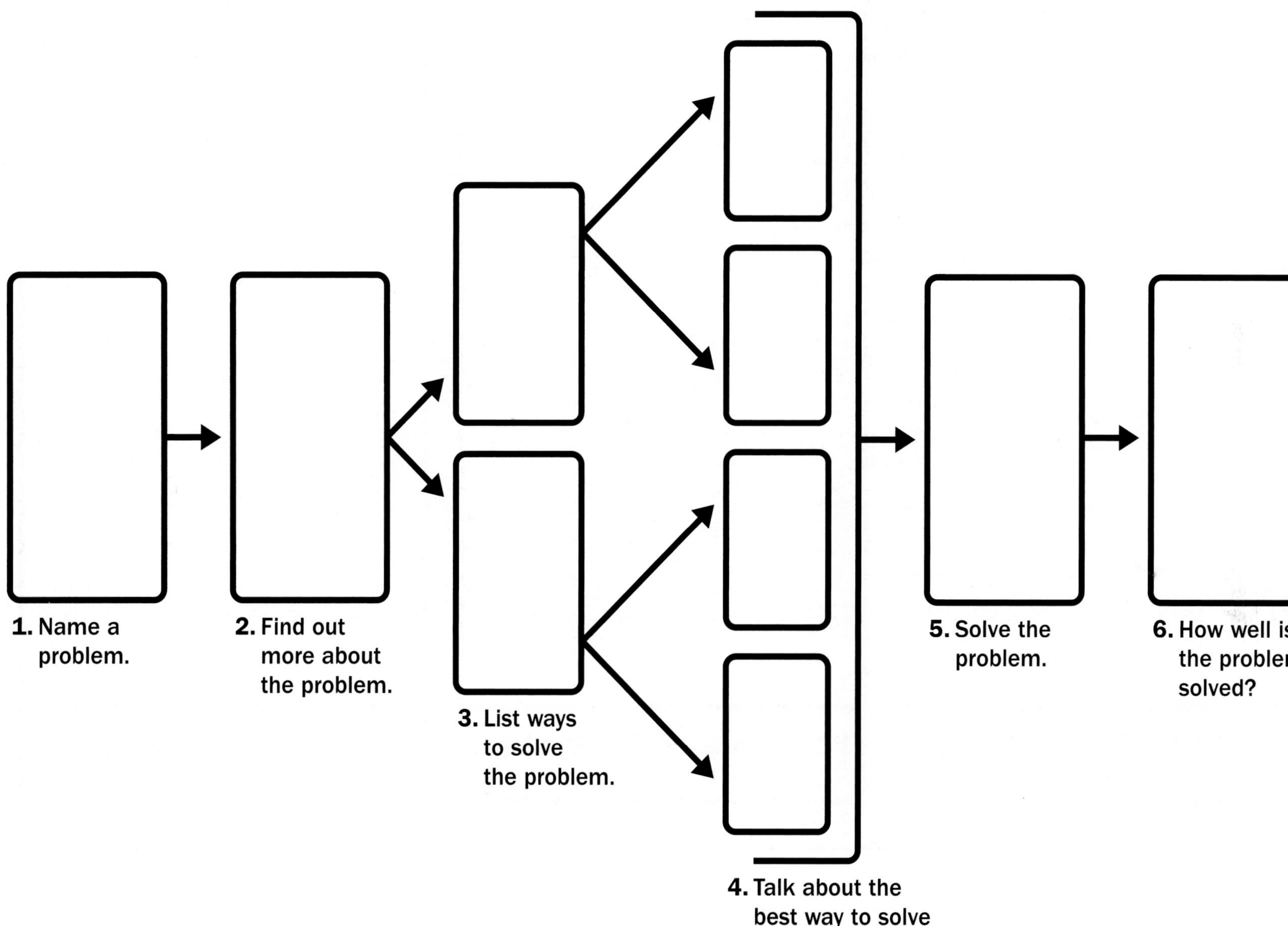

K-W-L Chart

Topic ______________________________

What We Know	What We Want to Know	What We Learned

K-W-L Interactive Reading Strategy was developed and is reprinted by permission of Donna Ogle, National-Louis University, Evanston, Illinois.

Unit 1

law	vote
community	history
urban	suburb
rural	capital

Vocabulary Words

Unit 2

geography	landform
ancestor	producer
consumer	natural resource
crop	conservation

Unit 3

income	goods
services	tax
factory	trade
transportation	barter

Vocabulary Words

Unit 4

government	mayor
citizen	governor
Congress	President
freedom	motto
monument	

Unit 5

shelter	tradition
explorer	colony
colonist	independence
pioneer	

Unit 6

immigrant	holiday
custom	landmark
artifact	invention
communication	

Dear Family:

Here is what we're learning in Social Studies!

Unit 1 Main Ideas

★ A group is a gathering of people or things.

★ A law is a rule that everyone must follow.

★ To vote is to make a choice about something.

★ A community is made up of many neighborhoods.

★ History is the story of people and places from the past.

★ An urban area is a city and the places around it.

★ A suburb is an area located near a city.

★ A rural area has small communities called towns that are far apart.

★ A capital is a city where the leaders of a state or country work.

Talk Together

Have your child tell you what he or she learned about your community and how rural, suburban, and urban areas are alike and different.

★ Activity ★

Help your child learn about where he or she lives.

✔ Drive or walk around your community with your child.

✔ Then make a large map showing stores, houses, public buildings, and other places.

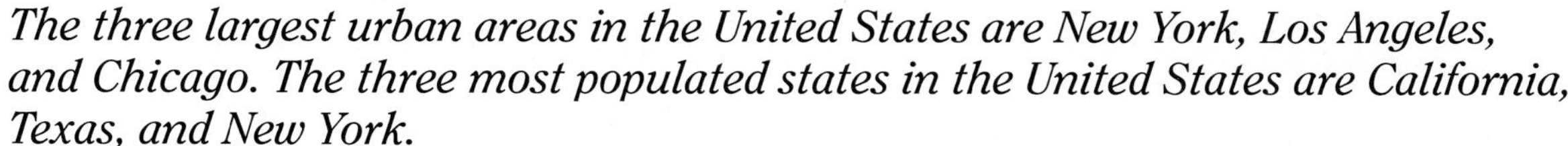

Fast Facts

The three largest urban areas in the United States are New York, Los Angeles, and Chicago. The three most populated states in the United States are California, Texas, and New York.

Thank you for supporting your child's Social Studies education!

Estimada familia:

¡Esto es lo que estamos aprendiendo en estudios sociales!

Unidad 1 Ideas principales

- ★ Un grupo es un conjunto de personas o cosas.
- ★ Una ley es una regla que todo el mundo debe respetar.
- ★ Votar es tomar una decisión sobre algo.
- ★ Una comunidad está compuesta de muchos vecindarios.
- ★ La historia trata del pasado de las personas y los lugares.
- ★ Un área urbana es una ciudad y los lugares que la rodean.
- ★ Un suburbio es un área ubicada cerca de una ciudad.
- ★ Un área rural tiene pequeñas comunidades llamadas pueblos que tienden a no estar cerca la una de la otra.
- ★ Una capital es la ciudad donde los líderes de un estado o país trabajan.

Para conversar

Pida a su niño o niña que le cuente lo que aprendió sobre su comunidad y las diferencias entre las áreas rurales, suburbanas y urbanas.

★ Actividad ★

Ayude a su niño o niña a aprender cosas sobre el lugar en el que vive.

- ✔ Conduzca o dé un paseo por su comunidad con su niño o niña.
- ✔ Luego hagan un mapa grande que incluya tiendas, casas, edificios públicos y otros lugares.

Datos curiosos

Las tres áreas urbanas más grandes de los Estados Unidos son Nueva York, Los Ángeles y Chicago. Los estados más poblados de los Estados Unidos son California, Texas y Nueva York.

¡Gracias por ayudar a su niño o niña con su educación de estudios sociales!

Dear Family:

Here is what we're learning in Social Studies!

Unit 2 Main Ideas

★ Geography is the study of Earth and the ways people use it.

★ Each kind of shape on the surface of the Earth is a landform.

★ A producer is someone who makes or grows something.

★ A consumer is someone who buys and uses goods.

★ A natural resource is a useful material that comes from the Earth.

★ Conservation is the care and protection of land, water, plants, and animals.

Talk Together

Ask your child to describe mountains, plains, and valleys. Then have your child choose one natural resource (air, water, sun, forests, soil) to tell you about and list ways to conserve, or protect, that resource.

★ Activity ★

Help your child learn about resources on Earth.

✔ List the following natural resources: water, air, trees, soil.

✔ Help your child identify where the resources are found, why they are important, and what can be done to help conserve them.

Fast Facts

The largest producer of apples in the world is China. The United States is the second largest producer of apples in the world. Washington produces more apples than any other state.

Thank you for supporting your child's Social Studies education!

Family Activities

Estimada familia:

¡Esto es lo que estamos aprendiendo en estudios sociales!

Unidad 2 Ideas principales

- ★ La geografía es el estudio de la Tierra y las formas en que la gente la usa.
- ★ Cada tipo de formación sobre la superficie de la Tierra es un accidente geográfico.
- ★ Un productor es alguien que fabrica, cultiva o cría algo.
- ★ Un consumidor es alguien que compra y usa mercancía.
- ★ Un recurso natural es material útil que procede de la Tierra.
- ★ La conservación es el cuidado y protección de la tierra, agua, plantas y animales.

Para conversar

Pida a su niño o niña que describa montañas, llanuras y valles. Luego pida a su niño o niña que elija un recurso natural (aire, agua, sol, bosques, suelo) para hablar de éste y de los modos en que se puede conservar o proteger.

★ Actividad ★

Ayude a su niño o niña a aprender cosas sobre los recursos de la Tierra.

- ✔ Cite los siguientes recursos naturales: agua, aire, árboles, suelo.
- ✔ Ayude a su niño o niña a identificar dónde se encuentran estos recursos, por qué son importantes y qué se puede hacer para conservarlos.

Datos curiosos

El principal productor de manzanas del mundo es la China. Los Estados Unidos son el segundo principal productor mundial de manzanas. Washington es el estado que más manzanas produce.

¡Gracias por ayudar a su niño o niña con su educación de estudios sociales!

Dear Family:

Here is what we're learning in Social Studies!

Unit 3 Main Ideas

★ The money that people earn is called income.

★ Goods are things people make or grow.

★ Services are jobs that people do to help others.

★ Money that is collected by a government is a tax.

★ A factory is a building where people produce goods.

★ Trade means to buy, sell, or exchange goods.

★ Transportation is a way of moving goods or people from place to place.

★ Barter means to trade goods or services for other goods or services without using money.

Talk Together

Ask your child to tell you what income is and how people earn income. Discuss the kinds of goods and services people buy. Have your child explain the difference between trading and bartering and name different ways that goods can be transported.

★ Activity ★

Help your child explore the world of transportation.

✔ Help your child make a transportation picture dictionary.

✔ Collect pictures of different types of transportation.

✔ Write *airplanes, buses, cars, ships, trains,* and *trucks* on sheets of paper.

✔ Staple the pages together.

✔ Then have your child paste the pictures on the correct pages.

Fast Facts

Dollar bills can usually be used for about one and one half years before they wear out. Most coins last about 25 years before they are too worn out to use. The United States Mint recycles old coins and uses the metal to make new coins.

Thank you for supporting your child's Social Studies education!

Estimada familia:

¡Esto es lo que estamos aprendiendo en estudios sociales!

Unidad 3 Ideas principales

★ El dinero que ganamos se llama ingresos.

★ La mercancía son cosas que la gente fabrica, cultiva o cría.

★ Los servicios son trabajos que hace la gente para ayudar a los demás.

★ El dinero que es recaudado por el gobierno es un impuesto.

★ Una fábrica es un edificio donde la gente fabrica productos.

★ Comerciar significa comprar, vender o intercambiar productos.

★ El transporte es una manera de trasladar productos o personas.

★ Trueque significa intercambiar productos o servicios por otros productos o servicios sin usar dinero.

Para conversar

Pida a su niño o niña que le explique lo que son los ingresos y cómo se obtienen. Hablen de los tipos de productos y servicios que compra la gente. Pídale que le explique la diferencia entre el comercio y el trueque y que mencione varias maneras de transportar productos.

★ Actividad ★

Ayude a su niño o niña a explorar el mundo del transporte.

✔ Trabaje con su niño o niña para hacer un diccionario ilustrado del transporte.

✔ Reúna ilustraciones de diversos tipos de transporte.

✔ Escriba *aviones, autobuses, automóviles, barcos, trenes* y *camiones* en hojas de papel.

✔ Grape las hojas.

✔ Luego, pida a su niño o niña que pegue las ilustraciones en las páginas correspondientes.

Datos curiosos

Los billetes de un dólar se pueden usar durante aproximadamente un año y medio antes de que se desgasten. Las monedas duran unos 25 años antes de que se desgasten demasiado. La Casa de la Moneda de los EE. UU. recicla las monedas viejas y usa el metal para producir monedas nuevas.

¡Gracias por ayudar a su niño o niña con su educación de estudios sociales!

Dear Family:

Here is what we're learning in Social Studies!

Unit 4 Main Ideas

- ★ A government is a group of people who work together to run a city, state, or country.
- ★ A mayor is the leader of a town or city.
- ★ A citizen is a member of a community, state, and country.
- ★ The governor is the leader of a state's government.
- ★ The Congress writes and votes on laws for all states.
- ★ The President is the leader of our country.
- ★ Freedom is every citizen's right to make choices.
- ★ A motto is a word or saying that people try to live by.
- ★ A monument is a building or statue that honors a person or event.

Talk Together

Ask your child to tell you about the current President of the United States. Then ask him or her to talk about any presidents who have special monuments in Washington, D.C. (George Washington, Thomas Jefferson, and Abraham Lincoln).

★ Activity ★

Help your child learn about our government.

- ✔ Help your child make a chart that shows the leaders of your community, state, and nation.
- ✔ Talk about the jobs these people do.

Fast Facts

The office of President of the United States is one of the most powerful offices in the world. There have been 43 Presidents. The youngest Presidents were Theodore Roosevelt—age 42, John F. Kennedy—age 43, and Bill Clinton—age 46.

Thank you for supporting your child's Social Studies education!

Estimada familia:

¡Esto es lo que estamos aprendiendo en estudios sociales!

Unidad 4 Ideas principales

- ★ Un gobierno es un grupo de personas que trabajan juntas para dirigir una ciudad, un estado o un país.
- ★ El alcalde es el líder de un pueblo o una ciudad.
- ★ Un ciudadano es miembro de una comunidad, un estado y un país.
- ★ El gobernador es el líder del gobierno de un estado.
- ★ El Congreso escribe y vota para pasar leyes para todos los estados.
- ★ El presidente es el líder de nuestro país.
- ★ La libertad es el derecho que tienen todos los ciudadanos a tomar decisiones.
- ★ Un lema es una palabra o dicho que inspira a la gente.
- ★ Un monumento es un edificio o una estatua que honra a una persona o un suceso.

Para conversar

Pida a su niño o niña que le hable del presidente actual de los Estados Unidos. Luego, pídale que le cuente de cualquier presidente al que se le haya dedicado un monumento en Washington, D.C. (George Washington, Thomas Jefferson y Abraham Lincoln).

★ Actividad ★

Ayude a su niño o niña a aprender sobre nuestro gobiernos.

- ✔ Ayude a su niño o niña a hacer una tabla donde se indiquen los nombres de líderes de su comunidad, estado y nación.
- ✔ Hablen del trabajo que realizan estas personas.

Datos curiosos

El cargo de presidente de los Estados Unidos es uno de los cargos más poderosos del mundo. Ha habido 43 presidentes. Los presidentes más jóvenes al momento de asumir el puesto lo fueron Theodore Roosevelt, a los 42 años, John F. Kennedy, a los 43 y Bill Clinton, a los 46.

¡Gracias por ayudar a su niño o niña con su educación de estudios sociales!

Dear Family:

Here is what we're learning in Social Studies!

Unit 5 Main Ideas

- ★ A shelter is a place where people live.
- ★ A tradition is something that is done a certain way for many years.
- ★ An explorer is a person who travels to a new place to learn about it.
- ★ A colony is a place that is settled by people from another country.
- ★ A colonist is a person who lives in a colony.
- ★ Independence means to be free from other people or places.
- ★ A pioneer is a person who goes first and prepares the way for others.

Talk Together

Ask your child to tell you about any of these people: Christopher Columbus, John Smith, the Pilgrims, Squanto, George Washington, Patrick Henry, Paul Revere, Thomas Jefferson, Lewis and Clark, Harriet Tubman, Sojourner Truth. Then have your child recall events related to Jamestown, Plymouth, Thanksgiving, the Declaration of Independence, or the Oregon Trail.

★ Activity ★

Help your child get a sense of the early history of our country.

- ✔ Ask your child to draw a picture of one of the people in the chapter.
- ✔ Then help your child write several sentences that tell what the person did and why he or she is important to our history.

Fast Facts

Children in the 13 colonies had many chores. For example, they helped milk the cows, fetch water from nearby streams or rivers, collect wood for the fire, wash dishes, and shake out dusty blankets and quilts. Children played games such as jump rope and tag.

Thank you for supporting your child's Social Studies education!

Estimada familia:

¡Esto es lo que estamos aprendiendo en estudios sociales!

Unidad 5 Ideas principales

- ★ Un albergue es un lugar donde viven personas.
- ★ Una tradición es algo que se hace de cierta manera durante muchos años.
- ★ Un explorador es una persona que viaja a un nuevo lugar para aprender sobre el mismo.
- ★ Una colonia es un lugar poblado por personas de otro país.
- ★ Un colono es una persona que vive en una colonia.
- ★ Independencia quiere diar ser libre de otras personas u otros lugares.
- ★ Un pionero es una persona que hace algo primero y prepara el camino para otros.

Para conversar

Pida a su niño o niña que le hable de cualquiera de estas personas: Cristóbal Colón, John Smith, los peregrinos, Squanto, George Washington, Patrick Henry, Paul Revere, Thomas Jefferson, Lewis y Clark, Harriet Tubman, Sojourner Truth. Luego pídale que recuerde sucesos relacionados con Jamestown, Plymouth, la Acción de Gracias, la Declaración de Independencia o el Camino de Oregón.

★ Actividad ★

Ayude a su niño o niña a aprender sobre la historia antigua de nuestro país.

- ✔ Pida a su niño o niña que haga un dibujo de uno de los personajes del capítulo.
- ✔ Luego, ayúdele a escribir varias oraciones que indiquen lo que hizo la persona y por qué es importante para nuestra historia.

Datos curiosos

Los niños de las 13 colonias tenían que hacer muchas tareas. Por ejemplo, ayudaban a ordeñar vacas, buscar agua de arroyos o ríos cercanos, recoger madera para el fuego, lavar platos y sacudir el polvo de cobijas y colchas. Los niños se divertían saltando a la cuerda y jugando otros juegos.

¡Gracias por ayudar a su niño o niña con su educación de estudios sociales!

Dear Family:

Here is what we're learning in Social Studies!

Unit 6 Main Ideas

★ An immigrant is a person who settles in a new country.

★ A holiday is a special day.

★ A custom is a special way that a group does something.

★ A landmark is a building or place that is important or interesting.

★ An artifact is an object made and used by people.

★ An invention is something new that someone makes or thinks of.

★ Communication is sharing ideas and information with others.

Talk Together

Ask your child to tell you about one of the places where immigrants to the United States arrived (Angel Island in San Francisco Bay or Ellis Island in New York Harbor). Then have your child tell you about his or her favorite holiday.

★ Activity ★

Help your child learn to appreciate people and events from the past.

✔ Help your child make a list of holidays, such as Memorial Day, Veterans Day, Independence Day, Labor Day, and Thanksgiving.

✔ Then talk about why each one is a holiday and how it is celebrated.

Fast Facts

Invention	*Year*	*Invention*	*Year*
microphone	*1827*	*compact disc (CD)*	*1972*
telephone	*1876*	*personal computer*	*1975*
pen	*1884*	*cell phone*	*1979*
copy machine	*1937*	*laptop computer*	*1987*

Thank you for supporting your child's Social Studies education!

Family Activities

Estimada familia:

¡Esto es lo que estamos aprendiendo en estudios sociales!

Unidad 6 Ideas principales

- ★ Un inmigrante es una persona que se establece en un nuevo país.
- ★ Un día festivo es un día especial.
- ★ Una costumbre es la forma especial en que un grupo hace algo.
- ★ Un sitio notable es una construcción o lugar importante o interesante.
- ★ Un artefacto es un objeto hecho y usado por personas.
- ★ Un invento es algo nuevo que alguien hace o se le ocurre que no existía antes.
- ★ La comunicación consiste en compartir ideas e información con otras personas.

Para conversar

Pida a su niño o niña que le hable sobre uno de los lugares a los que llegaban los inmigrantes a los Estados Unidos (la isla Ángel en la bahía de San Francisco o la isla Ellis en el puerto de Nueva York). Luego pida a su niño o niña que le hable de su día festivo favorito.

★ Actividad ★

Ayude a su niño o niña a que aprenda a apreciar a las personas y sucesos del pasado.

- ✔ Ayude a su niño o niña a que haga una lista de días festivos como el Día de los Caídos, el Día de los Veteranos, el Día de la Independencia, el Día del Trabajo y el Día de Acción de Gracias.
- ✔ Después, hablen de la razón por la que cada uno de estos días es festivo y cómo se celebran.

Datos curiosos

Invento	*Año*	*Invento*	*Año*
micrófono	*1827*	*disco compacto (CD)*	*1972*
teléfono	*1876*	*computadora personal*	*1975*
pluma	*1884*	*teléfono celular*	*1979*
fotocopiadora	*1937*	*computadora portátil*	*1987*

¡Gracias por ayudar a su niño o niña con su educación de estudios sociales!

ESSENTIAL KNOWLEDGE	K	1	2	3	4	5	6
History							
Understand human influence in shaping communities, states, and nations	★	★	★	★	★	★	★
Contributions of ordinary people	★	★	★	★	★	★	★
Historic figures and their lives		★	★	★	★	★	★
Understand the origins and significance of customs, holidays, celebrations, and landmarks in the community, state, nation, and world	★	★	★	★	★	★	★
Understand the concepts of time and chronology	★	★	★	★	★	★	★
Order of events	★	★	★	★	★	★	★
Past, present, future	★	★	★	★	★	★	★
Political, economic, and social change	★	★	★	★	★	★	★
Cause and effect		★	★	★	★	★	★
Understand how various sources provide information			★	★	★	★	★
Primary sources			★	★	★	★	★
Secondary sources			★	★	★	★	★
Understand how human needs, ideas, issues, and events influence past and present	★	★	★	★	★	★	★
Exploration, colonization, and settlement	★	★	★	★	★	★	★
Conflict and revolution	★	★	★	★	★	★	★
Immigration			★	★	★	★	★
Growth and expansion			★	★	★	★	★
Understand that the past influences the present	★	★	★	★	★	★	★
Connecting past and present	★	★	★	★	★	★	★
Comparing past and present	★	★	★	★	★	★	★
Geography							
Understand concept of location	★	★	★	★	★	★	★
Relative and exact	★	★	★	★	★	★	★
Factors influencing location		★	★	★	★	★	★
Understand concept of place	★	★	★	★	★	★	★
Landforms, bodies of water, vegetation, animal life	★	★	★	★	★	★	★
Climate, weather, and seasonal patterns	★	★	★	★	★	★	★
Understand human-environment interactions	★	★	★	★	★	★	★
Natural resources and land use	★	★	★	★	★	★	★
Human features (housing, roads)	★	★	★	★	★	★	★
Human adaptations to and modifications of their environments		★	★	★	★	★	★
Understand the concept of movement	★	★	★	★	★	★	★
Movement of ideas through cultural sharing	★	★	★	★	★	★	★
Colonization, immigration, settlement patterns (people)		★	★	★	★	★	★
Physical characteristics affect trade (products)			★	★	★	★	★
Physical characteristics affect human activities (culture)			★	★	★	★	★
Understand concept of region		★	★	★	★	★	★
Physical characteristics		★	★	★	★	★	★
Political characteristics			★	★	★	★	★

Scope and Sequence

ESSENTIAL KNOWLEDGE	K	1	2	3	4	5	6
Population characteristics			★	★	★	★	★
Economic characteristics			★	★	★	★	★
Time zones					★	★	★
Understand and use geographic tools to collect, analyze, and interpret information	★	★	★	★	★	★	★
Maps and globes	★	★	★	★	★	★	★
Comparison of world regions and countries		★	★	★	★	★	★
Read, interpret, and construct charts, maps, and diagrams		★	★	★	★	★	★
Economics							
Understand how scarcity of resources leads to economic choice	★	★	★	★	★	★	★
Basic human needs and wants	★	★	★	★	★	★	★
Goods and services	★	★	★	★	★	★	★
Production, distribution, and consumption	★	★	★	★	★	★	★
Work and income	★	★	★	★	★	★	★
Saving and spending	★	★	★	★	★	★	★
Opportunity cost	★	★	★	★	★	★	★
Understand markets and price	★	★	★	★	★	★	★
Exchange of goods and services	★	★	★	★	★	★	★
Impact of mass production and specialization			★	★	★	★	★
Supply and demand				★	★	★	★
Competition				★	★	★	★
Economic interdependence				★	★	★	★
Imports, exports, and trade				★	★	★	★
Understand economic patterns and systems	★	★	★	★	★	★	★
Effects of transportation and communication	★	★	★	★	★	★	★
Free enterprise			★	★	★	★	★
Entrepreneurship			★	★	★	★	★
Government							
Understand the purposes of government	★	★	★	★	★	★	★
Promotion of the common good	★	★	★	★	★	★	★
Order and security			★	★	★	★	★
Distribution of services			★	★	★	★	★
Protection of individual rights and freedoms			★	★	★	★	★
Understand the structure of government	★	★	★	★	★	★	★
Purpose of rules and laws	★	★	★	★	★	★	★
Roles and responsibilities of authority figures and public officials	★	★	★	★	★	★	★
Levels of government (local, state, and national)		★	★	★	★	★	★
Government services		★	★	★	★	★	★
Branches of government			★	★	★	★	★
Government documents			★	★	★	★	★
Political parties						★	★
Understand the functions of government	★	★	★	★	★	★	★

ESSENTIAL KNOWLEDGE	K	1	2	3	4	5	6
Making, amending, and removing laws	★	★	★	★	★	★	★
Enforcing laws		★	★	★	★	★	★
Financing of services			★	★	★	★	★
Understand types of governments		★	★	★	★	★	★
Citizenship							
Understand good citizenship	★	★	★	★	★	★	★
Historic figures and ordinary people	★	★	★	★	★	★	★
Citizenship traits (caring, respect, responsibility, fairness, honesty, courage)	★	★	★	★	★	★	★
Working for the common good	★	★	★	★	★	★	★
Believing in truth and justice	★	★	★	★	★	★	★
Treating all people equally	★	★	★	★	★	★	★
Solving problems	★	★	★	★	★	★	★
Making decisions	★	★	★	★	★	★	★
Understand state and national identities	★	★	★	★	★	★	★
Flags, symbols, anthems, pledges	★	★	★	★	★	★	★
Customs and celebrations	★	★	★	★	★	★	★
Mottoes		★	★	★	★	★	★
Understand the freedoms, rights, and responsibilities of citizens		★	★	★	★	★	★
Individual freedoms (choosing your associates, choosing where you live)		★	★	★	★	★	★
Economic freedoms (choosing your own work, owning property)		★	★	★	★	★	★
Political freedoms (joining a political party, running for office, purpose of and need for free elections)		★	★	★	★	★	★
Rights (free speech, voting rights, freedom of religion, equal protection and opportunity under the law)		★	★	★	★	★	★
Responsibilities/ participating, voting		★	★	★	★	★	★
Responsibilities/ keeping informed			★	★	★	★	★
Understand democratic principles		★	★	★	★	★	★
Due process and equal protection under the law				★	★	★	★
Majority rule with minority respect				★	★	★	★
Government by law				★	★	★	★
Culture							
Understand social groups and institutions	★	★	★	★	★	★	★
Family and community	★	★	★	★	★	★	★
Education	★	★	★	★	★	★	★
Religion		★	★	★	★	★	★
Politics			★	★	★	★	★
Understand similarities and differences among people	★	★	★	★	★	★	★
Culture and culture region	★	★	★	★	★	★	★
Language	★	★	★	★	★	★	★
Customs, holidays, and traditions	★	★	★	★	★	★	★
Similarities among diverse groups	★	★	★	★	★	★	★
Contributions of diverse groups	★	★	★	★	★	★	★

Scope and Sequence

ESSENTIAL KNOWLEDGE	K	1	2	3	4	5	6
Understand how the arts express cultural heritage	★	★	★	★	★	★	★
Literature	★	★	★	★	★	★	★
Music, drama, dance	★	★	★	★	★	★	★
Role of writers and artists		★	★	★	★	★	★
Art			★	★	★	★	★
Architecture			★	★	★	★	★
Science, Technology, and Society							
Understand how technology has affected life	★	★	★	★	★	★	★
Tools and appliances	★	★	★	★	★	★	★
Communication	★	★	★	★	★	★	★
Transportation	★	★	★	★	★	★	★
Recreation	★	★	★	★	★	★	★
Work, education, and learning	★	★	★	★	★	★	★
Medicine				★	★	★	★
Understand the significance of the inventions or creations of people in technology	★	★	★	★	★	★	★
Understand the changes brought about by scientific discoveries and technological inventions	★	★	★	★	★	★	★
Predict how future discoveries and innovations could affect life in the United States	★	★	★	★	★	★	★

ESSENTIAL SKILLS	K	1	2	3	4	5	6
Map and Globe Skills							
Understand directions		★	★	★	★	★	★
Cardinal directions		★	★	★	★	★	★
Intermediate directions			★	★	★	★	★
Understand globes	★	★	★	★	★	★	★
Purpose of globe	★	★	★	★	★	★	★
Equator			★	★	★	★	★
Hemispheres				★	★	★	★
Poles				★	★	★	★
Prime meridian/International Date Line				★	★	★	★
Arctic and Antarctic Circles				★	★	★	★
Latitude and longitude				★	★	★	★
Understand, use, and create maps	★	★	★	★	★	★	★
Location of cities, states, countries, continents, oceans	★	★	★	★	★	★	★
Comparison of map with photograph	★	★	★	★	★	★	★
Comparison of map with globe	★	★	★	★	★	★	★
Locator map		★	★	★	★	★	★
Routes and mental mapping		★	★	★	★	★	★
Grids			★	★	★	★	★
Inset maps				★	★	★	★

ESSENTIAL SKILLS	K	1	2	3	4	5	6
Map projections						★	★
Understand and use map symbols	★	★	★	★	★	★	★
Landforms and bodies of water	★	★	★	★	★	★	★
Symbols	★	★	★	★	★	★	★
Key and legend		★	★	★	★	★	★
Direction symbols and compass rose		★	★	★	★	★	★
Borders			★	★	★	★	★
Scale and distance				★	★	★	★
Lines of latitude and longitude					★	★	★
Elevation tints					★	★	★
Understand and use special purpose maps		★	★	★	★	★	★
Historical map		★	★	★	★	★	★
Political map		★	★	★	★	★	★
Physical map			★	★	★	★	★
Climate map				★	★	★	★
Product and resource map				★	★	★	★
Transportation map					★	★	★
Distribution map					★	★	★
Precipitation map					★	★	★
Elevation map					★	★	★
Population map					★	★	★
Population density map					★	★	★
Understand time zones					★	★	★
Understand cartograms							★
Chart and Graph Skills							
Understand charts and graphs	★	★	★	★	★	★	★
Charts	★	★	★	★	★	★	★
Diagrams	★	★	★	★	★	★	★
Calendars and time lines	★	★	★	★	★	★	★
Bar graphs	★	★	★	★	★	★	★
Pie (circle) graphs				★	★	★	★
Line graphs				★	★	★	★
Climographs						★	★
Critical Thinking Skills							
Problem solving	★	★	★	★	★	★	★
Identify a problem	★	★	★	★	★	★	★
Gather information	★	★	★	★	★	★	★
List and consider options	★	★	★	★	★	★	★
Consider advantages and disadvantages	★	★	★	★	★	★	★
Choose and implement a solution	★	★	★	★	★	★	★
Evaluate the effectiveness of a solution	★	★	★	★	★	★	★

ESSENTIAL SKILLS	K	1	2	3	4	5	6
Decision making	★	★	★	★	★	★	★
Identify a situation that requires a decision	★	★	★	★	★	★	★
Gather information	★	★	★	★	★	★	★
Consider the options	★	★	★	★	★	★	★
Predict the consequences	★	★	★	★	★	★	★
Take action	★	★	★	★	★	★	★
Analysis of information	★	★	★	★	★	★	★
Sequence	★	★	★	★	★	★	★
Categorize and classify	★	★	★	★	★	★	★
Compare and contrast	★	★	★	★	★	★	★
Identify main ideas and details	★	★	★	★	★	★	★
Predict		★	★	★	★	★	★
Identify cause-and-effect relationships			★	★	★	★	★
Summarize				★	★	★	★
Generalize				★	★	★	★
Make inferences and draw conclusions				★	★	★	★
Identify different points of view and frames of reference (detection of bias)				★	★	★	★
Fact and opinion				★	★	★	★
Evaluation of arguments and sources				★	★	★	★
Research Skills							
Tables and charts	★	★	★	★	★	★	★
Time lines	★	★	★	★	★	★	★
Bar graphs	★	★	★	★	★	★	★
Diagrams	★	★	★	★	★	★	★
Pie (circle) graphs				★	★	★	★
Line graphs				★	★	★	★
Flowcharts						★	★
Primary and secondary sources	★	★	★	★	★	★	★
Audio and video recordings	★	★	★	★	★	★	★
Art	★	★	★	★	★	★	★
Photographs	★	★	★	★	★	★	★
Biographies, autobiographies, and oral histories	★	★	★	★	★	★	★
Internet	★	★	★	★	★	★	★
Computer software	★	★	★	★	★	★	★
Artifacts and historical records		★	★	★	★	★	★
Atlases and gazetteers		★	★	★	★	★	★
News sources and current events		★	★	★	★	★	★
Speeches				★	★	★	★
Encyclopedias				★	★	★	★
Dictionaries and thesauruses				★	★	★	★
Almanacs				★	★	★	★

ESSENTIAL SKILLS	K	1	2	3	4	5	6
Political cartoons						★	★
Use appropriate math skills to interpret maps and graphs		★	★	★	★	★	★
Reading Skills							
Vocabulary	★	★	★	★	★	★	★
Context clues (synonym, antonym, definition)	★	★	★	★	★	★	★
Abbreviations and acronyms		★	★	★	★	★	★
Classification and categorization of words		★	★	★	★	★	★
Multiple meanings		★	★	★	★	★	★
Dictionary and glossary			★	★	★	★	★
Gazetteer				★	★	★	★
Comprehension	★	★	★	★	★	★	★
Order	★	★	★	★	★	★	★
Picture clues	★	★	★	★	★	★	★
Sequence	★	★	★	★	★	★	★
Compare and contrast	★	★	★	★	★	★	★
Use of visuals (pictures, maps, time lines, graphs, charts, models, graphic organizers)	★	★	★	★	★	★	★
Recall and retell	★	★	★	★	★	★	★
Main idea and details	★	★	★	★	★	★	★
Picture analysis		★	★	★	★	★	★
Prediction		★	★	★	★	★	★
Understand and use graphic and typographical features (boldface, headings, captions, phonetic respellings)		★	★	★	★	★	★
Summarize a chapter or section		★	★	★	★	★	★
Context clues			★	★	★	★	★
Understand and use book parts (table of contents, glossary, atlas, gazetteer, index, bibliography, appendices)			★	★	★	★	★
Scan for specific facts or ideas				★	★	★	★
Understand and use textbook study features (prereading questions, preview and focus statements, summary statements, postreading questions)				★	★	★	★
Make outlines				★	★	★	★
Cause and effect			★	★	★	★	★
Drawing conclusions				★	★	★	★
Summarize				★	★	★	★
Understand characteristics of text types (autobiography, biography, essay, expository, historical fiction, informational, journal/diary, legend, letter, narrative, poetry, speech)				★	★	★	★
Generalize				★	★	★	★
Take notes					★	★	★
Speaking and Listening							
Understand and use speaking and listening skills	★	★	★	★	★	★	★
Dramatization	★	★	★	★	★	★	★
Song	★	★	★	★	★	★	★
Poems	★	★	★	★	★	★	★

ESSENTIAL SKILLS	K	1	2	3	4	5	6
Stories	★	★	★	★	★	★	★
Oral directions	★	★	★	★	★	★	★
Interviews		★	★	★	★	★	★
Debates				★	★	★	★
Use standard grammar and sentence structure				★	★	★	★
Oral reports						★	★
Writing Skills							
Understand forms of writing	★	★	★	★	★	★	★
Descriptive	★	★	★	★	★	★	★
Narrative	★	★	★	★	★	★	★
Expository		★	★	★	★	★	★
Persuasive				★	★	★	★
Understand and use writing skills and processes	★	★	★	★	★	★	★
Lists	★	★	★	★	★	★	★
Captions and labels	★	★	★	★	★	★	★
Use standard grammar, spelling, sentence structure, and punctuation	★	★	★	★	★	★	★
Report		★	★	★	★	★	★
Letter		★	★	★	★	★	★
Collect, organize, and record information		★	★	★	★	★	★
Identify and use reliable sources		★	★	★	★	★	★
Use multimedia tools		★	★	★	★	★	★
Journal/diary			★	★	★	★	★
Essay				★	★	★	★
Research paper				★	★	★	★
Summary				★	★	★	★
News report and feature story				★	★	★	★
Editorials and opinion articles				★	★	★	★
Biography and autobiography						★	★
Speech						★	★
Bibliography						★	★
Historical fiction						★	★
Legend						★	★

Unit 1 Bibliography

Alphabet City, by Stephen T. Johnson (Puffin, ISBN 0-140-55904-3, 1999) **Easy** ***Caldecott Honor Book***

Communities, by Gail Saunders-Smith (Pebble Books, ISBN 1-560-65494-5, 1997) **Easy**

Last Dragon, The, by Susan Miho Nunes and Chris K. Soentpiet (illustrator), (Clarion Books, ISBN 0-395-67020-9, 1995) **Easy** ***Notable Social Studies Book***

Paperboy, The, by Dav Pilkey (Orchard, ISBN 0-531-07139-1, 1999) **Easy** ***Caldecott Honor Book***

Trashy Town, by Andrea G. Zimmerman and David Clemesha; Dan Yaccarino (illlustrator), (HarperCollins, ISBN 0-060-27139-6, 1999) **Easy** ***ALA Notable Book***

What Is a Community from A to Z? by Bobbie Kalman (Crabtree, ISBN 0-86505-384-7, 2000) **Easy**

Houses and Homes, by Ann Morris (Mulberry Books, ISBN 0-688-13578-1, 1995) **On-Level**

Lion Dancer: Ernie Wan's Chinese New Year, by Kate Waters and Madeline Slovenz-Low (Scholastic, ISBN 0-590-43047-5, 1990) **On-Level**

Mama & Papa Have a Store, by Amelia Lau Carling and Amelia Lau (illustrator), (Dial Books for Young Readers, ISBN 0-803-72044-0, 1998) **On-Level**

Smoky Night, by Eve Bunting and David Diaz (illustrator), (Harcourt Brace, ISBN 0-152-01884-0, 1999) **On-Level** ***Caldecott Medal Winner***

Century Farm: One Hundred Years on a Family Farm, by Cris Peterson and Alvis Upitis (photographer), (Boyds Mills, ISBN 1-563-97710-9, 1999) **Challenge**

City Green, by DyAnne DiSalvo-Ryan (Morrow, ISBN 0-688-12786-X, 1994) **Challenge**

Island Boy, by Barbara Cooney (Puffin, ISBN 0-140-50756-6, 1991) **Challenge** ***Boston Globe/Horn Book Award***

My Grandma's the Mayor: A story for children about community spirit and pride, by Marjorie White Pellegrino and John Lund (illustrator), (Magination, ISBN 1-557-98608-8, 1999) **Challenge**

Pioneer Church, by Carolyn Otto and Megan Lloyd (illustrator), (Henry Holt and Co., ISBN 0-805-02554-5, 1999) **Challenge** ***Notable Social Studies Book***

Uncle Willie and the Soup Kitchen, by DyAnne DiSalvo-Ryan (Mulberry Books, ISBN 0-688-15285-6, 1997) **Challenge** ***Reading Rainbow Book***

My Backyard History Book, by David Weitzman (Little Brown and Company, ISBN 0-316-92902-6, 1995) **Teacher Reference**

101 Social Studies Activities for Curious Kids, by Tracey Ann Schofield (Teaching and Learning Co., ISBN 1-573-18262-8, 2000) **Teacher Reference**

Look for this symbol throughout the Teacher's Edition to find **Award-Winning Selections**.

Unit Bibliographies

Unit 2 Bibliography

Bread Is for Eating, by David and Phillis Gershator (Henry Holt, ISBN 0-805-05798-6, 1998) **Easy**

I Am Water, by Jean Marzollo and Judith Moffatt (illustrator) (Cartwheel Books, ISBN 0-590-26587-3, 1996) **Easy**

Time Flies, by Eric Rohmann (Dragonfly, ISBN 0-517-88555-7, 1997) **Easy** ***Caldecott Honor Book***

Albert's Field Trip, by Leslie Tryon (Atheneum, ISBN 0-689-31821-9, 1993) **On-Level**

Blast Off to Earth!: A Look at Geography, by Loreen Leedy (Holiday House, ISBN 0-823-40973-2, 1992) **On-Level**

Butterfly House, The, by Eve Bunting and Greg Shed (illustrator), (Scholastic, ISBN 0-590-84884-4, 1999) **On-Level** ***Notable Social Studies Book***

Listen to the Desert/¿Qué dice el desierto? by Pat Mora (Clarion Books, ISBN 0-395-67292-9, 1994) **On-Level**

Water, Water Everywhere: A Book About the Water Cycle, by Melvin Berger and Gilda Berger; Bobbi Tull (illustrator), (Ideals, ISBN 1-571-02042-X, 1995) **On-Level**

Way to Start a Day, The, by Byrd Baylor and Peter Parnall (illustrator), (Aladdin, ISBN 0-689-71054-2, 1986) **On-Level** ***Caldecott Honor Book***

Child's Calendar, A, by John Updike and Trina Schart Hyman (Holiday, ISBN 0-823-41445-0, 1999) **Challenge** ***Caldecott Honor Book***

Somewhere in the World Right Now, by Stacey Schuett (Dragonfly, ISBN 0-679-88549-8, 1997) **Challenge**

Time of Wonder, by Robert McCloskey (Puffin, ISBN 0-140-50201-7, 1989) **Challenge** ***Caldecott Medal Winner***

Mapmaking with Children: Sense of Place Education for the Elementary Years, by David Sobel (Heinemann, ISBN 0-325-00042-5, 1980) **Teacher Reference**

Sense of Wonder, The, by Rachel Carson (Harper Collins, ISBN 0-06-757520-X, 1998) **Teacher Reference**

***Discovery Channel School* Videos**
Africa: People and Places 19 minutes.
China: People and Places 34 minutes.
Two Children, Two Cultures 25 minutes.

Look for this symbol throughout the Teacher's Edition to find **Award-Winning Selections**.

Unit 3 Bibliography

Frederick, by Leo Lionni (Knopf, ISBN 0-394-82614-0, 1987) **Easy** ***Caldecott Honor Book***

Gardener, The, by Sarah Stewart (Farrar, Straus & Giroux, ISBN 0-374-42518-3, 2000) **Easy** ***Caldecott Honor Book***

Joseph Had a Little Overcoat, by Simms Taback (Viking, ISBN 0-670-87855-3, 1999) **Easy** ***Caldecott Medal Winner***

Zin! Zin! Zin!: A Violin, by Lloyd Moss and Marjorie Priceman (illustrator) (Aladdin Paperbacks, ISBN 0-689-83524-8, 2000) **Easy** ***Caldecott Honor Book***

Community Helpers from A to Z, by Bobbie Kalman, Niki Walker (Crabtree Pub., ISBN 0-865-05404-5, 1997) **On-Level**

Ferryboat, by Betsy Maestro and Giulio Maestro (illustrator) (HarperCollins, ISBN 0-690-04520-4, 1987) **On-Level** ***Notable Social Studies Book***

Granddaddy's Street Songs, by Monalisa Degross and Floyd Cooper (illustrator) (Hyperion, ISBN 0-786-80160-3, 1999) **On-Level** ***Notable Social Studies Book***

Once Upon a Company: A True Story, by Wendy Anderson Halperin (Orchard Books, ISBN 0-531-33089-3, 1998) **On-Level**

School Principals, by Tracey Boraas (Bridgestone Books, ISBN 0-736-80074-3, 1999) **On-Level**

Tortilla Factory, The, by Gary Paulsen (Harcourt Brace, ISBN 0-152-92876-6, 1995) **On-Level**

We Need Mail Carriers, by Lola M. Schaefer (Pebble Books, ISBN 0-736-80392-0, 1999) **On-Level**

What Do Illustrators Do? by Eileen Christelow (Houghton Mifflin, ISBN 0-395-90230-4, 1999) **On-Level** ***ALA Notable Book***

From Tree to Paper, by Wendy Davis (Sundance Pub., ISBN 1-568-01494-5, 1995) **Challenge**

From Wheat to Pasta, by Robert Egan (Children's Press, ISBN 0-516-20709-1, 1997) **Challenge**

Love as Strong as Ginger, by Lenore Look and Stephen T. Johnson (illustrator) (Atheneum, ISBN 0-689-81248-5, 1999) **Challenge** ***Notable Social Studies Book***

Nim and the War Effort, by Milly Lee and Yangsook Choi (illustrator) (Farrar Straus & Giroux, ISBN 0-374-35523-1, 1997) **Challenge** ***ALA Notable Book***

Uncle Willie and the Soup Kitchen, by DyAnne DiSalvo-Ryan (Mulberry Books, ISBN 0-688-15285-6,1997) **Challenge** ***Reading Rainbow Book***

Economics and Children's Literature: Supplement, by B. Flowers and B. Meszaros (SPEC Publishing/ St. Louis, 1998) **Teacher Reference**

 Look for this symbol throughout the Teacher's Edition to find **Award-Winning Selections**.

Unit Bibliographies

Unit 4 Bibliography

America: My Land, Your Land, Our Land, by W. Nicola-Lisa (Lee & Low Books, ISBN 1-880-00037-7, 1997) **Easy**

Ballot Box Battle, The, by Emily Arnold McCully (Dragonfly, ISBN 0-679-89312-1, 1998) **Easy** ***Notable Social Studies Book***

Hooray for the Fourth of July, by Wendy Watson (Houghton Mifflin, ISBN 0-618-04036-6, 2000) **Easy**

Heartland, by Diane Siebert and Wendell Minor (illustrator) (HarperCollins, ISBN 0-064-43287-4, 1992) **On-Level** ***Notable Social Studies Book***

On the Day the Tall Ships Sailed, by Betty Paraskevas and Michael Paraskevas (illustrator) (Simon & Schuster, ISBN 0-689-82864-0, 2000) **On-Level** ***Notable Social Studies Book***

Our Elections, by Richard Steins (Millbrook, ISBN 0-761-30092-9, 1996) **On-Level**

So You Want to Be President? by Judith St. George (Philomel/Putnam, ISBN 0-399-23407-1, 2000) **On-Level**

Susan B. Anthony: A Photo-Illustrated Biography, by Lucille Davis (Bridgestone Books, ISBN 1-560-65750-2, 1998) **On-Level**

U.S. Treasury, by Jason Cooper (The Rourke Corporation, ISBN 0-865-93550-5, 1999) **On-Level**

It Happened in the White House: Extraordinary Tales from America's Most Famous Home, by Kathleen Karr and Paul Meisel (illustrator) (Disney Press, ISBN 0-786-81560-4, 1999) **Challenge**

Purple Mountain Majesties: The Story of Katharine Lee Bates and "America, the Beautiful," by Barbara Younger and Stacey Schuett (illustrator) (Dutton, ISBN 0-525-45653-8, 1998) **Challenge**

Scrambled States of America, by Laurie Keller (Henry Holt, ISBN 0-805-05802-8, 1998) **Challenge**

Uncle Sam & Old Glory: Symbols of America, by Delno C. West and Jean M. West with Christopher Manson (illustrator) (Atheneum, ISBN 0-689-82043-7, 2000) **Challenge**

My America: A Poetry Atlas of the United States, selected by Lee Bennett Hopkins. Illustrated by Stephen Alcorn. (Simon & Schuster, ISBN 0-689-81247-7, 2000) **Teacher Reference**

Seeing the Whole Through Social Studies, by Tarry Lindquist (Heinemann, ISBN 0-435-08902-1, 1995) **Teacher Reference**

Look for this symbol throughout the Teacher's Edition to find **Award-Winning Selections.**

Unit 5 Bibliography

Going West, by Jean Van Leeuwen (HarperCollins, ISBN 0-064-40693-8, 1997) **Easy**

I Have Heard of a Land, by Joyce Carol Thomas and Floyd Cooper (illustrator) (HarperTrophy, ISBN 0-064-43617-9, 2000) **Easy** ***Coretta Scott King Honor Book***

Minty: A Story of Young Harriet Tubman, by Alan Schroeder and Jerry Pinkney (illustrator) (Puffin, ISBN 0-140-56196-X, 2000) **Easy** ***Coretta Scott King Honor Book***

New Hope, by Henri Sorensen (Econo-Clad Books, ISBN 0-613-08432-2, 1999) **Easy** ***Notable Social Studies Book***

Aurora Means Dawn, by Scott Russell Sanders (Bradbury, ISBN 0-027-78270-0, 1989) **On-Level**

Freedom River, A, by Doreen Rappaport and Bryan Collier (illustrator) (Jump at the Sun, ISBN 0-786-80350-9, 2000) **On-Level** ***Coretta Scott King Honor Book***

Gift of the Sacred Dog, The, by Paul Goble (Aladdin Paperbacks, ISBN 0-020-43280-1, 1984) **On-Level**

Honest Abe, by Edith Kunhardt (Mulberry Books, ISBN: 0-688-15838-2, 1998) **On-Level**

Lewis and Clark: Explorers of the American West, by Steven Kroll (Holiday House, ISBN 0-823-41273-3, 1994) **On-Level**

Paul Revere's Ride, by Henry Wadsworth Longfellow, illustrated by Ted Rand (Puffin, ISBN 0-140-55612-5, 1996) **On-Level**

Pueblo Storyteller, by Diane Hoyt-Goldsmith and Lawrence Migdale (illustrator) (Holiday House, ISBN 0-823-41080-3, 1994) **On-Level**

Tapenum's Day: A Wampanoag Indian Boy in Pilgrim Times, by Kate Waters and Russ Kendall (photographer) (Scholastic Trade, ISBN 0-590-20237-5, 1996) **On-Level** ***Notable Social Studies Book***

Seaman: The Dog Who Explored the West with Lewis and Clark, by Gail Langer Karwoski and James Watling (illustrator) (Peachtree Publishers, ISBN 1-561-45190-8, 1999) **Challenge**

Sleds on the Boston Common, by Louise Borden (Margaret McElderry, ISBN 0-689-82812-8, 2000) **Challenge**

Ten Mile Day and the Building of the Transcontinental Railroad, by Mary Ann Fraser (Henry Holt, ISBN 0-805-04703-4, 1996) **Challenge**

Thunder from the Clear Sky, by Marcia Sewall (Aladdin Paperbacks, ISBN 0-689-82176-X, 1998) **Challenge** ***Notable Social Studies Book***

Kids' America, by Steven Caney (Workman Publishing, ISBN 0-911-10480-1, 1978) **Teacher Reference**

Pioneer Days: Discover the Past with Fun Projects, Games, Activities, and Recipes, by David C. King and Bobbie Moore (illustrator) (John Wiley & Sons, ISBN 0-471-16169-1, 1997) **Teacher Reference**

Look for this symbol throughout the Teacher's Edition to find **Award-Winning Selections**.

Unit 6 Bibliography

Grandfather's Journey, by Allen Say (Houghton Mifflin, ISBN 0-395-57035-2, 1993) **Easy** ***Caldecott Medal Winner***

Halmoni and the Picnic, by Sook Nyul Choi (Houghton Mifflin, ISBN 0-395-61626-3, 1993) **Easy**

Peppe the Lamplighter, by Elisa Bartone and Ted Lewin (illustrator) (Mulberry Books, ISBN 0-688-15469-7, 1997) **Easy** ***Caldecott Honor Book***

Day in the Life of an Architect, A, by Mary Bowman-Kruhm (Rosen Publishing Group, ISBN 0-823-95297-5, 1999) **On-Level**

Dreaming of America: An Ellis Island Story, by Eve Bunting and Ben F. Stahl (illustrator) (Troll, ISBN 0-816-76521-9, 2001) **On-Level** ***IRA Teachers' Choice***

Favorite Children's Stories from China and Tibet, by Lotta Carswell Hume (Tuttle Publishing, ISBN 0-804-83303-6, 2001) **On-Level**

Legend of Mu Lan: A Heroine of Ancient China, The, by Wei Jiang and Cheng An Jiang (Victory Press, ISBN 1-878-21714-3, 1997) **On-Level**

My Name Is Maria Isabel, by Alma Flor Ada (Aladdin Paperbacks, ISBN 0-689-80217-X, 1995) **On-Level**

Real McCoy: The Life of an African-American Inventor, The, by Wendy Towle and Wil Clay (illustrator) (Scholastic Paperbacks, ISBN 0-590-48102-9, 1995) **On-Level**

Rushmore, by Lynn Curlee (Scholastic, ISBN 0-590-22573-1, 1999) **On-Level** ***Notable Social Studies Book***

Vinnie in Egypt, by Elizabeth Bott, (Pageturner Books, ISBN 0-970-46780-X, 2000) **On-Level**

Wright vs. Wrong!: The True and Not-So-True Story of the Airplane, by Gigi Tegge (Greene Bark Press, ISBN 1-880-85126-1, 1997) **On-Level**

Ellis Island, by Patricia Ryon Quiri (Children's Press, ISBN 0-516-20622-2, 1998) **Challenge**

Freedom's Gifts: A Juneteenth Story, by Valerie Wilson Wesley and Sharon Wilson (illustrator) (Simon & Schuster, ISBN 0-689-80269-2, 1997) **Challenge** ***Notable Social Studies Book***

Through the Eyes of Your Ancestors, by Maureen Taylor (Houghton Mifflin, ISBN 0-395-86982-X, 1999) **Challenge**

Keepsakes: Using Family Stories in Elementary Classrooms, by Linda Winston (Heinemann, ISBN 0-435-07235-8, 1997) **Teacher Reference**

***Discovery Channel School* Videos**
Heroes of American History
25 minutes. (#730267)

Look for this symbol throughout the Teacher's Edition to find **Award-Winning Selections**.

Index

Index

W

Credits

Maps:

Mapquest.com, an America Online, Inc. company

Illustrations

1D Susan Tolonen; 1H, 49H, 97H, 133A, 147H, 165A, 195H, 243H Matt Straub; 49D Darryl Ligasan; 97D Lauren E. Simeone; 147D Karen Stormer Brooks; 243D Daniel Powers

Photographs

Every effort has been made to secure permission and provide appropriate credit for photographic material. The publisher deeply regrets any omission and pledges to correct errors called to their attention in subsequent editions.

Unless otherwise acknowledged, all photographs are the property of Scott Foresman, a division of Pearson Education.

Front Matter

SF12 (BR)Dennis O'Clair/Stone; **Unit 1:** 8A PhotoDisc; 24A Eyewire, Inc.; **Unit 2:** 49A (Bkgd)Frederick D. Atwood; 49B,C (T)Frederick D. Atwood; 49D,E (T)Frederick D. Atwood; 49F,G (T)Frederick D. Atwood; 49H (T)Frederick D. Atwood; 62A PhotoDisc; 68A PhotoDisc; 75A (BR)PhotoDisc; 76A PhotoDisc; 82A PhotoDisc; **Unit 3:**104A PhotoDisc; 120A PhotoDisc; 126A PhotoDisc; 134A (CR)PhotoDisc, (CL)Reuters NewMedia, Inc./, Corbis-Bettmann, (BR)Bruce Hands/Hulton Getty, (BL)Malcolm Fife/SuperStock; 139A PhotoDisc; **Unit 4:** 147A (Bkgd)John Neubauer/PhotoEdit; 147B,C (T)John Neubauer/PhotoEdit; 147D,E (T)John Neubauer/PhotoEdit; 147F,G (T)John Neubauer/PhotoEdit; 147H (T)John Neubauer/PhotoEdit; 154A Bob Daemmrich/Stock Boston; 160A Joseph Sohm/Corbis-Bettmann; 166A PhotoDisc; 171A Paul A. Souders/Corbis-Bettmann; 172A Bachmann/Rainbow; 180A (c) Leif Skoogfors/Corbis-Bettmann; **Unit 5:** 195A (C)Robert Glusic/PhotoDisc; 195B,C (T)Robert Glusic/PhotoDisc; 195C (BL)Archivo Iconografico, S.A./Corbis, (TC)Hulton Getty/Stone; 195D (B) Art Resource, NY; 195D,E (T)Robert Glusic/PhotoDisc; 195F,G (T)Robert Glusic/PhotoDisc; 195H (T)Robert Glusic/PhotoDisc; 202A Marilyn "Angel" Wynn/Nativestock; 210A SuperStock; 222A Corbis-Bettmann; 230A The Granger Collection, New York; **Unit 6:** 243A (C)M. Lee/Art Directors & TRIP Photo Library; 243B,C (T)M. Lee/Art Directors & TRIP Photo Library; 243C (B) Hulton-Deutsch Collection/Corbis; 243D,E (T)M. Lee/Art Directors & TRIP Photo Library; 243F,G (T)M. Lee/Art Directors & TRIP Photo Library; 243H (T)M. Lee/Art Directors & TRIP Photo Library; 250A The Granger Collection, New York; 256A SuperStock; 272A (BR)Araldo de Luca/Corbis-Bettmann

End Matter

TR46 (L)Austrian Archives/Corbis, (R) Horace Bristol/Corbis

Notes

Notes